ICTs for Mobile and Ubiquitous Urban Infrastructures:

Surveillance, Locative Media and Global Networks

Rodrigo Jose Firmino
Pontifícia Universidade Católica do Paraná, Brazil

Fabio Duarte
Pontifícia Universidade Católica do Paraná, Brazil

Clovis Ultramari
Pontifícia Universidade Católica do Paraná, Brazil

Information Science REFERENCE

INFORMATION SCIENCE REFERENCE
Hershey · New York

Director of Editorial Content:	Kristin Klinger
Director of Book Publications:	Julia Mosemann
Acquisitions Editor:	Lindsay Johnston
Development Editor:	Joel Gamon
Publishing Assistant:	Keith Glazewski & Milan Vracarich, Jr.
Typesetter:	Keith Glazewski
Production Editor:	Jamie Snavely
Cover Design:	Lisa Tosheff

Published in the United States of America by
Information Science Reference (an imprint of IGI Global)
701 E. Chocolate Avenue
Hershey PA 17033
Tel: 717-533-8845
Fax: 717-533-8661
E-mail: cust@igi-global.com
Web site: http://www.igi-global.com

Library of Congress Cataloging-in-Publication Data

ICTs for mobile and ubiquitous urban infrastructures : surveillance, locative media, and global networks / Rodrigo Jose Firmino, Fabio Duarte and Clovis Ultramari, editors.
p. cm.
Includes bibliographical references and index.
Summary: "This book investigates how a shift to a completely urban global world woven together by ubiquitous and mobile ICTs changes the ontological meaning of space, and how the use of these technologies challenges the social and political construction of territories and the cultural appropriation of places"--Provided by publisher.
ISBN 978-1-60960-051-8 (hardcover) -- ISBN 978-1-60960-053-2 (ebook) 1. City planning--Technological innovations. 2. Computer networks--Social aspects. 3. Community life--Technological innovations. I. Firmino, Rodrigo Josi. II. Duarte, Fabio, 1970- III. Ultramari, Clovis.
HT166.I38 2010
307.1'216--dc22

2010020103

British Cataloguing in Publication Data
A Cataloguing in Publication record for this book is available from the British Library.

Table of Contents

Detailed Table of Contents

This chapter invites the reader to suspect if global networks can be entirely explained by economic and financial flows leads the authors to confirm that it is also the result of local and global articulation that emerges around a wide variety of sociopolitical issues. Authors propose themselves to indentify the complexity and diversity of the emerging city networks by means of the methodology of Web Sphere Analysis.

This chapter criticizes the traditional way of understanding cities through the lens of financial, commercial, and industrials entities. At the same time, authors offer a different perspective: a combinative environment of interpersonal interaction, media landscape of spaces, places and communication texts. The result is a tacit agreement between traditional geographic community and a complex network of an enlarged one linked by virtual multimedia.

The main purpose of this chapter is to call attention to the "intangible" space of flows in order to better understand the characteristics of and relationships between world cities. Authors argue that Web represents an under-utilized database of information that is immense and updated in real time. To demonstrate that they bring to this book a research based on the Google search engine used to specify a dynamic, informational classification of North American cities.

Tai shows how control is made of a range of different and complex practices and technologies in a multilayered and multifaceted surveillance strategy mainly orchestrated by the Web Bureau of the Central Propaganda Department in the central government, and distributed through many other public and private institutions.

The focus of this chapter is more to analyze these devices as socio-technical systems that alter various practices, actions and processes of surveillance upon behavioural patterns of people and objects in public and private spaces.

The author interestingly points out the concepts of lateral surveillance (individuals surveilling other individuals), sousveillance (individuals observing observers), and synopticon (many watching the few) to deconstruct the idea that the use of personal surveillance devices by individuals constitutes an empowering practice.

Santaella argues about the importance of considering the social construction of surveillance technologies as opposite to a deterministic view that considers these technologies and surveillance itself either good or evil. The author uses the analogy to Thánatos and Eros to point out the extreme deterministic views that should be avoided in surveillance and media studies.

This chapter approaches projects of vehicle monitoring in a cross-national perspective (Europe and Brazil) to discuss previous preoccupation, discussions and legal instruments regarding the fundamental protection of personal data.

Botello questions the influence of the increasing use of Closed Circuit Television in the organization, form, experience and social practices in public and private places in two Mexican Cities. The author sustains that the myth created about CCTV systems as crime tacklers underpins most of the rationale for their application in public and private spaces in Mexico.

Foreword

THE NEW 'PLACE OF FLOWS'

Information and communication technologies have made a paradigmatic change from wired, fixed networks, devices and human interfaces to widely available, wireless networks and mobile devices which are integrated into activities unmoored from specific points. It made sense to talk about devices as terminals – gateways at the edges of communication networks. The teleprinter or later the fax machine merged the interface with the physical structure of the device and this appeared to be the most significant point of contact between human social life and communications within international networks. The place of bodies and community was similarly separate from the network, leading to the idea of a global telecommunications and transport space separate from fixed places of community as late as the 1990s. Manuel Castells' trilogy *Network Society* represented the pinnacle of this understanding with its signature idea of the 'space of flows' an idea in currency at the time (Castells, 1997; see Lash & Urry, 1994; Shields, 1997).

Mobile and ubiquitous communication and devices rely on wireless data networks that are spatial in their coverage despite the significance of fixed transceivers and antennas. These too have become more distributed around building rooftops than the towers of 1990s cellular technologies. A point has often been made about the physicality of wireless which depends on wired telephone company lines digital backbone infrastructures and a geography of undersea cables. Nonetheless, interfaces have been unbound from fixed points allowing communication activities to become moveable. This is almost the reverse of the fixing of plumbing into buildings in the late nineteenth and early twentieth centuries which fixed washing and ablution in specific rooms, literally attaching sinks to walls, creating bathrooms and modern kitchens (Roderick, 1998; Kaika, 2004). The result is an unbinding of individual activities related to information and knowledge such as looking up an address, and of social interactions via mobile technologies and around devices-made-mobile such as a GPS navigation, or game platforms which might combine local players, onlookers and remote players. Wireless devices are a new carapace for the mobile human in a localized space which is both concrete and informational.

Merging Space and Place

To suggest, as the contributors to this volume do, that information and communication technologies (ICTs) are ubiquitous, implies a merging of the global space of flows and the local place of everyday life (Duarte & Firmino, 2009). As an 'augmented reality' or augmented space, the local is extended in the same way that a look-out or vantage point offers a sense of an extended area by presenting a vista to the eyes. The binary dualism, a division of space and place, is still often found but even if it remains an meme, it is disabling and counter-productive except as a trope which is used for rhetorical purposes. Developments in programming and in the use of technologies no longer mark the edge of information and telecommunication networks at the teletypewriter.

The dualism of space of flows and everyday places turns on an outdated contrast between the ideal and the actual which imagines a purely abstract (capitalist, technological) space on the order of concepts and ideas. This matrix is contrasted with the materiality of the actually real. But left aside in this picture is the entire realm of intangibles or '*virtualities*' (Shields, 2003). They include intangibles such as a brand, community, medium, group, mathematical set and so on. These objects of contemporary science, technology, social and economic life are not physically concrete but have a reality which distinguishes them from abstractions such as ideas which are 'possible' but not 'real' objects. The material-abstract dualism similarly lacks an ontological category for probabilities, that is, for actual and possible entities conventionally described mathematically or in the language of risk and that serves as the basis for financial and insurance industries.

From Abstract Space of Capital into Virtual Spaces

In place of a network divided into nodes and linkages, we have a complex topology, a kind of rubber-sheet mapping where distance can be exaggerated or minimized to merge points together into new geographical unities. Similarly distant regions can be opened up to the needs of hegemonic places (Firmino & Duarte, 2010). The role of capital and power as operators in this virtual space must not be overlooked. This is a global-scaled and locally-determinant 'spatialisation' (Shields, 2006; R Shields, 1989) where a virtual, 'as-if' closeness can over-rule actual presence and proximity, marks the distinction between the sort of spaces and spatialities discussed by the authors in this text, and Lefebvre's uniformly-gridded Cartesian 'abstract space' of capitalism (Lefebvre, 1974). A virtual topology affords new opportunities for resistance and accepts new powers, while capitalism has had to transform itself and States have taken on new forms of governance, often focused on cities and regions. The editors and contributors lay the basis for exploring this new dynamics not only in global cities but in all centres where surveillance meets mobile and ubiquitous ICTs.

Military applications merge with civilian life in satellite-based services such as GPS or Iridium phones for which costly low-orbit satellites are paid for by State as part of their security infrastructure. If anything what is significant is this reversibility of national surveillance networks relied upon by citizens as much as by governments. Similarly, the contributors show that everyday communication continues to afford an irresistible opportunity for surveillance which expands from eavesdropping to locating individuals in real time by tracking mobile equipment by their identifying registration signatures. So-called 'push' services such as advertisements tends to be less adopted but these added features of mobile communications turn on allowing oneself to be tracked and identified. Like turning off the 'cookies' set by websites in the data caches of internet browsers, who would want to forego the usability of advanced features of websites (Elmer, 1998)?

With the exception of satellite-based services urban areas are the most privileged locales for affordable, widely consumed global ICTs. Coverage maps showing wireless service in countries such as Canada are remarkable for their regional qualities. Towns and regional centres are like pools on these maps. Signals extend like tributaries running into a great lake as they follow along major roadways.

High-speed, 3G data and better is even more limited – a kind of low-tide mark in this oceanography of data. Smaller towns may lack high speed data creating a digital divide in regional economic development options. The Place-based sites of everyday life, restricted to one locale on the planet's surface, are not nodes on this mapping, but the excluded outside, in the 'dry' regions without signals, where one imagines that they still speak of ancient radio receivers as 'the wireless' and do not interact with virtualities in any way. It is linguistically and information-technologically a world apart – or is it? Armed with a satellite phone or GPS, any Inuit or polar ecotourist interacts with this system and may even be able to phone or email friends. ICT's 'great outdoors' is an liminoid margin, not an exterior.

New Urbanities

In this sense, urbanity as a mode of conviviality and sociality beyond one's immediate circle extends beyond cities into rural areas and globally if one counts interest-based chat rooms, comment feeds and twitter postings. This is a virtual counterpart to the extension of the materiality of cities which Paul Virilio refers to as 'cities of the beyond'. The 'explosion of former geographical agglomerations follows not precedes 'cities of immateriality, or telecommunications, air corridors... an accelerated "*exurbanism*"'. But these are hardly 'cities of "foreigners"...urban up-rootedness...wherein no one feels at home, anywhere' (original italics Virilio in Armitage, 2009:109). We must resist such xenophobia against virtual Others, against the play of difference which ultimately is the achievement of cities which bring complementary functions together in space-time (cf. Lefebvre, 1970b) as the form of civility. We must demand what Lefebvre called our 'right to the city' as a right to urbanity, to difference, unmolested by moral dictates.

Rob Shields
University of Alberta, Canada

REFERENCES

Armitage, J. (2009). In the Cities of the Beyond: An Interview with Paul Virilio. *Open: 2030 War Zone Amsterdam, 18*, 100-111.

Castells, M. (1997). *Network Society* (Vol. 3). Oxford: Blackwell.

Duarte, F., & Firmino, R. J. (2009). Infiltrated city, augmented space: information and communication technologies and representations of contemporary spatialities. *Journal of Architecture, 14*(5), 545-565.

Elmer, G. (1998). Diagrams, maps and markets: The Technological matrix of geographical information systems. *Space and Culture - Theme Issue on Habitable Spaces*(3), 49-65.

Firmino, R. J., & Duarte, F. (2010). Manifestations and implications of an augmented urban life *International Review of Information Ethics*, 12(3).

Kaika, M. (2004). Interrogating the geographies of the familiar: Domesticating nature and constructing the autonomy of the modern home. *International Journal of Urban and Regional Research, 28*(2), 265.

Lash, S., & Urry, J. (1994). *Economies of Signs and Space*. London: Sage.

Lefebvre, H. (1970b). *Le Revolution urbaine*. Paris: Gallimard.

Lefebvre, H. (1974). La production de l'espace. *L'Homme et la société*, 31_32. 15_31.

Roderick, I. (1998). Habitable Spaces. *Space and Culture - Theme Issue on Habitable Spaces*(3.), 1-4.

Shields, R. (1989). Social Spatialisation and the Built Environment: The Case of the West Edmonton Mall. *Environment and Planning D: Society and Space, 7*(2, Summer), 147-164.

Shields, R. (1997). Flow. *Space and Culture - Theme Issue on Flow*(1), 1-5.

Shields, R. (2003). *The Virtual*. London: Routledge.

Shields, R. (2006). Knowing Space/Spatialization. *Theory Culture and Society, 23*(2-3), 146-149.

Preface

This book contributes to the discussion on how the world was transformed into an entire urban phenomenon. Impacts of such change are still to be clearly understood, but decisive tools to implement it are repeatedly said to be the means of information and communication technologies. This phenomenon is made concrete when space is intertwined with time, its scales are challenged, political and economic boundaries of territories are reviewed and social groups can kaleidoscopically appropriate parts of the world to turn them into their places. New ubiquitous and mobile technological urban infrastructures, essentially supported by ICTs, are crucial to provoke and to explain such changes. This is the main principle and reference to be found throughout this book.

By adopting a necessary multidisciplinary approach authors focus on ICTs and new urban infrastructures to discuss this topic. Discussions developed here, both theoretical and analytical, are all connected with global networks of signs, values and ideologies, locative media that gives us the freedom of spatial mobility and the possibility of creating and recreating places, and the surveillance artefacts which permeate our daily life and allow a hypothetical total control of space. These three types of technology constitute the three-section structure of this book. Sections may be read separately according to readers' interests on the book. Complex, multidisciplinary and unfinished character of the discussion brought here justify the expected interest it may arise among different researchers, either from a more sociological, psychological or anthropological point of view or from a more technological, urbanistic or public managerial perspective.

Each one of the three sections of the book, besides discussing three different but closely intricate aspects of the new urban world or of the new informational city, is introduced by a reference chapter. Each of these reference chapters guides and serves as a reference to the following chapters, which try, whenever possible, to engage in a conversation with the reference chapter of their respective section.

The first section presents six chapters (including the reference chapter) that have as their main theme what we are calling *global networks*. The intention of this section is to discuss the global networks of signs, values and ideologies, which break down the social and political boundaries of territories. The challenge presented in this section is to discuss both the roles of the global flows of information, social and cultural values, and – especially in this part of the book – the infrastructures that have been built as a global technological network. The reference chapter in this section, and hence the first chapter in the section, written by Peter Taylor, is *Measuring the World City Network: New Results and Developments*. Taylor proposes a model to measure what he calls the world city network, through the analysis of activities of advanced producer service firms. His intention is to show the possibility of precisely quantifying the connections between cities in a global scale.

In the second chapter in the section, *Policy-Oriented City Networks in Cyberspace: A Methodological Approach to the Understanding of Social and Political Articulations between Cities Based on the*

Concept of Policy Web Spheres, Klaus Frey, Mario Procopiuck and Altair Rosa invite the reader to suspect if global networks can be entirely explained by economic and financial flows by alerting that it is also the result of local and global articulation emerging from a wide variety of sociopolitical issues: the fight against poverty, the strengthening of human rights or protection of the environment, among others. The authors propose to indentify the complexity and diversity of the emerging city networks by means of the methodology of Web Sphere Analysis. In order to do so they take the example of a city in southern Brazil, Curitiba, and its position regarding other cities in the context of environmental policies.

Susan Drucker and Gary Gumpert, in *The Urban Communication Infrastructure: Global Connection and Local Detachment*, (the third chapter of the section) criticizes the traditional way of understanding cities through the lens of financial, commercial, and industrials entities. At the same time, authors offer a different perspective: a combinative environment of interpersonal interaction, media landscape of spaces, places and communication texts. The result is a tacit agreement between traditional geographic community and a complex network of an enlarged one linked by virtual multimedia.

In the fourth chapter, *City Networks in Cyberspace and Time: Using Google Hyperlinks to Measure Global Economic and Environmental Crises*, Andrew Boulton, Lomme Devriendt, Stanley Brunn, Ben Derudder and Frank Witlox call attention to the "intangible" space of flows in order to better understand the characteristics of relationships between world cities. Authors argue that the Web represents an underutilized database of information that is immense and updated in real time. To demonstrate this, they bring to this book a research based on the Google search engine used to specify a dynamic, informational classification of North American cities.

Chapter six is signed by Tan Yigitcanlar and Jung Hoon Han - *Ubiquitous Eco Cities: Infrastructure, Technology and Management* - where the main focus is on the search for tools to understand what is called Ubiquitous eco cities (U-eco cities). U-eco city is presented as a city that promises to provide a friendly environment, infrastructures and services, evidence in minimizing inputs trough ubiquitous technologies and sustainable principles. To do so, authors argue that it is necessary to take telecommunication infrastructure in high consideration. Thus, authors concentrate in the discussions about developments in telecommunication infrastructure and trends in convergence technologies and their implications on the management of Ubiquitous Eco Cities.

Social Networks on the Internet: Twitter Coverage of the Exile of the Peruvian Indigenous Leader Alberto Pizango to Nicaragua (chapter seven), by Débora de Carvalho Pereira closes the Global Networks section. This chapter discusses the use of the methodology of Social Network Analysis to systematize a network of relationships around the collective transnational flux of information via the micro-blog service Twitter. The case studied is the exile of Peruvian indigenous leader Alberto Pizango to Nicaragua, and the conflicts between Indians and the military in 2009. Information systems in geographically dispersed networks are discussed throughout this work as differential factors potentiating the practices, flow, and movement of information.

The second section of this book is based on the discussions around *mobile and locative media*, and as the intention to approach the technological and social implications of such instruments that give us the freedom of spatial mobility and the possibility of creating and recreating places. Divided in five chapters, this section is opened by chapter eight (the reference-chapter), titled *Locative Media and Surveillance at the Boundaries of Informational Territories*, where André Lemos advances on how location-based technologies (LBT) and location-based services (LBS), articulated through global information networks, have been used as new forms of surveillance – what shows an interdependency between the sections of this book. Lemos shows that small devices infiltrated in our daily life are the visible part of locative media. But they are dependent on ubiquitous though invisible information networks. Those networks have *hard* components (infrastructure and devices) but also *soft* components, such as the political, social and legal framework they are based on.

In chapter nine - *Mobile Telephony, Public and Private Planning and Regulation: A UK Perspective* - Deborah Peel and Greg Lloyd unveil how public and private planning and regulation are constituent parts of the mobile telephony in UK. The authors discuss attempts in Scotland "to design an appropriate regulatory regime to reconcile the environmental, economic, technocratic, and democratic considerations needed to support the physical distribution networks required to support mobile telephony".

Georgios Patris, Vassilios Vescoukis and Maria Giaoutzi in the chapter *Advances of the Location Based Context-Aware Mobile Services in the Transport Sector* (chapter ten) propose a theoretical model of location-based services for transit and transport. Using multiple locative technologies, they create a context-aware environment, where "services automatically adapt to the environment of a user". With this model authors show how urban space can be seen as an environment full of infiltrated information where people behave depending on which devices they have to establish an informative dialogue. Dialogues between users and urban environments are also explored by Thiago Falcão, Luiz Adolfo Andrade, Emmanoel Ferreira and Paolo Bruni, who analyse, in chapter eleven, different games developed in Brazil which use locative media to build a hybrid space, where electronic devices and the city constitute the environment where players must act. Thus, in *Locative Media and Playful Appropriations, or How Electronic Games Help to Redefine the Meaning of Space* author's main argument is that alternate reality games could "reconfigure the way we observe the city and interpret urban space".

This section closes with *Mobile Devices: Designing Hybrid Body-Spaces*, as chapter eleven, by Luísa Paraguai, who argues that the relationships between space and body, when mediated by mobile devices demand "new behavioural codes and evoke other communication patterns". According to the author, these devices, infiltrated in daily life, create new social bonds and boundaries which could enhance new spatialities. The artistic projects discussed by Paraguai in her chapter try to explore those new mobile urban spatialities.

The last section is also the biggest, with seven chapters. In the third section, authors focus their efforts on issues more directly involved with the application of *surveillance technologies*. In general, the chapters in this section discuss the technological and social implications of instruments that permeate our daily life, and which permit for those who control it a hypothetical total control of the space. The progressive relation between surveillance and new technologies, especially ICTs, coincides with a trajectory from the bodily, as seen in Foucault's panopticism to a surveillance society based on computerised and increasingly automated systems. The reference-chapter for this section, which is also chapter thirteen, is written by David Lyon: *Why Where You are Matters: Mundane Mobilities, Transparent Technologies, and Digital Discrimination*. Lyon shows how surveillance technologies have been used to increase the visibility of personal data through strategies of tracing bodies and artifacts. By associating mobile and traceable technologies to surveillance, Lyon also shows, indirectly, the interconnections between the three sections of the book, and hence, between the three types of technological applications which the approach of this book is based on.

In chapter fourteen, Zixue Tai, demystifies the idea that the efforts by the Chinese Government to control the Internet flow in the country is a single unified project based on filter technologies and network firewalls. In *Casting the Ubiquitous Net of Information Control: Internet Surveillance in China from Golden Shield to Green Dam*, Tai shows how control is made of a range of different and complex practices and technologies in a multilayered and multifaceted surveillance strategy mainly orchestrated by the Web Bureau of the Central Propaganda Department in the central government, and distributed through many other public and private institutions.

The pre-emptive characteristics of today's surveillance systems that rely on profiling software integrated to Closed Circuit Television is approached by is approached by Fernanda Bruno in chapter fifteen - *A Brief Cartography of Smart Cameras: Proative Surveillance and Control* - through a socio-technical standpoint, in order to understand these "intelligent" systems of control beyond its technological features. Although the author does describe recent developments of these technologies, her focus is more to analyze these devices as socio-technical systems that alter various practices, actions and processes of surveillance upon behavioural patterns of people and objects in public and private spaces.

Chapter sixteen, *Recording and Reporting: Camera Phones, User-Generated Images and Surveillance*, by Bilge Yesil, discusses the constitution of a "viewer society" with the intensification of the culture of visibility brought in by the increasingly widespread use of camera phones by individuals. The author interestingly points out the concepts of lateral surveillance (individuals surveilling other individuals), sousveillance (individuals observing observers), and synopticon (many watching the few) to deconstruct the idea that the use of personal surveillance devices by individuals constitutes an empowering practice. After Bilge's account on the "viewer society" through the use of camera phones, Lucia Santaella, in chapter seventeen, interestingly analyses the same kind of apparatuses (small, mobile and locative devices) to theorize what she calls the three regimes of surveillance: the panoptic regime, the scopic regime and the tracking regime. In *Mobile and Locative Media: In between Thánatos and Eros*, Santaella argues about the importance of considering the social construction of surveillance technologies as opposite to a deterministic view that considers these technologies and surveillance itself either good or evil.

The eighteenth chapter - *Notes about Vehicle Monitoring in Brazil and Europe from a Data Protection Perspective* - approaches projects of vehicle monitoring in a cross-national perspective to discuss previous preoccupation, discussions and legal instruments regarding the fundamental protection of personal data. Danilo Doneda and Mario Viola de Azevedo Cunha analyse some European and Brazilian regulations to build their argument and defend their concern about the widespread use of personal data in different kinds of (private and public) databases, especially in the case of projects for vehicle monitoring, by pointing out the risks of threats to individual privacy and data protection.

Finally, in chapter nineteen - *Urban Surveillance in Mexico* - Nelson Arteaga-Botello questions the influence of the increasing use of Closed Circuit Television in the organization, form, experience and social practices in public and private places in two Mexican Cities. In this analysis, the author shed light in the relationships between this specific kind of surveillance technology and the agency behind its implementation, acceptance, symbolic construction and organizational use for tackling crime and violence problems in urban public and commercial spaces.

This book is part of a greater contemporary effort to understand our own moment in history, characterized by a society both excited with its differences from predecessor moments and reluctant to easily accept artifacts and methods adopted to achieve it. By displaying side by side excitement and fear towards changes imposed by technological devices and digital procedures, this book is a contribution to make these feelings clear and proper, perhaps helping us to understand the moment in which we are witnessing the rising of the ubiquitous city, clearly marked by the relationships between space, place, territory, global networks, locative media, and surveillance practices and technologies.

Rodrigo Firmino, Fábio Duarte, Clovis Ultramari
Curitiba, Brazil, April 2010.

Acknowledgment

We would like to express our gratitude to CNPq (part of the Brazilian Ministry of Science and Technology) and *Fundação Araucária* (State of Paraná research funding agency) for sponsoring the studies coordinated by us, which indirectly contributed to form the ideas and stimulate the efforts that help us put this book together. We are grateful to the members of the editorial board and all contributing authors, but especially to Professors David Lyon, Peter Taylor and André Lemos, for kindly agreeing to write the papers that became the three thematic reference-chapters. Professor Rob Shields gave us the pleasure and the honour of having his words nar- rating the presentation of this book. And finally, our task would have been much more arduous if it was not the constant and competent help of Mr. Joel Gamon, Development Editor at IGI Global.

Rodrigo Firmino, Fábio Duarte, Clovis Ultramari
Editors

Chapter 1
The Rising of the Ubiquitous City:
Global Networks, Locative Media and Surveillance Technologies[1]

Rodrigo José Firmino
Pontifícia Universidade Católica do Paraná, Brazil

Fábio Duarte
Pontifícia Universidade Católica do Paraná, Brazil

Clovis Ultramari
Pontifícia Universidade Católica do Paraná, Brazil

ABSTRACT

In this chapter, the authors investigate how the shift to a completely urban global world intertwined by ubiquitous and mobile ICTs changes the ontological meaning of space, and how the use of these technologies challenges the social and political construction of territories and the cultural appropriation of places. The authors' approach to this conceptual debate will focus on what they consider to be more direct and tangible implications of this augmentation of urban life. Three types of manifestations will represent the core of the discussions presented here, both through theoretical approaches and analytical descriptions of some examples: surveillance artifacts which permeate daily life and allow a hypothetical total control of space; locative media that gives us the freedom of spatial mobility and the possibility of creating and recreating places; and the global networks of signs, values and ideologies, which break down the social and political boundaries of territories.

INTRODUCTION

"I've always been very careful never to predict anything that had not already happened". (Marshall McLuhan, 1970: 172).

DOI: 10.4018/978-1-60960-051-8.ch001

The idea that ICTs have been dramatically changing many aspects of contemporary society is no longer new. The influence of such technologies on our daily activities, and on the ways we perceive and use space, has attracted the interest of a wide variety of researchers from different backgrounds, and this has also in turn increased the inter- and multi-disciplinarity of studies about space, in particular urban space, and in different scales.

Recent references to the city predominantly relate the constant and rapid development of ICTs to the re-definition of notions of space, territory, place, time, mediation, presence, and immersion – virtual, physical and real. According to Moss and Townsend (2000: 31), "information systems are permitting new combinations of people, equipment, and places; as a result, there is a dramatic change in the spatial organization of activities within cities and large metropolitan regions".

It seems to be common sense, after more than three decades of speculation and studies about the intensification of communication through the use of increasingly sophisticated ICTs, that we have exponentially augmented our ability to interact and expand our personal and collective boundaries to a global scale – where Marshall McLuhan's known idea of a *global village* immediately comes to mind. As McLuhan puts it, "whenever a new technology develops, it creates a new environment for the whole culture, and that environment is totally invisible" (2003: 141). By demonstrating a concern to social appropriation of such new devices, he adds that "it is the environment that changes people, not the technology" (2003: 226).

The intangible relations between physical space and what Manovich (2002) calls dataspace contribute to the existence of what can be called augmented reality, and analogously, augmented city. Or, in other words,

'Contemporary augmentation of our immediate reality, differing from such experiences in the past (based on the fact that religion, magic, metaphysics and art have always provided means for augmenting the immediate material worlds of our existence), does not depend on specific and deliberate individual or collective beliefs. Augmentation takes place everywhere and anytime, regardless of our knowledge of what is indeed happening'. (Duarte and Firmino, 2009: 545-6)

This expansion of our ability to communicate has been compared to unlimited extensions of our own bodies and boundaries. It brings new perspectives to the perception and conceptual definition of space, to what are the political, physical and cultural boundaries that define a territory – or what are the strategies to break down these boundaries – and, to the subjective appropriation of portions of the space, called places. This shift in the perceptions of space deals, at the same time, with an urban world existing at a global scale and a fragmented world of mobile and mutant places and territories with no permanent relation with their position.

We argue that three kinds of technological applications can be used to discuss the contemporary meanings of space, territory and place in a world intertwined by ICTs. Firstly, if the background for this discussion is a world where anyplace, anywhere, is potentially connected to one another, we depart from a dependence of space upon *global networks* of services, signs and infrastructure to understand these global-local spatial relations. Second, and similarly, any kind of interaction (material or immaterial) in this real time global world is based on the use, interpretation and appropriation of signs, and *surveillance technologies* have been increasingly used to codify and mediate these signified spatial interactions. Third, as cultural attachments are still important to define individuals and groups, *mobile and locative media* have a dual relationship with global and local scales, as they rely on global networks of infrastructures and signs to exist and operate at the same time they empower the emergence of local manifestations, enriching spatial idiosyncrasies and allowing the valorization of place-based values.

Before entering in the discussion of these three kinds of technological developments or appropriations (which works as the basis for the three parts of this book), it is essential to bring about the idea that serves as a conceptual ground for any other discussion presented here, which are the notions of urban world and urbanized world.

THE IDEA OF AN URBAN WORLD

The contemporary world is completely urban. The idea of an urban world could be tracked back to Henri Lefebvre (1991), when he thought about the notion of urban as a manifestation of a way of life different from anything that had happened up until the 19th Century, before the second Industrial Revolution. According to Lefebvre, urban and city become two different and yet interdependent concepts. As Evelyn Ruppert (2003: 01) wrote in her review of the English translation of Lefebvre's *The urban revolution*, "urban society is not just in the 'city,' it is in and of all of society. The urban is a 'totality', a 'global' phenomenon, shaping and influencing all of society".

In this sense, the city is an object, while urban is a phenomenon – therefore, it could be understood as a culture, a way of economic and social life. So, urban is independent of the presence of what common sense sees as "urban" objects, or the existence of a city, of a bundle of buildings and people and infrastructure set together.

Urban is something intangible and subject to different scales (more or less urban), with much room for personal, historical, ideological comprehension, but at the same time widespread, consistent and contemporary.

Therefore, the urban phenomenon is not linked to the scale of the city as an object. And scale, here, should not be understood as a question of different dimensions of specific geographical units. As Neil Brenner (2009: 63) puts, based on and discussing the works by Lefebvre and Castells of the 1970s,

'Rather than conceiving the scalar constitution of modern capitalism – its differentiation among local, regional, national, supranational, and global geographical units – as a pregiven feature of social life, such scalar configurations are now understood as produced, contested, and therefore malleable arenas and products of political-economic relations'.

While the urban is a phenomenon (not an object) that tends to be global, and multi-scalar, the city is a concrete object, territorially delimited, and which can be seen trough the concentration of buildings, roads, public and private spaces, people, conflicts, and common efforts, altogether in a relatively concentrated area. While thinking about the concept of city, Patsy Healey takes into consideration the diverse interpretations made by different agents who live, build and use cities. She also considers the "imaginative", socially constructed concepts of city, those that are "locked into cultural inheritances and institutional practices" (Healey, 2002: 1777).

As far as ICTs are concerned, they have been connecting more and more places to the spatial idea of an urban world as they turn the physical differences and boundaries of concrete places into immaterial bumps of an interconnected world where every place is linked to the principal logics that moves the world. It is not to say that everything becomes part of a homogeneous singularity, but rather that everything becomes increasingly interconnected and interdependent, without losses in the particularities and idiosyncrasies of each part of this whole.

This idea of an interconnected urban planet announces an ethic issue: since any single part of the space is considered vital to the constitution of an urban society, this society assumes rights and responsibilities over the whole space – sometimes despite the values of people who live in particular places also directly or indirectly affected by a general way of life.

Even though the idea of a world completely urban relies in a fair share of immaterial perceptions and flows, as put by Lefebvre in the 1960s, and communication technologies of the 1960s were foreshadowing what McLuhan called a global village, this phenomenon has only become possible once the space is intertwined by ICTs in a global scale. Needless to say all this happens in a mesh of global infrastructures with mobile and ephemeral connection nodes enabling the exchange and transformation of shared values.

These increasingly infiltrated technologies challenge the scales of space, the boundaries of political and economic territories, and how social groups appropriate parts of the world to turn them into their places (Duarte and Firmino, 2009).

By presenting these ideas, we are arguing that the basic conceptual trilogy of any spatial study – space, territory and place –, are challenged by ICTs. Even if the way we develop and use these technologies do not influence these three concepts individually, we believe that the way they relate to each other are fundamentally being questioned or at the very least being brought to the core of the perceptions of what we call urban space in a global level.

Space, Territory, Place

Lucrécia Ferrara (2008: 150) points out that space is usually taken as an unspecific scientific object for two reasons: or the study of space is confounded with the study of some of its specific uses (i.e., when architecture is taken as a synonymous of space); or space is considered as an inert container of social practices. In this latter perspective, the main quality of space is precisely the absence of any quality, as observed Margaret Wertheim (2000) in her history of space seen trough religion, arts and sciences – a neutral container where the natural laws, given by God, could express themselves.

More recently, space (as an abstract philosophical category) has been denounced by Lefebvre as instrumental for capital and political powers. Brenner and Elden (2009: 358) argue that "in this way, abstract space permits continuous, rational economic calculation in the spheres of production and exchange, as well as comprehensive, encompassing control in the realm of statecraft".

The hard work of defining space was a main concern in Milton Santos's work. In *A Natureza do Espaço* (The Nature of Space), Santos defines space as a combination of "systems of objects" and "systems of actions." According to Santos objects and actions are reciprocally constituents:

'Systems of objects and systems of actions maintain a perpetual interaction. On one side, systems of objects drive the way in which actions are done and, on the other side, the systems of actions lead to the creation of new objects or affect already - existing objects. That is the way space finds its dynamism and changes itself'. (Santos, 1997: 52)

Hence, space can be considered as a multiple and heterogeneous entity, which primarily means that it is not defined only by the physical and topological aspects of geographic manifestations of humans and objects, denying the geometrical and Euclidian notion of space that sees it as a singular unit, an aseptic physical container for social interactions.

According to Doreen Massey (2005: 10), "identities/entities, the relations between them, and the spatiality which is part of them are all co-constitutive" – and, therefore, the space does precede those interrelations, it is not a repository, once it is co-constitutive of them. This argument echoes Derrida's essay on the Greek concept of *khôra*, which has become an important reference for architects and geographers as the understanding of the definition of space is part of its very essence. For Derrida, *khora* – which sometimes is translated as *place*, sometimes as *receptacle* – "is anything but a support or a subject which would *give* place by receiving or by conceiving, or indeed by letting itself be conceived" (Derrida, 1995: 95). Derrida never uses an article preceding *khora*, as he wants to make clear that it does not exist in itself, opposing the simplistic idea of an existing recipient to receive things – *khora* would be co-constitutive of the things it receives, which, on the other had, would only exist when received by *khora*.

And yet, Massey complements this notion by saying that multiplicity is the characteristic of those co-constitutive interrelations and that "the 'role' of space might be characterized as providing the condition for the existence of those relations which generate time" (Massey, 2005: 56).

When space is seen together with technological aspects, for example, the false understanding of space as mere container of actions exacerbates. Cuff (2003: 44) proposes the term cyburg as a "spatially embodied computing" to oppose the dread notion of the cyberspace as a "dematerialized space". At the same time Whittaker (2002: 136-7) points to the fact that many cyberspace theorists, for instance, increasingly "remove space from being simply the geometrization of symbolic mathematics and re-situate it within structures or webs of political and economic power".

Alongside with space, two other concepts are at the heart of any spatial logic – or of what Duarte (2002) calls the spatial matrix: territory and place. Space, territory and place are conceptually irreducible – their uniqueness denies the need for any kind of simplification or synonymous.

Space is the basic concept, the basis for the others, as it is at the same time the most theoretical and abstract of them ("a combination of systems of objects and systems of actions") and the only one that can be perceived or felt without considering specific cultural characteristics, meaning that space can be bodily perceived through the feelings related to physical manifestations such as shadows, lights, textures, wind, etc[2]. Territory and place are both portions of space – and the noun *portion* is important as it is not scale-dependent, or not intrinsic to physical dimensions. A portion is a part of the whole, but this part can easily represent the whole itself.

So, territory is a portion of space embedded with organizational and mainly hierarchical rules to which any entity, person, institution and even artifacts are forced to obey (Duarte, 2002). Commonly, territory is related to a state-space, as argued by Benner and Elden (2009: 363), based on the work of Lefebvre: "territory represents a historically specific political form of (produced) space – territorial space".

In a broader definition, Kärrholm (2007: 441) puts that these portions of space or "these areas do not necessarily have to be considered by any person or group as 'their own', but are nevertheless associated to by others as pertaining to a certain function or category of users". Haesbaert (2004: 97) remembers that *territorializing* "means create spatial mediations which give us 'power' to reproduce ourselves as social groups".

Therefore we could argue that rules and certain logic of exclusion characterize the territory – nobody needs to submit himself/herself to the rules of a territory, unless there is a need or desire (or obligation) to become part of it.

Places, for Yi-Fu Tuan (1977: 04), "are center of felt values". So, we could say that place is a portion of space appropriated by any person or group as "their own", but this appropriation does not involve rules or submissions (at least not written or imposed ones). It is defined by an affective appropriation or a projection of cultural values onto a certain portion of the space. This appropriation echoes what Edward Casey (1997: 06) has written as "the assurance offered by plenitude of place. The void of no-place is avoided at almost any cost".

A place is the kingdom of commonness, where some people or groups feel culturally attached to a geographical part of the space. If territory is characterized by rules and submission, place is characterized by affection and election. But it is important to make clear that this attachment is not perennial. Massey (2995) points out that place modifies us, not because of an imagined visceral attachment, but through its practice, where different trajectories meet together in a same portion of space for a certain time.

As cultural values of individuals and groups are intrinsic to the way they perceive and conceive space, territory and place, these concepts are completely interdependent and complementary. As Doreen Massey (2005: 12) puts it, "it is simply the principle of coexisting heterogeneity. It is not the particular nature of heterogeneities but the fact of them that is intrinsic to space". However, for the purpose of this essay, in the following sections we will separate them and link them to specific manifestations of ICTs.

ICTS AND THE CONNECTIONS BETWEEN SPACE, TERRITORY AND PLACE

The implications of ICT to the constitution of contemporary society seem to be a consensus (Castells, 1989). The same thing can be assumed about space, as ICTs have an essential role to the construction and understanding of spaces in contemporary society (Graham and Marvin, 1996; Coutard, Hanley and Zimmerman, 2005; Aurigi and De Cindio, 2008), and both are important to understand the redefinition of territories in global scales or for the cultural appropriation (sometimes ephemeral) of urban spots. But probably more than ever, in terms of macro- and micro-scales, ICTs are so intertwined to all aspects of contemporary urban life, to the point that it is not possible to differentiate technologies only through their geographical scale of action. Mobile phones, for example, have had a distinguished role in strengthening social ties in poor communities, and at the same time they are part of a mesh of global networks of communication technologies.

Evidently we are not naïf to embark in the notion of an immanent homogeneous global society, where all geographical positions would have equivalent importance. In some aspects what happens is almost exactly the opposite. Global hierarchies have been changing for the last twenty years, both economically and politically; but it is also noticeable that, at the same time in history, small communities are strengthening their position in their social context. Not coincidently, both opposite movements have ICTs as a key instrument.

What we are trying to present in this introductory essay for the book is almost a methodological way of thinking the implications of ICTs for the contemporary society. What we suggest is that it is possible to design a comprehensive panorama of these social transformations analyzing how the basic spatial concepts (space, territory and place) have been altered by many aspects related to the role that increasingly miniaturized and invisible technologies play in the construction, conception, use and appropriation of urban space.

To do so, we organized the next three subsections of this chapter in pairs of technologies and spatial concepts. Once place is a portion of space appropriated by cultural values, we have chosen a personal media. Locative and mobile technologies deal with the relationship between precise locations and global communication infrastructures, and are manipulated in an individual level. So, putting together place and locative and mobile technologies will allows us to discuss how ICTs may stimulate the way individuals or groups define their places.

As already known globalization is shaped according to economic, social, cultural and political phenomena. But underneath (or above, or in-between) these phenomena, globalization is dependent on global networks of signs and technological infrastructures to propel global interconnections. Therefore, the understanding of how territories (as portions of space appropriated with certain logics and rules with specific purposes) are defined and redefined over time, might likewise help us to understand how global forces try to maintain the dynamic equilibrium of economic and political globalization. As we argued, far from promoting a homogeneous space, globalization implies in the existence of changing heterogeneities and idiosyncrasies, which may well be reflected in territorial configurations.

Finally, space, as a combination of systems of objects and systems of actions filtered by biological and cultural aspects, depends on which objects and actions are apprehended and how they are articulated. Therefore, we could say that the existence and quality of a specific spatial configuration depend directly on which elements are apprehended and coded – remembering that codes are groups of signs syntactic organized – by a certain social group. Thus, to discuss space we make use of surveillance technologies. More than video cameras, what interest us here are the coded aspects of the objects and actions that are more and more fundamental to determine their own existence. So, there are invisible aspects of objects and actions which are becoming the most prominent constituents of contemporary spaces – and surveillance technologies are designed for tracking and organize them in a coded space, making invisible flows of information visible to very specific and determined purposes.

Mobile and Locative Media: The Sense of Place

Contemporary urban spaces are permeated by a multitude of electronic images and cultural and social signs embedded in the built environment and social context in many forms. In terms of technological infrastructure, on the one hand there is a space of ubiquitous computing, consisting of "interlinked capacities for memory and data storage, for perception and environmental sensing, and for the interpretation of contexts and situations" (Phillips and Wiegerling, 2007: 05). But on the other hand there is an explosion of mobile and locative media which are now part of a technological network of signs produced and accessed globally that, at the same time, allow a precise and instant positioning within geographical places and territories which, in turn, could lead to a meaningful link with specific locations.

The main differences from current mobile and locative media to former interfaces of instant connections within global networks are mobility and the relative unimportance of specific places for connection – despite an apparent incongruence with the very idea of locative media.

Some authors call 'hybrid spaces' this imbrication of infiltrated technological infrastructures, invisible but accessible information clouds and concrete space. As Sousa e Silva (2006: 262) puts is, "hybrid spaces are mobile spaces, created by the constant movement of users who carry portable devices continuously connected to the Internet and to other users".

This double role is essential for the re-signification of urban places, at the same time precisely positioned, even in movement (as in GPS technologies), and part of a global network of cultural and social values.

Recently, artists have been proactively using locative media with the intention to explore this hybrid space using all the potential of the global networks of signs but at the same time, anchoring them geographically by emphasizing local values. Once place is a culturally-appropriated portion of space, it cannot be considered, hierarchically, a small or submissive part of an alleged global space. Place has no physical dimension. Thus, locative media allows us to play equitably with the strengths of both the global networks of technologies and signs, and the cultural values of specific places – which are ephemeral and mobile.

Therefore, mobile and locative media are also addressed as a major manifestation of urban life augmentation, in the way that this kind of technology gives us the freedom of spatial mobility and the possibility of creating and recreating places.

Global Networks and Territories

Global networks of signs, values and ideologies, are intended to break down the social and political boundaries of territories. The flows and all kinds of relations (material and immaterial) that shape spaces and societies incessantly produce signs that intentionally promote the idea of a global interconnected society – or the dream of 'anything, anytime, anywhere'. But as Neil Smith (2005: 894) puts it, "it would indeed be nice if the world were flat and non-hierarchical. (...) But it is precisely the self-serving trick of neo-liberalism to assume that such a flat world is already here, hierarchy is gone, equality rules".

Indeed, the signs of an alleged global identity tend to disseminate a set of rules, beliefs, and technologies which are the support and conditions for the very existence of what can be recognized as a global world. Those global flows of signs are dependent, though, of a set of dense and interconnected infrastructures which work globally, from the telegraph to the internet. The illusion of a purposeless set of signs and values disseminated by the globalization finds a counterpart in a mostly necessary global infrastructure, named by Matt Ratto (2007: 21) as a 'seamless' infrastructure, which "emphasizes the erasure of the marks and boundaries between separate systems thereby creating an infrastructure whose individual parts blend transparently – without seams". The author makes clear that the seamless infrastructure can be positive when opening up access to technologies to non-experts; but he also argue that the abolition of seams is intended to avoid points of criticism or conflict.

Therefore, the challenge is to discuss both the roles of the global flows of information, social and cultural values, and the infrastructures which have been built as a global technological network to sustain such flows. The challenge is also in the unveiling – not necessarily to condemning beforehand – the seamless infrastructures that make this global network of material and immaterial facts and artifacts.

In this sense, studies produced by the Globalization and World Cities Research Network (GaWC) are seam-trackers and map-makers of the global systems and technological infrastructures that connects distant and close territories through the logics of a global interconnected economic networks. Putting in evidence the flights and airports hierarchies, the routes and hubs information dynamics, this research group claims its studies can help measuring global networks. This was already a concern to David Lyon (1997) in the first GaWC bulletin, when he argued that "world cities are the geographical entity that appear as the organizing nodes of world wide networks" and tried to collect data and design an empirical map for this organized world cities network. Yet, more recently, Devriendt, Boulton, Brunn, Derudder and Witlox have pointed out that "in a knowledge economy, there exists a need to apprehend the informational interconnections between cities of the world in ways that take into account the real-time and continuous production of urban places", and, with it, have tried to map the flows of information, based on the Google search engine, to show that information both reinforce some world cities hierarchies and overlap political and administrative territorial boundaries.

Surveillance: Hidden Dimensions of Space

According to Murakami Wood e Graham (2006), surveillance studies are part of a multidisciplinary field of Social Sciences which considerably neglects spatial issues in general. These studies have grown stronger with notorious works by Foucault, in Discipline and Punish (1977), which concentrates a great number of works that supports his theories about the panopticon. Although this has been derived from the spatial or architectural design of prisons by the English social theorist Jeremy Bentham in the 18th Century, Foucault and many other scholars after him were enthusiastic about the punitive and disciplinary systems involved in the idea of the panopticon rather than its spatial implications. This is not to say that Foucault's only preoccupation and major issue was the panopticon. In fact, he uses a great number of examples and issues relating architecture and city planning in order to link his evidences and to build his arguments about the inherently disciplinary characteristics of modern societies.

This vision of Foucault's works which goes beyond his ideas of the panopticon as an architectural and technological representation of power is a crucial approach to understand the notion of a surveillance society, and is well explored by Murakami Wood (2007) in Beyond the Panopticon:

Foucault and Surveillance Studies. Unfortunately there is no space in this paper to thoroughly assess and discuss the real implications of Foucault's works to the understanding of what now has been called the surveillance society, or as Murakami Wood argues, the different nuances of surveillance societies. In any way there is an essential difference between what has been explored by Foucault and what has been observed in present days in terms of the very meaning of surveillance.

The omnipresence of surveillance technologies in contemporary world has also its geopolitical basis on 9/11, almost as a landmark and definitely as a turning point. As mentioned by Zigmunt Bauman,

"les événements du 11 septembre ont souligné le fait que personne ne peut plus s'isoler du reste du monde. L'anéantissement de la capacité protectrice de l'espace est une arme à double tranchant: personne ne peut se cacher des coups adverses, et ceux-ci peuvent être planifiés de n'importe quelle distance" (Bauman, 2002: 60).

Empowered by a very large number of technologies more and more ubiquitous, invisible and small, nowadays surveillance has a decentralized, infiltrated and wide-spread nature, instead of the panopticon's original centralized surveillance perpetrated by Orwellian totalitarian (big brother like) State.

Boosted by ICTs, surveillance technologies are increasingly invisible and melted into the built space, and the material forms that sustain our current urban way of life. Thus, we can say that surveillance has become an intrinsic part of the space, and as such, it tends to make visible the invisible and immaterial components of places and territories. In other words, to rationalize the many flows of people, places, objects and actions for the sake of surveillance, these technologies organize information, bits and bytes for specific purposes, unifying and giving visibility to what was spread and intangible.

Therefore, there are at least two important characteristics of surveillance in relation to the discussions of space, place and territory, being its simultaneous antagonistic capability of disembodiment and materialization. These characteristics can also be understood as two different moments of the relationship between surveillance and space.

The first moment concerns the machinist manner in which surveillance systems turns persons and histories in numbers and codes of databases as part of various types of identification systems, which by definition are related to social sorting schemes (Lyon, 2009), used to point out who is eligible, who has access, who may claim or who is a suspect in the disperse and ever wary 'eyes' of the city. This divorce between identity and identification promoted by surveillance technologies can be illustrated by what happens to ants when scientists sprayed them with a pheromone that makes them smell dead to other ants – even though they are alive, they cannot communicate this effectively and keep being removed from the colony. In this case we have at once the immaterial codes that represent dead ants attached to the live bodies of real ants.

In a second moment, if some attention is paid to surveillance practices – assumed here as forms of objective and systematic attention to personal details for the purpose of generating influence, manipulation or control, as outlined by David Lyon (2001) –, one can say that while working in the rationalization of data through the sorting of many different kinds of information and immaterial flows captured and organized by devices programmed with surveilling functions, surveillance technologies are giving visibility to many of the invisible and intangible aspects of the contemporary augmented space, and also relating these information to people, facts and artifacts in places and territories.

'While many analysts focus on the fast-moving, fragmented, and disembodied aspects of contem-

porary cultures it is worth noting that those most affected by mobile technologies… use them in relation to very mundane aspects of life. Indeed, email addresses and phone numbers constitute fixed coordinates for relationships within the apparently blurred world of motion'. (Lyon, 2006: 210)

Therefore, what we are arguing is that, although it has been around for centuries, surveillance systems, technologies and practices have been empowered by ICTs and, as such, they represent clear manifestations of the ambiguous hybrid characteristics of space and technology in the contemporary urban world. Visible and invisible technologies and actions have been used in what can also be defined as spatial augmentation.

CONCLUSION

ICTs have a quick obsolescence. Nevertheless, their social and historical construction and implications to our life style change the concepts and experiences of urban spaces. In this sense, what we had tried here was to focus on how the influence of an emerging global urban infrastructure based on ICTs could enlighten and bring some ideas about the paradigmatic challenges upon space, the boundaries of political and economic territories, and how social groups appropriate parts of the world to turn them into their places.

The arguments that contemporary space is homogeneous because of globalization and its interdependent infrastructures, and that places are spots of cultural resistance are, at the very least, naïve. Doreen Massey (2007: 16) argues that "the idea that the local is a product of the global has become common currency (and this is indeed one aspect of what must be addressed) but it is less often recognized that the global is also, conversely, locally produced".

In this essayistic approach, we have used the examples of three kinds of technological manifestations – mobile and locative media, global networks and surveillance practices – to point out some of the ways in which ICTs are producing complex conflicts between traditional and new paradigms of space, territory and place, and creating some conceptual dilemmas for an integrative development of infrastructural technologies and cities. Therefore, what we have argued is that, although it has been around for centuries, the mechanisms for augmenting our spatial relations have been empowered by ICTs and, as such, they represent clear manifestations of the ambiguous hybrid characteristics of space and technology in the contemporary urban world. Visible and invisible technologies and actions as well as their intrinsic relations with the manifestations of space through territories and places (more evidently displayed in locative media, global networks and surveillance practices), have clear implications to the way we experience or think through the construction/production of space in the contemporary augmented urban world.

REFERENCES

Aurigi, A., & De Cindio, F. (Eds.). (2008). *Augmented urban spaces*. Hampshire, UK: Ashgate.

Bauman, Z. (2002). L'Etat face à la demande de sécurité. *Esprit (Paris, France)*, (décembre): 59–69.

Brenner, N. (2009). Restructuring, Rescaling, and the Urban Question. *Critical Planning, 16*(Summer), 61–79.

Brenner, N., & Elden, S. (2009). Henri Lefebvre on State, Space, Territory. *International Political Sociology, 3*, 353–377. doi:10.1111/j.1749-5687.2009.00081.x

Casey, E. (1997). *The fate of place*. Berkeley, CA: University of California.

Castells, M. (1989). *The Informational City: Information Technology, Economic Restructuring, and the Urban-Regional Process*. Oxford, UK: Blackwell.

Coutard, O., Hanley, R., & Zimmerman, R. (Eds.). (2005). *Sustaining urban networks*. New York: Routledge.

Cuff, D. (2003). Immanent Domain Pervasive Computing and the Public Realm. *Journal of Architectural Education, 57*(1), 43–49. doi:10.1162/104648803322336575

Derrida, J. (1995). *On the name*. Standord, CA: Stanford University.

Devriendt, L., Boulton, A., Brunn, S., Derudder, B., & Witlox, F. (2009). *Major Cities in the Information World: Monitoring Cyberspace in Real-Time*. GaWC Research Bulletin 308. Retrieved from www.lboro.ac.uk/gawc/rb/rb308.html

Duarte, F. (2002). *Crise das matrizes espaciais*. São Paulo, Brazil: Perspectiva.

Duarte, F., & Firmino, R. (2009). Infiltrated city, augmented space: information and communication technologies, and representations of contemporary spatialities. *Journal of Architecture, 14*, 545–565. doi:10.1080/13602360903187493

Ferrara, L. (2008). *Comunicação, espaço, cultura*. São Paulo, Brazil: Annablume.

Firmino, R. (2003). "Not Just a Portal" - Virtual Cities as a Complex Sociotechnical Phenomenon. *Journal of Urban Technology, 10*(2).

Foucault, M. (1977). *Discipline and Punish: The Birth of the Prison*. Harmondsworth, UK: Penguin.

Graham, S., & Marvin, S. (1996). *Telecommunications and the city*. New York: Routledge. doi:10.4324/9780203430453

Healey, P. (2002). On creating the city as a collective resource. *Urban Studies (Edinburgh, Scotland), 39*(10), 1777–1792. doi:10.1080/0042098022000002957

Kärrholm, M. (2007). The Materiality of Territorial Production: A Conceptual Discussion of Territoriality, Materiality, and the Everyday Life of Public Space. *Space and Culture, 10*(4), 437–453. doi:10.1177/1206331207304356

Lefebvre, H. (1991). *The Production of Space*. London: Blackwell.

Lyon, D. (2001). *Surveillance Society: Monitoring Everyday Life*. Buckingham, UK: Open University Press.

Lyon, D. (2006). Why where you are matters: Mundane mobilities, transparent technologies, and digital discrimination. In Monahan, T. (Ed.), *Surveillance and Security: Technological Politics and Power in Everyday Life* (pp. 209–224). New York: Routledge.

Lyon, D. (2009). *Identifying Citizens: ID Cards as Surveillance*. Cambridge, UK: Polity Press.

Manovich, L. (2002). The Poetics of Augmented Space. In Everett, A., & Caldwell, J. (Eds.), *Digitextuality*. London: Routledge.

Massey, D. (2005). *For Space*. London: Sage.

Massey, D. (2007). *World City*. London: Polity Press.

McLuhan, M. (2003). *Undestanding me. Lectures and interviews*. Cambridge, MA: MIT.

Moss, M., & Townsend, A. (2000). How Telecommunications Systems Are Transforming Urban Spaces. In Wheeler, J., Aoyama, Y., & Warf, B. (Eds.), *Cities in the Telecommunications Age: The Fracturing of Geographies* (pp. 31–41). London: Routledge.

Murakami Wood, D., & Graham, S. (2006). Permeable Boundaries in the Software-sorted Society: Surveillance and the Differentiation of Mobility. In Sheller, M., & Urry, J. (Eds.), *Mobile Technologies of the City* (pp. 177–191). London: Routledge.

Phillips, D. & Wiegerling, K. (2007). Introduction to IRIE Vol. 8. *International Review of Information Ethics, 8*(12/2007), 5-6.

Ruppert, E. (2003). Book review: Henri Lefebvre. The Urban Revolution. *Canadian Journal of Sociology*, (September-October), 1-3. Retrieved from www.arts.ualberta.ca/cjscopy/reviews/urbanrev.html

Santos, M. (1997). *A Natureza do Espaço: Técnica e Tempo, Razão e Emoção. São Paulo*. Brazil: Hucitec.

Smith, N. (2005). Neo-Critical Geography, or, the Flat Pluralist World of Business Class. *Antipode, 37*(5), 853–1094. doi:10.1111/j.0066-4812.2005.00538.x

Sousa e Silva, A. (2006). From Cyber to Hybrid: Mobile Technologies as Interfaces of Hybrid Spaces. *Space and Culture, 9*, 261–278. doi:10.1177/1206331206289022

Taylor, P. (1997). Hierarchical tendencies amongst world cities: a global research proposal. *Cities (London, England), 14*(6), 323–332. doi:10.1016/S0264-2751(97)00023-1

Tuan, Y. (1977). *Space and place*. Minneapolis, MN: University of Minnesota.

Wertheim, M. Pearly (2000). *Gates of Cyberspace: A History of Space from Dante to the Internet*. New York: W.W. Norton & Company.

Whittaker, J. (2002). *The Internet: The Basics*. London: Routledge.

ADDITIONAL READING

Batten, D. (1995). Networked Cities: Creative Urban Agglomerations for the 21st Century. *Urban Studies (Edinburgh, Scotland), 32*(2), 313–327. doi:10.1080/00420989550013103

Beaverstock, J. V., Derudder, B., Faulconbridge, J., & Witlox, F. (Eds.). (2010). *International business travel in the global economy*. Farnham: Ashgate.

Bruno, F. (2006). *Dispositivos de vigilância no ciberespaço: duplos digitais e identidades simuladas. Revista fronteira* (*Vol. VIII*, pp. 152–159). São Leopoldo/RS.

Castells, M., Fernandez-Ardevol, M., Qiu, J., & Sey, A. (2009). *Mobile Communication and Society: A Global Perspective*. Cambridge: MIT.

Deleuze, G. (1992). *Postscript on the societies of control*, October, 59, pp.3-7.

Drewe, P. (1998). *The Network City: How to Deal with It in Spatial Planning* (p. 16). Durham: Mimeo.

Foth, M. (Ed.). (2009). *Urban Informatics: The Practice and Promise of the Real-Time City*. Hershey: IGI Global.

Graham, S. (Ed.). (2004). *The cybercities reader*. New York: Routledge.

Graham, S., & Marvin, S. (2001). *Splintering Urbanism: Networked Infrastructures, Technological Mobilities and the Urban Condition*. New York: Routledge. doi:10.4324/9780203452202

Hall, P., & Pain, K. (Eds.). (2006). *The polycentric metropolis: Learning from mega-city regions in Europe*. London: Earthscan.

Kanashiro, M. M. (2008). Surveillance cameras in Brazil: exclusion, mobility regulation, and the new meanings of security. *Surveillance & Society, 5*, 270–289.

Kidd, T., & Chen, I. (2008). *Social Information Technology: Connecting Society and Cultural Issues*. Hershey: IGI Global.

Lianos, M. (2003). After Foucault (Trans. D. Wood). *Surveillance & Society*, *1*, 412–430.

Lyon, D. (2003). *Surveillance after September 11th*. Cambridge: Polity Press.

Lyon, D. (Ed.). (2003). *Surveillance as Social Sorting: Privacy, Risk and Automated Discrimination*. London: Routledge.

Marx, G. T. (1998). *Undercover*. Berkeley: University of California Press.

Marx, G. T. (2003). What's new about the 'new surveillance'? Classifying for change and continuity. *Surveillance & Society*, *1*, 9–29.

McLuhan, M. (1994). *Understanding Media: The Extensions of Man*. Cambridge, US: MIT.

Mostefaoui, S., Maamar, Z., & Giaglis, G. (2008). *Advances in Ubiquitous Computing: Future Paradigms and Directions*. Hershey: IGI Global.

Mulder, A. (2004). *Understanding Media Theory*. Rotterdam: V2.

Nusselder, A. (2009). *Interface Fantasy: A Lacanian Cyborg Ontology*. Cambridge: MIT.

Painter, J. (2001). *The Aterritorial City: Diversity, Spatiality, Democratization* (p. 47). Durham: Mimeo.

Ratto, M. (2007). Ethics of Seamless infrastructures: Resources and Future Directions. *International Review of Information Ethics*, 8 (12/2007), pp. 20-27.

Santos, M. (1985). *Espaço e Método*. São Paulo: Nobel.

Smith, N. (1996). *The New Urban Frontier: Gentrification and the Revanchist City*. New York: Routledge.

Smith, N. (2002). New Globalism, New Urbanism: Gentrification as Global Urban Strategy. *Antipode*, *34*(3), 427–450. doi:10.1111/1467-8330.00249

Spuybroek, L. (2008). *The Architecture of Continuity*. Rotterdam: V2.

Wood, A. (2009). *City Ubiquitous: Place, Communication, and the Rise of Omnitopia*. Creskill: Hampton Press Communication.

ENDNOTES

1 A short version of this text has been published on the *International Review of Information Ethics*, vol. 12, 2010.

2 It does not mean that the idea and perception of space do not change along history. In fact, its theoretical and perceptual transformations are the very basis of our arguments in this text. And also, we are not assuming the possibility of a sterile space without cultural or social characteristics. Our argument is based on the fact that the very definitions of territory and place depend on cultural, political and social aspects that designate the nature of these two concepts. On the other hand, however, although these cultural "filters" are important to understand the real meaningfulness of space, they are not necessary to perceive the limits of space.

Section 1
Global Networks

Chapter 2
Measuring the World City Network:
New Results and Developments

Peter J. Taylor
Northumbria University, UK[1]

ABSTRACT

Measuring the world city network is achieved by careful specification of a network model plus customised data collection to operationalize the model. The resulting interlocking network is described as advanced producer service firms in the role of city network-makers through their routine work across multiple offices. The basic measurement derived is the network connectivity of a city; this describes how well that city is integrated into the world city network. Selected results from the latest data collection (2008 – 175 firms, 526 cities) are presented with leading ('alpha') cities divided into connectivity strata. It is shown that compared to previous analyses in 2000 and 2004, the upper echelons of the world city network are becoming more and more integrated.

LISTS, RANKINGS, HIERARCHIES AND CITIES

We live in an age of 'list-mania'; there is so much information available that ordering selected topics has become popular entertainment. And so it is with cities, there are numerous rankings of cities available in both the commercial and academic spheres. People are interested in where their city ranks and this can be fun. Some years ago my city, Newcastle, was ranked above Rio as a 'world party city'; it made headlines in the local press. But beyond boosterism there has been a genuine concern for cities as business centres in a rapidly globalizing world economy. GaWC, with its measures of network connectivity, has contributed to this situation with its rankings of the importance of cities in the world city network. In fact, it appears that it is these rankings that most people want from GaWC. But there is a basic sense in which concern for city rankings operates against the spirit of the GaWC project. (Taylor, 2004)

City rankings fit into the approach to inter-city relations that emphasizes competition between

DOI: 10.4018/978-1-60960-051-8.ch002

cities. This is in keeping with the long-term, conventional theoretical approach to inter-city relations that described 'national urban systems' in each of which exists a 'national city hierarchy' broadly conforming to classical central place theory. The intellectual power of this theoretical framework can be appreciated through the fact that 'city hierarchies' appear almost natural (Taylor, 2009) – how else would cities relate to each other except through hierarchies? From this position ambitious cities are expected to 'climb the hierarchy' at the expense of rival cities. But there is an alternative position. I think that inter-city relations are inherently cooperative; cities exist in city networks and networks can only exist through collective complementarities (Powell, 1990; Thompson, 2003). Cities need one another; they grow through relations with one another, not by eliminating one another in a world of city competition. Thus one of GaWC's aims has been to reposition research on inter-city relations from the easy seduction of hierarchies to the complex subtleties of networks.

Of course, in practice, inter-city relations are both cooperative and competitive; it is a matter of where to begin. At GaWC we start with network so that we measure a 'world city network with hierarchical tendencies' (Taylor 2004). We treat network relations as generic to cities and hierarchical relations as contingent: city competitiveness varies in space and time with competitive relations being stronger locally and in cyclical downturns. Returning to theory, our starting point is the specification of a world city network to replace hierarchical theory in its various forms (Taylor et al 2010a).

THE INTERLOCKING NETWORK MODEL

Networks are relatively easy to understand. They usually consist of two layers, the net level and the node level. For instance, in a social network analysis of a gang, members are nodes, the gang is the net level and relations between the nodes (members) define the nature of the network. Formal city government associations work in this way with the cities (members) as nodes, the city association represents the net level, and the formal relations between members within the association define the network. Such networks can be an important component of global governance but this is not how cities operate as key components of the global economy. In the latter, it is advanced producer service firms that are the network makers; they create the world city network through their everyday practices linking offices across the world. This defines a different type of network, an interlocking network (Knoke & Kuklinski, 1982).

An interlocking network is unusual in having three layers. In the case of the world city network there is the net level of the global economy, the node level of cities, and an additional sub-nodal level of service firms. The latter are not just an additional level, they define the critical level: this is where the agents of network formation are found. In the global economy, it is firms who are the network makers not the cities themselves. Thus for studying the world city network it is service firms that are investigated in order to understand the city network as the outcome. In other words, it is through studying the locational strategies of firms that it is possible to describe and analyse the world city network: firms are the object of the research, cities are the subject of the research.

Why focus on these service firms? In the 1970s two separate industries, computers and communications, merged their technologies to enable work to be coordinated worldwide based upon simultaneous connections. Early on Sassen (1994) spotted two contrasting economic geography effects: first, a dispersal of production to cheaper labour locales, and second, a contrary trend towards concentration of management and business service industries. The latter were required to organize the new worldwide production and were concentrated in cities. As Sassen

(1991) originally argued, it is this concentration of management alongside financial, professional and creative services that characterises contemporary 'global cities'. Of course, service firms have always clustered in cities to provide such services to their clients but under conditions of contemporary globalization those specialised services became worldwide with fundamental implications for work practices. Firms need a multiple office policy across many cities to provide a seamless service to protect global brand integrity by keeping all work in-house.

This is how it came to be that from the 1980s onwards there have been hundreds of large service firms with trans-national office networks, many of them global in scope. Each firm had its own locational strategy – which cities to have offices in, what size and functions those offices will be, and how the offices will be organised. It is the work done in these offices that 'interlock' various cities in projects that require multiple office inputs. Thus the inter-city relations in these servicing practices are numerous electronic communications – information, instruction, advice, planning, interpretation, strategy, knowledge, etc., some tele-conferencing as required, and probably travel for face-to-face meetings at a minimum for the beginning and end of a given project. These are the working flows that combined across numerous projects in many firms to constitute the world city network (Taylor 2001, 2004).

So we have to study service firms to describe and analyse the world city network but, unfortunately, there is no feasible way that data could be collected from firms on these working flows. As well as the obvious confidentiality issues with competing private firms, there is also a feasibility issue: the degree of research collaboration that would be needed from a large number of firms makes such a data collection exercise beyond reasonable social science research logistics. However, this is not a particularly rare situation in measurement practices: where direct measures cannot be obtained, there is the fall back position of carrying out indirect measurement. This requires access to more easily available data plus credible assumptions about how the firms operate.

As mentioned previously, service firms offer a seamless service across their office networks. This means that the geographical distribution of their offices, and their scope and range, are important selling points in attracting new clients. Hence such information is commonly available on service firms' web sites. This has been the main source of data for measuring the world city network: for each firm, offices are assessed individually by asking what is the importance of this office in this city within the firm's overall office network? Answers to this question are termed the service value of a city to a firm. These values are coded and become the quantitative input into the study: the coding ranges from 0 (a firm having no office in a city) to 5 (a city housing the headquarters of a firm); standard or typical offices of a firm score 2, minor and major offices 1 and 3, respectively, leaving 4 for scoring cities housing exceptionally important offices such as regional headquarters. The credible assumption that is made is that the more important an office the more working flows it will generate. Therefore two important offices will generate a much higher level of flow between their respective cities than two minor offices between their respective cities. These data and this assumption are combined to generate estimates of inter-office working flow levels between cities for each firm; they are not actual working flows, but potential working flows, indirect measures derived from the data and the model assumptions. Aggregating all potential working flows for all firms located in a city generates estimates of its working flow relations with other cities; when this is done for all cities it constitutes the world city network.

Network connectivity is the main measure of importance of a city in this model (Taylor, 2001). It is computed from the products of service values for the city with each other city for all firms. Thus assuming m advanced producer service firms and

n cities we can define a service value for firm j in city i as v_{ij}. The basic relational unit of measurement is given by

$$r_{ab,j} = v_{aj} \cdot v_{bj} \tag{1}$$

which defines the relation between cities a and b in terms of firm j. This is an elemental interlock between two cities for one firm. The aggregate cities interlock between the cities is then given by

$$r_{ab} = \sum_{j} r_{abj} \tag{2}$$

For each city there are n-1 such interlocks and the network connectivity for a city is given by

$$C_a = \sum_{i} r_{ai} \quad \text{where } a \neq i \tag{3}$$

where C_a is the network connectivity of city a. This relates city a to all other cities within the network through its firms and measures the degree of integration of the city into the world city network.

This data collection and analysis exercise was carried out in 2000 utilizing 100 office networks of 'global service firms' in accountancy, advertising, banking/finance, insurance, law, and management consultancy (Taylor et al., 2002). Such firms were defined by having offices in 15 different cities or more including at least one office in each of the three main globalization arenas – northern America (USA plus Canada), western Europe, and Asia Pacific. Otherwise the firms were chosen pragmatically in terms of the quality of information on their websites, an important consideration given our research resources. Offices were traced across 315 cities worldwide. The result was a 315 cities x 100 firms matrix of 31,500 service values. Each column represents the locational strategy of a firm; each row represents the service mix of a city.

This exercise was repeated in 2004 (Taylor & Aranya 2008). However, because of corporate reorganizations and other changes, direct comparisons could only be made with 80 of the original 100 firms. The resulting 315 x 80 matrix of 25,200 service values was still deemed large enough to produce credible results. But this attrition of the original "GaWC 100" firms by a fifth made continuation of this approach problematic. Thus a revision in firm selection for the 2008 data collection was instituted.

THE REVISED, IMPROVED 2008 DATA COLLECTION

Collaboration between the Global Urban Competitiveness Project (GUCP) at the Chinese Academy of Social Sciences (CASS) and GaWC researchers at Loughborough and Ghent Universities made possible a much larger and complete data collection of advanced producer service firms. In order to put the data collection on a sustainable future trajectory, firms were simply chosen by their size not where there offices are located or the quality of their websites. For four of the previously studied services – accountancy, advertising, law and management consultancy – we included the top 25 firms. We combined banking/finance with insurance to define a financial services category and included the top 75 firms. Thus the number of firms was increased from 100/80 to 175. More important, this number will be retained in future data collection. Thus any future change recorded will be the result of both changes by individual firms and by firms entering and leaving the top 25/75 of the service sectors.

In addition we carried out a thorough review of cities and added many new cities from emerging markets to create a list of 525. The coding remained the same: CASS carried out the major data collection exercise between January and May 2008; the data were checked at Ghent University. The end result is a 525 cities x 175 firms matrix of 91,875 service values. These are the data used to produce the new results reported below. For a comprehensive analyses of these data, see Taylor et al (2010b).

A Digression: Return of Alpha, Beta, Gamma World Cities

When we first embarked on the GaWC project, we carried out a study of how London was connected to other world cities through its advanced producer service firms. As a starting point we needed a roster of 'other world cities' to begin our measurements of London's links. For this exercise we used a basic Adansonian taxonomy approach that eschews theoretical presumptions and just aggregates available empirical evidence, in this case presence of advanced producer service firms in cities (Beaverstock et al 1999). Simply summing city attributes allowed us to define world cities and categorise them into three levels: alpha, beta and gamma. To our continuing embarrassment, this very early work remains by far our most cited and quoted research output. That there was a demand for a roster of world cities in this research and policy community there can be no doubt, but this simple piece of crude empiricism was most certainly not the answer required.

It was only subsequent to this initial work that we specified the world city network as an interlocking network and derived measures of network connectivity to indicate how well a city was integrated into the network through its service firms. The resulting city connectivities are relational measures, the correct way of measuring the importance of cities in a network.

However, try as we may to forget or at least ignore our most cited paper, a decade later requests and queries continue to come in about alpha, beta and gamma world cities. We have decided to go with the flow and return to these categories but to treat them as levels of integration within the world city network. This means using the network connectivity results and recasting them as general categories. One advantage of this is that it eschews the individual ranking of cities and provides only ordinal classes. This is more in keeping with our 'network with hierarchical tendencies' position and is probably more in keeping with the degree of robustness in our aggregative measurements.

RESULTS: ALPHA CITIES IN THE WORLD CITY NETWORK, 2008

Not wanting to over-burden you with too many cities, I will keep the reporting of results to just the alpha cities. In addition I will compare the 2008 results with those for 2000 and 2004. Although the basis of firm selection has changed, I think comparing the results remains interesting and reflects genuine changes in the world city network.

Table 1 lists all alpha level cities identified in 2000, 2004 and 2008. The following empirical points are noteworthy:

1. London and New York define a duopoly that constitutes a case apart – 'NYLON' is the global cities dyad *par excellence*.
2. Hong Kong is consistently number 3 (NOT Tokyo) and is definitely gaining in importance and approaching the alpha++ level – if current trends continue, it is likely that the world city network will be dominated by a global cities triad – NYLOHK - in the very near future
3. The alpha ++/+ levels are over-represented by western Pacific Rim cities (50% in 2000 & 2004), a pattern strongly accentuated in 2008 by the rapid elevation of Sydney, Shanghai and Beijing (THIS IS THE KEY FINDING OF 2008)
4. Excepting New York, US cities are very distinctive in their positioning in the world city network: possibly under-represented with only 6 alpha cities in 2000, Miami and Atlanta drop out in 2004, and San Francisco is missing from the 2008 list. This leaves the US with just three alpha cities, New York plus Chicago and Los Angles, the latter hanging

Table 1. Alpha cities: 2000, 2004 & 2008

ALPHA++	**London**	**London**	**London**
	New York	**New York**	**New York**
ALPHA+	Hong Kong	Hong Kong	Hong Kong
	Paris	Paris	Paris
	Tokyo	Tokyo	Singapore
	Singapore	Singapore	Tokyo
			Sydney Milan
			Beijing
			Shanghai
ALPHA	Chicago	Toronto	Madrid
	Milan	Chicago	Moscow
	Los Angeles	Madrid	Seoul
	Toronto	Frankfurt	Toronto
	Madrid	Milan	Brussels
	Amsterdam	Amsterdam	Buenos Aires
	Sydney	Brussels	Mumbai
	Frankfurt	Sao Paulo	Kuala Lumpur
	Brussels	Los Angeles	Chicago
	Sao Paulo	Zurich	
	San Francisco	Sydney	
ALPHA-	Mexico City	Mexico City	Warsaw
	Zurich	Kuala Lumpur	Sao Paulo
	Taipei	Buenos Aires	Zurich
	Mumbai	San Francisco	Amsterdam
	Jakarta	Beijing	Mexico City
	Buenos Aires	Shanghai	Jakarta
	Melbourne	Seoul	Dublin
	Miami	Taipei	Bangkok
	Kuala Lumpur	Melbourne	Taipei
	Stockholm	Bangkok	Istanbul
	Bangkok	Jakarta	Rome
	Prague	Dublin	Lisbon
	Dublin	Munich	Frankfurt
	Shanghai	Warsaw	Stockholm
	Barcelona	Stockholm	Prague
	Atlanta	Mumbai	Vienna
		Miami	Budapest
		Budapest	Athens
			Caracas
			Los Angeles
			Auckland
			Santiago

Table 2. Average connectivities by alpha city levels

	2000	2004	2008
ALPHA++	0.988	0.992	0.998
ALPHA+	0.686	0.699	0.734
ALPHA	0.577	0.548	0.617
ALPHA-	0.455	0.446	0.513

on as a lowly alpha- city. I will return to this surprising result below.

5. The rise of cities from 'emerging markets' is very clear – in the plain alpha category they were represented only by Sao Paulo in 2000 and 2004 but despite this level reducing in number of cities, Seoul, Moscow, Mumbai, Buenos Aires and Kuala Lumpur have joined to constitute the majority of plain alpha cities in 2008.
6. The emerging cities' rise from 2004 to 2008 is largely at the expense of leading western European cities: Amsterdam, Frankfurt and Zurich move down to alpha- level. However, Madrid and Brussels consolidate their alpha level status, and Milan rises to alpha+.
7. In the ex-COMECON countries of eastern Europe whose economic privatizations in the 1990s led to their services-led integration into the world economy, Warsaw appears to be leading city by 2008; Berlin through its absence from the lists confirms the failure of its bid to become a major world city (see Kratke 2000)
8. Finally, the cities with relatively stable trajectories not mentioned so far should not be ignored: Paris and Singapore stay alpha+, Toronto remains alpha, and Mexico City, Taipei, Jakarta, Stockholm, Bangkok, and Dublin are alpha- cities in all three lists.

To aid in interpreting these results, I have provided average network connectivity scores in Table 2 for the different alpha levels. The connectivities are computed as proportions of the highest city connectivity (i.e. London's). The important point to make about this table is that 2008 averages are higher for all four levels. Thus, even though the alpha+ level is increased by four cities, this does not dilute the average; rather the new cities bolster the average. This indicates that globalization of services has been a dynamic process of growing bigger offices in many cities while extending office networks to new cities. The result has been an expanding and increasing integrated world city network. In these circumstances, cities with long established service offices in western Europe and the USA will decline relatively (standing still) while the rest of the world catches up.

But the USA is a special case with its cities being reported as under-represented in the world city network in 2000 (Taylor, 2004; Taylor & Lang, 2004) and 2004 (Taylor & Aranya, 2008). The 2008 results continue and perhaps accentuate this trend (Derudder et al., 2010). This appears to be a result of the US home market for advanced producer services being far greater than for any other country. This has two key effects. First, foreign firms find it hard to penetrate the market and often choose to represent clients through just a New York office. Second, US service firms have less reason to gamble on global expansion – compare a Chicago management consultancy company with an Amsterdam company, the former can make better profits through domestic expansion, the former can only expand in a big way through new cross-border work. Both effects lead to a tendency for US cities other than New York being less integrated in the world city network than might be expected.

Finally the all-important caveat: the GaWC method of measuring the world city network produces theoretically informed, empirically robust assessments of cities in globalization. But it measures just one process in city development: the servicing of global capital. As shown, London and New York are the supreme archetypal cities in this regard. But, as we have also seen, the failure of Berlin has shown that the world city network can never be a collection of mini-Londons and little New Yorks. All world cities will have mixtures of cutting edge economic functions but these need not just be advanced producer services. The key is to find economic niches but without being vulnerable to economic specialization (Turok, 2009). Milan and its design portfolio, Singapore and its logistics portfolio, Los Angeles and its entertainment portfolio and, outside the alpha cities, Houston and its energy portfolio, are each important examples of important world cities despite their contrasting positions in the world city network (Taylor, 2005). However, whatever the niches, cities WILL need to have a sufficiency of advanced producer services so as not to make them too overtly dependent on London, New York and their rare ilk. Thus within the world city network as conceptualised by GaWC, there will be 'global cities' in the original sense of Sassen (1991) focusing on advanced producer services, as well as numerous other cities with varying sufficiency in advanced producer services. GaWC network connectivities and the resulting levels of integration into the world city network represent just one process, albeit especially global in scope, among many that constitute contemporary cities in globalization.

REFERENCES

Beaverstock, J. V., Smith, R. G., & Taylor, P. J. (1999). A roster of world cities. *Cities (London, England)*, *16*, 445–458. doi:10.1016/S0264-2751(99)00042-6

Derudder, B., Taylor, P. J., Ni, P., De Vos, A., Hoyler, M., & Hanssens, H. (2010). Pathways of growth and Decline: connectivity changes in the world city network, 2000-2008. *Urban Studies (Edinburgh, Scotland)*, 47.

Knoke, D., & Kuklinski, J. H. (1982). *Network Analysis*. Beverly Hills, CA: Sage.

Kratke, S. (2000). Berlin: the metropolis as a production space. *European Planning Studies*, *8*, 7–27. doi:10.1080/096543100110901

Powell, W. W. (1990). Neither market nor hierarchy: network forms of organization. *Research in Organizational Behavior*, *12*, 295–336.

Sassen, S. (1991). *The Global City*. Princeton, NJ: Princeton University Press.

Sassen, S. (1994). *Cities in a World Economy*. Thousand Oaks, CA: Pine Forge.

Taylor, P. J. (2001). Specification of the world city network. *Geographical Analysis*, *33*, 181–194. doi:10.1111/j.1538-4632.2001.tb00443.x

Taylor, P. J. (2004). *World City Network: a Global Urban Analysis*. London: Routledge.

Taylor, P. J. (2005). Leading world cities: empirical evaluations of urban nodes in multiple networks. *Urban Studies (Edinburgh, Scotland)*, *42*, 1593–1608. doi:10.1080/00420980500185504

Taylor, P. J. (2009). Urban economics in thrall to Christaller: a misguided search for city hierarchies in external urban relations. *Environment & Planning A*, *41*, 2550–2555. doi:10.1068/a42235

Taylor, P. J., & Aranya, R. (2008). A Global 'Urban Roller Coaster'? Connectivity Changes in the World City Network, 2000-04. *Regional Studies*, *42*, 1–16. doi:10.1080/00343400601145202

Taylor, P. J., Catalano, G., & Walker, D. R. F. (2002). Measurement of the world city network. *Urban Studies (Edinburgh, Scotland)*, *39*, 2367–2376. doi:10.1080/00420980220080011

Taylor, P. J., Hoyler, M., & Verbruggen, R. (2010a). External urban relational process: introducing central flow theory to complement central place theory. *Urban Studies (Edinburgh, Scotland)*, 47.

Taylor, P. J., & Lang, R. E. (2005). *US Cities in the world city network. Metropolitan Policy Program Survey Series*. Washington, DC: Brookings Institution.

Taylor, P. J., Ni, P., Derudder, B., Hoyler, M., Huang, J., & Witlox, F. (2010b). *Global Urban Analysis: a Survey of Cities in Globalization*. London: Earthscan.

Thompson, G. F. (2003). *Between Hierarchies and Markets*. Oxford, UK: Oxford University Press. doi:10.1093/acprof:oso/9780198775270.001.0001

Turok, I. (2009). The distinctive city: pitfalls in the pursuit of differential advantage. *Urban Studies (Edinburgh, Scotland)*, *41*, 13–30.

ENDNOTE

1 In association with P. Ni, B. Derudder, M. Hoyler, J. Huang, F. Lu, K. Pain, F. Witlox, X. Yang, D. Bassens and W. Shen.

Chapter 3
Policy-Oriented City Networks in Cyberspace:
A Methodological Approach to the Understanding of Social and Political Articulations between Cities Based on the Concept of Policy Web Spheres

Klaus Frey
Pontifícia Universidade Católica do Paraná, Brazil

Mário Procopiuck
Pontifícia Universidade Católica do Paraná, Brazil

Altair Rosa
Pontifícia Universidade Católica do Paraná, Brazil

ABSTRACT

Whereas the academic debate on global networks used to be dominated by a focus on economic and financial flows, partially on strategies of technological or infrastructural integration, much less attention used to be dedicated to local/global articulations emerging around a wide variety of sociopolitical issues such as the fight against poverty, the strengthening of human rights or protection of the environment. In this chapter the authors endeavor to point out the limitations of traditional approaches in capturing the complexity and diversity of the emerging city networks and use the methodology of web sphere analysis to map and analyze new articulations of sociopolitical governance between different cities in the context of environmental policy as it is carried out in Curitiba, Brazil. The study is based on the mapping of Internet hyperlink connections and shows how a virtual transnational public space with the potential to support environmental governance processes in cities is emerging.

DOI: 10.4018/978-1-60960-051-8.ch003

INTRODUCTION

The importance of cities in the globalization process and the role they play in supporting the current global economic system have been the subject of a large number of studies in recent decades (Friedmann, 1986; Sassen, 2002, 2007; Taylor, 2010; Taylor, Walker, & Beaverstock, 2002). However, the activities of cities on a global scale, whether in the shape of local governments themselves or civil-society or private-sector organizations, are not limited to an economic dimension but take place in a wide variety of fields, such as the fight against poverty, the strengthening of human rights or protection of the environment. In this chapter we endeavor to point out the limitations of traditional approaches in capturing the complexity and diversity of the emerging city networks and use the methodology of web sphere analysis to map and analyze new articulations between sociopolitical governance in different cities in the context of environmental policy as it is carried out in Curitiba, Brazil. The study is based on the mapping of Internet hyperlink connections and shows how a virtual transnational public space with the potential to support environmental governance processes in cities is emerging.

CITY NETWORKS: TRADITIONAL APPROACHES AND THEIR LIMITATIONS

As Taylor (2010) points out in this collection of works, city rankings have become increasingly popular in the current context of neoliberalism, in which the principle of economic competitiveness is no longer limited to the economic field but invades all social sectors, which are also increasingly evaluated in terms of economic efficiency and their contribution to the global economic process.

Traditional studies of global city networks share the premise that these networks are formed essentially from the financial and economic relationships that exist between companies with offices in the cities in question and that any studies of these new network configurations must focus primarily on the economic and financial flows that connect the cities and support the current global economic system. Hence, according to Sassen (2007, p. 36), there are today around 40 cities that make up a "network of global cities [that] constitute a power space containing the infrastructure and capacities needed to manage the international operations of global companies and markets." The criterion for including cities in the category of global cities is the "intensity of the transactions between these cities, especially those related to finance, services and investment" (ibid., p. 41). Similar emphasis is also placed on economic, financial and service flows by Taylor, for whom the world city network is based on the working flows that connect companies in different cities. For Taylor, the position in the network occupied by each city is measured by the services it renders to global capital, i.e., an attempt is made to determine the "service value of a city to a firm" (Taylor, 2010; Taylor, Catalano, & Walker, 2002) in order to arrive at a "new economic geography of services" (Taylor, et al., 2002, p. 98). A similar leaning towards the economic dimension can also be observed in Friedmann, who highlights the economic variable as "likely to be decisive for all attempts at explanation" (Friedmann, 1986, p. 69) and therefore uses "the form and extent of a city's integration with the world economy" (ibid., p. 70) as the criterion for identifying the position of each city in the World City Hierarchy or, even more simplistically, posits "a cut-off point for identifying world cities in national economies of less than $200 billion GNP in 1989 prices" (Friedmann, 2001, p. 2536)[1].

Notwithstanding the methodological differences between Friedmann, who arrives at his World City Hierarchy by using attributes that characterize the cities themselves, Sassen, who focuses on the contributions made by cities to the global economic system in terms of finance, services and investments, and finally, Taylor, who measures the relationships between cities to identify "city connectivities" as indicators of the extent to which a city forms part of the world city network, the three authors share the same insistence on identifying global or world city networks by their role in the global economic system and consider "the resulting levels of [economic] integration into the world city network", because they are "especially global in scope" (Taylor, 2010), to be "the essence of globalization" (Sassen, 2007). The authors maintain their exclusively economic selection criteria even though they recognize, at least partially, the limitations of such measurements, which "represent just one process in city development" (Taylor, 2010) on the one hand, and the growing importance in the globalization process "of a range of institutional orders dedicated to various aspects of the common good in its widest sense, such as the international network of NGOs and the international human rights regime", on the other (Sassen, 2007, p. 47).

CITY NETWORKS BASED ON THE ACTIVITIES OF CIVIL SOCIETY

It is not our intention to question the central position occupied by economic and financial relationships in the configuration of urban networks as they relate to the economic globalization currently under way; however, we consider this approach to be inadequate to achieve an understanding of the new networked articulations between cities, which extend, as Sassen opportunely reminds us, to the fields of human rights and social, cultural and environmental policies. While economic integration is today driven by global capital, with the state increasingly playing a supporting role in this process or having new responsibilities and functions that are essentially at the service of global capital (Sassen, 2007), at the same time we are witnessing the emergence of an ever more transnational civil society dedicated to the promotion and inclusion on the global agenda of issues neglected by the current economically biased model. Symbolically speaking, the World Social Forum, which was first held in the Brazilian city of Porto Alegre and whose central motto is "another world is possible", has been questioning the practices and agreements negotiated as part of the World Economic Forum in Davos and in other arenas operating exclusively in favor of global capital since the alleged weakening of the liberal hegemony, which, according to Boaventura de Sousa Santos (2008), started in the mid 1990s.

The importance of place in this search for an alternative democratic path to development driven by forces originating in civil society can be observed, for example, in the process whereby local social forums are established in the different countries that provide important inputs for the global forum, but especially, according to Norvall (2009), in the patterns that can be observed in the way that ideas and concepts promoted at the global level are assimilated by local structures, "the still important national and local contexts where people make sense of it" (ibid., p. 460). The new social and political articulations that are developed in parallel with, or even in opposition to, political and economic articulations in favor of global capital generated by governments and transnational companies in global cities also reveal the central importance of certain places and cities in the development of these articulations. Boaventura de Souza Santos draws our attention to the global process of the formation of anti-establishment movements that depend on computer networks and for which place plays a fundamental role in globalizing processes: "Acts of resistance, together with the revolution in information and communication technologies, made it possible to create alliances in distant places of the world and articulate their struggles through local/global linkages" (de Souza Santos, 2008, pp. 248-249).

Although Saskia Sassen, for example, recognizes "the possibility of a space for a new transnational politics, at least partly contained within politics for culture and identity, [...that can] contribute to the formation of new types of 'citizenship' and a range of citizenship practices" (Sassen, 2007, p. 164), she locates the potential focus of these emerging protest processes in the global cities themselves, where "the contradictions of economic globalization materialize" (ibid., p. 163) and where "the multiculturalism of major cities" (ibid., p. 126) is supposedly concentrated. However, it is interesting to note that the cities that have so far hosted the World Social Forum — Porto Alegre, Mumbai, Nairobi and Belém — do not appear in the rankings of world and global cities, which should at least make us more cautious about wanting to simply transfer the concept of "the new geography of centrality" (ibid., ibidem) from the global economic system to the questioning structures in the emerging transnational civil society.

Network organization appears to have become the basic paradigm of ***civil society*** and its actions in the current context of the information society (Scherer-Warren, 2006). Despite the "permanent tension at the heart of the social movement between acting with and through the state to formulate and implement public policies and being an agent for pressure in civil society" (ibid., p. 114), the new network activism of social movements based on "the values of democracy, solidarity and cooperation" (ibid., p. 120) appears to be advancing inexorably towards cooperation with the state and even private initiative. On the one hand, civil-society movements and organizations seek to increase their capacity for collective action by forming associations with each other, creating inter-organizational networks and meetings in civil-society forums, such as the World Social Forum to mention but one, while on the other they are amenable to partnerships with the state and the market and look for a place in forums that act as intermediaries between the state and society, leading to new governance practices in the state sphere. In any case, these movements have their own dynamics, with new actors appearing on stage and new cities coming to the fore, making new mappings of the city networks both necessary and worthwhile.

UNDERSTANDING THE ROLE OF CITIES IN THE FORMATION OF TRANSNATIONAL PUBLIC SPHERES ON THE WEB

We start, like Sassen, from "the need to construct new data sets to be able to trace the movements in question" (ibid., p. 45). We understand that, analogously to the strategy adopted by the authors of global cities who used companies as the subject of their research to build city networks (Taylor, 2010), there is justification for using a perspective that investigates the relationships between institutions involved in movements to construct alternative spaces for the articulation of sociopolitical issues that can act as supports for the city networks resulting from such processes. Furthermore, it is our understanding that, unlike in global city networks, where relational structures are based on the flow of work, investments or services, forms of intermediation and cooperation in transnational civil society are based fundamentally on information and communication processes and the exchange of values, ideas and identities, as in the Habermasian supposition that socialization and political decision-making processes in civil society are fundamentally based on a communicative rationality (Habermas, 1998).

Consequently, from a methodological point of view it becomes necessary to reconstruct these informational and communicative structures, which mark the limits of public space in the sense of "a space for the communicative generation of public opinion" (Fraser, 2007, p. 7) or, in other words, "the space of communication of ideas and projects that emerge from society" (Castells, 2008, p. 78) and, supported by global communication networks, increasingly influence decision makers and public opinion at different societal levels in decisions of the state. In the case of global city networks, the centrality of cities is evaluated or measured by the potential contribution that the companies with offices in these cities can make to global capital. In this study, however, we start from the premise that city networks are formed based on communicational interactions between public and private institutions in these cities that shape public spaces, where public opinion is formed and which are usually oriented towards a particular sector, such as human rights, the fight against poverty or protecting the environment.

In view of the difficulty of mapping an enormous range of potential interactions between such institutions, we chose to map inter-institutional and, consequently, inter-city relations in the context of cyberspace. The methodological approach used was web sphere analysis (Foot, 2006; Schneider & Foot, 2005). Based on a survey of the hyperlinks connecting these institutions' websites, this approach allows one dimension of the emerging transnational and sectorial public spheres (which is undoubtedly of growing importance in the context of the information society) to be analyzed. We chose to carry out our analysis in the field of environmental protection policies as the environmental movement is emblematic of networked articulations supported by ICTs, all the more so because of its inherent need for local/global coordination. Supporting this approach,

Environmental networks show the potential that exists for increasing involvement of civil-society entities in the public sphere as questioning pluralist and multicultural actors who exert pressure and create environmental awareness but also put forward propositions aimed at reducing the risks of environmental degradation locally, regionally and transnationally (Jacobi, 2004, p. 219).

Starting, like Sassen (2007, p. 13), from the premise that globalizing dynamics must be detected "inside the institutional and social thickness of the national", we chose to map and analyze the environmental web sphere from a specific place (Curitiba, in Brazil). Our main objective was to gain an understanding of the local/global linkages that make up a "green public sphere" (Torgerson, 1999) as represented on the Internet and to highlight the city network that supports this emerging communicational space on the web.

THE POLICY WEB SPHERE AND ITS RELATIONSHIP WITH GOVERNANCE AND PUBLIC POLICY NETWORKS

A thematic web sphere or a network of hyperlinks related to a specific area of public policy (of which environmental policies are an example) only becomes politically important as sociopolitical actors take advantage of the information in it and use the infoways, i.e., the hyperlink tracks, to exchange ideas, concepts and strategies that have the potential to influence decision-making processes within the state sphere. The result of these processes is a policy web sphere supporting governance based on public policy networks. As a means of supporting social relations, the Internet has the peculiarity that it privileges open transverse relationships and more fluid structures more in line with the social and political processes underlying social or governance networks in more democratic societies (Frey, 2005, p. 193). The policy web sphere is an important support instrument for opinion forming and coordination in the sphere of policy networks.

The popularity of the network concept in the field of policy making is closely related to the neoliberal reforms of the state implemented in recent decades, which led to the "partial unbundling or at least weakening of the nation as a spatial unit [... and therefore] conditions for the ascendance of other spatial units and scales" (Sassen, 2002, p. 1) and even a general trend to decentralization of social organization and governance in favor of local cities and communities. Society is no longer conceived of as being controlled by a central intelligence, such as the (national) state; instead, control devices are spread out, and intelligence is distributed between a multiplicity of action (or processing) units. Coordination of these local action units is no longer the result of "central control" or some form of "pre-established harmony" but the result of intentional interactions between individual actors, who are each supported by parallel actions involving the exchange of information and other relevant resources (Kenis & Schneider, 1991, pp. 25-26; Klijn & Koppenjan, 2000).

From a network point of view, modern political decision-making processes cannot be fully understood if viewed exclusively from the perspective of classical political and institutional arrangements. Policies are in fact formulated in the increasingly informal context of structures outside the conventional legislative and executive channels and those represented by bureaucratic administrative organizations. Political processes start to emerge from complex constellations of agents and from the interdependence of resources, with decisions tending to be more decentralized and informal (Kenis & Schneider, 1991, p. 26).

With the emergence and strengthening of non-mechanistic technological paradigms, symbolic, technical and social networks become increasingly accepted as the natural way of viewing systems of social and political organization. They allow a better understanding of nonlinear relations between interconnected individuals, organizations or cities that overcome spatial barriers to share values, interests, ideas, information and resources freely and coherently. Incorporating the characteristics of live systems, networks tend to grow, evolve and expand in dynamic equilibrium as they differentiate and become more complex. The policy web sphere represents an increasingly important virtual sphere that supports such network governance processes; and cities, through the organizations located in them, are strategic central actors in the production of these articulations.

METHODOLOGY

Intertwined with economic, political and cultural interconnections, the issue of the environment has acquired increasing importance in the discussion of the phenomenon of globalization. It now becomes necessary to understand the relationships between institutions acting at different levels or on different scales. Thinking about the complexity of a globalized environment from the perspective of an individual requires that linear and mechanistic mental models be replaced by new conceptualizations that are able to encompass network logic and practice. Such conceptualizations can help us to understand better the multicausal and multiscale nature of actions that are undertaken, and hence provide a more comprehensive framework and greater detail to help interpret contexts whose essence resides in the complex polycentric nature of complex institutional structures. In the midst of these global institutional structures, as the linkages between the organizations that make up such structures are determined by the functional or operational relationships between them, organizational arrangements are formed that have the potential to define and influence the direction of broad global policies. The relationships between a global arrangement for the formulation of a policy (of which environmental policy is an example) and local contexts provide a point of reference and support for local initiatives, justifying innovation, providing an opportunity for important political directives and producing practical results.

In this case, to assume that a global context exerts an influence on, and has relationships with, local contexts does not mean that the different nuances and the importance of policies in terms of results obtained locally by the application of and interaction between different resources, knowledge and particular local relational abilities are being relegated to the background. Thus, insofar as the practical effects for local policies are concerned, the results of articulations by global arrangements can produce important directives for undertaking collective actions. In this sense, global articulations represent a prolific environment for evaluating different practices that yielded promising results in specific local contexts and, based on this evaluation, defining broad guidelines for thinking and acting that become commonplace and serve as new references for innovative actions and practices in these local contexts.

In light of this, an understanding of local and global social articulations takes on particular importance, particularly in the sphere of public policies. To achieve such an understanding, new approaches that allow the structures underlying the dynamics of social interactions to be visualized are required. Institutionalized in such structures may be important relational properties revealing unique organizational environments in which organizations and people try to express their identities and defend their interests to form a critical mass in an environment that on the one hand is permeated by conflict and divergences, and on the other has the potential for solidarity and, in turn, cooperation and collective action.

To gain a better understanding of the relationships between the contexts in which global and local arrangements exist and the actual interactions that take place between these arrangements on different scales, the perception of complex social phenomena and their representation closer to reality requires the use of new methodological strategies. The theoretical and methodological approach afforded by networks offers a way of gaining access to these relational structures and making them more explicit for analytical purposes. This innovative approach helps to understand, structure and interpret organizational qualities such as the fluidity with which processing patterns change, the nature and intensity of relationships between different actors, the interdependencies between the multiple levels inside and outside organizations and how they are reflected in inter-organizational contexts at the local, regional, national and international level. In methodological terms, network logic not only allows the global scope and structure of the relationships between constellations of actors to be understood, but also makes the analysis of individual relationships between agents possible. The methodology used in the network approach allows features ranging from the configuration of extensive arrangements to relational particularities between actors to be represented visually by means of graphs and mathematically by means of matrices.

In the specific context of relationships in the field of environmental policy as expressed by a network of hyperlinks, organizations whose values and intentions are manifested in their websites can be identified and associated with the social and political meanings that in turn give meaning to the environmental policy itself. In the context of the thinking that guides global directives or in the context of local practices, such values and intentionalities can be viewed as principals and standards that sustain reflection and action in this specific field of societal activity. These are the essential elements needed to define the particular policy web sphere profile and the relational logic of which the Curitiba environmental policy network is part and which is analyzed empirically in this study.

By investigating the content disseminated by institutions and the inter-institutional structure in the context of an environmental web sphere, with the essential aspects of interactions reconstituted and represented by a network of hyperlinks, both the symbolic meanings that drive the actors to pursue their shared interests and the influences exerted by the different actors or, in our case, institutions or cities, can be interpreted.

As far as the issue of the environment is concerned, social movements endeavor, by means of arrangements and practices articulated from a network perspective, to define and drive forward new ideas, conceptions and proposals that go beyond local limits and take on national, international and even global dimensions. Although it is difficult to isolate and evaluate specific practical results arising from information flows and articulations in virtual space in terms of concrete actions implemented locally, identification of these major movements and the directives they give rise to open up important possibilities for continually refining and reinventing local policies. In spite of this limitation, the fact that the global context within which policies are articulated locally can be identified is important as it allows other experiences and parameters to be sought out for comparison. In practical terms this means that efforts to produce innovative behavior and procedures in line with what is acceptable to the dominant opinion in such global spheres of interaction are encouraged.

In the present study, which was intended to provide an understanding of that part of global networks that have a perceptible influence on Curitiba's environmental policy by mapping the relationships between websites of organizations involved in environmental policy, we investigated the multiple levels of influences acting on this policy. Following the logic of interlocking networks described by Taylor (2010) and starting with the network of organizations acting in the web sphere, we arrived at the third network layer, i.e., the network of cities. In this part of the analysis, insofar as the relational representativity of the policy being studied is concerned, the importance of the different cities in the policy web sphere under analysis can be identified.

Following Rosa, Frey and Procopiuck (2007) and Procopiuck and Frey (2009a, 2009b), the analysis was carried out by means of policy web sphere analysis, which is based on Social Network Analysis and Hyperlink Analysis (Park, 2003; Park & Thelwall, 2003). This allows the relationships between institutions and, consequently, cities to be visualized by mapping Internet websites and offers great potential for improving the analysis of public policy articulations in the context of governance as they are expressed in cyberspace (Frey & Procopiuck, 2007).

Using policy web sphere analysis and data obtained in cyberspace, an understanding can be gained of concrete reality at a given moment. Concrete reality can be transcribed to the computational universe and, based on this, relational representations that express what actually happens in terms of influences when the policy is put into practice can be generated. In methodological terms, (deterritorialized) information expressed in cyberspace can thus be captured, filtered and organized to construct and represent an information and communication universe that allows the essential features of sociopolitical relationships and manifestations expressed by different actors in their respective *websites* to be identified. This information can then be used, as far as methodological aspects are concerned, to (re)territorialize the data with a view to understanding the processes undertaken in different local environments within the context of networks of social and political articulations (Procopiuck, 2007). The city networks generated demonstrate this reterritorialization, which is the result of web sphere analysis.

It should be stressed again that this study does not attempt, as, for example, Taylor (2010) or Sassen (1994) did, to measure or characterize the network of global cities as a whole. Our intention was to demonstrate, in general terms, the potential that new information and communication technologies offer for making inter-institutional and inter-urban relationships more dynamic, as well as to show how issues at a global level exert an influence at a local level. More specifically, we sought to discuss particular subjects or policies, producing specific interactive structures and patterns associated with different global social relationships that act as directives for local practices, not necessarily in accordance with relational structures that characterize the network of cities from a merely economic point of view. Faced, on the one hand, with the restrictions on the scope of the study imposed by operational limitations and, on the other, with the authors' fundamental interest in understanding the influence of supralocal spheres on urban policies, it was decided to investigate an environmental policy web sphere, using the main institutions involved in environmental policy in Curitiba as the starting point. Hence, rather than covering a global environmental policy web sphere, the scope of the study was chosen for its relevance to environmental policies, actions and projects undertaken in the city of Curitiba[2].

ANALYSIS OF RESULTS

The data and its graphical representation were analyzed at three distinct levels. At the first level, which is not addressed in detail in this chapter, a wide variety of public, private and third-sector organizations that were exchanging experiences and resources to draw up and implement actions and projects with practical consequences at a local level could be identified. At a second level of analysis, which covers the relationships between cities and is based on the relationships (represented by hyperlinks) between organizations in these cities, the results reveal a high level of activity between Brazilian cities and the involvement of important foreign ones. Lastly, at a third level of analysis, the relationships with the major global regions show the global dimension of discussions related to major environmental problems.

Starting at a global level, organizations from Brazil and 29 other countries were found to be involved directly or indirectly in the discussion and solution of problems located geographically in the Curitiba region, as can be observed in Figure 1. In this universe of 30 countries, the organizations involved with the environmental network are located in 220 cities. The relative importance of the relationships between the countries is ex-

Figure 1. Relationships between Brazil and other countries

1)Country of Origin	2)Direction of Relation	3)Country of Destination	4)Region	5)Number of relations	6)%	7)Number of Cities	8)%	9)Average of Relations for City
Brazil	⟷	Brazil	S. America	1477	82.19	140	63.64	10.6
Brazil	⟶	United States	N. America	159	8.85	27	12.27	5.9
Brazil	⟶	United Kingdom	Europe	20	1.11	7	3.18	2.9
Brazil	⟶	Canada	N. America	21	1.17	6	2.73	3.5
Brazil	⟶	France	Europe	17	0.95	5	2.27	3.4
Brazil	⟶	Argentina	S. America	13	0.72	3	1.36	4.3
Brazil	⟶	Australia	Oceania	11	0.61	3	1.36	3.7
Brazil	⟶	Netherlands	Europe	7	0.39	3	1.36	2.3
Brazil	⟶	Spain	Europe	5	0.28	3	1.36	1.7
Brazil	⟶	Mexico	N. America	6	0.33	2	0.91	3.0
Brazil	⟶	Switzerland	Europe	15	0.83	2	0.91	7.5
Brazil	⟶	Ecuador	S. America	3	0.17	1	0.45	3.0
Brazil	⟶	Colombia	S. America	2	0.11	1	0.45	2.0
Brazil	⟶	Peru	S. America	2	0.11	1	0.45	2.0
Brazil	⟶	Uruguay	S. America	2	0.11	1	0.45	2.0
Brazil	⟶	Chile	S. America	1	0.06	1	0.45	1.0
Brazil	⟶	Panama	C. America	2	0.11	1	0.45	2.0
Brazil	⟶	Portugal	Europe	7	0.39	1	0.45	7.0
Brazil	⟶	Italy	Europe	5	0.28	1	0.45	5.0
Brazil	⟶	Austria	Europe	3	0.17	1	0.45	3.0
Brazil	⟶	Germany	Europe	3	0.17	1	0.45	3.0
Brazil	⟶	Sweden	Europe	3	0.17	1	0.45	3.0
Brazil	⟶	Belgium	Europe	2	0.11	1	0.45	2.0
Brazil	⟶	Czech Republic	Europe	2	0.11	1	0.45	2.0
Brazil	⟶	Finland	Europe	2	0.11	1	0.45	2.0
Brazil	⟶	Denmark	Europe	1	0.06	1	0.45	1.0
Brazil	⟶	Greece	Europe	1	0.06	1	0.45	1.0
Brazil	⟶	Japan	Asia	2	0.11	1	0.45	2.0
Brazil	⟶	Egypt	Africa	1	0.06	1	0.45	1.0
Brazil	⟶	Kenya	Africa	1	0.06	1	0.45	1.0
Total				**1797**	**100.00**	**220**	**100.00**	**8.2**

Figure 2. Quantitative data for the environmental network

	Destination of Hyperlinks																							
Origin of Hyperlinks	Curitiba	Brasilia	Sao Paulo	Rio de Janeiro	Washington	Porto Alegre	New York	Belo Horizonte	Florianopolis	Salvador	Manaus	Niteroi	Campinas	Itajai	Belem	Campo Grande	Geneva	Goiânia	Londres	Cuiaba	Paris	Others 199 Cities	**Total**	**%**
Curitiba	298	133	115	122	62	34	23	14	25	17	12	6	10	12	6	9	8	10	11	8	7	353	**1,295**	72.06
Sao Paulo	9	19	49	20	4	7	-	8	3	4	-	1	-	3	1	2	1	-	-	1	-	57	**189**	10.52
Niteroi	9	23	26	6	6	9	5	4	1	2	3	7	4	1	2	-	1	-	-	-	-	40	**149**	8.29
Brasilia	7	62	6	9	1	3	1	-	-	-	1	1	1	-	4	-	1	1	-	-	2	15	**115**	6.40
Humaita	2	3	-	-	3	-	1	1	-	1	-	1	1	-	-	-	-	-	-	-	-	4	**17**	0.95
Porto Alegre	2	-	1	-	-	4	-	-	-	-	-	-	-	-	-	-	-	-	-	-	-	4	**11**	0.61
Viçosa	-	1	1	1	-	1	-	1	-	-	-	1	-	-	-	-	-	-	-	-	-	4	**10**	0.56
New York	-	4	-	-	-	-	1	1	-	-	1	-	-	-	-	-	-	-	-	-	-	1	**8**	0.45
Sao Jose dos Pinhais	1	1	-	-	-	-	-	-	-	-	-	-	-	-	-	-	-	-	-	-	-	-	**2**	0.11
Quatro Barras	1	-	-	-	-	-	-	-	-	-	-	-	-	-	-	-	-	-	-	-	-	-	**1**	0.06
Others 210 Cities	-	-	-	-	-	-	-	-	-	-	-	-	-	-	-	-	-	-	-	-	-	-	-	0.00
Total	**329**	**246**	**198**	**158**	76	**58**	**31**	**29**	**29**	**24**	**17**	**17**	**16**	**16**	**13**	**11**	**11**	**11**	**11**	**9**	**9**	**478**	1,797	
%	18.31	13.69	11.02	8.79	4.23	3.23	1.73	1.61	1.61	1.34	0.95	0.95	0.89	0.89	0.72	0.61	0.61	0.61	0.61	0.50	0.50	26.60		100.00

pressed by their intensity, which can be seen from the number of relationships given, represented by hyperlinks, in the websites of organizations involved with environmental causes.

In Figure 1, the first line, on a black background, shows the data for the relationships between Brazilian cities. The remaining lines in the table show the relationships between Brazil and other countries. The first four columns of the table show the relationships between Brazilian cities and cities in other countries in different geographic regions of the globe. Column 5 gives the number of relationships, represented by the hyperlinks connecting the organizations in each pair of countries. Column 6 gives the number of relationships between each pair of countries as a percentage of the total number of relationships in the global network. Column 7 shows the number of cities involved in each pair of countries. Column 8 expresses the number of cities for each pair of countries as a percentage of the total number of cities in the network. Finally, column 9 gives the average number of relationships between cities for each pair of countries.

Figures 3 and 4 show the 220 cities where the institutions that formed part of the virtual environmental network based on 51 core institutions with offices in Curitiba are located[3]. The difference between the two figures is that in the first the emphasis is placed on the way that the influence of organizations in the environmental web sphere is distributed by major global region, allowing international and transnational relationships to be identified, while the second figure allows the influence of specific cities — through the institutions located in them — on environmental policies and activities carried out locally to be identified and analyzed.

It should be stressed that the maximum number of relationships represented by a single link was limited to 12 in order to ensure that the figures in this chapter could be easily interpreted. To find out the actual number of cities that had more than 12 relationships, see Figure 2.

In Figures 3 and 4, the size of each shape is proportional to the number of links that leave or point to a particular city. The thickness of the links is proportional to the number of hyperlinks between cities that are directly connected because they are home to organizations with direct or indirect relationships in the context of the environmental network. In practical terms, the relationships mapped express the intensity and magnitude of the potential information and communication flows and exchanges[4], which in this case are made possible by hyperlinks connecting the institutions and cities. In these flows, the cities form nodes, with their own cultures and political and administrative stances. The relationships between these nodes in turn have the potential to exert an influence on the environmental web sphere as a whole, but also more specifically on policies and initiatives carried out locally, e.g., in Curitiba, as in our case. The elements that go to make up both the web sphere, as a space that symbolizes ideological and discursive representations, and the network, which is the result of the objective representation of the relationships between actors interacting in relation to environmental issues in different contexts, originate in the websites of public, private and third-sector organizations. These are organizations that influence the progress of local politics and the forming of public opinion either directly or indirectly.

Overall, it can be seen that the hyperlinks included by the organizations in their respective institutional sites show that the environmental network under discussion has its origins in locally rooted activities and policies. Environmental organizations in Curitiba connect with other organizations in Brazil and abroad according to whether they have projects or actions in common or just shared values and interests. As the aim was to identify articulations involving the immediate interests of cities, the data show a greater number of relationships between national organizations. A total of 82.19% of the relationships in the environmental network are between public, private and third-sector organizations with offices in Brazil (as per column 6 of Figure 1). Including Brazil, relationships with South American countries represented 83.47% (1500) of the total, while those with North American countries represented 10.46% (188), with European countries 5.18% (93), with countries in Oceania 0.61% and with African and Asian countries 0.11%. A spatial hierarchy can already be observed, reflecting the importance of the different regions for environmental policies and initiatives developed in Curitiba. The graphical representation in Figure 3 illustrates the unequal distribution of potential influences among the cities in the different regions of the world.

Although it is well known, particularly in the economic sphere, that cities located on the periphery, as shown in Taylor (2009) for example, have a limited role in world city networks, little information is available in this regard in relation to the environment. Figure 3 shows the relationships between the 220 cities identified and their classification according to the major regions of the globe where they are located geographically. The 148 cities (67.27%) in South America are represented by a circle. The 35 cities in North America (15.91%) and 30 cities in Europe (13.64%) are shown by squares and upward-pointing triangles, respectively. Africa is represented by two cities, shown by the circle-in-a-box symbol. Lastly, the only Asian city is shown as a box, the three Australian cities representing Australasia as a downward-pointing triangle, and the only city in Central America as a diamond. These results reflect two main findings regarding urban environmental issues. On the one hand, not surprisingly, there is a preponderance of articulations between institutions in Latin America itself, and on the other hand, as far as contacts outside the South American region are concerned, interests in terms of international cooperation are almost exclusively directed towards North America and Europe, supposedly because of the greater expectation of obtaining resources and support from the (economically stronger) institutions in these regions. We can deduce from this constellation of relationships that the concepts and discussions in economically and technologically more advanced countries exert a disproportionately strong

Figure 3. Environmental Web sphere – Cities and their distribution by Major Global Region

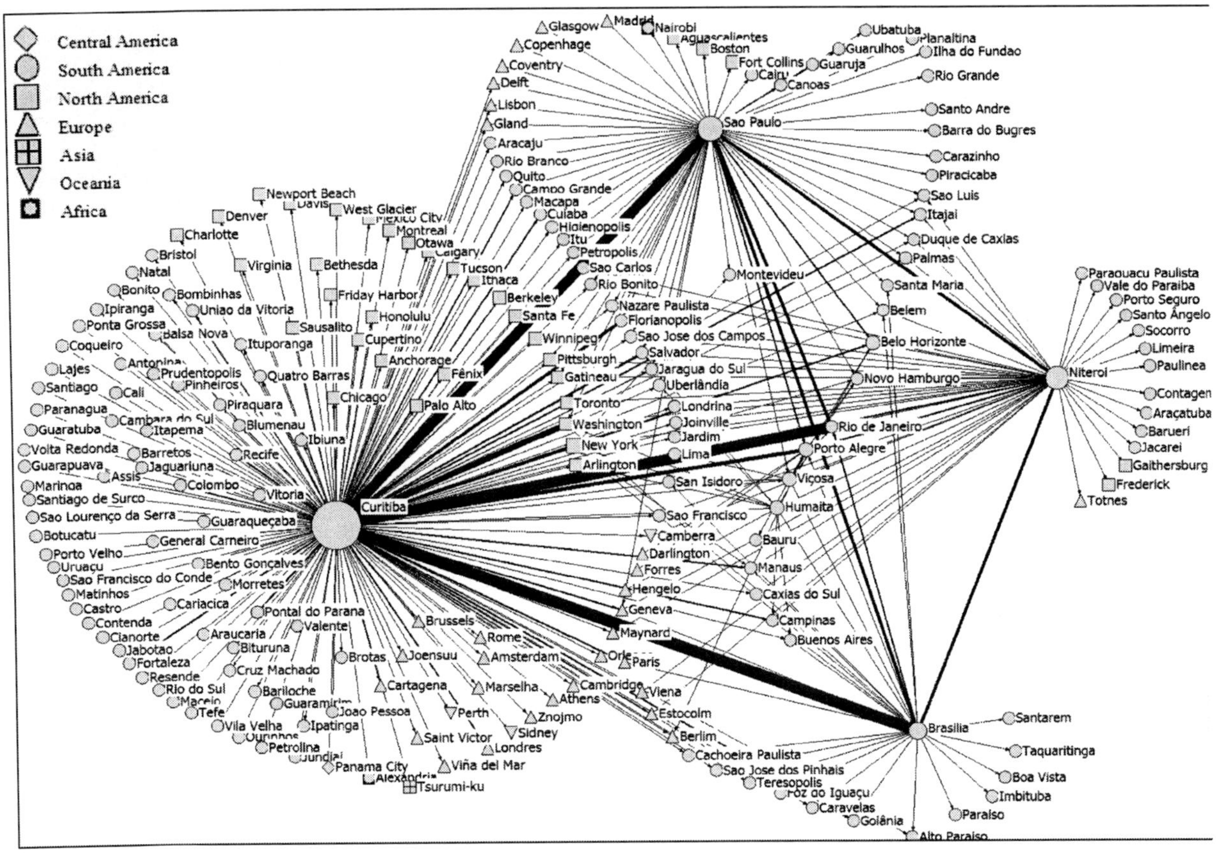

influence on the environmental debate in Latin America or, more specifically, Curitiba.

However, the possibility of the emergence of horizontal solidarity between less developed countries and cities in different continents or major intracontinental regions appears very remote, even in a potentially innovative field such as environmental policy. There can be little doubt that historical inheritance, i.e., the close historical links created between European countries and the Latin American continent and the global leadership of European and North American countries in the global environmental debate, both in the political and scientific field, is a significant factor. However, colonial inheritance and, associated with this, cultural affinities must play an important role in this situation as Asia, despite its growing importance in environmental issues, is only represented by two relationships, in the Japanese city of Tsurumi-ku, where "Environmentally Sound Technologies", an institution that operates exclusively over the Internet and provides an information system to support the transfer of environmental technology transfer, is located.

Curitiba, which was the starting point for the study, stands out in both figures as the city with the greatest local representativity. However, it should be stressed that in addition to being the point of entry to the network, Curitiba is also known as the ecological capital of Brazil. The importance of Curitiba in this discussion about sustainable urban development is confirmed by the significant number of both public bodies and non-governmental organizations in this environmental web sphere with offices in the city. Indeed, during the surveys, which took place between February and October 2006, the city hosted two conferences promoted by the United Nations (MOP-3, the Third Meeting of the Conference of the Parties to the Cartagena Protocol on Biosafety, and COP-8, the Eighth Meeting of the Conference of the Parties to the Convention on Biological Diversity), a fact that must have had a significant influence on the richness and diversity of the web sphere found.

Interestingly, closer examination of Figure 4, which shows the distribution of the cities by country, reveals the central role played by São Paulo, which was found to be the second most important city in the environmental web sphere because of its major importance as an economic center in Brazil. São Paulo not only attracts companies and economic interests, but has also, because of its own current environmental problems, become fertile ground for public sector and third-sector institutions involved in the struggle to achieve more sustainable cities and a healthier environment.

At a national level, it can be seen that Brasília, the capital of Brazil, is of particular importance, primarily because it is the political and administrative center of the country. It is home to a large number of national public bodies associated with environmental issues, which indirectly have an influence on local policies, both because they produce laws and directives and because they finance municipal and regional initiatives and projects. In terms of relationships, 13.7% of the relationships starting in Curitiba have Brasília as their destination, as can be seen from Figure 2. This shows that discussions at a federal level about

Figure 4. Environmental Web sphere – Cities and their distribution by Country

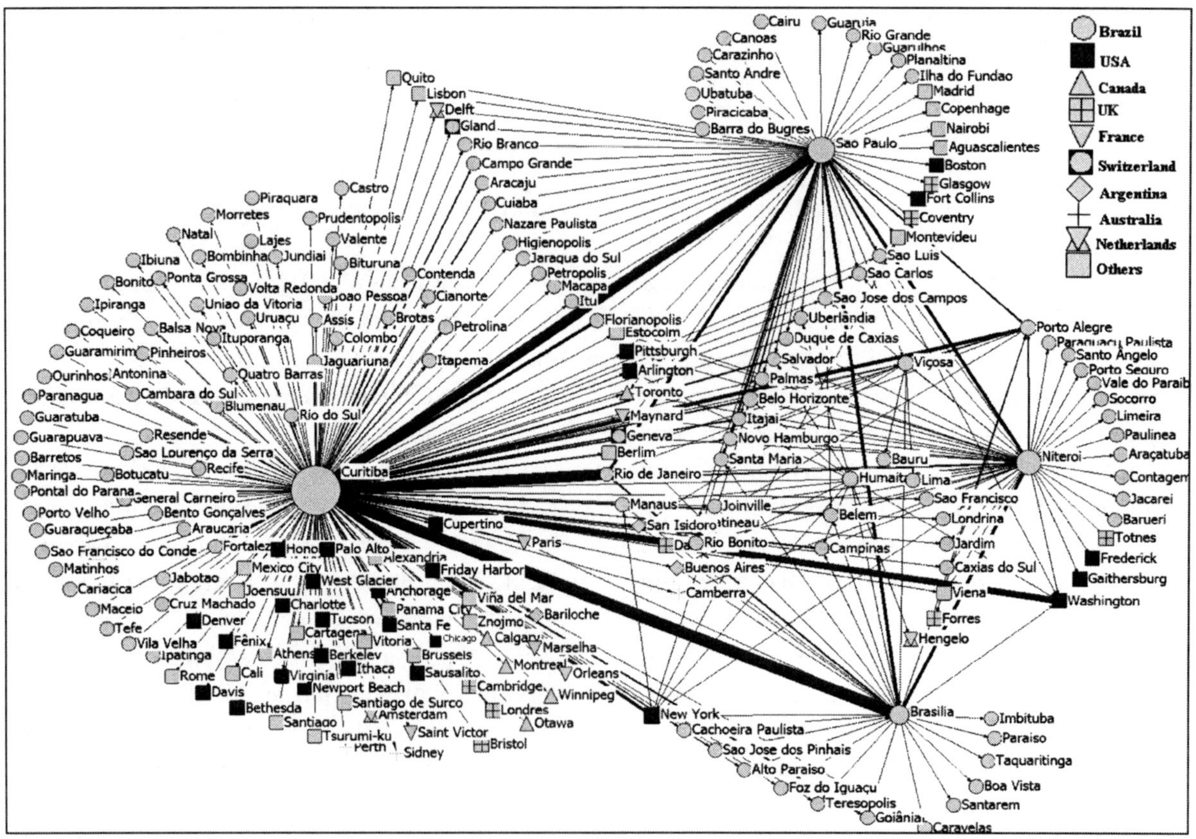

environmental issues involving conceptions, ideas promoted and, undoubtedly, incentive programs and financing funds still attract the attention of local governments and other local organizations seeking to fulfill their institutional objectives despite the greater economy achieved by municipalities following the 1988 Federal Constitution. Rio de Janeiro can also be seen to occupy a prominent position because it is home to important nongovernmental organizations that occupy a significant position at a national level.

At an international level, the first positions are occupied by Washington and New York, showing the importance of international development agencies and agencies for technical cooperation in the financing of environmental projects in developing countries. As can be seen in Figure 1, 82.19% (140) of the cities making up the environmental web sphere have offices in Brazil, 12.27% (27) in the United States and 3.18% (7) in the United Kingdom. These data show that, despite the increasing presence of international institutions, most articulations continue to occur at a local and national level.

Particularly noticeable was that the city of Niterói, in the state of Rio de Janeiro, emerged as the third most important city in the network and was more important than the state capital, Rio de Janeiro. This very central position occupied by Niterói is essentially the result of a particularly high out-degree of 149 references starting at the websites of institutions in the city and pointing to institutions with branches in other cities in the network. The importance of Niterói in the environmental network can be explained by the fact that the city is home to the Brazilian Network for Environmental Information (Rede Brasileira de Informação Ambiental), a civil-society organization whose mission, as stated in its website, is to "work to increase and strengthen socioenvironmental awareness and citizenship by ensuring the availability of channels for dialog and socioenvironmental information..." This illustrates the importance of organized civil society in forming virtual public spheres in different sectors, such as, in this case, the environmental sector. Such organizations, together with private companies specialized in environmental issues (for example, Portal Ambiente Brasil, which served as the starting point for our study), provide important information services for agents involved in environmental government processes and structures. These services, which are generally provided free of charge, are used not only by other non-governmental organizations, but also by representatives of state bodies and political actors, who make use of this information in their daily activities related to environmental issues.

On the whole, the preponderance — at least in numerical terms — of local organizations in the environmental web sphere mapped in this study was foreseeable in view of the method used, in which organizations in Curitiba were considered core institutions and the starting point in the mapping process. In the network in Figure 5, there are 298 local organizations, which correspond, according to Figure 2, to 18.3% of the relationships identified. This indicates that although we can observe the increasing importance of local institutions in the global environmental web sphere, from which they extract information and stimuli for local articulations, it is the density of local relationships that is a decisive factor in the local network's power for collective action as well as its ability to provide feedback to the global network.

An important point when analyzing a web sphere is the distinction between in-degree and out-degree relationships between pairs of cities, as shown in the data in Figure 2. The horizontal axis gives the number of hyperlinks to the institutions in the cities shown. The numbers on the horizontal axis thus represent the prominence of the city, i.e., recognition of the role played by institutions in these cities in sustaining the environmental web sphere. It should be noted that the table also shows the relationships between organizations in the same city. Examples of these

Figure 5. Network with degree greater than 1

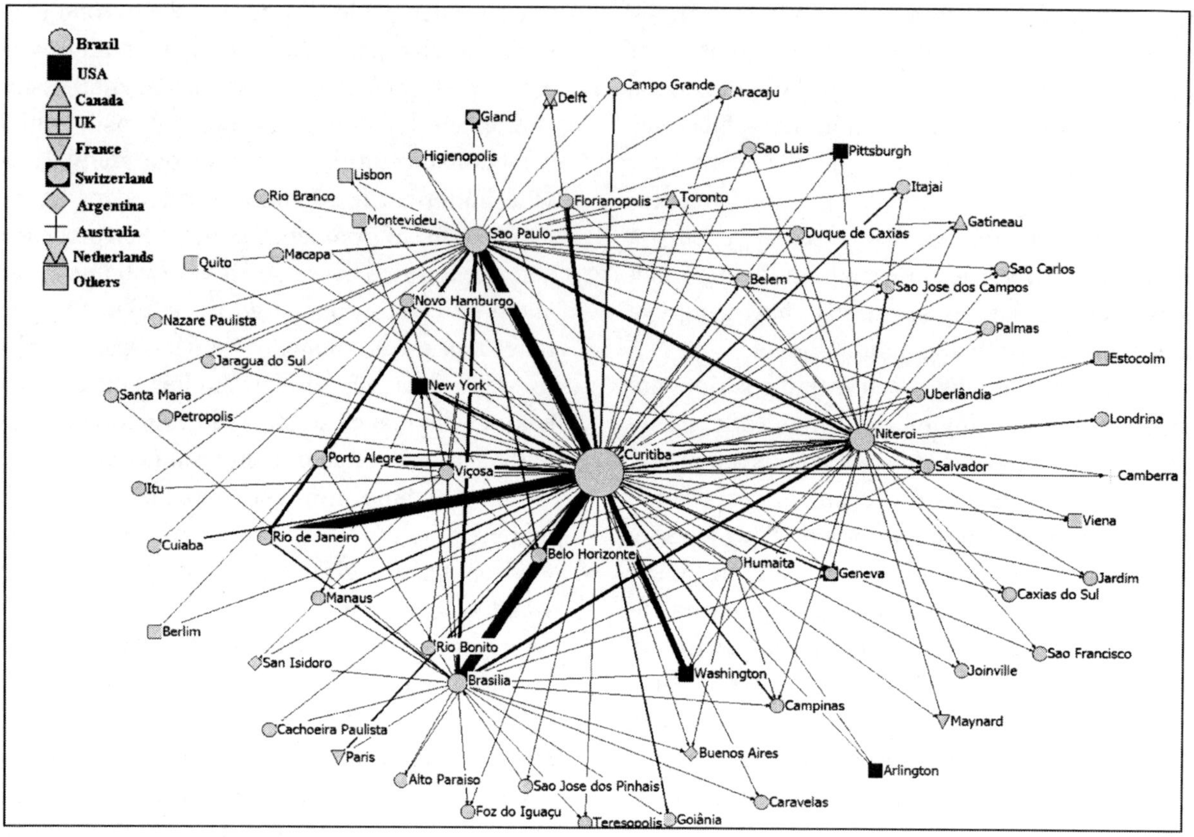

relationships within the same city, which cannot be seen on the network diagrams, can be seen at the intersections of the rows and columns for a given city; for example, Curitiba-Curitiba, with 298 relationships, and Brasília-Brasília, with 62.

Figure 2 shows that there is a significant difference between the percentage of hyperlinks leaving Curitiba (72.1%) and the percentage pointing to the city (18.3%). The opposite is true for Brasília, as the percentage of hyperlinks leaving it is 6.4% while the percentage pointing to it is 13.7%. This means that institutions in Curitiba are not necessarily points of reference for organizations in locations of greater national importance, such as Brasília, São Paulo or Rio de Janeiro, which tend to automatically attract the attention of institutions in cities on the periphery because of their importance in the environmental network, particularly as sources of finance for projects and policies. In the case of Brasília, for example, most of the hyperlinks pointing to the city are heavily influenced by the relationships between local organizations and federal bodies, such as the Ministry for the Environment, which is considered one of the most important references. This can be at least partly explained by the fact that the most powerful institutions do not feel it necessary to refer to the institutional websites of their partners or other institutions, which are perceived as being of secondary importance, while for organizations in peripheral cities it is an essential part of their institutional strategy to seek legitimacy and recognition by showing their involvement in the network of environmental organizations. Consequently, it is these peripheral institutions that make the greatest contribution to supporting the environmental web sphere on the Internet[5].

Lastly, Figure 5 shows only those cities that are important interconnection points, i.e., only those cities that have relationships with at least two other cities. A total of 66 (30%) of the 220 cities that make up the global network were found to satisfy this criterion when it was used as a filter.

Of the 66 cities shown in Figure 5, 45 (68%) are Brazilian and 21 (32%) are in other countries. For the global network as a whole, the number of Brazilian cities (according to the data in Figure 1) was 140 (63.64%), while the number in other countries was 80 (36.36%). These data show that, in terms of interconnectivity, the network has a large international component. Even in the network with greater interactivity (at least two relationships per city), the presence of international institutions (32% of the relationships) is still quite high. In practical terms, these data allow us to conclude that not only Curitiba but all the cities mapped are subject to the influence of large international bodies, which in turn act as points of reference, sources of information and even resources, thereby exerting an influence on local practices associated with environmental policy.

Analyzing the three figures globally, particularly in terms of the geographic dispersion of the institutions, the city network as expressed by these institutions illustrates the potential for exchanging information and experiences between different local areas both nationally and internationally. In fact, the network in question, which defines the main cities involved in the environmental network and the strength of the relationships between them, is a partial representation of the network of local environmental governance in Curitiba projected onto the global network of environmental governance through the intermediary of global cyberspace.

Inter-organizational networks, like those on which the networks of cities represented in the three figures are based, can be constructed because of the previously unseen levels of interaction between different societies, communities, organizations and individual agents. The degree of interaction now seen has only been made possible by the unprecedented advances in information and communication technology in different sectors. Such technologies have allowed information and ideas to be disseminated and channels for communicating sounds and images to be developed and expand geographically, opening up new opportunities for institutions and cities that had hitherto been located on the fringes of the major global urban — and economic — network to interact. At the same time as they bring governments and organizations closer together, these new technologies also allow citizens to establish instantaneous contact with individuals in other parts of the planet who are part of the environmental web sphere.

The interaction between these actors leads to new ways of thinking and behaving and, consequently, a new ability to act globally. The patterns that can be observed in these new ways of thinking and behaving can reveal relational structures based on different cultures, values, ideologies and interests. Considering the practical consequences of this growing potential for interaction, it is not unreasonable to suppose that this virtual space will tend to lead to a (re)structuring of identities based on the tension between dominant relational structures and recessive, or emerging, ones. Thus, the strong presence of foreign entities, particularly North American and European ones, the ideas, concepts and suggestions that they promote and the resources they offer leave their mark on local environmental policies and can even replace local perceptions and practices, creating conditions of relative dependence on external factors. Nevertheless, these locations should not just be seen as the objects or products of external structures and conditions, for they can also influence and shape global space (or the environmental web sphere) and emerging global networks, albeit to a different degree and to an extent that depends on their power and position in the network structure (represented by the links and relationships). It is this tension that gives rise to, on the one hand, the foundations and stimuli that can produce the inputs (ideas, principles and concepts) that in turn drive the latent thinking and behavior, making the network more dynamic and, on the other hand, the constant efforts by the institutions involved to maintain a presence in the web sphere and seek influence, recognition and legitimacy among those making up the network.

It is for this reason that institutions with the greatest number of hyperlinks pointing to them (i.e., the greatest in-degree) have the greatest recognition and legitimacy in the network and therefore also the greatest ability to influence the main actors in local environmental policy, in this case in Curitiba. The continual interaction between agents with different views of the world thus creates and recreates general concepts that start to influence local communities, which, because they interact with institutions/cities in different geographic locations, can influence and condition the behavior of other organizations, groups and individuals as a result of their own experiences and practices, which are made available on the network.

It should be stressed that the influence of the different institutions, cities, countries and regions on, or their involvement in, actual local policies tends to be only indirect or potential. However, as the channels opened in the web of hyperlinks start to be used effectively by the members themselves or by other individual or institutional actors to exchange information or experiences, a local environmental governance network can receive important stimuli for its day-to-day activities. Hence, it is not unreasonable to suppose that an important medium capable of exerting a concrete influence on policy in a particular network develops and that at the same time local dynamism has an important influence on the formation and evolution of the global network, which in turn has an impact on other locations. If, in the past, technological devices such as caravels represented an important means of disseminating information and ideas to different parts of the planet, in the information society hyperlinks are devices that have a similar, yet greater, potential. Because they are accessible anywhere by any individual who has the necessary resources and a basic knowledge, their communicative capacity is infinitely more democratic, even if in practice this democratic potential is not fully exploited.

This study has shown that various organizations either directly or indirectly involved in Curitiba's environmental governance system and environmental policies and projects are located in different cities that exert a global social and economic influence. In this sense, we can talk about interlocked networks or a network of networks on different scales connected and mutually influenced by the information and communication flows that determine their interactive dynamics. In the case of environmental policy in Curitiba, important organizations in different regions of the world act as suppliers of resources or lend legitimacy to an organization's behavior, as shown by the fact that these global organizations appear as references in the websites of core local institutions.

FINAL CONSIDERATIONS

In this work we have drawn attention to the lack of studies of global city networks that address emerging inter-urban articulations in a wide variety of social areas, from issues related to human rights through the valuing of diversity and the fight against poverty to environmental issues, which were the specific focus of the research described in this article. Even though nearly all research into, for example, major metropolitan regions focuses on the challenges posed by urban competitiveness and the need to attract external investments to these regions as fundamental reasons for new arrangements for governance in the metropolitan sphere (Rojas, Cuadrado-Roura & Güell, 2005), thus supporting the dominant notion that economic relationships are decisive in forming city networks, we should not ignore the growing effort by an increasing number of cities (i.e., their governments and the institutions acting in them) to strengthen the position on the global agenda of the previously mentioned non-economic issues, which are of growing importance for the quality of life in our cities. Even though such issues appear in large part as matters of secondary importance, municipal governments and their respective local organizations are increasingly taking part in global discussions, forming alliances to support the global climate and becoming involved in the World Social Forum. In the words of Saskia Sassen, what is happening is "the emergence of certain forms of the global centered on local actors and causes that are part of transborder networks. It is a case of a type of global political activity that is channeled through local rather than global institutions." (Sassen, 2007, p. 31). These alliances and local/global articulations strengthen the local causes themselves through multiscale negotiations, and information and communication technology acts as a facilitator for these emerging relationships.

The interaction between these actors leads to new ways of thinking and behaving and, consequently, a new ability to act globally. This study has endeavored to capture such trends by means of web sphere analysis, while at the same time recognizing the limits inherent to this approach by reducing an enormously complex set of potential (virtual and real) connections to those connections based on hyperlinks, which can be captured more easily.

In spite of these limits, we believe that the regular nature of these patterns can reveal structural relationships based on different cultures, values, ideologies and interests. Considering the practical consequences of this growing potential for interaction, it is not unreasonable to suppose that this virtual space will tend to lead to a (re) structuring of strategies and identities based on the tension between dominant relational structures and recessive, or emerging, ones. Thus, the strong presence of foreign entities, particularly North American and European ones, the ideas, concepts and suggestions that they promote and the resources they offer supposedly leave their mark on local environmental policies and can even replace local perceptions and practices, creating conditions of relative dependence on external factors. Just as countries such as Great Britain and the United States are responsible for producing new legislation for accounting practices or international trade that is in the end imposed, either voluntarily or not, on other countries (Sassen, 2007, pp. 49-50), so in the case of structures identified in the environmental web sphere, on the one hand there are opportunities for strengthening inter-institutional relationships based on equal rights between institutions and cities in the North and South, while on the other there is also the possibility of classical environmentalism, the dominant form of environmentalism in rich countries, being imposed, voluntarily or not, on poor cities in the South, making the search for endogenous solutions in line with the particular conditions in these countries more difficult (Lee, 2006). To learn more about the mutual influences that are exerted through such web spheres, new methodological approaches for analyzing the contents of these information and communication channels are required.

However, these locations should not be seen just as the objects or products of external structures and conditions, for they can also influence and shape global space (or the environmental web sphere), albeit to a different degree and to an extent that depends on their power and position in the structure (represented by the links and relationships). It is this tension that gives rise to, on the one hand, the foundations and stimuli that can produce the inputs (ideas, principles and concepts) that in turn drive the latent thinking and behavior, making the network more dynamic, and on the other hand, the constant efforts by the institutions involved to maintain a presence in the web sphere and seek influence, recognition and legitimacy among those making up the network. Web spheres are therefore emblematic manifestations of a phenomenon known as "glocalization" (Beck, 1998), a condition characterized by the "transcultural production of worlds of cultural meanings and symbols" (ibid., p. 88) in which what is local needs to be seen as part of the global and "the typical duality between the national and the global, or the local and the global" (Sassen, 2007, p. 17) becomes undone. Virtual space, in this sense, becomes a potential space for the interactive production of meanings transcending multiple scales.

In this study we have taken some initial steps towards a broader perception of the phenomenon of global urban networks, going beyond their economic manifestations to include the broad spectrum of activities at the local/global interface where local organizations and governments are increasingly dedicated to "various aspects of the common good in its widest meaning" (ibid., p. 49). A number of approximations to this new emerging reality have been described. However, these need to be refined through the use of complementary qualitative methodological approaches, investigation on a global scale and the inclusion of a temporal dimension by investigating changes in these relational structures over time.

REFERENCES

Castells, M. (2008). The New Public Sphere: Global Civil Society, Communication Networks, and Global Governance. *The Annals of the American Academy of Political and Social Science*, *616*(1), 78–93. doi:10.1177/0002716207311877

De Souza Santos, B. (2008). The World Social Forum and the Global Left. *Politics & Society*, *36*(2), 247–270. doi:10.1177/0032329208316571

Foot, K. (2006). Web Sphere Analysis and Cybercultural Studies. In Silver, D., Massanari, A., & Steve, J. (Eds.), *Critical Cyberculture Studies* (pp. 88–96). New York: New York University.

Fraser, N. (2007). Transnational Public Sphere: Transnationalizing the Public Sphere: On the Legitimacy and Efficacy of Public Opinion in a Post-Westphalian World. *Theory, Culture & Society*, *24*(4), 7–30. doi:10.1177/0263276407080090

Frey, K., & Procopiuck, M. (2007). *Policy Websphere Analysis: Uma abordagem para se (re) pensar a transformação estrutural da esfera pública na era da Internet. Revista Brasileira de Ciências Sociais*. Artigo Submetido.

Friedmann, J. (1986). The world city hypothesis. *Development and Change*, *17*(1), 69–83. doi:10.1111/j.1467-7660.1986.tb00231.x

Friedmann, J. (2001). World Cities Revisited: A Comment. *Urban Studies (Edinburgh, Scotland)*, *38*(13), 2535–2536. doi:10.1080/00420980120094641

Kenis, P., & Schneider, V. (1991). Policy networks and policy analysis: Scrutinizing a new analytical toolbox. In Marin, B., & Mayntz, R. (Eds.), *Policy Networks. Empirical Evidence and Theoretical Considerations* (pp. 25–59). Frankfurt: Campus.

Klijn, E.-H., & Koppenjan, J. F. M. (2000). Public management and policy networks: Foundations of a network approach to governance. *Public Management: an international journal of research and theory*, *2*(2), 135-158.

Nordvall, H. (2009). Making Sense of the Social Forum: On the Local Framing of a Fashionable Global Symbol. *Journal of Contemporary Ethnography*, *38*(4), 435–464. doi:10.1177/0891241608330355

Park, H. W. (2003). Hyperlink network analysis: a new method for the of social structure on the web. *Connections*, *25*(1), 49–61.

Park, H. W., & Thelwall, M. (2003). Hyperlink Analyses of the World Wide Web: A Review. *Journal of Computer-Mediated Communication*, *8*(4).

Procopiuck, M., & Frey, K. (2009a). Articulações organizacionais em *redes de políticas públicas* no ciberespaço: o caso da política de difusão social de TICS em Porto Alegre e Curitiba. *Revista Organizações & Sociedade, 16*(51).

Procopiuck, M., & Frey, K. (2009b). Redes de Políticas Públicas e de Governança e sua Análise a partir da *Websphere Analysis*. *Revista de Sociologia e Politica, 17*(34), 131–144. doi:10.1590/S0104-44782009000300006

Rosa, A., Frey, K., & Procopiuck, M. (2007). Redes virtuais de governança ambiental: análise de uma websphere ambiental a partir da cidade de Curitiba. *Revista Tecnologia e Sociedade, 5*, 79–102.

Sassen, S. (2002). Locating cities on global circuits. In Sassen, S. (Ed.), *Global networks, linked cities* (p. 368). New York: Routledge.

Sassen, S. (2007). *Una sociología de la globalizacón*. Buenos Aires: Katz.

Schneider, S. M., & Foot, K. (2005). Web Sphere Analysis: An Approach to Studying Online Action. In Hine, C. (Ed.), *Virtual Methods: Issues in Social Science Research on the Internet* (pp. 157–170). New York, NY, USA: Berg Publishers.

Taylor, P. J. (2010). Measuring the world city network. In Firmino, R., Duarte, F., & Ultramari, C. (Eds.), *ICTs for Mobile and Ubiquitous Urban Infrastructures: Surveillance, Locative Media and Global Networks*. Hershey, PA: IGI Global.

Taylor, P. J., Walder, D. R. F., & Beaverstock, J. V. (2002). Firms and their global service networks. In Sassen, S. (Ed.), *Global networks, linked cities*. New York: Routledge.

ADDITIONAL READING

Albrechts, L., & Mandelbaum, S. J. (Eds.). (2005). The network society: a new context for planning? Abington: Routledge.

Appadurai, A. (2001). Deep democracy: urban governmentality and the horizon of politics. *Environment and Urbanization, 13*(2), 23–43. doi:10.1177/095624780101300203

Axford, B. (2004). Global Civil Society or 'Networked Globality': Beyond the Territorialist and Societalist Paradigm. *Globalizations, 1*(2), 249–264. doi:10.1080/1474773042000308596

Bach, J., & Stark, D. (2004). Link, Search, Interact. The Co-evolution of NGOs and Interactive Technology. *Theory, Culture & Society, 21*(3), 101–117. doi:10.1177/0263276404043622

Beaumont, J., & Loopmans, M. (2008). Towards Radicalized Communicative Rationality: Resident Involvement and Urban Democracy in Rotterdam and Antwerp. *International Journal of Urban and Regional Research, 32*(1), 95–113. doi:10.1111/j.1468-2427.2008.00780.x

Bingham, L. B., Nabatchi, T., & O'leary, R. (2005). The New Governance: Practices and Processes for Stakeholder and Citizen Participation in the Work of Government. *Public Administration Review, 65*(5), 547–558. doi:10.1111/j.1540-6210.2005.00482.x

Borja, J., & Castells, M. (2000). *Local y global. La gestión de las ciudades en la era de la información*. México: Taurus.

Börzel, T. A. (1998). Organizing Babylon - on the different conceptions of policy networks. *Public Administration, 76*(2), 253–273. doi:10.1111/1467-9299.00100

Brenner, N. (1999). Globalisation as Reterritorialisation: The Re-scaling of Urban Governance in the European Union. *Urban Studies (Edinburgh, Scotland)*, *36*(3), 431–451. doi:10.1080/0042098993466

Capello, R. (2000). The City Network Paradigm: Measuring Urban Network Externalities. *Urban Studies (Edinburgh, Scotland)*, *37*(11), 1925–1945. doi:10.1080/713707232

(1996). InCastells, M. (Ed.). The Information Age. Economy, Society, and Culture.: *Vol. 1. The Rise of the Network Society. Oxford, and Malden*. MA: Blackwell Publishers.

Castells, M. (2001). *The Internet Galaxy: reflections on the Internet, business and society*. Oxford: Oxford University Press.

Castells, M. (2008). The New Public Sphere: Global Civil Society, Communication Networks, and Global Governance. *The Annals of the American Academy of Political and Social Science*, *616*(1), 78–93. doi:10.1177/0002716207311877

Chadwick, A. (2003). Bringing E-Democracy Back In: Why it Matters for Future Research on E-Governance. *Social Science Computer Review*, *21*(4), 443–455. doi:10.1177/0894439303256372

Coe, A., Paquet, G., & Roy, J. (2001). E-Governance and Smart Communities: A Social Learning Challenge. *Social Science Computer Review*, *19*(1), 80–93. doi:10.1177/089443930101900107

Conway, J., & Singh, J. (2009). Is the World Social Forum a Transnational Public Sphere?: Nancy Fraser, Critical Theory and the Containment of Radical Possibility. *Theory, Culture & Society*, *26*(5), 61–84. doi:10.1177/0263276409106350

Crang, M. (2000). Public Space, Urban Space and Electronic Space: Would the Real City Please Stand Up? *Urban Studies (Edinburgh, Scotland)*, *37*(2), 301–317. doi:10.1080/0042098002203

Evans, P. (2008). Is an Alternative Globalization Possible? *Politics & Society*, *36*(2), 271–305. doi:10.1177/0032329208316570

Garton, L., Haythornthwaite, C., & Wellman, B. (1997). Studying Online Social Networks. *Journal of Computer-Mediated Communication*, *3*(1).

Granovetter, M. (1983). The strength of weak ties: a network theory revisited. *Sociological Theory*, *1*, 201–233. doi:10.2307/202051

Hampton, K., & Wellman, B. (2001). Long Distance Community in the Network Society: Contact and Support Beyond Netville. *The American Behavioral Scientist*, *45*(3), 476–495. doi:10.1177/00027640121957303

Hanneman, R. A., & Riddle, M. (2005). *Introduction to social network methods. Riverside*. CA: University of California.

Licoppe, C., & Smoreda, Z. (2005). Are social networks technologically embedded? How networks are changing today with changes in communication technology. *Social Networks*, (27): 317–335. doi:10.1016/j.socnet.2004.11.001

Matusitz, J. (2010). Collapsing the Global and the Local through Interscalar Strategies: a Glurbanization Perspective. *Planning Theory*, *9*(1), 6–27. doi:10.1177/1473095209342608

McCarthy, H., Miller, P., & Skidmore, P. (Eds.). (2004). *Network Logic: Who governs in an interconnected world?* London: Demos.

Mclaughlin, L., & Pickard, V. (2005). What is bottom-up about global internet governance? *Global Media and Communication*, *1*(3), 357–373. doi:10.1177/1742766505058129

Moran, M., Rein, M., & Goodin, R. E. (Eds.). (2008). *The Oxford Handbook of Public Policy*. Oxford: Oxford University Press. doi:10.1093/oxfordhb/9780199548453.001.0001

Moriset, B. (2003). The New Economy in the City: Emergence and Location Factors of Internet-based Companies in the Metropolitan Area of Lyon, France. *Urban Studies (Edinburgh, Scotland)*, *40*(11), 2165–2186. doi:10.1080/0042098032000123231

Mutzel, S. (2009). Networks as Culturally Constituted Processes: A Comparison of Relational Sociology and Actor-network Theory. *Current Sociology*, *57*(6), 871–887. doi:10.1177/0011392109342223

Rifkin, J. (2001). *The age of access. The new culture of hypercapitalism where all of life is a paid-for experience*. New York: Penguin Putnam.

Sassen, S. (Ed.). (2002). *Global networks, linked cities*. New York, London: Routledge.

Schuler, D., & Day, P. (Eds.). (2004). *Shaping the network society. The new role of civil society in cyberspace*. Cambridge, Massachusetts; London, England: The MIT Press.

Scott, J. (2000). Social Network Analysis: a handbook (2ª ed.). Thousand Oaks, California: Sage Publications.

Shatkin, G. (2007). Global cities of the South: Emerging perspectives on growth and inequality. *Cities (London, England)*, *24*(1), 1–15. doi:10.1016/j.cities.2006.10.002

Siegel, D. A. (2009). Social Networks and Collective Action. *American Journal of Political Science*, *53*(1), 122–138. doi:10.1111/j.1540-5907.2008.00361.x

Torgerson, D. (1999). *The promisse of green politics: environmentalism and the public sphere*. Durham, Londres: Duke University Press.

Torrance, M. I. (2008). Forging Glocal Governance? Urban Infrastructures as Networked Financial Products. *International Journal of Urban and Regional Research*, *32*(1), 1–21. doi:10.1111/j.1468-2427.2007.00756.x

Van Bueren, E. M., Klijn, E.-H., & Koppenjan, J. F. M. (2003). Dealing with Wicked Problems in Networks: Analyzing an Environmental Debate from a Network Perspective. *Journal of Public Administration: Research and Theory*, *13*(1), 193–212. doi:10.1093/jopart/mug017

Volkmer, I. (2003). The Global Network Society and the Global Public Sphere. *Development*, *46*(1), 9–16. doi:10.1177/1011637003046001566

Wasserman, S., & Faust, K. (Eds.). (1994). *Social Network Analysis: Methods and Applications*. Cambridge: Cambridge University Press.

Wasserman, S., & Faust, K. (1997). Social Network Analysis in the Social and Behavioral Sciences. In Wasserman, S., & Faust, K. (Eds.), *Social Network Analysis: Methods and Applications* (pp. 3–27). Cambridge: Cambridge University Press.

Wellman, B. (2001). Physical Place and Cyberplace: The Rise of Personalized Networking. *International Journal of Urban and Regional Research*, *25*(2), 227–252. doi:10.1111/1468-2427.00309

Winkler, I. (2006). Network Governance Between Individual and Collective Goals: Qualitative Evidence from Six Networks. *Journal of Leadership & Organizational Studies*, *12*(3), 119–134. doi:10.1177/107179190601200308

Woods, P. A. (2003). Building on Weber to Understand Governance: Exploring the Links Between Identity, Democracy and `Inner Distance'. *Sociology*, *37*(1), 143–163. doi:10.1177/0038038503037001391

Yeoh, B. S. A., & Chang, T. C. (2001). Globalising Singapore: Debating Transnational Flows in the City. *Urban Studies (Edinburgh, Scotland)*, *38*(7), 1025–1044. doi:10.1080/00420980123947

KEY TERMS AND DEFINITIONS

Global City Networks: Should be understood not only as based on financial and economic flows that connect the cities and support the current global economic system, but include city-based inter-institutional articulation in the fields of human rights and social, cultural and environmental policies.

Network Activism: A current pattern of civil society cooperation based on the principles of democracy and solidarity that allow social movements to engage collectively in processes of public governance and cooperation without necessarily resigning to traditional movement practices of social protest and critical contestation.

Public Space: In the information society has to be considered as a space of communication, increasingly shaped by the technological resources of new ICT, above all the Internet, where symbols, values, ideas and knowledge are generated and disseminated, contributing to the formation of public opinion and, consequently, exerting influence on political and societal decision-makers.

Web Sphere Analysis: A methodological approach that, based on the mapping of hyperlinks connecting institutional websites, allows to represent, illustrate and analyze inter-institutional and, consequently, inter-city relations as they are expressed in cyberspace.

Environmental Web Sphere: Represents the overall structure of local/global linkages amongst environmental institutions, agents and/or cities as expressed through hyperlink connections in cyberspace, revealing besides these structural relations a virtual space for the dissemination of symbolic meanings, the consolidation of a green identity and the preparation of projects and strategies, as important common resources for collective action in favor of a sound environment.

Environmental Governance: Represents a complex set of formal and informal institutional arrangements and cooperative practices aiming to approximate governmental and non-governmental agents in the pursuit of environmental improvements.

Glocalization: The idea is highlighted that contemporary society cannot be considered as the sheer result of global forces inflicting hegemonic societal and economic models or cultural identities upon local communities, but that localities play a meaningful role in shaping processes on the global scale; particularly in the course of an ongoing strengthening of virtual spaces and communication trans-cultural and trans-scale production of meaning and identity becomes a common trace of global networks and society.

ENDNOTES

1 The approach mentioned by Friedmann in this article was initially suggested in FRIEDMANN, J. (1998) World city futures: the role of urban and regional policies in the Asia–Pacific region, in: Y. M. YEUNG (Ed.) *Urban Development in Asia: Retrospect and Prospect*, ch. 2. Hong Kong: Hong Kong Institute of Asia–Pacific Studies, The Chinese University of Hong Kong.

2 To prepare this article we used data gathered as part of Altair Rosa's Master's dissertation on environmental governance in Curitiba (Rosa 2007) as, compared with initiatives related to digital inclusion (PROCOPIUCK, 2007), the environmental area proved to have a greater presence in global space. For more detailed information regarding specific methodological procedures, see Rosa (2007).

3 The figure of 51 core institutions acting in the environmental area in Curitiba was arrived at after consulting http://www.ambientalbrasil.com.br. This site is maintained by a company with offices in Curitiba and proved after an initial exploration to be the most important site for environmental information, with a very extensive record of institutions involved in environmental issues. Using the snowball

method, only those institutions that satisfied previously established cutoff limits, i.e., only organizations that were referred to by the core institutions as partners on projects or ideological or subject-related partners, that had their own web page and that were actually involved in urban environmental policy were included in the global network. While the different types of relationships were used to carry out specific analyses of the respective subnetworks identified, for the purposes of the analysis in this article, all the different types of connections observed in the hyperlinks were used to create the global network of institutions involved in some way with local environmental governance in Curitiba.

4 It should be stressed that the mapping of virtual space does not correspond to a representation of the real flows connecting institutions/cities; rather, it corresponds to the channels, the infrastructure as an essential requirement for movement in the web sphere, although it does not allow us to determine the volume or the importance of the traffic circulating in these channels.

5 A similar situation was observed in the relations between institutions that were active in Curitiba itself. It was mainly the non-governmental organizations that were responsible for supplying and maintaining the web of hyperlinks related to the environment, whereas the different town council departments, such as the Department of the Environment, did not insert any hyperlinks pointing to their partners or to other institutions that are important for environmental policy in Curitiba. In other words, the town council departments become "dead ends" in the environmental web sphere "road network".

This work was previously published in International Journal of Advanced Pervasive and Ubiquitous Computing (IJAPUC), edited by J. Symonds, pp. 18-38, copyright 2010 by IGI Publishing (an imprint of IGI Global).

Chapter 4
The Urban Communication Infrastructure:
Global Connection and Local Detachment

Susan J. Drucker
Hofstra University, USA

Gary Gumpert
Communication Landscapers, USA

ABSTRACT

Does Wi-Fi, the Internet, the mobile phone, satellite communication, the I-Pod, flat screen television, wireless devices, Skype, Face Book, Twitter, virtual communities, laptops, Kindle, alter a sense of place and attachment? This area of exploration is absent not only in the areas of urban planning and design, but also other types of places such as schools and even the home where communication technologies are especially varied and proliferate. This chapter will propose a taxonomy of the relationship of people to places in a media rich environment suggesting a continuum ranging from place attachment through a sense of a-location. The taxonomy offers a classification system clarifying the need to examine the impact of media technologies on the people/environment relationship. This reflects not only how people's use of space and place have changed as a result of the proliferation of laptops and I-phones, but also what this means in terms of how they connect or disconnect with their physical surroundings.

INTRODUCTION

"The city, the city my Dear Brutus – stick to that and live in its full light. Residence elsewhere, as I made up my mind in early life, is mere eclipse and obscurity to those whose energy is capable of shining in Rome."

Marcus Tullius Cicero

DOI: 10.4018/978-1-60960-051-8.ch004

The introduction of innovation is associated with sense of apprehension and uncertainty. In the 15th century uncertainty surrounded the impact of moveable type upon the nature of knowledge and worship. Each new medium is perceived by some as a threat to the more traditional political, religious, economic and media institutions. Simultaneously, each new media invention altered the form and function of cities and communities. Cities function as a medium of communication in so far that messages are carried through communication in those spaces. These spaces are arguably among the oldest forms of communication and media. Yet cities have fallen on hard times. The detrimental impact of suburban sprawl can be seen on the economic, environmental and vibrancy of social life in cities. Cities struggle with the rise of privatization of formerly public spaces including streets and parks; increasing surveillance, the demise of public space, decreasing tax base along with aging infrastructure, the loss of the small shop, the rise of the mall, and increasing fear of life on the street. Harold Innis saw a continual process of decentralization and recentralization with small communities trying to outrun metropolitan influences only to be absorbed back into it later (Carey, 1992, p. 155). Digital media arise at a critical time for cities. In 1900, only 10% of the human population lived in cities, while today it's 50%. Added to that the expectation that it will reach 75% by 2050, and there's just cause for a thorough reevaluation of our urban environments.

URBAN COMMUNICATION

The city as an economic, social, and iconic symbol of national prosperity has been and continues to be under scrutiny by economists, geographers, sociologists, urbanists, planners and environmental psychologists. Traditionally, cities have been viewed as financial, commercial, and industrials entities. There is, however, a growing body of scholarship examining urban, suburban, and rural communication. This work reflects both an emergent and interdisciplinary field. The advantage of this perspective is that it provides a fresh perspective from which to view the city and its transformation. The communication perspective provides a parallax or different way of observing and analyzing the urban environment. Foregrounding communication in the study of urban landscapes is not revolutionary given that the essence of the city is community, a relationship to communication underscored by the etymology of the words.

Communication studies offer valuable perspectives and methodologies for the examination of the urban and suburban life conceptualizing the city as a combinative environment of interpersonal interaction, media landscape of spaces, places and communication texts. Communication scholars have addressed how the understanding of urban and suburban life are reflected in and shaped by media coverage or representations in factual or fictional contexts. Some have turned to the close analysis of media texts to learn about urban and suburban life.

Two volumes, in particular, *The Urban Communication Reader* (Burd et al, 2007) and *Urban Communication: Production, Text, Context* (Gibson & Lowes, 2006) typify the direction of the communication perspective. *The Urban Communication Reader* represents research in rhetoric, media studies, political communication, health communication, organizational communication, legal communication, visual communication, conflict resolution, and cultural studies. The driving force of this volume is a tacit agreement for the increasing need "for balance between the traditional geographic community and the newer virtual multimedia-constructed communities, and the unintended and dysfunctional consequences of the new communication technologies and digital environments" (Burd et. al, p. 2).

Gibson and Lowes show how urban communication grows from interdisciplinary specialties of communication and urban studies. This volume seeks to bridge the research of two very specific areas of scholarship, (Gibson & Lowes, 2006, p 5). The city as text is featured, as are the rhetorical dimensions of city. The relationship between urban growth and consumerism of "fantasy cities" is a contrasted with urban growth rooted in cultural institutions or vibrant "no-bohemian" art-filled neighborhoods.

Andrew Wood, Professor of Communication at San José State University explores iconic signage and the move away from idiosyncratic environments in *City Ubiquitous: Place, Communication, and the Rise of Omnitopia (2009).* Steve Macek's *Urban Nightmares: The Media, The Right, and the Moral Panic Over the City,* (2006) deals with "discourse on the urban crisis." Macek's argument that the coverage of the urban landscape found in television and print news portrayed the city as "terrifying and crime-filled, confirmed suburbia's racist fantasies about ghetto culture, and embraced conservative mystifications (and exaggerations) of the cities' problems" (xvi). *Where The Ball Drops: Days and Nights in Times Square* by Daniel Makagon (2004), explores issues of urban revitalization, commodity culture, and social isolation in his detailed ethnographic study of Time Square. Times Square is viewed as symbolic communication and as a site of communication.

Significantly, communication scholars now address the relationship of media and conceptions of the city. Eric Gordon's *The Urban Spectator: American Concept-Cities from Kodak to Google* (2010) addresses how conceptions of the American city changed in response to new media technologies. He explores how new technological practices challenge accepted notions of urban life which he argues have been shaped by photography, cinema and now the database city. *Adriana de Souza e Silva and Eric Gordon* continue this examination of the implications of embedded media technologies in urban landscape through their forthcoming work on net-local public space in which people move between the immediately proximate and the mediately distant that ultimately serves to extend the purview of local space. Others have examined the municipal Wi-Fi movement (Jassem, 2007) In *Digital Cityscapes: Merging Digital and Urban Playspaces,* Adriana de Souza e Silva and Daniel M. Sutko explore urban games, location-based mobile games (and hybrid reality games as these games merge experience in cities and encounters between players who move in and between digital and real world environments (2009). Of particular note is Scott McQuire's *Media City* (2008). In this volume McQuire argues media are not separate but are part of what makes a city producing a distinctive social experience in those environments. He focuses on the power of mobile, pervasive and instantaneous media. McQuire highlights the significance of digital networks, surveillance and digital architecture, webcams and public screens in shaping the experience and meaning of cities.

MEDIA AND THE CITY

The urban landscape is in a state of change as civics and community are altered through the proliferation of mobile media, broadband technology, escalating expectations of global connection and the increasing requirement of data accessibility. Because connection is expected and probable, the value placed on physical place has been redefined. Humans have always dreamed of transcending the shackles of place. The accelerating development of communication technology is a testament to that desire. From print on, the technologies of communication emancipate the individual from the boundary of place. With each technological increment the human being is connected further and faster from the location in which he/she is physically bound (Innis, 1951; McLuhan, 1964; Carey, 1992). Yet there is a conflict between territorial emancipation and the attachment to place, between community and civic obligations.

A World Charter on the Right to the City was proposed at the Social Forum of the Americas (Quito) meeting in July 2004 and at the World Urban Forum (Barcelona) meeting in September 2004. The proceedings emerged without explicit recognition of the significance of media and technologies even though there was discussion of the relationships of globalization and cities. The Preamble states: "The Charter on the Right to the City is an instrument intended as a contribution to the urban struggle and as an aid in the process of recognition of the right to the city in the international human rights system." Among the 23 articles of the Charter, two address dimensions of communication. Article VI underscores the importance of the right to public information from city administrations, or from the Legislative or Judicial authorities: - this in an age when e-government and digital cities offer "one-stop" public access for local information. While the city has always connected people, always served as a means of communication, the city has long been neglected, overlooked, or ignored even by those engaged in examining the landscape as it relates to the protection of human rights, justice and well being of communities.

This approach is quite distinct from that of Taylor (2010) in the reference chapter with its focus upon world city literature and the implications of globalization as a new spatial organization. Taylor deals with world city literature focusing on the implication of emphasizing that globalization is a new spatial organization. The concerns of diverse disciplines lead to assessment at different levels of analysis. Sociologists deal with the society level, urban planners address the neighborhood level, economists the global level. This communication studies approach highlights the individual and community level This is attributable to the significance placed on the concept of community and its impact on human interaction and meaning (Jeffres et al, 2010).

Rethinking Urban Communication Environment

This essay makes the following argument: That cities are being shaped by the contradicting forces of connection and disconnection; by technologies available to the citizen enabling social and psychological movement. Contemporary existence is located in the interstices of physical location and virtual development. We argue a degree of media determinacy in which any development in the media landscape forecasts a change or configuration of the person/environment relationship. We suggest a continuum running from attachment to physical place, at one end, to the a-located citizen at the other end.

In order to understand present-day modifications in the relationship of people to place, changes in the experience of place should be placed in the foreground. Scott McQuire suggests the need to consider not the "city" but the "media city" to highlight the critical role media play in the creation of contemporary urban space. Significantly, the experiential dimensions of the city are featured as he argues, "modern social life emerges through a complex process of co-constitution between architectural structures and urban territories, social practices and media feedback. The contemporary city is a media architecture complex" (McQuire, 2008).

Communication technologies are not simply superimposed upon the environment of city, street, home, and office; rather they are reciprocal agents of symbiotically related change. As the invention of glass windows changed the psychology of being inside, the integration of the telephone into the home and later into the street as a constant companion is not simply an extension of social interaction, but a change in the nature of being outside. The space for living, working, shopping, and playing is redefined on the basis of the extant technological cornucopia. At the same time the needs and demands of space and place are altered by communication possibilities.

VARIATIONS ON A THEME OF DETACHMENT

A. Detachment from Center City

Each increment of communication technology alters the urban landscape. Every additional mode of communication changes the social and psychological relationship of individual to physical location. Much of the urban population has moved away from the center carried outward by the power of mobility. The automobile and the tentacles of high-speed highways plus the hypervelocity of mobile communication technology extend and transform the urban into the suburban. Beyond suburbia lies sprawl. Sprawl is accompanied by detachment away from the former pull of the city center.

As technology erases the distance of space, the character of place is altered. The probability of connection is always expected thereby redefining the value placed on physical place. It is an imposed sense of contraction that permeates the relationship of person and place. Every medium functions either ***centrifugally*** and/or ***centripetally*** – that is moves information inward or outward. The urban/suburban landscape is inexorably linked by the technical, multi-directional, attributes and character of the accompanying media landscape. Historically the urban centripetal force was powerful, drawing people towards city centers. The relationship of center to suburb, of transportation to suburban development and communication to sprawl are mutually interdependent. The centripetal force of cities has been diminished with the increasing centrifugal outward pull away from urban center and the centrifugal pull of suburbia and sprawl.

Sprawl is the result of policy, particularly zoning policy, and those policies and priorities that elevated the automobile and the highway as its prime role of transportation. Overlooked is the acceleration of communication technology that allows the individual to escape from their dependence on location. The laws of gravity are defied as the individual becomes electronically transportable.

At the May 1998 Transportation Research Conference, Policy analyst Anthony Downs, identified ten "traits" associated with sprawl:

- Unlimited outward extension
- Low-density residential and commercial settlements
- Leapfrog development
- Fragmentation of powers over land use among many small localities
- Dominance of transportation by private automotive vehicles
- No centralized planning or control of land-uses
- Widespread strip commercial development
- Great fiscal disparities among localities
- Segregation of types of land uses in different zones
- Reliance mainly on the trickle-down or filtering process to provide housing to low-income households (http://www.plannersweb.com/sprawl/define.html)

Suburbs are not new, they existed since there have been cities. Early suburbs could be seen in the areas outside of ancient walled cities. However, the modern version of the suburb provides a combination of non-urban amenities without the loss of urban benefits.

A place-based perspective, focused on the physical environment, is reflected in a popular planning model that posits that the relationship of urban and suburban may be viewed as points on a continuum (transect). The conceptual path of the transect, introduced in the 1790 work of Von Humboldt, is based upon urban density. It proposes a linear route – natural, rural, suburban, general urban, urban center, and urban core and identifies a set of habitats that "vary by their level and intensity of urban character" (Bohl and Plater-Zyberk, 2006). It is based upon on an undeniable emotional and physical bond between person and place inherent in the concept of place attachment (Low & Altman, 1992).

There is a growing body of literature arguing that the clear gradations of the transect, once so clear, are blurring (Kotkin, 2000). These studies focus on qualitative dimensions of quality of life and introduce a "life-stage oriented scenario" for the future of relations between telecommunication and cities. For example, Kotkin (2000) depicts different design attributes for decentralized and centralized scenarios of human settlements in the digital era. He describes a hi-tech archipelago in the countryside made possible by two variables: (1) the desire of key players to operate outside the urban environment, and (2) media technology. In the process, the relentless pull of the urban center weakened and altered in part by the liberating impact of media connection. Disconnection is substituted for connection as cyber-bonds achieves priority over physical environment. In 1964, urban designer and theorist Melvin M. Webber described "community without propinquity." 46 years later Webber observed: "The concept of 'urbanism' and the concept of 'city' were no longer coterminous." His reasoning was foreboding:

"The metropolis is a massive communications switchboard, all right. It exists only because interdependent persons and groups have to be accessible to each other and because the cost of overcoming space has not yet reached zero. If location theorists have it right, and if time and dollar costs were zero, there'd be little reason for urban settlements to exist. People and firms would be in immediate contact with friends and associates even though they were in distant places."

Urban settlements persist, but are newly configured – zero cost leads to community dilettantism – a commitment to the ease of the present, without the obligations of community. In *The Death and Life of Great American Cities*, Urbanist Jane Jacobs said, "The point of cities is multiplicity of choice." (1961, p. 340). But choice today is no dependent upon "downtown" as a place.

B. Technologically Assisted Detachment

The physical and social structures of the city are intimately intertwined. In *Pattern Language* Christopher Alexander wrote, "Cars give people wonderful freedom and increase their opportunities. But they also destroy the environment, to an extent so drastic that they kill all social life." (Alexander, *et al*, p 64, 1977).

"The effect of this particular feature of cars on the social fabric is clear. People are drawn away from each other; densities and corresponding frequencies of interaction decrease substantially. Contacts become fragmented and specialized, since they are localized by the nature of the interaction into well-defined indoor places – the home, the workplace, and maybe the homes of a few isolated friends." (p. 65).

Add telegraph, telephone, radio, television, computer, Internet and Wi-Fi to car and Christopher Alexander's perceptions gain momentum and import.

While physical spaces become more restricted, privatized, threatening or expensive, media spaces become more available, mobile, omnipresent and digital. Digitalization alters and irrevocably modifies the nature of relationships between individuals and their environment (Gumpert & Drucker, 2004). It is this sense of contraction that permeates the relationship of person and place when a medium of communication is interposed. The contradictions of increased connection accompanied by a greater sense of disconnection can be characterized by the following series of paradoxes:

The more we extend our connection, the more insular we become. The more we control our communication environment, the less is surprise or chance a daily expectation. The more we connect, the more we seek to control the connection. The more we detach from our immediate surroundings, the more we rely upon surveillance of the environment. The more communication choice offered, the less we trust the information we receive. The more information and data available, the more we need. The more individuality we achieve, the more communities we seek. The more we extend our senses, the less we depend upon our sensorium (Gumpert, 1996. p. 41).

Not only does technology have the capacity to disconnect people from place, but also those planning and designing the physical environment have practiced detachment by dividing technology from place and behavior. The apparent non-planning of disconnection has resulted. If the symbolic relationship of place and human behavior has been recognized by some, place has been disconnected from communication technology by most. Communication technology displaces and relocates functions within a community (Gumpert & Drucker, 2004). We have argued "One is left with a strange conception of civic involvement - the informed citizen disconnected from community, connected with others without physical connection. The detached citizen resides in a place of their choosing, but in a variety of distant communities, which in turn reshape their physical spaces in paradoxical ways" (Gumpert & Drucker, 2001).

The psychological, cultural, social, and structural connection of communication technology and urban/suburban planning has been grossly neglected. There is a reciprocal and defining interdependence of place modified by communication technology. The perception of urban public space is changed through the experience of mobile and wireless networks (Willis, p. 11) "Euclidian or topological understanding of space can be interpreted in terms of physical separation, bounded-ness, linkage, temporality and presence (Willis, 2008, pp. 11-12).

An individual's state of consciousness is redefined through media use and in so doing; person/environment relations are restructured. The media of mobility alter the perception of time and place (Rettie, 2005). "Presence" describes the feeling of being in a situation. Blascovich (2002, p. 129) defines presence as "a psychological state in which the individual perceives himself or herself as existing within an environment." Media use re-distributes the experience of presence between parallel interactions, creating absent presence in the face-to-face interaction (Rettie, 2005). Media have the capacity to reconstruct our sense of connection to things local. Presence online or in phone space reduces physical presence even though one may be simultaneously interacting with co-present people (Rettie, p.21). Gergen described this phenomenon by the term "absent presence" (2002, p. 227).

This approach is extremely individualistic, stressing psychological or emotional connectedness. Distinguishable from P.J. Taylor's concern with the connectedness of cities themselves neglects the people-place connection. Measuring connectivities and assessing the stability of the world city network is dissimilar from consideration of the people environment relationship.

The paradigm of the "good city" should be reconsidered in light of the influence of communication technology that invaded every sector of modern life from the ubiquitous mobile telephone to Internet, Wi-Fi, I-Pod and broadcast connection. The mobile phone is the quintessential medium encouraging "absent presence" as one moves through the urban environment oblivious to that environment.

The history of telephone numbers is quite revealing in regard to presence and place. Relatively early in the history of urban telephony the first three letters of telephone numbers included letters stood for a particular group of phones located in a specific location. Later the letters were replaced by numbers, but the numbers, nevertheless, grouped together users of a particular location. A call to 212 – xxxxxxxx indicated a call to some one in New York City. 404 indicated the Atlanta, Georgia area. The mobile phone changed that completely by allowing the user to take a number to any place or location. Unless it is volunteered in the course of the conversation, talking to some one on a mobile phone provides no information regarding the place from where the call is initiated or received. The mobile caller is without location or presence.

William Mitchells' "The City of Bits Hypotheses" suggests a new urban typology with traditional place-based communities made up of physical spaces and organized around traditional public spaces at one end of the spectrum. At the other end of the spectrum are virtual communities composed of widely and randomly scattered disconnected physical places together with many virtual places including virtual public places (Graham, 2004, p. 127-8). In between are numerous possible hybrid spaces, where both physical and virtual places play significant roles, and in which linkages are formed both by transportation and electronic connections. These hybrid spaces include augmented spaces, physical spaces filled with ubiquitous/pervasive computing, and mobile, wireless connectivity. To understand contemporary physical space one must appreciate that communication media are powerful agents of change for an environment filled with electronic and visual information. It is experientially a different physical environment. Aurigo amd De Cindio point out that "In the augmented city, 'virtual' and 'physical" spaces are no longer two separate dimensions, but just parts of a continuum, of a whole. The physical and the digital environment have come to define each other... (Aurigi & De Cindio, 2008, p. 1). The introduction of media into physical public spaces brings with it remarkable change in our experience of place. The perception of urban public space and place is changed through the experience of mobile and wireless communication (Willis, p. 11).

PLACE ATTACHMENT

The literature of people/environment studies emphasizes the significance of place making and place attachment. A person's sense of identity is associated with a sense of belonging to a place and is useful in understanding the choices made by people. Milligan (1998) articulated an interactionist theory of place attachment. Rooted in the premise that all interaction is spatially located, place attachment occurs when a particular interaction is accompanied by significant meaning. The interactional past and interactional potential of a place are seen as components of a person's feelings about place. When interactions past and future are emancipated from place, attachment is changed.

Expanding on the studies on place attachment, we suggest a continuum of people/environment relationship rooted in *place detachment* – modifying and even replacing the concept of *place attachment*. This continuum ranges from attachment to non-attachment to disconnection, to re-allocation, to replacement, and ends with a-location.

Attachment – Place attachment is a concept embraced by scholars from diverse areas including social ecology, geography, psychology, and family studies. Place attachment helps explain the bonds between people and their physical settings (Brown & Perkins, 1992). Physical settings are expressive, creating messages about resident identity, neighborliness and obligation to others. From the media studies perspective Scott McQuire notes, the "displacement of 'substantive, continuous and homogenous space inherited from classical geometry' in favor of what Virilio (1991, p. 35) calls the 'relativity of an accidental, discontinuous and heterogeneous space, of electronic media which deals the final blow to the spatial paradigms of classical architecture and urbanism." (McQuire, p.20).

Non-attachment – Non-attachment is an emotional state associated with never having been attached. Non-attachment provides control and the ability to maintain an emotional distance. Non-attachment, a lack of engagement, provides potential autonomy or a sense of independence. Never having been attached suggests no need to extricate oneself from the emotional pull of place.

Disconnectedness – refers to the choice of not spatially dependent connections. There is a difference between non-attachment and disconnection, the latter involves the detaching or disengaging from an emotional connection. Increasingly information and interaction disengaged from place is an attractive choice. Scott Lash argues that the information society mush be understood on the basis of the nature of information disembedded from place. He asserts (2002, p. 206) that distant communicational bonds are displacing older social bonds organized on the basis of spatial proximity - either communication coming from a distance or people coming from a distance in order to meet face to face. He asserts these communication bonds are different than older forms of social bonds embedded in spatial proximity (McQuire, p. 23). An associated concept has been referred to as the "digital sublime" (Mosco, 2004), transcending matter, overcoming the constraints of place, communication spaces of cyberspace may offer liberation and options.

Re-allocation – the time spent in media fundamentally alters the amount of time available for other non-mediated events. The reciprocal and defining interdependence of place modified by communication technology is a temporal concept, defined by a difference in time or time usage. The amount of time spent in media activity fundamentally alters the amount of time available for other events. The contemporary individual spends an increasing amount of time electronically connected with others in lieu of physical interaction on a face-to-face basis.

Replacement – the substitution or alteration of one or more locations for another. Mediated connection brings with it a degree of 'replacement' as well as some degree of 'displacement'. 'Replacement' is a spatial concept, a difference of environment, the substitution and/or alteration of one or more locations for another. Both displacement and replacement portend significant consequences on the nature and use of public space.

A-location – the redefining of social space and psychological presence with potential emancipation from physical space. "A-location," the severing or de-connection of event from location, forms the basis of relationships to some physical environments as a person moves from place to place. A-location reflects transcendence of the constraints of place.

As previously mentioned psychological presence in physical space is easily altered through ubiquitous media connection. Presence refers to the illusion of being there, whether 'there' exists in physical space or not (Biocca, 1997). Telepresence refers to the sense of being transported to a mediated environment through radio, film, television, and cyberspace. As mobile connection beckons, people become immersed or absorbed in media connection, altering their awareness and interaction with the physical environment. At heart of the matter is the phenomenon of the human communicator gliding and shifting between physical and media environments. It is this sense of contraction and expansion that permeates the relationship of person and place when a medium of communication is interposed.

DIGITAL MEDIA

Digital media supplant communities of space with communities of interest or communities of place. While space and place are terms often used interchangeably, they are distinct. The difference is defined in the literature of environmental psychology. In his book *The Psychology of Place,* David Canter (1977), puts forward three components constituting 'place'. They are *the physical attributes* of the environment, the *activities* within and the *conceptions of* the person(s) making sense of all those."

The meaning an individual associates with a space refers to place. Meaning is not part of the space itself: it is an added quality created by, personal interpretation, lived experience, interaction, memories, conceptions and behaviors of the users of a space. 'Place-ness' results from the activities and ideas of those inhabiting the space. Place is a *psychological* phenomenon. Place has *meaning* based on what individuals associate with physical sites, based on social interactions, culturally based understandings. Such associations change space to *place*. Communities selected in an age of choice can be either physical or aspatial with a shared sense of personal meaning and connection. The significance of this unobserved shift is suggested by cultural historian and communication theorist James W. Carey who cautioned that while technology "overcomes many boundaries (of space and time, politics and economics), other social borders may be created at the same time. It is easier to see old boundaries coming down than to see new ones being erected" (Carey, 2005).

ATTACHMENT AND SURVEILLANCE

One strand of place attachment research reveals a connection between attachment and potential crime. Physical settings are communicative and the characteristic physical signs of place attachment have been said to supply some protection from crime (Brown, 2004). Low levels of attachment and weak social ties are expressed by very different indicators, such a deteriorated looking house exterior, litter and unkempt lawns. These are referred to as incivilities (Brown 2004). According to Brown and Altman (1983) personalized and well-kept residences may put potential offenders on guard. They found that "burglars in a suburban neighborhood were more likely to avoid personalized homes (those with prominent signs of resident names and/or addresses) in favor of less personalized neighboring homes" (Brown & Altman, 1983). In one study subjects examining photos of homes were able to distinguish whether the resident had high or low levels of place attachments (Harris & Brown, 1996). Environmental psychologist Barbara Brown's work links observed incivilities and weak place attachments. Her research supports the argument that the relative strength or weakness of place attachment is an important variable in crime rates.

Is level of attachment linked to the need for CCTV? More attached residents may be better territorial guardians (Felson, 1987), exhibiting greater vigilance and protectiveness toward their own and neighbors' residences" (Brown, p. 36-361). Jane Jacobs argued for "eyes on the street" surveillance methods." Many neighborhood watch programs took up the phrase. Elaborate surveillance camera systems now blanket cities around the globe. CCTV cameras are embedded in cities infrastructures as expected as traffic lights, and outdoor lighting.

Does reliance on CCTV cameras suggest an affordance allowing residents to detach further? One is faced with a chicken and egg situation. Which comes first, the place detachment leading to the need for CCTV cameras or CCTV cameras enabling residents to detach thereby relinquishing the need to be connected with obligation to one's neighbor? Community cohesion is based upon social relationships, obligation, dependence upon others, and trust.

Surveillance is defined as the close observation of a person or group, especially one under suspicion, or simply as the act of observing or the condition of being observed. On the other hand, further distinction must be made between non-electronic and electronic surveillance. Gary Marx (2002) has contrasted traditional surveillance with new surveillance. Traditional surveillance was visible while new surveillance less so or invisible. Sensing is unaided in traditional environments but extended by new surveillance technology. Traditional data collection was a human activity while new surveillance is mechanical. Significantly, the location of the data collector was on the scene in traditional surveillance and remote in new surveillance (Marx, 2002, p. 28).

Non-electronic surveillance is based on community of place rather than on virtual or digital community. Historically, community meant mutual obligation, an unwritten contract governing people physically located in proximity that stipulated that commitment. It is an obligation from which many have sought to escape.

With the rapid acceleration and adoption of communication technology we have accepted and embraced the cult of surveillance that places trust in the electronic tools of safety and risk reduction. Powerful cameras, sensors, global positioning satellite technology, biometrics, data mining technologies, powerful subpoenas, warrantless government programs are building the surveillance infrastructure. Surveillance has become the favored solution to stave off fear and insecurity. The embedding of surveillance technology into the urban infrastructure alters the person/environment relationship.

Reactions range from compliance to resistance but ultimately in our day to day lives the awareness of that blanket of public/private surveillance is manifest in several possible behaviors: (a) reactive conduct—behavior tailored to the surveillance; (b) The suspension of awareness—the disregard or pretense that observation is not occurring (studies support the fact that we forget the cameras are there). (c) Non-reactive behavior—based upon the assumption and acceptance that surveillance is a cultural and technological norm. (Gumpert & Drucker, 2002)

Each of these possible psychological states shapes the perception of public space. Today, the gaze of others, both public and private is expected and becomes part of the internal state, the psyche, of the in the community.

INFRASTRUCTURE

The infrastructure of a city shapes and is shaped by the need for communication. The infrastructure creates communication. The original infrastructure of cities consisted of the physical environment; paths, roads, streets, market places, meeting places, and city walls (Gumpert & Drucker, 2008). The infrastructure has evolved to include towers, poles, fiber optics, coaxial cable, and Wi-Fi. In *A Nation Transformed by Information* (2000), Chanler and Cortada demonstrate the continuities and differences between the infrastructure of the Industrial Age and the infrastructure of the Information Age. They argue the centrality of the telegraph as the critical development. "The telegraph became and essential handmaiden to the operation and management of railroads" (p. 282). In his examination of the telegraph James Carey asserted that the telegraph was built on previous frameworks and infrastructure. He noted '...[it] twisted and altered but did not displace patterns of connection...'(p. 204). He develops the idea by extending it through an analogy of the infrastructure of telegraph wires following the physical and natural patterns of geography. Today we read about the need to explore the interplay between the city and the infrastructures and the city as communication infrastructure.

In their important volume on *Telecommunications and the City* (1996), Stephen Graham and Simon Marvin said:

The growing use and significance of telecommunications throws up many profound and fundamental questions which go to the heart of current debates about cities and urban life both today and in the future. For example, how do cities and urban life interrelate with the proliferation of electronic networks in all walks of life and at all geographical scales? ...Are cities being affected physically by advances in telecommunication as many claim they were in previous eras by the railway and the automobile...And what do all these changes imply for the ways in which cities are planned, managed, and governed? (pp. 4-5).

There has been a great deal of conjecture about component of the telecommunications infrastructure considering complex communications systems networks, regional and long distance systems, but little research has been done about the relationship of these communications systems to each other and to the overall pattern of urban development and urban life. There is a striking continuity in the infrastructural evolution that begins with the postal system in the eighteenth century, and then moves to the railway and the telegraph, the telephone, radio and television, and then computers. That continuity will probably have a significant impact on the ongoing evolution of the information age infrastructure (Chandler & Cortada, 2000, p.282).

MEDIA ECONOMICS AND PLACE

Economic historian and political economist Harold A. Innis "saw technological developments, particularly in the fields of transportation and communication (roads, canals, shipping, railroads, telegraph, postal systems), as interacting with geography and staples to disrupt established patterns of social interaction" (Babe, 2006, p 43). For Innis the most critical factor in a society is its communication: not the content as much as the form or how specific communications media operated. Innis argued that *any* form of communication possesses a bias; by its nature in terms of the organization and control of information resulting in a dialectic between media with a time-bias and those with a space-bias: Key is the medium's weight or mass, its durability, and ability to store and transmit messages facilitate either control of society through time or over space (Innis 1971, 33). For Innis, development of communication media was the key to social change. Any empire or society is generally concerned with *duration over time* and *extension in space.* Spatially biased media obliterate space and temporally biased media obliterate time. Innis recognized that the speed and distance of electronic communication enlarged the possible scale of social organization and greatly enhanced the centralization and imperialism in political and cultural terms. Media that are durable and difficult to transport, and possessing limited capacity he called *time-biased or time binding*. Time-binding media "favored relatively close communities, metaphysical speculation, and traditional authority" (Carey, 1992, p. 134). Media that are easy to use and transport, that are not durable, easy to work with and have ample capacity, he called *space-biased* or *space-binding.* Such media support *space-bound cultures*, which are secular, present-minded, individualistic, space-binding media such as print and electronic media facilitate expansion and control and favor "the establishment of commercialism, empire and eventually technocracy" (Carey, 1992, p. 134).

Canadian cultural ecologist Robert E. Babe has stated: "For people in time-bound cultures space is where the community lives, where its roots are, and how it maintains its connections with the past, and where its future will unfold " (Babe, 2006) In space-bound cultures, the conquest of new lands, enlargement of markets and organization of labor are motivating forces. The spatial bias of modern media was initiated by print and extended by film and broadcasting as the power of space in modern world wanes. The traditional spatial dimensions of place are obliterated in cyberspace as increasingly geography becomes irrelevant. Transportation and inexpensive media connection make distance inconsequential. "As global is perceived as local, global is homogenized. We are coupled to sources of information with no location and we find ourselves in non-physical relationships constructed in the new geography of connections" (Gumpert & Drucker, 2004).

Electronic technologies enhance spatial bias and lead to more urban and secular cultures. Over the past several years we have attempted to articulate the paradigm of the "the city' and its evolving form as it has been reshaped and redefined by the accelerating impact of new communication technology. For Innis, the medium is the critical factor that reshapes cultures. Digital technologies provide new opportunities for participation, new forms of experience, and ecologies of knowledge. New space-time boundaries are being created. Digital environments offer opportunities for pseudonymity or the illusion of anonymity, each provides the opportunity to hide or fabricate identity fostering a sense of freedom or liberation from accountability.

COMMUNITY

We have witnessed the rise of the digital city. "The city in which obligation and responsibility to the immediate community was a requirement gave way to different social structures facilitated by newer modes of communication. Communities of "connection" rather than "obligation" have become the focus of much attention - from Melvin N. Webber's consideration of "community without propinquity" or "non-place communities" back in 1964 (Webber, 1964, p.116) to Howard Rheingold's seminal "Virtual Community" (1993) onward there has been a growing literature examining online community construction, community networks, and the fabrication of digital communities (Barnes, 2001, Schuler & Stone, 1996).

In the digital media environment the individual blocks, filters, monitors, scans, deletes and restricts while constructing a controlled media environment. The individual functions in a multi-media environment characterized by "detachment." Enhanced control of the media environment brings greater community choice. The "I" can select community with distant others. Traditional community reflected a time bias, community meant to endure and bind people over time. The space bias of electronic media extends community over distance, but physical space retains relevancy.

Digital media promote supplanting communities of space with communities of interest or communities of place. Could it be said that the "me" bias of digital media allow for "place-making" based on personal meaning and resulting in the elevation of communities of place? "Place–making is the conscious process of arranging or appropriating objects and spaces to create an environment that supports desired activities, while conveying the social and cultural conceptions of the actors and their wider communities (Canter, 1977).

Spatially biased media obliterate space and temporally biased media obliterate time. The "me" biased digital media enable, to a degree, the obliteration of the unwanted, the detachment from place and, in extreme cases, the choice of a-location.

SOLUTIONS AND RECOMMENDATIONS

We are living on an "urban planet" (Brugman, 2009) with more than half the world's population now living in cities of diverse sizes, shapes, populations and economies. Cities are being built and rebuilt and will need to accommodate an additional 2 billion people new urbanites in the next 25 years.

It took 80 years from the start of mechanized production in the 1760s until the realization in the 1840s that Britain was undergoing an "Industrial Revolution." People didn't discuss and plan "industrialization" until the 1880s. In the same way, we only partially understand the revolutionary event of our times: the re-engineering of society, economics and Earth's ecology into a global city.

Most city planning, investment and governance debates still explore the city in mid-20th century terms. Back then, cities were viable jurisdictions, working within the framework of nation states. It was an orderly world. Nations had "primary," "secondary" and "tertiary" cities. In today's economic development jargon, cities are still ranked as "alpha" and "beta" cities, and they "compete" with one another as if they were distinct and manageable corporations (Brugman, 2009).

Future cities will be smart cities, wired cities, virtual cities, digital cities and perhaps most significantly, global cities. Manuel Castells views the modern global city as a consequence of the shift to an information-based economy. In his conception, global cities are key nodes in a 'space of flows' that structure the international economic and social relations of production. But flows alone do not capture the essence of a global city that struggles to retain its sense of community or more accurately, communities. Communication is at the heart of both To understand and plan for growing urban environments dominating the world that recognizes that our daily lives are shaped by the design of place intertwined and co-existing with electronic means of connection, that the two fuse and are determinants of the other, we begin to approach design through a different and perhaps more complex but unified model. A contemporary approach to the city should account for the influence of the physical environment augmented by embedded and mobile technologies and influenced by the larger media environment. In so doing, the person/environment relationship is increasingly characterized by a degree of place detachment.

FUTURE RESEARCH DIRECTION

The increasing development of convergent technology, in which a variety of media are integrated in a single platform or protocol has enormous implications both on the nature of community and planning, and upon the relationship of individuals within a global network. We live in increasingly convergent cities. With the development of the "wired" or "smart" city, the increasing role of telecommuting, the ambiguity of "public" and "private" space, the rise of cyberspace and virtual environments, the spatial and ecological consequences require the attention of planners, designers, and architects.

Convergence is an in-vogue concept recently applied to the coming together of a variety of media through the platform of the computer and digitalization thereby transforming it into an instrument capable of transmitting and receiving sound and image simultaneously and serially. The daily lives of individuals are experienced in multiple and diverse psychological and social zones. Increasingly we function across overlapping and simultaneous boundaries of place–some physical, others mediated, some public, others private. We could see the rise of the convergent city.

P.J. Taylor has noted that urban policy now transcends boundaries and with this change comes the necessity to consider relational overlapping spaces. However, in emphasizing the measurement of inter-city relations in urban policy development the interpersonal and inter-media relations are lost. To study the future of the city with adequate consideration of the media environment fueling the move to a convergent city future research ought address the following questions:

- What is community in a technological age?
- Is it possible to retain vibrant place-based communities while recognizing the increasing significance of digital communities and global connection?
- How might policies and practices of urban design and planning best address the changing nature and experience of urban space by integrating information and telecommunication technologies into their views of the world?
- What is the relationship of suburbia and the center city?

Valuable future directions in empirical research are suggested by Jeffres et. al (2010) looking at how effective different community communication systems are in enhancing a personal sense of community or neighborhood attachment. Research directions underscore the potential in measuring indicators of instrumental communication patterns for learning about identification and place attachment when communication through mediated channels can pull people from attachment to community and place.

In an age of increasing place detachment the words of George Simmel resonate. He said: "We are at any moment those who separate the connected or connect the separate?"

REFERENCES

Alexander, C. (1977). *Pattern Language: Towns, Buildings, Construction*. New York: Oxford University Press.

Aurigi, A., & De Cindio, F. (2008). Introduction. In Aurigi, A., & De Cindio, F. (Eds.), *Augmented Urban Spaces* (pp. 1–4). London: Ashgate Publishers.

Babe, R. E. (2006). Innis and the News. *Javnost—The Public, 13*(3), 43-56.

Barnes, S. B. (2001). *Online Connections: Internet Interpersonal Relationships*. Cresskill, NJ: Hampton Press.

Biocca, F. (1997). The cyborg's dilemma: Progressive embodiment in virtual environments. *Journal of Computer-Mediated Communication, 3*(2). Retrieved from www.ascusc.org/jcmc/vol3/issue2/biocca2.html accessed Sept. 12, 2009.

Blascovich, J. (2002). Social influence within immersive virtual environments. In Schroeder, R. (Ed.), *The Social Life of Avatars* (pp. 127–145). Berlin: Springer-Verlag.

Boler, M. (2008). *Digital Media and Democracy Tactics in Hard Times*. Boston: MIT Press.

Brown, B., Perkins, D., & Brown, G. (2004). Incivilities, place attachment and crime: Block and individual effects. *Journal of Environmental Psychology, 24*, 359–371. Retrieved from http://www.observatoriodeseguranca.org/files/sdarticle.pdf accessed August 30, 2009. doi:10.1016/j.jenvp.2004.01.001

Brown, B. B., & Altman, I. (1983). Territoriality, defensible space, and residential burglary: An environmental analysis. *Journal of Environmental Psychology, 3*, 203–220. doi:10.1016/S0272-4944(83)80001-2

Brown, B. B., & Perkins, D. D. (1992). Disruptions in place attachment. In I. Altman, & &S. Low (Eds.), *Place attachment,* (pp. 279–304). New York: Plenum.

Brugman, J. (2009, May 5). *Living on Urban Planet Forbes.com*. Retrieved September12, 2009 from http://www.forbes.com/2009/05/05/state-of-the-city-opinions-contributors-urban-planet.html

Burd, G., Drucker, S. J., & Gumpert, G. (Eds.). (2007). *The Urban Communication Reader*. Cresskill, NJ: Hampton Press.

Canter, D. V. (1977). *The Psychology of Place*. New York: Architectural Press.

Carey, J. W. (1992). *Communication As Culture: Essays on Media and Society*. New York: Routedge.

Carey, J. W. (2005). Historical Pragmatism and the Internet. Retrieved September 1 5, 2009 from http://nms.sagepub.com/cgi/content/abstract/7/4/443

Castells, M. (2000). *The Rise of the Network Society* (2nd ed.). New York: Blackwell Publishing.

Chandler, A. D., & Cortada, J. W. (Eds.). (2000). *A Nation Transformed by Information. How Information Has Shaped the United States from Colonial times to the Present*. New York: Oxford University Press.

De Souza e Silva, A., & Sutko, D. M. (2009). *Digital Cityscapes: Merging Digital and Urban Playspaces*. New York: Peter Lang Publishing.

Duany Plater-Zyberk. (2003). Retrieved from http://www.smartcodecentral.org/smartfilesv9.html, accessed 16 April 2007.

Felson, M. (1987). Routine activities and crime prevention in the developing metropolis. *Criminology, 25*, 911–931. doi:10.1111/j.1745-9125.1987.tb00825.x

Gergen, K. J. (2002). The challenge of absent presence. In Grant, C. A., & Ladson Billings, G. (Eds.), *Dictionary of multicutural education* (pp. 227–241). New York: Oryx Press.

Gibson, T. A., & Lowes, M. A. (2006). *Urban Communication: Production, Text, Context*. New York: Rowman & Littlefield Publishers.

Goldberger, P. (n.d.). *Cities, Place and Cyberspace*. Retrieved March 21, 2005, from http://www.paulgoldberger.com/speeches.php?speech=berkeley#articlestart

Gordon, E. (2010). *The Urban Spectator: American Concept-Cities from Kodak to Google*. Dartmouth, MA: Dartmouth.

Graham, S. (Ed.). (2004). *The Cybercities Reader*. New York: Routledge.

Graham, S., & Marvin, S. (1996). *Telecommunications and the City*. London: Routledge. doi:10.4324/9780203430453

Gumpert, G., & Drucker, S. (2001). A Plea for Chaos. *Qualitative Research Reports in Communication, 2* (2, Spring), 25-32.

Gumpert, G., & Drucker, S. (2004). The Perfections of Sustainability and Imperfections in the Digital Community: Paradoxes of Connection and Disconnection. In Tanabe, M., Van den Besselaar, P., & Ishida, T. (Eds.), *Digital Cities III* (pp. 369–379). Berlin: Springer-Verlag.

Gumpert, G., & Drucker, S. (2008). Communicative Cities. *The International Communication Gazette, 70* (3-4, June), 195-208.

Gumpert, G., & Drucker, S. (2008). The City and the Two Sides of Reciprocity. In Aurigi, A., & De Cindio, F. (Eds.), *Digital Cities: the Augmented Public Space*.

Harris, P. B., & Brown, B. B. (1996). The home and identity display: Interpreting resident territoriality from home exteriors. *Journal of Environmental Psychology, 16*, 187–203. doi:10.1006/jevp.1996.0016

Innis, H. A. (1950). *Empire and Communications*. Oxford, UK: Oxford University Press.

Innis, H. A. (1951). *The Bias of Communication*. Toronto: University of Toronto Press.

Innis, H. A. (1971). *The Bias of Communication. Introduction by Marshall McLuhan*. Toronto: University of Toronto Press.

Jacobs, J. (1960). *The Death and Life of Great American Cities*. New York: Vintage Books.

Jassem, H. (2007). Municipal Wi-Fi-ing of the United States. In Burd, G., Drucker, S., & Gumpert, G. (Eds.), *The Urban Communication Reader* (pp. 219–235). Cresskill, NJ: Hampton Press.

Jeffres, L., Lee, J., & Jian, G. (2010). Modeling Neighborhood Attachment Influence. In Jassem, H., Drucker, S., & Burd, G. (Eds.), *Urban Reader II* (pp. 103–131). Cresskill, N.J.: Hampton Press.

Macek, S. (2006). *Urban Nightmares: The Media, the Right, and the Moral Panic over the City*. Minneapolis, MN: University of Minnesota Press.

Makagon, D. (2004). *Where the Ball Drops: Days and Nights in Times Square*. Minneapolis, MN: University of Minnesota Press.

Marx, G. (2002). What's New about the "New Surveillance"? *Surveillance & Society, 1*(1), 9–29.

McLuhan, M. (1964). *Understanding Media: The Extensions of Man*. New York: Mentor.

McQuire, S. (2008). *The Media City: Media, Architecture and Urban Space*. London: Sage.

Milligan, M.J. (). *Interactional Past And Potential: The Social Construction Of Place Attachment, 21* (1), 1–33.

Mitchell, W. J. (1995). *City of Bits: Space, Place, and the Infobahn*. Cambridge, MA: MIT Press.

Mosco, M. (2004). *The Digital Sublime: Myth, Power, and Cyberspace*. Cambridge, MA: MIT Press.

Rettie, R. M. (2005). Presence and Embodiment in Mobile Phone Communication. *PsychNology Journal*, *3*(1), 16–34.

Rheingold, H. (1993). *The Virtual Community: Homesteading on the Electronic Frontier*. Reading, MA: Addison-Wesley Pub Co.

Schuler, D., & Stone, T. (Eds.). (1996). *New Community Networks: Wired for Change*. Reading, MA: Addison-Wesley Pub Co.

Taylor, P. J. (2010). Measuring the world city network. In Firmino, R., Duarte, F., & Ultramari, C. (Eds.), *ICTs for Mobile and Ubiquitous Urban Infrastructures: Surveillance, Locative Media and Global Networks*. Hershey, PA: IGI Global.

Virilio, P. (1991). *The Lost Dimension* (trans. D. Moshenberg), New York: Semiotext(e).

Webber, M. N. (1964). The Urban Place and the Nonplace Urban Realm. In *Explorations into Urban Structure*. Philadelphia: University of Pennsylvania Press.

Willis, K. S. (2008). Places, Situations, and Connections. In Aurigi, A., & De Cindio, F. (Eds.), *Augmented Urban Spaces* (pp. 9–26). London: Ashgate Publishers.

Wood, A. (2009). *City Ubiquitous: Place, Communication, and the Rise of Omnitopia*. Cresskill, NJ: Hampton Press.

World Charter on the Right to the City. (2004). Retrieved September 12, 2009 from http://v1.dpi.org/lang-en/resources/details.php?page=124

ADDITIONAL READING

Aurigi, A. (2005). *Making the Digital City: The Early Shaping of Urban Internet Space*. UK: Ashgate Publishing Ltd.

Bagdikian, Ben. 1990. The Media Monopoly. 3d ed. Boston: Beacon Press.

Bates, B. "Information as an Economic Good: Sources of Individual and Social Value". The Political Economy of Information. eds. Vincent Mosco and Janet Wasko. 1988. Madison: University of Wisconsin Press.

Carey, J. W. (1988). *Communication As Culture*. New York: Routledge.

Duany, A., Plater-Zyberk, E., & Speck, J. (2001). *Suburban nation*. New York: North Point Press.

Fernandez, R. R., & Dillman, D. A. (1979). The influence of community attachment on geographic mobility. *Rural Sociology*, *44*, 345–360.

Florida, R. (2008). *Who's Your City?: How the Creative Economy Is Making Where You Live the Most Important Decision of Your Life*. New York: Basic Books.

Graham, S. (2004). *Cybercities Reader*. London: Routledge.

Graham, S., & Marvin, S. (1996). *Telecommunications and the City: Electronic spaces, Urban Places*. London: Routledge. doi:10.4324/9780203430453

Granovetter, M. (1982). The strength of weak ties. A network theory revisited. In P.V. Marsden & N. Lin (Eds.), *Social structure and network analysis* (pp. 105-130). Newbury Park, Sage.

Gumpert, G., & Drucker, S. J. (1992). From the Agora to the Electronic Shopping Mall. *Critical Studies in Mass Communication*, 9.

Hays, R. A., & Kogl, A. M. (2007). Neighborhood attachment, social capital building, and political participation: A case study of low- and moderate-income residents of Waterloo, Iowa. *Journal of Urban Affairs*, *29*, 181–205. doi:10.1111/j.1467-9906.2007.00333.x

Horan, T. A. (2000). *Digital places: Building Our City of Bit*. Washington, D.C.: Urban Land Institute.

Jeffres, L. W. (2002). *Urban communication systems*. Cresskill, N.J.: Hampton Press, Inc.

Kasarda, J. D., & Janowitz, M. (1974). Community attachment in mass society. *American Sociological Review, 39*, 328–339. doi:10.2307/2094293

Katz, J. E. (Ed.). (2006). *Magic in the air: Mobile communication and the transformation of social life*. New Brunswick, NJ: Transaction Publishers.

Katz, J. E. (Ed.). (2008). *Handbook of mobile communication studies*. Cambridge, MA: The MIT Press.

Katz, J. E., & Aakhus, M. (Eds.). (2002). *Perpetual contact: Mobile communication, private talk, public performance*. Cambridge: Cambridge University Press. doi:10.1017/CBO9780511489471

Katz, J. E., & Rice, R. (2002). *Social consequences of Internet use: Access, involvement and expression*. Cambridge, MA: MIT Press.

Kleinman (ed.). In *Displacing place: Mobile communication in the 21st cCentury,* Peter Lang Publishing, 2007, 7-20.

Kunstler, J. H. (1993). *Geography of nowhere*. New York: Touchstone.

Maslow, A., & Lowery, R. (Eds.). (1998). *Toward a psychology of being* (3rd ed.). New York: Wiley & Sons.

McKenzie, E. (1996). *Privatopia: Homeowner associations and the rise of residential private government*. New Haven, CT: Yale University Press.

McLuhan, M. (1964). *Understanding Media: The Extensions of Man*. New York: McGraw-Hill.

Mesch, G. S., & Manor, O. (1998). Social ties, environmental perception and local attachment. *Environment and Behavior, 30*, 504–519. doi:10.1177/001391659803000405

Meyerowitz, J. (1985). *No Sense of Place*. New York: Oxford University Press.

Mitchell, W. J. (1999). *E-topia*. Massachusetts: MIT Press Cambridge.

Moores, S. (1993). *Interpreting Audiences: The Ethnography of Media Consumption*. London: Sage Publishing.

Mosco, V., & Wasko, J. (1988). *The Political Economy of Information*. Madison, Wisconsin: University of Wisconsin Press.

Mumby, D. K. (1989, Fall). Ideology and the Social Construction of Meaning: A Communication Perspective. *Communication Quarterly, 37*(4).

Mumford, L. (1960). *The Culture of Cities*. New York: Harcourt, Brace.

Poole, Ithiel de Sola Pool. 1983. Technologies of Freedom. Cambridge: Harvard University Press.

Putnam, R. D. (1995). Bowling alone: America's declining social capital. *Journal of Democracy, 6*, 65–78. doi:10.1353/jod.1995.0002

Riger, S., & Lavrakas, P. J. (1981). Community ties: Patterns of attachment and social interaction in urban neighborhoods. *American Journal of Community Psychology, 2*, 55–66. doi:10.1007/BF00896360

Rotenberg, R., & McDonogh, G. (Eds.). (1993). *The Cultural Meaning of Urban Space*. Westport, Connecticut: Bergin and Garvey.

Sennett, R. (1990). *The Conscience of the Eye: The Design and Social Life of Cities*. New York: Norton.

Soja, E. (1990). *Postmodern Geographies: The Reassertion of Space in Critical Social Theory*. London: Verso.

Stamm, K., Emig, A. G., & Hesse, M. B. (1997). The contribution of local media to community involvement. *Journalism & Mass Communication Quarterly, 74*, 97–107.

Tonnies, F. (1963). *Community and society*. New York: Harper & Row.

Tuan, Y. (1990). *Topophilia: A Study of Environmental Perception, Attitudes, and Values*. New York: Columbia University Press.

Tuan, Y. (2001). *Space and Place: The Perspective of Experience*. Minneapolis: University of Minnesota Press.

KEY TERMS AND DEFINITIONS

Augmented Spaces: Spaces enriched with media and information technologies. Augmented spaces are enhanced by both connectivity and content.

Place Attachment: Refers to the emotional bonds between people and their physical settings. Meanings are given to places since they function as a setting for experiences. The concept of place attachment is is studied from across diverse disciplines including psychology, geography, social ecology.

Presence: The feeling or psychological state in which an individual perceives as being in a situation.

Time-Binding Media: Communication media that unifies widely separated times as articulated in the work of Canadian economist Harold Innis. Time-binding, such as hand copied manuscripts, clay tablets and oral communication are have limited distribution but have the ability to facilitate social continuity over time.

Transect: A model for regional planning based on separation of six zones, moving from rural to urban which vary by the degree of natural and built features. The transect a feature of the New Urbanism movement.

Space-Binding Media: Unifies widely separated places by extending communication over distance. Space binding media such as printing, telegraph, broadcasting enable the development of cohesion across space.

Urban Communication: The study of communication patterns in the urban environment. Urban Communication scholars use established communication studies approaches/methodologies; to explore the historical and philosophical perspectives along with case studies of the interpersonal and media landscape of spaces, places and communication texts.

Zoning: Zoning is a way governments control land use and development. Originating in Europe during the 19th century, New York City developed the first formal zoning ordinance in 1916. Zoning typically segregates land uses into three main categories - residential, commercial, and industrial.

Chapter 5
City Networks in Cyberspace and Time:
Using Google Hyperlinks to Measure Global Economic and Environmental Crises

Andrew Boulton
University of Kentucky, USA

Lomme Devriendt
Ghent University, Belgium

Stanley Brunn
University of Kentucky, USA

Ben Derudder
Ghent University, Belgium

Frank Witlox
Ghent University, Belgium

ABSTRACT

Geographers and social scientists have long been interested in ranking and classifying the cities of the world. The cutting edge of this research is characterized by a recognition of the crucial importance of information and, specifically, ICTs to cities' positions in the current Knowledge Economy. This chapter builds on recent "cyberspace" analyses of the global urban system by arguing for, and demonstrating empirically, the value of Web search engine data as a means of understanding cities as situated within, and constituted by, flows of digital information. To this end, the authors show how the Google search engine can be used to specify a dynamic, informational classification of North American cities based on both the production and the consumption of Web information about two prominent current issues global in scope: the global financial crisis, and global climate change.

DOI: 10.4018/978-1-60960-051-8.ch005

INTRODUCTION

The lexicon surrounding cyberspace, the Internet and "new" technologies is replete with spatial metaphors and analogies (Adams, 1997): e.g., online *community*, web *site*, information *gateway*, *portal* site, chat *room*. At one level, the reading of this spatial language is straightforward. Spatial/territorial analogy superimposes upon the otherwise intangible (and unintelligible) sphere of bits and bytes a determinate and visible/visualizable *representational* surface. Cyberspace, so imagined, becomes knowable; written in "geographical language" (Kellerman, 2002, p. 31) it becomes definable, mappable and understandable in terms of standard spatial rubrics of distance and proximity, connection and flow (see, in relation to virtual worlds, Hudson-Smith et al. 2007). But an alternative reading of this spatial language suggests a problematization of the supposed separation between underlying reality (intangible/unintelligible) and overlaid representation (tangible/visible) (see Cicognani, 1998). This second reading recognizes that the "virtual" world of cyberspace is already fundamentally imbricated with the "real", material life of the contemporary city (Crutcher & Zook, 2009). It is this more nuanced conceptualization of the relationship between the "virtuality" of cyberspace and the "reality" of cities that we seek to build on in this chapter.

Hyperbolic claims that distance—and with it, place, city, and geography—is, or soon will be, "dead" (e.g., O'Brien, 1992; Negroponte, 1995; Kaba, 1996) belie an important paradox of the contemporary information-based economy: even as ICTs become accessible "everywhere", demand for the physical, corporeal transportation between places, and for prime, proximate real estate within "core" urban locations continues to grow (Denstadli & Gripsrund, 2010). The vision of so-called "post-industrial" theorists of a world without distance, where "everyplace is everyplace" (Abler, 1974), remains entirely unmet in several key respects. Society and technology shape each other in complex ways. While, at the most basic level, ICT implies a decoupling of simultaneity in time from contiguity in space (Castells, 1996), informational flows—the informational "cloud" of ubiquitous communications—are in fact, underpinned and enabled by a vast, *physical* (placed) ICT infrastructure. Thus, rather than rendering place irrelevant, cities' economic performance and their prominence within the global urban network becomes, increasingly, a product of their positions vis-à-vis all other places in relation to ICT networks. Electronic communication has not and cannot be substituted for the social, cultural and economic advantages of urban agglomeration. Or, as Goldsmith and Wu (2006, p. 56) put it, very simply: "[f]ar from destroying cities by making place irrelevant, the production and consumption of Internet content, and the infrastructure to support it, are concentrated in cities."

This chapter seeks to unpack this question of the positions cities occupy in relation to ICT networks, meaning that we seek to understand "cyberspace" as an *object* of study in the context of global urban networks. In contrast to earlier ICT-based urban research in which analyses tend to trace out a 'cyber' geography via *physical* infrastructure and *material* connection, we suggest two ways cyberspace can be incorporated into global urban network research. First, we consider cities as lived places with attributes—experiential, economic, representational, infrastructural—which are represented in and produced by their cyberspaces. And, second, we consider cities as nodes in transnational networks of capital, ideas, representations, and information. Our focus on cyberspace offers a new take on the methodological question of how to study cities' positions within urban networks, especially, in the context and under the aegis of the information-based Knowledge Economy.

The remainder of this chapter proceeds as follows. We first turn to debates within the literature on the conceptualization of "hierarchies" versus "networks", "world cities", and "cyberspace". We examine the nature of the global urban network in order to problematize the ontological assumption of horizontality and mutuality between cities. We argue that the world city network of information flows/exchanges presents itself as an altogether messier and dynamic amalgam of hierarchical and networked characteristics wherein cities position themselves simultaneously in terms of both. Given this understanding, we put forward the thinking that the use of "cyberspace" (i.e. placed and georeferenced informational data) is essential in producing meaningful characterizations of the dynamism of cities and their connections. We examine the relationship between "cyberspace" and world cities[1] literature in more detail and review the ways in which flow information has been used in empirical World Cities Network (WCN) research. Thereafter, we evaluate two different approaches to apprehending empirically cities' relative positions within omnipresent ICT networks, detailing the contributions of both infrastructural (or "cyberplace") and informational (or "cyberspace") approaches (Devriendt et al., 2008). While we argue that infrastructure-based accounts of inter-city connection (e.g., Moss & Townsend, 2000; Rutherford et al., 2004; Malecki & Wei, 2009) are valuable, we show that there exists a need to study not only tangible informational infrastructures and their associated material flows between places, but also the evolving cyberspaces of cities in relation to digital information. These cyberspace-based approaches offer new ways of comparing world cities in the knowledge-based "Information Age" based on the nature of their respective cyberspaces.

In order to illustrate this "new way" of comparing cities, we build on our ongoing search engine based project using Google data (Devriendt et al., 2009). We distinguish this contribution by making use of Google's Insights tool to introduce an innovation in world city analysis, viz., a means of operationalizing "dynamism" in WCN inquiry via the introduction of a "real-time" temporal component to our analysis. The largest cities in the United States are used as our empirical case as an empirical "first cut" using this methodology. Similar analyses, for other cases, and in other languages represent fruitful ground for future cybserspace research. The major question we ask, in the empirical analysis, is: which U.S. cities are leaders (and laggards) in terms of the popular awareness of/interest in key cultural, political and environmental issues? The largest 51 cities, in terms of population, in the United States (Demographia, 2008), and the global financial and environmental crises will be used to address this central question. A two-pronged approach focusing on information consumption (i.e., Web search activity) *and* information production (i.e. Web information availability) provides additional information about the *nature* and *temporality* of these cities' cyberspaces. Finally, we summarize our main findings and suggest some avenues for further research.

WHAT FLOWS? NETWORKS, HIERARCHIES, CYBERSPACE AND CYBERPLACE

In this section we review relevant aspects of the world cities literature to examine critically the ways in which "networks", "world cities" and "cyberspace" have been and can be conceptualized. What are some of the implications for regarding world cities as networked horizontally rather than nested vertically (for example, see Taylor, this volume)? While in some ways—specifically, in terms of the distribution of particular economic functional specialization—the world city network might appear as a horizontal network predicated on the mutuality of cities' functions (i.e. complementarity, rather than competition), this is a rather narrow view of a much more amorphous, complex space of power and connection. Following through this argument—that cities present themselves not just as hierarchically arranged, or just as networked, but simultaneously both (or neither)—leads us to specify a means of capturing something of the less tangible connections and identities of places using Google search engine derived data.

Hierarchies and Networks

Fundamental to the trajectory of world city research in recent years has been the shift from treating global space as a hierarchical arrangement of city-entities to a flattened, networked ontology of complementarity. Intuitively, "hierarchy" is held in contradistinction from "network" (Thompson, 2003). While the former—the staple of early world cities literature—implies verticality, a ranking of more-or-less powerful places, the latter (network) suggests horizontality, a flattened space of mutuality and cooperation (Taylor, 2008). Certainly, this view is implicit in Manuel Castells' work on "flows". In his seminal work, Castells (1996) argues that qualitative changes in the nature of contemporary society necessitate a "new spatial logic," that is, one based on networks of informational flows: "flows of technology, flows of organizational interaction, flows of images, sounds and symbols" (Castells, 1996, p. 412). But, even though discussions of urban *hierarchy*—where "senior" cities have power over and control those below them—might be unfashionable or unhelpful (Taylor, 2009), we argue that it makes some sense to examine cities in terms of urban *rank*. That is, some cities are, we observe, simply more important than others in terms of the production and consumption of discourse on definitive world (city) issues such as financial and environmental crises, cultural trends, etc.

"List-mania" (Taylor, this volume) is, undoubtedly, a popular international pastime (or affliction) of geographers and others. The top 10 party cities; top 20 weekend getaways: cities are popular subjects to rank. The ordering of cities in such ways, however specious the methodologies and however lacking in rigor the methods, speaks to an underlying political economy of boosterism, but also of information production and consumption. While to some extent these rankings are 'just for fun', the "top 10 party city" headlines (Ibid.) are just the tip of an economic-cultural iceberg beneath the ranking surface: a political economy incorporating press releases, public relations, traditional marketing, Web traffic solicitation, newspaper circulation and so forth. Lists are meaningful to information consumers, and not only a "lay" readership. Peter Taylor laments that, of all the subtle and complex work produced under the ambit of the Global and World Cities (GaWC) Group and Network (http://www.lboro.ac.uk/gawc), it is the list of alpha, beta and gamma cities that is most frequently sought out—and referenced by—urban scholars (Taylor, this volume)[2]. Once categorized, and once ranked, cities, like sports teams, may assume a particular more-or-less impressive status among the peers with which they are competing. *Forbes* magazine's "most livable city in the US" accolade, for instance, is touted on the official tourism Web site of Portland, Oregon long after the actual methodology, or purpose, of the ranking exercise is forgotten (http://www.travelportland.com/media/portland_in_news.html).

Given an initial 'league table', the impulse to monitor that table through time seems irresistible. Giving consumers—whether urban scholars in the case of the GaWC, or city planners in the case of "livability" rankings—what they want is one (economically sound) argument for producing rankings. Another is to claim that cities are, in fact, related hierarchically to other cities. The so-called "NY-LON" (New York and London) or "NY-LON-KONG" (New York, London and Hong Kong) phenomenon is, perhaps, the classic illustration offered in favor of the argument that global financial centers are oriented towards carving complementary niches within the global economy rather than simply competing for dominance. The qualitative work of Karen Lai (2009) on the often complementary relationships between China's financial centers (Shanghai, Beijing and Hong Kong) is useful in drawing attention to the complexity of actually existing connections between places. Treating cities as networked places, rather than as placeless nodes, requires us to note that places are peopled with diverse actors with diverse agendas, and are associate too with different "types" of flow (people, information, capital). This complicates notions of agency and claims to unproblematically assert a city's identity/function/type (etc.). As Ranjit Hoskote's (2008) account of the complexities surrounding Mumbai's development and emergence as (among many other things) a "world city" and a "cultural center" makes clear, cities are by no means "unities", or unified actors. That is, the contiguity of actors in space does not necessarily entail commonality of purpose, shared allegiance, or shared understanding of place.

Ranking cities, implicitly ordering them hierarchically might, as Peter Taylor suggests (this volume) emphasize competition rather than cooperation, running against the "spirit" of the GaWC Network but—less optimistically—it also reflects that cities are locked into complex and uneven networks of power. While it is possible to gain a handle, empirically, on aspects of a city's identity, especially in terms of components of its economic activity and specific types of material connection between cities, we would seek to stress differences and, specifically, the less-than-tangible representations and flows of information that represent, mediate and produce place. It is because of, and not in spite of, the dynamism of cities and their connections that the task of producing meaningful characterizations—including rankings—of cities, using informational data (specifically, cyberspace) becomes important. A network ontology of world cities should, in other words, accommodate cyberspace-based city rankings, not because such rankings unproblematically and intuitively reflect a structural ordering of cities in global political-economic space (though, durability of cities' relative rankings might be suggestive), but because they present instantaneous snapshots of dynamic interrelations.

Indeed, the rise of the Internet and the increasing ubiquity of ICTs, especially in the form of portable devices and personal computers, have transformed and complicated the relationship between the materiality of urban places and the virtuality of digital information. While "cyberspace", like informational flows, is, from one perspective, place-less, that is, a horizontal "network" of flows or an informational cloud above (or apart from) material reality, from another perspective, cyberspace is inextricably linked to material reality. Cyberspace reflects/represents and mediates material reality, but it also in part constitutes that reality (Crutcher & Zook, 2009). That which flows (capital, ideas, etc.) is embodied in people and in the enabling material infrastructure of cyberspace, but it also entails decentered patterns of production and consumption of information about cities untethered in respect of physical/absolute space. Central to this way of thinking about an interurban network of connection is the need to complicate (in order to comprehend) concepts such as "cyberspace" and "networks" in ways that recognize the twin qualities of cities as *both* lived places with attributes—experiential, economic, representational, infrastructural—*and* nodes in transnational networks of capital, ideas, representations, and information.

A legitimate question at this juncture then arises, viz., how, can we examine the relationships between "cyberspace" and "world cities" in ways that acknowledge both the importance of placed attributes, infrastructures and concentrations of power *and* the autonomy of a dis-placed cyberspace? In section 2.4 below we consider the insights of both the *cyberplace approach*—concerned with tangible informational infrastructure that facilitates "virtual" flows—and the (here advocated) *cyberspace approach* which is more concerned with the effects and content of information and how these change through time.

ICT Networks and World City Research

The current revival in interest in classifying cities and characterizing the links between them can be placed on a long trajectory in the social sciences. As we have already noted, the "ranking" impulse is strong, and, indeed, has been a prominent component of the "world cities" literature, defined broadly, from the outset of modern inquiry into the global urban system in the first half of the twentieth century. Here we locate current cyberspace/information-based analyses of cities within a genealogy of literature examining the interactions between cities.

Concepts such as "primate cities" (Jefferson, 1939) and, later, millionaire cities (Davis, 1959) stressed the hierarchical arrangement of global space. Writing in the context of a globalizing world urban system and, more pertinently to these authors, rapidly urbanizing populations, scholarly interest turned to the question of understanding and theorizing the relationship between cities and their hinterlands, and between cities and other cities. And as change continues apace, especially in terms of the transportation and, more dramatically, ICTs connecting and reconfiguring cities, interest has once again been piqued in respect of how scholars can begin to get a handle on qualitative changes in the nature of the world city network.

Where population was key, in classic central place theory studies, to determining the "threshold" for certain service functions and thus defining hierarchy, the theoretical underpinnings and empirical validation of such models soon came into question. The inadequacy of population size as a proxy for cities' relative positions and importance in the information world is obvious. For example, in terms of current population, more than half of the world's 30 largest cities are located in Asia, yet few of these rank among the commercial, political and cultural centers of gravity in the global city system (Williams & Brunn, 2004). Few analysts would deny the very real importance of population size, or how the rate of population change influences the nature and intensity of the economic and social challenges and opportunities a city faces. Indeed, such issues as resource sustainability, quality, affordable housing, infectious disease, as well as governance, and disaster preparedness, are more prominently the concern of scholars and policymakers alike in the present era.

Thus, from the 1960s onwards, a succession of geographers and sociologists moved on from the population focus to make use of other proxies for cities' importance/centrality at local, national, regional and global scales. They included: the number of headquarters of major corporations; banking and financial institutions; quantity of NGOs, etc. (Hall, 1966; Friedmann, 1986; Knox, 1994). Derivatives of these studies, especially work on corporate organization (Taylor, 2001, 2004), provide valuable insights into the complex nature of contemporary economies. Taylor's work, and that of the GaWC Group more generally, represent the clearest illustration of the ways in which recent research on world cities has moved beyond the attribute-based comparative research model[3]. In other words, earlier classificatory schema treated cities as discrete entities with attributes, analyzing the internal "structure" of individual cities, or comparing their attributes. This mode of inquiry has come under sustained scrutiny only recently, and most prominently following the work of Castells (1996 & 2000). Today, the "standard" mode of inquiry in the world cities literature is, as we have identified, a variant on the "network" approach, characterizing the WCN as, if not a system, then certainly an interconnected assemblage. Although the earlier world cities literature did not seek to imply that cities exist in a vacuum, apart from and unconnected with other cities, it is only with the advent of the "new" knowledge economy, and within the context of rapid and far-reaching economic fluctuations, that the necessity of dynamic approaches emerges. The quickening and deepening connections—that is, flows—between places, held to be characteristic of the contemporary globalizing world, called for and calls for new ways of apprehending the relative importance of cities in an "Information Age" (Castells, 1996). In the present "Knowledge Economy" it is crucial that measures of global urban linkages take into account the flows of knowledge and informational between, and about, cities.

Specifying "Connection"

Manuel Castells' (1996) call for a "new spatial logic" based on networks of informational flows is, perhaps, the founding battle cry of the "new" network approaches to world cities. For Castells, flows were defined as: "flows of technology, flows of organizational interaction, flows of images, sounds and symbols" (Castells, 2000, p. 442). In this section, we draw out the major implications of this flow-based "spatial logic" for the study of world city networks. Perhaps the most striking feature of the Castellian approach—which rapidly established itself as central to world cities literature—was the gulf, until relatively recently, between the theoretical complexity of world city research and the absence of empirical elucidation. We, therefore, consider the (types of) data that can and have been used in world cities research. The inquiry into cities' cyberspaces, via search engine data—the method illustrated here—begins to introduce the intangible flows of information which at once bear traces of cities' qualities, and work to produce and mediate the experience and (therefore) material reality of cities.

According to Castells, physical proximity and face-to-face interaction were definitive of industrial society, whereas the (present) Information Age entails the fundamental reconfiguration of previously taken-for-granted relationships between time and space. At the most basic level, the Information Age, enabled by ICTs, entails a decoupling of simultaneity in time from contiguity in space (Sheller & Urry, 2006). Castells (1996) suggests that the global urban system should be apprehended not as a *space of places,* but as a *space of flows*. In the former, "place"—as constituted by Castells' space of places—is defined as the historically rooted spatial organization of common experience, fixed in space and invariant through time. The latter, the focus of "network" approaches to world cities, acknowledges both the multiple, overlapping spatialities of information in material and "virtual" spaces, and their continuous reconfiguration through time. Mindful of charges of a globalist hyperbole, we would note that change is a constant in the global economy and (thus) in the relations between world cities, even outside of "crisis" moments such as global recessions and credit crises. Friedmann's noting of this basic fact of continuous change in the global urban system led him to conclude that establishing hierarchy is futile (1995, p. 24):

"Establishing such a hierarchy [...] may, in any event, be a futile undertaking. The world economy is too volatile to allow us to fix a stale hierarchy for any but relatively short stretches of time. Assigning hierarchical rank may therefore be a less compelling exercise than recognizing the existence of differences in rank without further specification and, based on this rough notion, investigating the articulations of world cities with each other."

Friedman's call anticipated the present shift towards network based analysis in world cities research. His cautionary note against "stale' hierarchies is well-stated. But investigating the "articulations of world cities with each other" also entails, we would suggest, characterizing the quality and type of connections between cities in terms of their relative importance (rank), *and* the qualities of cities as places in and of themselves.

Friedmann (1986), Sassen (1991), and Castells (1996) all advocated using "flow" (or relational) data in the study of the global urban system. But the challenge of operationalizing this prioritization of networks—flows and relationality—over place—entities with attributes—was rarely addressed (Derudder, 2006). The absence of empirical elaboration that we note here has not gone unnoticed in previous studies. The so-called "data deficiency problem" (Taylor, 1997) is described by Short et al. (1996) as "the dirty little secret of world cities research". It is a truism of the Information Age that information is everywhere, but when it comes to information relevant to world cities scholars, finding and utilizing "good" data are relatively new developments. Indeed, one of the founding premises of the GaWC Network was precisely this observation: "although there has never been as much data for describing the world as exists today, the vast majority are collected for states and are about states and as such facilitate international comparisons but not the study of trans-state processes" (http://www.lboro.ac.uk/gawc/mission.html). Leading examples of the ways in which scholars have transcended the limitations of these "*state*-istics" to generate meaningful information about city (rather than nation-state) linkages include the outcomes from the GaWC group on corporate organization in advanced producer service firms (e.g., Taylor, 2001, 2004), along with infrastructure-based studies on "global reach" such as Internet infrastructure (e.g., Rutherford et al., 2004; Malecki & Wei, 2009) and airline networks (e.g., Zook & Brunn, 2005, 2006; Derudder et al., 2007). These are important studies that address in some detail various dimensions of the physical connections between cities in the global urban system. Further, they comprise part of the ongoing information-based research agenda that contributes to our understanding of the extent and complexity of inter-city connections.

The further challenge, spinning off from the discussion of Castells (1996), is how to acknowledge that among the connections between cities are flows that are intangible and *not* simply embodied in people (in the case of airline network analysis) or places (in the case of studies that focus specifically on the physical, enabling infrastructure of electronic communications). Partially addressing this "absence" are studies that use content analysis to examine news sources (e.g., Pred, 1980; Beaverstock et al., 2000) or analyses of conference proceedings in respect of the changing salience of specific topics through time. Beaverstock (2000) argues that "by recording place mentions in a sample of business news stories one can derive a surrogate measure of a city's external relations." Earlier studies based on hyperlinks between cities—operationalized as the number of web pages jointly referencing city pairs—conceptualized city relationships in similar ways, while pointing towards the potential of additional search engine data for world city research (Brunn & Williams, 2003; Brunn, 2004). We reiterate the importance of up-to-date information, and particularly the focus on "information" in its own right—in the case of Beaverstock et al (2000), the newspaper. Popular publications undoubtedly function as a barometer of issues' salience—at least insofar as their editors have access to sufficient information, and we trust their abilities to judge "salience". However, newspapers represent a tiny and declining slice of the political economy of knowledge production and consumption, and the information selection decisions of an editor represent the partial views of one person (or very small group). By contrast, the World Wide Web, accessed by one in four of the world's population (internetworldstats.com), entails millions of decisions by millions of "editors" daily—all of them gatekeepers of information. People make selection decisions both in terms of information production, by choosing what information to publish (via blogs and personal web pages) and, more frequently, in terms of information consumption, by searching. Web search engines provide us with up-to-date, detailed documentation of these decisions regarding information production and consumption. This information database is updated continuously; it is not a static time slice. In section 3 we return in detail to a consideration of the specific methodological challenges and implications of utilizing search engine data—a little-used (in the world cities literature) resource.

Cyberspace and Cyberplace

Against the backdrop of the a shift towards a Knowledge Economy or "Information Age" it is, as we have suggested, both desirable and necessary that digital communications and their enabling networks—the very "stuff" of the Knowledge Economy—should have entered into the purview of world city scholars' concerns. There is, of course, more than one way to examine such information networks. Indeed, following Devriendt et al. (2008), we can identify two broad typologies into which Information-based descriptions of the trans-national city network fit. We label and describe these approaches as CP (cyberplace) and CS (cyberspace), both of which offer promise in examining world city networks. Both, however, have some associated limitations.

Cyberplace. Here, we consider the body of work dealing with physical interconnections and material flows, viz., capital flows, corporate organization, and the distribution of airline passengers on a trajectory towards more recent work on Internet infrastructure. Infrastructural approaches are concerned with the physical infrastructure, such as fiber optic cables on which electronic communications depend and provide the framework in which to examine how high tech service and quaternary sector firms choose their locations. These physical connections can be considered reasonable proxies for the relative importance of cities in relation to digital flows as they reflect the architecture of the transnational infrastructure enabling ICT communications across the globe. In other words, global (tele)communication technologies are largely "tied to" key cities (Derudder, 2006), making a persuasive case that the flows of information and knowledge between these key cities defines the global urban network.

Always lurking in the background of infrastructure-based (CP) studies is the question of the proper conceptualization of cities both terminologically and in terms of "scale". As Derudder (2006) points out, there are methodological consequences of defining cities in particular ways, for example, as "world cities" (Friedmann, 1986) or "global cities" (Sassen, 1991). The "world cities" terminology is used typically to signal an approach to urban hierarchy based on the definition of a city as a territorially defined and "spatially integrated economic and social system at a given location or metropolitan region" (Friedmann, 1986, p. 70). Couched in the language of world systems theory, world cities literature classically emphasizes the international division of labor as materialized in and through the reproduction of core, peripheral, and semi-peripheral zones (cities) at the global scale.

By contrast, the sign "global cities" (Sassen, 1991) denotes a more explicitly knowledge-based focus, often concerned with agglomerations of advanced producer service firms (e.g., banking, law, accountancy, advertising, management consultancy, etc). Here power is reconceptualized not as the command-and-control power of world cities theory—in which more powerful core cities exert economic, ideological, and symbolic/representational control over their subordinates (Derudder, 2006)—but as practiced through intercity networks. The global city perspective is based on the active production of economic power via flows of knowledge and information. The adoption of a global cities perspectives has major implications for studies of inter-city linkages. First, the focus on knowledge flows implies an untethering of cities' economic functions from their physical location. In other words, major agglomerations of service functions such as downtown New York City are more connected with other similar agglomerations throughout the world than they are with their own metropolitan and suburban hinterlands. Second, and related, the patterns of hierarchy between cities are not necessarily fixed, and do not necessarily reflect "old" spatial/territorial hierarchies between North and South or core and periphery. That is, as telematics and ICTs more generally gain still further in importance, the most successful (and "powerful") cities will be those that are best placed with respect to ICT networks. These new "centers" might be in the developing or developed worlds. As Derudder (2006) flags, for example, Jakarta would not, perhaps, rank highly from a world city perspective, but its critical mass of high-technology, highly-connected financial and service functions downtown make it more prominent from a global cities perspective. Thus, even if one does not necessarily "buy" fully the more excitable post-industrial hype about the transformative potential of technology, the global cities approach is undoubtedly useful in identifying explicitly the importance of knowledge and information flows in the contemporary urban system. It is this information focus that the cyberspace approach seeks to build upon.

Cyberspace. In contrast to the cyberplace approaches in which knowledge/information flows are measured, by proxy, in terms of the physical connections between places, cyberspace approaches seek to deal with the virtual/digital world as an object of study in itself. It is a cyberspace approach to the study of world city networks that we seek to develop in this paper. Broadly, cyberspace approaches are based either on the structure of cyberspace or the content of cyberspace. Structural approaches to cyberspace are concerned with mapping out the hyperlinks between Web sites. For Web users, hyperlinks are the most obvious way in which two Web sites—and thus two pieces of information, two corporations, two places—are linked together, aiding navigation. Further, as Devriendt et al. (2008) point out, organizations must be extremely careful about which external Web sites they link to given that hyperlinks to external sites often denote endorsement of the external entity. Companies might, therefore, choose not to link to external sites for this very reason—a decision not without consequences. Indeed, search engine algorithms examine the structure of hyperlinks between Web pages, and rank pages, in part, on the importance of other Web sites with which they are connected (Zook & Graham, 2007). The structural approach to cyberspace is, therefore, useful for tracking the connections between corporations within the global knowledge economy. The structural approach is also a key component of search engine algorithms—the procedures by which the Web is "mapped" and Web pages ranked—and thus of the "optimization" of Web pages on the part of content-producers. The basic argument in favor of a structural approach to cyberspace is the expectation that, as more and more "business"—including social interaction via social networking services and the like—takes place online, the structure of hyperlinks (and equivalent digital connections) between people, corporations, and cities, will ever more closely approximate—and constitute—"real" interconnections.

In addition to structural approaches to cyberspace, content-based approaches to cyberspace are concerned with the material contained within Web sites. Centrally, content-based approaches to cyberspace are concerned with the textual content of Web pages. Web users seek information by inputting keywords into search engines such as Google. For example, in the context of the current study, Web users seeking information about the global financial crisis and its effects on the economy of New York City might enter "global financial crisis New York" into a search engine in order to return a listing of pages containing information on this topic. Which Web pages appear or, rather, the order in which they appear, is, as we have seen, partly a product of the hyperlinked structure of the World Wide Web as interpreted by the opaque algorithms of the search engine. But content-based analyses do not necessarily make reference to the underlying structure of hyperlinks or to the rank of pages (though see Devriendt et al., 2009 for a discussion of qualitative content analysis of highly ranked Web pages). Rather, they are concerned—as is the search algorithm—with the actual content of Web pages. Connections between topics are made textually within "pages" rather than contextually via hyperlink structures.

A CYBERSPACE ANALYSIS OF U.S. CITIES

The present study builds, in particular, on the content-based approach to cyberspace analysis. Previously, content-based analysis of cyberspace has been used to trace out the dyadic interconnections between cities by obtaining counts of Web pages jointly referring to those cities (Brunn & Williams, 2003; Brunn, 2004; Devriendt et al., 2008). An innovation to this approach is the inclusion of topical information in hyperlink analysis (Devriendt et al., 2009). We build upon the content-based analysis of Web information by asserting the importance not just of information production/availability (how much information is "out there"?) but also information consumption (what information is actively being sought?). [4]

In the discussion of "global cities" literature above, we noted that it is to be expected that cities' "ranks" vary according to which criteria are used. That is, the world airline network differs in some respects from the world fiber optic network, which in turn is not a straightforward reflection of the locations of producer service firms (Taylor et al. 2007). Likewise, in terms of content-based cyberspace analyses, it is to be expected that different cities would be positioned differently with respect to different informational measures. In this section we introduce, based on data from the leading and de facto standard Web search engine Google, two dynamic, informational city classifications, which we label the "Web content" and "Web activity" analyses, both exploring the production and the consumption of Web information about two prominent current issues global in scope: the global financial crisis, and global climate change.

The *Web Content Analysis* (WCA) illustrates some of the latest ways in which knowledge/information is produced *about* urban places. That is, we examine the information prominence on the two above-mentioned global issues for the 51 largest US cities (in terms of population, Demographia.com, 2008). The *Web Activity Analysis* (WAA), on the other hand, illustrates the urban *interest* in knowledge/information on these topics *over time*. That is, we investigate which cities (of the 51 largest) have the highest reported levels of search interest—based on the number of user searches made from each city—between January 2004 and August 2009. In short, we argue, this empirical section provides real time "snapshots" of the U.S. space of informational flows taking into account the *content*, the *spatiality* (geography), and the *temporality* of global Web information.

Web Content Analysis

Method. In seeking to understand the U.S. cities' positions within the space of informational flows, we first ranked the cities via a quantitative hyperlink analysis (for more information, see Devriendt et al., 2009). That is, we recorded the absolute numbers of hits or hyperlinks, according to Google.com, for each of the 51 largest US cities, in terms of (a) population (Demographia.com, 2008), (b) the combination of the city name and two financial terms ('economic slowdown' and 'global financial crisis') and (c) the city name in combination with two environmental topics ('climate change' and 'global warming'). For example, querying Google for the number of Web pages that jointly mention "Seattle" and "climate change" resulted in 1,750,000 entries. This search procedure resulted in four data entries for each city: that is, the number of hits for the city name in conjunction with, in turn, each of the four topical search terms. Given the high degree of correlation between the two financial and the two environmental search terms is high (Pearson's r value exceeds 0.97), we derived a Global Financial Score (GFS) and a Global Environmental Score (GES) based on the average hyperlink volume of the pairs of financial and environmental terms respectively. The cities with the twenty highest urban hyperlink volumes in terms of GFS and GES are shown in Figures 1 and 2.

Figure 1. 20 most important US cities in terms of GFS (Source: Google.com, 21 September 2009)

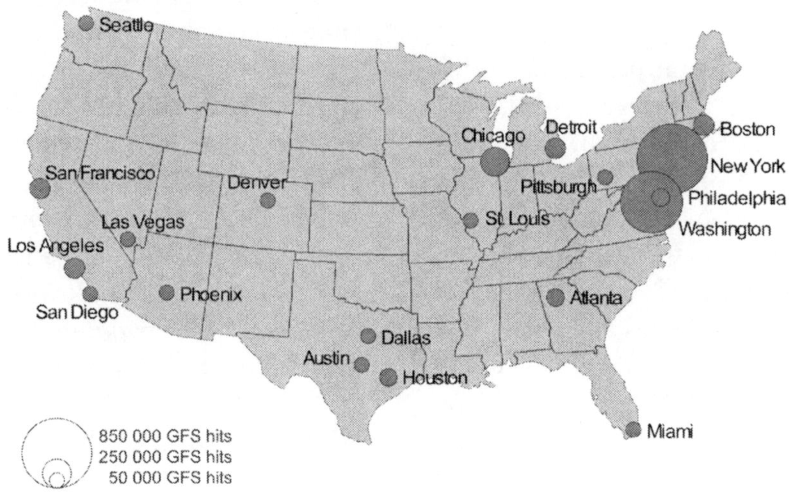

The U.S. cities that were/are most highly ranked in terms of GFS are New York, Washington, Chicago, Los Angeles, Detroit, Boston, and San Francisco. Ranking on GES, we obtain the highest GES scores for New York, Washington, San Francisco, Los Angeles, Chicago, Boston, and Orlando. A casual examination of Figures 1 and 2 suggests that while both have similar patterns, there are some differences in terms of information volumes between the two indices when proceeding down the urban hierarchy. For instance, Las Vegas, St. Louis, and Pittsburgh are in the top-twenty in terms of GFS scores only, while Orlando, Portland, and New Orleans appear in Figure 2. In order to understand these ranking differences, we examine, in contrast to the separate GFS and GES rankings/mappings above, the relationship between both measures (see Figure

Figure 2. 20 most important US cities in terms of GES (Source: Google.com, 21 September 2009)

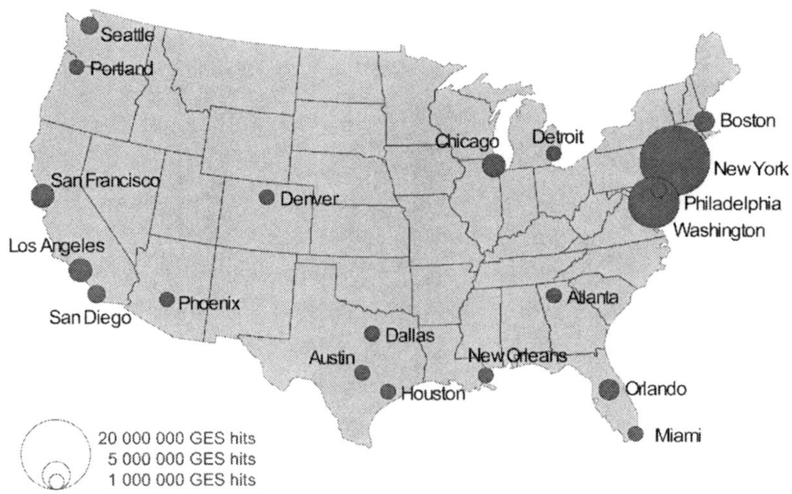

3). Through an assessment of the differences from the regression line, the cities' positions in terms of GES and GFS scores—that is the relative prominence of environmental and financial Web information—can be illustrated. This so-called regression residual analysis is a powerful yet simple tool for understanding cities' positions. It can be used readily to identify which cities do not "fit" the generalized model of the relationship between GES and GFS (GES=21,195GFS + 29099, Pearson r = 0.97), thus indicating the relative position of a city in the two information spaces represented by the GFS and GES variables. Figure 3 below shows the position of the 51 largest US cities according to both scores.

This "cloud" of cities can be, heuristically, divided in three main parts. First, there is an absolute domination of New York and Washington in terms of both information topics (not surprising given the many reports, conferences, meetings (e.g. UN data) associated with these cities). Next, at the opposite end of the graph are two lower-ranked cities, that is, Virginia Beach and Bridgeport (part of the New York metro area). In order to understand the rest of the cities' positions within the central cluster of the "cloud" we look in this regression model at the residuals (vertical distance between a point and the regression line). The largest residual values (absolute value above 1.5) in this model are for Detroit (negative residual, placing the city well below the regression line), Orlando (positive), and New Orleans (positive).

Potential explanations for some of these interesting outliers are rather easier to suggest than others. In the case of Detroit, the higher than "predicted" (by the regression) GFS score is likely based on the plethora of new Web information/commentary relating the financial crisis to slowdowns in the auto industry (Chrysler, GM, Ford), as well as home foreclosures and unemployment which hit this city particularly hard during the period of this study. New Orleans, by contrast, was ranked "unexpectedly" highly in terms of GES—most likely as a result of the volume of climate/environmental information referencing Hurricane Katrina. However, other (large) residuals are less easy to explain which makes meaningful analysis useful, but also difficult. For example, Las Vegas, a city with ongoing and well-document water and

Figure 3. Position US cities in terms of GES/GFS (Source: Google.com, 21 September 2009)

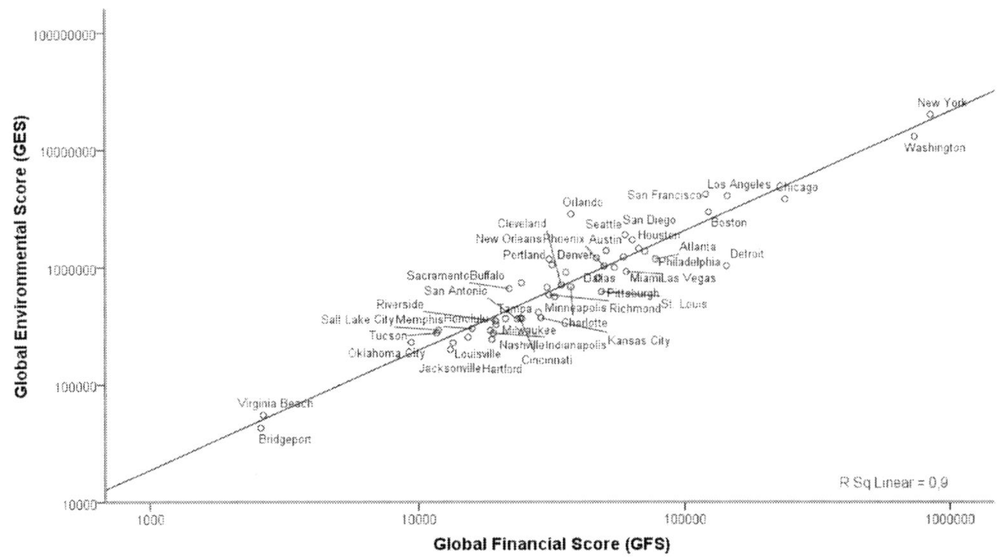

resource issues also has a housing market that was hit particularly hard first by the bursting of the real estate "bubble", then the more generalized mortgage crisis (see Table 1).

Given the relative rankings based on economic and environmental "importance"—particularly as evidenced in Table 1—it seems that a division might usefully be made between the two lists. Rustbelt or Manufacturing Belt cities, where joblessness increased rapidly in 2008 and 2009, appear in general in the right column of Table 1 (exceptions being San Jose, Jacksonville, San Antonio, Tampa, Las Vegas, and Atlanta). The left column, on the other hand, contains predominantly Sunbelt cities (except for Seattle and Buffalo which have, arguably, characteristics of Sunbelt economies). In general, these "higher GES" cities did not suffer as dramatically from the recent global economic upheaval but are facing, because of their geographical locations, particular problems such as water shortages (Woods, 1981). Furthermore, large coastal or port cities are, not surprisingly given the amount of material speculating on climate change, water supply and so forth, ranked more highly for GES than GFS. Future work needs to explore these differences in greater detail. The here-presented preliminary results merely suggest the value of Web information-based research for understanding change as experienced in cities.

Table 1. GFS and GES residuals

CITY	Pos Residuals (more GES)		CITY	Neg Residuals (more GFS)
Orlando	3.630		Detroit	-2,900
New Orleans	1.750		St. Louis	-1.238
San Francisco	1.466		Kansas City	-1.197
Portland	1.361		Hartford	-1.172
Seattle	1.220		Indianapolis	-0.873
Sacramento	1.142		San Jose	-0.835
Buffalo	1.136		Atlanta	-0.803
Los Angeles	0.842		Tampa	-0.781
Austin	0.835		Las Vegas	-0.768
San Diego	0.776		Cincinnati	-0.735
Denver	0.682		Jacksonville	-0.732
Baltimore	0.649		Chicago	-0.711
Salt Lake City	0.617		San Antonio	-0.687
Oklahoma City	0.608		Providence	-0.650
Tucson	0.500		Washington	-0.502

(Source: Google.com, 21 September 2009)

Web Activity Analysis

In order to grasp the *geographical* and *temporal* dimension of the space of informational flows, we turn from a consideration, in the previous section, of the information *available* about cities to the information sought by Web users *in* cities. These data illustrate the changing urban interest in these key informational issues *over time*. That is, we seek to merge both the temporality and spatiality of the U.S. cities' Web search activity. In this effort, we take advantage of a relatively recently developed search engine tool: "Google Insights for Search" (http://www.google.com/insights/search). This tool has not been used before by urban scholars looking at global hierarchies or networks. The possibilities of the use of Google Insights for gaining real-time insights into public engagement with key issues have, however, been recognized in the medical field and elsewhere. Google.org—the "part of Google" that aims to make good on the corporation's commitment to donate time and resources towards addressing "some of the world's most urgent problems"—is funding a Web site that tracks worldwide influenza outbreaks in real-time (http://www.google.org/flutrends/) and maps that data. This project, reported in the journal *Nature* (Ginsberg et al., 2009) finds a strong relationship between the

Figure 4. Web search activity (global) of financial and environmental topics over time (Source: Google Insights for Search, 29 September 2009)

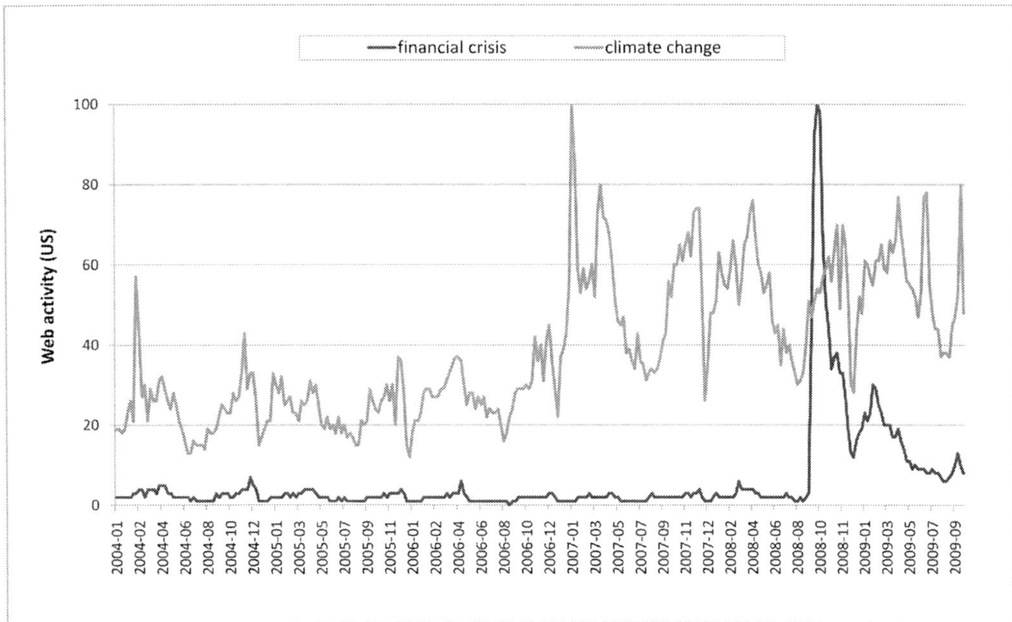

geography of "flu"-related search activity, and the underlying geography of flu incidents. The Insights tool analyzes a portion of the worldwide Google web searches from all Google domains and reports the volume of searches for a given term relative to the total number of searches carried out in Google (Google.com, 2009). It should be noted, however, that the reported results only reflect search terms that receive a significant amount of traffic. That is, only search terms that exceed a minimum threshold of search volume are made available within the tool. For our purposes, we investigate the fluctuations of Google search volumes originating within US cities pertaining to the above-mentioned (and sufficiently popular/heavily-trafficked) global issues, i.e. the global financial crisis and global climate change.

Figure 4 presents on a weekly basis the US search trends for the most frequently used 'global financial crisis'-related and 'global warming'-related search terms (i.e. 'the financial crisis' and 'climate change') over the period January 2004 – August 2009.[5] The actual search volumes are normalized in such a way that the maximum search volume for a time slice (a one week window) within the time period in question is fixed at 100. Thus, a search frequency of 60 represents a weekly search volume of 60 percent of the peak (long-term) search volume. We also recognize that the peaks and troughs in the search frequency could be correlated in more detail with the ebb and flow of news stories, political campaigns, published scientific data, and stock market fluctuations.

The search volumes during this 300-week period for climate change information fluctuates (and sometimes rather widely) in contrast to financial crisis information. Financial crisis-related queries are relatively insignificant and stable in the years 2004, 2005, 2006 and 2007 (where "Asian financial crisis" and "Asian crisis" account for most of the observed financial crisis-related search activity). The skyrocketing in financial crisis-related search terms occurs in August 2008, and begins to refer explicitly to the onset of the present global crisis. Search volumes for climate change information have fluctuated since 2004, reaching a peak in January 2007,the week that the IPCC (International Panel on Climate Change) report Executive Summary hit the international news media.

In order to understand the *spatiality* of these two sets of indicators—financial and environmental information— we extract from the generalized timeline of overall US search activity (Figure 4) a spatially disaggregated "snapshot" of where the "hot spots" for search interest in the two sets of terms were located. For the climate change term, we selected the 36 month period from August 2006 through August 2009; for the financial crisis data, we selected the period from August 2008, when financial crisis search activity began to relate explicitly to the global financial crisis, and August 2009. Table 2 shows the cities with the highest Web search activity for the two sets of search terms over the selected periods. Again, the reported results are normalized such that the city with the highest search volume is allocated a score of 100.

Clearly, different cities populate the rankings on search interest related to the two key issues: note the "popularity" of the "climate change" issue in Denver, Minneapolis, and Seattle in contrast to their rankings on the "financial crisis" topic. Conversely, we see higher rankings for New York, San Francisco, Boston, Miami, and Los Angeles on the latter issue. Distinguishing between coastal versus inland cities and Rustbelt versus Sunbelt cities (see above) suggests that the search activity *within* cities is rather strongly correlated with Web information *about* cities. That is, those cities about which there exists a large quantity of information related to a particular topic tend also to be the cities where Web users are disproportionately interested in that topic. The above-mentioned differences between interest levels in environmental and financial topics are summarized graphically for New York and Denver in Figure 5 below, which presents search volumes for the period 2004-2009. Exploring the small (but important) differences in temporality between search activities in different places presents a complex but exciting avenue for further research.

Table 2. Web search activity at US cities over time

Web search activity at US cities			
for "Climate Change" in period Aug 2006 - Aug 2009		for "Financial Crisis" in period Aug 2008 - Aug 2009	
City	Search Activity	City	Search Activity
Washington	100	Washington	100
Denver	45	New York	80
Sacramento	43	Boston	56
New York	41	San Francisco	55
Seattle	40	Philadelphia	49
Portland	40	Chicago	47
San Francisco	38	Seattle	46
Reston	37	Reston	46
Boston	35	Pleasanton	44
Pleasanton	34	Los Angeles	42
Minneapolis	29	Miami	42
Chicago	25	Houston	40
San Diego	24	Atlanta	39
Los Angeles	24	Minneapolis	39
Miami	24	Denver	38

(Source: Google Insights for Search, 28 September 2009)

CONCLUSION

The work of Saskia Sassen (1991) and Manuel Castells (1996) introduced to urban scholars the idea that cities should primarily be conceived of as centers of knowledge within transnational networks of *information* and *corporeal* flows. While recent research has, to a large extent, heeded these calls by studying the myriad "informational" interactions between major cities across the world, the focus has been predominantly on tangible

Figure 5. Web activity at Denver/New York (Source: Google Insights for Search, 13 October 2009)

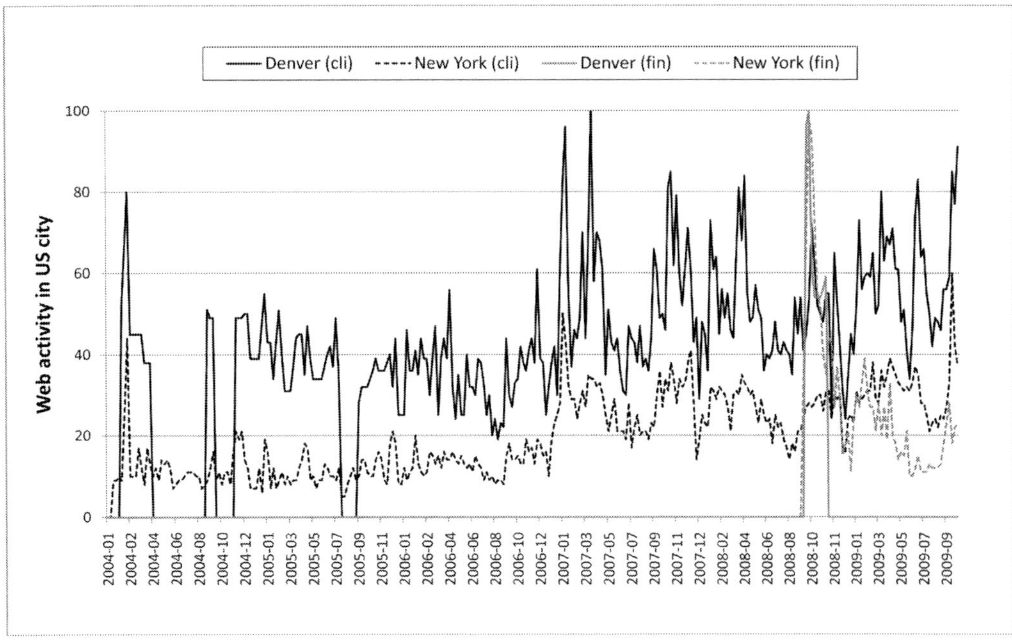

networks (e.g., corporate geographies, air passenger traffic). The main purpose of this chapter is to suggest why urban researchers should pay attention to the "intangible" space of flows in order to (better) understand the characteristics of and relationships between (world) cities. Specifically, the Web represents an under-utilized database of information that is i) immense and ii) updated in real time, offering a wealth of data that can be used by urban, economic, environmental and social geographers, and others, interested in the spatial and temporal patterns of information surrounding the current economic and environmental crises at regional and international scales. The "cyberspace approach" demonstrated here builds on earlier hyperlink-based studies such as those by Brunn (2003) and Devriendt et al. (2008) by examining Web information *consumed in* and *produced about* cities, trough time and in relation to issues which are global in scope.

To this end, we illustrated how cyberspace can be interrogated to specify a dynamic classification of the global urban system. Central to this way of thinking is the recognition of the "twin" qualities of cities as *both* lived places with attributes—experiential, economic, representational, infrastructural—*and* nodes in transnational networks of capital, ideas, representations, and information. In section 2 we related the "cyberspace approach" more explicitly with longer-run "world city research". In the empirical section, we showed how the Google search engine can provide valuable insights (and, indeed, "Insights") into both the production and the consumption of information about key global issues. Specifically, we examined the information availability about, and Web activity in, US cities based on two issues: the global financial crisis, and climate change. What is most striking in the results is that there is no clear population- or economy-size basis to the observed variations in knowledge production and consumption. While cities such as New York and Washington are the most important "knowledge" centers—according to these results—there are important processes and experiences affecting the positions within the information "cloud" (Figure

3) of each city. Furthermore, the Web Activity Analysis demonstrates the fluctuating salience through time of the keywords in and about US cities. In other words, the space of informational flows varies dramatically through time illustrating very clearly the inadequacy of one-time "snapshot"/slice analyses of cities' positions in information networks.

The Google Insights tool offers new and exciting windows onto the geography of information consumption and, as such, is of immense potential use to geographers and other scholars (as well, of course, as commercial interests). In other words, the data and theoretical frameworks of "cyberspace" await further study by geographers and others interested in the positions and experiences of cities in the context and under the aegis of the information-based Knowledge Economy. Popular culture, the diffusion of disease, flows of knowledge and information (and misinformation), new social movements, etc.: all phenomena represented in (and in some cases enabled by) digital communication. All are influencing and (re)producing the relationships between places. All are suggestive of new and creative takes on the global urban system.

REFERENCES

Abler, R. (1974). The geography of communications. In Hurst, M. E. (Ed.), *Transportation Geography* (pp. 327–346). New York: McGraw Hill.

Adams, P. (1997). Cyberspace and Virtual Places. *Geographical Review*, *87*, 155–171. doi:10.2307/216003

Beaverstock, J., Smith, R., Taylor, P., Walker, D., & Lorimer, H. (2000). Globalization and world cities: some measurement methodologies. *Applied Geography (Sevenoaks, England)*, *20*(1), 43–63. doi:10.1016/S0143-6228(99)00016-8

Brunn, S. (2003). A note on the hyperlinks of major Eurasian cities. *Eurasian Geography and Economics*, *44*(4), 321–324. doi:10.2747/1538-7216.44.4.321

Brunn, S. (2004). An e-classification of the world's capital cities: URL references to websites. In Kehal, H. (Ed.), *Digital Economy: Impacts, Influences and Challenges* (pp. 200–216). Hershey, PA: Idea Group, Inc.

Brunn, S., & Williams, J. (2005). Cybercities of Asia: measuring globalization using hyperlinks. *Asian Geographer*, *23*(1/2), 121–147.

Castells, M. (1996). *The Rise of the Network Society*. Oxford: Blackwell.

Castells, M. (2000). *The Rise of the Network Society* (2nd ed.). Oxford: Blackwell.

Cicognani, A. (1998). On the linguistic nature of cyberspace and virtual communities. *Virtual Reality (Waltham Cross)*, *3*, 16–24. doi:10.1007/BF01409794

Crutcher, M., & Zook, M. (2009). (in press). Placemarks and waterlines: racialized cyberscapes in post-Katrina Google Earth. *Geoforum*. doi:10.1016/j.geoforum.2009.01.003

Davis, K. (1959). *The World's Metropolitan Areas*. Berkeley, CA: University of California Press.

Demographia. (2008). *Largest Urban Areas in the World*. Retrieved October 4, 2009, from http://www.demographia.com/db-wlargestua.pdf

Denstadli, J., & Gripsrund, M. (2010). Face-to-face by travel or picture: the relationship between travelling and video communication in business settings. In Beaverstock, J., Derudder, B., Faulconbridge, J., & Witlox, F. (Eds.), *International Business Travel and the Global Economy*. London: Ashgate.

Derudder, B. (2006). On conceptual confusion in empirical analyses of a transnational urban network. *Urban Studies (Edinburgh, Scotland)*, *43*(11), 2027–2046. doi:10.1080/00420980600897842

Derudder, B., Devriendt, L., & Witlox, F. (2007). Flying where you don't want to go: an empirical analysis of hubs in the global airline network. *Tijdschrift voor Economische en Sociale Geografie, 98*(3), 307–324. doi:10.1111/j.1467-9663.2007.00399.x

Devriendt, L., Boulton, A., Brunn, S., Derudder, B., & Witlox, F. (2009). Major cities in the Information World: monitoring cyberspace in real-time. *GaWC Research Bulletin 308*. Retrieved June 23, 2009 from http://www.lboro.ac.uk/gawc/rb/rb308.html.

Devriendt, L., Derudder, B., & Witlox, F. (2008). Cyberplace and Cyberspace: two approaches to analyzing digital intercity linkages. *Journal of Urban Technology, 15*(2), 5–32. doi:10.1080/10630730802401926

Friedmann, J. (1986). The world city hypothesis. *Development and Change, 17*, 63–83. doi:10.1111/j.1467-7660.1986.tb00231.x

Ginsberg, J., Mohebbi, M., Patel, R., Brammer, M., & Brilliant, L. (2009). Letter: Detecting influenza epidemics using search query data. *Nature, 457*, 1012–1014. doi:10.1038/nature07634

Goldsmith, J., & Wu, T. (2006). *Who Controls the Internet? Illusions of a Borderless World*. Oxford, UK: Oxford University Press.

Gorman, S., & Malecki, J. (2000). The networks of the Internet: an analysis of provider networks in the USA. *Telecommunications Policy, 24*(2), 113–134. doi:10.1016/S0308-5961(00)00005-7

Hall, P. (1966). *The World Cities*. New York: McGraw-Hill.

Hoskote, R. (2008). Versions of a postcolonial metropolis: competing discourses on Bombay's image. In Segbers, K. (Ed.), *The Making of Global City Regions: Johannesburg, Mumbai/Bombay, Sao Paulo, and Shanghai* (pp. 258–287). Baltimore, MD: JHU Press.

Hudson-Smith, A., & Milton, R. Dearden, J. & Batty, M. (2007). Virtual cities: digital mirrors into a recursive world. *UCL Working Papers Series, 125*(December 2007), 1-24.

Jefferson, M. (1939). The law of the primate city. *Geographical Review, 29*, 226–232. doi:10.2307/209944

Kaba, S. (1996). Building the future: an architectural manifesto for the next Millennium. *Web Architecture Magazine, April*.

Kellerman, A. (2002). *The Internet on Earth. A Geography of Information*. West Sussex, UK: John Wiley & Sons, Ltd.

Knox, P. (1994). *Urbanization: An Introduction to Urban Geography*. Englewood Cliffs, NJ: Prentice Hall.

Lai, K. (2009). Global Cities in Competition? A Qualitative Analysis of Shanghai, Beijing and Hong Kong as Financial Centres'. *GaWC Research Bulletin,* 313. Retrieved October 4, 2009 from http://www.lboro.ac.uk/gawc/rb/rb313.html.

Malecki, E., & Wei, H. (2009). A wired world: the evolving geography of submarine cables and the shift to Asia. *Annals of the Association of American Geographers. Association of American Geographers, 99*(2), 360–382. doi:10.1080/00045600802686216

Moss, M., & Townsend, A. (2000). The Internet backbone and the American metropolis. *The Information Society, 16*(1), 35–47. doi:10.1080/019722400128310

O'Brien, R. (1992). *Global Financial Integration: the End of Geography*. London: Pinter.

Ohmae, K. (1990). *The Borderless World: power and strategy in the interlinked economy*. London: HarperCollins.

Pred, A. (1980). *Urban Growth and City Systems in the United States, 1840-1860*. London: Hutchinson.

Rutherford, J., Gillespie, A., & Richardson, R. (2004). The territoriality of Pan-European telecommunications backbone networks. *Journal of Urban Technology*, *11*(3), 1–34. doi:10.1080/10630730500064166

Sassen, S. (1991). *The Global City: New York, London, Tokyo*. Princeton, NJ: Princeton University Press.

Sheller, M., & Urry, J. (2006). The new mobilities paradigm. *Environment & Planning A*, *38*(2), 207–226. doi:10.1068/a37268

Short, J., Kim, Y., Kuss, M., & Wells, H. (1996). The dirty little secret of word city research. *International Journal of Regional and Urban Research*, *20*, 697–717. doi:10.1111/j.1468-2427.1996.tb00343.x

Taylor, P. J. (2001). Specification of the world city network. *Geographical Analysis*, *33*, 181–194. doi:10.1111/j.1538-4632.2001.tb00443.x

Taylor, P. J. (2004). *World City Network: A Global Urban Analysis*. London: Routledge.

Taylor, P. J. (2008). World Cities in Globalization. *GaWC Research Bulletin 263*. Retrieved April 28, 2008 from http://www.lboro.ac.uk/gawc/rb/rb263.html.

Taylor, P. J. (2009). Urban Economics in thrall to Christaller: A Misguided Search for City Hierarchies in External Urban Relations. *GaWC Research Bulletin 311*. Retrieved June 30, 2009 from http://www.lboro.ac.uk/gawc/rb/rb311.html

Taylor, P. J. (2010). Measuring the world city network. In Firmino, R., Duarte, F., & Ultramari, C. (Eds.), *ICTs for Mobile and Ubiquitous Urban Infrastructures: Surveillance, Locative Media and Global Networks*. Hershey, PA: IGI Global.

Taylor, P. J., Derudder, B., & Witlox, F. (2007). Comparing airline passenger destinations with global service connectivities: a worldwide empirical study of 214 cities. *Urban Geography*, *28*(3), 232–248. doi:10.2747/0272-3638.28.3.232

Thompson, G. F. (2003). *Between hierarchies and markets*. Oxford, UK: Oxford University Press. doi:10.1093/acprof:oso/9780198775270.001.0001

Woods, M. (1981). Desert-like conditions hurt Sun Belt. *The Blade (Toledo, OH)*, 18 January 1981.

Zook, M., & Brunn, S. (2005). Regions, hierarchies and legacies: European Cities and global air travel. *Journal of Contemporary European Studies*, *13*(2), 203–220. doi:10.1080/14782800500212459

Zook, M., & Brunn, S. (2006). From podes to antipodes: positionalities and global airline geographies. *Annals of the Association of American Geographers. Association of American Geographers*, *96*(3), 471–490. doi:10.1111/j.1467-8306.2006.00701.x

ADDITIONAL READING

Borja, J., & Castells, M. (Eds.). (1997). *Local and Global: The Management of Cities in the Information Age*. Earthscan.

Brunn, S., & Leinbach, T. (Eds.). (1991). *Collapsing Space and Time: Geographic Aspects of Communication and Information*. London: Harper Collins.

Dodge, M., & Kitchin, R. (2001). *Mapping cyberspace*. London: Routledge.

Dodge, M., & Kitchin, R. (Eds.). (2002). *Atlas of Cyberspace*. Pearson.

Dogan, M., & Kasarda, J. (1988). *The Metropolis Era: A World of Giant Cities*. Sage.

Graham, S. (Ed.). (2004). *The Cybercities Reader*. London: Routledge.

Graham, S., & Marvin, S. (1996). *Telecommunications and the City: Electronic spaces, Urban Places*. New York: Routledge. doi:10.4324/9780203430453

Janelle, D. And Hodge, D., editors (2000). *Information, Place, and Cyberspace: Issues in Accessibility.* Heidelberg: Springer

Kehal, H. And Sing, V., editors (2005). *Digital Economy: Impacts, Influences and* Challenges. London: Idea Group

Kellerman, A. (2002). *The Internet on Earth. A Geography of Information*. West Sussex, England: John Wiley & Sons Ltd.

Knox, P., & Taylor, P. (1995). *World Cities in a World System*. Cambridge, UK: Oxford University Press. doi:10.1017/CBO9780511522192

Kotkin, J. (2006). *The City: A Global History*. Random House.

Massey, D. (2007). *World City*. Polity.

Miller, H. (2007). *Societies and Cities in the Age of Instant Access*. Springer. doi:10.1007/1-4020-5427-0

Mitchell, W. (1995). *City of Bits: Space, Place, and the Infobahn*. Cambridge, MA: MIT Press.

Segbers, K. (Ed.). (2007). *The Making of Global City Regions: Johannesburg, Mumbai/Bombay, Sao Paulo, and Shanghai*. JHU Press.

Susser, I. (2002). *The Castells Reader on Cities and Social Theory*. Oxford: Wiley-Blackwell.

Wheeler, J., Aoyama, Y., & Warf, B. (Eds.). (2000). *Cities in the Telecommunications Age: The Fracturing of Geographies*. New York: Routledge.

Wilson, M. And Corey, K. (2000). *Information Tectonics*. New York: Wiley

Zook, M. (2005). *The Geography of the Internet Industry: Venture Capital, Dot-Coms and Local Knowledge*. Oxford: Wiley-Blackwell.

ENDNOTES

1 Hereafter, "world cities" and "World Cities Network" are used interchangeably to refer to the cities of the world, and in particular those "major"/most-connected cities. See section 2.1 for an overview of the "world cities" literature and the nuances of "world" versus "global" cities as they have been used in the literature. Taylor (2008) provides an account of the lineage of "world city" as a term and as a concept.

2 Based in the geography department at the University of Loughborough, UK, the Globalization and World City (GaWC) Research Network was established as a central place for scholars studying the relations between cities.

3 GaWC-researchers have developed a methodology for studying transnational urban networks based on the assumption that advanced producer service firms 'interlock' cities through their intra-firm communications of information, knowledge, plans, directions, advice, etc. to create a network of global service centres (Beaverstock et al. 2000).

4 Another shortcoming of previous hyperlink studies is that there is not any critical reflection or discussion on the merits of using search engine data: while there are clearly great advantages to using the Google Search Engine—especially size (over one trillion unique URLs trawled), and timeliness (the index is continuously updated by its distributed network of "spiders")— cautions are required. For example, searching via Google.com (the US/international version of Google), and the spelling of search terms and city names in English limits our analysis to the English language Web. This and other "problems" with these methods are discussed, and how these are addressed in the subsequent analysis, in Devriendt et al. (2009). We refer readers to this publication for a more detailed discussion of these methodological challenges.

5 In each case, we used the Google Insights service to identify the two most frequently searched keyword terms related to each topic.

Chapter 6
Ubiquitous Eco Cities: Infrastructure, Technology and Management

Tan Yigitcanlar
Queensland University of Technology, Australia

Jung Hoon Han
Griffith University, Australia

ABSTRACT

Efficient and effective urban management systems for Ubiquitous Eco Cities require having intelligent and integrated management mechanisms. This integration includes bringing together economic, socio-cultural and urban development with a well orchestrated, transparent and open decision-making system and necessary infrastructure and technologies. In Ubiquitous Eco Cities telecommunication technologies play an important role in monitoring and managing activities via wired and wireless networks. Particularly, technology convergence creates new ways in which information and telecommunication technologies are used and formed the backbone of urban management. The 21st Century is an era where information has converged, in which people are able to access a variety of services, including internet and location based services, through multi-functional devices and provides new opportunities in the management of Ubiquitous Eco Cities. This chapter discusses developments in telecommunication infrastructure and trends in convergence technologies and their implications on the management of Ubiquitous Eco Cities.

INTRODUCTION

During the last few decades across the globe urban system and structures have been changed dramatically by rapid urbanisation trends (Yeung, 2000). As a result of this urbanisation process urban systems have become increasingly complex and large in scale. At the moment sustainable and efficient usage of scarce resources together with competing economic and social priorities are parts of everyday decisions required to be made by local governments, which are obliged to employ a sound urban management system that increases the understanding of, and capacity to undertake, the strategic management of urban areas (Teriman et al., 2009). Urban management is basically a process of deliberately directing and facilitating urban development, and also an

DOI: 10.4018/978-1-60960-051-8.ch006

integration of the traditional ideas of planning, with its physical, economic and social concerns, and recently latched to management with its emphasis on efficiency (Davey, 1993). The application of innovative systems to support urban management and collaborative decision-making offers considerably new opportunities for the 21st Century cities, particularly for Ubiquitous eco cities (U-eco cities).

U-eco city is a city that promises to provide an environmentally friendly urban milieu with advanced ubiquitous infrastructures and services for residents and visitors (Yigitcanlar, 2009a). Beyond this a U-eco city is claimed to be a sustainable city with an entire city dedicated to minimising the required inputs, of energy, water and food, and waste outputs, of heat, air and water pollution, by benefiting from ubiquitous technologies and sustainable urban development principles (Galloway, 2003). In U-eco cities urban and infrastructure planning, development and management require complex information and input from institutions, stakeholders and users to deal with spatial, social, economic, multi-dimensional and complex characteristics of urban and environmental phenomena and problems (Lee et al., 2008).

In U-eco cities telecommunication infrastructure forms the backbone network system of the management (Warf, 1998). Over the past few decades, telecommunications networks have become important infrastructure players and information and communication technologies (ICTs) form the basis of telecommunications infrastructure for U-eco cities (Hackler, 2003a). In the information era, ICTs play an increasingly important role in the planning, provision and management of urban infrastructure. Moreover, ICTs as telecommunication networks are major infrastructure management systems, and rapidly evolving and transforming into a network supported by convergence technologies that supports urban management. Telecommunication and infrastructure networks are rapidly moving from systems based on wired technology to those that are wireless and seamless digital network systems (Dourish, 2004). Although ubiquitous computing network systems have become one of the major phases in many contemporary agendas in terms of the design and engineering of computer systems, their economic, social and environmental implications are yet to be explored (Weiser, 1991). Additionally, complexity of urban management in U-eco cities requires a new understanding including intelligent systems and tools to deal with this complexity. Given this significance, there is limited research that focuses on the implications of developments in the fields of telecommunication infrastructure, technology convergence and urban management on U-eco cities.

This chapter aims to investigate developments in telecommunication infrastructure, trends in convergence technologies and their implications on the management of U-eco cities. This chapter is organised in six sections. Following this introduction, secondly, we introduce U-eco cities as a new city form that aims to bring sustainability, efficiency and quality of life into cities. Thirdly, we present telecommunication infrastructures as the backbones of U-eco cities and their services that play an important role in monitoring and managing activities via wired and wireless networks. Then, we discuss technology convergence and its impacts on U-eco city formation that creates new ways in which information and telecommunication technologies are used and formed the base for urban management. Fifthly, we explore the need and potentials for intelligent systems as revolutionary urban management systems of U-eco cities. Lastly, we conclude by summarising the key findings of the research.

UBIQUITOUS ECO CITIES: A NEW CITY FORM

Eco and ubiquitous cities constitute the two distinctive facades of a contemporary city. Eco city forms the visible facade, where ubiquitous city is the hidden infrastructure facade supporting information flow and services. The integration of eco city and ubiquitous city is important to improve the sustainability and quality of life in cities. Therefore, the traditional quartet of urban planning, human-architecture-city-society, needs to be evolved into human-architecture-digit-city-society, where information management plays a key role in such cities (Wang, 2001; Wang et al., 2002). The modern eco city concept originates from Ebenezer Howard's theory of garden city. The theory of garden city reveals the ecological charms of harmonious joint development of built and natural environments. A good example of such development is the Letchworth garden city in England designed by Ebenezer Howard and built in 1903. Still after over a century, it remains to be one of the most desirable living spaces. Since the early garden city examples urban planners have tried to integrate ecological ideologies and principles into urban design and development by considering cities as artificial ecosystems (Wang et al., 2002). For instance, Yanitsky (1987) sees an eco city as a perfect living space and an ideal pattern for urban development. Similarly, Roseland (1997) advocates the idea of eco city concept that coexists with and contains others, rather than existing independently.

The eco city theory views urban development from a point of ecosystem interactivity. The basic idea of city development is to fully exploiting the potentials of ecological construction under the existing resource environment for the purpose of building up efficient, harmonious, healthy and wealthy cities. It rejects the traditional way of low productivity and the modern way of excessive resource-consuming. Thus the eco city ideology solves urban problems by considering an ecological point of view, this is to say, it aims to change a city into a low-entropy regular structure with perfect functionalities, sustainable efficiency and high-level environmental quality. An eco city also aims to be panacea for the problems caused by urbanisation activities and urban environmental transition. The eco city development process benefits from ecological, environmental and social systems. Therefore, in a broad sense an eco city is a sustainable city that establishes a harmony between built and natural environments. In a more specific sense, an eco city is a city based on the improvement of productivity, using modern science and technologies such as eco-engineering, system engineering and information technology including technological systems of digital or ubiquitous cities (Wang et al., 2002). There are several management and information technology related challenges exist in developing eco cities. These issues and challenges bring the discussion of the need for merging ubiquitous and eco city concepts with each other. Some of the major challenges include: building a comprehensive database for ecological elements of a city; decision, information and management systems for an eco city; managing and monitoring infrastructure and services, and; establishing a collaborative process and active public participation (Wang et al., 2002).

As Lee et al. (2008) define ubiquitous cities (u-cities) as cities that provide ubiquitous infrastructure (u-infrastructure) and ubiquitous services (u-services) for their residents, workers and visitors by utilising a range of ubiquitous technologies (u-technologies). O'Connell (2005) exemplifies life in an u-city by imagining "public recycling bins that use radio-frequency identification technology (RFID) to credit recyclers every time they toss in a bottle; pressure-sensitive floors in the homes of older people that can detect the impact of a fall and immediately contact help; cell phones that store health records and can be used paying for prescriptions" (p. 1). Similar to just-in-time delivery system, which saves time and cost by delivering materials when they are needed and by eliminating storage space otherwise needed to be stockpiled, urban resources could be conserved in u-cities by delivering and receiving services right on time with support from wired and wireless integrated networks equipped with digital home and intelligent building systems (Kim, 2008).

In recent years a shift from u-city to U-eco city has occurred and a number of integration frameworks have been developed (Yigitcanlar, 2009). The U-eco city concept creates environments in cities where residents can enjoy access to high-speed networks and enhanced information services at anytime regardless of location through a ubiquitous computing network (Lee and Leem, 2009). The U-eco city concept has taken root in contemporary urban planning as a new technology and ecology model. The U-eco city concept enhances global competitiveness and connectivity of the public and private sectors through the combination of the hardware construction industry, ICT and their ubiquitous interaction with residents and the natural environment. This ubiquitous interaction and the resulting form of the U-eco city are expected to overcome the limitations of current city development approaches and physical city implementation and ongoing management by municipal entities. Current city development approaches to organise the urban fabric use formal spatial patterns for buildings, open space, transportation and infrastructure. The U-eco city concept uses open technological systems and with an urban management centre sitting at its very core, it controls and manages the entire city (Kirkwood, 2008). The significance of U-eco cities are elaborated by Kirkwood (2008) as "the significance of a U-eco city project for private and public sectors as well as government agencies is in providing the ubiquitous infrastructure itself thus enabling U-eco city concept to advance, generating a larger service market for next-generation communication technologies as well as establishing a range of cities of good life and happiness for citizens. A further area of significance would be the establishment of an industry world benchmark in ubiquitous city design and holistic environmental planning of the u-city. This is important to capture the future global market in U-eco city planning as well as to establish a set of metrics to describe and evaluate the legislative framework, performance activities and capacity for change and evolution of the U-eco city" (pp. 13-14).

In a U-eco city, urban land, modern technology, industry and people create a mutually supportive and holistic environment for the 21st Century's new urban development. Primary characteristics of a U-eco city includes but not limited to the five key aspects (5Es): ecological integrity; economic security; enhanced quality of life; empowerment with responsibility, and; electronic infrastructure (Kline, 2000). This new, U-eco city, urban form has a number of challenges and opportunities and technological self-sufficiency and advancement of the U-eco city concept at the same time must also be dynamic, not static, changing to meet the challenges of each new generation. According to Yigitcanlar (2009a) major challenges for a U-eco city include: "development cost; retrofitting; more technology and mobility, more energy use; too much transparency, limited privacy; digital security, smart mobs; technology upgrades and dependency and collapse; urban privileged, and; managing complex and high-tech urban environments" (p: 25). Besides these challenges a U-eco city presents a unique opportunity to foster an alternative model of city and urban development, one that is holistic, environmentally conscious and humane. Some of the major opportunities for a U-eco city include: zero emission, zero car, waste and water are recycled; compact urban development; improved quality of life and services; sustained eco-system, better use of energy and natural resources; more legible and accessible built and natural environments; opportunities to build new social spaces, and; new socio-cultural and economic interactions (Yigitcanlar, 2009a).

To address abovementioned challenges and opportunities planning and development of a U-eco city require an integrated and sustainable mechanism. Therefore, linking strategy (planning) and practice (development) is crucial for the development of successful U-eco cities. Strategic visioning and planning of U-eco cities need to consider knowledge-based development in order to establish a strong economic, social and spatial base. Additionally management of a U-eco city requires an intelligent urban management system which is based on a sound telecommunication infrastructure benefiting from the convergence of ICT and infrastructure networks.

INFRASTRUCTURE: TELECOMMUNICATIONS INFRASTRUCTURE

Not so long ago telecommunications infrastructure was not considered in business or household location decisions. Our lifestyles have been changed dramatically during the past few decades, due to rapid technological advances, the convergence to digital forms of computing, media, and communications, and also globalisation. Consequently, telecom has become a complex menu of choices and providers from which business and households choose (Malecki & Bous, 2003). Modern economic productivity benefits from the proliferated use of telecommunications networks and information technologies such as computers and software. This trend has not only altered the business practices of all industries that use these as inputs but also sponsored the growth of new businesses that we now refer to as high-tech industry (Hackler, 2003a). Today firms and also households, many of which rely on constant high-speed, or broadband, connections among far-flung operations, demand not only fast connections, but also redundant links that prevent any downtime or discontinuities, in service. Telecommunications is the leading factor in location decisions of companies today and is accounted as among the top criteria for locating a facility (Lawless & Gore, 1999). Many cities around the world today highly take advantage of advanced telecommunications infrastructure and such infrastructure has become a growing concern of local government and industry. From computer manufacturing to software development and from biotechnology to aviation industries, many cities seek high-tech growth, where advanced telecommunications infrastructure supports such development, which is associated with prosperous urban regions (Yigitcanlar et al., 2008a). The Silicon Valley in Northern California, Route 128 surrounding Boston, the Silicon Hills in Austin, Texas, and One-North in Singapore are the most prominent examples of advanced telecommunications infrastructure hardwired in high-tech locations (Yigitcanlar et al., 2008b). As mediators of all aspects of the reflexive functioning and development of aforementioned cities, convergent media, telecommunications and computing grids, known collectively as telematics, are thus basic integrating infrastructures underpinning the shift towards intensely interconnected planetary urban telecommunications networks (Graham, 1999).

Infrastructure networks such as telecommunications support not only cities to develop networks within themselves, but also provide a vehicle to get connected with other cities and join in the world city network. Beyond this telecommunications infrastructure also supports cities in the tough global competition and helps them develop their competitiveness further (Yigitcanlar & Velibeyoglu, 2008). According to Rutherford (2005) "in the same way as the supply of producer services in world cities can be seen largely to reflect demand for those services from multinational corporations, in a competitive market environment, the supply of telecommunications infrastructure in and between world cities comes from expressed or anticipated demand for high performance telecommunications network connections to interlink multinational corporate and producer service firm headquarters and offices in cities around the world" (p. 2391). Basically without a quality infrastructure, a city would become pretty much disconnected from or less connected to the rest of the world city network and, therefore, would lose much of its competitiveness and world city status. Taylor (2003) sees the connections between offices and cities as the skeleton upon which contemporary economic globalisation has formed, and Rutherford (2005) following up on this analogy argues that measures of intercity relations should include the infrastructural backbones which form the actual basis of the skeleton. Moreover, technological advances play a key role in the provision of telecommunication infrastructure or in other words backbones and skeletons, for example fibre optic network development, which is according to Walcott and Wheeler (2001) "hair-thin threads of glass utilizing laser light pulses in digital computer code, with multiple glass fibres in each cable – some sending messages from A to B and others from B to A – are the standard physical paths for global internet telecommunications for major numeric data and word and graphic information" (p. 321). The infrastructure particularly plays a crucial role in the development and management of U-eco cities.

For attracting industries, chiefly knowledge-based or high-tech ones, being able to meet the telecommunications service requirements is a necessity. Wiemann (1998) argues that "broadband information infrastructure is now as important to a growing array of high-tech firms as railroads were to nineteenth-century steel and textile mills" (p. 22). Similarly, cities that are vying to be silicon havens are using tactics to enhance their telecommunications assets, from developing smart buildings to increasing bandwidth available to business. For the latter case, some cities even lobby telecommunications service providers to improve existing infrastructure, and some are building their own improved one. These local communities perceive that an improved telecommunications infrastructure is a necessity in the new information economy as an economic and social advantage. As Dwyre (1998) views "a solid telecom network is key to economic development: building industry and manufacturing, improving agriculture, education, health, social services, transportation, and other crucial elements that make up a nation's economy" (p. 47). Telecommunications is an important ingredient to cities, particularly U-eco cities, wanting to have a knowledge economy growth. Basically telecommunications infrastructure is attractive to high-tech industry; locations with large concentrations of high-tech industry are more likely to have greater telecommunications capacity. In many cases the relationship between telecommunications infrastructure and economic development are also mutually reinforcing. This is to say economic growth can spur telecommunications investment because of the increase in demand from new business, and telecommunications investment provides a foundation for further economic growth (Hackler, 2003b). Beyond creating the necessary conditions for a robust economic structure and stimulating the growth of productive activity telecommunications infrastructure in U-eco cities also can produce substantial public benefits, such as social welfare and development, and e-democracy (Guild, 2000).

Some advanced telecommunications can be advantageous, particularly, to remote areas, although not necessarily for use directly by business. The major applications are likely to be for delivering higher quality education and health services. Better education, training, and health services can help upgrade the human resource capacity that is often the greatest problem in remote areas (Fox & Porca, 2001). However, opportunities to use new electronic technologies to extend users' social and economic actions across space are thus being configured highly unevenly within and between the material geographies of contemporary cities. For instance, the wiring of cities with the latest fibre optic networks is also extremely uneven. On that point Graham (1999) writes "it is characterised by a dynamic of dualisation. On the one hand, seamless and powerful global-local connections are being constructed within and between highly valued spaces, based on the physical construction of tailored networks to the doorsteps of institutions. On the other hand, intervening spaces – even those which may geographically be cheek-by-jowl with the favoured zones within the same city – seem, at the same time, to be largely ignored by investment plans for the most sophisticated telecommunications networks. Such spaces threaten to emerge as network ghettos, places of low telecommunications access, and concentrated social disadvantage" (p. 929). In terms of social implications of telecommunications network Hanafizadeh et al. (2009) highlight the digital divide as one of the key issues to be dealt with in telecommunication infrastructure provision. The digital divide is the differences between individuals, households, companies, or regions related to the access to and use of ICT (Vehovar et al., 2006). The various factors may cause the divide such as historical, socio-economic, geographic, educational, behavioural, generation factors, or the physical incapability of individuals (Curtin, 2001). Whitacre and Mills (2007) argue that as residential internet access shifts toward high-speed connections, a gap emerges in rural high-speed access relative to urban high-speed access, and the potential causes of this high-speed digital divide include rural–urban differences in people, place, and infrastructure. Digital exclusion is among the major challenges that u-eco cities experiencing and they are heavily criticised places of and for urban elites and wealthy people.

Recent developments in both technology and conceptualisation of the needs of the economy and people provide new opportunities for cities and their administrations to develop new generation telecommunications networks. Particularly ubiquitous urban infrastructure developments are among the significant moves in this direction. In the light of global connectivity and increasing communication options available for accessing and exchanging information, the vision for future communications is information anytime, anyplace and in any form, based on the idea of an open electronic market of services, where an unlimited spectrum of communication and information services is offered, ranging from simple communication services up to complex distributed multimedia applications. In this ubiquitous context the instant provision of services and the customisation and configuration of existing services become fundamental issues (Magedanz et al., 1996). Ubiquitous urban infrastructure, particularly in the field of telecommunication, as stated by Arseni et al. (2001), is witnessing the impetuous evolution and expansion of two kinds of systems. The first is the universal wireline network that is now able to provide sophisticated multimedia services. The second comprehends the cellular or wireless network and is able to satisfy user mobility demand, providing standard telephone services and low-speed data transmission. Especially in U-eco cities the new generation telecommunication systems are integrating these wireline and wireless networks in a single, advanced infrastructure. On top of this network integration, the convergence of technology also revolutionises the way telecommunications infrastructure is delivered and accessed. And beyond this it contributes to the formation of the next generation telecommunications infrastructure for U-eco cities.

TECHNOLOGY: CONVERGENCE OF TECHNOLOGY

U-eco cities and their u-infrastructure depend on intelligent planning support, monitoring and management systems that heavily benefits from ICTs and technology convergence. U-infrastructure in the areas of education, transport, power supply, sewerage and waste treatment, and water supply constantly rely on the ICT convergence to enhance its quality and customer service delivery. As Britchie et al. (1987) point out "a shift, from land, material, and energy to knowledge, information, and intellect as key factors of production, increased the interdependence between manufacturing, commerce, and consumption and the new information channels and transport systems" (p. 449). The convergence technologies used in urban infrastructure help local economic growth through u-business, improve local service delivery through u-government, advanced connectivity to local and global networks through wireline and wireless devices, and provide access to education through u-education. It is argued that these technologies minimise unnecessary travels and contribute to reducing greenhouse gas emissions by offsetting material and energy consumption and expediting more efficient use of current form of physical infrastructure (Lee et al., 2008). However, some also argue that on the contrary they encourage productivism and consumerism as a consequence of the technological ubiquity conditions. Many local governments have been investing in the latest telecommunication convergence such as wireless internet network technologies (WiMAX) in order to improve a shift from polluting manufacturing industries to clean knowledge industries. An example is the intelligent streetlights that are being provided with RFID, wireline and wireless communication technologies in order to minimise the energy consumption (Lee & Leem, 2009). This intelligent streetlight system benefits from the convergence technology of construction and information and communications (C-ICT).

Internet is one of the most powerful technologies to access information in our modern society. Internet provides a channel for users to undertake many tasks including doing business, studying online, communicating with others, entertaining and so on (Cunningham & Turner, 2005). For instance people can easily access the latest audiovisual data, for instance from youtube.com, anytime if they have access to internet. Internet and media convergence allow people to access information regardless of time and space using a converged digital device referred as black box. Jenkins (2006) describes the technology convergence as a black box, which is made of multiple integrated products taking technical advantages of each others. Convergence leads a technological shift or a new technological process. The convergence impacts the way in which individuals interact with each other and use various media platforms in order to create new experiences, new forms of media and content (Cunningham & Turner, 2005). To date technology convergence of internet media and contents significantly improve learning activities. For example, a number of primary schools in Australia use Nintendo DS and Wii with a touch-panel interface for mathematics education. Students of these schools show higher performance than those who do not use such innovative education tools (Moses, 2006). These innovative devices are converged technologies that integrate a games console, moving sensor and internet browser. Integrated activities are visible in U-eco cities using these converged technologies, for instance, the programmable street is provided with multiple functions such as lighting, security monitoring, commercial advertisement, solar energy and audio-visual objects.

During the last decade, convergence of ICTs created new urban spaces. Public telephone booths and public transport ticketing offices are disappeared and replaced as a result of converged technology use. New generation mobile phones are now equipped with more advanced features such as touch screen, video recording, global positioning system (GPS) navigation, internet and emailing, data storage and security mechanisms. Today it is possible to access to information on urban utilities and real-time monitoring of the environment via a mobile phone (Yigitcanlar, 2009b). Although excessive technology use and sustainability may look conflicting concepts, ubiquitous devices have potential to be used in real-time planning and management and contribute to conservation of urban natural resources, urban growth management and sustainable urban development (Yigitcanlar et al., 2008c). Technology convergence also occurs in the area of marketing and business. The notion of multi-play is used in a convergence of ICT services and products and often adopted to U-eco city planning. The multi-play is needed when people access many different telecommunication services, such as broadband internet access, cable television, telephone, and mobile phone services at once. The multi-play technology convergence consists of dual-, triple- or quadruple-play options depending on the specific application area (Cunningham & Turner, 2005). A dual-play service provides two ICT services such as high-speed internet (ADSL) and telephone service over a single broadband connection. High-speed internet (cable modem) and TV service provided by a single broadband connection is an example for this type (ANSI, 1998). In a triple-play service, the convergence can be accompanied by the underlying telecommunications infrastructure, where communication services are bundled, which allows consumers to access TV, internet and telephone through a single subscription (Flew, 2008). A quadruple-play service is similar to the triple-play service of broadband internet access, television and telephone, but is based on wireless technologies (Baumgarter, 2005). The next level of service used in U-eco cities is the integration of RFID into the quadruple-play, which adds the capability for home equipment to communicate with the outside world and schedule maintenance of its own (Fisher & Monahan, 2008). RFID tags are applied to an object incorporated into a product, an animal or a person for the purpose of identifying, reading and tracking information by using radio waves.

Convergence is a key concept in coordinating a range of urban network services such as physical networks or components thereof that channel fluxes through conduits or media to their nodes such as receivers (Neuman, 2006). Technology convergence required of supporting super ordinate systems connected to networks. These networks include transportation, pipes, wires and cables in the channels through, which their products are sold and serviced. A highly mobile nature of portable technology provides immobile physical networks with convergence incorporating telecommunication devices such as portable video and media, GPS navigation, portable internet surfing, and mobile telecommunications devices into a single device, a black box, designed to remove the need to carry multiple devices. Telecommunication infrastructure is interconnected by web of sensors, actuators, wireline and wireless communications networks, and computer systems benefit from convergence in a form of combination of different telecommunication media in a single operating platform (O'Brien & Soibelman, 2004). Fixed, mobile, and internet protocol (IP) service providers can offer content and media services, and hardware and software providers can offer services directly to users (Telecom Media Convergence, 2007). These days most of the content or service providers are consistently looking for new digital infrastructure and more effective distribution channels. For instance, the new G3 mobile phone technology uses technology convergence that provides the combination of telecom, data processing and imaging technologies. Previously separate technologies such as audio including telephone features, data including productivity applications, and video including teleconferencing now share resources and interact with each other (Jenkins, 2006). In U-eco city environment voice over IP (VoIP) and Bluetooth technologies are merged into a wireless internet network so called WiMAX for seamless mobility between VoWiFi and cellular networks (Telephony Online, 2009). This mobile service provision gives rise to the ability to access to most of the telecommunications channels including audio, internet, video and content without requiring tethering to the network via cables (Williams, 2008). Given the recent advancements in WiMAX and other leading edge technologies, the ability to transfer information over a wireless link at combinations of speed, distance and none line of sight conditions is rapidly developing. Therefore, the whole range of technology conversion becomes increasingly invisible, intangible, pervasive and user-friendly (Firmino et al., 2008).

The implementation of convergence technologies on urban infrastructure is already understood clearly and somehow the development is underway in most parts of the developed world. Rapid new economic growth associated with new technology and new infrastructure is clearly now taking its roots in the global knowledge economy (Wieman, 1998). Managing and monitoring the urban infrastructure could be relatively easy by deploying appropriate wireless infrastructure, making it accessible and inexpensive to users, and refining software, portals and so on (Aurigi, 2006). Convergence technology solutions including performance monitoring, distance working and seamless production can be incorporated into broad planning initiatives focusing on improving the efficiency of existing urban infrastructure planning, provision and management of U-eco cities. According to Jenkins (2006) due to the speedy progress of technology conversion, eventually, users will access all services and information from urban infrastructure networks and services through one single mobile device, such as a black box. The development of multi-level technology convergence and black box devices can be problematic due to their complexity (Neuman, 2006). The major problems of the implications of black box are grouped under three categories.

First of all, black boxes are often in and out of popularity, and the consumers are left with numerous technologies to choice from that can perform the same task. For example, a consumer may own both a smart card and a credit card with a microchip to use in public transport, subsequently owning two e-cards. This is for sure does not comply with the streamlined goal or spirit of the black box theory, and instead creates a clutter (Rheingold, 2000). Secondly, technological convergence tends to be experimental in nature. This leads consumers purchasing technologies with many functions that are sometimes harder, or impractical, to use compare to a device specifically designed for each function (Jenkins, 2006). For instance, Nokia, iPhone and other brands have mobile phones in the market with an in-built GPS navigation. However, many users find more practical to use an automobile built-in GPS rather than these mobile phones with GPS capabilities. In some cases technology convergence might be unnecessary or unneeded; however, still an advanced and specialised device for each task might not be affordable for all users (Cheskin Research, 2002). Lastly, technology convergence provides a single platform or system to access and use urban infrastructure. However, the physical infrastructure is instead diverging whilst the platforms on the infrastructure are converging. Urban services can offer the same content in a number of forms. An example of this is subways, although, subways are public transport zones, they are also spaces for socialising, shopping, advertising and delivering fluxes such as goods, services, information, energy and people.

MANAGEMENT: INTELLIGENT URBAN MANAGEMENT SYSTEMS

The traditional idea of urban management consists of the good management and planning of a city, entrusted to institutional actors (UNDP, 1997). Increasing awareness of the complexity of the modern urban setting has led to the questioning of management approaches founded on institutional, administrative and geographical compartmentalisation (Stubbs et al., 2000). The concept of urban management is extensive. Borja and Castells (1997) reveal five main challenges of managing an urban community as to: provide an economic base; build urban infrastructure; improve the quality of life; ensure social integration, and; guarantee governance. The quality of the management depends not only on how well each of these challenges is met, but also on their integration to create coherence in urban development. The changing context, in which our societies are evolving, places new pressures on all professionals engaged in managing development and built and natural environments. Today, and into the future, planners and managers of urban and regional development face, on the behalf of our governments and communities, the complex demands of societies (Neilson, 2002).

Handy (1994) states "life will never be easy, nor perfectible, or completely predictable, it will be best understood backwards but we have to live it forwards" to underline the importance of foresighted views in place making and urban management (p. 18). In their research Stubbs et al. (2000) find that a new conceptualisation of management for responding to complex urban issues that confound bounded problem-solving is necessary. Around the globe, increasing awareness of the complexity of the modern urban setting and aforementioned demands have led to questioning of management approaches founded on traditional institutional, administrative and geographical compartmentalisation (Stubbs et al., 2000). Urban environments act as crucibles, where a multitude of interactions not only take place, but also make place for individuals (Giddens, 1984) and, therefore, managing such places plays a critical role in establishing sustainable cities. It has been proved that traditional urban management practices lack of comprehensively tackling urban, economic, social and environmental problems (Jones et al., 2002).

Starting from late 1970s it is clearly accepted that automated information systems or intelligent management systems in local governments contribute significantly to the decision process of top policy-making and management teams by providing them with accurate information and decision directions (Dutton & Kraemer, 1977). In recent years, the growing need for an effective urban management approach led into the development of the notion of intelligent urban management. This new urban management approach rises from improving communication within and between agencies and the public about the highly connected and emergent nature of problems which management responsibility has been assumed (Stubbs et al., 2000). One of the characteristics of the intelligent urban management is that it improves the communication within and between agencies about the highly connected and emergent nature of problems by benefiting from digital technologies. The most recent view of intelligent urban management is shaped by the principles of real-time, effective, efficient, reliable and responding to the emerging issues of sustainable development in urban environments. There are not much comprehensive intelligent urban management systems available at the moment, and the big challenge is to make such systems work in ambitious U-eco cities.

Regardless of whether intelligent or not a sound urban planning and management system should provide: safe, healthy and cohesive communities; sustainable natural resource management; a supportive environment within which business can develop and which assists in opportunities for economic growth; and appropriate urban structure and form so as to provide equitable access to service and amenities. Jones et al. (2002) summarise the important aspects of shaping the new or intelligent planning and urban management systems, and these key aspects include: changing attitude and understanding in urban development and economic growth; coordinating and planning the development through a professional and resourced single body; increasing participation in the planning process; providing equal access to services such as education and health; supporting systems for service planning and delivery; strengthening and providing coordinated urban management services between key infrastructure providers; meeting the demands of varying interest groups; operating a regulatory framework for the control, monitoring and assessment of the development; considering the costs of urban growth such as financial, social and environmental, and; bringing transparency and accountability to the management system. Additionally, much like in the case of U-eco cities an intelligent urban management system as support systems highly benefits from the state of the art technologies in planning, decision-making and management. These advanced technologies include u-technologies, ICTs, decision support systems, digital information systems, strategic choice tools, and e-service technologies. In recent years such technologies made online and web-based platforms and decision support systems accessible for technicians, policy-makers and the public for urban planning, development and management purposes. Although technologies ease the decision-making process, it is still complex by nature, particularly at a large city context. For example the range of factors needs to be taken into consideration in decision-making, which include different agencies to develop awareness on the aspects of the complex phenomenon of air quality.

The literature points out that the complexity of an urban management system could be simplified by using a set of indicators for urban management constitutes an instrument for observation and decision (Joerin et al., 2001). This simplification gives urban stakeholders a model of city development at a given time and for a definite territorial space (Allen, 2001). Indicators used as a common base of comparison between the territorial entities have three key strategic purposes in urban management: monitoring; controlling, and; benchmarking (von Stokar et al., 2001; Spangenberg et al., 2002; Repetti & Desthieux, 2006). So far there are a number of intelligent urban management systems are developed in dealing with various urban issues. One of the most common application areas of these management systems for U-eco cities is the urban environmental management. Intelligent environmental management systems are broadly defined as computer-based technologies that support environmental management systems. The main benefit of intelligent environmental management system adoption is that it provides a systematic process to address comprehensively all major environmental issues. Tasks that intelligent environmental management systems support include tracking activities, tracking waste, monitoring emissions, scheduling tasks, coordinating permits and documentation, managing material safety data sheets, conducting cost/benefit analysis, and choosing alternative materials, to name a few. An intelligent environmental management system integrates monitoring and simulation for environmental decision support in urban areas. The establishment of clear procedures and responsibilities, environmental management programmes, audits and other tools lead to the effective monitoring of environmental issues and solution of problems in a timely manner. An intelligent environmental management system is a set of interacting processes or elements. Each process or element of the environmental management system takes one or more inputs and creates one or more outputs to be passed onto one or more process or elements (DEWHA, 2009). Another common application area of intelligent management systems for U-eco cities is the urban transport management, which is necessary for solving problems caused by traffic congestion through a synergy of new information technology for simulation, real-time control, and communications networks. More specifically, this term refers to the application of advanced information processing, communications, sensing and computer control technologies to the driver-vehicle-road infrastructure system with the aim of improving travel efficiency and mobility, enhancing safety, conserving energy, providing economic benefits and protecting the environment (Regan et al., 2001). Urban transportation planning and management is facing challenges and opportunities in the rapid developments of intelligent transportation systems. Such systems are characterised by real time information feedback in their operations and management, and by increasing levels of automation of their various components. The challenges to planning and management stem from the increased range and added complexity of the choices available to transportation planners (Kanafani et al., 1993).

The main aim of an intelligent urban transport management system in a U-eco cities is to strengthen public transport systems to reduce the negative impacts of air pollutants through advanced traffic management, to directly involve citizens in planning their own trips based on environmental friendly routes and finally, to train young citizens and increase the environmental awareness of citizens in general to develop a new urban mobility culture. It also aims is to coordinate transport infrastructure and demand management through the highest possible use and integration of information and its real time processing, based on the principle of environmental protection in the degraded areas. The operation of numerous key components of intelligent urban transport management systems, such as real-time traffic surveillance and management, incident management, traveller information, and natural and human hazard evacuation, heavily relies on the support of an effective and efficient communication system (Boxill & Yu, 2000).

In response to the evolution of the urban context, during the last decade we have witnessed radical changes in management and communication (Geertman & Stillwell, 2003). The new urban management techniques are highly dynamic and derived from economic management principles and information technologies. In the light of current changes the key challenges for the management of U-eco cities can be grouped under three groups. Firstly, as urban management is becoming more flexible, based on the integration of a strategic global scheme and local management dynamics, the management of highly complex U-eco cities are expected to respond both local and global concerns (Carmona & Burgess, 2001; Ingallina, 2001). Urban management generally addresses a number of urban projects (Borja & Castells, 1997) or spatial or territorial planning (von Stokar et al., 2001), which are flexible tools for management and communication established at the metropolitan level. The rising sustainability concerns and more and more transparency for public participation are making the management process of U-eco cities even more complicated than they already are (Borja & Castells, 1997; le Gales, 1998; Shafer et al., 2000). Secondly, urban management deals more with powerful databases and information systems. To face a considerable volume of data, tools are needed to establish overviews of the goals and provide an appropriate level of synthesis. In an U-eco city actors must be able to access all relevant data without getting lost in details, nor swamped with information that does not provide a clear picture and is not directly useful for decision-making (Allen, 2001; Joerin et al., 2001). Lastly, the evolution of management approaches requires new instruments and tools for strategic development, for information update and transmission, and for monitoring the development, and managing the whole planning and delivery process. At this point new generation intelligent urban management systems are needed to be developed particularly to be able to cope with the complexities of U-eco cities.

CONCLUSION AND FUTURE RESEARCH DIRECTIONS

In the 21st Century global and local forces, such as climate change, resource consumption and depletion, energy security, oil vulnerability, globalisation, knowledge economy, global financial crisis, and technological developments, are rapidly reshaping our cities. In this reshaping process developing pathways towards sustainable urban development is crucial. In this regard U-eco city infrastructure, technology and management system developments offer new opportunities. Telecommunications infrastructure in U-eco cities contributes to the sustainability and quality of urban environments by using eco-friendly materials, employing cutting edge technologies, accumulating wealth, control, and power, and providing a backbone network for delivery and management of urban service and utilities. Technology convergence develops new standards for sustainability performance assessment, improves the accessibility to urban amenities, provides enhanced and fast connection opportunity to urban features through a single device, and helps lifecycle planning and management of U-eco cities. Along with infrastructure and technology developments U-eco city management systems revolutionise urban planning, development and management by providing a new direction for intelligent urban management and contribute to the formation of healthy U-eco cities.

Along with the infrastructure, technology and management system opportunities provided for U-eco cities, there are also a number of challenges. These challenges include: strategically planning every stage of the U-eco city development process; significant financial commitment to invest on developing, equipping and retrofitting new U-technologies to urban environments; developing a system that is resilient to adopt new technological changes quickly, and; securing and safe guarding the whole system from external and internal security treats. Beyond addressing these challenges several key instruments are also required, which include: a strong administration and will to plan and develop sound policies; legislations and regulations to legitimise and empower the process; a fiscal system based on user pays principle rather than tax payers funding of all services, excluding key social services; adoption of a bottom-up and grass roots approach in the decision making;` strong financial and institutional structure to realise and coordinate u-infrastructure and services; capability to manage both assets and knowledge that is key for the knowledge-based and sustainable development of U-eco cities, and; embracing an advocating, transparent and participatory approach for development. Further research needs to be undertaken in order to clearly investigate the interaction of the trilogy of infrastructure, technology and management of the U-eco cities. This investigation will also be useful to depict a lucid picture of the opportunities and prospects that U-eco cities will provide in the 21st century, and to discover solutions to the major challenges we are facing today.

REFERENCES

Allen, E. (2001). INDEX: software for community indicators. In Brail, R., & Klosterman, R. (Eds.), *Planning Support Systems* (pp. 229–261). Redlands, CA: ESRI Press.

American National Standards Institute (ANSI). (1998). *Network and Customer Installation Interfaces: Asymmetric Digital Subscriber Line (ADSL)*. Metallic Interface.

Arseni, P., Boggia, G., & Camarda, P. (2001). Modeling telecommunication infrastructures integrating wideband wireless and wired networks. *Simulation*, *78*(3), 173–184. doi:10.1177/0037549702078003528

Aurigi, A. (2006). New Technologies, yet same dilemmas? Policy and design issues for the augmented city. *Journal of Urban Technology*, *13*(3), 5–28. doi:10.1080/10630730601145989

Baumgartner, J. (2005). Cable consortium mobilizes quad-play with Sprint. *CedMagazine.com*, November 02.

Borja, J., & Castells, M. (1997). *Local and global: management of cities in the information age*. London: Earthscan.

Boxill, S. A., & Yu, L. (2000). *An Evaluation of Traffic Simulator Models for Supporting ITS*. Houston, TX: Development Centre for Transportation Training and Research, Texas Southern University.

Britchie, J., Hall, P., & Newton, J. (1987). The Transition to an Information Society. In Brotchie, (Eds.), *The Spatial Impact of Technological Change*. London: Croom Helm.

Carmona, M., & Burgess, R. (2001). *Strategic Planning and Urban Projects*. Delft, The Netherlands: Delft University Press.

Cheskin Research (2002). *Designing Digital Experiences for Youth*, (Market Insights Series, Fall).

Cunningham, C., & Turner, G. (2005). The Media and Communications in Australia. In Flew, T. (Ed.), *New Media: an Introduction* (2nd ed.). Sydney: Allen & Unwin.

Curtin, J. (2001). *A digital divide in rural and regional Australia? Current issues brief 1*. Australia: Information and Research Services, Department of the Parliament Library.

Davey, K. (1993). *Elements of urban management*. New York: World Bank. doi:10.1596/0-8213-2424-1

DEWHA. (2009). *Environmental Management System Tool. Department of the Environment, Water, Heritage and the Arts*. Sydney, Australia: DEWHA.

Dourish, P. (2004). What we talk about when we talk about context. *Personal and Ubiquitous Computing*, *8*(1), 19–30. doi:10.1007/s00779-003-0253-8

Dutton, W., & Kraemer, K. (1977). Technology and urban management: the power payoffs of computing. *Administration & Society*, *9*(3), 305–340. doi:10.1177/009539977700900303

Dwyre, D. (1998). Newsatellite services to bridge the gap. *Telecommunications*, *32*(12), 47–49.

Firmino, R., Duarte, F., & Moreira, T. (2008). Pervasive Technologies and Urban Planning in the Augmented City. *Journal of Urban Technology*, *15*(1), 77–93. doi:10.1080/10630730802401983

Fisher, J., & Monahan, T. (2008). Tracking the social dimensions of RFID systems in hospitals. *International Journal of Medical Informatics*, *77*(1), 176–183. doi:10.1016/j.ijmedinf.2007.04.010

Flew, T. (2008). *New Media: An Introduction* (3rd ed.). Melbourne, Australia: Oxford University Press.

Fox, W., & Porca, S. (2001). Investing in Rural Infrastructure. *International Regional Science Review*, *24*(1), 103–133. doi:10.1177/016001701761012971

Galloway, A. (2003). *Resonances and everyday life: ubiquitous computing and the city*. Accessed on 6 Oct 2003 from www.purselipsquarejaw.org/mobile/cult_studies_draft.pdf

Geertman, S., & Stillwell, J. (2003). Planning support systems: an introduction. In Geertman, S., & Stillwell, J. (Eds.), *Planning Support Systems in Practice* (pp. 3–22). Berlin: Springer.

Giddens, A. (1984). *The constitution of society: outline of the theory of structuration*. Cambridge, UK: Polity Press.

Graham, S. (1999). Global grids of glass: on global cities, telecommunications and planetary urban networks. *Urban Studies (Edinburgh, Scotland)*, *36*(5-6), 929–949. doi:10.1080/0042098993286

Guild, R. (2000). Infrastructure Investment and Interregional Development: Theory, Evidence, and Implications for planning. *Public Works Management Policy*, *4*(4), 274–285. doi:10.1177/1087724X0044002

Hackler, D. (2003a). High-tech growth and telecommunications infrastructure in cities. *Urban Affairs Review*, *39*(1), 59–86. doi:10.1177/1078087403253054

Hackler, D. (2003b). Invisible infrastructure and the city: the role of telecommunications in economic development. *The American Behavioral Scientist*, *46*(8), 1034–1055. doi:10.1177/0002764202250493

Hanafizadeh, M., Saghaei, A., & Hanafizadeh, P. (2009). An index for cross-country analysis of ICT infrastructure and access. *Telecommunications Policy*, *33*(1), 385–405. doi:10.1016/j.telpol.2009.03.008

Handy, C. (1994). *The Empty Raincoat: Making Sense of the Future*. London: Hutchinson.

Ingallina, P. (2001). *Le Projet Urbain. Presses*. Paris: Universitaires de France.

Jenkins, H. (2006). *Convergence Culture: Where Old and New Media Collide*. New York: New York University Press.

Joerin, F., Rey, M., Nembrini, A., & Desthieux, G. (2001). Information et participation pour l'am'enagement du territoire. *Revue Internationale de Geomatique, 11*(3/4), 309–332.

Jones, P., Tauleelo, T., & Kohlhase, J. (2002). Growing pacific town and cities: Samoa's new planning and urban management system. *Australian Planner, 39*(4), 186–193.

Kanafani, A., Khattak, A., Crotty, M., & Dahlgren, J. (1993). *A planning methodology for intelligent urban transportation systems*. California Partners for Advanced Transit and Highways (PATH). Research Reports: Paper UCB-ITS-PRR-93-14.

Kim, T. (2008). Planning for knowledge cities in ubiquitous technology spaces. In Yigitcanlar, T., Velibeyoglu, K., & Baum, S. (Eds.), *Creative Urban Regions: Harnessing Urban Technologies to Support Knowledge City Initiatives* (pp. 218–230). Hershey, PA: Information Science Reference.

Kirkwood, N. (2008). *Research on U-eco city. Final consultancy report*. Boston, MA: Centre for Technology and Environment, Harvard University.

Kline, E. (2000). Planning and creating eco-cities: indicators as a tool for shaping development and measuring progress. *Local Environment, 5*(3), 343–350. doi:10.1080/13549830050134275

Lawless, P., & Gore, T. (1999). Urban regeneration and transport investment: a case study of Sheffield 1992-96. *Urban Studies (Edinburgh, Scotland), 36*(1), 527–545. doi:10.1080/0042098993510

Le Gales, P. (1998). Regulation, territory and governance. *International Journal of Urban and Regional Research, 22*(3), 482–506. doi:10.1111/1468-2427.00153

Lee, S., & Leem, Y. (2009). *Philosophical and Conceptual Characteristics of Ubiquitous City Strategies and Projects*. CUPUM'09, Hong Kong, 16-19 June 2009.

Lee, S., Yigitcanlar, T., Han, J., & Leem, Y. (2008). Ubiquitous urban Infrastructure: Infrastructure Planning and Development in Korea. *Innovation: Management. Policy & Practice, 10*(3), 282–292.

Magedanz, T., Rothermel, K., & Krause, S. (1996). Intelligent agents: an emerging technology for next generation telecommunications. In *INFOCOM '96*, March 24-28, San Francisco.

Malecki, E., & Bous, C. (2003). Telecommunications Infrastructure in the South-eastern United States: Urban and Rural Variation. *Growth and Change, 34*(1), 109–129. doi:10.1111/1468-2257.00201

Moses, A. (2006). Wii breaks Xbox 360 sales record. *The Sydney Morning Herald,* 14/12/2006.

Neilson, L. (2002). Instruments of governance in urban management. *Australian Planner, 39*(2), 97–102.

Neuman, M. (2006). Infiltrating infrastructures: On the nature of networked infrastructure. *Journal of Urban Technology, 13*(1), 3–31. doi:10.1080/10630730600752728

Nolmark, H. (2007). *Re-thinking Sustainable Urban Development in an Era of Globalisation, Resource Constraints and Climate Change*. Centre for Sustainable Urban and Regional Futures, University of Salford, November 2007.

O'Brien, W., & Soibelman, L. (2004). Technology and Engineering Dimensions: Collecting and interpreting new information for civil and environmental infrastructure management. In Zimmerman, R., & Horan, T. (Eds.), *Digital Infrastructures: Enabling Civil and Environmental Systems through Information Technology*. London: Routledge. doi:10.4324/9780203357125_chapter_TWO

O'Connell, P. (2005). Korea's high-tech utopia, where everything is observed. *New York Times, 5 October 2005.* Retrieved from http://www.nytimes.com/2005/10/05/technology/techspecial/05oconnell.html?ex=1286164800&en=4a368c49e8f30bd2&ei=5088

Regan, M., Oxley, J., Godley, S., & Tingvall, C. (2001). *Intelligent Transport Systems: Safety and Human Factors Issues*. Victoria, Australia: Royal Automobile Club of Victoria.

Repetti, A., & Desthieux, G. (2006). A Relational Indicator set model for urban land-use planning and management: methodological approach and application in two case studies. *Landscape and Urban Planning, 77*(1), 196–215. doi:10.1016/j.landurbplan.2005.02.006

Rheingold, H. (2000). *Smart Mobs: the next social revolution* (pp. 157–182). Cambridge, MA: Perseus.

Rutherford, J. (2005). Networks in cities, cities in networks: territory and globalisation intertwined in telecommunications infrastructure development in Europe. *Urban Studies (Edinburgh, Scotland), 42*(13), 2389–2406. doi:10.1080/00420980500379529

Shafer, C., Lee, B., & Turner, S. (2000). A tale of three greenway trails: user perceptions related to quality of life. *Landscape and Urban Planning, 49*(1), 163–178. doi:10.1016/S0169-2046(00)00057-8

Spangenberg, J., Pfah, S., & Deller, K. (2002). Toward indicators for institutional sustainability: lessons from an analysis of Agenda 21. *Ecological Indicators, 2*(1), 61–77. doi:10.1016/S1470-160X(02)00050-X

Stubbs, M., Lemon, M., & Longhurst, P. (2000). Intelligent urban management: learning to manage and managing to learn together for a change. *Urban Studies (Edinburgh, Scotland), 37*(10), 1801–1811. doi:10.1080/00420980020080421

Taylor, P. J. (2003). *World city network: a global urban analysis*. London: Routledge.

Taylor, P. J. (2010). Measuring the world city network. In Firmino, R., Duarte, F., & Ultramari, C. (Eds.), *ICTs for Mobile and Ubiquitous Urban Infrastructures: Surveillance, Locative Media and Global Networks*. Hershey, PA: IGI Global.

Telecom Media Convergence. (2007). *Telecom Media Convergence*. Retrieved on 15 June 2009 from http://www.tmforum.org/TelecomMediaConvergence/4645/home.html

Telephony Online. (2009). *Simplifying fixed/mobile convergence (FMC) for businesses.* Retrieved on 15 June 2009 from http://telephonyonline.com/global/commentary/simplifying-fixed-mobile-convergence-0330/?cid=hcom

Teriman, S., Yigitcanlar, T., & Mayere, S. (2009). Urban sustainability and growth management in South-East Asian city-regions: the case of Kuala Lumpur and Hong Kong. *Planning Malaysia, 7*(1), 47–68.

UNDP. (1997). *Participatory local governance*. New York: United Nations Development Programme Publications.

Vehovar, V., Sicherl, P., Husing, T., & Dolnicar, V. (2006). Methodological challenges of digital divide measurements. *The Information Society, 22*(5), 279–290. doi:10.1080/01972240600904076

Von Stokar, T., Frick, R., Schultz, B., Keiner, M., Rey, M., & Mettan, N. (2001). *Planification Directrice Cantonale et Developpement Durable*. Berne, Switzerland: Publications de l'Office du Developpement Territorial.

Walcott, S., & Wheeler, J. (2001). Atlanta in the telecommunications age: the fiber-optic information network. *Urban Geography, 22*(4), 316–339.

Wang, H. (2001). Digital City and Urban Sustainable Development. *China Population Resources and Environment, 11*(2), 114–118.

Wang, L., Wu, H., & Song, H. (2002). *A framework of integrating digital city and eco-city*. Wuhan, China: School of Business, Hubei University.

Warf, B. (1998). Reach out and touch someone: AT&T's global operations in the 1990s. *The Professional Geographer*, *50*(1), 255–267. doi:10.1111/0033-0124.00119

Weiser, M. (1991). The computer for the twenty-first century. *Scientific American*, *265*(3), 94–10. doi:10.1038/scientificamerican0991-94

Whitacre, B., & Mills, B. (2007). Infrastructure and the rural–urban divide in high-speed residential internet access. *International Regional Science Review*, *30*(3), 249–273. doi:10.1177/0160017607301606

Wieman, C. (1998). The high-tech transition: technology and the prospects for improving infrastructure performance. *Journal of Urban Technology*, *5*(2), 21–46. doi:10.1080/10630739883895

Williams, I. (2008). *Huawei pushes fixed-mobile convergence*. Retrieved on 15 June 2009 from http://identitymanagement.itweek.co.uk/vnunet/news/2230131/huawei-pushes-fixed-mobile

Yeung, Y. (2000). *Globalization and networked societies: urban-regional change in Pacific Asia*. Hawaii: University of Hawaii Press.

Yigitcanlar, T. (2009a). *Ubiquitous eco cities: a new sustainable city form?* Paper presented at the Urban Design Seminar, 11 February 2009, Gold Coast City Council, Australia.

Yigitcanlar, T. (2009b). Planning for smart urban ecosystems: information technology applications for capacity building in environmental decision making. *Theoretical and Empirical Researches in Urban Management*, *3*(12), 5–21.

Yigitcanlar, T., Han, J., & Lee, S. (2008c). Online Environmental Information Systems. In Frederic, A. (Ed.), *Encyclopaedia of Decision Making and Decision Support Techniques*. Hersey, PA: IGI Publishing.

Yigitcanlar, T., & Velibeyoglu, K. (2008). Knowledge-based urban development: local economic development path of Brisbane, Australia. *Local Economy*, *23*(3), 197–209. doi:10.1080/02690940802197358

Yigitcanlar, T., Velibeyoglu, K., & Baum, S. (Eds.). (2008a). *Knowledge-based urban development: planning and applications in the information era*. Hersey, PA: Information Science Reference.

Yigitcanlar, T., Velibeyoglu, K., & Baum, S. (Eds.). (2008b). *Creative urban regions: harnessing urban technologies to support knowledge city initiatives*. Hershey, PA: Information Science Reference.

ADDITIONAL READING

Anderson, B., Brynin, M., Gershuny, J., & Raban, Y. (Eds.). (2007). *Information and Communication Technologies in Society. E-living in a digital Europe. Routlege Studies in Innovation, Organization and Technology*. New York: Routledge Taylor & Francis Group.

Baum, S., Haynes, M., Gellecum, Y., & Han, J. (2006). Advantage and disadvantage across Australia's extended metropolitan regions: A typology of socio-economic outcomes. *Urban Studies (Edinburgh, Scotland)*, *43*(9), 1549–1579. doi:10.1080/00420980600831759

Beaverstock, J., Smith, R., & Taylor, P. (2000). World-city network: a new meta-geography? *Annals of the Association of American Geographers. Association of American Geographers*, *90*(1), 123–134. doi:10.1111/0004-5608.00188

Bin, H., & Bo, H., JiZheng, W., Huilan, N., and Chongzhi, Z. (2009). Safe river water: A ubiquitous and collaborative water quality monitoring solution. *Pervasive and Mobile Computing*, *5*(5), 419–431. doi:10.1016/j.pmcj.2009.07.019

Chhetri, P., Han, J., & Corcoran, J. (2009). Modelling Spatial Fragmentation of the Brisbane Housing Market. *Urban Policy and Research*, *27*(1), 73–89. doi:10.1080/08111140802468291

Engwicht, D. (1992). *Towards an Eco-City: Calming the Traffic*. Sydney, Australia: Envirobook.

Gottman, J. (1983). *The coming of the transactional city*. College Park: Institute of Urban Studies, University of Maryland.

Hak, L., Sun, L., Kyoo, H., Hak, C., Woo, C., & Ju, Y. (2009). Ubiquitous healthcare service using Zigbee and mobile phone for elderly patients. *International Journal of Medical Informatics*, *78*(3), 193–198. doi:10.1016/j.ijmedinf.2008.07.005

Han, J. (2008). U-eco city Philosophy, Vision and Demand, invited research paper. *International Symposium on Land, Transport and Marine Technology: New Growth Engine for the Future*, Seoul, South Korea, November 5-6th 2008.

Hancock, T. (1997). Healthy, sustainable communities: concept, fledgling practice and implications for Governance. In Roseland, M. (Ed.), *Eco-city Dimensions: Healthy Communities, Healthy Planet*. New Society Publishers, Gabriola Island.

Jacobs, M. (1991). *The Green Economy: Environment, Sustainable Development and the Politics of the Future*. London: Pluto Press.

Kwon, O., Yoo, K., & Suh, E. (2005). UbiDSS: a proactive intelligent decision support system as an expert system deploying ubiquitous computing technologies. *Expert Systems with Applications*, *28*(1), 149–161. doi:10.1016/j.eswa.2004.08.007

Landsbergen, D., Shiang, J., & Byrnes, P. (1994). Fiber optic highways and network bridges: Planning for the telecommunications infrastructure needs of the city in the 21st century. *Telematics and Informatics*, *11*(3), 255–274. doi:10.1016/0736-5853(94)90010-8

Maurseth, P. (2001). Convergence, geography and technology. *Structural Change and Economic Dynamics*, *12*(3), 247–276. doi:10.1016/S0954-349X(01)00022-4

McManus, P., & Halighton, G. (2006). Planning with ecological footprints: a sympathetic critique of theory and practice. *Environment and Urbanization*, *18*(1), 113–127. doi:10.1177/0956247806063963

Newton, P. (2008). *Transitions: pathways towards sustainable urban development in Australia*. Melbourne: Springer.

Pierre, S. (2001). Mobile computing and ubiquitous networking: concepts, technologies and challenges. *Telematics and Informatics*, *18*(2-3), 109–131. doi:10.1016/S0736-5853(00)00024-1

Register, R. (1994). Eco-cities: rebuilding civilization, restoring nature. In Aberley, D. (Ed.), *Futures By Design: The Practice of Ecological Planning*. Gabriola Island, BC: New Society Publishers.

Rinne, M. (2004). Technology roadmaps: infrastructure for innovation. *Technological Forecasting and Social Change*, *71*(1), 67–80. doi:10.1016/j.techfore.2003.10.002

Roseland, M. (Ed.). (1997). *Eco-city Dimensions: Healthy Communities, Healthy Planet*. Gabriola Island, BC: New Society Publishers.

Sadik, J. (2008). Technology adoption, convergence, and divergence. *European Economic Review*, *52*(2), 338–355. doi:10.1016/j.euroecorev.2007.02.005

Tuominen, A., & Ahlqvist, T. (2010). Is the transport system becoming ubiquitous? Socio-technical roadmapping as a tool for integrating the development of transport policies and intelligent transport systems and services in Finland. *Technological Forecasting and Social Change*, *77*(1), 120–134. doi:10.1016/j.techfore.2009.06.001

Wackernagel, M., Kitzes, J., Moran, D., Goldfinger, S., & Thomas, M. (2006). The ecological footprint of cities and regions: comparing resource availability with resource demand. *Environment and Urbanization, 18*(1), 103–112. doi:10.1177/0956247806063978

Wang, H., Zhang, Y., & Cao, J. (2008). Access control management for ubiquitous computing. *Future Generation Computer Systems, 24*(8), 870–878. doi:10.1016/j.future.2007.07.011

Yasunaga, Y., Watanabe, Y., & Korenaga, M. (2009). Application of technology roadmaps to governmental innovation policy for promoting technology convergence. *Technological Forecasting and Social Change, 76*(1), 61–79. doi:10.1016/j.techfore.2008.06.004

Yigitcanlar, T., & Han, H. (2009). Managing ubiquitous eco cities: telecommunication infrastructure networks, technology convergence and intelligent urban management systems. Research Monograph, Queensland University of Technology, School of Urban Development, August 2009, Brisbane, Australia.

Yilmaz, S., & Dinc, M. (2002). Telecommunications and regional development: evidence from the U.S. States. *Economic Development Quarterly, 16*(3), 211–218. doi:10.1177/08942402016003002

KEY TERMS AND DEFINITIONS

Ubiquitous City: A city that provides ubiquitous infrastructure and ubiquitous services for their residents, workers and visitors by utilising a range of ubiquitous technologies.

Ubiquitous Eco City: A city that promises to provide an environmentally friendly urban milieu with advanced ubiquitous infrastructures and services for residents and visitors.

Urban Management: A process of deliberately directing and facilitating urban development, and also an integration of the traditional ideas of planning, with its physical, economic and social concerns, and recently latched to management with its emphasis on efficiency.

Intelligent Management Systems: Are management support tools that are used in institutions including local governments and contribute significantly to the decision process of top policy-making and management teams by providing them with accurate information and decision directions.

Technology Convergence: A black box, which is made of multiple integrated products taking technical advantages of each others. Convergence leads a technological shift or a new technological process.

Information and Communication Technologies: Are technology tools that allow users to participate in a rapidly changing world in which work and other activities are increasingly transformed by access to varied and developing technologies.

Urban Telecommunication Infrastructures: Are the backbones of urban communication networks and provide necessary communication and business channels for public and private sectors and residents.

This work was previously published in International Journal of Advanced Pervasive and Ubiquitous Computing (IJAPUC), edited by J. Symonds, pp. 1-17, copyright 2010 by IGI Publishing (an imprint of IGI Global).

Chapter 7
Social Networks on the Internet:
Twitter Coverage of the Exile of the Peruvian Indigenous Leader Alberto Pizango to Nicaragua

Débora de Carvalho Pereira
Universidade Federal de Minas Gerais, Brazil

ABSTRACT

Social Network Analysis – SNA is a hybrid research method used here to systematize a network of relationships around the collective transnational flux of information via the micro-blog service Twitter. The case studied is the exile of Peruvian indigenous leader Alberto Pizango to Nicaragua, and the conflicts between Indians and the military in May and June 2009 in Bagua, in the Amazon. To historically and politically contextualize the object of this case study in the so-called "Network society", concepts about globalization, ubiquity, and spatial and informational connectivity are employed. The method of Social Network Analysis is described in detail, with attention to the possibilities of visualization and of patterns of connections and identification of ideological values of actors in the network.

INTRODUCTION

This chapter presents, using the method of Social Network Analysis - SNA, a case study on collective media coverage, via the micro-blog server Twitter,[1] of the exile of Indian leader Alberto Pizango, after the massacre of Indians of the Peruvian Amazon in June 2009. It is possible to identify a network of social relations through comments posted about the subject. For a conceptual understanding of the issue, reflections are made about the shape of the emerging socio-technical culture, something called by many authors the Network Society. (Castells, 2002, 2003; Santos, 2002A and 2002B; Bauman, 1999, 2005). Thus it can be seen how informational flows engender cultural changes in society.

To understand these flows, two aspects of networks are examined: they are considered as social (symbolic, economic, political) networks, and as a socio-technical networks (because they are organized on the Internet). This leads to the following questions: (a) Does the field of Information Science note the importance of networks of

DOI: 10.4018/978-1-60960-051-8.ch007

informational practices? (b) Is it attentive to new forms of social interaction employed by companies and entities, and to the institutional, cultural and ideological[2] identities present in these networks? In a time when everyone wants to be 'seen to be something' in the virtual world, it seems that the issue of legitimacy of information issue is somewhat shaky. In this context, on one hand, elements such as 'community', 'identity', 'personality', and 'sociability' are discussed, while on the other hand, questions of 'authority', 'dispersed participation', 'control', and 'collaboration' are raised.

Information systems in geographically dispersed networks are discussed throughout this work as differential factors potentiating the practices, flow, and movement of information. Semantic Web tools (Berners-Lee et al 2001) offer mechanisms to search for specific terms, and to monitor the degree of interest arising in them on the network. They are available on the front page of Twitter, which made it possible to locate the term 'Pizango' in posts, and from this a social network around the Indian leader's name.

Web Semantics structure data to allow those searching to identify content pertinent to their subjects (Breitam, 2005; Pickler, 2007; Feitosa, 2006; Mika, 2006). In this way, this quantitative and qualitative analysis of data from a case study demonstrates the links between communicators and diverse social actors, which make a flow of information through the network possible.

To understand a society full of technical and social webs, it is necessary to bring together knowledge in the form suggested by the Social Network Analysis method. From the perspective of the SNA, research is a transdisciplinary proposition that converges upon the goals of the field of Information Science, allowing the researcher access to different disciplinary matrices.

Social networks are not new objects of study; what is novel is how technologies of information and communication can potentiate its flows. This phenomenon promotes an exchange of knowledge concerning global problems left unsolved by postmodern Enlightenment perspectives. Pollution, global warming, environmental destruction, uncontrolled urbanization, human rights issues and the massacre of indigenous populations are complex and radical issues that reach society in various guises. However, they are usually simplified, with each researcher, in the context of his/her disciplinary beliefs, viewing the subject through his/her own particular lens. Against this process of fragmentation of the truth into traditional scientific fields, the interdisciplinary methodology observed in the practice of Information Science requires the hybridization of different viewpoints to understand the phenomena of information mediated by computer use, through the prism of complexity (Morin, 2002).

When bringing together several fields of knowledge, "sailing is necessary, but you need to know where you are going "[3], to produce insightful science in a critical spirit, or inquiry that goes beyond the market logic of permanent urgency, producing scientific programs devoid of profound concepts.

In the spirit of transdisciplinary research, this chapter tackles the spatiotemporal and cultural paradoxes of network society (1). The SNA method is described in detail (2), and applied to a case study (3). Note that the network is initially defined not with reference to the actors but to the keyword 'Pizango'. That, by itself, indicates local social capital, but it is also implemented as a global cause for human rights and the management of the Amazon. The conclusions also present opportunities for further analysis (4).

SOCIAL NETWORKING TECHNOLOGY: CULTURAL PARADOXES IN INFORMATION SYSTEMS

Nowadays, technical innovations lead us to believe in the functionality of "all-in networking". This metaphor is indeed appropriate, emphasizing connections between geographically dispersed elements organized into social, economic and political networks. It is, therefore, a better representation of contemporary society than *mechanistic* metaphors or the Fordist perspective used to represent work processes in the Industrial Revolution.

Networks form around various hubs, including cities, corporations, supermarkets, churches, banks, restaurants, social movements, and virtual personalities. As a phenomenon observed in several fields of scientific knowledge, note that the concept of a network varies with the perspective of analysis, whether of architecture (design), of types of interaction, of content, or flows of information. In fact, technological networks perform a function that language has always performed in human societies, but in a more potent manner. As well as conveying meaning from one place to another, they organize network action. If we consider the network as a means of communication, all that is manifested through it will be viewed as the flow of information according to certain parameters. In this sense, a network can be "any infrastructure allowing for the transport of matter, energy or information, which is carved out upon the territory characterized by the topology of their circles of transmission, their nodes of bifurcation or communication" (Cruein, apud Santos, 2002B, p. 262).

Santos (2002B) believes in networks as facilitators of everyday contact, or as entities guided by social practices that cause impacts on our everyday lives, not only in a technical sphere, but also in the 'real world'. The author (Santos, 2002b) identifies three stages of 'network life', developing from a simple to a more complex level. This depends on evolving technology, necessitating the deliberate planning of the constitution of a network. At first, the constitution is formed spontaneously, through small daily relationships, with little human engineering needed to facilitate natural data flow among actors, because the amount was small. As a civilization advances, more 'roughness'[4] arises, and the network territory must be improved *i.e.*, the second stage is characterized by increased usage, which requires the establishment of functional units of relationships across borders, dealing with economic, fiscal, diplomatic, military and political issues. In the third stage, the network becomes absolute and ubiquitous. Social life is possible at a distance, potentiated by technologies, bringing together the social tempo with the tempo of technical devices, where social memory, which is continually changing, is almost totally objectified in technical devices (Lévy, 1993).

Businesses organized themselves in networks through offices in fluid relationship with urban areas. Indeed, Taylor (2010) notes that financial markets in cities across the world provide the best illustrations of *business* in globalization. By this logic, cities have different potentials to meet the demands of transnational corporations, and this potential varies due to the strategic location of an urban center and its commercial value. In addition, Taylor (2008) agrees with Doreen Massey (1997, *apud* Taylor 2008), viewing the sites less according to their physical limits, and more in terms of the flows running through it, transcending geographical boundaries. That is, through flows of information and capital, 'global' standards mix into 'local' norms, they transcend state borders, and engender new cognitive and social values.

This experience of the *totality of idea* is concomitant with the weakening of borders, and it undermines the authority of nations. Other social phenomena are involved: the fragmentation of knowledge (much criticized by transdisciplinary researchers), and intensified specialization; the increase in asymmetry of relationships between actors, facing the need to deal with so-called 'social roughness'; and the ubiquitousness of technique, which increases the circulation of pragmatic (operational) information. There is a voracious search for more fluidity (in terms of condition, cause and effect), in which the rotation of ideals determines production and consumption (Santos, 2002b).

Other authors (Bauman, 2005; Castells, 2003) also agree with Santos (2002AB), noting that networks have always existed. For them, what has changed is down to technical improvement, that enhances the number of interactions, while simultaneously emptying the relationship of social depth: as face-to-face relationships decrease, involvement between actors becomes superficial, built upon weak ties. Actually, it is easier to protest and be a part of a 'social movement' through the Internet, because it does not require a profound political and social commitment, this way an individual can belong to different tribal communities. But could it be that the idea of belonging to communities and the notion of absolute ubiquity erode the quality of our relationships?

"At airports and other public spaces, people with cell phones equipped with earphones walk up and down, speaking aloud alone, like paranoid schizophrenics, blind to their surroundings. Introspection is a dying virtue" (Hargreaves *apud*Bauman, 2005, p.31-32). The condition of modern man affirms some paradoxes, according to Augé (2006); the unified and divided world, the populated solitude of connections, and places devoid of any cultural context related to their geographical position – such as shopping centers, airports, international hotels, highways – what the author calls 'non-places' (Augé, 2006, p. 101). These generic urban spaces make it impossible for visitors to identify any sense of history, since these places were transformed by 'planetarization'. These places do not allow people to engage in sustained social relations. As Santos (2002b) says, "the networks are a vehicle of a dialectical movement that both oppose territory and place in the world, whilst also meaning that place and territory be taken as a whole" (Santos, 2002b, p. 270).

Weissberg (2004) reflects upon this aspect in his article "Paradoxos da Teleinformática" (Tele-informatics Paradoxes), saying that borders are denied, and at the same time, territorial communities use networks and technology to strengthen their ties. Another ambiguous factor is that presence at distance does not dispense with transportation; on the contrary, it is intensified. Geographic Information Systems promote in an intelligent manner 'the specialization of information' on hybrid maps of territory and informational space, in which geostrategic procedures are crossed with traditional topographic data of abstract information, of historical, economic, or psychological character). Between proximity and distance, the network does not dissolve the notion of place, but re-contextualizes it, mixing 'physical uni-presence with mediated multi-presence' (Weissberg, 2004, p. 121). This phenomenon, that some authors call *glocalization*, (Antoun, 2001; Weissberg, 2004), concerns information systems and global media, but its use is local, marking out the nature of space by the social location of actors engaged in the remote exchange of information.

This flow of data is catalyzed, according to Santos (2001), by the coming together of three distinct possibilities: (1) Perfect universal forms, a result of new technology making information ubiquitous and instantaneous, (2) Universal standards (treaties, protocols and agreements between countries and diverse institutional actors), and (3) Universal Information[5] or the alleged intention of universal discourse. Santos (2002a) interprets globalization – and his concept of a network comes from this conception – as resulting from standardized technologies, functional interdependence, convergence of moments, and increasing information exchange. Unipolar domination of space is therefore made possible by new communication and technology links, which are information networks and capital flows. Santos (2002a) proceeds from the judgment of globalization as 'perverse', to a vision or hope that the common idea of fairness awakens hope of 'a possible new world':

From these transformations, it is possible to think about the local production of a progressive understanding of the world and of place, with the indigenous production of images, discourses, and philosophies, along with the development of a new ethos, new ideologies, and new political beliefs, supported by the idea and rebirth of the practice of solidarity. (Santos, 2002a, p. 167-168)

Although the author announces a common idea, resulting from a progressive understanding of the planet, it is the connectivity that reveals content, from groups that are in contact despite different cultural and ideological profiles. It is this interaction which structures a network. In this sense, establishing a connection between institutions and their agents means establishing lines of communication, where experiences are exchanged. In a participatory and collaborative manner, people build up encyclopedic platforms of knowledge (such as Wikipedia) they rewrite classical works (*fanfictions*). In this way, foreign environmentalists collectively created a movement on Twitter to make the Peruvian government abandon the implementation of developmental policies in the Amazon, culminating in the exile of the indigenous leader Alberto Pizango to Nicaragua.

To study this case, it is first necessary to understand the methodical propositions of Social Network Analysis.

THE METHOD OF SOCIAL NETWORK ANALYSIS

Social Network Analysis - SNA identifies and seeks to span the abysses of knowledge between different fields, working with interactive possibilities between various fields. Thus, SNA is not only used in different epistemological fields to produce new data, but also to re-frame existing perspectives to investigate specific issues of networks. It is common in this analysis to bring together anthropology, economics, sociology, computer science, social communications and other fields, and can bring new knowledge to light.

The researcher must be sensitive in choosing the tools of data collection, to unify complex viewpoints, to establish methods that objectify the area as a well-defined epistemological pillar. It is necessary to know more than the context of the analysis (the place being observed), but also its context (the place of observation), which can affect lines of enquiry in the field. Transdisciplinarity is not the denial of disciplines; rather, it is the intelligent interaction between them.

Social Network Analysis supposes that social relations constitute the basic units of society, because they help identify various indices. These should not be treated in isolation; on the contrary, the focus should be on the interdependence between them (Wasserman, 1994; Lazega, 2007; Hanneman, 2008; Pizzaro, 2004; Marteleto, 2001).

It is a rigorous sociological method of modeling, which can reveal the structures of relations in society. It is also flexible, because it hybridizes several matrices, bringing together a set of conceptual elements in search of new novel and instructive permutations(Caballero, 2005).

The method is used to contextualize behaviors and display systematically the invisible dimension of social connections within society. Caballero (2005) considers it a tool in the service of collective action theory, which helps to redefine concepts within the disciplines and produces new knowledge, contextualized with the researcher's individual perspective. Each researcher's 'epistemological identity', carries a theoretical heritage, which determines the nature of his/her research, the goals and direction of his/her inquiry, the methodology and collection of data, and also their reading and influences. The personal and academic profile of the researcher influences many of his/her choices, as do his relationships. The weight of this disciplinary legacy sometimes means that the complexity of the object (in the case of social networks) is mutilated in the name of simplification and reductionism. The SNA method counteracts this influence, combining a structural approach (display, generation, and automated interpretation of graphs) with other methods of contextualizing action in network.

This does not disregard the theories particular to each field; it uses the best that each field offers.

The complex social interdependence of networks, therefore, cannot be read from mathematical formalization alone, but also in elaborating of relevant sociometric questions. The nature of the question must be considered in an organized way, because you cannot promote eclecticism without considering the theoretical basis of each matrix. Production of knowledge regarding the context of social relations within networks is not only a prerogative of universality or research centers. It is also a process to identify the character of relations in constant negotiation and mutation.

Social networks, for their part, are considered important partners in the construction of knowledge about themselves. In the systematization of the network in this case study, only participative observation was used, this being the limit of the study.

Visualizations

To objectify and make transparent those processes, SNA describes and visualizes social groups in terms of relational and structural properties (which consist of a pattern of relationships between sets of social actors, identified in units of analysis). The networks can be described, therefore, in metaphorical, descriptive or essayistic (simulated) forms, observing the interdependence between members of actors in an organized social context. It is important not to isolate obtained data, and to focus on indicators that represent transference and exchange channels, as intentional, circumstantial and underlying engagements. The socio-technical networks make use of technological devices to potentiate these engagements, as they help to organize a level of rationality (rules) pertaining to actors involved.

As indexes of these engagements, the visualizations are a useful tool in understanding the structure of a network. The figures show patterns of connections from specific points of inquiry (Welser *et al*, 2007, Dekker, 2005). A network is usually represented in various forms. When this occurs, it is important to treat different categories of actors in different sub-graphs, since the figures are fundamental to understanding the operation of the network.

The visual treatment of information allows the exploration, understanding and explanation of the dynamics of the network. It facilitates the proposal and denial of hypotheses, and suggests new subjects for analysis. Two approaches can inform the generation of graphs for visualization: entire networks and ego-centered networks (Recuero, 2009, p.69). The ego-centered network (or personal network) describes connections from a particular node, *i.e.*, it is drawn from a central actor, and the data are collected from information emitted by this center.

The entire networks can also be measured as starting from a pre-existing point, deliberately chosen by the researcher as a reference, which could be geographical, thematic, institutional, or set by other limits. In this case, it is important to know how the network is defined, aware that this choice influences its parameters.

Units of Analysis

According to Garton *et al.* (2007), SNA is not only attentive to the attributes of specific actors in networks, but also relationships and social exchanges between them, considering the kind of ties, their multiplicity and composition.

In more detail[6]:

- Relationships are characterized by content (type of resource or information exchanged through the network), its direction (recipient and emitter), and strength (according to various indices of different types of social capital). They can also be classified as direct or indirect, considering that actors can be linked to others through third parties, in a symmetric or asymmetric fashion.

- Ties have the function of connecting actors in one or more relationships. They vary in content (according to the social capital that drives the connection), direction and strength. Actors who are considered strong ties are more representative of the motives and resources of the network itself, while those considered weak, with less representation within a network, are useful for connecting the network to other social groups, because they generally span more than one sphere of relations.
- Multiplicity refers to the amount of wires that connect the actors within a network, according to the degree of interactivity (if there are many changes, many wires, for example). Multiple ties tend to be more intimate, voluntary and durable.
- The composition of a relationship or tie is derived from social attributes such as gender, hierarchy, age and others.

Types of Networks

A network can be centralized, decentralized or dispersed, according to the flow of communication (Baran, 1964, *apud*Recuero, 2009, p.56). A network can also present these three characteristics at the same time. Recuero (2009, p. 59-67) defines two other types of dynamics in networks of communication, which are in constant movement and evolution, like Twitter:

- Small world networks: characterized by having high clustering coefficients[7] and short distances between nodes. This model demonstrates that through ties made randomly between close people, the distance between people on the planet is reduced.
- Scale-free networks: in which few nodes have more connections than others. This model describes the dispersal of ties along nodes (degrees of dispersal), with low clustering coefficients.

Twitter, as a socio-technical device works as a technical support for social networks. According to 'State of the Twittersphere'[8], published by Hubspot (2008) there is a new media area based on this socio-technical network, with 4.5 million users as of December 2008. In first six months of 2008, Twitter was in the top thousand most highly visible websites throughout the Internet.

The nature of Twitter relationships is as follows: all users can post up to 140 text characters. There is no space to display images, besides the User Profile picture, and the user can write a mini-biography. Users can choose people to follow and read only their posts, or read posts of the website's entire usership (general).

It appears that Twitter is usually accessed via mobile platforms, mobile phones and PDA's, such as Blackberrys, Palmtops and Apple I-Phones. According to another survey by the Social Networking Blog[9], the most observed applications in the interaction between social networks happen via mobile phone, converging on platforms such as Facebook, Myspace and others. The research[10] (2008) predicts increasing use: 63 million users worldwide in location-based services (LBS) in 2009, and 486 million in 2012, which will move around $3.3 billion in the economy. It is expected that in 2012, 18% of mobile phone users will access social networking, something like 950 million users.

CASE STUDY

The tag markings in Twitter micro-blog present new perspectives for treating of information, with the emergence of a new semantic dimension of communication flow in online social networks. The network was identified by monitoring posts containing the word 'Pizango' on Twitter from June 5th to 23rd, *i.e.*, from the date of the main Indian massacre. Searching for this keyword in the tool that tracks all Twitter posts returned 262 results, originating from 137 users including bloggers, journalists, activists, companies, mass media firms, environmental campaigners and others. Most are in Spanish, but there are also posts in English, Portuguese, German and Russian.

This diversity of languages indicates that this network is in the third stage of the 'life of networks', cited by Santos (2002B), in the first section of this chapter. In other words, socializing at a distance between actors who have no relationships between them except those pertaining to the technical gadgets. Even though there are semantic connections between the actors, represented by the occurrence of the term 'Pizango' in their posts, it cannot be inferred that these actors have any kind of ties or social involvement with each other. It is a loneliness full of connections (Augé, 2006) between actors who are geographically distant but close in their interest in the subject of the massacre of Indians (one of the paradoxes of teleinformatics described in section 1)

A network with 50 connections linking these 137 users was identified, represented by 50 *retweets* – RTs. This means that the post is being passed on to another user, or comes from another information source, that is it was read, judged to be of value, and therefore passed on. RTs were considered as a network relation. This suggests, however, that 84 users of the network are not connected with other actors. In fact, the visualization shows that there is a large area sprayed with unconnected points, confirming that social relations are degraded in this medium, tending to be superficial in socio-technical networks (Bauman, 2005). Even though there are semantic connections between the actors represented by the term 'Pizango' in the posts, it cannot be inferred that they include some tie or social involvement.

Paradoxically, the symbolic constructions around the issue emphasize the Peruvian indigenous theme as social capital. Although the massacre of Indians was an event geographically restricted to Peru, the issue crosses borders – it is 'transnational', *i.e.*, values of a causal nature determine the exchange and engagement of foreign actors. Events around Alberto Pizango constitute the network's cognitive link. To clarify this statement, the social and historical context of the situation must be elucidated.

The indigenous policies of the Peruvian government are criticized by non-governmental organizations (such as Survival International, Greenpeace and WWF), because they do not recognize the rights of Amazonian tribes to live in and from their original territories. As a result, since 2008, Survival International[11] has constantly complained on its website about migration tracked by satellite of indigenous people to lands in the Brazilian state of Acre, and violence against tribes resisting deforestation. These informational and political dynamics centered around the theme of environmental conservation, transcending national sovereignty, demonstrating that regional events involve the interests of foreign actors.

The global action of these entities strengthens Santos' argument (2002AB), in which the increase in exchange of information in the world, which characterizes sociability in networks, is possible because of the emergence of universal norms, or rather, international agreements and protocols between diverse institutions, which legitimize universal discourse, principally in questions of environmental action. For example, in May 2009, the Peruvian government implemented a new development program for management of the Peruvian Amazon, which foresees exploitation of timber and mineral deposits in indigenous lands in partnership with multinational companies. This project was created, consulting neither the NGO's acting in the region nor the indigenous tribes, who responded with protests, blocking roads, disrupting airports and other essential services, and leading to armed conflict with the army and police. The Peruvian President Alan García said in the media that all citizens should benefit from the country's natural resources, not just a small group of Indians: "It has to be understood that natural resources, such as oil, gas and timber, do not belong exclusively to the people who had the luck to be born there"[12]. According to the Peruvian Constitution, the state owns any mineral abundance and hydrocarbons in the country.

In reaction to this statement, on May 15th, 2009, Alberto Pizango, the leader of the Peruvian Amazon Indian Organization (AIDESEP, its acronym in Spanish), said that dialogue with the government had broken down. According to him, territories were being handed over to multinationals without consulting the indigenous populations. In a statement, Pizango denied that AIDESEP – an umbrella organization for 65 indigenous groups – is against progress. He said: "what we want is development, as we judge it from our perspective"[13]. Since then, Indians supported by the technicians and executives of transnational environmental organizations, disrupted transport services, including airports and bridges. Their aim was to overturn several laws that they considered harmful, especially those providing concessions to foreign companies exploiting the Peruvian Amazon.

The use of local information by transnational NGOs, and the spreading of such in critical reports through social networks proves that the hope of Santon (2002A) that 'a new world is possible' is viable. Preserving the memory and culture of indigenous tribes, and recognizing their territories, with the help of international organizations, indicates the progressive understanding of the world generated locally, described by the author as one of the faces of globalization (Santos, 2001).

The Peruvian Amazon is the largest area of intact forest outside Brazil. It is the geographical center of the western part of the forest, and is rich in terms of unexplored mineral assets and timber. There are great interests at stake. The French oil company Perenco[14] has promised to invest US$2 billion in just one oil field. Indigenous communities complain that about 70% of the Peruvian Amazon territory is being "rented" to exploit oil and gas, endangering both their lives and the biodiversity of the region.

On June 5th, there was a confrontation in Bagua between police and Indians, resulting in the death of at least 34 people, according to government figures. It began when the police tried to suppress a protest that had been blocking the Fernando Belaunde Terry Road for ten days. Although the government stated that most of the victims were policemen, indigenous leaders accused the police of "genocide", and reported more than 500 missing Indians[15]. Although not usually guided by the media, blogs and micro-blogs started a disseminating a growing number of images and testimonials, with videos showing government helicopters throwing bagged bodies into rivers. The National Ombudsman of Peru did not find any bodies, but it was only authorized to inspect the sites two days later.

Faced with transnational media mobilization around the issue, the Peruvian Congress[16] decided to interrupt, but not repeal, the pro-investment legal package launched by García, arguing that the country needed to adjust its legislation to the FTA (Free Trade Agreement) with the USA. The protesters argued that the government should have consulted the communities of the forest before creating the laws, as required by Peruvian law. Currently, 72% of the Peruvian forest is divided into lots destined for exploitation by oil companies, 90% of which is on indigenous land, according to a study at Duke University[17] (USA). Many companies have acquired rights to these areas, but they face resistance from local communities. AIDESEP president, Alberto Pizango, was charged with sedition, and was granted political asylum[18] in Nicaragua on June 17th, 2009. He intends to continue leading indigenous people against the Peruvian government from there.

The support of transnational environmental organizations for the indigenous struggle in Peru, through publications on institutional websites and through social networks, indicates that there is a juxtaposition of physical and informational dimensions, through the influence of transnational actors, catalyzing changes in the local environment, as shown in the following example of visualization of the network around the term 'Pizango' on Twitter.

Figure 1. Entire network

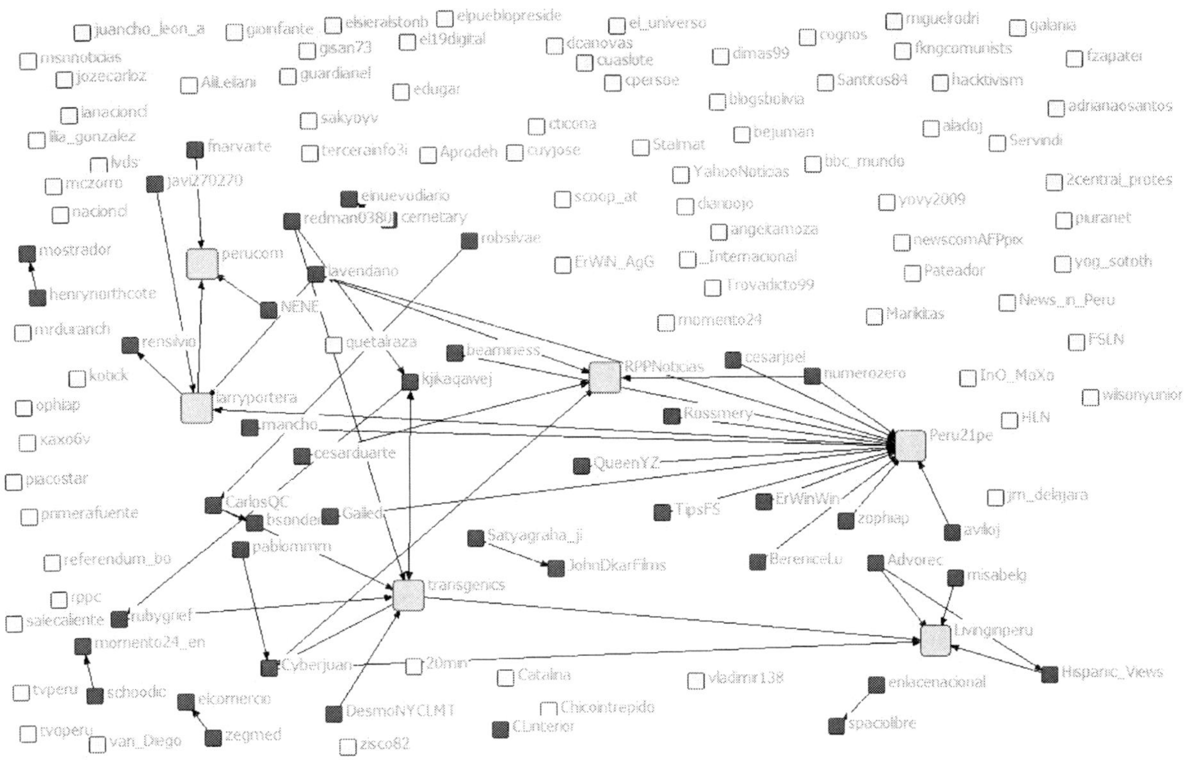

Pizango on Twitter

By assigning values of attributes, the network was divided between actors who posted positive, negative or neutral material about Pizango. It can be seen here that groups with different interests are in contact through the micro-blog.

Figure 1 shows how *clusters* form around central players in the network, identified by the Ucinet 6.0 tool for measuring centralization. We see that these profiles can be considered *informational centers*, and this is confirmed by Table 1, which demonstrates the centrality. In descending order related to the most cited in RT, there are: *Peru21pe*, *transgenics*, *RPPNews*, *larryportera*, *perucom*, *kjikaqawej*, *Cyberjuan*, *lavendano* and *CarlosQC*.

The centralization of information of the top six players in Table 1 is highlighted in Figure 2. The visualization suggests that the identified network is decentralized and dispersed, though not equal, because each central actor evidences the formation of a cluster. It can still be considered a 'scale-free' network, as few nodes have more connections than the majority, and many nodes are unrelated to other actors. To facilitate differentiation, unconnected actors are represented by floating points, the leaders of information are represented by squares, and the others (forming clusters) are represented by triangles.

The network can also be split according to the value of information, into posts "in favor of Pizango" (Figure 3), posts "against Pizango" (Figure 4) and "neutral" posts (Figure 5). Note that among leaders of information, the neutral pattern is most common – three – where two other leaders are pro and one against Pizango. These neutral posts do not assign value to the facts; they 'inform' without expressing an opinion.

Examples of neutral posts:

Table 1. Measures of network centrality. (All actors not cited had a number less than 1)

Profile	Output Grade Level	Input Grade Level	% Total Input	% Total Output
1 *Peru21pe*	2.000	13.000	1.471	9.559
2 *transgenics*	4.000	5.000	2.941	3.676
3 *RPPNoticias*	0.000	4.000	0.000	2.941
4 *larryportera*	2.000	3.000	1.471	2.206
5 *perucom*	0.000	3.000	0.000	2.206
6 *Kjikaqawej*	2.000	2.000	1.471	1.471
7 *Cyberjuan*	2.000	2.000	1.471	1.471
8 *Lavendano*	3.000	1.000	2.206	0.735
9 *CarlosQC*	2.000	1.000	1.471	0.735

- *avilioj* RT *@Peru21pe* Alberto **Pizango** estaría dejando el país entre mañana y pasado, informó Tasha del Pozo, funcionaria de la Embajada de Nicarágua
- *CarlosQC* Indigenous leader Alberto **Pizango** arrived to Nicaragua / lider indigena Alberto **Pizango** llego a Nicaragua! http://tinyurl.com/lbh5
- *'transgenics* RT *@rubygrief* amazon protest leader Alberto**Pizango** has left Peru on a plane headed for Nicaragua, where he has been granted political...

Examples of posts against Pizango:

- *Chicointrepido* Indígena MENTIROSO!!! a través de su raza quiere manipular a to-

Figure 2.

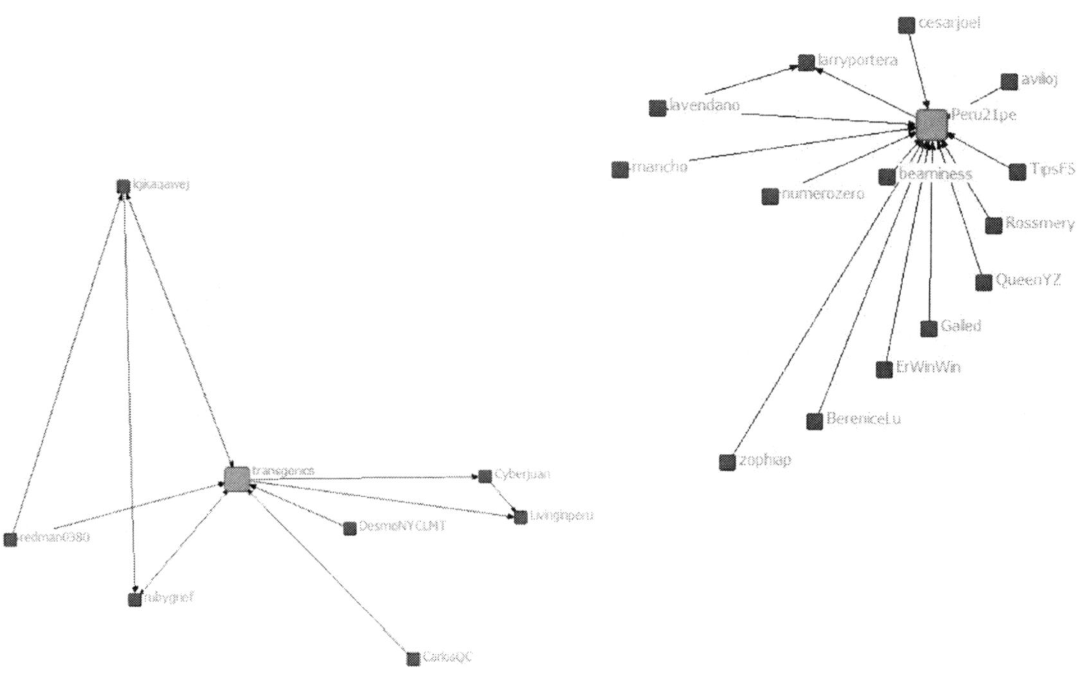

Figure 3.

dos los incautos extranjeros!!!! Qué tal tomada de pelo por dios!!! **Pizango**!!

- *fzapater* Q'orianka Kilcher, para evitar el ridiculo hay que informarse primero. **Pizango** no es ningun ejemplo a seguir. Ojala q alguien te instruya

Examples of posts in favor of Pizango:

Figure 4.

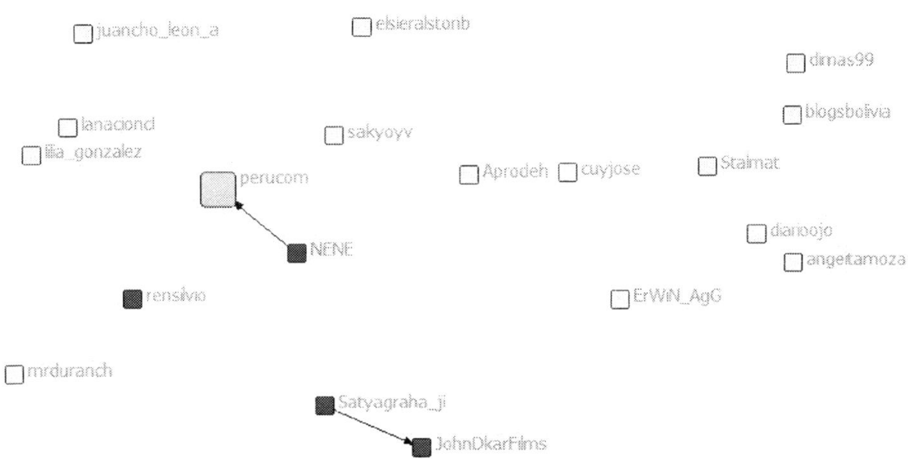

Figure 5.

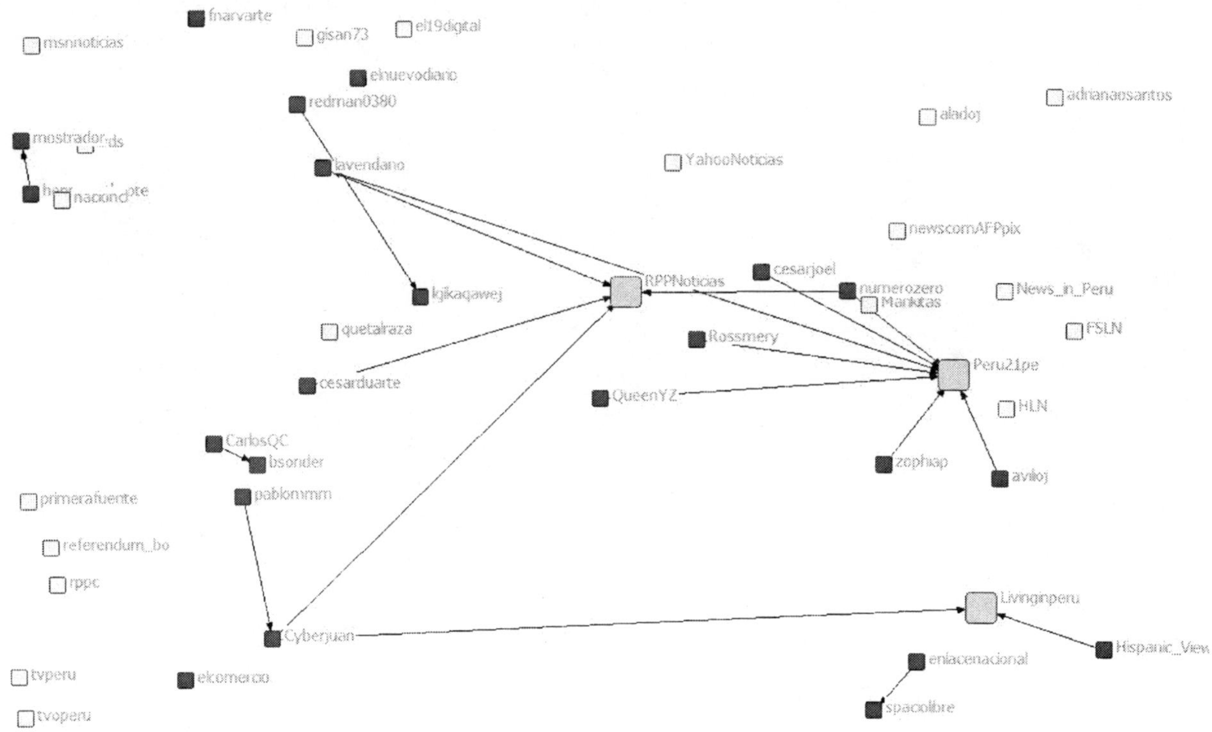

- *transgenics* RT *@CarlosQC* Indigenous hero Alberto **Pizango** about to leave assailed Peru for Nicaragua - WILL HE BE THE FUTURE PERU'S EVO MORALES?
- *yog_sototh* Manuin: "Los verdaderos interlocutores están en la selva y los dirigentes y jefes están allá(...)**Pizango** no era suficiente." http://ir.pe/f5

In addition to technical operations involving the exile (such as leaving the embassy by car, going to the airport, contacting the press and so on), there was a protest in favor of Pizango, supported by the Indian actress Q'orianca Kilcher (known as 'Pocahontas'), who said that Pizango "lives in her heart", and earned the following commentary on the network:

- *dimas99* Desubicada Q'orianca: " **Pizango** está en mi corazón". No, linda, **Pizango** esta corrido en la Embajada de Nicaragua.
- *van_Diego* Q'orianka Kilcher: "Alberto **Pizango** está en mi corazón" http://is.gd/10449 Bien desubicadita esta chica! *10 days ago from web*

It is true, therefore, that these posts can be considered media threads running through informational flows related to the theme.

POSSIBILITIES FOR FURTHER ANALYSIS

The identification and visualization of this network of meanings, showing the transnational nature of the Peruvian indigenous movement on Twitter, could be analyzed from different perspectives. For example, new clusters could be identified from the links to other websites in the posts. This way, other actors or informational persons that produce content on these websites could be identified.

These websites could be also separated into two categories: 'mass media' and 'niche media' (bloggers, activists, and alternative websites), or divided between professionals in the field of information and amateurs. And by understanding the dynamic of information between them, we could investigate feedback between different sources of information that use the micro-blog publishing tools.

Another possibility for analysis is to situate data collected on geographical maps, creating Geographic Information Systems, overlaying the places connected with the profiles with the location of the conflict.

This could demonstrate the degree of transnationality of the issue, and the social place of information. Being such a niche subject, it is clear that Peruvian actors use local media, but when the issue becomes global, it presents new parameters that can be pictured on hybrid maps. It is interesting to observe whereabouts in the world this issue is of concern.

Entire networks can be further split into ego-centered networks around the main actors, generating graphs for each cluster, analyzing separately the dynamics of the chains.

When designing visualizations of connections between a concrete and virtual group, the study can be enriched by a transdisciplinary approach, with quantitative and qualitative (anthropological and sociometric) analysis, with spontaneous interviews, with mathematical, spatial, psychological data crossing.

CONCLUSION

New Semantic Web tools, or technical devices that enhance interaction between social networks, allow the association of local and global information. Specifically in the case of Twitter, the tool to search for specific terms within posts allowed a case study based on the exile of Indian leader Alberto Pizango. Monitoring revealed the centrality of some actors in the flow of information through the network. The attributes representing the values were related to social context, and the visualizations inferred that the network identified is decentralized and disperse, even though it cannot be considered an equal network: each central actor, in differentiated clusters, has around him/her self followers that amplify his/her material. Regarding this amplification, it is not only reproducted literally, as the information can be edited and altered according to the actor's opinions.

The network of interactions around the exile is therefore a 'scale-free' network, since only a few nodes have many more connections than the majority do. Many nodes are unrelated to other actors. From this we can conclude that even though there are clusters, most of the information is fragmented; that is they are punctual emissions without connection to other actors in the network. They are, however, connected via semantic content that motivates the analysis: the indigenous issue in Peru.

Even though there are more neutral posts from the informational leaders, a greater number than the posts 'against' or 'in favor' of Pizango, we must consider this neutrality a fallacy (in the *comteano* positive sense), since there is no communication without intention. The motivation to log in to a social network and publish something related to the indigenous conflict indicates an intention to make the issue visible. In other words, the issue is of public interest, both on a regional and a transnational level.

Visualizations of the network allow one to infer that other events cluster around environmental conflicts in the Peruvian Amazon, such as the interview by Indian actress Q'orianca Kilcher's, that reverberated around Twitter. Specifically in this case, we can understand that a 'spectacle' is made of the indigenous conflict in the media.

The actress' declarations caused reactions and debates in the semantic network, as the data shows. Furthermore, the statements' echoing through the network show that there is feedback between different media nowadays, as in the Pizango network on Twitter there are references to newspapers and television channels.

Systematized by the graphs, the formation of clusters could be identified in the networks, where information flows come together. Although Twitter only allows texts of up to 140 characters, the interactive tools of this social network promoted social convergence among dispersed actors, who interact through comments and posts.

The analysis also made clear that the transnational flow of contents about this theme from a region that is not much urbanized, but has in its cultural diversity valuable ecological and social capital (which attracts environmental activists). Peru attracts economic capital from the multinational companies that wish to exploit natural resources, and which are connected to governments which favor progress – *i.e.* urbanization and migration of native populations (like Indians) to cities (Pereira, 2007, 2008). And this can be perceived in the analysis of the content of messages in the indentified network.

Globalization, therefore, manifests in market flows between cities via the connections of multinational offices in urban environments ('international financial centers'), proposed by Taylor (2008), and can be extended to the current connections in the Amazon region, because of its natural and cultural biodiversity. Global non-governmental organizations, alongside local communities, stimulate public policies, promote links between Indian tribes and environmental associations, and streamlining flows of information about forest conservation through socio-technical networks. If the Indian issue is regional, it is also transnational, in that 'save the forest' is a global issue. The result is a transnational network of information, involving the conflict between two different political sides.

This method of analysis, used here to measure and monitor a specific term through trails through the Twitter system, can be used in various cases, to monitor the formation of ideologies through social networks. That is because SNA shapes itself to the problem, analyzing it from a transdisciplinary perspective. This methodology raises new subjects for analysis, construction, re-construction, and deconstruction of social and personal networks, formalized by different perspectives. The contribution of related disciplines, triangulating methods to enrich our understanding of the phenomena, encourages cross-disciplinary Information Science researchers to apply their findings to extended programs, thereby promoting not only the dissemination of scientific knowledge, but even more than that, social interventions in fields beyond the university.

REFERENCES

Antoun, H. (2001). *Jornalismo e ativismo na hipermídia: Em que se pode reconhecer a nova mídia*. Porto Alegre, Brazil: EDIPUCRS.

Augè, M. (2006). *Sobremodernidade: Do mundo tecnológico de hoje ao desafio essencial do amanhã*. Rio de Janeiro, Brazil: Mauad.

Bauman, Z. (1999). *Comunidades: A busca por segurança no mundo atual*. Rio de Janeiro, Brazil: J. Zahar Editor.

Bauman, Z. (2005). *Identidade: Entrevista à Benedetto Vecchi*. Rio de Janeiro, Brazil: J. Zahar Editor.

Bicalho, L. M., & Oliveira, M. (2005) *Transdisciplinaridade nas ciências: o lugar da Ciência da Informação*. I EBEC - Encontro Brasileiro de Estudos da Complexidade – Curitiba, Brasil, July 11th to 13th, 2005.

Breitman, K. K. (2005). *Web semântica: a Internet do futuro*. Rio de Janeiro, Brazil: LTC.

Bulik, L. (1990). *Doutrinas da informação: No mundo de hoje*. São Paulo, Brazil: Loyola.

Caballero, E. G. *Pluralidad teórica, metodológica y técnica en el abordaje delas redes sociales: hacia la "hibridación" disciplinaria*. REDES - Revista hispana para el análisis de redes sociales Vol.9#1, Dic.2005. Avaiable at: http://revista-redes.rediris.es.

Castells, M. (2002) *A sociedade em rede*. (6ª Ed.). São Paulo, Brazil: Paz e Terra.

Castells, M. (2003). *A galáxia da internet: Reflexões sobre a internet, os negócios e a sociedade*. Rio de Janeiro, Brazil: J. Zahar Editor.

Debray, R. (1995). *Manifestos Midiológicos* (Teixeira, J. F., Trans.). Petrópolis, Brazil: Vozes.

Dekker, A. *Conceptual Distance in Social Network Analysis*. Journal of social structure, vol. 6. Available at: http://www.cmu.edu/joss/content/articles/volume6/dekker/, Accessed July 5th, 2009.

Feitosa, A. (2006). *Organização da informação na Web: das tags à web semântica*. Brasília: Thesaurus.

Garton, L. (n.d.). Studying Online. *Social Networks*. Available at http://jcmc.indiana.edu/vol3/issue1/garton.html#References Accessed on July 5th, 2009.

Hanneman, R. (n.d.). *Introduction to social network methods*. Available at: http://wizard.ucr.edu/~rhannema/index.html#news. Accessed on May 1st, 2008.

Keck, M. E., & Sikkink, K. (1998). *Activists beyond borders: Advocacy networks in international politics*. Ithaca, NY: Cornell University Press.

Lazega, E. (2007). *Réseau sociaux et strutures relationnelles*. Paris: PUF.

Lee, T. Berners, Hendler, J. & Lassila, O. (2001). The Semantic Web. *Scientific American*, May.

Lemos, A. (2008). *Ciberespaço e Tecnologias Móveis: Processos de Territorialização e Desterritorialização na Cibercultura*. COMPÓs, 2008. Available September 2008, at [http://www.facom.ufba.br/ciberpesquisa/andrelemos/territorio.pdf

Lévy, P. (1993). *As tecnologias da Inteligência: o futuro do pensamento na era da informática,* (pp. 34). Rio de Janeiro, Brazil, Ed.

Marteleto, R. (2001) Análise de redes sociais – Aplicação nos estudos de transferência da informação. *Ci. Inf., Brasília, 30*(1, jan./apr), 71-81.

Mattelart, A. (2006). Para que "Nova Sociedade Mundial da Informação.". In de Moraes, D. (Ed.), *Sociedade Midiatizada*. Rio de Janeiro, Brazil: Mauad.

Mika, P. (n.d.). *Social Networks and the Semantic Web*. Disponível em wrg.upf.edu/WRG/seminarios/260407_aMika.pdf

Morin, E. (2002). *O método 3 – Conhecimento do conhecimento*. Porto Alegre, Brazil: Sulina.

Nicolescu, B. (1999). *O manifesto da transdisciplinaridade*. São Paulo, Brazil: Ed. Triom.

Pereira, D. C. (2007). *Amazônia Transnacional: As redes ambientais na internet e a padronização da natureza*. Dissertation in Agricultural Extension, Department of Rural Economy, Federal University of Viçosa.

Pereira, D. C. (2008). *O encadeamento da imagem dos índios isolados da Amazônia na internet e a padronização da natureza*. In 1° Colóquio de Comunicação e Sociabilidade 'Comunicação Midiática: Instituições, Valores e Cultura', novembro de 2008.

Pizzaro, N. (2004). *Un nuevo enfoque sobre la equivalência estructural: lugares y redes de lugares como herramientas para la teoría sociológica*. Redes: Revista hispana para el análisis de redes sociales.

Recuero, R. (2009). *Redes Sociais na Internet*. Porto Alegre, Brazil: Sulina.

Santos, M. (2002a). *Por uma outra globalização: do pensamento único à consciência universal*. Rio de Janeiro, Brazil: Record.

Santos, M., & Marques, M. C. (2002b). *A natureza do espaço: Técnica e tempo, razão e emoção*. São Paulo, Brazil: Editora Science.

Taylor, P. J. (2008). World Cities in Globalization. *GaWC Research Bulletin 263*. 28th April 2008. Available at http://www.lboro.ac.uk/gawc/rb/rb263.html

Taylor, P. J. (2010). Measuring the world city network. In Firmino, R., Duarte, F., & Ultramari, C. (Eds.), *ICTs for Mobile and Ubiquitous Urban Infrastructures: Surveillance, Locative Media and Global Networks*. Hershey, PA: IGI Global.

Wasserman, S., & Faust, K. (1994). *Social network analysis: Methods and applications*. Cambridge, UK: Cambridge Univ. Press.

Weissberg, J. L. (2004). Paradoxos da Teleinformática. In Parente, A. (Ed.), *Tramas da rede: novas dimensões filosóficas, estéticas e políticas da comunicação* (pp. 113–141). Porto Alegre: Sulina.

Welser, H. T., Gleave, E., Fisher, D., & Smith, M. (2007). Visualizing the signatures of social roles in online discussion groups. *Journal of Social Structure*, *8*(2).

ADDITIONAL READING

Alain, D., & Michel, F. *Les réseaux sociaux. Une approche structurale en sociologie*. Paris: Armand Colin, coll. "U", 2004, 263 p.

Barzilai-Nahon. Karine. *Gatekeeping in Virtual Communities: On Politics of Power in Cyberspace*. Proceedings of the 39th Hawaii International Conference on System Sciences, 2006.

Borgatti, S. P., Everett, M. G., & Freeman, L. C. (2002). *Ucinet for Windows: Software for Social Network Analysis*. Harvard, MA: Analytic Technologies.

Brandes, U., et al. *La explicación a través de la visualización de redes*. REDES- Revista hispana para el análisis de redes sociales. Vol.9,#6, Diciembre 2005. http://revista-redes.rediris.es

Burt, R. (1987). Social contagion and innovation: Cohesion versus structural equivalence. *American Journal of Sociology*, *92*, 1287–1335. doi:10.1086/228667

Chelton, M. K., & Cool, C. (2007). *Youth information-seeking behavior II: context, theories, models, and issues*. Lanham, Md.: Scarecrow Press.

Cohen, S., Doyle, W. J., Skoner, D. P., Rabin, B. S., & Gwaltney, J. M. (1997). Social ties and susceptibility to the common cold. *Journal of the American Medical Association*, *277*, 1940–1944. doi:10.1001/jama.277.24.1940

Dias, L. C. Silveira, Rogério Leandro da (orgs.). *Redes, sociedades e territórios*. Santa Cruz do Sul, 2007. Ding, Li et al. *Analyzing Social Networks on the Semantic Web*. Available: http://ebiquity.umbc.edu/_file_directory_/papers/126.pdf

Doreian, P. Stokman, Frans N. *Evolution of social networks*. Amsterdam: Gordon and Breach Publishers, c1997. 261 p.

Faust, K., & Wasserman, S. (1992). Blockmodels: Interpretation and evaluation. *Social Networks*, *14*, 5–61. doi:10.1016/0378-8733(92)90013-W

Ferlander, S. *The Internet, social capital and local community*. Thesis submitted for the degree of Doctor of Philosophy at the University of Stirling, Scotland, January 2003. http://www.crdlt.stir.ac.uk/Docs/SaraFerlanderPhD.pdf

Freeman, L. (1979). Centrality in social networks: Conceptual clarification. *Social Networks*, *1*, 215–239. doi:10.1016/0378-8733(78)90021-7

Freeman, L. C. *Visualizing Social Networks*. Journal of Social Structure, 2000. http://www.cmu.edu/joss/content/articles/volume1/Freeman.html.

Granovetter, Mark. *The strength of weak ties*. American Journal of Sociology, 1973. 78-1361-1381.

Hine, C. (2000). *Virtual ethnography*. London: SAGE.

Hummel, J. *Social Profiles of Virtual Communities*. Proceedings of the 35th Hawaii International Conference on System Sciences, 2002.

Jeanneret, Y. *La relation entre mediation et usage dans les recherché en information-communication*. In: *1er.Colloque mediations et usages des savoirs et de l'information; un dialogue France – Brésil*. Rio de Janeiro: Fiocruz, 2008. p. 37-59.

Katz, J. S., & Martin, B. R. *What is the research collaboration?* Research Policy, 26, 1997, pp 1-35.Disponível em: <http://www.sussex.ac.uk/Users/sylvank/pubs/Res_col9.pdf>. Acesso 16 Abril 2008.

Katz, J. S., & Smith, D. *Collaborative Approaches to Research*. Final report for the HEFCE Fundamental Review of Research Policy and Funding, April 2000. Leeds/Brighton: HEPU/SPRU, 119p Disponível em: <http://www.hefce.ac.uk/research/review/consult/collc.doc>. Acesso 16 Abril 2008.

Laine, M. O. J. *Key success factors of virtual communities*.2006. Available in: http://users.tkk.fi/~molaine3/ml_mastersthesis_310506_public.pdf (tese)

Law, J. MOL, Annemarie. *Complexities: social studies of knowledge practices*. Durham: Duke University Press, c2002. 295 p. (Science and cultural theory)

Lomas, J. (1998). *Social capital and health: Implications for public health and epidemiology*. Social Science and Medicine.

Mamas, E. *Collection, evaluation, and diffusion of information in online commmunities*. 2005. http://dspace.mit.edu/bitstream/handle/1721.1/35108/71358883.pdf?sequence=1

Matheus, Renato Fabiano, et al. *Análise de redes sociais como metodologia de apoio para a discussão da interdisciplinaridade na ciência da informação*. Ci. Inf., Brasília, v. 35, n. 1, p. 72-93, jan./abr. 2006.

McCarty, C., & Killworth, P. (2007). Impact of Methods for Reducing Respondent Burden on Personal Network Structural Measures Social Networks. *Social Networks*, *29*, 300–315. doi:10.1016/j.socnet.2006.12.005

McGrath, C., Krackhardt, D., & Blythe, J. (2003). *Visualizing Complexity in networks: Seeng both the forest and the trees*. Connections.

Eve Michael. *Deux traditions dans l'analyse des réseaux sociaux*, Réseaux, n° 115, 2002.

Miller, D. Slater, Don. *The Internet: an ethnographic approach*. Oxford; New York: Berg, 2000 (2001 printing) 217 p.

Moura, Maria Aparecida. *Informação e conhecimento em redes virtuais de cooperação científica*: necessidades, ferramentas e usos. (no prelo) Perianes-Rorigues. Antonio. *Analysis and visualization of networks applied to study of scientific collaboration in research groups*. (dissertation) http://www.scimago.es/perianes/Archives/Long_abstract_Perianes_Dissertation.pdf

Peter, D. (1984). Killworth, H. Russell Bernard and Christopher McCarty. *Measuring Patterns of Acquaintanceship. Current Anthropology*, *25*, 381–397.

Schweizer, T. (1997). Embeddedness of ethnographic cases. *Current Anthropology*, *38*, 739–760. doi:10.1086/204665

Scott, J. *Social network analysis: a handbook*. 2nd ed. London; Thousands Oaks, Calif.: SAGE Publications, 2000. 208 p.

Sonnenwald, D. H., & the Scientific Collaboration. A Synthesis of Challenges and Strategies. Annual Review of Information Science and Technology, Vol. 4, Blaise Cronin, (Ed,), Medford, NJ:Information Today. 2004.

White Harrison, C., Boorman Scott, A., & Breiger Ronald, L. (1976). *Social Structure from Multiple Networks*: I. Blockmodels of Roles and Positions. *American Journal of Sociology*, *81*, 730–780. doi:10.1086/226141

Xu, W., Kreijns, K., & Hu, J. *Designing Social Navigation for a Virtual Community of Practice*, 2004. http://citeseerx.ist.psu.edu/viewdoc/summary?doi=10.1.1.60.5962

KEY TERMS AND DEFINITIONS

Social Network Analysis: SNA is a hybrid research method used here to systematize a network of relationships around the collective transnational flux of information.

Alberto Pizango Chota: The current president of AIDESEP, the premier indigenous rights organization in Peru. Most notably, Pizango has been actively resisting the government of Peru's selling of petroleum concessions to foreign companies of lands legally titled to indigenous people.

AIDESEP: The Interethnic Association for the Development of the Peruvian Rainforest (Spanish: Asociacion Interetnica de Desarrollo de la Selva Peruana - AIDESEP) is a Peruvian national indigenous rights organization, presided by a decentralized National Council based on 6 organisms found in the North, Center and South of the country. The organization is composed by 57 federations and territorial organizations, which represent the 1 350 communities where 350 000 indigenous men and women live, gathered in 16 language families. Its current president is Alberto Pizango.

Twitter: A social networking and microblogging service that enables its users to send and read messages known as *tweets* (posts of up to 140 characters) displayed on the author's profile page and delivered to the author's subscribers who are known as *followers*. Senders can restrict delivery to those in their circle of friends or, by default, allow open access. Since late 2009, users can follow lists of authors instead of following individual authors.

Information Science: An interdisciplinary science primarily concerned with the analysis, collection, manipulation, storage, retrieval and dissemination of information.

Semantic Web: An evolving development of the World Wide Web in which the meaning (semantics) of information and services on the web is defined, making it possible for the web to "understand" and satisfy the requests of people and machines to use the web content. It derives from World Wide Web Consortium director Sir Tim Berners-Lee's vision of the Web as a universal medium for data, information, and knowledge exchange.

Information Systems: In this research is generally concerned with the study of the effects of information systems on the behavior of individuals, groups, and organizations.

ENDNOTES

1 Twitter is a social network and micro-blog server founded on March, 2006 by Obvius Corporation in San Francisco - USA. It allows users to send texts up to 140 characters by the official website, mobile phones, SMS, e-mail or specialized programs.

2 Although the term 'ideology' can be used in different ways, from philosophy to sociology, we here use the concept as "a set of values that follows the action in a given society" (Bulik, 1990, p.17), which coincides with

what Keck and Sicking (1998, p.3) call the 'common frame of meaning'.

3 In a lecture on Informational Literacy, given by the Portuguese Professor Armando Malheiro, who says that Librarianship 'plasters' its epistemological view when it doesn't look at users and multiform communication processes under the light of complexity. UFMG, 06/10/2009.

4 Social "roughness" can be considered as all difficulties that prevent a kind of tranquil relation, that is, prevent the free flow of a global economy.

5 Armand Matterlart (2006) uses the expression "New World Information Order" to a "civil society extended worried with inserting the technique issue in the future of democracy. (Matterlart, 2006, p. 246)

6 Although not all these categories are used in the presented analysis, they are essential for the understanding of a social network operation in the Internet, and to the understanding of the future analysis possibilities about the theme.

7 Cluster are groups of nodes densely connected to the network.

8 HubSpot, North-American Web 2.0 marketing company, made a research called *State of the Twittersphere*, with collected data by their tool, Twitter Grader. Available on: http://cdnqa.hubteam.com/State_of_the_Twittersphere_by_HubSpot_Q4-2008.pdf. Last access on January 12, 2009.

9 Available on: http://www.sociableblog.com/2008/12/27/top-mobile-social-networks-2009/. Last access on January 1st, 2009.

10 Available on: http://www.sociableblog.com/2008/10/10/mobile-location-based-services-on-the-move/. Last access on January 1st, 2009.

11 See http://www.survival-international.org/campaigns/uncontactedtribes, last access on June 13th, 2009.

12 Available on: http://www1.folha.uol.com.br/folha/bbc/ult272u567185.shtml, last access on June 12th, 2009.

13 Ibid.

14 Available on http://www1.folha.uol.com.br/folha/mundo/ult94u580992.shtml. Last access on June 12th, 2009.

15 Information available at: http://www1.folha.uol.com.br/folha/mundo/ult94u579966.shtml. Last access on June 15th, 2009.

16 Available on: http://www1.folha.uol.com.br/folha/mundo/ult94u579480.shtml. Last access on June 20th, 2009.

17 Information available at: http://www1.folha.uol.com.br/folha/mundo/ult94u584392.shtml. Last access on July 5th, 2009.

18 Information available at: http://noticias.terra.com.br/mundo/interna/0,,OI3831408-EI8140,00.html. Last access on June 18th, 2009.

Section 2
Mobile and Locative Media

Chapter 8
Locative Media and Surveillance at the Boundaries of Informational Territories

André Lemos
Universidade Federal da Bahia, Brazil

ABSTRACT

This chapter aims to understand new forms of surveillance raised with location-based technologies (LBT) and location-based services (LBS). LBS and LBT are used under the label "locative media". Locative media are media where digital information is bounded to a specific context, and are used for locating, controlling, monitoring and tracking people, places and objects. Here the authors investigate how ubiquitous and pervasive technologies are creating informational territories and digital bubbles or virtual walls that can protect privacy and anonymity of a "sujet insecure", or "insecure individual". To illustrate their goal, the authors will see some systems that use locative media to controling, monitoring and tracking people and objects and some art project showing souveillances or critical actions vis à vis the "control society". They will show informational territories involving surveillance cameras, Bluetooth networks and RFID tags.

INTRODUCTION

Location-based technologies (LBT) and location-based services (LBS) are a product of military research into technologies for locating, controlling, monitoring and tracking people, places and objects. Authors have drawn attention to the dangers of the "Internet of Things" (Kuitenbrouwer, 2006, van Kranenburg, 2008) as personal information can be easily disseminated and/or stored in databases. Ubiquitous computing invades places and transforms everything and everybody into sources of data. Digital footprints emanate invisibly, providing information about the *sujet insécure*, or insecure individual (Rosello, 2008), in the subtlest form of surveillance in our control society (Deleuze, 1992). Pervasive environments create informational territories (LEMOS, 2007) and require digital bubbles (Beslay & Hakala, 2005) or virtual walls (Kapadia et al., 2007) to

DOI: 10.4018/978-1-60960-051-8.ch008

protect privacy. Artists and activists have addressed these questions through the critical use of LBT and LBS. The term locative media was created by them to differentiate their work from commercial projects. The objective of this article is to show how the concepts of the digital bubble and virtual wall prove the existence of informational territories and raise questions related to new (diffuse and invisible) forms of surveillance. To illustrate this we will give examples from life and art involving surveillance cameras, Bluetooth networks and RFID tags.

PRIVACY AND ANONYMITY AMONG LOCATIVE MEDIA

We have entered the era of informational mobility. Location-based services and technologies are expanding with the dissemination of mobile devices (cell phones, smartphones, GPS), wireless computer networks (Wi-Fi, Wi-Max, Bluetooth, GPS) and sensors (mainly RFID) that allow location, surveillance and physical and informational mobility (the ability to consume, produce and distribute information) to be combined for the first time.

Locative media can be defined as the combination of LBS and LBT, such as devices, sensors and digital networks (and the services associated with them) that react to their local context (Kellerman, 2006; Benford, 2005, Benford et. al, 2006; Pope, 2005). The term is an expression created by artists to differentiate their work from commercial projects and to highlight the ambiguities of current issues such as mobility, location, public space and surveillance. The expression was proposed by Karlis Kalnins in 2003, and this terminology has since been used by various authors. One of the pioneers was Russel (1999), who launched a manifesto in which he said that "the internet has already started leaking into the real world".

The mobility offered by ubiquitous networks implies greater informational freedom in urban spaces, but also greater exposure to (subtle and invisible) forms of control, monitoring and surveillance.

A control mechanism that could constantly give the position of an element in an open medium, an animal in a reserve or a man in a company (electronic collar) can be imagined without the need for science fiction. [...] what matters is not the barrier, but the computer that locates each one's position (whether licit or illicit) and operates a universal modulation. (Deleuze, 1992, p. 225).

According to Gow (2005, p.4), "the essential qualities of the ubiquitous network society vision are invisibility and pervasiveness". Invisibility and pervasiveness have been the focus of contemporary debates about locative media and the "Internet of Things"[1], and it is in this area that serious threats to privacy and anonymity arise.

Although they often appear to be synonymous, it is important to distinguish between informational control, monitoring and surveillance so that the problem can be better understood. We consider control to be the supervision of activities, or actions normally associated with government and authority over people, actions and processes. Monitoring can be considered a form of observation to gather information with a view to making projections or constructing scenarios and historical records, i.e., the action of following up and evaluating data. Surveillance, however, can be defined as an act intended to avoid something, as an observation whose purposes are preventive or as behavior that is attentive, cautious or careful. It is interesting to note that in English and French the two words "vigilant" and "surveillance", each of which is spelt the same way and has the same meaning in both languages, are applied to someone who is particularly watchful and to acts associated with legal action or action by the police intended to provide protection against crime, respectively. We shall define surveillance as actions that imply control and monitoring in accordance with

Gow, for whom surveillance "implies something quite specific as the intentional observation of someone's actions or the intentional gathering of personal information in order to observe actions taken in the past or future" (Gow, 2005, p. 8).

According to this definition, surveillance actions presuppose monitoring and control, but not all forms of control and/or monitoring can be called surveillance. It could be said that all forms of surveillance require two elements: intent with a view to avoiding/causing something and identification of individuals or groups by name. It seems to me to be difficult to say that there is surveillance if there is no identification of the person under observation (anonymous) and no preventive intent (avoiding something). To my mind it is an exaggeration to say, for example, that the system run by my cell phone operator that controls and monitors my calls is keeping me under surveillance. Here there is identification but no intent. However, it can certainly be used for that purpose. The Federal Police can request wiretaps and disclosure of telephone records to monitor my telephone calls. The same can be said about the control and monitoring of users by public transport operators. This is part of the administrative routine of the companies involved. Once again, however, the system can be used for surveillance activities (a suspect can be kept under surveillance by the companies' and/or police's safety systems). Note the example further below of the recently implemented "Navigo" card in France. It seems to me that the social networks, collaborative maps, mobile devices, wireless networks and countless different databases that make up the information society do indeed control and monitor and offer a real possibility of surveillance.

The question I would pose is whether the term surveillance can be generalized to cover ALL these actions and systems. I do not believe that when I use Facebook I am under surveillance (the information is protected and there is no intent). But Facebook can be used for surveillance (if there is unauthorized access to my personal data and intent with a view to avoiding or causing something). I am not convinced that control, monitoring and surveillance are the same thing or that systems (social networks) that collect non-nominal data and cross these with other non-nominal data in databases in other systems inherently constitute surveillance. To my mind these systems monitor and control, which is dangerous precisely because such monitoring and control can give rise, *a posteriori*, to a form of individual or group surveillance.

It should be noted that locative media pose a threat to private life and anonymity. Privacy can be defined as the control and possession of personal information, as well as the use that is made of it subsequently. Anonymity in turn implies an absence of information about an individual and an absence of control over the collection of personal information (GOW, 2005). Privacy is one of the pillars of democratic societies, as it:

"[...] empowers people to control information about themselves; protects people against unwanted nuisances, or the right to be left alone; [...] is related to dignity in the reciprocal obligations of disclosure between parties; [...] is also a regulating agent in the sense that it can be used to balance and check the power of those capable of collecting data" (Lessig in Gow, 2005, p. 7).

Although related, privacy and anonymity are affected in different ways by the action of locative technologies[2]. These can collect personal data and transmit other data previously generated without the consent or even knowledge of the user in actions involving supervision (control), follow-up and evaluation (monitoring) and prevention and watchfulness (surveillance). Individuals can lose control over the circulation of existing data and the generation of new data. Hence, their anonymity or privacy is being restricted:

There is an urgent need for sophisticated mobile marketing techniques based on detailed knowledge of customer profiles, history, needs, and preferences. Information existing in customer databases developed by retailers like Amazon.com, for example, can be used in parallel with location-based information'" (Gow, 2005, p. 12).

Locative media can in fact be tools to invade privacy and violate anonymity for commercial, military, political and police purposes. As the access to, distribution of and freedom of movement of information grows, so the new invisible regime of databases, of locating and cross-referencing information and of monitoring consumer profiles and movements through urban space grows. It is not by chance that these services and technologies, which are an extension of the state, police, commercial and industrial surveillance going back to the 18th century, are a product of military research. Companies and governments have been using these technologies to collect personal data, not always with the person's knowledge or consent[3]. Effective measures to protect individuals from (state, military and commercial) surveillance systems that might violate their rights are only possible if new informational territories are recognized.

As I have insisted in other papers, the ever more apparent intersection between physical and electronic space creates informational control zones that I call "informational territory". This can be thought of as a new heterotopia (Foucault, 1984) that creates (digital/computer network-based) informational functions in physical space from databases and electronic devices. This informational territory is perceived by some authors as "digital territory or a digital bubble" (Beslay & Hakala, 2005), "interstitial space" (Santaella, 2008), "increased hybrid reality or cellspace" (MANOVICH, 2005) or a "virtual wall" (Kapadia, et al. 2007). In all of these conceptions what is at play is informational control (territorialization) and, consequently, a new function for (public and private) spaces. It is here that the place at which privacy and anonymity can be violated, but also protected, emerges. To understand the ontology and new meanings of places, I propose a concept of informational territory that emphasizes the control of borders[4].

Understanding new territories is fundamental to visualize the impact of locative media on privacy and anonymity, which are under threat from new forms of control, monitoring and surveillance. To that end, I first of all take the idea of the "insecure subject" proposed by Mireille Rosello as a major element of the contemporary surveillance regime. I then explain the concepts of "digital territory or digital bubble" and "invisible wall" to make the new borders of informational territories clear. I also give some concrete examples of surveillance and "sousveillance"[5].

THE INSECURE INDIVIDUAL

Mireille Rosello (2008) supports the thesis of the existence in the present age of the insecure individual ("*sujet insécure*"). First, she discusses the concept of a "culture of insecurity", placing the emphasis on the idea of culture, that is, the social, communicational and political dimension in which we are immersed. For her it would be impossible for us to place ourselves outside this dimension, a fact that we must take into account. However, the feeling of collective fear is not new. The difference is that the culture of fear, under the generic name of culture of insecurity, is taking on planetary dimensions. For Rosello, the "mode" of insecurity becomes an ontology, a way of being, knowing and reading in the present age. For her, we must agree to be part of this culture to transform it; this is the first observation and the back-drop to understanding the problem of surveillance today.

Analyzing the current ubiquitous surveillance cameras in the public space, Rosello shows that they are part of the discourse on security and, at the same time, create a culture of insecurity. They cannot be avoided, and even systems that divert and appropriate these devices (with artistic experiments under the title of "*sousveillance*", as we shall see later) are part of the same cultural dynamic. Cameras and other public and private surveillance devices are part of the way of life of advanced societies. It is in this context that technologies, services and the use of locative media are expanding. The very emphasis on locating and indexing everything with coordinates and tags seems to reflect the culture of fear and insecurity: a fear of drift and disorientation transformed into a rationalizing action.

Rosello develops three postulates that are usually present in current debates about surveillance and the invasion of privacy: (1) "there are reasons to be afraid"; (2) "citizens are caught between two fears: the fear of someone who is under surveillance" (a perspective which she calls right wing); and (3) "fear of the person watching us" (a perspective which she calls left wing). This last postulate is complemented by: "the feeling of insecurity is undesirable". According to Rosello, this leads to a vulnerable subjectivity that is reflected in dichotomies and simplistic oppositions. The individual wants to react to the cameras in the struggle between, on the one hand, the right to privacy and individual freedom, and on the other, social security and the visible control reflected in the movement of the ever-threatening other. When looked at in this light, the debate leaves us clinging to ideologies without being able to analyze the problem and move forward. Furthermore, many of those who are against current surveillance cameras are so because of their ineffectiveness in the fight against crime.

The perspective of the left, to use Rosello's terminology, is that surveillance cameras pose a threat to privacy and anonymity, while failing to solve the problems of criminality. Similarly, the discourse of the right asserts that if we live in a society we must give up some privacy in order to have more security. However, the extent to which citizens' rights have been violated and attacked has far exceeded the effects of any reduction in criminality. It could be said that the use of these instruments has been increasing worldwide and that the discourse on security through surveillance is present everywhere (the police, the academic world and the media). While there has been massive growth in the use of surveillance cameras, little progress has been made in the debate in this polarized ideological context.

To resolve this problem, Rosello renounces these arguments and proposes that the analysis be undertaken from a different angle. For her — and this appears to me to be the strong point of her argument — the solution is to recognize not only the ideologies, but also the materiality of the object, the camera (and we can include the sensors, the wireless networks and the locating devices) and its relationship with space, the phenomenology of the device. Based on studies of CCTVs, Rosello presents data that show that the mere installation of a camera causes users to feel afraid, vulnerable and insecure, irrespective of whether the problem of criminality has been solved or not. On the one hand, the camera stimulates a positive reaction, generating the idea that there is a security problem in the area and that the camera will solve it. However, the materiality of the device changes the relationship with the space/place, producing a feeling of insecurity. It matters little whether the issue of insecurity is solved or not. The fear is in the present ("the camera is there to provide protection from something"), in updating of the past ("I should have been afraid before") and in the future ("problems will happen or will be prevented"). The interesting thing when the analysis is approached from this angle is that the problem no longer revolves around the issue of solving/not solving but instead involves three principles arising from the existence of the camera: phenomenological (the device), topological (the place) and genealogical (fear and insecurity). One way or another, anguish is generated, increasing fear and paranoia. Therein lies the essence of the modern "insecure individual". The presence of the camera does not so much create fear of surveillance, according to studies quoted by Rosello, as create the sensation that we must feel afraid, as the camera is there.

Rosello (2008) proposes that the camera should be viewed and accepted as an "uncivilized citizen." Based on the literature on forms of incivility in society (ways of occupying space that are not accepted norms, verbal violence, lack of respect for others, impoliteness in day-to-day life), Rosello shows that these forms were always combated because they led to more violence. Cameras or other surveillance devices should always be considered something upsetting, something that leads to uncivil relationships and violates respect for others. We can therefore understand why they are violent, as their intrusive gaze produces a feeling of fear caused by constant observation and surveillance. A fear, as we have seen, that is in the present, past and future at the same time. Invading the present, evoking a frightening past and producing a future catastrophe, cameras are, for Rosello, "uncivil" and should be recognized as such. They produce violence and, rather than solving anything, only film: they are forms of uncivilized social "premediation".

Returning to the third postulate ("the feeling of insecurity is undesirable"), Rosello states that insecurity is the result of a specific cultural context and that the events of September 11 served as an excuse to try to solve the problem from a technocratic or ideological angle, creating differences and stigmas and increasing fear of the "other". Surveillance, violence and incivility occur not only with cameras but also with satellites, cell phones, the monitoring of profiles on the Internet and radio frequency tags; hence, it becomes more diffuse, more performative (electronic database) and invisible. Uncivilized individuals have increased in number and acquired new forms and more performative properties, as they can now be easily located, are mobile on computer networks and are fitted with memories in databases. In this global regime of insecurity, there are some (the "other") who must be kept under surveillance and others who must not. For Rosello it is fundamental that all of us can put ourselves in the place of that "other" and accept the regime of insecurity. Not passively, but comprehensively, dialogically and socially. Developing what she herself calls a more "optimistic" view, the author goes on to state that suffering is not so much the result of being looked at too much, but rather of not being looked at enough. If I am afraid, as a human, I can put myself in the place of the other who is frightening me. The problem is not so much to eliminate the other (not to see), but to be concerned about it, to recognize its vulnerability, which is also ours. Thus, for Rosello, accepting vulnerability can produce sociability and "compassion". The individual must consider the cameras (and other devices) as another individual who is watching him but also needs help. It is not so much a question of avoiding the gaze as of reinforcing it to be able to see not so much the differences as what makes us similar. Insecurity and vulnerability can be ways of getting closer to the other, a means of social reinforcement.

To conclude, Rosello calls for recognition of this "insecure individual", a vulnerable individual whom we accept as based on insecurity, since total and complete security is an illusion. This "insecure individual" must have the capacity to accept the relationship of vulnerability and insecurity and not to cling to dichotomies that make the former a personal issue and the latter a social fact. The "insecure individual" is aware of the illusion of security created by surveillance cameras and knows that they generate fear and intolerance and, instead of solving the problem, only worsen it, producing more feelings of insecurity. This "insecure individual" would be better able to move around in the current regime of diffuse locative visibility and surveillance and could, with greater clarity, report perverse attempts to solve the "universal insecurity" of which he or she is a victim. It is in this context that we should consider not only surveillance cameras, but also the other portable, mobile and networked devices (Wi-Fi networks, Bluetooth, cell phones, GPS, sensors and radio frequency tags) that greatly increase the different forms of control, monitoring and surveillance. The examples related to surveillance cameras are important both to put the debate in context and to show that a culture of insecurity is emerging. Locative characteristics are only found in the new IP cameras that combine the use of digital wireless networks to communicate with control, monitoring and mobile surveillance systems (police cars, for example) with localization by GPS. The widespread availability of cell phones with cameras has taken this culture of insecurity (of witnessing events, of voyeurism, of the invasion of privacy and anonymity) to a new, even more acute phase by placing the power of surveillance into everybody's hands.

Next, we discuss (1) the relationship between locative media and the insecure or control society and (2) notions of a "digital bubble" and "virtual wall", the boundaries of "informational territories".

ON THE RELATIONSHIP BETWEEN LOCATIVE MEDIA AND THE INSECURE SOCIETY

The control society is everywhere. Going beyond the panopticon, which keeps watch over the confined, surveillance cameras, smart cards, Internet profiles, GPS systems and sensors control the increasingly mobile "insecure" individual. And mobility is indeed the key word when thinking about the masses, about how information is used and about the possibilities for recognizing and locating things in space. More movement also means greater possibilities for controlling, monitoring and keeping watch over people, information and objects. Locative media, where location and mobility represent possibilities for producing meaning in space and places, are also instruments for controlling, monitoring and keeping watch over places, spaces and individuals now caught up in modulatable databases, ubiquitous sensors, fluid and intelligent wireless networks, and locating devices that are "attentive to things". Because they associate mobility and location, such technologies, which are of military origin, can be used to monitor movements, keep watch over people and control day-to-day actions.

Deleuze's idea of a control society started from the observation that the panoptical surveillance of Foucault and the disciplinary society of confinement had been superseded. In fact, the two regimes coexist today, although there is a change in direction to a more subtle, modular, invisible surveillance. For Deleuze, the control society was what Foucault had announced as our near future, which in practical surveillance terms means that technologies are no longer visible and fixed but ubiquitous, pervasive, "in things" and diffuse and do not require the individual to be confined but instead require exactly the opposite, mobility that allows dynamic control.

In a control society, the new surveillance is everywhere and, at the same time, nowhere. Unlike in structures of confinement, surveillance no longer occurs in closed spaces, but in structures of control in profiles on the Internet, in databases in interconnected social networks, in movements where the cell phone is monitoring the user's "roaming", in GPS tracking, in tracks left by the use of electronic cards, in smart cards used on public transport, in signals transmitted and received by Bluetooth networks, in radio frequency tags that come with products and buyers... Everything is undoubtedly less visible and more diffuse, making this watchful invisibility more performative and the control of movements more effective. It is no longer a question of enclosing and immobilizing in order to place under surveillance, but of letting movement flow, of controlling and keeping watch over people and information to prevent consequences and exert control over the "modulations": "rather, control man undulates, working in orbit, in a continuous beam" (Deleuze, 1992, p. 222).

Databases, portable electronic devices, satellite or wireless Internet or cell phone networks, mobile social networks, Wi-Fi triangulation with cell phone masts and sensors all do the job very well. These media, which have locative functions, are instruments that produce the fear and insecurity that Rosello discusses. The "insecure individual" must recognize them to be able to face the new instruments of the culture of insecurity responsibly. Following are some concrete examples of this threat.

Surveillance Cameras

On arriving at Montreal airport, the French artist Renaud Auguste-Dormeuil, who is interested in the processes of surveillance and militarization, was given a city guide with five proposed tourist itineraries. The aim of these itineraries was to show a beautiful, dynamic, multicultural Montreal. The place was thus invested with "myths and dreams" and became a place conceived by institutions. For Renaud, the role of the artist is to "inject reality" into the dreams produced by those who control a space[6]. After receiving the guide, Renaud followed the itineraries, noting down all the surveillance cameras (with exact addresses and the names of the owners) and produced a map of these. He then placed an "errata" in the free guides and placed them in a pile. Another interesting project is "Mabuse", where the artist creates a tourist itinerary that the tourists follow in a minibus to see the city's surveillance cameras (the most important ones that have been seen and filmed are the camera at the obelisk at the Place de la Concorde and the camera at the Hotel Ritz, which caught the last pictures of Dodi and Diana).

In the same spirit of "sousveillance", the iSee project maps the CCTVs in a city (London, New York) to produce an interactive map of alternative itineraries. When an address is chosen, the system indicates the streets that a pedestrian should use to avoid being seen by the cameras. The objective is for users to achieve anonymity in their itineraries. As the project website explains: "iSee enables users to avoid CCTV surveillance cameras. Some UK-based artists working on ideas of counter-surveillance for the broad public have discovered that in fact most people are totally comfortable with the idea of surveillance in public space." [7]

Another interesting project is "Life: A User's Manual" by the Canadian Michelle Teran. The project detects videos transmitted by CCTVs that use Wi-Fi networks and displays them in the street. The artist developed a device that intercepts these images and, in an inversion of logic, displays them to passers by in the public space. There is an explicit reference here to the work "Life, A User's Manual" by Georges Perec. What is internal, private and watched by a few becomes external and visible to many. This is explained on the artist's website[8].

Bank Password Generators

For Deleuze, one of the characteristics of the control society is not a signature, which identifies the individual and their position in the masses, but a password, the numerical language that guarantees access to information. One example of this control by codes is the password generators used by banking institutions. Moving from molding (a disciplinary society) to modulation (a control society):

"[...]in control societies, on the other hand, what is important is no longer either a signature or a number, but a code: the code is a password [...].Individuals have become 'dividuals', divisible, and the masses, samples, data, markets or 'banks'". (Deleuze, 1992, p. 223)

Bank password generators make the use of access passwords compulsory (for greater control over the customer's signature and personal identification number) and, more recently, modulatable access passwords (in some cases the password generators come in the form of key fobs that produce a different combination each time they are used – hypermodulation and hypermobility) for improved security and control for both the bank and the user. The use of password generators is compulsory, reflecting control that is growing and expanding as a result of the greater physical mobility of the user and greater informational mobility (a "mobile" password). This modulation is a strategy of the banks to increase the user's responsibility for stolen passwords. The "codes" of the "dividuals" appear to allow the user to control his account better, although it is in fact the system that is controlling the account holder while at the same time giving the impression of greater mobility and freedom.

Life-Logs

Another example of surveillance combining mobility and freedom is life-logs. They can be defined as personal information that is generated and stored daily as data in computer networks in the form of an electronic record of an individual's life. Martin Dodge and Rob Kitchin (2007) show that surveillance of personal data increases with increasing use of social networks and Internet profiles (BRUNO, 2008) and that these are in effect instruments of surveillance. Every action, movement, conversation and piece of content produced (text, photos and video) is stored in electronic databases spread all over the planet, representing a threat to privacy and anonymity. It should be noted that much of this data is generated as a result of the user's own initiative, leading to a conflict between free production, mobility and the threat to privacy and anonymity. In their day-to-day activities in cyberspace, individuals take part in and use blogs, microblogs, social software, forums, photo and video publishing systems, digital maps and other Web 2.0 tools. This information is captured automatically to produce a record of the individual's life. It is a question of recognizing not so much the "data", which represents what is given (supplied), as the "capta", the digital information that is removed or captured by the various electronic systems that are available at no cost on the Internet.

"To date, recording regimes have generated capta from an `exterior' position, generally through one dimension and held by an organization which is external to an individual and which they do not control (eg, they constitute surveillance). A life-log will generate capta from an `interior' (or first-person) perspective, from which the individual watches themselves through intimate technologies (ie, technologies in service to the individual - eg, phones, car, wearable computing), with the capta pooled into a unified, multimedia archive which they control [eg, it constitutes sousveillance - sousveillance being the internal counter to external surveillance (Mann et al, 2003)". (Dodge & Kitchin, 2007, p. 432)

An ever increasing number of capta are integrated into systems that bring information together and constitute real databases of peoples' lives. The basic problem is that life-logs never forget the inputs captured in a very wide range of actions, events or conversations or other expressions of daily life on the network. All this movement through cyberspace with portable devices, networks and sensors generates data and capta. To escape from these systems, the authors propose an ethics of forgetting as a way of protecting privacy and inhibiting different forms of control and vigilance. To prevent data and capta creating an absolute memory, where nothing is forgotten and everything, absolutely every step is remembered, the authors suggest that, as in the real world outside the Internet, forgetting should be a form of survival and should be built into electronic memories in the system. It is not so much a question of building virtual "bubbles" and "walls" that protect the borders of informational territory but of data and capta being eliminated (forgetting).

"To counter the potentially pernicious effects of pervasive computing we have suggested the

development of an ethics of forgetting that is materialized through the `loss of memory' in a life-log. While building fallibility into the system seemingly undermines life-logging, it seems to us the only way to ensure that humans can forget, can rework their past, can achieve a progressive politics based upon debate and negotiation, and can ensure that totalitarian disciplining does not occur". (Dodge & Kitchin, 2007, p. 431)

Mobile Social Networking

An example of mobile social networking is the Google Latitude[9] service launched by Google for locating people. The system finds users and shows their location on a map on the screen of a smartphone. This type of tracking, known as mobile social networks, lets users know where their friends are so that they can meet them in the urban space. The system allows the privacy level (who you want to see you) and anonymity level (how accurately your location is given) to be adjusted. Google does not keep a log of locations. Here are informational "bubbles", "walls" and "territories", as we shall show later on. Nevertheless, possibilities for control, monitoring and surveillance will arise. A recent article in PC World, "Spy on Your Workers With Google Latitude" by David Coursey (2009), shows how companies can use the service to spy on employees:

"It's easy to think of business uses for Latitude, such as tracking service people as they move from call-to-call. Delivery vehicles might also be tracked, and the service could also be used to make certain the closest resource is always sent to a customer's request. [...] The downside of Latitude is the amount of extremely personal information, such as the details of all a person's travels that is sent to Google. I know people who simply don't trust Google to not become evil, if the company hasn't already. They wonder why the company offers so many free applications unless it has some way to monetize them that isn't obvious to the user."

"Privacy International"[10], which is headquartered in London, says that this kind of surveillance is already being used on mobile devices by companies without the knowledge or consent of their users. While Google Latitude offers features to ensure privacy and anonymity, as we have seen above, "Privacy International" warns that the system can be used without users knowing they are being followed. According to the organization:

"The only means of minimizing this threat might be a regular message sent to a phone advising that it has been Latitude-enabled. [...] However, according to Google, this function is available only in certain circumstances" and may only apply to "certain unspecified phone types."[11]

Radio-Frequency Identification (RFID)

Examples of violation of privacy can be found in experiments with radio frequency identification tags (RFIDs), commonly known as spy chips. Albert and McIntyre (2006) give countless examples of violation of privacy where RFID tags have been used for police, political or commercial purposes. These micro-tags are becoming widespread (they can be found in clothes, car number plates, products and passports) and are intended to improve the efficiency and safety of companies by helping to monitor people and products, combining physical and informational mobility

"in a future world laced with RFID spy chips, cards in your wallet could 'squeal' on you as you enter malls, retail outlets, and grocery stores, announcing your presence and value to businesses. Reader devices hidden in the doors, walls, displays, and floors could frisk the RFID chips in your clothes and other items on your person to determine your age, sex, and preferences. Since spy chip informa-

tion travels through clothing, they could even get a peek at the color and size of your underwear". (Albrecht & McIntyre, 2006, p. 3)

Various companies place RFID tags in their products without telling their customers so they can keep watch on their purchasing habits and even monitor customers at home. Every product will soon have an RFID tag in place of existing (static) bar codes[12]. For example, when you buy a product with your credit card, you will be associating the number of your credit card with the product and the tag stuck on it (such as a shoe that only you use or a loyalty card for that shop that only you have). Whenever you pass a reader with that product (in posts, on the ground, in traffic lights, in shops etc.) you will be identified and your movements can be monitored for various purposes, such as marketing, focused advertising or police work.[13] RFID tags are already used in car number plates, an application that is justified on the basis of greater safety, improved traffic and better control over the payment of taxes. However, there can be little doubt that such tags represent a threat to privacy and anonymity as your car (you) will be identified and monitored whenever you pass a reader (a traffic light, for example), and when the data is cross-checked between databases, you may, for example, receive focused advertising, provide information to update your profile for future use or be stopped by the police for not having paid your taxes.

Another example is the RATP Navigo card in France, which is a threat to the anonymity of people who use the transport system. The RATP (Paris transit authority) intends to change the analog "carte orange" (a monthly pass that can be used on the subway and bus system) to Navigo (a contactless transit card). This new digital card will allow the company to know where and when a person is travelling and what form of transport they are using. The Navigo card contains the user's photograph, name, surname and address and an RFID tag that associates a person's trips on the transport system with a unique number. The CNIL, "Commission Nationale de l'Informatique et des Libertés", believes that the new card is a real threat to anonymity and peoples' private lives. Once again we see an example of the tension between the new culture of mobility and the control society in the shape of specific threats. With Navigo and the whole chain of readers, RFID tags and cell phones, users can move more easily but leave footprints wherever they go.

However, there are alternative uses for RFID that go beyond corporate, police or political use, and some artists have developed interesting countersurveillance projects. Commercial projects include the Alcatel-Lucent Tikitag project (2008) and the Nokia 3220 (2005). Both are based on RFID tags, which can be placed on anything and allow users to create connections with the Internet and link an object to historical information, for example. In this way, blogs of things can be created and updated automatically. Another similar project is the Symbolic Table by Mediamatic, ThingLink[14], Helsinki.

Artistic/activist countersurveillance projects include actions by the American group "Preemptive Media", which created the "Zapped" project, in which cockroaches with RFID tags were set loose in a Wal-Mart store to play havoc with the database. Other interesting actions include the Dutch project "z25's Data" (2005) or the "Attention Please" project in Liverpool (KUITENBROUWER, 2006)[15]. For Kuitenbrouwer it is important to make use of another aspect of RFIDs: their creative potential. The problem is to know how to negotiate privacy (not whether one has privacy or not, but the degree of privacy) and manage its use. It may be advantageous at times to make certain personal data available in order to receive personalized information. For example, by saying what my personal taste in music, books, films or food is I gain by receiving information that interests me directly. The same applies to RFID tags. I can attach them to certain personal objects so that they have a history and memory in the network. They can be useful platforms for bottom-up projects, as they can be organized in creative ways and transformed into communication media rather than just surveillance devices.

"An 'internet of things' can also increase the experienced value of objects. Things that are tagged can start preserving their own history. [...] Opposition to it from consumer organizations mainly has to do with the ease with which everyone can invent privacy-threatening scenarios in a world crawling with RFIDs. At the same time, the complete disregard by the major market parties of a possible say on the part of consumers and citizens concerning the introduction and applications of RFID is also an important factor. [...] We can leave this to market forces, but it would be better to do it ourselves. Just as the Internet after the dotcom implosion has still managed to become the domain of democratic media production, so too can a large-scale implementation of RFID (after the stumbling of RFID 1.0 over privacy issues) become a terrain for a public sphere developing from bottom-up. Not all its content will be relevant, but what's more important is that RFID 2.0 offers a network for new relations between people and things". (Kuitenbrouwer, 2006, p. 59)

It is, of course, a political dispute to minimize current (commercial and governmental) use, according to which the user is merely a passive target who, without his/her knowledge, is at the service of marketing, advertising and insurance companies, as well as the police. The development of RFID 2.0, with which users can produce their own content and indexing, should be encouraged.

Bluetooth Cell Phones

Cell phones can also be a point of entry used to violate privacy or anonymity. Artists in the London group "LOCA", raising questions about the use of Bluetooth networks and cell phones, put on a performance called "Set to Discoverable"[16], where passersby received unusual messages as they moved along streets where Bluetooth sensors were installed. The system detected cell phones with open Bluetooth networks and sent the users messages like "Why have you left the square?" or "How long are you going to spend sitting on that bench?" The LOCA artists watched the passersby and sent these messages directly to cell phone users. It is interesting to note that the passersby looked up or to either side for surveillance cameras. The aim of the performance was to question the invasion of privacy while users were mobile and to draw attention to the fact that the users were unaware of the potential invader of the Bluetooth networks.

This short description of projects involving Bluetooth cell phones has shown how locative media can violate information borders and pose a threat to privacy and anonymity through electronic control, monitoring and surveillance. These borders are invisible, and many users do not perceive the true dimensions of this aspect of the control society: a subtle, diffuse surveillance that leaves the user with the sensation that they have freedom to produce information and be mobile. The examples using surveillance cameras, bank password generators, life-logs, mobile social networking, RFID tags and Bluetooth cell phones show that ubiquitous computing, the Internet of Things and its associated technology, networks and electronic sensors transform panoptic surveillance into invisible, modular, distributed control that is everywhere and nowhere at the same time.

Before, the threats to privacy were visible in the form of immobility or the breaking of very clear material borders (home, work, the body, prison, hospital, school…). Now, locative surveillance is invisible and subtle, as it is generally the users themselves who deliberately produce the data (data and capta) while under the impression that they are free, mobile information producers. This violation of borders is no longer material but is instead electronic and digital and flows through the porous membranes of the new informational territories. Instead of movement being inhibited in clearly visible confinements, personal information is collected, stored and circulated in a cloud of fully mobile data. The permeability of information cannot be observed by looking at the concrete physical borders of rooms, homes, hospitals, companies or prisons. Surveillance using locative media takes place in invisible informational territories by the violation of invisible electronic borders in the form of "digital bubbles" or "virtual walls". Control by citizens of personal information needed to ensure the right to privacy and anonymity in the present cyberculture can only be guaranteed by recognizing informational territories and borders.

THE BOUNDARIES OF INFORMATIONAL TERRITORIES

A control society, mobile media and location-based services interfacing with the urban space – these all make up the current surveillance environment. The information produced by devices and sensors that is circulating in networks does so increasingly at the intersection between electronic and physical spaces. It is not just a question of information circulating in cyberspace, but of information transiting through day-to-day objects and places, transmitting and collecting personal information in an urban space that is hyperconnected as a result of the development of ubiquitous computing, the Internet of Things. Privacy will only be effectively protected when this new ontology of places is recognized, when it is understood that physical places now contain new digital informational heterotopias, involving automatic processing of data, memory in databases and the circulation of this data in global computer networks - in other words, informational control zones in the urban space. This hybridization creates a new territoriality known as informational territories that are similar to electronic boundary and border control zones. This concept is clarified by Lemos (2008, p 221): "By informational territories we mean areas where the flow of digital information in the intersection between cyberspace and the urban space is controlled."

It is precisely by territorial interrelationships that places are characterized: social, cultural, imaginary, subjective, economic and political functions and their rules, standards and social rites. To understand the emerging informational threats in urban spaces, we must therefore recognize a new informational territoriality that interfaces with the other territorialities of places. It is not the end of places, but a resignification with new border tensions.

Access to and control of information is achieved with mobile devices and wireless networks. Informational territory is not cyberspace but the moving, hybrid space formed by the relationship between electronic and physical space. For example, the area where a Wi-Fi network can be accessed in a park is an informational territory, which is different from the physical space of the park and the electronic space of the Internet. When users access the Internet over the Wi-Fi network they are in an informational territory overlapping the physical (and political, cultural, imaginary...) territory of the park and computer network space. Informational territory creates a space that is dependent on the physical and electronic spaces that it is linked to." (Lemos, 2008, p. 221)

When we sit in a coffee shop, talk on the cell phone or use a notebook to send or receive information on a Wi-Fi network, we are making personal information transit through invisible borders, and this information can be captured and used without our knowledge or consent. Of course, we are only in a coffee shop, but it has acquired new informational functions. We can observe here a new control tension, a new informational territory created by wireless networks and digital devices in places.

Such a situation allows us to be monitored, controlled or placed under surveillance in the coffee shop simply by using our cell phone or notebook or if there is a reader that can activate the RFID tag in my pen. Without this informational layer, this informational territory, digital information cannot circulate and the coffee shop would only be an ordinary place where one can have coffee or read a newspaper. But now it is a cybercafé. It is by recognizing invisible informational territories that we perceive the new heterotopias of informational control. This recognition of informational territories is fundamental for an awareness of the threats posed by the era of ubiquitous computing and locative media. Indeed, the new phase of ubiquitous computing, with cyberspace "leaking" into things (Russel, 1999), opens up new possibilities for violating the electronic borders through which personal data circulate; therefore, unless informational territory is recognized, it will not be possible to establish a privacy policy or an agreement covering surveillance, monitoring and control in this age of mobile locative distributed computing.

Let us see then how the borders of informational territories can take the form of "digital bubbles" or "virtual walls". At both boundaries, what is under discussion is control by the user of the information that enters or leaves the bubble through the walls. The invasion of privacy, the control of movement, the monitoring of actions, in short, the new electronic and digital surveillance, takes the form of the invasion of informational territories through their boundaries, whether these are considered bubbles or walls, as discussed below.

It is in informational territories that control is exercised over the flow of information. Control is achieved by, among other things, access passwords; firewalls; access permissions for data and personal tracking; and control of information transmitted based on devices and sensors. The invisible boundaries of informational territories should be controlled by the users themselves to guarantee the desired level of privacy and anonymity. It is by negotiating the permeabilities of the boundaries of (invisible and electronic) informational territories that we maintain our privacy and prevent unwanted forms of control, monitoring and surveillance. Beslay and Hakala (2005) use the image of a bubble, which they suggest is the digitization of a personal space, to define the boundary of what they call "digital territory": "a temporary defined space that can be used to limit the information coming into and leaving the bubble in the digital domain." (Beslay & Hakala, 2005, p. 2).

Thinking in terms of digital or informational territory allows us to visualize borders and boundaries that may or may not be permeable to the flow of information and to define and maintain policies related to privacy. The bubble represents an image of social protection, a way of isolating the place electronically: for Beslay and Hakala, digital territory is "a place of information and communication" (2005, p. 1). The concept of territory and the image of a bubble help to recognize the existence of control (a territory) and borders (a bubble) through which personal information passes. Users are not always aware of this dimension, and data have been collected in this invisible daily space unbeknown to users and then used without their knowledge as the borders between private and public spaces have been electronically blurred: "without digital boundaries, the fundamental notion of privacy or the feeling of being at home will not take place in the future information society" (Beslay & Hakala, 2005, p.1).

The purpose of the image of a bubble is to create an isolating layer, a layer of informational control, giving the users power over what comes in and goes out. Beslay and Hakala are concerned that information should not leak out of personal space, space at home, space at the workplace or any other space without users' authorization and knowledge. Thus, creating a digital bubble ensures privacy and anonymity[17]. Digital territory must be conceived at various levels, with different permeabilities. Informational bubbles can prevent information, in the words of Russel (1999) once again, leaking out of these levels.

The first territory would be personal (the body and subjectivity). The home is the second level of isolation and border control, and public space the third territorial level, where people negotiate proximity and distance. The design of the digital territory would isolate the three types of spaces protecting the individual.

"[...] the vision of digital territory offers the opportunity to introduce the notion of territory, property and space in a digital environment. The objective is to provide a tool that enables users to manage proximity and distance with others in this future ambient intelligence space, both in a legal and a social sense, as is the case in the physical world". (Beslay & Hakala, 2005, p. 2)

With its ubiquitous computing, the new informational environment collects, processes and distributes large amounts of information: think about how you use your cell phone; the payments you make by credit card; your access to the Internet at home, at work or in the street using 3G or Wi-Fi networks; your insurance company collecting data about your consumer profile on the Internet; your position being tracked in systems like Google Latitude; and the exchange of SMS messages between you, your friends and members of your family.

These are commonplace examples that show the different "bubbles" and the respective porosities of the public and private spheres to informational data. Recognizing the new informational territories (that allow the actions mentioned above to be carried out) is the starting point for developing effective ways of protecting the data that is transmitted, stored and circulated during these actions. For Beslay and Hakala, "in the information society, the crucial issue will be to design this digital territory" (Beslay & Hakala, 2005, p.2).

In these examples the bubbles should be seen as borders of informational territories, as control zones that ensure privacy, security and protection. The threat to privacy and anonymity in the age of locative media arises from violation of the borders of informational territories, of bubbles.

"[...] a growing number of emerging technologies, such as location-based services, fourth generation mobile telephones, closed circuit television, biometrics, etc., tend to establish links and bridges between a specific physical location and digitised knowledge and information. If the added value for the user is obvious, the potential new threats are not always highlighted. [...] Location-based services, radio frequency identification tags, body implants, ambient intelligence sensors, etc. will permit the implementation of a trustworthy environment and therefore the domestication of the ambient intelligence space by the individual. The vision will facilitate the transition through a traditional society that coexists with an information society, to a single society whose citizen have accepted and adopted the fusion of physical and digital realities. In this future society, people will still be able to control and manage distance from others with new tools provided by ambient intelligence space technologies". (Beslay & Hakala, 2005, p. 7)

It is worth repeating that territories, digital bubbles and, as we shall see, virtual walls must be recognized to ensure people's privacy and the inviolability of personal data as well as to protect unsuspecting citizens from the excesses of control and surveillance made possible by LBT and LBS.

The concept of virtual walls is similar to that of digital bubbles. Once again, it is a matter of recognizing and claiming borders of informational territories in a ubiquitous computing environment with a view to protecting privacy in the age of locative media. Kapadia et al. (2007) discuss pervasive environments and the risks to privacy posed by locative sensors and devices that make users leave "digital footprints". Virtual walls, which can be thought of as interface systems (a GUI or graphical user interface), must allow users to control their digital footprints (generation, storage and distribution). These virtual walls, like digital bubbles, show the new territoriality of places in the form of an informational control zone. By controlling the electronic boundaries that make up spaces, privacy, anonymity and freedom should be guaranteed in ubiquitous environments.

"[RFID] can record a user's activities and personal information such as heart rate, body temperature, and even conversations. Users may unwittingly leave 'digital footprints' (information about users derived from sensors) that can threaten their privacy. These footprints can be disseminated to applications, or stored for later retrieval, giving rise to useful context-aware applications". (Kapadia et al., 2007, p.162)

The idea of the virtual wall is concerned with the confidentiality of information exchanged between the various environments and captured by wireless networks, devices or sensors. The authors start with the observation that confidentiality and privacy must be managed by users. Here, confidentiality is understood to be the access to or use of information only by authorized people or systems. The authors prefer the term "digital footprint" because it is more accurate than "context" and allows one to anticipate the monitoring, control and surveillance of footprints. For the authors, "users will be more motivated to protect the privacy of their 'digital footprints' rather than their 'context'" (Kapadia et al., 2007, p.163). Protecting footprints and fingerprints (digital trails) therefore leads to new ways of controlling information between borders in the heart of new territories. Here, the borders of informational territories take the form of "virtual walls"[18].

"We propose a policy framework based on the intuitive concept of 'virtual walls' that extends the notion of privacy provided by physical walls into the virtual realm. For instance, users are aware of their physical privacy in a closed room — outsiders cannot see or hear them. In a pervasive environment, however, their virtual privacy could be quite the opposite. Digital footprints from a video camera and a microphone could expose their privacy in the virtual world, where other users can see and hear them by accessing their footprints [...] Using virtual walls, users can 'bolster' physical walls by specifying intuitive policies that control access to all their personal footprints in a way that is consistent with their notion of physical privacy. Virtual walls also relieve the burden of specifying separate policies for several footprints, which would be cumbersome in sensor-rich environments". (Kapadia et al., 2007, p.163)

Technically, a virtual wall is an interface that can be used in a number of electronic systems[19] whose porosity to information (or ability to negotiate what information passes through it or not) is defined in levels — transparent, translucent and opaque — that allow controlled exchanges between users through the membranes. Transparent means permission to see all the data, translucent only some data, and opaque, none. Levels of privacy and confidentiality are thus defined, showing that users can choose the level of control of what information enters or leaves their informational territories according to the permeability levels:

"In keeping with the metaphor of privacy afforded by physical walls, transparent virtual walls allow queries to access any footprints, even a user's personal information (such as their heart rate or whether they are speaking); opaque walls block access to all footprints originating from within the wall; and translucent walls allow queriers to access only general information such as room temperature and the presence of motion. To add flexibility, users may create walls of varying transparencies for different queriers". (Kapadia et al., 2007, p.166)

It is interesting to note how the concepts of "place", "footprints", "survey" and "virtual walls" are defined in the authors' model. They use "place" to refer to the physical spaces where users are: rooms and buildings with identification tags. The users "put" virtual walls in specific places according to the permission levels discussed above. This shows once again how informational territories redefine and give new meanings to places. A virtual wall can be used anywhere. "Footprints or fingerprints" originate with electronic sensors or devices that collect data. For example, a recording of a voice in a bedroom is a "digital footprint" that originated in the "place" bedroom. The authors categorize them into (1) general footprints, which do not give any personal information, such as the temperature of the bedroom; and (2) personal footprints, which contain data that identify the user in some way. The "survey" model assumes that the user can investigate footprints based on a number of different variables: place, time, movement, owner… Lastly, virtual "walls" can be defined as electronic protection that allows users to control the visibility of their digital footprints in places:

"Virtual walls protect the privacy of users by allowing them to control the visibility of their personal footprints and general footprints in their vicinity. In our implementation, users create virtual walls through a GUI. The context server records walls in a persistent database and uses them to enforce the user's access control policies". (Kapadia et al., 2007, p.168)

The system was tested with a number of social-software users. The authors concluded from their study that the virtual-wall model is easy to use and understand and that users are able to translate their privacy preferences into virtual walls.

CONCLUSION

We have shown in this article how locative media and the development of the "Internet of Things" pose a threat to private life by providing performative possibilities for monitoring, surveillance and control.

The ubiquitous-computing environment, which transforms everything into "digital footprints", forms the backdrop to insecurity and the emergence of the "sujet insécure" (Rosello, 2008). Recognition of informational territories thus becomes a technical and political barrier (legal protection) against the diffuse, invisible surveillance found in the current phase of cyberculture. The concepts of the "digital bubble" (Beslay & Hakala, 2005) and "virtual wall" (Kapadia, et al., 2007) and projects related to these concepts illustrate the boundaries of informational territories and represent ways of protecting privacy in the technical, regulatory and sociological domains. The examples given in this article show the extent and seriousness of current forms of surveillance — they are locative, mobile, invisible and subtle. Surveillance systems flourish on greater informational freedom and mobility for users rather than on the confinement and immobility of a disciplinary society, although the latter has not completely disappeared. To respond to this threat, we conclude that it is important to understand how such surveillance systems work, what their consequences for society and individuals are, and how they can compromise human dignity and social justice.

"The chain of events that connects Cartesian disengagement with the amoral actuarial surveillance of the twenty-first century can be broken. The first step is to understand how such surveillance systems operate and with what social and personal consequences. Articulated with this, the second step is to find agreement on what constitutes the human dignity and the social justice that may be compromised by those systems. I suggest that embodied, social, personhood provides such a starting point. Until the body is brought back in, and the face is recalled to its rightful place, surveillance systems will continue to haunt us

with Cain's impertinent and fateful question". (Lyon, 2001, p. 181)

We therefore agree with Lyon, who suggests that we should seek an ethical view of privacy that considers the individual as a whole, counteracting the trend towards the digitization of "representations" of subjects in computer systems, data mining and the violation of the borders of informational territories in different ways. A global concept of the individual would involve more effective control of the boundaries, bubbles and virtual walls of informational territories, recognition of the "insecure individual" and the need to guarantee the individual's independence in terms of what is being done and what information is being produced that concerns him.

REFERENCES

Albrescht, K., & Mcintyre, L. (2006). *Spychips: How Majors Corporations and Government Plan to Track Your Every Purchase and Watch Your Every Move*. New York: Plume Book.

Benford, S. (2005). Future Location-Based Experiences. *JISC Tech Report (TSW0501)*.

Benford, S., Flintham, M., & Drodz, A. (2006). The Design And Experience of The Location-Based Performance Uncle Roy All Around You. *Leornardo, 14*(3). Retrieved May 10th 2008, from http://leoalmanac.org/journal/ Vol_14/ lea_v14_n03-04/roy.asp

Beslay, L., & Hakala, H. (2005). *Digital territory: Bubbles*. Draft Publication, European Community. Retrieved 10th May 2008 from http://cybersecurity.jrc.es/ docs/DigitalTerritoryBubbles.pdf

Bruno, F. (2008). Monitoramento, classificação e controle nos dispositivos de vigilância digital. In *Compós 2008, Proceedings*. Retrieved 15th August 2008 from http://www.compos.org.br/data/biblioteca_365.pdf

Coursey, D. (2009). Spy on Your Workers With Google Latitude. *PC World*, Business Center, 5th February 2009. Retrieved 5th February 2009 from http://www.pcworld.com/businesscenter/article/158975/ spy_on_your_workers_with_google_latitude.html

Deleuze, G. (1992). *Post-Scriptum sobre as Sociedades de controle.* In Deleuze, G., (Ed.), *Conversações: 1972-1990*, (Ed. 34, pp. 219-226). Retrieved 21st April 2008, from http://netart.incubadora.fapesp.br/ portal/midias/controle.pdf

Deleuze, G., & Guatari, F. (1980). *Mille Plateaux. Capitalisme et Schizophrénie*. Paris: Les Editions de Minuit.

Dodge, M., & Kitchim, R. (2007). Outlines of a world coming into existence: pervasive computing and the ethics of forgetting. *Environment and Planning. B, Planning & Design*, *34*, 431–445. doi:10.1068/b32041t

Foucault, M. (1984). Des espaces autres (conférence au Cercle d'études architecturales, 14 mars 1967). *Architecture, Mouvement, Continuité*, (5, octobre), 46-49. Retrieved 21st April 2008, from <http://foucault.info/documents/heteroTopia/foucault.heteroTopia.fr.html

Gow, G. A. (2005). Privacy and ubiquitous network societies. *ITU Workshop on Ubiquitous Network Societies*, April, Geneva, Switzerland.

Kapadia, A., Henderson, T., Fielding, J., & Kotz, D. (2007). Virtual Walls: Protecting Digital Privacy in Pervasive Environments. In *Proceedings International Conference on Pervasive Computing 2007*, (pp. 162-179). Berlin: Springer-Verlag.

Kellerman, A. (2006). *Personal Mobilities*. New York: Routledge.

Kuitenbrower, K. (2006). The Cultural and Social Possibilities of RFID. *Open, 11*. Retrieved 21st April 2008, from http://www.skor.nl/id.php/KUITENBROUWERENGELSOPEN11

Lemos, A. (2007). Cidade e Mobilidade. Telefones Celulares, funções pós-massivas e territórios informacionais. *Matrizes. Revista do Programa de Pós-Graduação em Ciências da Comunicação, 1*(1), 121–137.

Lemos, A. (2008). Mídias Locativas e Territórios Informacionais. In Santaella, L., & Arantes, P. (Eds.), *Estéticas Tecnológicas: Novos Modos de Sentir* (pp. 207–230). São Paulo, Brazil: EDUC.

Lyon, D. (2001). Facing the future: Seeking ethics for everyday surveillance. [from http://csalt.education.ecu.edu.au/projects/ cyberspace/lyon/ethics_surveillance.pdf]. *Ethics and Information Technology, 3*, 171–181. Retrieved May 10th, 2008. doi:10.1023/A:1012227629496

Manovich, L. (2005). The Poetics of Augmented Space: Learning from Prada. *Noemalab*. Tecnologie e Società. Retrieved 10th May 2008, from http://www.noemalab.org/sections/ideas/ ideas_articles/manovich_augmented_space.html

Meyrovitz, J. (1985). *No Sense of Place: The impact of Electronic Media on Social Behavior*. London: Oxford University Press.

Pope, S. (2005). The Shape of Locative Media. *Mute Magazine, 29*. Retrieved 21st April 2008, from http://www.metamute.com/look/article.tpl?IdLanguage=1& IdPublication=1&NrIssue=29NrSection=10NrArticle=1477

Rosello, M. (2008). *Culture de L'insecurité*. Keynote speech gave at Séminaire transdisciplinaire Cultures de l'(in)sécurité, Université de Montréal, Montréal. Retrieved 21st April 2008, from http://www.cerium.ca/Insecurite- linguistique-et

Russel, B. (n.d.). *Headmap Manifesto*. Retrieved 17th June 2007, from http://www.headmap.org/headmap.pdf

Santaella, L. (2008). A Estética Política das Mídias Locativas. *Nómadas, 28*, April 2008. Universidad Central, Colombia. Retrieved 21st July 2008 from <http://bibliotecavirtual.clacso.org.ar/ar/libros/colombia/iesco/nomadas/28/12-estetica.pdf

Scientific America. (2008, September). Who's watching you: The Future of Privacy. Retrieved 20th January 2009 from http://www.scientificamerican.com/ sciammag/?contents=2008-09

Van Kronenburg, R. (2008). *The internet of things: A critique of ambient technology and the all-seeing network of RFID*. Amsterdam: Waag Societt/Institute of Network Cultures.

ENDNOTES

1 "The term 'Internet of Things' has come to describe a number of technologies and research disciplines that enable the Internet to reach out into the real world of physical objects. Technologies like RFID, short-range wireless communications, real-time localization and sensor networks are now becoming increasingly common, bringing the Internet of Things into commercial use. They foreshadow an exciting future that closely interlinks the physical world and cyberspace - a development that is not only relevant to researchers, but to corporations and individuals alike." Ver http://www.the-internet-of-things.org/

2 Privacy and anonymity should be understood in terms of three domains: technical, regulatory and sociological. The technical domain can be said to refer to the design of network security systems and interfaces, such as the proposal for virtual walls, which we shall look at later; the regulatory domain refers to privacy in the context of data protection and regulatory policies; and the sociological domain considers privacy as something that

must be understood within a specific social, ethical and institutional context. See Gow, 2005.

3 In the Carnet de Notes (http://andrelemos.info) and other articles (Lemos, 2007 and 2007a), we give examples of the creative, free use of locative media: the collective construction of histories, urban electronic notes, pervasive games, GPS writing... Here we show the other side of the question: the threats to freedom, privacy and anonymity.

4 New functions emerge from the relationship between the (cultural, personal, historical, economic, imaginary...) characteristics of spaces and the informational function added by the digital layer in cyberspace. Place is now the result of a set of physical, cultural and economic characteristics: physical dimensions and a database.

5 Sousveillance is a term used to refer to countersurveillance processes. Locative technologies make countersurveillance actions possible, as a result of which issues relating to this subject in contemporary society become more complex. Remember the pictures of Rodney King being beaten, the photographs taken with cell phones in Abu Ghraib prison, the pictures of Saddam Hussein's death taken with a cell phone... Artists like Steve Mann, who coined the phrase as an inversion of surveillance, repeatedly show new possibilities for this type of response.

6 In a lecture at the "Espace Mobile" event in the Vox gallery, Montreal, in May 2008.

7 http://www.appliedautonomy.com/isee/info.html

8 http://www.ubermatic.org/life/

9 See http://www.google.com/latitude/intro.html and http://www.pcworld.com/businesscenter/article/158909/google_latitude_service_lets_you_track_your_friends_how_it_works.html

10 See http://www.privacyinternational.org/

11 See http://www.sci-tech-today.com/news/Misuse-of-Google-Latitude-Feared/story.xhtml?story_id=012001GSW8JC

12 The tag has two components: a silicon chip, which contains a unique identification number, and an antenna connected to the chip, which transmits information by means of radio waves. RFIDs can be passive or active. The former only communicate when they are activated by a reader (they do not need a battery and can work forever), while the latter, which are larger and more expensive, require a battery and can transmit signals without being activated by a reader. A reader activates the chip so that it transmits data. The reader than connects to databases in computers and/or to the Internet.

13 There have been protests against companies such as Benetton, Gilette, Procter & Gamble and a shopping mall that tested the system in Rheinberg, Germany. See Albrecht and McIntyre, 2006

14 See http://www.thinglink.org

15 See the projects at: http://www.zapped-it.net; http://dat-a.z25.org; http://attentionplease.wordpress.com/tag/exhibition/

16 See http://www.loca-lab.org/

17 There is a difference between the digital bubble/territory and what I call informational territory (although the terms are similar). Informational territory should be thought of not just as a bubble but as a new functionality of a space. It is a hybrid, which changes the dimensions of a space, rather than a bubble, which is created and isolates an individual in a space. Digital territories and bubbles isolate places. However, as far as the discussion about surveillance is concerned, both notions reinforce the political dimension of the inviolability of electronic borders.

18 The material metaphor of a wall is not very appropriate as this material element does not exist in the digital world. However, it evokes a picture of borders being controlled to pro-

tect territory. The image portrays personal territoriality as privacy maintained behind walls. Once again we must stress that the concept of informational territory — the fusion of physical and electronic dimensions — shows clearly that walls are no longer enough to ensure privacy and prevent different forms of surveillance. Nowadays, homes, bedrooms and prisons are all permeable to the new informational layer.

19 "Our system consists of a context server, which collects and disseminates digital footprints; clients, who instantiate walls or request footprints; and a sensing infrastructure that extracts footprints from sensor inputs. Users instantiate virtual walls by contacting the context server, which then uses the virtual walls to regulate access to footprints." (Kapadia, et. al, p.165)

Chapter 9
Mobile Telephony, Public and Private Planning and Regulation: A UK Perspective

Deborah Peel
University of Ulster, Northern Ireland, UK

Greg Lloyd
University of Ulster, Northern Ireland, UK

ABSTRACT

The global connectivity, experience and opportunities afforded by the expansion of modern informational mobility is particularly evident in the sustained expansion of mobile, cell and smart phones which are held to offer important social and economic benefits to individuals, businesses and governments. In practical terms, these are held to provide greater spatial mobility and connectivity, whilst potentially contributing to economic competitiveness, social emancipation, and territorial cohesion. Yet, the invisible connectivity afforded by such devices necessitates a visible physical infrastructure in rural and urban localities. This chapter discusses the technological, environmental and socio-economic implications of providing a mobile telephony infrastructure through a case study of the land use planning regulatory framework in the UK. Specific reference is made to Scotland which introduced statutory planning regulation in the public interest. This chapter explores the theoretical dimensions of the regulatory challenge of mobile telephony from a public and private perspective.

INTRODUCTION

Information and Communication Technologies are generally held as critical in meeting the needs of a modern information society, better enabling nation states compete in a global economy, and offering opportunities for promoting improved social cohesion (Castells, 1996). The vision of an 'E-topia' articulated by Mitchell (1999) highlights, for example, the changes that were expected to take place in different places and spaces as a consequence of the anticipated digital revolution. In practice, technological change in the communications sector has been rapid, certainly instrumental and potentially transformational. The specific development of high capacity broadband networks, the use of the Internet, and high-speed information networks have combined in various

DOI: 10.4018/978-1-60960-051-8.ch009

complementary ways to generate new patterns of networking, and to open up and expand novel potentialities for information gathering and knowledge exchange.

Digital networks have emerged as an important component of urban and rural infrastructure, leading Mitchell (1995), for example, to argue that digital telecommunications technology both extends and intensifies the reach and impact of earlier transportation networks, such as the mail, telegraph and telephone systems, thereby providing for economic and social integration on a larger geographic scale. This ambition necessarily cuts across established political borders. Extending this logic to the present, the emergent concept of ubiquitous infrastructure technologies (U-infrastructure) is held to represent a new paradigm of intelligent infrastructure provision, comprising a complex of inter-connected urban infrastructures that combine and facilitate information and communication technologies and digital networks (Lee *et al.*, 2008). This predominantly Korean perspective chimes with related debates around the need to establish a secure urbanism and the provision of a resilient infrastructure which can respond to emerging ecological constraints and environmental challenges in modern metropolitan areas (Hodson & Marvin, 2009a). This in turn raises questions for the institutional frameworks and multi-layered governance arrangements for managing the transition to accommodate and manage the new technologies (Hodson & Marvin, 2009b). This is particularly the case where competitive regimes exist and where unanticipated impacts of new technologies remain unknown.

Significantly, Gow (2005) argued that the essential characteristics of a ubiquitous network society were its 'invisibility and pervasiveness' (p. 4). Yet, the perspective of this chapter is that such "invisible" technological activity requires a physical and material supporting infrastructure. Here, Graham and Marvin (1995), for example, argued that the underlying complexities associated with the required utilities infrastructure risked becoming a 'missing link' in debates concerned with urban redevelopment and restructuring, and made a case for more appropriate empirical research into the relationship between utility, infrastructure and regulation. Notwithstanding the evident miniaturisation and portability of different communications media, the devices still require a communications network. The necessary supporting facilities and structures are likely to be relatively more visible and material in character and, as a consequence, bring with them the possibility of creating different contestations around the ownership, use and development of spaces and places.

In effect, the supporting infrastructure for the invisible technology is very much more visible and potentially intrusive in different social, political and environmental contexts. Indeed, its very physicality has potentially cumulative and tangible impacts on different localities and communities. Such effects are likely to feature, or indeed be concentrated at specific points, in defined urban neighbourhoods, rural environments, or along linear transport and infrastructure corridors. Specifically, this chapter is concerned with the strategic mediation and site-specific facilitation of the necessary infrastructure development for mobile telephony through the UK statutory land use planning system.

In practical terms, this chapter examines attempts in Scotland to design an appropriate regulatory regime to reconcile the environmental, economic, technocratic, and democratic considerations needed to support the physical distribution networks required to support mobile telephony. In many ways, this wider environmental perspective is not a new concern. During the 1920s, for example, campaigning groups in the UK militated against the perceived intrusion of urban paraphernalia, including the erection of telegraph poles and advertising hoardings (Gallent *et al.*, 2008). Notably, the Campaign for the Protection of Rural England, and the equivalent body for Wales, were amongst those most active and influential in the debates which eventually culminated in the Town and Country Planning Act of 1947. This legislation was designed to regulate development in the wider public interest, yet, following Murdoch and Lowe (2003) the construction of this spatial division requires a sophisticated form of relational understanding. Indeed, this may be implied by the very title of that Act which emphasises the active and integrated connectivities between urban and rural locales – town and country. This clearly invokes a range of potential developmental impacts across territorial spaces.

In theoretical terms, the objective of this chapter is to advance contemporary understandings of the role of regulation as it responds and reformulates to emerging technological developments. It addresses an issue relating to the concept of the public interest with respect to new technological forms, paralleling and complementing the ethical concerns of the implications for the private individual (Lemos, 2010). Here, an appropriate regulatory apparatus represents another dimension to the informational territory. Significantly, this sits in very visible space yet raises new challenges to private and public domains. The chapter draws on applied research undertaken in relation to regulation through statutory land use planning controls over the infrastructure required to support the development of mobile telephony (Lloyd *et al.*, 2004; Askew *et al.*, 2009). Specifically, it locates land use planning in the mixed economy of regulation that has been devised in the UK for the mobile telephony sector. At the site specific level this comprises a blended arrangement comprising the statutory land use planning system itself alongside the self-regulation put in place by the competitive operators involved. In considering both the private and public perspectives on planning for mobile telephony infrastructure, this chapter draws attention to the regulatory layering and intricate relations associated with the development of mobile telephony infrastructure.

BACKGROUND

In the UK, the growth of the mobile telephony sector may be explained in terms of a sequence of rapid technological innovations which commenced in the 1980s. The first wireless networks to be deployed were broadcast networks in relation to radio and, later, television. Developments within the industry mean that wireless technology is now used in a range of ways for home and business networking, including computer and mobile phone communication, Bluetooth for personal, portable, and handheld electronic devices, games consoles, remote sensors, and smart cards. Notwithstanding the apparent similarities between the use of wireless technologies, however, the infrastructure requirements for mobile phone networks differ from more conventional broadcast networks, such as radio and television, as they (currently) necessitate a more extensive and visible national network of radio base stations, masts, and antennas to support the effective delivery of the technology.

In consumer terms, the first generation of analogue-based mobile phones was generally considered to be cumbersome and unreliable. The introduction and development of the Global System for Mobile Communications / Universal Mobile Telecommunication System subsequently resulted in the analogue technology being phased out. It was replaced by a second generation of mobile phones which were held to be relatively more convenient for consumers, being smaller and easier to handle. As reliability continued to improve, and the geographical coverage of the technology increased, consumer demand and expectations grew. A third generation (3G) of mobile telephony subsequently provided mobile broadband internet access, full motion multimedia, and colour video footage, as part of a range of new consumer services, including photo-messaging, e-mail, games, and information services. Consumer interest in these media continued to grow in the UK. Recent statistics, for example, show that the total mobile revenues increased to £15.4 billion; that there were almost 77 million mobile subscriptions; but that whilst smartphones and applications ("apps") offer a relatively more sophisticated use of the mobile internet, take-up is highly differentiated, and, more importantly, there is a general lack of awareness of the functionalities available; in effect, this means that the relatively more advanced technology has not yet entered the consumer mainstream (Ofcom, 2009). Nevertheless, this potential and sustained expansion of mobile telephony will likely carry with it further physical development requirements.

Reflecting the evident portability, increased miniaturisation, mobility, intensification and enhanced capacity of information and communication technologies, there has been a roll-out of the necessary infrastructure. This has had a concomitant impact on the use and development of land in a range of urban and rural localities. The provision of the necessary facilities creates different sets of strategic, regional, and site-specific conflicts and related political matters. The required strategic networks and site-specific installations for individual mobile telephony operators involve a set of related material considerations. In particular, the roll-out of infrastructure generally involves, for example, the erection of masts to support antennae, cabins to house equipment, access routes for installation and maintenance, and potential landscaping for screening purposes, in addition to the essential base stations. As demand increases, further infrastructure is required. In parallel, however, technological developments risk rendering existing infrastructure obsolete, requiring a mechanism to control the management of redundant equipment. These features triggered a number of substantive community concerns, prompting wider political and governance debates. As a consequence, attention has been paid to the appropriate forms of governance which are involved in the different decision-making arenas relating to these scales and territories.

RETHINKING REGULATION OF MOBILE TELEPHONY

The particular political economy context to the technological and consumer revolution in mobile telephony in the UK is important in understanding the design of the regulatory framework. In effect, a neoliberal economic policy regime generally militated against the then established state ownership arrangements for the provision of telecommunications in the UK. This led to a broad shift from state to market provision. On the one hand, the ensuing institutional realignment to a competitive market context was intended to enable further technological advance and market penetration of the sector. Yet, on the other hand, it resulted in a set of emerging societal concerns associated with the increased physical infrastructure to support the new mobile telephony services. This created evident tensions between the state, market and civil interests involved in mobile telecommunications policy and this led to the recasting of the regulatory arrangements for the industry.

At the core of the debates about the regulation of mobile telecommunications infrastructure is devising an appropriate institutional design for reconciling the trade-offs between a range of technological, environmental, consumer, economic and social conditions. Central to this is an important question relating to what constitutes – or is perceived to constitute – the public interest within specific spatial jurisdictions. Following Wilsdon *et al.* (2005), for example, the concept of public value in science and technology is highly contested. It involves a complex layering of individual and collective experiences and expectations, and requires active and informed public engagement to reach an appropriate outcome. Critically, the concept of public value encompasses an intricate shifting balance of private, public, and common property rights which can evolve in different dynamic combinations over time and place (Webster and Lai, 2003). It further invokes contestation around the nature of the intrinsic, instrumental and institutional values at stake (Holden, 2006). In addition, perceptions of value are mediated by (potentially competing) professional, political, policy-maker, and public interests (*ibid.*). Serving the wider social interest is then a sensitive political, policy, institutional and democratic process and requires appropriate governance arrangements. In the context of this chapter, defining the public interest suggests a need to design an effective institutional frame which can secure the appropriate balance of public and private interests in order to sustain collective well-being in relation to the emergent technology. Appropriate regulatory design forms part of that institutional frame.

It follows that devising arrangements to attain or reflect the public interest in evolving circumstances must involve an appropriate alignment of state, market, civil relations and understandings, and the design, implementation and enforcement of specific institutional forms. Here it is important to acknowledge that this assertion clearly represents a normative perspective on securing the public interest, which is itself a normative assertion of a perspective on the material world. From this stance, the public interest is not considered to be a spontaneous and naturally occurring event or process – it is a political assertion at a given point in time. It is thus dynamic and, following Hannigan (2006), is socially constructed.

Securing the public interest has traditionally fallen to the state to articulate and enforce. Conventionally, state intervention to secure its construction of the public interest has been articulated through regulation of market and civil behavior. In general terms, such state regulation of market activity, for example, seeks to monitor and control private sector activities, transactions or market behaviours that involve the public interest or are considered to be of broader social value (Selznick, 1985). The concept of regulation, however, is layered and may be articulated to secure different political and policy outcomes. In practice, the state can deploy regulatory intervention to influence, direct, and control social and market behaviours in a number of ways so as to secure different facets of the public interest (Baldwin *et al.*, 1998). The ensuing layering of regulation is important as it can also involve complementary self-regulation within the industrial and corporate sectors. Reconciling state and self-regulation, however, poses a set of management questions and capacity issues around ensuring that there is an efficient and effective meshing of the different regulatory codes. Regulation measures and instruments can thus take different rationales and forms, operate at different institutional scales, and involve cross-sector and policy regimes. This is the case with mobile telephony in the UK.

MOBILE TELEPHONY IN THE UK

Under the Telecommunications Act 1984, the telecommunications sector in the UK was privatised and, as a consequence, its operational structures and players were dramatically changed. As a result, the provision of telecommunications services, which had been dominated by state provision through a single statutory undertaker, British Telecom, was replaced by a relatively more open market. Initially, this comprised a duopoly of British Telecommunications plc, the former state-owned operator, and one other fixed-link provider (Parker, 1999). This phase of relatively restricted competition was changed in 1991 following the publication of a Government White Paper, *Competition and Choice: Telecommunications Policy for the 1990s* (Department of Trade & Industry, 2001), which sought to encourage a more deliberate opening up of the communications market to competition. The primary driver for market openness in this sector was a consequence of the UK Government's strategy to increase greater competition in telecommunications. This initially led to the market being populated by a number of new fixed and mobile telecommunications operators, prompting the Department of

Trade and Industry (2001) to describe the UK's telecommunications market as being one of the most open in the world.

Institutional privatisation of the telecommunications sector required new sector specific regulatory arrangements. Following Baldwin *et al.* (1998) these were likely intended to provide for economic and social well-being and to create the context for further scale economies in the sector. Regulation was originally achieved through the setting up of a new body, the Office of Telecommunications (Oftel), which was established under the Telecommunications Act, 1984. This body was concerned only with telecommunications, however, and with providing the appropriate regulatory safeguards for the industry. Its remit was principally to ensure effective competition and to secure the best possible outcomes for customers in terms of quality, choice and value for money. The two licensed operators were required to comply with defined obligations to meet reasonable consumer demand, provide for geographical coverage across the UK, and to ensure the delivery of a high quality service. Substantial investment in mobile services culminated in the subsequent auctioning and granting of five 3G licences in 2000.

The further liberalisation of the market was accompanied by increasing convergence and a relatively greater integration of telecommunications, IT and broadcasting, through developing and using common networks and platforms. In 2003, the UK Government responded to these emerging structural changes in technological and market conditions by recalibrating its regulatory arrangements. A new second phase authority, the Office of Communications (Ofcom), became the unitary regulator for a broader communications portfolio. This comprised the UK's telecommunications and television, radio, and wireless communications services. Ofcom's wider regulatory remit embraced the promotion of choice and competition, balanced with a duty to foster plurality and informed citizenship, protect viewers, listeners and customers, and promote cultural diversity; serving the interests of the citizen-consumer in the digital age; supporting innovators, creators and investors; and encouraging the evolution of electronic media and communications networks. This particular form and scale of regulation was primarily concerned then with the industrial efficiency and consumer well-being associated with the expanding sphere of communications, and of which telecommunications is an essential part. It provided the conditions within which both technological innovation and market size and coverage increased. Notwithstanding the relatively conventional focus on regulating a privatised industrial sector, particularly in relation to consumer protection, the interests of investors, and attempts to avoid sector capture by a particular interest (Parker, 1999), a number of unintended effects emerged which prompted additional layers of regulation.

MOBILE TELEPHONY AND HEALTH

A very significant yet unintended consequence of the expansion of the new mobile telephony and its related infrastructure turned on fears about the possible health impacts involved. Indeed, there was a clearly articulated public and political expression of concern with respect to the location of the mobile telephony infrastructure and the perceived health impacts on communities and specific groups, such as young children. In response, in 1999, the UK Government directed the National Radiological Protection Board to set up the Independent Expert Group on Mobile Phones (IEGMP) to examine the possible effects of mobile phones, base stations and transmitters on health. Its report, *Mobile Phones and Health* (IEGMP, 2000), commonly referred to as 'The Stewart Report', made a number of specific recommendations on the measures to be followed in order to reduce public concerns.

The Stewart Report concluded that, in general, exposure to radio frequency radiation below defined guideline levels would not cause adverse health effects to the general population, whilst proposing a 'precautionary approach' to the use of mobile phone technologies (IEGMP, 2000). The findings were confirmed by research undertaken by an independent Advisory Group on Non-Ionising Radiation, and the National Radiological Protection Board. The Stewart Report (IEGMP, 2000) had, nevertheless, asserted the need for further scientific evidence. This resulted in the setting up of the Mobile Telecommunications and Health Research Programme which subsequently (2007) confirmed the findings that neither mobile phones nor base stations have been found to be associated with any biological or adverse health effects. Importantly, however, the deliberations and advocacy of a precautionary approach to the development of mobile telephony in the Stewart Report, led to the design of *de facto* regulation to address health concerns. This turns on industrial compliance guidelines.

One of the issues considered in The Stewart Report related to potential health risks in the vicinity of mobile network base stations. Whilst the Independent Expert Group on Mobile Phones concluded that the balance of evidence indicated that there was no general risk to the health of people living near to base stations, as exposures were expected to be lower than the International Commission on Non-Ionizing Radiation Protection (ICNIRP) guidelines, the Stewart Report (IEGMP, 2000) pointed to a general need to give the public reliable and openly available information about the location and operating characteristics of base stations. This led to the setting up of *Sitefinder*, a database hosted by Ofcom, which holds information on the location and operating characteristics of individual base stations. This information is delivered voluntarily by the mobile network operators, suggesting a deliberate attempt to demonstrate the sector's commitment to addressing public concerns.

Since this chapter is principally concerned with the regulation of the land and property infrastructure implications of providing mobile telephony in the UK, it is useful here to observe that the land use planning system (the principal means for regulating land development) is not the appropriate forum for determining health safeguards relating to mobile telephony. If a proposed mobile phone base station meets the ICNIRP guidelines for public exposure, the government has stated that it should not then be necessary for a local planning authority to consider further the health aspects in determining individual planning applications. This would, in effect, have resulted in the statutory land use planning system replicating (and duplicating) controls which already exist under separate health and safety regimes and other bodies. There is, however, a regulatory requirement for all statutory land use planning applications to include a formal statement that certifies that the operating of a mobile phone station, or the addition of equipment to a station, will comply with the ICNIRP guidelines. The need for compliance with this health regulatory dimension is confirmed in the mobile telecommunications industry's own code of conduct (MOA, 2006) which may be seen as adding another layer to these arrangements.

SELF-REGULATION: THE MOBILE OPERATORS ASSOCIATION

In 1999, the Mobile Telecoms Advisory Group, which subsequently became the Mobile Operators Association (MOA) was formed to represent the best interests of the mobile telephony industry. The MOA deals with radio frequency and health and safety issues, and land use planning matters. Following the publication of the Stewart Report (IEGMP, 2000), it subsequently launched The Ten Commitments in 2001 (MOA, 2006) and a Code of Best Practice (Office of the Deputy Prime Minister, 2002). The code is intended to support the operations of the five mobile network operators in the UK – 3, O2, Orange, T-Mobile and Vodafone – so as to improve the transparency of the process of developing mobile telephony networks; provide more information to the public; and increase the role of the public in the decisions relating to the siting of base stations. This voluntary form of self-regulation has subsequently been complemented by practical guidance on different types of community consultation, notably through a Traffic Light Model (MOA, 2004).

Together with the Code of Best Practice, the Traffic Light Model seeks to enhance communication and consultation at all stages of network development between operators, local authorities and local people; to improve consistency of practice and procedures through a standardisation of forms and actions; to develop a greater understanding by explaining important technical features of mobile systems; and to provide good practice guidance on the siting and design of telecommunications development (Office of the Deputy Prime Minister, 2002). The industry anticipated that the introduction of the Ten Commitments would thereby enhance a broader and deeper understanding of the physical infrastructure requirements of mobile phone technology and complement a relatively more light-touch implementation of the statutory land use planning system, as is the case in England and Wales.

The Ten Commitments cover a range of aspects which are concerned with (i) developing clear standards and procedures and enhancing consultation with local communities; (ii) engaging the industry in obligatory pre-roll-out and pre-application consultation with local planning authorities; (iii) subscribing to measurable criteria for cross-industry good practice, such as mast- and site-sharing; (iv) providing professional development workshops on technological developments for local authority officers and elected members; (v) providing a locational database of radio base stations; (vi) complying with the ICNIRP requirements; (vii) submitting certification of compliance with ICNIRP public exposure guidelines as part of formal planning applications; (viii) providing customer care services in the immediate aftermath of the erection of a base station; (ix) contributing financially to the Government's research programme on mobile communication health issues; and (x) developing standardised supporting documentation for all types of planning submission (Office of the Deputy Prime Minister, 2002). This catalogue represents a detailed and comprehensive expression of self regulated behaviours for the member operators. It offers a parallel framework to the land use planning system and goes beyond the regulatory confines of that statutory function.

The Traffic Light Model of community consultation seeks to provide a structured programme for bringing together local issues. This includes ascertaining views and attitudes of local groups and residents, understanding associated social and political considerations, including the ownership of the land and extent of media interest. These aspects must be mediated with land use planning and environmental management issues, such as questions relating to site sensitivity, siting and appearance considerations and the broader spatial planning context. Here, detailed land use designations and policies come into play. The Traffic Light Model has been specifically designed as a generic practical guide to ascertaining the amount and type of public consultation required for an individual proposed site. The consultations associated with this approach are then intended to supplement those carried out by the local planning authority in discharging its statutory responsibilities. In effect, the Traffic Light Model sets out what may be considered to be a health-check procedure to guide operators and their agents in progressing the development of individual sites to support mobile phone technology and its market.

Understanding the rationale for the mobile network operators' decision to introduce this voluntary approach to self-regulation is critical. It was based on a clear view by the industry that the popularity and benefits of mobile services could only serve to contribute to the UK economy and meet consumer expectations and demand if sufficient infrastructure and coverage were provided.

Articulating their individual views through the MOA, it was therefore clear that the operators considered that potentially restrictive regulation, principally through the land use planning system, would serve to affect adversely the operators' capacity to meet their license obligations, reduce their ability to retain a competitive edge in a global market, and would likely fail to address any public concerns adequately. Specifically, the MOA argued that local planning authorities were ill-equipped to assess health concerns and that making the regulation of mobile telephony infrastructure a matter for the planning system would serve to raise public expectations. This line of reasoning suggested that, on the one hand, such arrangements might imply a local public veto on base station siting; and, on the other hand, the necessary arrangements would result in an unnecessary administrative burden on the statutory land use planning system.

An evaluation of the implementation of the Ten Commitments by the operators for the MOA (Deloitte & Touche, 2003) asserted that demonstrable progress has been made in implementing the objectives of the essential and optional components of the Ten Commitments. Moreover, the MOA committed itself to respond to the recommendations for continuous improvement following a second evaluation study of the industry's implementation of the Ten Commitments (Deloitte & Touche, 2005). Yet, this self-regulatory approach has not been accepted unilaterally. Johnston (2001, p. 13), for example, described the telecommunications industry's approach as a 'charm offensive to break down suspicions over mast development among local authorities and the general public'. More importantly, perhaps, the nature of the planning controls of mobile telephony development in the UK have continued to attract government attention and to evolve as the permitted development rights regime has been subjected to an on-going critical evaluation (Askew *et al.*, 2009).

In practical terms, the locational and public aspects of developing the necessary telecommunications infrastructure lie directly at the interface of the sector with the statutory land use planning system. Significantly, then, within the UK Government's broad policy objective of facilitating the growth of new and existing telecommunications systems, the individual devolved administrations of Scotland, Northern Ireland and Wales have variously sought to better address the developmental and environmental impacts of the mobile telephony infrastructure through their land use planning regulatory systems.

STATUTORY LAND USE PLANNING IN THE UK

In the UK, the statutory land use planning system finds its origins in the perceived need to manage the orderly development of land in the aftermath of the industrial and urban revolutions in the late 18th and early 19th centuries. Over time, a concern with public health, housing standards, and providing infrastructure came together in a discretionary regulatory land use planning system. The purposes of planning are to regulate proposed land and property development proposals to ensure they fall within the public interest; to anticipate future social, environmental and economic needs, and to allocate the required land accordingly, and to provide for the necessary supporting infrastructure; and, to guide, at a strategic level, land use and development in the wider public interest.

The intellectual rationale for a land use planning system is to support, enable, and facilitate private sector land and property development whilst reconciling this with the broader community agenda. On the one hand, the public regulation of private land and property rests on ensuring the comprehensive, consistent and coherent management of development. On the other hand, this statutory framework seeks to facilitate sustainable development which is sensitive to a more holistic perspective, including issues of environmental justice, social inclusion, intra-generational equity, and territorial cohesion. The implementation of the statutory land use planning system rests on the legal definition of development. This involves material changes of use (in land or property) and operational development, such as the erection of physical structures.

Throughout its history, land use planning has directly engaged with the provision of urban and rural infrastructure. This has involved securing the necessary supporting services and facilities for land development. Examples include matters relating to roads and transport, water and sewerage, energy utilities, open space, community facilities, and, in more recent times, the roll-out of mobile telecommunications. A common characteristic of modern infrastructure tends to turn on its site-specific location, the competing priorities over the use and development of the land resource in that locality, and its very material and visible physical manifestation. This may be illustrated with respect to motor-ways and bridges, telegraph-poles and telephone-boxes, pylons and pipe-lines, or reservoirs and roads. In principle, and although these are supporting services and structures, they are still generally subject to some form of planning regulation.

In the late 1990s, the operation of the statutory land use planning system in the UK was transformed as a consequence of political innovation around devolution and the creation of new political administrations in Scotland, Northern Ireland and Wales, alongside those put in place in England. Devolution has gradually resulted in the articulation of different interpretations of land use planning structures and processes as each political administration has devised institutional forms considered appropriate to the prevailing and anticipated social, economic and environmental conditions. Whilst telecommunications legislation and regulation is a reserved matter, and rests with Westminster as a UK-wide strategic matter, land use planning policy is a devolved responsibility. Caution must then be exercised in considering the relationship of individual land use planning regulations to development across the devolved UK as variegated arrangements exist.

The evolving regulatory differentiation is of particular significance to mobile telephony since new regulatory regimes now co-exist in the UK as the individual devolved administrations have sought, variously, to address the unexpected, unintended and unanticipated consequences of the privatisation of the telecommunications sector (Walton, 2002a). Together with consumer demand and technological innovation, the design and proliferation of the supporting infrastructure has resulted, over time, in a set of new issues and controversies. This has principally turned on addressing the question of permitted development rights and identifying the appropriate responses to their definition and management in the individual devolved administrations. Development rights obtain in particular circumstances and sectors, including certain agricultural activities and particular developments carried out by statutory undertakers, and may be curtailed in defined circumstances, such as in areas or sites of special designation, conservation areas and listed buildings, and Sites of Special Scientific Interest.

An unintended impact of the privatisation of telecommunications in the late 20th century may be considered to be a direct consequence of the permitted development rights regime in relation to the mobile operators. This permissive arrangement was intended principally to facilitate the roll-out of the required infrastructure in the new market economy. Yet, the proliferation and extent of the infrastructure under the permitted development rights regime, led to widespread public disquiet, particularly in relation to the siting and design of the necessary masts.

The differentiated devolved planning responses to these concerns resulted in what may be considered to form a continuum of controls from models of full planning in Northern Ireland and Scotland to those relatively less stringent prior approval arrangements in England and Wales (Lloyd *et al.*, 2004). In the case of telecommunications, prior approval procedures relate to defined types of development which are permitted, subject to an operator making a prior approval application. This enables the local planning authority to consider the siting and appearance of the proposed development with a presumption that the development will go ahead. Here, the prior approval offers an administrative check on the exercise of permitted development rights. Yet, this relatively light-touch arrangement was held not to provide sufficient development control and management. The next section concentrates on documenting and understanding the construction of the particular regulatory regime in Scotland which was then put in place to address the land use and development implications of mobile communications.

REGULATING MOBILE TELEPHONY INFRASTRUCTURE DEVELOPMENT IN SCOTLAND

Scotland is located to the north of the UK. It is a devolved nation-region of some five million population. There are four city regions - Edinburgh, Glasgow, Aberdeen and Dundee. The remainder of the population is located in small- to medium-sized settlements. The north and west of Scotland is generally characterised as a relatively remote rural, and sparsely populated area. Much of Scotland is acknowledged internationally as being of high environmental quality, with 26% of the land area covered by natural heritage designations, including two national parks (Scottish Executive, 2004). The major cities each have relatively long histories of industrialisation, urbanization, and development. As a result, the built environment is rich in its built and cultural heritage and this is reflected in the extensive catalogue of listed building and conservation area designations, for example, which serve to protect or encourage enhancement of the built form. The particular settlement patterns and population densities, and the nature of the terrain and topography, particularly to the north, provide demanding contexts for the roll-out of the necessary mobile telephony infrastructure in Scotland.

The *National Planning Framework for Scotland* (Scottish Government, 2009) provides the strategic context for development. Significantly, the Framework pays particular attention to the variety of infrastructure needs across rural and urban areas. This serves to reinforce their close relationship, both in terms of meeting local requirements and in securing and supporting mobility of people and services, and also in ensuring greater spatial connectivity within and between the cities and their sub-regions. In addition to emphasising the importance of roads, ports and air infrastructure to facilitating improved internal and external connectivity, for instance, the *National Planning Framework* also addresses the specific needs of information and communications technologies. As a national statement of intent, the *National Planning Framework* asserts the importance of promoting technology and telecommunications with respect to enhancing employment, global networks, and wider economic and social development opportunities.

The *National Planning Framework* is an important element in the evolving modernisation of the statutory land use planning system which seeks to provide a more hierarchical, proportionate, and facilitative approach to land use and development in Scotland. Here, it is important to recognise that, just as the mobile telephony sector has innovated and extended its market coverage, so too has the statutory land use regulatory framework within which the telecommunications infrastructure is developed and managed. The following sub-sections trace the reasons for, and responses to, the need for establishing a new form of enabling regulatory framework for mobile telephony in Scotland.

LAND USE PLANNING REGULATION FOR MOBILE TELEPHONY

Prior to 2001, a permissive regime for the control and regulation of the physical and fixed infrastructure for mobile telephony existed in Scotland. Here, the exercising of a range of permitted development rights by the licensed mobile network operators was a consequence of the UK-wide Telecommunications Act 1984 which, in replacing British Telecom with a small number of private licensed companies, also transferred the associated permitted development rights which previously rested with the single statutory undertaker. In subsequently meeting their licence requirements under Oftel, and in responding to a rapidly changing market demand, the privatised – and now competitive – mobile network sector moved to implement a rapid roll-out of the necessary infrastructure. An unintended consequence of this intense period of policy and private sector development was considerable public and local elected representative concern about the proliferation of masts. In parallel, there was a concerted media campaign drawing attention to this perceived urban and rural *malaise*, encapsulated in one popular newspaper headline as 'the plague of the phone masts' (Pyatt, 2002). This particular commentary noted a paradox, for example, that whilst, on the one hand, there was growing public enthusiasm to use and own a mobile phone, on the other hand, the related infrastructure was held to represent a health hazard and eye-sore, leading to both fear and anger in local communities. This was partly a consequence of a lack of wider public understanding about the nature of the new technology but it was also due to a public participation deficit in locales where the immediate physical environment was being altered. Moreover, it was also a consequence of the type of development appearing in urban and rural localities and the scientific or technological processes involved.

In practice, the strategic rollout of the 3G infrastructure in the 2000s led directly to the rollout of the necessary radio-base stations, and, often more controversially, to the erection of communication masts. This infrastructure was concentrated in areas of relatively high population where demand tended to be higher. Moreover, the technological requirements of mobile phone technology, which is dependent upon the transmission and reception of radio signals, places particular siting demands on the built and natural environments. In simple terms, the UK is divided into thousands of individual geographic areas which are known as cells. A radio base station lies at the heart of each cell and these overlap to improve coverage, particularly since users may be on the move (MOA, 2006). Critically, where the physical terrain consists of trees and hills, for example, or in a built-up area, radio signals may be obstructed by natural or man-made features. In addition, in spaces of high consumer use, such as a shopping centre or railway station, use may exceed the capacity of a cell. Where coverage is obstructed or incomplete there is a case for additional cell coverage and infrastructure to support consumer expectations.

The necessary infrastructure, however, involves developmental impacts on land and property. Masts, for example, are free-standing structures which are required to support antennas at a specific height where they can transmit and receive radio waves. Technical solutions to address issues of coverage and reception then tended to involve, for example, the erection of masts on sky-lines to avoid any obstructions, or the installation of further antenna on existing structures, potentially resulting in what was perceived as cumulative clutter. Yet, such responses led to criticism on siting and design grounds. As local people and their locally elected representatives discovered that such operational development did not require the submission of a formal land use planning application due to the provisions of the General Permitted Development Order, a number of deep concerns arose around local communities' perceived lack of ability to influence the nature of the developments taking place in their localities.

The controversies associated with the physical presence of mobile telephony infrastructure may be summarised in terms of the siting and visual concerns in the different landscapes in which the masts are erected; the associated effects on the social enjoyment of the natural heritage setting (including the erosion of visual amenity); and the various ecological impacts, particularly local habitat loss and disturbance. These may be caused not only by the construction works but the associated maintenance activities at sensitive environmental sites which would be necessary over the longer term. Attempts to address these matters by disguising the equipment were perceived in some quarters as representing development by stealth (Walton, 2002b) which illustrates how the credibility of the sector was subject to question. Newspaper coverage also showed that attempts to use church towers and steeples, for example, to support and conceal the necessary equipment were contentious due to the potentially sensitive nature of the information being transmitted by the technology, and the sanctity of such buildings.

In certain localities there was a cumulative infrastructure impact on the natural landscape due to a reluctance by individual operators to engage in collaborative mast-sharing. Notwithstanding the Government's policy and regulatory position on the potential health risks associated with mobile telephony masts, there remained an enduring concern with health which communities sought to channel and address through the planning system. Here, attention was drawn to human rights. Moreover, in addition to site-specific concerns, there were issues relating to the strategic roll-out plans of individual operators and the nature of the lines of communication open to local elected members and planning officials to be aware of the corporate position regarding appropriate locations for base-stations and masts. Taken together, this raised matters relating to calls for improved mast design, more sensitive siting in appropriate locations, issues associated with minimum distances of masts from sensitive sites such as schools, and improved mast- and site-sharing between the operators.

The unexpected level of public concern prompted the setting up of a Parliamentary Inquiry into the possible case for introducing more stringent controls over mobile telecommunications developments. This was conducted by the Scottish Parliament's Transport and Environment Committee which reported in April 2000. This resulted in the Scottish Government amending the General Permitted Development Order in 2001 so as to bring telecommunications developments within the scope of full land use planning control. Policy and design guidance were set out in the publication of a new National Planning Policy Guidance (Scottish Executive, 2001a) and an accompanying Planning Advice Note (Scottish Executive, 2001b) on Radio Telecommunications. This policy framework and siting and design guidance provided clear and deliberate support for the development of mobile telephony, whilst highlighting the need to be sensitive to social and environmental concerns. Whilst representing a relatively more stringent regulatory regime the purpose was to provide greater clarity, certainty and consistency to both the mobile telephony operators and to local communities. In effect, the land use planning system was seeking to mediate strategic, technocratic and democratic aspects of facilitating the technology and its required infrastructure by enabling debate around the relevant material considerations. In Scotland, the (non-statutory) Ten Commitments work informally alongside this statutory decision-making environment. Importantly, then, the national guidance, which in some areas is supplemented by locally produced guidelines and electronic information, provides an array of publicly available information on the nature and needs of telecommunications development.

In its evidence to the Transport and Environment Committee of the Scottish Parliament in February 2003, however, the MOA took particular issue with the implementation of the revised legislation, and the apparent lack of preparedness of planning authorities in terms of its implementation. At a general level, the MOA was concerned about the effects of moratoria on the installation of infrastructure and equipment on local authority owned land and buildings. At another level, and whilst noting a growing co-operation, in practice, between operators and planning authorities in terms of the land use planning arrangements, the MOA pointed to a general increase in the time taken to process telecommunications infrastructure. It highlighted the fact that the time-frame associated with the planning regulations excluded the time taken up in the pre-application phase. This was clearly a matter that also affected the workload and therefore the overall efficiency of planning authority decision-making. More specific concerns raised by the MOA included the apparent misunderstanding of the complex nature of the legislation, the poor response by planning authorities to licensed operators' strategic roll-out demands, the degree of inconsistency in determining planning applications by different local authorities, the imposition of what the industry perceived as the unnecessary and unreasonable conditions in planning permissions with which they were required to comply, and the removal of permitted development rights for new ground-based masts. These arguments clearly point to the transaction costs associated with the new regulatory regime.

The relatively more stringent planning regime in Scotland was the subject of independent evaluation conducted on behalf of the Scottish government (Lloyd *et al*., 2004). This evaluated the impact of the new regulatory framework on a full range of stakeholders, including elected members, local planning authorities, central government, the planning appeals inspectors, local communities, and, importantly, the mobile network operators. This study concluded that subjecting development proposals to the rigours of full planning permission had improved decision-making and development outcomes, and not overly burdened the planning system. A separate study for the Welsh Assembly Government (Askew *et al.*, 2009) as to the need to revise the permitted development rights in relation to mobile telephony in Wales provided a further opportunity to review the impacts of the 2001 regulations in Scotland and again indicated that the Scottish arrangements were perceived as working effectively by securing an appropriate balance between enabling the necessary roll-out, protecting the land resource, minimising adverse impacts on the built form, and facilitating democratic engagement. What lessons can be taken from this experience of mobile phones and physical fixtures in understanding regulation of emerging urban and rural mobile and ubiquitous infrastructures in order that the visible land and property dimensions of new technologies receive adequate attention?

THEORISING A REGULATORY FRAMEWORK FROM MASTS AND MOBILES

Traditionally, regulation has fallen to the state to manage the activities of markets and to secure the well-being of civil society (Baldwin *et al.*, 1998). This arrangement implies a hierarchical framework of controls and guidelines which seek to secure desired political and policy outcomes. Reflective studies of regulation, however, suggest adopting a more heterogeneous approach which encourages a relatively more qualitative dimension to be incorporated into the more instrumental approach conventionally associated with state intervention. Here, for example, it is argued that the scope of regulation can be extended to that of an enabling mechanism as much as a controlling activity on the part of the state (Baldwin and Cave, 1999). In other words, regulation can be crafted in more flexible ways to reflect the nature of the activity and the desired public interest outcomes. This interest in promoting a greater sensitivity in designing regulatory frames is supported by insights drawn from the new institutional economics (Webster, 2005). Webster and Lai (2003), for example, point to the design of conventional regulatory institutions and instruments in terms of their constituent property rights and associated economic incentives. This attention to detail seeks to promote more effective, efficient and transparent governance and regulation arrangements (Needham and Louw, 2006). Here, there is a primary concern with devising more cost effective governance which can facilitate a positive business environment which is conducive to private sector investment and development (Geuting, 2007). In essence, this approach is a new attempt to reconcile the private and public interests in appropriate arrangements for regulation.

The potential for a new form of regulation is highly appropriate in seeking to understand the regulatory arrangements and relations which are now associated with mobile telephony. On the one hand, the state has asserted its strategic economic ambitions for promoting innovative telecommunications technology through the privatisation of the sector. This policy imperative at a national scale was supported by appropriate industrial level regulations to ensure an appropriate balance between market efficiency and consumer well-being. The subsequent debates associated with health concerns led to a similar national level response through the introduction of new regulatory arrangements. The principal driver, however, at the national scales was that of the economic advantages perceived to be associated with the continuing development and competitiveness of mobile telephony.

On the other hand, different regulatory responses emerged at the local and operational scales as a response to the perceived impacts on land, property and the environment and related effects on local communities. This level of regulation has received relatively less academic and critical attention. Yet, scope to address this dimension was influenced by the constitutional agendas associated with devolution, the mediation through local democratic and community mechanisms, and the introduction of local regulations. Integral to this level of governance was the attempt to self-regulation by the industry to inform communities and local authorities of the development agendas for mobile telephony. This approach suggests the construction of a more nuanced potential for regulation in facilitating technological innovation.

Yet, central to the call for a re-balancing of statutory land use planning ideas and practices was the explicit attention given to strengthening involvement and enhancing participation in decision-making processes in relation to mobile telephony infrastructure. Within this re-working of patterns of engagement was an active interest in improving channels of communication and widening a societal understanding of the role of land use planning. This was nevertheless caught up with the industry concern with minimising the perceived adversarial character of planning decisions and addressing the attendant perceived inefficiencies of the planning system. In addition, however, arguments for bringing telecommunications under full planning controls were driven by a wider political interest in promoting a more participatory form of decision-making that better provides for the necessary legitimacy, resource allocation and measurement of service outcomes (Horner *et al.*, 2006). This cuts to the quick of what constitutes public value and the public interest, and the need at least to debate competing views on the appropriate course of action.

In the specific context of land use planning, it is argued that conventional notions of private and public values have led to a false dichotomy between economic progress and environmental sustainability. Conducted in the intellectual vein of public value in contemporary policy making, a recent study (Bradwell *et al.*, 2007) asserted that the problems of land use planning as a regulatory activity, stem, in part, from a wider failure or inability to integrate planning's ambitions within this broader network of market-state interactions. Specifically, this is held to have 'led to a critical gap between the regulatory and legal framework planners work from, and the wider context they must operate within' (Bradwell *et al.*, 2007, p. 4). It follows then that new expressions of public value require new professional relationships, and different contributions and methods of involvement from the private and public sectors. Such technocratic and democratic imperatives demand a search for new opportunities and spaces for 'conversations' and dialogue around the key issues associated with reconstructing public value in planning. Here, the public value tensions inherent in U-infrastructure are no different.

Competing interpretations of the nature of the public interest in land use planning, and how such an interest might be articulated and safe-guarded, are not new (Campbell and Marshall, 2002; Moroni, 2004). It remains, however, an elusive concept that requires continual re-articulation as societal pressures and expectations change (Grant, 2005). This perspective is further articulated by Marris (1998, p. 10), for example, who observed that: 'Disillusioned with naïve assumptions that planning serves to represent the public interest, and dissatisfied with the ambiguities of planning as advocacy, we are constantly looking for better ways to articulate the relationship between planning and the constituencies and values it should ideally represent'. This would appear to open up a number of rich vistas for research in encouraging relatively deeper understandings of the potential implications and unintended impacts and consequences of emergent technologies and their cumulative impacts; for promoting new interpretations of the public interest, and for revisiting the relationships between the state, market and civil society in relation to ubiquitous infrastructures, whether these relate to mobile or surveillance technologies; and for ensuring that the research agenda is more sensitive to the urban and rural implications of these developments.

CONCLUSION

In the context of this book, mobile telephony provides a clear example of a portable and itinerant communicative medium that traverses place and space, public and private realm, and local and global relations. Yet, such wireless connectivity which is apparently facilitated by an invisible transmission and reception of radio signals, does have certain ethical and private interest strings attached (Lemos, 2010). There is also a public interest dimension as the development of the technology traverses the wider public domain. Indeed, in practice, an individual mobile phone user travelling across the devolved UK and who expects continuous and good reception, may be unaware of the differentiated regulatory frameworks for the ubiquitous supporting infrastructure. Yet, clear differences exist in order to mediate the physical and visible impacts that this type of technology involves

In examining the development and refinement of the legislation in Scotland in order to secure the better regulation of this particular wireless technology and mediate its physical presence as the market extends over geographical space, this chapter has highlighted the regulatory risks that potentially lie behind a market incentivising political agenda and, related to this, the contested nature of the public interest. Further, in identifying the iterative regulatory responses to different sets of public concerns, the chapter also serves to alert policy makers and inventors, for example, to the potential unintended, unexpected and unanticipated effects such technological innovations may create. These may require particular state intervention and specific regulatory responses. The experience in Scotland suggests that the new institutional and regulatory designs required to mediate the impacts on place and space of emergent global networks and their celebrated mobility, necessitated the implementation of appropriate state regulation and an associated democratic debate to control the fixed and visible physical developments at the local scale and to ascertain the public value. Importantly, in this instance the regulations put in place worked alongside the interests of the private sector whilst serving the wider public interest. In effect, the regulations prompted the private operators to modify their behaviours to ensure the sustained roll out of the supporting infrastructure. The evidence suggests that the overall effect has been a private and social gain at large. This highlights the need to enhance the collective understandings of how public value is interpreted and represented with respect to the tangible and intangible constructions of mobile networks, for example, and how these competing values may best be served by the statutory land use planning system. This paradox of contested values to be mediated is particularly relevant where constructions of sustainable development may privilege economic growth to the (perceived) detriment of the relatively more ephemeral or spiritual qualities of place-shaping. Here, in responding to the challenges of new technologies, the planning process has a role in mediating the different international, national, regional, and neighbourhood scales of the built, natural and cultural environments.

REFERENCES

Askew, J., Sheppard, A., Dalton, A., Baker, N., Appleby, T., & Peel, D. (2009). *Research Project for a Review of Mobile Phone Operators Permitted Development Rights*. Cardiff, UK: The Wales Planning Policy Development Programme Cardiff, Welsh Assembly Government.

Baldwin, R., & Cave, M. (1999). *Understanding Regulation: Theory, Strategy, and Practice*. Oxford, UK: Oxford University Press.

Bradwell, P. Johar. I., Maguire, C. & Miner, P. (2007). *Future Planners: Propositions for the Next Age of Planning*. London: Demos.

Campbell, H., & Marshall, R. (2002). Utilitarianism's bad breath? A re-evaluation of the public interest justification for planning. *Planning Theory*, *1*, 163–187. doi:10.1177/147309520200100205

Castells, M. (1996). *The Rise of the Network Society, The Information Age: Economy, Society and Culture* (*Vol. I*). Oxford, UK: Blackwell.

Deloitte & Touche. (2003). *Implementation Review of the Ten Commitments to Best Siting Practice for the UK Mobile Industry, September*. London: Deloitte & Touche.

Deloitte & Touche. (2005). *Implementation of the Ten Commitments to Best Siting Practice for the UK Mobile Industry, January*. London: Deloitte & Touche.

Department of Trade & Industry. (2001, March). *Communications Liberalisation in the UK. Key Elements, History & Benefits*. London: DTI.

Department of Trade and Industry. (1991). *Competition and Choice: Telecommunications Policy for the 1990s. Cm 1461*. London: HMSO.

Gallent, N., Juntti, M., Kidd, S., & Shaw, D. (2008). *Introduction to Rural Planning*. London: Routledge.

Geuting, E. (2007). Proprietary governance and property development: using changes in a property-rights regime as a market based policy tool. *The Town Planning Review*, *78*(1), 23–40. doi:10.3828/tpr.78.1.3

Gow, G. A. (2005). *Privacy and ubiquitous network societies*. ITU Workshop on Ubiquitous Network Societies, April, Geneva, Switzerland.

Graham, S., & Marvin, S. (1995). More than Ducts and Wires: Post-Fordism, Cities and Utility Networks. In Healey, P., Cameron, S., Davoudi, S., Graham, S., & Madani-Pour, A. (Eds.), *Managing Cities: The New Urban Context* (pp. 169–189). London: John Wiley.

Hodson, M., & Marvin, S. (2009b). Urban Ecological Security': A New Urban Paradigm? *International Journal of Urban and Regional Research, 33*(1), 193–215. doi:10.1111/j.1468-2427.2009.00832.x

Hodson, M., & Marvin, S. (2009b). Cities mediating technological transitions: understanding visions, intermediation and consequences. *Technology Analysis and Strategic Management, 21*(4), 515–534. doi:10.1080/09537320902819213

Holden, J. (2006). *Cultural Value and the Crisis of Legitimacy: Why culture needs a democratic mandate*. London: Demos.

Horner, L., Lekhi, R., & Blaug, R. (2006). *Deliberative Democracy and the Role of Public Managers*. London: The Work Foundation.

Independent Expert Group on Mobile Phones [IEGMP]. (2000). *Mobile Phones and Health*. Didcot, UK: Oxon.

Johnston, B. (2001). Mobile firms act on message. *Planning, 1432*, (17 August), 12-13.

Lee, S.-H., Yigitcanlar, T., Han, J.-H., & Leem, Y. T. (2008). Ubiquitous Urban Infrastructure: Infrastructure Planning and Development in Korea. *Innovation: Management. Policy & Practice, 10*(2/3), 282–292.

Lemos, A. (2011). Locative media and surveillance at the boundaries of informational territories. In Firmino, R., Duarte, F., & Ultramari, C. (Eds.), *ICTs for Mobile and Ubiquitous Urban Infrastructures: Surveillance, Locative Media and Global Networks*. Hershey, PA: IGI Global.

Lloyd, M. G., Peel, D., Roberts, P. M., & Riley, J. (2004). *An Evaluation of Revised Planning Controls over Telecommunications Development*. Edinburgh, UK: Scottish Executive Social Research.

Marris, P. (1998). Planning and civil society in the twenty-first century: An introduction. In Douglass, M., & Friedmann, J. (Eds.), *Cities for Citizens: Planning and the Rise of Civil Society in a Global Age* (pp. 9–17). New York: J. Wiley.

Mitchell, W. J. (1995). *City of bits: space, place, and the Infobahn*. Cambridge, MA: MIT Press.

Mitchell, W. J. (1999). *e-topia. 'Urban Life, Jim - But Not as We Know It.'* Cambridge, MA: MIT Press.

Mobile Operators Association. (2004). *Guide to Using Traffic Light Rating Model for Public Consultation*. London: MOA. Retrieved from http://www.mobilemastinfo.com/planning/UK-Guide-to-using-TLM-version-2-1.pdf

Mobile Operators Association. (2006). *Developing Mobile Networks Ten Commitments to best siting practice*. London: MOA. Retrieved from http://www.mobilemastinfo.com/planning/MOA_10_Commitments.pdf

Mobile Operators Association. (2006). *Mobile Phones and Base Stations*. London: MOA.

Mobile Telecommunications and Health Research Programme. (2007). *Report 2007*. London: MTHR Management Committee.

Moroni, S. (2004). Towards a Reconstruction of the Public Interest Criterion. *Planning Theory, 3*, 151–171. doi:10.1177/1473095204044779

Murdoch, J., & Lowe, P. (2003). The preservationist paradox: modernism, environmentalism and the politics of spatial division. *Transactions of the Institute of British Geographers, 28*(3), 318–332. doi:10.1111/1475-5661.00095

Needham, B., & Louw, E. (2006). Institutional Economics and Policies for Changing Land Markets: The Case of Industrial Estates in the Netherlands. *Journal of Property Research, 23*(1), 75–90. doi:10.1080/09599910600748675

Ofcom. (2009). *Communications Market Report 2009*. Retrieved September 13, 2009, from http://www.ofcom.org.uk/research/cm/cmr09/cmr09.pdf

Office of the Deputy Prime Minister. (2002). *Code of Best Practice on Mobile Phone Network Development*. London: ODPM.

Parker, J. (1999). Regulation of privatised public utilities in the UK: performance and governance. *International Journal of Public Sector Management*, *12*(3), 213–235. doi:10.1108/09513559910267387

Pyatt, J. (2002). The plague of the phone masts. *The Sun (Baltimore, Md.)*, *15*(July).

Scottish Executive. (2001a). *National Planning Policy Guideline NPPG19: Radio Telecommunications*. Edinburgh, UK: Scottish Executive.

Scottish Executive. (2001b). *Planning Advice Note: PAN 62 Radio Telecommunications*. Edinburgh, UK: Scottish Executive.

Scottish Executive. (2004). *National Planning Framework for Scotland*. Edinburgh, UK: Scottish Executive.

Scottish Government. (2009). *National Planning Framework 2 for Scotland*. Edinburgh, UK: Scottish Government.

Selznick, P. (1985). Focussing organizational research on regulation. In Noll, R. G. (Ed.), *Regulatory Policy and the Social Sciences*. Berkeley, CA: University of California Press.

Walton, W. (2002a). The changing regulation of mobile-phone mast development in a devolved United Kingdom. *Environment and Planning. B, Planning & Design*, *29*(5), 687–705. doi:10.1068/b12849

Walton, W. (2002b). Out of sight, out of mind? (mobile phone antennae). *Town and Country Planning*, *71*(12), 300–301.

Webster, C. (2005). The New Institutional Economics and the Evolution of Modern Urban Planning. *The Town Planning Review*, *76*(4), 455–484. doi:10.3828/tpr.76.4.5

Webster, C., & Lai, L. W.-C. (2003). *Property Rights, Planning and Markets. Managing Spontaneous Cities*. Cheltenham, UK: Edward Elgar.

Wilsdon, J., Wynne, B., & Stilgoe, J. (2005). *The Public Value of Science (Or how to ensure that science really matters)*. London: Demos.

ADDITIONAL READING

Askew, J. (2006). Mobile phone masts: the role of planners in resolving conflict. *Journal of Planning and Environment Law,* pp. 929-938.

Barnett, J., Timotijevic, L., Vassallo, M., & Shepherd, R. (2008). Precautionary advice about mobile phones: public understandings and intended responses. *Journal of Risk Research*, *11*(4), 525–540. doi:10.1080/13669870802086430

Choudrie, J., Weerakkody, V., & Jones, S. (2005). Realising e-government in the UK: rural and urban challenges. *Journal of Enterprise Information Management*, *18*(5), 568–585. doi:10.1108/17410390510624016

Consulting, O. V. U. M. (2007). *GSM Europe Health and Environment - Building Mobile Networks: European Mobile Operator Responses to Public Concerns*. London: GSM Europe.

Curwen, P. (2009). The licensing and launch of high-speed mobile telecommunications networks in Europe. *Info - The journal of policy, regulation and strategy for telecommunications*, 12(1), pp. 54-66

European Commission. (nd) *Regulatory framework for telecoms in the EU today.* Available: http://ec.europa.eu/information_society/policy/ecomm/current/index_en.htm

Floyd, D., & Mercado, S. (2003). European Briefing. *European Planning Studies*, *11*(5), 585–594. doi:10.1080/0965431030365

Gruber, H. (1999). An investment view of mobile telecommunications in the European Union - Multimarket contact and cross-ownership in the mobile telephone industry. *Telecommunications Policy*, *23*(7), 521–538. doi:10.1016/S0308-5961(99)00042-7

Harno, J. (2009) Techno-economic analysis of beyond 3G mobile technology alternatives. *Info - The journal of policy, regulation and strategy for telecommunications,* 11(3), pp. 45-63

Kwiatkowska, M. (2008). From computers to ubiquitous computing by 2020, in M. Kwiatkowska And Rodden, T. And Sassone, V., (eds). *Royal Society Discussion Meeting,* 17 - 18 March 2008, pp.3665-3668.

Local Government Ombudsman. (2007). *Special Report - Telecommunications masts: problems with 'prior approval' applications*. London: The Commission for Local Administration in England.

Maicas, J. P., Polo, Y., & Francisco, J. (2009). The role of (personal) network effects and switching costs in determining mobile users' choice. *Journal of Information Technology*, *24*(2), 160–171. doi:10.1057/jit.2008.35

Nathaniel Lichfield and Partners. (2003). *Review of Permitted Development Rights for the Office of the Deputy Prime Minister*. London: Office of the Deputy Prime Minister.

Nathaniel Lichfield and Partners. (2003). *Review of Permitted Development Rights. Report to Department of the Environment Planning Service of Northern Ireland*. Belfast: Planning Service.

NRPB. (2005). *Mobile Phones and Health 2004: Report by the Board of NRPB.* Volume 15, Number 5. Didcot, NRPB.

OFCOM. (2006). *Nations and Regions - Statement on the policy implications arising from the Communications Market: Nations and Regions Research*. London: Ofcom.

Park, J., Jorgensen, A., Swanwick, C., & Selman, P. (2008). Relationships between Environmental Values and the Acceptability of Mobile Telecommunications Development in a Protected Area *Landscape Research*, 33(5), pp. 587-604

Park, J., Jorgensen, A., Swanwick, C., & Selman, P. (2008). Perceived landscape impacts of mobile telecommunications development in the Peak District National Park, England. *Journal of Environmental Planning and Management*, *51*(5), 679–699. doi:10.1080/09640560802218529

Patricelli, F., Beakley, J., Carnevale, A., Tarabochia, M., & von Lubitz, T. (2009). Disaster management and mitigation: the telecommunications infrastructure. *Disasters*, *33*(1), 23–37. doi:10.1111/j.1467-7717.2008.01060.x

Scottish Executive. (2000). *Transport and the Environment Committee Third Report (2000) Report on inquiry into the proposals to introduce new planning procedures for telecommunications developments - interim response by the Scottish Executive*. Edinburgh: Scottish Executive.

The University of Reading and Arup. (2006). *Review of the Code of Best Practice on Mobile Phone Network Development: Final Report*. London: Office of the Deputy Prime Minister.

Troshani, I., & Hill, S. (2009). Linking stakeholder salience with mobile services diffusion. *International Journal of Mobile Communications*, *7*(3), 269–289. doi:10.1504/IJMC.2009.023672

Tsai, Wen-Hsien., Lo, Hsueh-Wei. and Chou, Wen-Chin. (2009). Evaluation of mobile services for the future of 3G operators. *International Journal of Mobile Communications*, *7*(4), 470–493. doi:10.1504/IJMC.2009.023695

Chapter 10
Advances of the Location Based Context-Aware Mobile Services in the Transport Sector

Georgios Patris
National Technical University of Athens, Greece

Vassilios Vescoukis
National Technical University of Athens, Greece

Maria Giaoutzi
National Technical University of Athens, Greece

ABSTRACT

The present chapter focuses on the Location Based Context-aware Mobile Services (LBCAMS) in the context of the most recent technological advances in Decision Support Systems for the transport sector. The chapter demonstrates the rationale for the introduction of the Location Based Context-aware Mobile Services and the state of the art of the location-based services in the field of transport. In addition, a typology of market orientations is developed, including the demand side of context-ware mobile services in the field of transport. The chapter also introduces the theoretical outline of a five-layer model, studying the Location Based Context-aware Mobile Services, in a Decision Support System context, for applications in the transport sector. In order to advance understanding, some indicative applications are presented, on road safety and urban parking management and finally conclusions are drawn and future research orientations are explored.

INTRODUCTION

As computing becomes increasingly mobile today, applications and services need to be able to adapt to dynamic environments. Within a suitable framework, context-aware mobile services constitute a market-oriented technological development that could potentially meet end-user needs.

In this framework a *"context"* can be defined as any set of information and/or status of elements, obtained either explicitly or implicitly, that can be used to characterise a certain aspect of an *entity* or an *event* involved in a specific application or network service. The term "*entity*" can be

DOI: 10.4018/978-1-60960-051-8.ch010

defined as a person, a place, or an object that is considered relevant to the interaction between a user and an application, including user and application themselves. Similarly, the term "*event*" is denoted as any happening produced by or related to an application, which takes place under certain assumptions. A context-aware service is one that uses such a context for the provision of value to its user.

Context-aware services automatically adapt to the environment of a user, for instance to the location, time, or physical condition of a person (e.g. heart rhythm and blood pressure). The social context of the users is an important determinant in the creation of the information requirements and well being of people. An essential function of these services is the Context-aware computing, which deals with the ability of computer systems to take advantage of information in a dynamic environment in order to provide added-value services in a "best-fit" way for each particular user and time, or to execute more complex tasks. Context-awareness has received attention, in recent years, with the development of mobile computing and the appearance of a new generation of mobile devices as well as in application domains such as e-learning where the term "adaptive" is more relevant. With most cars of the future likely to be equipped with multiple embedded computing platforms, we shall witness the development of a variety of context-aware mobile services and applications with significant commercial potential.

In recent years, vehicle manufacturers have been developing advanced technologies to improve the standards of driving, to make driving easier, safer, less stressful and more comfortable. Many of these technologies are also applied to facilitate public and freight transport in order to increase the efficiency of transport networks and maximise their utilisation. These technologies, when properly applied, can potentially make the transport system more sophisticated, safer, more efficient and with less environmental impacts. In a time when major infrastructure investments are reaching their limits, the use of technology and its applications can be seen as a viable solution to make the mobility of people and goods more efficient for all transport modes.

Various terms are used to describe, nowadays, existing technologies, services, systems and functions such as (Abele, 2005):

- **ITS** (Intelligent Transport Systems and Services),
- **ADAS** (Advanced Driver Assistance Systems),
- **AVG** (Automated Vehicle Guidance),
- **AVCSS** (Advanced Vehicle Control and Systems),
- **IVSS** (Intelligent Vehicle Safety Systems)

In a different way of clustering, these systems could be presented as follows:

- Vehicle-based systems
- Infrastructure-based systems (primarily roadside sensors which collect information along with roadside equipment which issues warnings and advice)
- Cooperative systems (utilise both infrastructure-based and vehicle-based systems with communication links between them).

The above-mentioned transport and vehicle oriented systems, can contribute to the minimisation of the negative effects of transport on society, mainly road traffic accidents, congestion and pollution. According to the European Commission (EC, 2006) there are around 300 million drivers in the EU Member States, wishing to have had easier driving with less trouble, less delay, and lower probability for accidents. Within the spectrum of transport problems, safety is the aspect with the most serious impacts on citizens' daily lives, with a high impact on most socio-economic indicators. Despite the continuous efforts of the past years there are still over 40.000 fatalities on the Euro 27 roads every year, with 1.4 million accidents at a cost around 200 billion €/year representing 2% of the EU GDP (EC, 2006). Concerning the causes of accidents, human error is involved in almost 93% of accidents and in almost three-quarters of the cases, the human mistake is solely to blame. In addition, traffic congestion has an important impact on the transport system, the economy and the environment. In the EU, congestion costs amount up to 50 billion € per year or 0.5% of the Community GDP, and by 2010 this figure could go up to 1% of EU GDP. The environment is also heavily influenced by road transport. Around 50% of all road-related emissions are concentrated in urban areas. It is estimated that up to 30% of urban traffic is due to the so-called "search traffic", which is the traffic generated when searching for parking spaces (Ramirez, 2003). Among the many applications around today, context-aware systems may provide the most efficient mobile solutions for parking space management (Caliskan, 2006) that contribute towards sustainable urban mobility, and clean urban transport

These intelligent context-aware systems assist the driver and prevent or avoid accidents. They also provide drivers with real time information about the road network thus avoiding congestion, and they optimise a journey or the overall automobile performance by improving overall energy efficiency. These systems require the interaction between the driver, the vehicle and the road conditions, in an integrated approach where the autonomous on-board systems are complemented by vehicle-to-vehicle and vehicle-to-infrastructure co-operative technologies and improved traffic network management.

The present paper focus is on the Location Based Context-aware Mobile Services (LBCAMS) placed in the context of a framework benefiting from the introduction of most recent technological advances in Decision Support Systems (DSS) for the transport sector. More precisely, the paper will elaborate on a 5-layer model as a reference for explaining and categorising the context-aware services. The paper firstly presents the state of the art of the location-based services in the field of transport, as well as a typology of market orientations, exploring the demand side of context ware mobile services in transport. Then the paper focuses on the theoretical outline of a five layer model. This will be used as a reference model for studying the LBCAMS as part of the DSS in applications in the Transport sector. Indicative applications are presented, on road safety and urban parking management. These will focus on the potential offered by and the barriers involved in the advances discussed above. An analysis is then developed of the policy challenges that are faced when pursuing the goal of supporting such applications on a larger scale.

Finally conclusions are drawn and future research orientations are explored.

STATE OF THE ART OF LOCATION-BASED SERVICES IN TRANSPORT

Modern automobiles provide new intelligent solutions, dealing with the main negative effects of transport and traffic, by developing applications that increase road safety, overall efficiency of the transport systems and efficiency in the use of fuel (Chang, 2009). Such applications, in mobile distributed environments, often need to dynamically obtain information that is relevant to their current location. The transport sector is a suitable environment for such technologies, with a great variety of applications available and promising market potential. Due to the emerging nature of this market, new services and applications are evolving at a constant rate. Most of these applications can be grouped into the following categories (Lacy, 2001):

- Road safety (and other emergency services)
- Tracking (including traffic/ parking management)
- Navigation

Road Safety

A number of applications have been developed aimed at reducing the road accident rates (Yang, 2004). These applications either assist the driver when performing difficult manoeuvres or warn the driver for possible danger situations. A demonstrating example with purely location context, concerns the EU initiative for the development of "Emergency Call" (e-Call). In cases where a vehicle is involved in an accident, an Emergency Call, or e-Call can be initiated automatically, and accurate vehicle location and additional safety-related information can be passed to the Public Service Answering Point. Such information cuts down dramatically the emergency response time, saves lives and reduces the consequences of serious injuries.

Tracking

Wireless location technology provides a cost effective solution for tracking valuable assets. Applications include business uses such as tracking of a firm's fleet, such as taxis, busses or trucking vehicles (Velaga, 2009). Wireless tracking could also be used to detect traffic congestion. These applications are briefly described below.

Fleet Management

Fleet management services enable the tracking of the location and status of mobile assets. Location and status information is received via existing wireless infrastructure and compiled in a central location to be matched to a GIS database. This information is then used centrally but also through remote access by authorized parties.

Fleet Management helps to manage a fleet of vehicles by gaining control of travel records and time. These advanced systems could also help to manage fuel consumption, speed, load balancing and vehicle positioning. Once data collection of the fleet activity is automated and accurate, depicting it in comprehensive reports is straightforward, enabling effective management and business efficiency in a highly competitive industry situation like at present.

Traffic Monitoring

Traffic Congestion can be detected by wireless location technologies using a system that detects many mobile devices clustered in a row (Gallagher, 2006). The success of this system relies on a sufficient penetration of location-enabled wireless devices among vehicle and/or drivers. Traffic monitoring using the location of cellular devices is significantly cheaper than installing and maintaining fixed monitoring systems along roads, and enables a broader network of roads to be monitored.

Navigation

By combining the knowledge of current location, desired location and map or guidance data, navigation is made possible for the traveller. Current location would be determined automatically by the system and desired location would be entered by either plain text or a voice activated system. The route would then be determined in conjunction with the base map data and possibly, the route optimization software that takes into account current available traffic data. TMC is a typical example of such a system. The output could be presented in the form of a symbol based map on a screen (PDA or enlarged mobile handset screens highly preferred), plain text or verbally.

In all cases, the rationale for the provision of services is based on the identification of the user's exact location by use of various techniques. The most popular is currently the use of the US Global Positioning System (GPS) (Boertien, 2002). The development of an EU equivalent system (Galileo) is expected to improve the services provided as more accurate information on location becomes available for civilian use.

When the information on space location is combined with various Geographical Information Systems' techniques, such as digital maps and other geographical information, a number of value-added services can be provided, to the benefit of the individual user and the transport network.

An emerging trend is the integration of in-vehicle computer systems with off-vehicle communications capabilities (Fitzgibbons 2004). These systems offer the potential of much lower dependence on government maintained IT (Information Technology) infrastructure, by exploiting equipment that will be continually upgraded and maintained as new vehicles are purchased and existing vehicles are upgraded. In-vehicle systems allow coverage to extend beyond areas where roadside equipment has been installed. In-vehicle sensors offer the potential for much more detailed, accurate information (e.g., vehicle emissions) than would otherwise be possible, enabling thus new ways to improve and optimize the transportation system. In-vehicle computing systems facilitate the customization of information services to the needs and characteristics of individual travellers. For example, driver assistance and safety applications exploit upstream traffic information to help users avoid congestion or use information concerning nearby vehicles to provide early warning of hazards.

A developing field, at present is inter-vehicle communication. Inter-vehicle communication (IVC) and vehicle to infrastructure communication are amongst the most promising applications of mobile ad hoc networks (Biswas, 2006; Palazzi, 2009). Many applications are being discussed in this context, but road traffic related messaging and local danger warning remain among the most prominent (Aijaz, 2005). Such developments assume that all (or at least a minimum number of) participating vehicles are equipped with on-board computing and wireless communications, a GPS device enabling the vehicle to track its spatial-temporal trajectory, a pre-stored digital map, and other sensors reporting crashes, engine statistics, etc. Under these circumstances vehicles could communicate directly with each other on a peer-to-peer basis, and data could be partially evaluated while moving from vehicle to vehicle.

Such systems would provide valuable services to end users, bringing together technologies ranging from one-way communication applications and basic location-based services, to interactive sophisticated routing, optimisation and advanced communications such as in-vehicle internet access. The range of solutions and applications offered is so broad, that the need for a reference framework for classifying such services becomes quite an imperative, as is the case of the OSI (Open Systems Interconnection) reference model for digital networks that will be discussed below.

A REFERENCE MODEL

The focus of this part of the chapter is on the theoretical outline of a five layer model. This will be presented as a reference model for studying the LBCAMS in applications in the Transport sector.

The evolution of the information and telecommunication technologies has created a variety of services influencing the every day life and has affected the traditional urban environment (Giaoutzi & Vescoukis, 2006). The application of digital technology has evolved in mobile contexts, taking advantage of the rapid development of telecommunication networks that aim to provide users with high quality services in real time conditions. The relevant available services are sometimes difficult to be adopted by users, especially due to their rapid development and certain fuzziness as to the technical context they evolve. In order to facilitate the understanding of the likely impacts of such services and their applications on spatial structures a layered reference model has been introduced based on previous work by Giaoutzi and Vescoukis (2006) and Shiode (2000).

Figure 1. The OSI reference model for digital network communications

OSI Layer 7: **application**
OSI Layer 6: **presentation**
OSI Layer 5: **session**
OSI Layer 4: **transport**
OSI Layer 3: **network**
OSI Layer 2: **data link**
OSI Layer 1: **physical**

Such a 5-layer Context-Aware Services Reference Framework (CAS-RF), that can be used as a reference for the representation of the interactions between the urban environment and the digital services, has been proposed (Giaoutzi & Vescoukis (2008) (see Figure 2). According to this framework, each of the five layers represents a step in the evolutionary process from the physical world to the cyber-environment. Context-aware applications can be classified in any of the 5 layers of CAS-RF, in a comprehensive and implementation-independent way. This framework can be better understood when compared to a similar approach, which has been followed by the technical community to classify digital communication network services and applications; the outcome of this effort was the 7-layer Open System Interconnection (OSI) reference model introduced by the International Standards Organization (ISO), shown in Figure 1.

Layer 1 (physical) in the OSI model, consists of the physical network, that is, the media on which data is actually transferred in any form (electrical signal, optical, radio wave, etc). It is responsible for activating, maintaining and deactivating the physical link between communicating parties. **Layer 2** (data link) provides transparent network services to the Network layer (layer 3). It is responsible for reassembling bits, taken of the wire by the Physical layer, to frames and for

Figure 2. The CAS-RF 5-layer framework

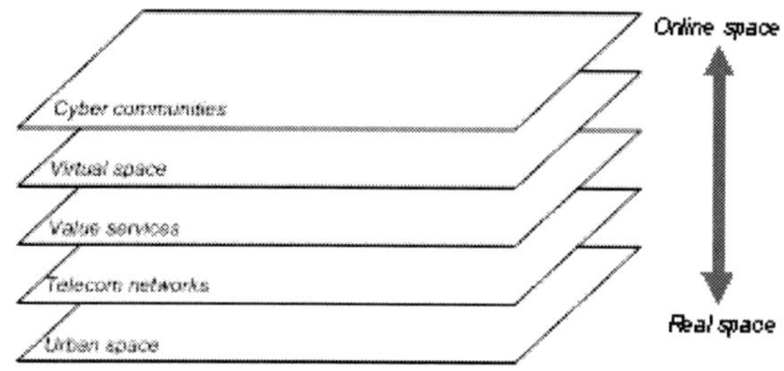

error correction. **Layer 3** (network) converts the segments from the Transport layer (layer 4) into packets (or datagrams) and is responsible for path determination routing and the delivery of packets across networks, without recognizing any relationship between those individual packets. **Layer 4** (transport) converts the data received from the upper layers into segments and prepares them for transport; this layer is responsible for end-to-end delivery of entire messages. **Layer 5** (session) establishes, maintains, and terminates end-to-end connections (sessions) between two applications on two network nodes. It controls the dialogue between the source and destination node. **Layer 6** (presentation) 'represents' the data in a particular format to the Application layer. It defines encryption, compression, conversion and other coding functions. Finally, **layer 7** (application) provides network services directly to the user's application such as a web browser or email client. This layer is said to be "closest to the user".

As the OSI model serves as a reference for communications network equipment, services and applications, so can the CAS-RF model be used as a reference for LBCAMS.

Returning to the CAS-RF reference model, the **first layer** refers to the physical environment of the urban space, which is the real-world location. There is no correspondent layer in the OSI 7-layer reference model, since the orientation the OSI model is network-oriented. The **second layer** refers to the tangible infrastructure and basic service of the modern telecommunication

Figure 3. Relation of the OSI reference model to the CAS-RF reference framework

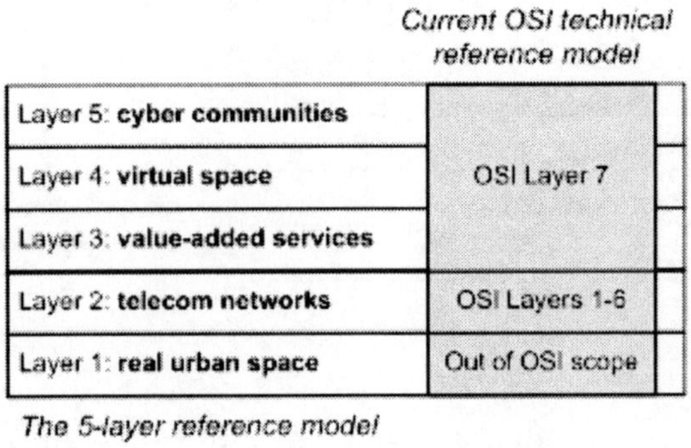

networks used for data, voice and media delivery. With reference to OSI, this corresponds to layers 1-6 of the OSI reference model. The **third layer** of CAS-RF is the layer of the "*value added services*" which are offered using services from the "*telecom networks*" layer. End-user services such as web application services, data services, content services, as well as peer-to-peer communication services are some examples of services on this layer. The **fourth layer** is the layer of the virtual space. The services provided on this layer make use of the value added services of the previous layer to create "*non-real-space entities*", such as a virtual classroom, a special interest discussion service and more. Many similar virtual space services form the basis for the creation of the "*cyber communities*" in the **fifth layer**. Putting together virtual classrooms and other services in order to create integrated, space-independent educational structures is a typical example. A more "trendy" case is social networking where virtual communities co-exist with value-added services by third parties, as is the case with Facebook, linked-in, and many other services.

In regard to the OSI model, layers 3 to 5 of CAS-RF correspond to layer 7 of the OSI model (figure 1). It is clear that the representation of physical space, as well as a more refined representation of high-level user services, which is exactly the motivation for introducing the CAS-RF, falls out of the scope of the OSI reference model. Although the motivation for the definition of both models is very different, figure 3 shows a rough correspondence between the OSI reference model and the 5-layer CAS-RF model.

Based on the reference framework described above, the context-aware services can be classified in the "*value-added services*" layer and above, namely in layers 3, 4 and 5. Taking advantage of the modern telecommunication services, the context-aware mobile services can combine information gathered from the surrounding environment and provide important (value-added) assistance to the driver in order to improve the road safety of his/her vehicle, to avoid congested routes, to easily locate available parking places and to improve the overall driving performance.

Some of the value added services and applications of context-aware mobile services for vehicles are described in the following section.

TRANSPORT APPLICATIONS: THE VEHICLE AS A CONTEXT-AWARE SYSTEM

The present section will present some indicative applications for road safety and urban parking management. The focus will be on the potential offered and the barriers faced by the advances discussed in the above context. To this extent an analysis of the policy challenges is developed, focusing on the goal of supporting these applications on a broader scale.

The Context

Vehicles continue to gain intelligence (Biswas, 2006). Advanced driver assistance systems are gradually acquiring new functions, while extended use of electronics offers the benefit of ultra fast reactions and the unwavering alertness of sensors. Combined with ever increasing intelligence and speed of data processing, this opens up the possibility of actively supporting the driver and (in the future) even to take over certain driver functions in order to enhance safety. Safety technologies already available include (Miles, 2006) traction control, adaptive cruise control, intelligent speed adaptation, collision warning and avoidance systems, driver drowsiness detectors, night and bad weather visions systems and truck roll-over warning systems. The development of such systems, assisting the driver, addresses the fact that driving is a complex human function influenced by a wide range of factors in space and time. Factors include goals, distraction, errors, expectancies, workload, attention, traffic, vehicle safety features, fatigue, memory, skills, training and experience. In order to better understand these related factors, these can be categorised according to their requirements for communication and information exchange as those related to intra-vehicle functions and those related to vehicle-to-vehicle and vehicle-to-infrastructure functions (Gallagher, 2006).

The development of context-aware services relies on the efficient and timely dissemination of the information acquired. Without this information sharing, context has little or no power to influence decision-making in vehicle driving. In this respect, the main difference between the categories referred to above is the range of dissemination of any given information and consequently the number of parties involved. In this context the intra-vehicle communication involves the specific vehicle and its driver, while the vehicle-to-vehicle and vehicle-to-infrastructure communication is more complicated and involves other vehicles and drivers as well as infrastructure elements.

Context-aware systems aim to improve driving behaviour. However, the inclusion of a context-aware system in a complex system such as driving does not warrant safe behaviour regardless of how well designed the context-aware system is. This is mainly due to the fact that the emerging property of a complex system such as the driver behaviour cannot be easily predicted.

In the following, these factors will be examined, in order to determine how a context-aware system can best use them to its advantage.

Factors Related to Intra-Vehicle Functions

Vehicles are complicated systems and their operation includes a great number and variety of functions and parameters, which are difficult to be controlled by the driver while driving. In order to assist the driver in this complicated task, various services have been developed. Among others, an area for such applications is the monitoring of the car's "health". While this gives rudimentary information, it can be expanded to make the system software itself aware of the car's components and their individual health. Models can be used to predict how long a component is still safe to use, after which the likelihood of a failure increases. The driver can be informed so that he/she may take the necessary actions previous to any mechanic failure. In this way road safety is enhanced, while vehicle maintenance costs can be reduced. Other applications in this field may include the state of the driver him/herself. Special sensors can detect for example if the driver is intoxicated (by alcohol) or too tired to drive and even decline to start the vehicle's engine. Such functions require of course a complex monitoring system.

Factors Related to Vehicle-to-Vehicle and Vehicle-to-Infrastructure Functions

While the previous category of services provides an important aid to efficient driving, it has limited capabilities due to the fact that is confined to factors inside the vehicle, isolated from useful or even crucial information related to the road network, on which the vehicle is moving. The development of telecommunications especially in the field of wireless networks has provided significant potential for services and applications that can assist the driver not only in the operation of the vehicle but also in the efficient use of the whole infrastructure (Aijaz, 2005). To this extend there are various options for mobile communication such as the GSM (Global System for Mobile communications) and the GPRS (General Packet Radio Service) standards. Alternatively (or complementarily) roadside transmitters can communicate over short distances by microwave or infrared with vehicles fitted with suitable on-board equipment, while coded messages can be sent via the RDS TMC (Radio Data System Traffic Message Channel) to an in-vehicle radio. A more expensive option is Satellite Communications, which offer additional services such as in-vehicle mobile telephony and internet access. All categories of Location Based Services (i.e. road safety, tracking, navigation) mentioned earlier can find remarkable applications when enhanced with real-time exchange information systems.

More specifically:

Navigation applications are among the most popular LBS. With the help of digital maps and on-line information services, the user can find his/her route to the desired destination or even pose questions such as "which is the shortest way to ...?" or "where is the nearest ...?". Such interactive services can be realised via SMS and mobile phones, PDAs or other similar devices. Special applications have been developed for tourists (tourist guidance systems) including useful information for this purpose.

Another application in this category concerns intelligent speed adaptation, which aims to increase road safety levels by urging drivers to drive according to speed limits. Vehicles equipped with intelligent speed adaptation (ISA) warn or prevent the driver from exceeding the local speed limit. Information on speed limits is obtained either by comparing vehicle location to an in-vehicle speed limits database or by transmission of speed limits to the vehicle by roadside beacons. It is anticipated that such systems will genuinely influence driver behaviour to the benefit of road safety.

Traffic management is another area where a context-aware system can really make a difference. In addition to the navigational assistance which is available today, accurate real-time information about traffic conditions ahead on the road can be presented to the driver via the windshield. Such information can include detours due to accidents or roadworks, the distance to the nearest cars, and whether or not there is oncoming traffic (is it safe to overtake or not?). Probably the easiest way this could be communicated in real time to the software is an inter-vehicle communication link. This allows vehicles to communicate important information to each other, so that a driver may for example "see" around a corner which he/she has never seen before. The use of this function would require special driver training. In addition, the behaviour of other cars can be analyzed so that those posing a danger to safety (through erratic or drunk driving) can be marked as such. Also, the inter-car communication network allows the announcement of approaching priority vehicles such as police and ambulance vehicles, so that drivers are easily able to get out of their way.

Parking is also an area that can be significantly assisted by the use of a context-aware system. Modern urban areas suffer from severe problems due to vehicle traffic congestion which are intensified by drivers searching for an open parking space in the city centres; this contributes to about 30% to the congestion during peak hours. A context-aware system can assist the drivers finding a parking space both on the roadside and in car-parks, in order to reduce: average travel time, atmospheric pollution, wasted energy consumption and stress experienced by drivers. The service can combine sensors, a central control station and a communication network, guiding drivers to the nearest available parking place.

In the end, LBCAMS can be used both as a helpful tool for the driver when operating his/her vehicle without any information exchange with other vehicles or sources and as a tool for infor-

Figure 4. The classification of a simple vehicle routing service using the CAS-RF reference model

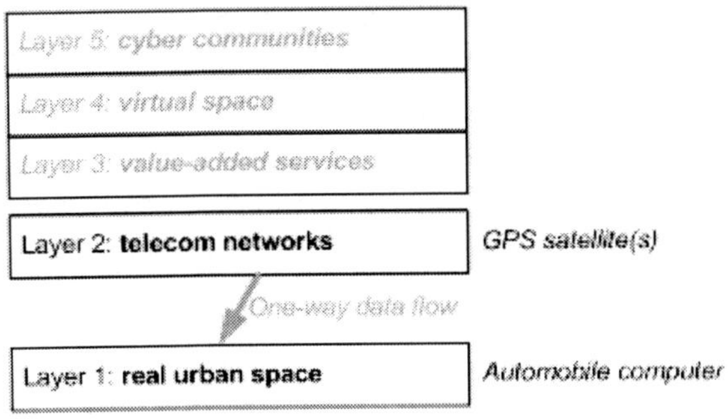

Figure 5. A more sophisticated (and expensive) version of the vehicle routing service

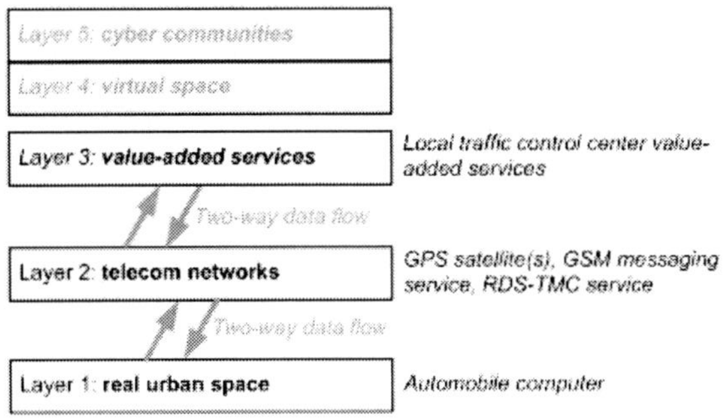

mation management and data exchange aimed at improving the overall system performance.

Referring to the CAS-RF Model

In the following, an example of using the 5-layer CAS-RF model for classifying two variants of in-vehicle navigation will be given, in order to show how the concept works. Indeed, the classification mechanism offered by CAS-RF for services such as the one mentioned below is useful in at least two reasons: first to support analysis of current practice and applications. Second, to support the development of the context-aware services as a new open market with heavy user involvement.

The first variant of the routing service is limited by the available communication services: a GPS system is installed in the vehicle and the driver may use its interface to enter the required destination, assuming that the current vehicle position is the starting point. The software embedded into the vehicle will implement some routing algorithms and provide guidance to the driver to follow a route leading to the destination. In this variant, no two-way communication or any service such as RDS-TMC is available. The above is a typical, low-cost and low added-value, yet very useful service, which is available even in low-cost car models. This service can be classified using the CAS-RF model as shown in figure 4. As discussed earlier, the car navigation computer is responsible for providing the navigation service, using only the GPS satellite data.

The second variant of this example is an improved version of the simple routing service, in which the current traffic conditions, as well as some routing guidelines provided by a local traffic control center, are also taken into consideration. In this case, the routing guidelines are value-added services offered by a local application server and as such, they are classified in layer 3 of CAS-RF. Information flows both ways, assuming that the vehicle needs to state its position and destination to the local traffic control center in order to be better guided. This involves the use of communication services such as GSM messaging and RDS-TMC. The difference from the simplified version of the routing service discussed earlier, is that in the simple version all computation takes place into the vehicle computer while, in the latter case, a local application server offers useful routing information and a part or even all of the routing service to the vehicle computer. This example is shown in Figure 5.

This example could be taken even further, assuming that drivers have a means to interact with the routing service host, so drivers can give their own opinions regarding routing in a particular area at a certain time. For example, drivers could create a virtual space by stating, for example, that SUVs (Sport-Utility Vehicles) can follow route X from point A to point B, while classic cars cannot, due to the poor road conditions, and should better follow route Y. This would be classified using layer 4 of the CAS-RF framework, because user-involvement would take place in a virtual space. It would, however, be difficult, though not impossible, for such applications to reach the level of a cyber-community, in layer 5 of the CAS-RF framework. This, for example, could be the case when vehicle drivers on a specific route at a given time are able to exchange information in a way that a cyber-community requests.

The description above reveals the potential of LBCAMS to offer services of different value-added levels, according to user needs. This could be extremely useful for commercial applications and it can be adequately understood via a suitable reference model, which is necessary for the classification of the various services.

CHALLENGES FACED

The type of applications and services described above are not always easy to perform in real conditions. The primary issue that must be dealt with in the construction of this type of system is the complexity of manufacturing a highly intricate system with heavy safety, real-time and fail-safe requirements. Coping with this will undoubtedly require the development of new software and hardware engineering techniques, which must be thoroughly tested and trusted to take such a central role in the operation of a vehicle. Problems can be faced regarding the accuracy of the sensors used, especially in applications requiring the analysis of the driver behaviour or some environmental conditions. Another difficult aspect is the prediction of other drivers' or pedestrians' behaviour.

There are also legal issues surrounding a safety system possibly taking autonomous actions, since it will be difficult to allocate responsibility in the case that the system fails to properly warn the driver, or worse, is the cause of an accident and loss of life. Moreover the sharing of personal driving-related information such as driving behaviour, origin and direction of travel and so on between cars creates privacy issues. Consumers may not be willing to share such information with everyone else, which requires some form of control over its distribution. This constitutes a general "*threat*" to private life and anonymity (Lemos, 2010).

Another important aspect is financing. The cost for the deployment of such systems at a large scale is a factor that policy makers have to take into account. Quantifying the monetary value of reduced congestion, accident rates, or pollution, or of social benefits such as reduced traveller stress or improved general health, presents a challenge. Existing schemes can at best provide a rough guide to the impact of similar systems in different locations. Moreover, since many applications rely on the existence of physical or virtual infrastructure which is common to a number of applications (such as roadside traffic monitoring or communication equipment, digital maps of road networks, or a database of traffic information), quantifying the infrastructure costs for individual applications is difficult. Hence evaluation of the costs and benefits of any given project can be challenging. Decision-makers may be reluctant to deploy LBCAMS systems without quantitative data on costs and benefits. One of the challenges for Government in LBCAMS deployment is how and whether it facilitates development of the supporting infrastructure. Revenues from a single LBCAMS application will often be insufficient to justify infrastructure investment. Moreover, private sector operators may be concerned that public sector developments could make their services redundant. For example, publicly available sources of traffic information already compete with private commercial applications. On the other hand much LBCAMS infrastructure development may depend on public-private ventures. Public-private arrangements inevitably raise complex questions of responsibility for maintenance, repair and upgrading of the system, revenue sharing arrangements, reliability and ownership of the system, use of data, and liability in the event of failure. Resolving these questions may prove more difficult than the technical aspects of any given project.

Moreover, the current lack of common standards for many aspects of LBCAMS may also discourage investors. Developments in LBCAMS are rapid and often technology driven. As a result many systems have evolved ahead of current standards. With the potential introduction of a multitude of LBCAMS systems there is a need to try to integrate these services and provide common means of payment, communication, vehicle location and information delivery. Without these, public transport users could be put off LBCAMS' applications by the need to learn to use several new systems. Operators of bus or truck fleets could require different in-vehicle equipment to interact with charging or vehicle location systems in different areas. For example, the truck-charging schemes currently under development in a number of EU countries use a variety of different technological approaches. A lack of common standards and system interoperability could act as a barrier to private investment in LBCAMS, and to commercial and public sector use of such systems. A particular challenge in this area may be the interoperability of in-vehicle systems, typically designed by vehicle manufacturers to rapid timetables, with road infrastructure, typically provided by public authorities to longer timescales. For example, in-vehicle dynamic route guidance systems may currently receive up-to-date traffic information from a private sector operator but might be unable to take advantage of any future publicly available in-vehicle traffic information service. Although some in the industry have argued that Government-imposed standards would provide a rapid stimulus to industry, others believe that industry's self regulation would be more effective.

CONCLUSION

Despite its rapid development in recent years, road transport is facing significant problems especially in relation to road safety and capacity issues. In a time of limited resources for infrastructure investment, information systems and context-aware services in particular, can provide ways for a more efficient use and management of existing transport facilities.

Dynamic developments in the field of ITS and LBCAMS offers new possibilities and better exploitation of technology, where communication networks have a vital role. The way forward seems to include in-vehicle devices capable of communicating with one another as well as with certain infrastructure components. In this way, aspects like enhanced road safety and traffic monitoring are expected to overcome many of today's difficulties and limitations.

LBCAMS can be developed at various levels of interaction between the user and the system's components, according to individual needs and the desired level of service. The categorisation of LBCAMS in the context of a specific framework can contribute to the better understanding of their role in the urban-cyber environment and make their development potential more comprehensive.

There is already a significant number of context-aware applications that can improve driving especially in the field of road safety, traffic and parking management. These applications can provide viable solutions to confront the daily traffic problems.

Nevertheless, there are still technical and institutional issues that need to be tackled for a reliable development of those applications to take place. Policy makers should make clear decisions on the legal, institutional and financing context in which LBCAMS will be developed and implemented in the future. There are still many issues pending, with challenges for more research and better understanding.

REFERENCES

Abele, J. et al. (2005). *Exploratory study on the potential socio-economic impact of the introduction of intelligent safety systems in road vehicles.* SEiSS Final Report, eSafety Forum.

Aijaz, A., Bochow, B., Dotze, F., Festag, A., Gerlach, M., Kroh, R., & Leinmuller, T. (2005). Attacks on Inter Vehicle Communication Systems - an Analysis. In *Proceedings of the 3rd International Workshop on Intelligent Transportation (WIT 2006).*

Biswas, S., Tatchikou, R., & Dion, F. (2006). Vehicle-to-vehicle wireless communication protocols for enhancing highway traffic safety. *IEEE Communications Magazine, 44*(1), 74–82. doi:10.1109/MCOM.2006.1580935

Boertien, N. (2002). Location based services: services and technologies, *Virtuele Haven report series T3.D9, Telematica Instituut.* Retrieved March 5, 2006, from https://doc.telin.nl/dscgi/ds.py/Get/File-19920

Caliskan, M., Graupner, D., & Mauve, M. (2006). Decentralized discovery of free parking places. In *VANET - Proceedings of the Third ACM International Workshop on Vehicular Ad Hoc Networks*, (pp. 30-39).

Chang, B. R., Tsai, H. F., & Young, C.-P. (2009). (Article in Press). Intelligent data fusion system for predicting vehicle collision warning using vision/GPS sensing. *Expert Systems with Applications.*

European Commission. (2006). *Communication from the Commission to the Council, the European Parliament, the European Economic and Social committee and the Committee of the Regions On the Intelligent Car Initiative - "Raising Awareness of ICT for Smarter, Safer and Cleaner Vehicles" COM/2006/0059final.* Retrieved July 17, 2006, from http://eur-lex.europa.eu/LexUriServ/LexUriServ.do?uri=COM:2006:0059:FIN:EN:HTML

Fitzgibbons, B., Fujimoto, R., Guensler, R., Hunter, M., Park, A., & Wu, H. (2004). Simulation-Based Operations Planning For Regional Transportation Systems. In *Proceedings of the 5th Annual Nat. Conf. on Digital Government Research: New Challenges and Opportunities*, Seattle.

Gallagher, B., Akatsuka, H. & Suzuki, H. (2006). Wireless communications for vehicle safety: Radio link performance & wireless connectivity methods. *IEEE Vehicular Technology Magazine, 1*(4), 4-16+24.

Giaoutzi, M., & Vescoukis, V. (2006). The Context of IST Impacts on Urban Policy-Making: the Case of Integrated Mobile Spatial Information Systems. In Giaoutzi, M., & Nijkamp, P. (Eds.), *Transport and Information Strategies for Emerging European Networks.* London: Ashgate.

Giaoutzi, M., & Vescoukis, V. (2008). Integrated Mobile Spatial Information Systems and Urban Services. In In Giaoutzi, M., & Nijkamp, P. (Eds.), *Network Strategies in Europe, Developing the Future for Transport and ICT.* London: Ashgate.

Lacy, I., Quarles, A., Stokes, T., & Tabuchi, L. (2001). *Location, Location, Location. Will Location – Based Services be the Next Golden Child? Technical report.* Kellogg Tech Venture.

Lemos, A. (2010). Locative media and surveillance at the boundaries of informational territories. In Firmino, R., Duarte, F., & Ultramari, C. (Eds.), *ICTs for Mobile and Ubiquitous Urban Infrastructures: Surveillance, Locative Media and Global Networks.* Hershey, PA: IGI Global.

Miles, J. C., & Walker, A. J. (2006). The Potential Application of Artificial Intelligence in Transport. *IEE Proceedings Intelligent Transport Systems, 153*(3), 183–198. doi:10.1049/ip-its:20060014

Palazzi, C. E., Ferretti, S., & Roccetti, M. (2009). Communities on the road: Fast triggering of interactive multimedia services. *Multimedia Tools and Applications, 44*(2), 229–247. doi:10.1007/s11042-009-0292-x

Ramirez, C. (2003). *E-Parking: User friendly e-commerce to optimise parking space*. Paper presented at 10th World Congress and Exhibition on Intelligent Transport Systems and Services, Madrid.

Shiode, N. (2000). Urban planning, information technology, and Cyberspace. *Journal of Urban Technology*, *7*(2), 105–126. doi:10.1080/713684111

Velaga, N. R., Quddus, M. A., & Bristow, A. L. (2009). Developing an enhanced weight-based topological map-matching algorithm for intelligent transport systems. *Transportation Research Part C, Emerging Technologies*, *17*(6), 672–683. doi:10.1016/j.trc.2009.05.008

Yang, X., Liu, J., Zhao, F., & Vaidya, N. H. (2004). A vehicle-to-vehicle communication protocol for cooperative collision warning. In *Proceedings of MOBIQUITOUS 2004 - 1st Annual International Conference on Mobile and Ubiquitous Systems: Networking and Services*, (pp. 114-123).

ADDITIONAL READING

Akkhara, P., Sekiya, Y., & Wakahara, Y. (2009). Efficient alarm messaging by multi-channel cut-through rebroadcasting based on inter-vehicle communication. *IAENG International Journal of Computer Science*, *36*(2), 132–147.

Asakura, Y., & Hato, E. (2001). Behavioral monitoring of public transport users through a mobile communication system. *Journal of Advanced Transportation*, *35*(3), 289–304. doi:10.1002/atr.5670350307

Beatty, C. (2002). Location-Based Services: Navigation for the Masses, At Last! *Journal of Navigation*, *55*, 241–248. doi:10.1017/S0373463302001790

Chen, W., Yu, M., Li, Z. -., & Chen, Y. -. (2003). "Integrated vehicle navigation system for urban applications". *Proceedings of the 7th International Conference on Global Navigation Satellite Systems (GNSS)*, 15-22.

Fujimoto, N., Moriya, M., Ishizuka, A., & Goto, M. (2002). Intra- and inter-vehicle communication network using low-cost POF links. *IEICE Transactions on Information and Systems. E (Norwalk, Conn.)*, *85-D*(11), 1839–1850.

Grakovski, A., Kabashkin, I., & Ressin, A. (2008). Intelligent transport system for intra-city logistics based on www technologies. *Transport and Telecommunication*, *9*(3), 30–38.

Hattori, M., Kase, N., Ohsuga, A., & Honiden, S. (1999). Agent-based drivers' information assistance system. *New Generation Computing*, *17*(4), 359–367. doi:10.1007/BF03037242

Holton, A. E., & Fisher, D. L. (1998). Advanced parking management systems: Models of drivers' parking strategies. *Proceedings of the Human Factors and Ergonomics Society*, *2*, 1237–1241.

Kase, N., Hattori, M., Ohsuga, A., & Honiden, S. (1999). InfoMirror - agent-based information assistance to drivers. *IEEE Conference on Intelligent Transportation Systems, Proceedings, ITSC*, 734-739.

Kato, A., Sato, K., & Fujise, M. (2001). Technologies of millimeter-wave inter-vehicle communications - propagation characteristics. *Journal of the Communications Research Laboratory*, *48*(4), 99–110.

Kato, A., Sato, K., Fujise, M., & Kawakami, S. (2001). Propagation characteristics of 60-GHz millimeter waves for ITS inter-vehicle communications. *IEICE Transactions on Communications. E (Norwalk, Conn.)*, *84-B*(9), 2530–2539.

Kim, J. S., Lee, J. H., Kang, T. H., Lee, W. Y., & Kim, Y. G. (1996). Node based map matching algorithm for car navigation system. *Proceedings of the 29th ISATA Symposium, 10*, 121-126.

Ku, W., Chen, Y., & Zimmermann, R. (2009). Privacy protected spatial query processing for advanced location based services. *Wireless Personal Communications, 51*(1), 53–65. doi:10.1007/s11277-008-9608-9

Li, J., & Fu, M. (2003). Research on route planning and map-matching in vehicle GPS/dead-reckoning/electronic map integrated navigation system. *Proceedings of IEEE Conference on Intelligent Transportation Systems,* 1639-1643.

Mokhtarian, P. L. (1990). A typology of relationships between telecommunications and transportation. *Transportation Research Part A, General, 24*, 231–242. doi:10.1016/0191-2607(90)90060-J

Mokhtarian, P. L. (2002). Telecommunications and travel: The case for complementarity. *Journal of Industrial Ecology, 6*, 43–57. doi:10.1162/108819802763471771

Munaka, T., Yamamoto, T., Kuroda, M., Mizuno, T., & Watanabe, T. (2002). A reliable multicast mechanism for location dependent data in DSRC-based ITS networks. *IEICE Transactions on Information and Systems. E (Norwalk, Conn.), 85-D*(11), 1809–1821.

Nagaosa, T., & Hasegawa, T. (1998). Code assignment and the multicode sense scheme in an inter-vehicle cdna communication network. *IEICE Transactions on Fundamentals of Electronics, Communications and Computer Sciences. E (Norwalk, Conn.), 81-A*(11), 2327–2333.

Ogiwara, M., & Inaba, K. (2001). Intelligent parking system - parking reservation system. *NTT R and D, 50*(9), 721–726.

Ohmori, S., Yamao, Y., & Nakajima, N. (2000). Future generations of mobile communications based on broadband access technologies. *IEEE Communications Magazine, 38*(12), 134–142. doi:10.1109/35.888267

Okada, Y., Wada, T., Horie, M., Nakase, F., & Okada, H. (2007). Experimental performance evaluations of reflect-transmission control schemes for vehicle-pedestrian communications (VPEC). *IEICE Transactions on Communications. E (Norwalk, Conn.), 90-B*(10), 2931–2939.

Ozawa, S. (1999). Image processing for intelligent transport systems. *IEICE Transactions on Information and Systems. E (Norwalk, Conn.), 82-D*(3), 629–636.

Quddus, M. A., Noland, R. B., & Ochieng, W. Y. (2006). A high accuracy fuzzy logic based map matching algorithm for road transport. *Journal of Intelligent Transportation Systems: Technology, Planning, and Operations, 10*(3), 103–115. doi:10.1080/15472450600793560

Quddus, M. A., Ochieng, W. Y., & Noland, R. B. (2007). Current map-matching algorithms for transport applications: State-of-the art and future research directions. *Transportation Research Part C, Emerging Technologies, 15*(5), 312–328. doi:10.1016/j.trc.2007.05.002

Rappaport, T. S., Reed, J. H., & Woerner, B. D. (1996). Position location using wireless communications on highways of the future. *IEEE Communications Magazine, 34*(10), 33–41. doi:10.1109/35.544321

Rybicki, J., Scheuermann, B., Kiess, W., Lochert, C., Fallahi, P., & Mauve, M. (2007). Challenge: Peers on wheels - A road to new traffic information systems. *Proceedings of the Annual International Conference on Mobile Computing and Networking, MOBICOM,* 215-221.

Salomon, I. (1985). Telecommunications and travel - substitution or modified mobility? *Journal of Transport Economics & Policy*, *19*, 219–235.

Salomon, I. (1986). Telecommunications and travel relationships: a review. *Transportation Research Part A, General*, *20*, 223–238. doi:10.1016/0191-2607(86)90096-8

Schwanen, T., & Kwan, M.-P. (2008). The Internet, mobile phone and space-time constraints. *Geoforum*, *39*, 1362–1377. doi:10.1016/j.geoforum.2007.11.005

Scott, S., & Kealy, Y. (2002). An Intelligent Navigation Solution for Land Mobile Location-Based Services. *Journal of Navigation*, *55*, 225–240.

Shiode, N. (2003). A geographical interpretation of cyberspace: preliminary analysis on the scaling tendency of information spaces. In Boots, B. N., Okabe, A., & Thomas, R. (Eds.), *Modelling Geographical Systems: Statistical and Computational Applications (Geojournal Library, 70)* (pp. 275–293). Amsterdam: Kluwers.

Srinivasan, D., Cheu, R. L., & Chuan, W. T. (2003). Development of an improved ERP system using GPS and AI techniques. *IEEE Proceedings on Intelligent Transportion Systems*, *1*, 554–559.

Stefancić, G., Presecki, A., & Andrić, S. (2002). In-vehicle information systems. *Promet - Traffic - Traffico*, 14(2), 67-69.

Syed, S., & Cannon, M. E. (2004). Fuzzy logic-based map matching algorithm for vehicle navigation system in urban canyons. *Proceedings of the Institute of Navigation (ION) National Technical Meeting*.

Taylor, G., Steup, D., Car, A., Blewitt, G., & Corbett, S. (2001). Road reduction filtering for GPS-GIS navigation. *Transactions in GIS*, *5*(3), 193–207. doi:10.1111/1467-9671.00077

Thompson, R. G., Takada, K., & Kobayakawa, S. (1998). Understanding the demand for access information. *Transportation Research Part C, Emerging Technologies*, *6*(4), 231–245. doi:10.1016/S0968-090X(98)00017-5

Tokuda, K. (2001). Applications of wireless communication technologies for intelligent transport systems. *Wireless Personal Communications*, *17*(2-3), 343–353. doi:10.1023/A:1011258622298

Tseng, Y., Ni, S., Chen, Y., & Sheu, J. (2002). The broadcast storm problem in a mobile ad hoc network. *Wireless Networks*, *8*(2-3), 153–167. doi:10.1023/A:1013763825347

Widodo, A., & Hasegawa, T. (1998). A vehicular driving assistant system using spread spectrum techniques. *IEICE Transactions on Fundamentals of Electronics, Communications and Computer Sciences. E (Norwalk, Conn.)*, *81-A*(11), 2334–2340.

Widodo, A., & Hasegawa, T. (1998). Evaluations of traffic safety improvement using an autonomous traffic flow simulator including inter-vehicle communications. *Conference Record / IEEE Global Telecommunications Conference*, *5*, 2629-2634.

Xu, Y. (2000). Development of transport telematics in europe. *GeoInformatica*, *4*(2), 179–200. doi:10.1023/A:1009876223822

Chapter 11
Locative Media and Playful Appropriations, or How Electronic Games Help to Redefine the Meaning of Space

Thiago Falcão
Universidade Federal da Bahia, Brazil

Luiz Adolfo Andrade
Universidade Federal da Bahia, Brazil

Emmanoel Ferreira
Universidade Federal do Rio de Janeiro, Brazil

Paolo Bruni
Universidade Federal da Bahia, Brazil

ABSTRACT

This chapter presents an investigation on how the ludic incorporation of locative media modifies the creation of meaning in urban spaces. In this sense, the authors try to understand how electronic games reinforce the relationship between the urban space and the digital media, allowing the creation of intelligent informational territories. The authors' hypothesis is based on the fact that these specific types of digital games – known as ubiquitous, pervasive games – develop new spatiality forms, producing – to the players – other types of use and appropriation of the urban space. In order to develop this discussion, they propose an analysis of some alternate reality games (ARGs) developed in Brazil.

INITIAL APPROACH

Ubiquitous and pervasive games appeared in the beginning of the 21st century as a result of the combination between experimental game design, mobile digital technologies, wireless networking, location-based systems and ubiquitous and pervasive computing. In Brazil, the *alternate reality games* (ARGs) are the most relevant examples of games inscribed in those categories, being experimented in a growing scale since around

DOI: 10.4018/978-1-60960-051-8.ch011

year 2004. In contrast with their growing popularity, most ARGs related researches lack a more thorough theoretical approach, being limited to the discussion of how to use these games as part of companies' marketing strategies.

In order to expand the reflection about alternate reality games, particularly in Brazil, this chapter presents an investigation on how locative media has been used alongside these new appropriations of ludic forms to modify the way individuals actually relate to urban space. In this sense, we seek to apprehend the way these electronic games – those which are played with the assistance of locative media, strengthening the relationship between urban and digital/informational space – bring forth the possibility of creation of new meanings for the urban space.

Our hypothesis is that the relationship between the development of these alternate reality games and the notions of mobility and spatiality gives birth to new forms of appropriation – use and adaptation – of urban space, producing new senses of meaning to places people are used to. As an unfolding of this central hypothesis, we believe that locative media can go back and forth on a two way road: at the same time that they work as an in-game communication device, between players and characters, they serve as a tool to the players' articulation in the urban space quests, in the game context. To elaborate our discussion, we propose an analysis of the Brazilian play phenomena which are contained in this category – known to researchers by the title of pervasive and ubiquitous games, which in Brazil are most represented by the genre of the alternate reality games.

The analysis corpus featured on this chapter comprises some of the offspring of the convergence between ubiquitous computing and experimental game design, which reconfigured the way by which the electronic games are related to ordinary life and urban spaces in the "normal" life, as game theorist Johan Huizinga (1950) would name it. Ubiquitous computing is the field of computer science responsible to enhance the latent potential of objects and physical environments with the application of the same functionalities networks uphold, according to computer theorist Mark Weiser (1991; 1994). Experimental game design is the field of interactive arts that aims at developing new and revolutionary platforms and contexts to digital games, according to ubiquitous games theorist Jane McGonigal (2006; 2007). Finally, our understanding of locative media is related to those media which combine informational data provided by wireless networks to a specifically considered urban space, according to Tuters & Varnelis, (2006), Santaella (2008a, 2008b, 2008c), and Lemos (2007, 2008a, 2008b, 2009, 2010).

Our choice, then, was to focus on a specific genre of ubiquitous games, the Alternate Reality Games (ARGs) – which are games that blurs the boundaries between fiction and reality, creating a sense of a 'new reality' experienced by its players. The criteria used to choose these games among the variety of ubiquitous and pervasive games experienced worldwide was the fact that this is the only genre with a proper representation in Brazil. We have chosen to analyze five of these games: (i) *Instituto Purifica* (2006, MTV), (ii) *O Tambor* (2007, MTV), (iii) *Zona Incerta* (2007, Guaraná Antártica / Superinteressante - Abril Jovem), (iv) *Desenrola* (2009 Raccord/OiFuturo), and (v) *A Fórmula do Conhecimento* (2009, Engenhonovo/Realidade Sintética/Unijorge), aiming specifically at judging how the use of locative media helped – or not – these games to create a new sense of place. These five specific titles were chosen because of the fact that they represent the biggest games – both in quantity of players and amount of budget spent – developed in Brazil. We propose the premise that alternate reality games force their players to experience urban space through new signifying lenses, giving new meaning to objects (in a broader sense of the word, representing both people, places and things) both determined by their interaction with the urban space *per se* and the informational layer in the form of wireless networks of any kind. In this sense, we believe that this typical game structure transforms physical bodies and spaces into interactive platforms that can respond to the players' stimuli.

In this category of games, the player must interact with the urban space, completing quests and challenging/fighting against other non-player characters – often hired performers – among another myriad of ludic-proposed tasks. These games are experienced by a great number of players, who must use several media platforms to accomplish the game goals. In addition, most of these games contests' comprise a wide time span, encapsulating months, sometimes.

In order to develop our argument, we start by discussing the relationship between space, place and meaning. Then, we present the discussion about locative media and their relationship with ubiquitous and pervasive computing. In a third moment, we approach the idea of intelligent environments, articulating it with the *bubble* metaphor and with the concepts of *hybrid spaces*, *informational territory* and *interstitial space*. All these concepts feed the idea of *magic circle*, or playground, which in the case of the games we analyze in this chapter, is the urban space itself. After discussing the logic of the ubiquitous, pervasive and alternate reality games, we present a table with all the ARGs developed in Brazil and the analysis of the five chosen cases.

OF SPACE AND MEANING

There are many ways by which individuals relate to each other through space (Osborne & Rose, 2004) – be it for communicational purposes or any other one. One aspect is exactly the way by which each one of these relations occurs – working as a vector of meaning between individual and physical space. Following this argumentative line, therefore, we can point to two paths that allow different – although related to each other – forms of understanding space (Lefevbre, 1991, Dourish and Harrison, 1996; Dourish, 2006, Santaella, 2008a; 2008b; Lemos, 2009): the first (i) is related to the geometrical aspect of space – the physical aspect, the way space is occupied by a body – and how another body cannot occupy the same space. The second way of understanding (ii) is related to the space as a social construct, a place that is 'practiced' by people. One particular street, for example, which is geometrically defined by urban design, has its meaning transformed by passers-by and by the activities performed by them.

Such synergy between one understanding more related to the matter and another more abstract, related to meanings, brings us to Lefevbre's (1991) argument about the idea of *social production of space*, that assumes that the activities of individuals and collectives in specific spaces, transform those spaces in *places*, due to the performing of social actions (pp. 33-34). The term *spacialization*, therefore, can be defined as a process of fluxes, created by changes in spaces and by the production of places, resulting in a sense of *belonging* (Lemos, 2009). Therefore, the main argument of this chapter is that the *alternate reality games* are efficient operators of this type of spacialization, because, like games in general, ARGs are related to the creation of a specific domain – a territory that is, at the same time, guided by the laws of physics and also by a series of specific laws, the rules of a game. When an ARG event takes place, what we have is a overlapping of several layers of meaning – some of them simply related to the urban space; others related to the informational space that overlaps to the physical space[1]; and others related to the behavior modes unleashed by the interaction between individual/player and the game activity (Ferreira & Falcão, 2009).

As observed by Santaella (2008b, 2008c), there is not an agreement between theorists about the concept of place, especially about the conceptual distinction between place and space. The word place is used in many day-by-day situations to refer, for example, to a building or a meeting place, endowed by meaning. In several moments, the word is related to something that goes beyond a space referential: it becomes an expectation about the behavior related to the position of an individual in a social structure and her actions in space, combining spatial and social aspects, resulting in what Croswell (1996) calls *social space*.

Paul Dourish, in two occasions, makes an effort to help defining the concepts of place and space (Dourish & Harrison, 1996; Dourish, 2006). In a first moment, space represents the world structure, it is the three-dimensional environment in which objects and events happen and in which they uphold a certain position and relative direction. In another, place is the space endowed by meaning, which reflects how that space can be used. We are located in space, but all actions are performed in places, which transforms the meaning of space. Places are created and sustained by their use patterns, representing the way one particular space is used, reconfiguring its meaning (Santaella, 2008a, 2008b, 2008c). The same way that the general (mathematical, abstract) aspect of space was already demonstrated, there is a social aspect, produced by the people dynamics, in society (Lemos, 2009). When discussing the space as a social production, we should consider the many activities performed in the urban space.

Being Locative: How Space does relate to Media

As Mark Tuters and Kazys Varnelis say:

Locative media emerged over the last half decade as a response to the decorporealized, screen-based experience of net art, claiming the world beyond either gallery or computer screen as its territory. Initially coined as a title for a workshop hosted by RIXC, an electronic art and media center in Latvia during 2002, the term is derived from the "locative" noun case in the Latvian language, which indicates location and vaguely corresponds to the English prepositions "in", "on", "at", and "by." A report produced during the workshop outlined the scope for locative media: "Inexpensive receivers for global positioning satellites have given amateurs the means to produce their own cartographic information with military precision... As opposed to the World Wide Web the focus here is spatially localized, and centred on the individual user; a collaborative cartography of space and mind, places and the connections between them (2006, p. 357).

Locative media should be understood as a result of the combination between location-based services and technology (McCullough, 2004; Lemos 2007, Santaella, 2008a), such as sensors, electronic devices, digital networks and the services associated with them, which react to their local context (Lemos, 2010). Thus, they favor the idea that the cyberspace is not separated from the physical world (Dourish, 2006); conversely, what we see is that the electronic space is – day-by-day – more intrinsic to the physical space. This discussion was originally proposed by Ben Russel (1999) in his famous *headmap* manifesto, in which he perceives that the Internet has already started "leaking" into the real world. Some years later, this debate tend to be expressed by metaphors that rescue the importance of location and mobility to the understanding of the cyber culture scene of today, as *Internet of Things* (Tuters & Varnelis, 2006) and *cyberspace download* (Lemos, 2009).

Such expressions sustain the argument that information can be produced, distributed and consumed in different places in the physical space, and solve two problems evoked by the cyberspace culture. Firstly, (i) the 'de-territorializing' myth, characterized by the argument that the electronic space would transcend physical space and that geographic issues would no longer make sense, was completed discarded. Secondly, (ii) the existence of a particular connection point, a place to which we should move to in order to connect to the Internet – like a *hotspot* – tends to be, in the future, not essential, as connection points would be everywhere. All these notions make a critique to the same idea, that cyberspace would be *another* place in which one could get in and out, free from geographic conditions, where social relations, companies, people and institutions would be represented by a disembodied avatar; it seems that these notions have been – at some extent – left to the past.

In Brazil, some theorists discuss the relationship between the digital locative media and the devices that aggregate informational content to a specific location (Lemos, 2007, 2009; Santaella, 2008a; 2008b, 2008c). In this sense, locative media include wireless digital networks and devices equipped with sensors, which are 'aware' to places, people and objects (Lemos, 2009). In another work, Lemos (2007) proposes a classification of locative media, taken from their perceived functions: augmented reality, mapping and monitoring, geo-tags and urban notes. Later, when analyzing our corpus, we will show how alternate reality games can use one or more of these functions, producing *spacialization*. The production of space we refer is sustained by the idea of spatial expansion, featured in these games (Montolla, Stenros and Waern 2009), which can appropriate from everyday environments and, therefore, turns them into content and context for a game.

Locative media reflect the pervasive and ubiquitous computing (*ubicomp*) paradigm, proposed by Mark Weiser (1991, 1994), former scientist in chief in the Palo Alto Research Center (PARC). In his time, Weiser was considered a visionary, because even before the appearance of the World Wide Web, he proposed a model called "The Computer of the 21st Century". According to the scientist, the technologies that really evolve are the ones that have the capacity of *disappearing* in the human environment, infiltrating through objects located in the physical space. According to Weiser, computers will follow the same course taken by electric engines, which got downsized day after day, until 'disappearing' inside objects. Weiser points that this same situation will happen to computers, which will also infiltrate inside the human environment and inside the real world objects, interweaving to day-by-day life; thus, the use of computers would become much more 'natural' to human beings.

Mark Weiser's proposition could be proved in the turn from the 20th to the 21st century, considering the new devices developed under the scientist's paradigm, for instance, sensitive computing and pervasive computing. The first refers to the possibility of interconnection between computers, bodies and objects, which can recognize one another in an autonomous way. It is the case, for example, of automatic doors and lights, RFID sensors and also the Bluetooth technology. On the other hand, the expression *pervasive computing* was created in 1998 by IBM, and serves to name a series of products that carry internal microchips, for example *smart phones*.

Thus, in the 21st century, ubiquitous computing has been reaffirmed as an emergent field to computer science, with the goal of adding computer networks functionalities to day-by-day objects and to physical world environments (McGonigal 2006; 2007), integrating computer processes to different objects located on the physical world (Lemos, 2009). Ubiquitous and pervasive computing, alongside the 'Internet of Things', feed the debate about new territorialities, which would represent new forms of spacialization, new contexts created from experimentations that take place in the physical space, as the relation between utopias and heterotopias, as traced by Michel Foucault (1984). The 'Internet of Things' age is also the age of mobility, of intelligent environments and of informational territories.

Intelligent Environments and Informational Territories

According to the common sense, the idea of territory relates to the idea of political control; it is related to the promotion of piece through security, therefore defining and delineating the power functioning. Territories are also social creations in which human relations – culture, society and community – organize themselves in a specific space (Gottman, 1973). Along the 21th century first decade, new territorialities – created by the information flux that leaks from the cyberspace – arose, thus following the logic of the 'second moment' of cyberculture, as described above. This 'data cloud' gets infiltrated in the urban space and becomes part of the human environment, thus reconfiguring the original sense of places, producing new territorialities. According to André Lemos (2010), understanding these new territories is fundamental to visualize the impact of locative media on society.

Informational territories are areas of control of digital information fluxes in an intersection zone between cyberspace and urban space. Access and informational control occur by means of mobile devices and wireless networks. The informational territory is not the cyberspace itself, but rather the space that is formed by the relationship between physical space and electronic space (Lemos, 2007).

This new type of territory occupies a central position in many discussions about how these territorialities – classified as informational – transform, modify or amplifies the original function of places – cafés, squares, streets, public buildings, for example. According to Lemos (2009), places equipped with sensors, wireless devices and networks, are transformed by the emergent informational territoriality, which can be understood as a digital-electronic 'skin' attached to places, feeding a particular relationship between the real world with databases and wireless and electronic devices, which are, by their turn, inlayed in things.

The *bubble* metaphor is used by Beslay and Hakala (2005) to illustrate this informational exchange zone that occurs between places, objects and users in the informational territories, feeding the idea of *intelligent environment* – a place, in the future, where human beings will be in a central position in relation to knowledge, society, information and communication technologies. In this same sense, Adriana Souza e Silva (2006) proposes the concept of *hybrid spaces* to illustrate this new type of territory:

Hybrid spaces are mobile spaces, created by the constant movement of users who carry portable devices continuously connected to the Internet and to other users. A hybrid space is conceptually different from what has been termed mixed reality, augmented reality, augmented virtuality, or virtual reality (...) The possibility of an "always-on" connection when one moves through a city transforms our experience of space by enfolding remote contexts inside the present context This connection is related both to social interactions and to connections to the information space, that is, the Internet (p. 262)

Lucia Santaella calls this an *interstitial space*, because it tends to dissolve the boundaries between physical and virtual spaces: it belongs neither to the former, nor to the latter. This would be, actually, a *third* space, which refers to the boundaries between the physical and the digital domain, resulting in a connected space, breaking the traditional distinction between those spaces. An interstitial (or hybrid) space, as pointed by Santaella, happens when it is no longer necessary to jump out from the physical domain to get in contact with digital environments (Santaella, 2008a).

Lúcia Santaella points as a key problem which is present in the hybrid-space terminology the fact that the 'hybrid' adjective has become an expression used in many and different contexts. Looking for a precise terminology, which emphasizes not only the information fluxes that circulate through physical space in direct connections, but in the emergent socializing forms, the author proposes the concept of interstitial spaces to refer to these new domains. This term is a metaphor that is able to characterize the multiple faces of the recent changes in communication and culture, among which are included the activities performed under the 'locative media' umbrella (Santaella, 2008a).

Nevertheless, both terms apparently shows the same meaning, for they relate both to the connection between space and information as well as the social interactions that occur between the system actors, considering the ways these processes can transform the experience between man and urban space. However, the idea elaborated by Santaella, besides reinforcing the sociability links that can be perceived in these situations, can comprise the interaction processes between users and devices, tempering the scope the adjective 'hybrid' has acquired.

DIGRESSION ABOUT THE ACT OF PLAYING

It is curious to realize that there is a certain agreement between the various aspects of media when it comes to treating both the spheres of work and play as separate poles of the same dichotomy. Such framing has received wide support, along the course of history, figuring also in the ideas of some of the classic game theorists: Johan Huizinga (1950) and Roger Caillois (1961), for instance, believed that in order to play a game, the individual had to consciously step outside "normal life" (Huizinga, 1950) and voluntarily engage into an activity considered "not serious" – suppressing both time and space.

This place in space and time in which the play activity happens received a thorough theoretical treatment – and a proper terminology – when Katie Salen and Eric Zimmerman (2003) published their treatise on general analysis and development of the constitutive processes of the game – from their analogical components, commonly represented by cards and boards, to their convergence with hypermedia, where is located the essence of the video game – and has been recently known as 'magic circle', being inspired by a passage in Huizinga's classic *Homo Ludens*. According to the authors, "Although the magic circle is merely one of the examples in Huizinga's list of "play-grounds", the term is used here as shorthand for the idea of a special place in space and time created by a game" (Salen & Zimmerman, 2003).

The central idea would not be to consider the magic circle as something that necessarily encapsulates the player, suppressing space-time and projecting her into an alternative zone. Instead, the magic circle would work as a mediation symbolic system, which helps the dialogue between player and game and also between player and reality, working on the relationship between the individual and the duo game/reality. Such mediation may be presented both as a fluid form – drawing blurred borders, in the sense that they cannot be plainly identified, which allows fiction and reality to meet; and in a harder, more defined – solid – form, which really enables the sense of displacement – space-time suppression.

Such proposition finds support on the ideas of Jesper Juul (2008), who points that, to Huizinga, the space in which the game develops is as separate as other daily spaces, as court houses, churches and classrooms – places that are integrated to the flow of life, but that ensue on a different behavior – which explains the fact that Caillois (1961) refers to these places as "separate". As Juul (2008) points out: "For Huizinga, the space of game-playing is but one type of space governed by special rules, and as with other types of space, the space of game-playing is social in origin. People make special spaces, be they court houses, religious spaces or game spaces".

This proposition takes us to two specific understandings: the first one, which legitimates and supports Huizinga's idea that, in the game – in the ludic object – one would find some origins of culture. The second understanding suggests that although we can refer to the game as an object – that is, as a symbolic good that is produced and commercialized – we cannot forget a fundamental aspect of the ludic space: the interaction between games and people. The formation of the space-time *other*, which is inherent to the game, is actually inherent to *play the game* – it demands the interaction between people and object. Hence Juul's proposition that the magic circle is formed not only by the rules structure but requires the players to construct its functional and logic space.

Although, essentially, the game space is constituted by rules, some games (like the ones analyzed in this chapter) also project a fictional world to which the characters, sceneries and actions developed during gameplay are subordinate. According to Juul (2005), as in any fiction, the space created in electronic games follows the *possible worlds* logic (Dolozel, 1998), taken from analytical philosophy. According to the author, "In its most basic form, possible worlds can be understood as abstract collections of states of affaires, distinct from the statements describing those states" (Juul 2005, p. 122). The idea the author tries to unveil is that in a work that uses a fictional world – a book, for example – the scenery described is much smaller than the world in which it is circumscribed.

Even if we have the conscience that a fictional world is bigger than the one is given to us, as "readers", we can say that these lacunas work, actually, according to the production of meaning by the players, as they get in contact with such world. This happens because those worlds are, according to Juul, (2005, p. 122), incomplete. Such incompleteness comes from the fact that authors have the power to decide what is or what is not true in the world they create, at the very moment they create it – and it happens simply because it is not possible to specify all the details about whatever is the world. To deal with this issue, Marie-Laure Ryan (2001, pp. 48-60) created the theoretical concept called "principle of minimal departure", which proposes that when a piece of information about a determined fictional world is not specified, we usually fill in the blanks with our understanding of the world to which we are used. This explanation provides liberty for the authors to ignore certain descriptive aspects – such as the gravity, for instance – of their worlds.

Because games – generally speaking – are directly related to the formation of a domain on its own – the magic circle – they can be considered great spacialization operators. The games we refer to in this chapter produce a domain that reconfigures our perception of "game board" or "place to play", through the use of new communication technologies and the application of game design creative process in the urban space (McGonigal, 2006). Montolla notices that there are great possibilities to spatially expand the "playground" in this kind of game. They can connect the cyberspace to the urban space; allow social playing in many locations; take games to places where they are not usually supposed to be; ideologically, it can be seen as a way of reclaiming public spaces for people (2005, p. 02).

Montolla, Stenros and Waern (2009, pp. 77-79) expand this discussion and call this phenomena *spatially expanded games*, because they are not experienced in restricted zones, as a TV monitor or a game board, for example. Because they can circulate in public places, the social conventions and also the meaning of these places are reconfigured by the application of game design techniques. In the same way, they can be considered as a natural way to facilitate people to understand the city in a new perspective, because these games feed other types of appropriations of public space environments, different from their original purpose. All places have their original purposes – sidewalks are meant to allow people to walk; roads allow people to drive; restaurants allow people to eat. Nevertheless, by the installation of a ubiquitous and pervasive game, this meaning is modified by the game activities dynamics.

Games and the Urban Space

At the turn of the 21st century, as observed by McGonigal (2006, 2007), ubiquitous computing has converged with experimental design – a field from interactive art that looks forward to find out new platforms and new contexts to electronic games.

Today, there is a significant corpus composed by many game projects, which expands the notions of where, when and with whom we play. In these cases, the challenge goes beyond the online environments and bursts into public spaces of big cities, as museums, squares, streets and buildings, thus connecting social networks, communication technologies and urban space.

There is not, though, a formal consensus to refer to these phenomena. Björk et al. (2002) call them *ubiquitous games*, referring to electronic games that explore the possibilities of application of functionalities taken from ubiquitous computing. Schneider e Kortuem (2001) adopt the expression *pervasive games* to refer to games which purpose can be defined as the hybridization between Live Action Role Play (LARPs) and the ubiquitous and pervasive logic. To the authors, ubiquitous and pervasive technology is not the game focus, but its support, because it allows users to interact while moving, in a network world that offers many intelligent and interconnected services.

Nevertheless, Bjork advise that Weiser's perspective makes reference to computers inscribed in ordinary life, and not to devices that contain assembled chips, as is the case of IBM's pervasive computing. These authors consider pervasive games as games that articulate mobile technologies with location-based services, as, for instance, the game *pervasive clue*[2], described by Schneider and Kortuem. In Brazil, this opinion is expanded by André Lemos (2009), who understands pervasive games as those that combines mobile digital technologies and location-based services, resulting in an interface between physical and electronic spaces.

Jane McGonigal (2006) tries to stress this discussion and proposes a taxonomy to the analysis and identification of these games, created from three different ways of playing. Firstly, McGonigal considers the *ubiquitous computer games*, prototypes created by ubiquitous computing researchers. The second model comprises the *pervasive games* – perform-related interventions that use electronic games to break the formal conventions of public spaces and private technologies. According to McGonigal, *pervasive games* are those that concentrate the user's focus onto a device, which is a fundamental piece to challenge solving (usually these challenges are shared by a defined number of players within a specific domain – playground). Finally, the third model comprises the *ubiquitous games*, which contains the greatest number of players around the world. These games are electronic games created with commercial goals, which comprise thousands of participants and operate through the replication – in the real world – of techniques taken from *game design*.

On the other hand, Montolla, Stenros and Waern (2009) adopt the expression *pervasive games* to make reference to the category of games created from Weiser's paradigm. The adjective *pervasive* means *infiltrated*, *penetrating*, reflecting the way by which these games can burst into urban space. The authors' argument is based in two perspectives from the Nieuwdorp's philosophical analysis (2007). The first one is the technological perspective, related to the ways that the gameplay can use the IBM's pervasive computing proposal. The second one is the cultural perspective, which focus on the ways these games relate to ordinary life. Those authors believe that Nieuwdorp's cultural perspective is the best way to understand the phenomenon and its way of appropriating urban space. The *pervasive games* category, according to these researchers, could be divided into another four genres, which would reflect four ways of playing: *treasure hunts*, *assassination games*, *pervasive larp* and *alternate reality games*, the latter being the most popular.

Jane McGonigal (2006) points that the alternate reality games comprise the most representative genre of ubiquitous games, which format is close to pervasive games. Both formats make reference to the Weiser's paradigm and evoke a new way of playing, configuring a new gameplay pattern. The reason we have chosen the *alternate reality games* to construct our analysis on the use of locative media and their playful appropriations in the urban space, and how they reconfigure the meaning of space, was because they uphold all those common features of ubiquitous and pervasive games, according to the authors referred in this chapter.

ON ALTERNATE REALITY GAMES, THEIR STRUCTURES AND FEATURES

The recent history of alternate reality games was set off by the development of the pioneer *The Beast*[3], produced by Microsoft aiming at the marketing campaign of Steven Spielberg's science fiction film *A.I. – Artificial Intelligence* (2001), which was then followed closely – in the year of 2003, two after the launch of the film and its marketing campaign – by a first sequence of theoretical efforts on trying to engender a series of analysis of that innovative game structure (McGonigal, 2003a).

Involved both academically and at the core of the production's sphere – author of the hits *I Love Bees* (2004) e *The Lost Ring*[4] (2008) – Jane McGonigal adopted a study perspective focused on the relationship between the aspects of performance and the game structure (2006; 2007). McGonigal (2006, 2007) treats ARGs as a specific phenomena attached to the pervasive computing cultural appropriations. To the theorist, alternate reality games are contained by a general category of games addressed as *ubiquitous games* (Bjork, 2002).

McGonigal (2007) argues that these games blur the borders between real and virtual worlds, taking over services, softwares and communication technologies available on our daily existence and applying them as game design procedures which modify behaviors and uses – puzzles and quests, then, become items that redefine our understanding of places and objects, people and social contexts. ARGs are, then, experienced both on physical and online environments, lasting weeks, sometimes months, and involving dozens of social network engaged players working collaboratively to solve the given puzzles – especially, these games are also composed physically and materially, in a phenomenological and ontological order; distributed through a variety of platforms, temporalities, localities and media forms (McGonigal 2006, 2007).

Although, in what concerns this chapter, Jane McGonigal figures as the most important theorist thinking about alternate reality games, a host of researchers also figure as contributors to the built up of the theoretical notion of ARGs. Szulborski (2005) address the category as a genre of fictional story that brings together treasure hunting, role-playing, games and online communities, and not only as mere electronic games whose gameplay embodies the ordinary life substances. Christy Dena (2007, p. 200) believes ARGs are projected to the collective consumption – they demand a variety of abilities and knowledge that only collective intelligence may provide. Dena argues that they provide unique elements in a variety of media platforms. All components are delivered through so-called real world media such as email, fax, SMS and websites. It is the task of players to collaborate to uncover clues and plot points, solve puzzles, create content, converse with and rescue characters in the urban landscape.

Finally, Örnenbring (2007), as much as Hall (2009), think of alternate reality games as multimedia games that use the communication tools – Internet, mobile phones, mail, etc – to supply the players' immersion in a fictional world in which they should solve puzzles, explore mysteries and so on.

In Brazil, the first ARG-like recognized experiences began in 2004, in a project of mobile phone operator *Vivo* called *Vivo em Ação*[5] that transformed the operator clients in detectives, challenging them to solve a mystery and prevent the firm of being targeted by sabotage. In 2005, *The Project*[6] and *Prenoma*[7] were created as grassroots ARGs, which means they were "designed by individuals either as a bit of fandom work, or as a standalone work of fiction" (IGDA, 2006). The genre, then, became popular and much more frequent by the year. In the brief moment that this chapter is being written, there are about thirty Brazilian alternate reality game projects already finished.

Just as so we could, *grosso modo*, behold the relationship between market and academy concerning the worldwide production of ARGs, it is nothing but obvious that such type of game would also be interesting for the Brazilian theorists to think about. In 2006, then, the first papers having alternate reality games as their substance started to appear, even if in a limited number, in academic peer-reviewed journals and dissertations. Brazilian theorist Vicente Mastrocolla (2006) understands alternate reality games as intense series of enigmas involving websites, clues in newspapers and phone calls – he posits that in this category of games, the player embodies a character to live the plot in a vivid way, therefore, the playground of an ARG is the real world, and there are no synthetic avatars, as is the case of video games, and the character aesthetics are related to the physical bodies of the players.

It is, then, on the attempt of establishing a dialogue with this body of research concerning ARGs that we seek to contribute to the above cited works by expanding the notion of alternate reality games as specifically focusing on its narrative aspects. We should, then, address ARGs as puzzle structured narratives, encrypted both in the online environment (through the use of the Internet, specially) and in the real world. Solving these puzzles, then, is a premise of the game, since the narrative cannot develop otherwise. To solve such puzzles, then, players need to work as a group – or as many groups, given the context or the specific dynamics in play, operating through what is commonly addressed as collective intelligence.

The specificity of alternate reality games, therefore, is observed when analyzing its gameplay: the technical characteristics of videogames design – puzzles, quests, interfaces and a narrative progressive system – are then transported to the urban space, modifying the meaning of its contents – re-signifying the whereabouts of a player. Simultaneously, real and virtual elements – characters, sceneries, props – establish a dialogue, which works on a synergy to improve the storytelling feature of the game. In sum, there is a convergence of (i) the playful element – hence the puzzles and enigmas – (ii) the communication technologies – through ubiquitous and pervasive computing, making use of gadgets that enable mobile gameplay – and more importantly (iii) fiction, that gives meaning to elements both created and stationary – be it either an element crafted especially in order to enable gameplay or a piece already existent of the urban life.

Brazilian ARGs and their Locative Media Use

Concerning the universe of alternate reality games produced in Brazil, we chose five of them in order to structure our analysis of their locative media use – and how this feature help redefine the meaning of urban space. The chosen games were, as follow: (i) *2084*, (ii) *Teoria das Cordas*, (iii) *Zona Incerta*, (iv) *Desenrola*, (v) *A Fórmula do Conhecimento*. The first three were chosen because of the amount of investment related to them: *2084*, *Teoria das Cordas* and *Zona Incerta* were the biggest ARGs ever produced in Brazil concerning budget issues, while the two latter, *Desenrola* and *A Fórmula do Conhecimento* were chosen because of the highly detailed database access provided for the sake of this chapter.

The information on these games was collected through structured interviews with members of the two most representative player communities, *Resistenza* and *Cúpula*, during the year of 2009. The point of the interviews was to try and identify whether the ARG made use of locative media and, being this the case, how the production of place was affected by the use of the mobile technologies. The answers support the fact that locative media works not only as a resource to the production of enigmas – but also that they serve the players as vectors of orientation and articulation through the urban space.

Zona Incerta[8] was an ARG produced by Editora Abril, a press agency responsible for some of the most important magazines published in Brazil, and was used as a marketing piece of a soda brand known as *Guaraná Antarctica*. Categorized as the biggest ARG project to figure in Brazilian lands, *Zona Incerta* lasted for five months and its live actions were played in fourteen different cities. The game was responsible for memorable facts[9], as when Brazilian senator Arthur Virgílio, member of Brazilian Social Democrat Party (PSDB-AM) proffered a speech in full session, against the fictional firm controlled by the game's base[10], *Arkhos Biotech*. Without the knowledge that all the actions upheld by the firm were fictional, part of a game, the senator, outrageously spoke against the privatization of Amazônia, south American rain forest.

The plot was centered on a Brazilian scientist named Miro Bittencourt, kidnapped by agents related to the above-mentioned firm[11] – that besides speaking against the rain forest, supposedly was responsible for corporate espionage, stealing the beverage's formula. The goal of the game was to help Gastão and Olívia, Miro's brother and former fiancée, to find the scientist and recover the stolen formula. After solving the series of puzzles, the players were able to free Miro Bittencourt and help him denounce and arrest the *Arkhos Biotech* CEOs.

The point in which the description of this specific game converges with the argumentation of this chapter is clarified by the uses of communication technologies and location based services on its gameplay. One of the central challenges of this ARG was to locate a series of twenty-four fragments of a map that stood hidden inside bottles at different Brazilian cities. The characters – controlled by the base of the game – then used the Global Positioning System (GPS) in order to hide the bottles and, consequently, inform the coordinates of every one of them to the player's community.

Another mission[12], this one played exclusively in the city of São Paulo – though in a different variety of points – required the use of the WAP (*Wireless Application Protocol*) network so that the players could navigate the game space. It is visible, then, how the locative media – represented here by the mobile phone, figuring as the device, the interface between the urban space and the informational flux of the network – acted as a bridge that clearly turned possible that subway stations, streets and abandoned warehouses acquired fictional, narrative value.

Our argument here points towards the fact that perhaps, on an ordinary treasure hunt, the final spot of the hunt has its perception both of space and of social context re-signified by the rules of the game, regardless of the use of technologies. Mobile and Location Based Technologies allow the entire way from one spot to another to be turned in a sequence of places – places, not simply spaces – the city, the urban path is then transformed in a giant board, in which "pieces" can slide one way or another – except these pieces are people – and that their relationship to these places is determined by whether or not the narrative aspect of the game is salient (Falcão and Ferreira, 2009).

Brazilian television channel MTV Brasil was responsible for two of the ARGs that figure amongst our corpus: *2084* and *Teoria das Cordas*. Although *2084* was the official name of the game, it is commonly known to the players' communities as *Instituto Purifica* – which is the name of the central firm that works as the fiction antagonist. The referred firm is a fictional piece that claimed to help on human orientation and preached a new world order, intending to recruit the highest possible number of followers through its website.

Gradually, the players found the evidence that framed the church-like firm, especially in subliminal messages broadcasted with MTV Brasil's shows. After four months of online and geo-located – in São Paulo, from October, 2006 to January, 2007 – the firm was taken over by players and the game ended.

MTV Brasil's second game was entitled *Teoria das Cordas*, but spread commonly referred as *O Tambor*. It happened from May to December, in 2007, and was also location-centered in São Paulo. *O Tambor* was initially related to a series of seven television short films also broadcasted by the channel. As the days went by, though, audience – that soon became players – found out that the short films were only a door, players should step through to enter the game world. What is worth pointing here is that even if we simply watched the videos gradually telling us about Delfim, the main character whose mission was to spread traps through São Paulo's urban space, the story would have its closure – the videos were a form of media that could be, itself, independent, even though they were interconnected to the "real", locative aspect of the gameplay – that audiovisual pieces do not traditionally have.

The locative aspects of this title were related to the traps Delfim spread through the urban space – these items were a part of a much larger plan of a mafia group called *Humes Publis*. As soon as the short videos stopped being broadcasted, the drum phase began, that comprised about a dozen[13] different missions spread through the streets of São Paulo. Both ARGs sponsored by MTV Brasil were successful, and naturally, the locative medias offered a big repertoire of opportunities that could be explored in the live actions of these games. The interviews we conducted with some of the players from these ARGs revealed the use of these devices. The players described moments in which they had to execute the triangulation of a certain person through its cell phone signal, for instance – which is a clear appropriation of, not only the urban space, but also the technology involved in the process – that transformed cell phones, computers and the urban space in vectors of a transformation in the meaning of the specific place. Another clear example related to *2048* had players use Google Maps to find stickers that resembled a giraffe spread through some points of São Paulo. Later in the game, such stickers were used to identify a secret password relevant to the game.

The next game in which we can clearly see the action of the locative media is the ARG *Desenrola*, that had its plot to develop at Rio de Janeiro during January and February, 2009. It was one of the narrative pieces used to tell the story of *Orelha*[14], main character of the game. The central challenge of the game was to help Celo and Paola, two teenagers, to release their friend Orelha from drug dealer Formiga's grasp. The dealer demanded a ransom to release its hostage and threatened Celo and Paola with their deaths. In fear, they hid and set up an Internet website that framed Formiga. This content should then be discovered by the players, that giving sequence to the game's story, would be delivered to the police.

Locative media had its way into *Desenrola* as well: At the website, Celo and Paola concealed *podcasts* that framed Formiga and took the players to locations pointed by photos pointed by a Google Maps user from the duo. These files were hidden in links created at places, on the map, that informed where the dealer had business. This way, the base – the people responsible by the flow of the game – offered a way to map the route taken by Formiga – which involved both Brazil and other South America countries. Another lead was also related to Google Maps: Celo and Paola informed where was located, considering Rio de Janeiro's urban space, another photo that would frame the drug dealer. After making this transition between the informational flux and the urban space, leaving their homes to chase little objects through the corners of Rio, the players, following a GPS coordinate imprinted in one of the clues, were directed to the building of the Instituto Oi Futuro – the moment where the branding associated to the game was revealed – and could use both wireless networks and Bluetooth devices (provided by the base) to access the building blueprint and find a number of clues hidden in the building[15].

The last ARG being considered in this paper was *A Fórmula do Conhecimento*, which was played in Salvador, Bahia. This ARG meant to be part of the marketing campaign of a university – and the players needed to help a damsel in distress to find her grandfather, that supposedly was abducted to a criminal corporation. Turns out the old man was hiding, afraid of what might happen to him if the bandits got to him, for he discovered a formula that could power up one's knowledge.

Three were the opportunities, between May and June, 2009, where the players went downtown in Salvador to find clues that would lead them to the formula – and the end of the game. First, they had to find a map in one of Salvador most famous piazzas; next, they had to find a book lost inside one of Salvador's public libraries; last, they were taken to an old harbor to find the chemical equation that corresponded to the formula. Blogs and social network sites were responsible for providing the GPS coordinates once the players were already at the urban space – that required both the use of locative media, since the players had to check the coordinates at Google Maps live from the place they were, or even communicate with people who were at their desktops, watching the game roll.

FINAL THOUGHTS

According to what was previously exposed, alternate reality games can reconfigure the way we observe the city and interpret urban space. Buildings, squares, museums, among other places, are appropriated by the ARGs' gameplay and become the *play space*. In order to accomplish this goal, these games are aided by locative media, which become important tools, for they allow that the game content, available in the cyberspace, be *poured* into physical space. Thus, one layer of information can be indexed in certain city points, reconfiguring the original meaning of these places. Therefore, a control zone is created, an informational territory, a "bubble" over the space where the ARG is experienced, resulting in a resignification of that place. Locative media help to expand the original meaning of real world places, connecting electronic games to urban spaces through informational territories.

In the cases previously mentioned, it was possible to confirm these prerogatives. As in the case of the *A Formula do Conhecimento*'s live action, in Campo Grande Square, in which players stood around a monument to connect to the wi-fi network and search for clues to solve the puzzle. In the case of *Desenrola*, the Oi Futuro building structure, in Rio de Janeiro, allowed the information exchange between mobile devices operated by players and characters, through locative media.

Locative media had also a important role as a facilitator in the dialogue between characters and players, especially when transmitting confidential information, as the bottles' hiding places in Zona Incerta and the chemical components in *A Fórmula do Conhecimento.* Encrypted numbers in social networks websites or hidden in source codes of specific blogs were interpreted and transformed in coordinates, which, after being analyzed through GoogleMaps, directed players to these hiding places. In the case of *Desenrola*, on the other hand, the game characters printed GoogleMaps screens to inform the route to reach the drug dealer Formiga and to hide podcasts in order to put him in jail.

Finally, we come to the conclusion that locative media can be appropriated by players and used as a tool for orientation in urban space, when searching for game items, as seen in the games *2084* and *Teoria das Cordas*. In these cases, players simulated a position mapping to search for players characters and, consequently, the game clues. In the case of *Desenrola,* players had to use the location blueprints[16], available on the Internet. Once more, by means of interpreting numbers, which were accessed through social networks profiles, like Orkut and Twitter, players unveiled the points in which the items were hidden.

The purpose of this chapter was to analyze how locative media have been used alongside these new appropriations of ludic forms to modify the way individuals actually relate to urban space. To accomplish this goal, we made a research on the most popular ubiquitous (or pervasive) games – the alternate reality games – and came to the conclusion that these games can expand their ludic space through the use of locative media, resulting in a resignification of places in real world. Alongside, we noticed that locative media are efficient tools used for internal communication between characters and players, and, finally, that these media are also powerful tools for the in-game players' articulation. Evidently, this study does not finish the issue on the possibilities of appropriation of locative media in electronic games. The arguments we presented in this chapter are intended to help to the construction of a knowledge foundation on these issues; to contribute to the understanding of other alternate reality games related aspects, which can help on the elaboration of further works on the ludic appropriations of locative media.

REFERENCES

Beslay, L., & Hakala, H. (2005). *Digital Territory: Bubbles*. Vision Book.

Bjork, S. (2002). Designing ubiquitous computing games. *Personal and Ubiquitous Computing*, *6*, 442–458.

Caillois, R. (1961). *Man, Play and Games*. Chicago: University of Illinois Press.

Croswell, T. (1996). *In Place/Out Place: Geography, Ideology, and Transgression*. Minneapolis: University of Minnesota.

Dena, C. (2007). Creating Alternate realities. In Borries, F., Walz, S., & Bottger, M. (Eds.), *Space Time Play: Computer Games, Architecture and Urbanism: the Next Level*. Basel, Switzerland: Birkhauser Verlag AG.

Dolozel, L. (1998). *Heterocosmica. Fiction and Possible Worlds*. Baltimore: Johns Hopkins University Press.

Dourish, P. (2006). Re-Shape-ing Place: "Place" and "Space" Ten Years On. In [Banff, Alberta, Canada.]. *Proceedings of CSCW*, *06*(November), 4–8.

Dourish, P., & Harrison, S. (1996). Re-Place-ing Space: The Roles of Place and Space in Collaborative Systems. In *Proceedings of CSCW*. New York: ACM.

Ferreira, E., & Falcão, T. (2009). Through the Looking Glass: Weavings Between the Magic Circle and the Immersive Processes in Video Games. In *Digital Games Research Association 2009 Conference Proceedings*, London, September 2009.

Foucault, M. (1984). De Outros Espaços. In *Architecture, Mouvement, Continuité*. Retrieved August 2009, from http://www.rizoma.net/interna.php?id=169secao=anarquitextura

Gottmann, J. (1973). *The Significance of Territory*. Charlottesville, VA: University Press of Virginia.

Hall, A. (2009). "I am Trying to Believe": Dystopia as Utopia in the Year Zero Alternate Reality Game. *Eludamos. Journal for Computer Game Culture*, *3*(1), 69–82.

Huizinga, J. (1950). *Homo Ludens: A Study of the Play-Element in Culture*. Boston: Beacon Press.

IGDA. (2006). *Alternate Reality Games White Paper*. IGDA ARG SIG.

Juul, J. (2005). *Half-Real: Video Games between Real Rules and Fictional Worlds*. Cambridge, MA: The MIT Press.

Juul, J. (2008). The Magic Circle and the Puzzle Piece. In S. Günzel, et al (eds.), *Conference Proceedings of the Philosophy of Computer Games*. Potsdam, The Netherlands: Potsdam University Press.

Lefevbre, H. (1991). *The Production of space*. Oxford, UK: Blackwell Publishers.

Lemos, A. (2007). Comunicação e práticas sociais no espaço urbano: as características dos Dispositivos Híbridos Móveis de Conexão Multirredes (DHMCM). *Revista Comunicação. Mídia e Consumo*, *4*(10), 23–40.

Lemos, A. (2008a). Mídias Locativas e Territórios Informacionais. In Santaella, L., & Arantes, P. (Eds.), *Estéticas Tecnológicas: Novos Modos de Sentir* (pp. 207–230). São Paulo: EDUC.

Lemos, A. (2008b). Mobile Communication and new sense of places: a critique of spatialization in cyberculture. [PUCSP]. *Galáxia*, *16*, 91–108.

Lemos, A. (2009). Pervasive Games and Processes of Spacialization Communication, Informational Territories and Mobile Technologies. In *Canadian Journal of Communication*.

Lemos, A. (2010). Locative Media and Surveillance at the Boundaries of Informational Territories. In Firmino, R., Duarte, F., & Ultramari, C. (Eds.), *ICTs for Mobile and Ubiquitous Urban Infrastructures: Surveillance, Locative Media and Global Networks*. Hershey, PA: IGI Global.

Mastrocolla, V. M. (2006). ARGS: Uma nova ferramenta de entretenimento, comunicação e Marketing. *Revista da ESPM, 13*(12-5), 94-103.

McCullough, M. (2004). *Digital Ground: Architecture, Pervasive Computing, and Environmental Knowing*. Cambridge, MA: MIT Press.

McGonigal, J. (2003a, November). A real little game. The performance of belief in pervasive play. In Raessens, J.R., Copier, M. (Eds.). *Proceedings of the Level Up DiGRA Conference,* Utrecht.

McGonigal, J. (2003b). *This is not a game: Immersive aesthetics and collect play*. Presented at the 5th International Digital Arts and Culture Conference (Melbourne, May).

McGonigal, J. (2006). *This Might be a Game*. Unpublished doctoral Dissertation, Berkeley University, Berkeley, CA.

McGonigal, J. (2007). Ubiquitous gaming. A vision for the future of enchanted spaces. In Borries, F. (Eds.), *Space Time Play: Computer Games, Architecture and Urbanism: the Next Level*. Basel, Switzerland: Birkhauser Verlag AG.

Montolla, M. (2005). *Exploring the Edge of the Magic Circle. Defining Pervasive Games.* DAC 2005 conference, December 1-3, IT University of Copenhagen. Retrieved September 2008 from http://users.tkk.fi/mmontola/exploringtheedge.pdf

Montolla, M. Stenros & Waern. (Eds.). (2009). *Pervasive Games: Theory and Design*. San Francisco: Morgan Kaufmann.

Nieuwdorp, E. (2007). The pervasive interface. Tracing the magic circle. In S. De Castell & J. Jensen (Eds.). *Proceedings of the DiGRA Conference*, Vancouver, June 2007.

Örnenbring, H. (2007). Alternate reality gaming and convergence culture: The case of *Alias. International Journal of Cultural Studies*, 10.

Osborne, T., & Rose, N. (2004). Spatial phenomenotechnics: making space with Charles Booth and Patrick Geddes Environment and Planning D. *Society and Space*, *22*, 209–228.

Russel, B. (1999). *A Headmap Manifesto*. In Headmap.Org. Retrieved August 28, 2009, from http://www.mutateweb.com/library/headmap.pdf

Ryan, M.-L. (2001). *Narrative as Virtual Reality: Immersion and Interactivity in Literature and Electronic Media*. Baltimore: The Johns Hopkins University Press.

Salen, K., & Zimmermman, E. (2003). *Rules of Play. Game Design Fundamentals*. Cambridge, MA: MIT Press.

Santaella, L. (2008a). *A Estética Política das Mídias Locativas*, Nómadas, 28, April, Universidad Central, Colombia. Retrieved August 2009, from http://bibliotecavirtual.clacso.org.ar/ar/libros/colombia/iesco/nomadas/28/12-e stetica.pdf

Santaella, L. (2008b). *A ecologia pluralista das mídias locativas Revista FAMECOS nº 37*. Porto Alegre, Brazil: Programa de Pós-Graduação em Comunicação Social da Faculdade de Comunicação Social / PUCRS.

Santaella, L. (2008c). *Mídias Locativas: A Internet Móvel de Lugares e Coisas Revista FAMECOS nº 35*. Porto Alegre, Brazil: Programa de Pós-Graduação em Comunicação Social da Faculdade de Comunicação Social / PUCRS.

Schneider, J., & Kortuem, G. (2001). *How to host a pervasive game. Supporting face-to-face interactions in live-action role-playing*. Presented at the Workshop on Designing Ubiquitous Computing Games. Ubicomp, Atlanta, GA, September/October 2001.

Souza e Silva, A. (2006). From cyber to hybrid: mobile technologies as interfaces of hybrid spaces. *Space and Culture*, *9*(3), 261–278. doi:10.1177/1206331206289022

Szulborsky, D. (2005). *This Is Not A Game: A Guide to Alternate Reality Gaming*. New Fiction Publishing.

Tuters, M., & Varnelis, K. (2006). Beyond Locative Media: Giving Shape to the Internet of Things. *Leonardo*, *39*(4), 357–363. doi:10.1162/leon.2006.39.4.357

Weiser, M. (1991). The computer for the 21st century. *Scientific American*, *265*(3), 66–75. doi:10.1038/scientificamerican0991-94

Weiser, M. (1994). The world is not a desktop. *Interaction*, (January): 7–8. doi:10.1145/174800.174801

ADDITIONAL READING

Andrade, Luiz Adolfo de (2009). Alternate Reality Games e Espacialização Novos lugares, fluxos e negócios através dos jogos eletrônicos. In: Revista Universitária do Audivisual (RUA) Edição Especial #05. São Carlos: UFSCar.

Bogost, I. (2007). *Persuasive Games: The Expressive Power of Videogames*. Cambridge: MIT Press.

Borries, F., & Watz, S. Böttiger (Eds.) (2007). Space Time Play: Computer Games, Architecture and Urbanism: the Next Level. Basel: Birkhauser Verlag AG.

Consalvo, M. (2007). *Cheating. Gaining Advantage in Videogames*. Cambridge: MIT Press.

Ferreira, E. M., & Falcão, T. (2009) 'Through the Looking Glass: Weavings Between the Magic Circle and the Immersive Processes in Video Games', paper presented at Digital Games Research Association Conference, London, September, 2009.

Fine, G. A. (1983). *Shared Fantasy: Role-Playing Games as Social Worlds*. Chicago: University of Chicago.

Harrigan, P., & Wardrip-Fruin, N. (2009). *Third Person: Authoring and Exploring Vast Narratives*. Cambridge: MIT Press.

Juul, J. (2008) 'The Magic Circle and the Puzzle Piece', in S. Günzel, M. Liebe and D. Mersch (ed.) Conference Proceedings of the Philosophy of Computer Games, Potsdam, Potsdam University Press.

Latour, B. (2005). *Reassembling the Social. An Introduction to Actor-Network Theory*. Oxford: Oxford University Press.

McGonigal, J. (2006). This Might be a Game Ubiquitous Play and Performance at the Turn of the Twenty-First CenturyUnpublished doctoral Dissertation, Berkeley University. Berkeley, CA/EUA.

McPherson, M., & Smith-Lovin, L. (2002). Cohesion and membership duration: Linking groups, relations and individuals in an ecology of affiliation. *Advances in Group Processes*, *19*, 1–36. doi:10.1016/S0882-6145(02)19002-3

Mead, G. H. (1934). *Mind, Self and Society*. Chicago: University of Chicago Press.

Montolla, M., & Stenros, J. Waern. A. (Eds.). (2009). Pervasive Games: Theory and Design. Oxford: Morgan Kaufmann.

Ryan, M. (1994) 'Immersion vs. Interactivity: Virtual Reality and Literary Theory', Postmodern Culture, 05.

Taylor, T. L. (2006). *Play Between Worlds. Exploring Online Game Culture*. Cambridge: MIT Press.

Van Kranenburg, R. (2008). *The Internet of Things. A Critique of Ambient Technology and the All-seeing Network of RFID*. Amsterdan, Network Notebooks.

Wolf, M. J., & Perron, B. (2009). *The videogame theory reader 2*. London: Routledge.

Yee, N. (2006). The Labor of Fun: How Video Games Blur the Boundaries of Work and Play. *Games and Culture*, *01*, 68–71. doi:10.1177/1555412005281819

KEY TERMS AND DEFINITIONS

Alternate Reality Games: Are games that mix the essential substance of the normal life to the diegetic patterns found out in fiction, therefore making them potentially capable of blurring the borders between the real and virtual aspects of the world.

Informational Territories: Are areas of control of digital information fluxes in an intersection zone between cyberspace and urban space.

Locative Media: Should be understood as the result of the combination between location-based services and technology such as sensors, electronic devices, digital networks and the services associated with them, which react to their local context.

Places: Can be defined as geographic spaces infused by meaning, which is conferred by people continuously stablishing social relationships in such space.

Spatialisation: A process that points out to changes in a given space created by processes of flux that produce meaning. Fluxes are events in mobility that posses and are controlled by time, space and matter.

The Magic Circle: Is created when a game takes place. It represents the feeling that one is in a sacred, rule-governed space, outside of the ordinary life.

ENDNOTES

1 For Brazilian theorist André Lemos, "It is plausible to think that the information society produces new territories. Informational territories can be understood as areas where informational flow in the intersection between cyberspace and urban space is digitally controlled. Here uses can either control inputs and outputs of information date. The informational territory creates a new function of place, a heterotopy. For informational territory I understand the area of control (and to be controlled by) of digital information flow in an intersection with a physical area. So place, as a result of territorialization (geographic delimitation, laws, and regulations) gains a new layer of information that's a new territory created by electronic networks and mobile devices" (LEMOS, 2009, p. 5).

2 http://www.turbulence.org/blog/archives/001365.html

3 http://en.wikipedia.org/wiki/The_Beast_(game)

4 http://www.thelostring.com/

5 http://www.argbrasil.net/wiki/Vivo_em_A%C3%A7%C3%A3o_1

6 http://www.argbrasil.net/wiki/O_Projeto

7 http://www.prenoma.com

8 http://www.zonaincerta.com.br/

9 http://www.revistaparadoxo.com/materia.php?ido=4411

10 In Brasil, 'base' is the term used to address the team behind the veil of the illusion, including the puppetmasters and the game producers.

11 http://www.arkhosbiotech.com

12 http://www.youtube.com/watch?v=sTpamZZWPPM

13 http://semanapassada.wordpress.com/missoes-de-campo/

14 http://www.desenrola.com

15 http://www.youtube.com/watch?v=csEn9dc4kgc

16 http://www.oifuturo.org.br/museu/#2_visita.asp

Chapter 12
Mobile Devices:
Designing Hybrid Body-Spaces

Luisa Paraguai
Universidade Anhembi Morumbi, Brazil

ABSTRACT

The chapter is concerned with the mobile technology and its interventions on the perception of the body and the space, demanding new behavioural codes and evoking other communication patterns. This technology enables users to be always connected, creating other practices of sociability and composing the urban landscape and the body space with digital contexts. So, the space occupied by mobile users is no longer physical or virtual, but hybrid. After a brief introduction about hybrid spaces, some theoretical references configure the idea that mobile technology determines specific modes of interaction, emphasising a ritual dimension. The mobile users have started to perform the same body gestures and bounded intimacies in a social context that configure a specific new bodily spatiality. Some artistic projects will be presented pointing out some aspects of significant social mobile uses, transforming users bodily states and spatial domains.

INTRODUCTION

If the 1990s were about the virtual, it is quite possible that this decade of the 2000s will turn out to be about the physical – that is, physical space filled with electronic and visual information. (Manovich, 2005: 2)

DOI: 10.4018/978-1-60960-051-8.ch012

The computer as a communication tool has transformed the means of human interaction profoundly, providing a social space that has been individually and/or collectively explored, accessed, and developed through different devices. The computing technologies and networks have effectively contaminated the physical space. To understand the materiality and effect of mobile devices on everyday life is the main concern of this text. The mobile technology enables users to be always connected, helping them to create other practices of sociability, composing the urban landscape and the body space with informational spaces. This process has transformed the comprehension of the communication space, that it is no longer physical nor virtual, but an emerging dynamic configuration of different spatial matrices – distinct dimensions organised by cultural, economic, social and technological elements. The space is no more determined by the physical contiguity, and according to Castells (1999) it is the space of flux, a circulation space, not any more restrict to geographical frontiers.

Manovich (2005: 2) has proposed the term "cellspace" to point out the physical space filled with data, in which users can access any information through personal wireless communication devices, working on local and/or global digital networks. Comprehending that,

cellular networks are, technologically, digital networks. However, the term "digital network" is used in this work as a reference to the network shaped by personal computers, which constituted, mainly, what was analyzed as cyberspace. Conversely, mobile networks are characterized by nomadic technology devices. (De Souza e Silva, 2006b: 121)

For Manovich (2005: 3) "cellspace is an invisible layer of information which is overlaid over the physical space and which is customized by an individual user". According to Hayles as cited by De Souza e Silva (2004: 135) "the context is becoming enfolded, so that there is no longer a homogeneous context for a given spatial area, but rather pockets of different contexts in it." A hybrid space, thus, is not only related to the layering of digital data on physical reality; it is a conceptual space created by the merging of the borders between the physical and the digital space due to the use of mobile technologies (De Souza e Silva, 2004). Then, the hybrid space can become local, not only thorough geographical inputs, but every time someone actualizes any live communication activity, such as MSN, twitter, email, on the web; it can be understood as a process of virtualization, making emerge distinct realities in real time. According to Santaella (2007: 224), the "interstitial space" is another term that comprehends users actions combining urban spaces and digital contexts through mobile technologies. Lemos (2010: 4) affirms that "place is now the result of a set of physical, cultural and economic characteristics: physical dimensions and a database". These configurations have enabled a dynamic perspective of our interactions, combining face-to-face and mediated relationships through synchronous and asynchronous exchanges.

Those artefacts are sensitive to people, other devices and the physical space around, creating other states of attention and configuring different bodily movements to the users perceive and experience the world around them. But, what is important to emphasize is that social practices and mobility are responsible and determinant to qualify those spaces as hybrid with a dynamic flux of information. By interfacing those different codes simultaneously, it is possible to consider a re-configuration of our bodily spatiality, and a negotiation of other boundaries for our perceptions. As Negroponte (1995: 2) says "the modulation of signals processed from wearable accessories can constitute the 'bodynet', a personal area of web communication that establishes connections through the body itself". So, body can be understood as a physical reality technologically mediated, elaborating its activities, which take place either locally or remotely, in constant juxtaposition of space and time dimensions not related.

Some data can be embedded in objects and places, involving the users in the reconfiguration of global, local and personal networks. Then, "the garment, the home, and the public space become sites of processing and mediation" (Greenfield, 2006: 26). It is necessary to comprehend that other user/artefact relations have been evoked. Designing new actions and behaviours will reconfigure our understanding of daily life. The computing systems become interwoven with the existing rituals of everyday life. Usually, cognitive models and feedbacks are conformed by recognising "the objectives and intentions" at the context of people's privileged actions (Norman, 2006: 71). For the author, there is a continuous flux among objective, intention, action, perception, interpretation and evaluation that have determined a reading and comprehension of the world without forgetting the existence of executing lacunas, characteristic of any activity.

In antagonistic way, the technological context of wireless communication and embedded processors has evoked a non-usual negotiation between the user and the information-processing system. There can be no intention in the users' action or even consciousness of what is taking place, differently from saving or deleting a doc file, although we will still have feedbacks from the artefacts as computing systems; because of the technology of sensors the objects have become aware of how people use them or react to them. The lacunas on that context are more frequent, potentializing the uncertainty of the exchanges and the understanding, and complexifying the attempts of control and/or management. It is possible to affirm that the knowledge can recognise patterns of information, distributed in the world and dependent of the users physical and corporeal relations. For Greenfield (2006: 26) those artefacts can be called "everyware" and understood as "information processing dissolving in behaviour". Another dynamic of interactions has emerged from that hybrid context, changing daily routines and transforming the social relations and movements. So, the space being occupied depends on physical and informational inputs, which reconfigure dynamically the materiality of gestures and behaviours. Users have elaborated different states of perception while interfacing the boundaries between the physicality of action/reaction and the virtuality of connections.

Several theorists have written about the phenomenon of wireless communication and its consequent social mobility - a fluid organization with holes not so rigid and social spaces constantly changeable. According to Meyrowitz (2004) the contemporaneous culture is creating "the global nomads", and to Urry (2000) the actual culture can be comprehended only by the concept of "a mobile sociology". So, the actual process of urban mobility, despite creating body and information displacements, has evoked other ways of space and time control by the juxtaposition of digital and physical spaces.

A new spatial context and a new time dimension in which the communication takes place. It is the space and time of the communicating individual, that is a material form, as material as any other space and time, but this is chosen by the communication subject. (Castells et al, 2004: 241)

For example, someone who travels constantly, but still remains connected on the Web, can be recognised by the flux of information produced and transmitted by his/her choices of subjects. Every access implies on the attempt of keeping the control of the local space. What suggests that our incursions on the Web are still a matter of occupying, engaging and a feeling of belonging.

That comprehension of the body can be understood according to Merleau-Ponty (1999: 336)

it doesn't matter as the way in fact it is, while something in the objective, real, space, but my body as a system of possible actions, a potential body, which has its circumstantial space defined by its activities and situation. ... my body is there where he has something to do.

Then, the body has created other bodily zones, limits of power and privacy, which can be thought of as possible presences beyond relationships established by possibilities of interactions - actions and reactions. It cannot be sustained by an identity, or a physical domain only, it expands itself as potential connections, accessing and being accessed. The constant possibilities of interfacing with other spatial and time dimensions have established a constant renegotiation of the body's boundaries.

MOBILE DEVICES AND MODES OF INTERACTION

Communication is a symbolic process whereby reality is produced, maintained, repaired, and transformed. (Carey, 1985: 23)

Assuming the relation between communication and culture to comprehend mobile technologies, we bring the concept of ritual dimension to understand the mobile users' usual performance, embodying the same corporeal gestures and intimacies in distinct social contexts. For Licoppe (2003) the communicational exchanges among mobile users have assumed, in some way, a discreet and continuous way of performing the dialogues; those interactions are recurrent, small and punctual dosages, that point out and, by the end, determine a kind of unity. It means that users actions belong to the present time. Those everyday events are constant and can create another understanding of the world and of the other, mediated by the users' gestures and movements.

According to Greene (apud Castells et al, 2004: 234) those connections between mobile space and time, articulated in multiple and heterogeneous places and rhythms, can be defined in three main contexts: "rhythms of device use; rhythms of everyday life; and rhythms of institutional change." For the author, rhythms of device use refer mainly to the interaction between any person and the device – individual difficulties and facilities in using a technological interface; the rhythms of everyday life refer to the social and cultural interferences in which a specific device use is embedded; and finally, the rhythms of institutional change refer to the historical and infrastructural elements that enable mobile use – any technological development to establish and maintain network technologies.

The social interferences, according to Carey (1985), can have two distinct views approaching the communication process: transmission and ritual. The transmission view refers to the communication as "a process whereby messages or signals are transmitted and distributed in space for the control of distance and people. It is defined by terms such as imparting, sending, transmitting, or giving information to others" (Carey, 1985: 15). It is composed from physical references, a geographic or a material goods circulation metaphor.

For the same author, the ritual view refers to the communication "not toward the extension of messages in space but toward the maintenance of society in time; not the act of imparting information but the representation of shared belief" (IBID: p.18). He assumes that reality is not given but is shaped and moulded through communication: "...a ritual view conceives communication as a process through which a shared culture is created, modified, and transformed" (IBID, p.19). According to Ling (2008: 57), "the ritual interaction implies on participants sharing a common mood and recognizing their mutual entrainment". The transmission view of communication implies on the extension of messages across geography with the purpose of control, while the ritual view draws people together in fellowship. Taking an example described by Carey:

If one examines a newspaper under a transmission view of communication, one sees the medium as an instrument for disseminating news and knowledge in larger and larger packages over greater distances. Under a ritual view, then, news is not information but drama. It does not describe the world but portrays an arena of dramatic focus and action; it exists solely in historical time; and it invites our participation on the basis of our assuming, often vicariously, social roles within it. (Carey, 1985: 20-21)

For the author, the ritual view does not exclude the processes of information transmission, but both are cast within an essentially ritualistic view of communication and social order.

More and more, the mobile devices use has been included in our daily life, and what is observed are the stylized social behaviours being repeated frequently everywhere, establishing other social bonds and personal boundaries. That assumption can be understood by Goffman's thoughts about ritual interaction and everyday activities; Goffman, cited by Ling (2008: 60-61), suggests that individuals can develop the sense of being part of a social group when they recognize their movements, with the use of various artefacts, into the context of their everyday lives. The mutual engagements actually presented during any mobile call or SMS sessions, can suspend the time perception during the occurrence of those exchanges. The synchronic time for these exchanges - texts, images, videos, and sounds, can establish the sense of cohesion and organize a spatial condition to be occupied by the mobile users.

Reflecting about the mobile communication way of operating, we bring Licoppe (2003: 180-182), who has examined the contrast between what he calls "the conversational and the connected modes of interaction". The conversational form is a style wherein the telephone call is a routine procedure, such as the weekly call to one's parents. The call is a part of the regular interactions among people and it generally takes place on a specific day and time, usually from the same place. For the connected form of interaction, the interaction among individuals takes place in short sessions through the day perhaps using a variety of media (phone, SMS, email, IM, etc.).

For Chan (apud Manovich, 2008: 40) "all cultures practice the exchange of tokens that bear and carry meanings, communicate interest and count as personal and social transactions". For him, even the gestures can become a sort of cue or signal that indicates users' interests in one another. For instance, as the author notes, the use of tokens is often

... accompanied by ambiguity of intent and motive (the token's meaning may be codified while the user's motive for using it may not). This can double up the meaning of interaction and communication, allowing the recipients of tokens to respond to the token or to the user behind its use. (IBID, p.40-41)

We can assume the messages as tokens, since their original meaning is less important than their function as tokens – to be available for those friends and keeping them in touch no matter what has taken place. It is possible to recognize a specific code in those standardized communications protocols that allow the interchange between mobile users and other specific applications on the web.

In some cases, the new forms of written expression are signs of subcultures, and expression of innovation from the users. In fact, creative uses of language become a form of personal and group expression. But in most cases, it is the simple adaptation of language to the format and limits of the technology, including strategies to reduce the cost of transmission. (Castells et al, 2004: 246)

The connected form is a continual flux of small interactions characterized by a specific code. The individuals update each other on their progress through the day and perhaps make small requests and provide small bits of exchanges and gossips. According to Ling (2004a: 8) "Licoppe's point is that this form of interaction is becoming pervasive. Rather than occurring at a specific time and place, it is happening everywhere, at all hours and in homeopathic doses".

The capacity of wireless communication technology displays a multimodal form of communication, with text, image, and audio being used from different stations – on the web and mobile devices.

The observation shows that the combination of these different modes of communication, particularly by the young users, are creating new forms of meaning, characterized by the mixture of methods of assigning meaning, e.g. using text only for the personal commentary or for emphasis, while sound and images are supposed to be self-explanatory. (Castells et al, 2004: 246)

So, it is possible to say that different levels of disconnection and interconnection, running cyclically, can characterize the context of nomadic technology use. Mobile phones users can cut themselves off from their environments or stay engaged with the actual world while making or receiving phone calls. Those devices do take people out of their actual context, but also bring remote people and information to the nearby space. They combine both, the centre and the periphery of our attention, and in fact provoke the constant movements of forward and back between the two conditions. They operate simultaneously in different contexts and spatial dimensions, not related, working as several folds of existence.

According to Ling (2008: 148) the establishment of a common mood is decisive for those interactions to mark social boundaries. The movement of in and out evokes new types of sociability and communication patterns and transforms the senses of public and private space, external and internal, creating distinctions in the behavioural dimensions. The notion of time, is therefore, becoming more flexible with these easy calls and easy appointments, and, in most of times, the mobile phone actually "immobilizes" young people within these existing social networks. (Castells et al, 2004)

MOBILE DEVICES AND INFORMAL RITUALS: SHARING BODILY GESTURES AND BEHAVIOURS

In French it is called le portable, or le G, which stands for GSM. The Finns have adopted the term kanny, which refers to an extension of the hand. In German it is the handy. In Spanish it is el movil. Americans still call it a cell phone. In Arabic it is sometimes called el mobile, but often a telephone sayaar or makhmul (both of which refer to carrying) or a telephone gowal (air telephone). In Thailand it is a moto. In Japan it is keitai denwa, a carried telephone, or simply keitai, or even just ke-tai. In China it is sho ji, or hand machine. (Plant, 2001: 23)

The phone calls have always occurred in the interior of buildings, specific rooms, and historically, have moved to the exterior locations with the design of phone booths. That gradual movement toward to the public space still keeps some kind of privacy, but the personal and public relation has changed a lot with mobile calls coming at any time, at any place, and in the company of any number of onlookers and eavesdroppers.

The first mobile phone was introduced only twenty years ago and its popular diffusion dates back to the early 90's. Where borders and physical walls were used to define space, mobile technologies and new means of communication have created hertzian space, an evolving overlay of wireless technology and other layers of data that modify the urban space, creating new structures and systems for people to navigate. Jenny L. Chowdhury created the piece "Cell Atlantic CellBooth" [http://jennylc.com/cellbooth/] to make visible that talking on the phone is no longer a private exchange. Jenny asked herself about the possibility of carrying a phone booth and setting it up when she needed to converse in private, emphasizing the changes in human behaviour due to the ubiquitous use of mobiles. Her project is concerned with the enquiry into everyday life situations, evolving product experiences.

Some recent researches have re-discussed a number of topics such as the emergence of a new body language, the definition of private space versus public space, the concepts of presence, telepresence and attentiveness, as well as the appearance of new social codes, behaviours, and etiquettes. According to Ling (apud Ling 2002: 5-6) "when talking, there is the general exchange of words. Beyond this, there is an equally important back channel flow of gestures, interjections and glances that allow for the management and the pacing of interaction." His comprehension is that the mobile users and their personal conversations and bounded intimacies have been determined and formatted by characteristic bodily gestures and postures.

According to Plant (2001), the receipt of a public call can be seen as a ritual component that evokes different levels of user's attention and disconnection from the physical context, characterized by three distinct situations described as

flight, in which users immediately move to absent themselves from their social situation; suspension, in which recipients stay put, but stop whatever they are doing for the duration of a call and effectively cut themselves off from their environment; and persistence, in which users stay put and engaged with the actual world, as far as possible carrying on with whatever they were doing before they made or took the call. (Plant, 2001: 31)

The author divides the mobile phone-using world into "innies" and "outies". The "innies" group use their phones unobtrusively, often leaving venues like the supper table to answer a call. Their basic response is "flight". The "outies", who "readily and smoothly integrate" the mobile phone into their lives, will arrive at a table and place them out in the open, claiming a bit of territory and signalling, "my mobile and I are here." Their primary mode is "persistence". (Ibid, p.32-33)

The mobile phone users are really trying to live in two contexts, frequently riding bikes, eating, drinking, carrying packages while talking on their mobiles - receiving and making phone calls. The artefact and the actions that people might engage in with it have meaning, both for the people engaged in those actions and for members of the social group of practice.

Those devices do take people out of their actual context, but also bring remote people and information to their nearby physical space. They have to combine both the centre and the periphery of users' attention and in fact provoke the constant movements of forward and back between those conditions. Plant (2001) uses the word "bi-psyche" to conjure this cognitive ability of operating on two spatial dimensions.

Other consequence can be described as a physical bodily manifestation: a whole new set of postures adopted by mobile phone users. The researcher describes the "speakeasy" posture - head thrown back and neck upright, "giving out an air of self-assurance and single-minded refusal to be distracted by the outside world", and the "spacemaker" posture with the head bowed, often walking around in a circle trying to carve out an imaginary private space – a bubble space (Plant, 2001: 51-52).

Another difference on that body gestuality of mobile users, when walking on the streets is that they usually avoid eye contact with people around, often ignoring them (Castells et al, 2004); this body language differs from the usual pedestrians and emphasizes that bodily gestures have not being determined any more by local demands only; people have to negotiate the actual and remote interactions and reconfigure their bodily zones for this new spatial condition.

Nowadays, there is a common rule of mobile etiquette that is talking in a low voice in public places, such as the theatre, the cinema, trains, buses, and even airplanes. There is what has been called m-etiquette (Lacohée, Wakeford and Pearson, 2003) or mobile etiquette (Crabtree et al, 2003; Licoppe and Heurtin, 2002), which can be defined as the collection of rules that establish the public use of mobile telephony. But, according to Castells et al (2004: 229) there is a non-written set of rules that, indeed, is still under construction, it means that people have to learn how to deal with permanent availability – "the era of perpetual contact".

This social learning process, which can also be identified as the social appropriation or domestication process, has two sides. One refers to manners, because people have learned how and when a mobile phone could be used and, moreover, some old embarrassments are not usually happening nowadays thanks to the generalization of some technical features. New design of devices has evolved in this direction, and vibration or silent modes are commonly used. (Ibid, p.229)

For Rheingold (2005) the mobile phone use and ritual interaction are interconnected and able to create social changes and social capital. The understanding of mobile devices does not reside in the technology itself, but it is determined by its social use – its capability on extending and modelling human activities and relationships over time and space. So, the body can be understood as an entity, technologically mediated to operate simultaneously in different, not related, contexts and dimensions, like several folds of existence. Therefore, those artefacts do shape and transform, proposing other ways in which people interact with, and perceive the world.

MOBILE DEVICES AND EXPERIENCES OF PERCEPTION: ARTISTIC PRACTICES

The mobile phone has become associated with the common question: 'where are you?' and common answers: 'on my way', 'on the bus', 'on the train' might be changed for 'on the mobile'. For these mobile users, it does not matter so much the geographical location but rather the possibility of reaching someone and to be answered by him/her. So, the idea of local has been constantly determined and updated by the possibility of being accessed, and this can be perceived by the warbles, beeps and tunes, emerging around us and transforming the background sound of the cities. Nowadays, someone talking, shouting or laughing to him/herself on the street is not weird and it does not cause any sort of embarrassments. According to Santos (1999: 148-149)

the techniques participate on the creation of spatial perception and also the temporal perception, as for its physical existence, what registers the sensation before the velocity, as its imaginary. ... The same space can be understood as where the people can process their individual and collective procedures, or as reality perceived. ... The logic of the device and the human relations affect the human behaviours.

The mobile devices have created possible concomitant digital and physical spaces of information – databases and actions, in which the user is constantly negotiating and establishing their connections to create meaning and knowledge. It is possible to reaffirm the assumption of Merleau-Ponty (1999: 328) about space, that it "... is not the real or logical environment where the things take place, but the way as the person can establish and do possible connections." He thought about the space as a universal potential of connections - a system established through the experience, where the meaning has been elaborated from the object relations with and onto the space.

Thinking about those changes associated with mobile communication, some poetic procedures and sensorial experiences were chosen and described below with their different proposals, recreating, in some way, and questioning the relations between public and private spaces, the perception of body and space and their contours for that dynamic configuration. The artists invite users/participants to internalise what they are experiencing, to make new connections, in other words, to re-map their own nervous systems (De Kerckhove, 1997: 24). Those works are able to produce an open and engaging experience that manifests the actual cultural changes; trying to escape the constraints of the body through technological interfaces in order to reach a better understanding of our own capabilities and to create other ways of being.

Social Mobiles[1]

This mobile phone behavior exploration project is a collaboration project between global design and innovation firm IDEO and artist and designer Crispin Jones. This project presents five prototypes of mobiles (electric shock mobile, speaking mobile, musical mobile, knocking mobile, catapult mobile) that in different and provocative ways modify their user's behaviour to make it less disruptive (see Figure 1). The intent of the project was to provoke discussion about the social impact of mobile phones.

The electric shock mobile delivers a variable level of electric shock depending on how loudly the person at the other end is speaking. As a result the two parties are induced to speak more quietly. A sound level, monitored by the interface, determines the engagement of both. The catapult mobile can been used to launch sounds into other people's phone conversation. This provides a direct yet discreet way of invading their space. The man sense of space is quite dynamic because it is related to "action – what can be done in a given space, rather that what is seen by passive viewing" (Hall, 1982: 115). The spatial discussion proposed by the social mobile project have evoked reflexions about physical territories and the "proxemic distances" introduced by Hall (1982). He determined the limits of proxemics zones to designate the interrelated observations and theories of man using of the space as a specialized elaboration of culture. According to him there are four areas for this informal space: "intimate distance" for embracing or whispering (15-46cm), "personal distance" for conversations among good friends (0.5-1.2m), "social distance" for conversations among acquaintances (1.2-3.6m) and "public distance" used for public speaking (3.6m or more). The concept of those interpersonal spaces can be redefined by the occurrence of users sensory mediated experiences.

Figure 1. Social mobiles

Agoraphone[2]

Kelly Dobson project consists of a communication sculpture installed as an element of urban intervention. From any touch-tone phone anywhere, people can call agoraphone's number and be connected to the public place (see Figure 2). Even not using a mobile device, the project is concerned with behavioural aspects involved in mobile phone calls.

Most of us have been acculturated to not express ourselves in public. But at the same time in our culture we have talk shows, reality TV, and online chat rooms through which we tell all. Those scenarios, characterized by extreme sacrifice of privacy, seem to take advantage of the seeming safety of media culture and mediated communication. AgoraPhone combines mediated communication with public space, to evoke a new domain of sensory-motor interactions and learning processes, leading the user to rediscover his/her own space and the perception of his/her presence. These

Figure 2. Agoraphone

possible artistic expressions change the contemplative and interpretative behaviour of users' actions, and therefore demand a different attitude from users to handle the space and their sense of presence. According to the artist, Kelly Dobson (2002),

there occurred two distinct changes in the space. Firstly, as expected, people who have never spoken with each other gather at the sculpture in conversation groups. The second major change in the physical public social space also occurs quite frequently - groups of people hang out nearby and call from cell phones while watching people at the sculpture. (http://web.media.mit.edu/~monster/AgoraPhone/webcam/index.html)

An example taken from the website describes a woman talking about her experience at the sculpture,

I was just walking by and someone said, 'Hey, anybody there?' so, I said, 'hello,' and they asked me how my day was going... But I felt kind of weird... Yeah, kind of self conscious, because I am talking to this person and I do not even know who they are and people are walking by seeing me talking to this thing... It is like talking to yourself in public if people do not know what it is... It is kind of like when you are talking on a cell phone in public only this is really big and out loud like your conversation is on speaker phone! I think if it were well known what it was, you know, if it was socially acceptable, and then it would feel less weird. (http://web.media.mit.edu/~monster/AgoraPhone/at-site/index.html)

At least one frequent caller made the AgoraPhone a personal radio station. He called every afternoon and made requests while broadcasting music into the public space. The constancy of those calls plays and maintains the mutual engagement among participants, evoking issues that are central to the definition of any social group. Then, the work, not even using the mobile interface, can make the participants reproduce and think about some characteristic behaviours and expectations, by playing with the social context and individual attitudes, not worried about sharing with others personal conversations.

Plesiophone Series[3]

Sidney Fels and Sachiyo Takahashi developed in 2001 the PlesioPhone series as a set of four interactive artworks (AirPhone, PhysicalPhone, String Phone, SMS-Phone) that comment on the evolution of human communication and its cultural implications. The context of the telephone and mobile phone medium is recreated, assuming the private and public zones as a blurring experience of boundary-maintaining communicational tendencies. The project literally means close-phone or close-voice. Each piece provides an original communication experience: the idea of a private communication space is redefined; virtual distance between people who are physically closed is created; the idea of collaborative communication is highlighted and the concept of phone communication as a contemporary art form is proposed.

People interact with the pieces in PlesioPhone series using their voice and body through various communication channels and systems of perception. Each piece in the series involves at least two people in the interaction, providing an original communication experience. They encompass some aspects of the face-to-face communication, reminding the fragility of voice communication both in public and in private spaces. The concepts of intimacy and embodiment are explored by the work, linking physically the human and the machine. The intimacy and the consequent level of embodiment can be measured by the behaviour and control of the object. (Fels, 2002)

The "PhysicalPhone" needs two computers for processing the voice channel and acting upon the touch sensor. It creates virtual distance between people who are physically close. Users have freedom to exchange their voice and thoughts in virtual space, but also maintain their physical intimate channel. The suggestion of a new physical experience can make us reflect about the tactile and communication dimension. In a variation of PhysicalPhone, the physical channel can be made remote, so talkers can be anywhere in the world. For this project, the body touch becomes a digital input but stays physical to link people through the two channels. The "StringPhone" needs a computer for displaying the graphics associated with the string tension, as well as controlling the audio. The "SMS phone" needs two computers for doing the voice-to-text and text-to-voice translation as well as answering and redirecting phone calls. The "Airphone" connects two people, which talk to each other through plastic masks, connected by a plastic tube. Their talk is private because their voices are meant only for the recipient and are not public property. The distance between them is always close and intimate. In a sense, it is the opposite of the public mobile call. What people are exploring now is no longer the distance but the different qualities of communication.

CONCLUSION

The actual configuration between the human and the computer has profoundly transformed the means of social interaction, providing a hybrid space that has been explored and accessed through different devices. More and more, people have incorporated the mobile devices to perform formal and informal everyday activities, and what is observed are the stylized social behaviours being repeated frequently everywhere, which have established other social bonds and personal boundaries – new cultural spaces and territories. According to Hall (1982: 101) there are three different basic spaces, "the first is fixed-feature space", which consists of unmovable elements such as walls and rooms in conventional occidental buildings and streets in the layouts of cities. The second is "semi-fixed feature space"; moveable objects such as furniture. The third is "the informal space" that is an individual's personal territory around his/her body, a spatial experience dependent of personal and social interactions. By establishing those limits and contours, people have configured an invisible bubble, usually determined by comfortable distances and dependent on cultural aspects. The uses of space and the behaviours within this domain, mediated by those artefacts, have to be negotiated by each person. He/She has to redefine and recreate those personal distances of engagement and interaction, since

human bodyhood is always the bodying forth of the ways of being in which we are dwelling and which constitute our existence at any given moment... They are in fact at any given time identical, though they are always changing with the fluid expansion and contraction of my relationship to the world. (Boss apud Robbins, 1999: 7)

The mobile devices can extend the ritual domain of society beyond physical distances and co-presence, representations and mediations, and model folds of existence. We perform to and for another that bears the sense of the group and we make part of it.

People start to coexist in the threshold, moving, shaping, behaving, and designing themselves. The body expanded as a body-in-connection, reconstructing the limits of the space, the conditions of our behaviours, and our measure of the things (Anders, 2001). The communication act mediated by mobile devices has assumed different corporeal configurations accepted socially as an extension of the subjectivity, combining tactility and intimacy. The vibracall command is an example of that assumption that materializes the design of the device as an interface quite close to the body (De Sá, 2004). The users have developed other gestures while they try to keep the connection despite the non-signal areas. According to Locke (apud Manovich, 2005: 13) "the mobile networks have to negotiate the architecture of their occupied space since the radio waves can be reflected and refracted by some obstacles, creating not a continuous but a pulse network."

Observing the artistic projects and their proposals, body movements have been experienced by participants as a constant negotiation; the different ways of access and being accessed have created other physical boundaries to perform visibility. So, it is possible to ask: can the constant possibilities of interfacing simultaneously with different codes and realities generate a reconfiguration of our bodily spatiality, and a renegotiation of other boundaries for our perceptions?

Another consideration for the creation of new behaviour patterns can be the tendency of modulation the devices – the development of pervasive networked objects. A computing and information distribution among different objects, wearable or not, can demand new functionalities, and, therefore, the need of new behaviours patterns elaborated by the users. According to Sterne, cited by De Sá (2004), there is a contemporaneous way of hearing that is articulated to the technical objects of audition, such as telephone, telegraph, phonograph, and even to the medical devices, such as stethoscope. The needs of the learning process of these objects use have transformed our way of hearing.

Reflecting about the embodiment of mobile devices in our daily life and the behaviours described on Plant's research, it is possible to affirm that users have been performing not common bodily movements, but trying to recreate an appropriate personal space for being "on my phone". Those movements can be understood as physical inscriptions on the body, formatting social and cultural subjectivities. Assuming the body as a construct of texts layers, the technology and its mobile interfaces of communication have determined a new bodily frame that users have tried to combine with old ones. The everyday body, as an eternal chameleon play, reveal and show, among diverse odours and flavours, its lots of masks.

REFERENCES

Anders, P. (2001). Anthropic Cyberspace, Defining Electronic Space from First Principles. *Leonardo*, *34*(5), 409–416. doi:10.1162/002409401753521520

Carey, J. (1985). *Communication as Culture: Essays on Media and Society*. Boston: Unwin Hyman.

Castells, M. (1999). A sociedade em rede. In *A era da informação: economia, sociedade e cultura*, (Vol. I). São Paulo: Editora paz e Terra.

Castells, M., Fernandez-Ardevol, M., Qui, J. L., & Sey, A. (2004). *The mobile communication society: A cross-cultural analysis of available evidence on the social uses of wireless communication technology.* Research Report. Retrieved July 08, 2009, from http://arnic.info/WirelessWorkshop/MCS.pdf

De Sá, S. (2004). Telefones Móveis e Formas de Escuta na Contemporaneidade. *Razón y Palabra*. n.41. October-November. Retrieved January 16, 2006, from http://www.cem.itesm.mx/dacs/publicaciones/logos/anteriores/n41/spereira.html.

De Souza e Silva, A. (2004). *From multiuser environments as (virtual) spaces to (hybrid) spaces as multiuser environments: Nomadic technology devices and hybrid communication places. Tese de Doutorado*. Rio de Janeiro, Brazil: UFRJ/CFCH/ECO.

De Souza e Silva, A. (2006a). From cyber to hybrid: mobile technologies as interfaces of hybrid spaces. *Space and Culture*, *9*(3), 261–278. doi:10.1177/1206331206289022

De Souza E Silva, A. (2006b). Re-conceptualizing the mobile phone: From Telephone to collective interfaces. *Australian journal of emerging technologies and society, 4*(2), 108-127.

Dobson, K. (2002). *AgoraPhone*. Retrieved April 08, 2008, from http://web.media.mit.edu/~monster/AgoraPhone/webcam/index.html

Fels, S. (2002). *PlesioPhone series*. Retrieved April 08, 2008, from http://hct.ece.ubc.ca/research/plesiophone/plesiophone.pdf

Goffman, E. (1967). *Interaction ritual, Essays on face-to-face behaviour*. New York: Pantheon Books.

Greenfield, A. (2006). *Everyware: The dawning age of ubiquitous computing. Berkeley, CA: New Riders Press. De Kerckhove, D. (1997). Connected Intelligence: the arrival of the Web society*. Toronto: Somerville House Publishing.

Hall, E. T. (1982). *The hidden dimension* (2nd ed.). Garden City, New York: Anchor Books Editions.

Hayles, K. (1999). *How we became posthuman—virtual bodies in cybernetics, literature, and informatics*. Chicago: The University of Chicago Press.

Kleinrock, L. (2000). On some principles of nomadic computing and multi-access communications. *IEEE Communications Magazine*, (July), 46–50. Retrieved April 08, 2006, from http://www.comsoc.org/~ci/public/2000/jul/index.html

Lemos, A. (2010). Locative media and surveillance at the boundaries of informational territories. In Firmino, R., Duarte, F., & Ultramari, C. (Eds.), *ICTs for Mobile and Ubiquitous Urban Infrastructures: Surveillance, Locative Media and Global Networks*. Hershey, PA: IGI Global.

Licoppe, C. (2003). Two modes of maintaining interpersonal relations through telephone: from the domestic to the mobile phone. In Katz, J. (Ed.), *Machines that become us: the social context of personal communication technology* (pp. 171–185). New Brunswick, New Jersey: Transaction Publishers.

Ling, R. (2000). Direct and mediated interaction in the maintenance of social relationships. In Sloane, A., & Van Rijn, F. (Eds.), *Home informatics and telematics: Information, technology and society* (pp. 61–86). Boston: Kluwer.

Ling, R. (2002). *The social juxtaposition of mobile telephone conversations and public spaces*. Chunchon, Korea, July. Retrieved May 15, 2008, from http://www.richardling.com/publications.php.

Ling, R. (2004a). Where is mobile communication causing social change? In Lim, S.D., (ed.), *Mobile communication and social change*. Seoul, South Korea. Retrieved June 17, 2006, from http://www.rheingold.com/texts/Ling_2004_Socialchange.htm#_ftn9

Ling, R. (2004b). *The mobile connection: the cell phone's impact on society*. San Francisco: Elsevier; Morgan Kaufmann Publishers.

Ling, R. (2008). *New tech, new ties: how mobile communication is reshaping social cohesion*. Cambridge, MA: The MIT Press.

Manovich, L. (2005). *The Poetics of Augmented Space: Learning from Prada*. Retrieved May 15, 2008, from http://www.manovich.net/

Manovich, L. (2008). The practice of everyday (media) life. In Lovink, G. & Niederer, S. (Eds.), *Video Vortex Reader,* Responses to Youtube, (pp. 33-44). Amsterdam: Institute of Network Cultures. Retrieved May 15, 2006, from http://www.networkcultures.org/publications

Merleau-Ponty, M. (1999). *Fenomenologia da Percepção. 2a. Edição.* São Paulo, Brazil: Martins Fontes.

Merleau-Ponty, M. (2005). *The Poetics of Augmented Space: Learning from Prada.* Retrieved May 27, 2006, from http://www.manovich.net/DOCS/augmented_space.doc.

Negroponte, N. (1995). Wearable computing. *OBS "Being Digital" Cyberdock.* Retrieved May 27, 2006, from http://www.obs-us.com/obs/english/books/nn/bd1201.htm

Norman, D. (2002). *The design of everyday things.* New York: Basic Books.

Plant, S. (2001). *On the mobile. The effects of mobile telephones on social and individual life.* Motorola Inc. Retrieved May 27, 2006, from http://www.motorola.com/mot/documents/0,1028,296,00.pdf.

Rheingold, H. (2005). *Mobile Phones, Ritual Interaction and Social Capital.* Retrieved June 01, 2006, from http://www.thefeaturearchives.com/topic/Culture/Mobile_Phones__Ritual_Interaction_and_Social_Capital.html.

Robbins, B. D. (1999). *Emotion, Movement & Psychological Space: A Sketching Out of the Emotions in terms of Temporality, Spatiality, Embodiment, Being-with, and Language.* Retrieved June 16, 2006, from http://mythosandlogos.com/emotion.html.

Santaella, L. (2007). *Linguagens líquida na era da mobilidade.* São Paulo: Paulus.

Santos, M. (1999). *A Natureza do espaço: Técnica e Tempo. Razão e Emoção, (3a Edição).* São Paulo, Brazil: Editora Hucitec.

Weiser, M., & Brown, J. S. (1995). *Designing Calm Technology.* Xerox PARC. Retrieved May 16, 2006, from http://www.ubiq.com/weiser/calmtech/calmtech.htm

ADDITIONAL READING

Castells, M. (2009). *Communication power.* New York: Oxford University Press.

Castells, M., Fernandez-Ardevol, M., Qiu, J. L., & Sey, A. (2007). *Mobile Communication and Society.* Cambridge: The MIT Press.

Dourish, P. (2004). *Where the action is: the foundations of embodied interaction.* Cambridge: The MIT Press.

Duarte, F., & Firmino, R. J. (2009). Infiltrated city, augmented space: information and communication technologies, and representations of contemporary spatialities. *Journal of Architecture, 14*(5), 545–565. doi:10.1080/13602360903187493

Ferrara, L. D'A. (org.) (2007). *Espaços Comunicantes.* São Paulo: Annablume; Grupo ESPACC.

Goffman, E. (1967). *Interaction ritual, essays on face-to-face behaviour.* New York: Pantheon Books.

Green, N. (2002). On the move: technology, mobility and the mediation of social time and space. *The Information Society, 18*(4), 281–292. doi:10.1080/01972240290075129

Hansen, M. B. N. (2006). *Bodies in Code: interfaces with digital media.* New York, London: Routledge.

Ito, M., Okabe, D., & Matsuda, M. (2005). *Personal, Portable, Pedestrian: Mobile phones in japanese life.* Cambridge, MA: The MIT Press.

Jones, C. A. (2006). *Sensorium: embodied experience, technology, and contemporary art*. Cambridge, London: The MIT Press.

Karrholm, M. (2007). The materiality of territorial production: a conceptual discussion of territorial materiality, and the everyday life of public space. *Space and Culture*, vol.10, n.4, p.437-453. Disponível em <http://sac.sagepub.com/cgi/content/abstract/10/4/437>.

Katz, J., & Aakhus, M. (2002). *Perpetual contact: mobile communication, private talk, public performance*. Cambridge: Camnridge University Press. doi:10.1017/CBO9780511489471

Levinson, P. (2004). *Cellphone: the story of the world's most mobile medium and how it has transformed everything!*New York, N.Y.: Palgrave Macmillan.

Low, S. M. (2003). Anthropological theories of body, space, and culture. *Space and Culture*, *6*(1), 9–18. doi:10.1177/1206331202238959

Luciani, A., & Cadoz, C. (Eds.). (2007). *Enaction and enactive interfaces, a handbook of terms*. Grenoble: Enactive Systems Books.

Meyrowitz, J. (2003). Global nomads in the digital veldt. In Nyíri (ed.). Mobile democracy. *Essays on Society, Self and Politics*. Vienna: Passagen Verlag, p.91-102.

Munster, A. (2006). *Materializing New Media: embodiment in information aesthetics*. Hanover, New Hampshire: Dartmouth College Press.

Rheingold, H. (2003). *Smart Mobs*. Cambridge: Perseus Publishing.

Urry, J. (2007). *Mobilities*. Cambridge, UK: Polity Press.

Varela, F. J. (1998). *Las ciencias cognitivas: tendencias y perspectivas. Cartografía de las ideas actuales. 2ª reimpresión*. Barcelona: Editorial Gedisa.

Varela, F. J., Thompson, E., & Rosch, E. (2000). *The embodied mind, cognitive science and human experience. 8a edição*. Cambridge, London: The MIT Press.

KEY TERMS AND DEFINITIONS

Hybrid Bodyspace: Not only do people use technology for their own purposes, but technology also transforms people according to its own rules of functioning. Mobile technologies can introduce synchronous and asynchronous experiences in which the body can be understood as a physical reality technologically mediated, elaborating its activities, which take place either locally or remotely, in constant juxtaposition of space and time dimensions not related. From those relations, established by a dynamic flux and exchange of information, emerge present body spatialities, articulated between the physical and the virtual, but both real. The body, compounding infinite aesthetical and lived approaches, can expand the territorial physical limits and transform each negotiation as a subjective event. On the mobile, people have to manage the local and the remote context, developing the ability to immerse in the conversation and to be present with the partners close physically.

Mediated Interactions: the communication act mediated by technological devices and interfaces. More and more, the mobile devices use has been included in our daily life, and what is observed are the stylized social behaviours being repeated frequently everywhere, which have been establishing other social bonds and personal boundaries.

Mobile Technologies: The mobile technology combines different interfaces and devices, such as cellular, pagers, wearable computers, GPS, enabling users to be always connected and to create other practices of sociability, composing the urban landscape and the body space with informational spaces.

Ritual Dimension: the ritual view refers to the communication toward the maintenance of society in time through the exchanges and the construction of social codes, behaviours, and etiquettes. These bodily gestures have not being determined any more by local demands only; people have to negotiate the actual and remote interactions and reconfigure their bodily zones for this new spatial condition. The ritual interaction implies on participants sharing these common gestures and behaviours and recognizing them as part of the communication process.

ENDNOTES

[1] http://www.ideo.com/work/item/social-mobiles

[2] http://web.media.mit.edu/~monster/Agora-Phone/top.html

[3] http://hct.ece.ubc.ca/research/plesiophone/plesiophone.pdf

This work was previously published in International Journal of Advanced Pervasive and Ubiquitous Computing (IJAPUC), edited by J. Symonds, pp. 39-52 , copyright 2010 by IGI Publishing (an imprint of IGI Global).

Section 3
Surveillance Technologies

Chapter 13
Why Where You are Matters:
Mundane Mobilities, Transparent Technologies, and Digital Discrimination

David Lyon
Queen's University, Canada

ABSTRACT

The traceability of bodies and goods has become a central feature of surveillance systems in the twenty-first century. This heightened visibility is made possible by numerous technical means but among the most important is the global expansion of mobile telephony. By this means, for example, employers may trace the location of employees, parents of children, marketers of consumers and police of suspects. How this happens involuntarily, how it builds on the 'mundane mobilities' of voluntarily acknowledging the location of the caller, what its consequences are for the increased transparency of, and digital discrimination among, mobile telephone users, is discussed in the context of broad theories of surveillance today. These technologies are in constant development, that simultaneously renders them more effective as surveillance devices and they are thus of more than mere academic interest.

KEEPING TRACK, IN TRANSIT

Howard Boyle, the president of a fire sprinkler installation company in Woodside, New York, sends his workers out to sites where systems are established or serviced. In 2003 he gave five such workers company phones with a GPS feature, though he did not tell them about the latter. He can now check if they have arrived at a site, and whether they are moving around or are sitting still. He hopes that he will be able to sort out billing queries where installation times are disputed, and boasts that he can call his workers to ask "where are you now?" while looking at a screen that tells him just that (Harmon 2003).

Such applications of "location technologies" are fairly well known in the world of work but perhaps the largest changes in this field have been in commercial domains, especially using combinations of internet and mobile phone technologies. Here, the question of why where you are matters – to whom? – becomes more significant. It is

DOI: 10.4018/978-1-60960-051-8.ch013

obvious that employers would want to keep track, but why would ordinary people use machines that permit their location to be known to anyone with the right software? The iPhone, for instance, has an application called "WhosHere" that knows where you are, shows you other users nearby and allows you to chat with them. For one user, Mathew Honan, who wrote about his experiment with a location-aware lifestyle (Honan 2009) the consequences are very mixed. He found himself in contact with at least as many people with whom he did not want to communicate as ones about whom he was positive. And he mentioned almost nothing about the marketers who are very keen indeed to get hold of location data.

Keeping track of where people are has always been important for families, employers, authorities. They want to know that children are safe, workers are busy, and that citizens are living lawfully. In the modern era, with its bureaucratic organizations and high mobility rates, schools, government departments, marketers, law enforcement and emergency services also want to know where people are – as students, claimants, consumers, offenders and accident victims. In fast-moving mobile societies, too, people simply want to keep in touch with friends, acquaintances, family. Hence the popularity of devices that permit constant contact. Anxiety, care, distrust and opportunism can be strong incentives to find ways of finding people, of locating them at specific times.

Since the turn of the twenty-first century especially, the ability to trace people's whereabouts while in transit has grown enormously, and very fast. Howard Boyle simply would not have been able to keep track of his sprinkler employees by mobile (or cell) phone[1] in the early 1990s. Nor would parents have been able to fit monitoring devices in their children's cars, or in the pockets of their own Alzheimer's-afflicted parents. Tracing parolees by satellite would have sounded like science fiction, and posting invitations by text message to potential customers passing near to Starbucks like a marketer's fantasy. All these things now happen.

However, these tracking technologies develop, not because of some supposed "logic of technology" but because of an ongoing negotiation between social entities – cultural, economic, political – and social-technical systems. While many analysts focus on the fast-moving, fragmented, and disembodied aspects of contemporary cultures it is worth noting that those most affected by mobile technologies (above all I have in mind the mobile or cell phone) use them in relation to very mundane aspects of life. Indeed, email addresses and phone numbers constitute fixed coordinates for relationships within the apparently blurred world of motion.[2]

It is a truism that some earlier technical innovations have contributed in extraordinary ways to fresh patterns of social relationship. The clock and the computer, mundane though they seem today, are paramount examples of such 'exotic' technologies. Publicly coordinated synchronic time permits all manner of convenient meetings and management procedures, from school schedules to train timetables. Clocks became a vital part of the capitalist enterprise, particularly for measuring labour time down to the minute and thus for controlling workers. Computers, too, have contributed enormously to the surveillance capacities of all major social institutions, as an aspect of increasing efficiency and productivity.[3] These taken-for-granted technologies have far-reaching implications for power relations within the modern, bureaucratic, capitalistic contexts where they were developed.

In some similar ways, mobile technologies already show signs of being singularly significant within emerging patterns of "liquid" social life (Bauman 2001, 2005). Mobile technologies enter the empty gaps in social life, areas once thought of as "dead" time used for travel, and bring them back to life. As Nicola Green (2002: 290) says, such "Lazarus time" may be resurrected for family or business purposes. But it can equally be resurrected for surveillance purposes. Indeed, the surveillance aspects are the hidden side of what appear on the surface to be new freedoms – to be in touch anywhere, and to make positive uses of those "dead" moments. Paradoxically, mobility was seen by modern sociologists, such as Georg Simmel, as liberating. You could stroll the streets of the big city anonymously, freed from the constraints of the villagers' watchful eyes (Simmel 1971 [1903]). Today, movement in urban spaces is no longer a means of evading the gaze.

Mobile technologies both facilitate and inhibit mobility by easing open or closing-off the channels of flow of persons, objects, and data. While they may be linked with global systems, these mobile technologies are triggered or activated by their users. John Urry suggests, creatively, that in the twenty-first century it is appropriate to think of "inhabited machines" such as cars and mobile phones, that "come to life" as people use them (Urry 2002). To inhabit such machines is to be connected with sites across the world, which is an important aspect of globalization, helping to make the world feel like "one place." What Urry observes but does not elaborate is that "… simultaneously such sites can monitor, observe and trace each inhabited machine." In the process, the transparency of all participants to each other, or to organizations, becomes more pronounced.

It is such "monitoring, observing and tracing" that is explored in this chapter. "Where you are" matters increasingly from the point of view of contemporary regimes of governance, whether of commerce, policing or government. Mobile phones, in conjunction with other technologies such as GPS (Global Positioning Satellites) may be used to monitor, observe and trace their users continuously, and in real time. In this way, surveillance capacities are enhanced in various systems (intended to map the travels of consumers, employees or citizens, for example). In particular, the number of points of contact between systems and subjects grows, with consequences for power relations between the two (Rule 1973, Lyon 1994: 51-52). While mobiles may have unforeseen positive consequences for democratic processes, they may equally offer opportunities for the enhancement of other kinds of power. Surveillance – as "monitoring, observing, tracing"—is not necessarily negative, but power relations are always present, for better or for worse.

A further question is, in what ways do power relations alter as mobility is monitored more and more? Let me put the question of "privacy" on one side at the outset. Some of the issues surrounding mobile telephony have to do with overheard conversations and in this sense "privacy" seems to be a relatively trivial matter for many. Public places and mass transit systems are often alive with uninhibited "private" conversations. Other issues, more seriously, may relate to the extent to which the content of calls may be intercepted by unauthorized (or even authorized) others. This raises "privacy" questions of an informational, rather than a "place-based" type. In this case, expectations and legal requirements – "lawful access"—are also significant. But the focus in this chapter is different again, and does not start with "privacy" questions.

Beyond the "privacy" of mobile communications lie questions of governance. Most broadly, governance refers to modes of governing populations whether or not the nation-state is involved. Social order is achieved and maintained in myriad ways in contemporary societies and what I refer to as "surveillance" has to be considered as one of these. Conventionally, surveillance was thought of as the practices of watching specific persons for specific purposes in specific, usually bounded, places (such as the "Panopticon" prison). Today, in part due to its reliance on electronic technologies, surveillance is generalized across populations, for numerous, overlapping purposes, and in virtual and fluid "spaces" (see e.g. Haggerty and Ericson 2000). As Majid Yar suggests, these now include "…mobile, nomadic forms of control that utilize coded information to monitor, predict and direct the behaviour of individuals…" (Yar 2003: 257) that are outside the old fixed panoptic spaces in what Giorgio Agamben calls "zones of indistiction" (Agamben 1997).

Although this chapter began with an example from production, it is more likely to be in the realm of consumption that mobile surveillance will be most manifest. As Mark Andrejevic argues, it is "m-commerce" that is becoming a dominant site of mobile surveillance, where the most mobile are also likely to be the most surveilled (Andrejevic 2004). At the same time, two other features should also be noted. One, while the analytic distinction between production and consumption may still hold, the processes discussed here help to blur those boundaries. Surveillance moves increasingly freely across and between those once more distinct realms. Two, the fact that commercial data may be most prominent in mobile surveillance, this does not exclude their use for law enforcement and other "state-related" purposes. Indeed, to take a current example, the "war on terror" frequently uses "commercial" data in sorting for suspects (see O'Harrow 2005, Lyon 2003).

MUNDANE MOBILITIES

Many people, young and old, women and men, in many countries now use mobile phones more than they use the internet. The mobile phone offers person-to-person contact based on assumed constant availability (Wellman 2001). There is a sense of ordinariness of life with mobile phone use, especially if these devices are commonly visible – and audible – on the streets and in public transport in urban areas. Overheard conversations – or split conversations – are often about very mundane matters. People report their progress in traffic or at stations, or arrange meetings, or simply discuss exactly the same kinds of things that are discussed on landline phones. Indeed, they often offer information about where they are, as reassurance, or as a reason why they will miss the meeting.

The content of mobile calls may at times be of interest to other parties than the caller and called, but this does not seem to produce much care about what is said, even when intimacies are shared in very public places. Being audible and overheard by others is clearly an issue that relates to the context, so one might ask why location data matters in one setting but not another. The answer suggested here is that location data as consciously revealed by the phone user is unlikely to be thought of in surveillance terms, unless a fear – such as stalking – is brought into the picture. But locational data revealed by the device (rather than consciously by the person) is more likely to be regarded negatively when it is known about.

Much social analysis of mobile phones has examined behaviours and etiquette surrounding mobile culture. Sadie Plant (2001), for instance, compares several cities around the world, looking at uses of the mobile. The constant question (over)heard is, "where are you?" but this is a personal, not usually a surveillance question. She comments on the truism that landlines connected urban areas and nations of modernities, whereas mobiles appeared for a new – perhaps late- or postmodern – world of movement, of tourists and travelers, businesspersons and refugees, students and workers. While this could be dismissed as soft technological determinism – it is mobile phones, *inter alia*, that help constitute the "postmodern" world as such -- there is also an important sociological point here. In a general sense, in situations of lower mobility than those of the affluent and technologically advanced countries today, it is assumed that we know (more or less) where people are. Key means of communication today, such as email and the mobile phone, do not yield any clues to the called party about the location of the person communicating. But such data are of interest to third parties; indeed, as we shall see there is potential economic (and other) benefit associated with those data.

Mobiles are used for mundane purposes. One could argue that the technologies are socially shaped by an era of growing mobility, even as that mobility is further enabled by them. In a world in which travel has become easier, quicker, and over larger terrains, and in which many things are done at a distance, corporations are in a constant quest for the means of connectivity. Customers are grateful when developing devices offer the chance to stay in touch despite dislocations of distance and schedules. If for some analysts the world is one of increasing disintegration and fragmentation, mobile technologies offer opportunities for holding things together, even if they require new skills to operate them (Agar 2004). This may mean that places change their meaning and significance, or, possibly, that the means of communication become more significant.

What this assumes, however, is that the means of "holding things together" is created for the benefit of the consumer, the mobile user. However, the market for consumer data has grown hugely in recent decades, such that today the industries seeking to process personal data for a variety of purposes are valued in the multi-billion range. With respect to locational data some optimistic market analysts expect a large scale growth in traffic over the next few years, although as with any such market forecasts considerable variation appears (Lyon, Marmura and Peroff 2005, O'Brian 2008). The aim of these is to use locational data for mainly economic purposes, to exploit them for more precisely targeted marketing. In other words, it is above all marketers who will be better enabled to "hold things together" as they use locational data to coordinate their contacts with potential consumers.

It could be objected that in the case of GPS-enabled mobile telephony in the USA, user benefit was intended when ordinary devices became traceable for location by emergency services (the essential move that enabled commercial services to build on such traceability).[4] No doubt users may be more quickly reached in an emergency using such techniques. Yet in the USA, despite considerable opposition by civil liberties groups, such devices are legally required to be switched on at all times (rather than having an emergency call trigger the switch). This means not only that emergency services have continual access and tracking affordances, but that commercial enterprises do as well. This immediately places users in a situation in which information about their locations are available by default. The power relations embedded in such surveillance capacities are clearly unequal.

Many studies of new mobile telephony have remarked the ways in which concepts of time and space are undoubtedly altering in relation to the new mobile technologies although it does seem that small-scale, local, and immediate time-space paths are still vitally important to most people. As Boden and Molotch (1994) say, a "compulsion of proximity" still exists that encourages the ongoing persistence of face-to-face meeting, despite the potential for remote and now mobile communication. Anthony Townsend puts it neatly when he comments that "The use of mobile phones offers an even finer level of identifying and exploiting minute variations in conditions between locations, the micromanagement of space as a result of the micromanagement of time and the always-accessible individual" (Townsend 2000, cf. Fortunati 2002). Townsend puts an optimistic spin on this, suggesting that even as individuals struggle to sustain order and coherence in the face of accelerating time and compressing space, they also have the means of managing these forces, and manipulating them as large-scale institutions tend to do.

However, there are other ways of thinking about the micromanagement of space-time. The "mundane" mobile may actually have some more "exotic" aspects to it (Michael 2003) that relate to more radical kinds of social change. But this idea cannot be discussed further until we have considered some ways in which the "exotic" aspects of mobile phones emerge. The device that is bought and sold with the promise of a reordering of opportunities and life pathways for the individual user (the mundane aspects) may also have a role in reordering such opportunities and everyday activities *of* that user (the exotic, surveillance aspects). Neither of these is stable, however. The exotic and the mundane are likely to emerge together and in relation to one another.

TRANSPARENT TECHNOLOGIES

When a mobile phone is switched on, and every few minutes while it is working, it sends out a signal. All network base stations respond, and the provider allocates a phone to a station. On the highway, this may be up to 35 km away, but in cities it is more likely to be within 500m. Picocells, with 50m radius, exist around shopping malls or office blocks. Which station the mobile uses is recorded, even if the call is simply to retrieve voicemail. The UK company, Orange, for example, keeps this location information from the beginning and end of each call, whether outbound or inbound, for six months. Another UK company, BT Cellnet, offers traffic news based on which station is nearest to the caller, and other such services are planned. But the data may be revealed to others, on application, under the Regulation of Investigatory Powers Act (2000) for a wide range of reasons: national security, crime, preventing disorder, public health and safety, emergency protection of mental or physical health, and assessing or collecting taxes or other charges relating to government departments (Mathieson 2001).

One striking feature of almost every sociological and cultural examination of mobile phones is that the transparency of these technologies is unremarked. As I noted above, John Urry points out but does not discuss the ways that the "sites" to which people are connected by mobile devices also have the capacity to check up on them. Leslie Haddon and others (2001) mention the fact that there is a potential for surveillance, using audit trails that reveal location, combined with databases to which service providers have access. And more than one author has noted that children and parents use mobile phones in contradictory ways. Teenagers may think that they can find more privacy out of their parents' earshot by using a mobile. At the same time, parents may use mobiles as "electronic leashes" – means of keeping tabs on where children are, either for their safety or because they do not trust them to act in an appropriate way when they are beyond range of their vision or hearing (Dong Kim 2002:73).[5] However, existing research has yet to place mobile phones firmly within the context of contemporary surveillance practices and processes.

Social science focus, by and large, is on the activities of the end user and how his or her direct social relationships are affected by mobile phone use (important exceptions include Gow and Ihnat 2004, Green and Smith 2004). A key assumption is that the mobile puts in the hands of individuals new means of communication, connection, and of the "micromanagement" of time and space. The emphasis is frequently on the liberating aspects of the new technologies that permit the "quicker, cheaper, convenient" connections, which free the individual from time-and-place constraints, or give those with no established landlines the chance to communicate by phone. All these features of the emerging social landscape no doubt exist, and it is perfectly proper to draw attention to them.

But as we have seen, mobile phones have other kinds of capacities in addition to those from which users benefit. They send signals as well as transmitting the messages of their users. Third parties may discover where mobile users are at a given time, and may under certain circumstances listen in to some messages.[6] It may well be the case that social movements are able to mobilize faster using mobile phones – as happened for instance in the anti-WTO protests in Seattle in 1999 and the democracy movement that was mobilized during the Iranian elections during June 2009 – but it is also the case that mobile technologies are used to keep track of such protesters, in some countries in quite a detailed manner. The same technologies that provide the medium for coordination and micromanagement of individual activities can also provide the medium for institutional coordination and micromanagement, in ways that far transcend what may have been possible with landline phone systems.

Today, the transparency of mobile communications is becoming increasingly evident, and as this happens it will become clear why "where you are" matters to others as well as to friends, family and colleagues. Three examples of this follow, relating to emergency services, marketing techniques, and anti-terrorist activities. In each case, it is not so much the content of calls as their location that matters, although in policing and law enforcement contexts phone tapping may also occur. In each case, too, an important feature of "mobile surveillance" is evident, namely that location is continuously traceable, in real time. This is not the case with technologies such as RFID (Radio Frequency Identification) that require some kind of scanning device to obtain the locational data. It is useful to distinguish, then, between these "location technologies" and others that do not have quite the same capacities, for this distinction also has sociological and surveillance consequences (see Lyon *et al* 2005).

In the USA and Canada, as well as in Europe, emergency calls from mobiles have become the focus of some attention from privacy advocates, due to their surveillance capacities and implications. Under so-called E-911 ("E" for "enhanced" and 911 for emergency calls, as 999 in the UK) systems in the USA, and their equivalents elsewhere, emergency calls can be traced quickly. Conventional landline phones reveal their number and location to public services when an emergency number is called. But this used not to apply to mobile users, who had to give verbal information and instructions about how they could be reached. So the systems are being extended to mobile users, such that calls are traceable to within 20-50m of the phone (Bennett and Regan 2002). It remains to be seen how this will affect the "anonymous Samaritan" who calls on behalf of others but who does not want to be identified.

In September 2003 a European Union directive (E112) came into force, requiring mobile phone networks to provide emergency services with any and all location information they can, again to try to speed up response times. By February 2004 the London Ambulance Service became the first to benefit from an initiative which is in line with the European directive, giving ambulance drivers accurate location information about the origin of emergency calls.[7] This is part of a process, the first stage of which was established at the start of 2004, to offer full coverage of the Enhanced 999 service in the UK. The five mobile networks, plus BT and Cable & Wireless, which connect emergency calls from mobiles, worked together with Ofcom, the regulator of UK communications, to provide the new services.[8]

For various reasons, network operators plan to take further such developments. If phone locations are traceable in an emergency, what is to prevent their being traceable in other circumstances as well? Commercial interests are evident in cases such as geography-sensitive traffic news services, and the (celebrated but not very fully exploited) Starbucks coffee example. It seems that Starbucks has yet to take up on a large scale this opportunity for mobile marketing – as with a number of other companies, there is some hesitation about which is the best means of exploiting the mobile phone for consumer purposes. Some operators wish to recoup costs of making their systems comply with the emergency services directives while others simply see other possibilities for using locational data. In the UK Vodaphone customers can use their phone to find the nearest ATM, restaurant or cinema, and another company, Zingo, offers to connect you with the nearest taxi.[9] Other companies are offering specialized services, particularly for tracking employees and children. While these systems are in their infancy, and thus have yet to be studied empirically, it is clear that they are of great interest to some companies in particular (Doward 2003).

Last but not least, the 'anti-terror' initiatives introduced since 9/11 have also included mobile phone location and message tracing as a means of both investigating and even pre-empting violent acts. To many observers, the dynamics of al-Qaeda pointed up the changed rules of global guerilla activities, and perhaps of warfare, too. So far from the "state-sponsored terrorism" feared by many governments, al-Qaeda represents a network that operates independently of any state (and may in fact have states in its power rather than vice-versa). Ease of travel, of funds transfers, and of communications, particularly using the internet and mobile phones, enable this new *modus vivendi* (Neuman, 2004). Hardly surprising, then, that post-9/11 anti-terrorist tactics include these three areas: travel, focusing on security at airports and borders; financial systems, focusing on curtailing the flow of funds to "terrorists;" and communications, focusing on the interception of suspicious messages.

Such concerns became even more pronounced after the Madrid bombings in March 2004. The EU has appointed an "anti-terror czar" who will, among other things, deal more diligently with the matter of sharing communications data. The idea is to track the activities of suspected conspirators, using their internet and mobile phone logs (Brand, 2004). It may be that the relative neglect of the surveillance aspects of mobile technologies is also related to the nature of these third party uses. Questions of safety in relation to emergency calls have some *prima facie* priority over civil liberties or privacy questions (Black 2001). Questions about the uses of personal technologies for marketing and commercial surveillance are often deemed to be individual concerns, at worst of nuisance value, as in unwanted or repeat advertising calls. And in a climate of rising media-amplified fears and suspicions about the threat of "terrorism," matters of national security appear to outweigh any queries about the necessity or efficacy of general surveillance sweeps for combating violence against civilians (Lyon, 2003).

Mobile phones are increasingly likely to be used for tracking purposes, in relation to both public and private services. Revealing timed locations is important, especially in an era of growing mobility. The systems described above are all transparent technologies in the sense that they permit a greater "visibility" – as traceability – of their users to others. Some of those others have the public interest and personal safety in mind; others have profitability or personnel coordination in mind. Either way, the process of tracing and tracking people through devices they carry with them is likely to grow. What we do not yet know with any certainty is what the consequences will be, simply because of the newness of the systems described. However, several other factors should be noted.

One, mobile phones themselves have multiplying functions. The ongoing integration of functions in one machine – voice, text, image, sound – is occurring at a very rapid rate. Some increased traceability relates to these proliferating combined functions. A Cambridge (UK) company, for instance, now offers to find you when you're lost, if you can send a photo and one UK pound to their database. The image should depict a building or street where you are "lost," which the company will identify using image recognition software, and send back instructions on how to get back on track or further information about the buildings or street (Edward 2004: 5).

Two, mobile phones are only one mobile technology among others; their combined use is more significant than just telephone use. Other mobile technologies are rapidly coming on stream, which also have significant social aspects. These include various applications available on iPhones or via Google, that offer "collective intelligence" kinds of services to locate and connect users near or far (see Markoff, 2008). Much surveillance speculation attends such developments, but little is known as yet about their use, let alone their unintended consequences (but see Blumberg & Eckersley, 2009). On-board navigation systems for cars, transponders for electronic tolls at bridges or tunnels or on private highways, and the increasing use of "black box" sensors in cars offer multiple possibilities for generating mobile data. California resident Scott Knight, for example, was convicted in 2001 after a hit-and-run death when his OnStar system reported an airbag inflation. And Acme Rent-a-Car in New Haven fined drivers $150 when their GPS system showed they had been consistently speeding (Schwartz, 2003).

Three, the capacities of mobile technology surveillance are currently limited in significant ways. Legal requirements, though contradictory in some contexts place limits on the extent to which mobile surveillance – relating to message content only -- occurs. Tapping, for instance, still requires a warrant in most countries, and there are also curbs on the passing of data to third parties in privacy and data protection legislation. The technical capacity to engage in mobile surveillance is also limited. When it comes to message interception, this is particularly true. Only a fragment of the total messages of potential interest to surveillors is likely to be intercepted (Clarke 2003). Lastly, mobile surveillance is costly. Even enhanced emergency services are expensive to establish, so it is not surprising that networks attempt to defray costs by considering other services as well as emergency ones.

Four, different kinds of transparency are produced by different kinds of mobile technology. Roger Clarke (2003) helpfully summarizes some of the differences, starting with the obvious self-disclosure of location data in the course of a conversation. Landline phones have utilized versions of caller-ID for some years now, and the prefix of the calling number discloses location to within a few kilometers in urban areas. Mobile phones disclose the cell from which the phone is operating, and this has now become a sought-after datum for law enforcement and anti-terror purposes. There are also business incentives for obtaining access to this. Crisis-story-led E-911 initiatives lead to more precise location of calls, using GPS, triangulation, and directional antennae methods. Lastly, Clarke points to a further source of location data, self identification by devices as they pass detectors. These would include smart-cards, transponders (for example, for highway or bridge tolls) and RFID (Radio Frequency Identification) systems. As I observed earlier, however, such devices do not meet the criteria of location technologies as defined here.

Having pointed out various limits on locational surveillance, it should also be said that the trend is towards increasing traceability. The transparent technologies discussed here now help constitute everyday life in the affluent, technologically advanced societies. So all users can expect to become more traceable (if not more audible) to third parties, the more we use such devices. This may mean that people find ways of reducing their visibility (not using their devices, or encrypting them to prevent unauthorized or unwanted use), or possibly that they choose to go on using them in the belief that their benefits outweigh the possible negative aspects. Those who entertain doubts about mobile surveillance are likely to do so because they have strong views about their privacy, or possibly because they believe that their civil liberties are jeopardized. However, there are further reasons for thinking carefully about mobile devices, that have to do with their place within a bigger picture of surveillance and governance in the twenty-first century.

DIGITAL DISCRIMINATION

Accounts of mobile technologies that highlight how ordinary people reorder their daily time-space paths must be placed in a broader context. While individual patterns of social life are constantly changing as people use new devices to coordinate their activities, the same devices are used by third parties, who also wish to have a say in coordinating those activities. The use of mobile technologies may also be considered as a new – locational – element within processes of governance. This may be rather obvious, as in the case of Howard Boyle, surreptitiously tracking his sprinkler system employees, or more likely, rather subtle, seen within a larger frame of digital discrimination. It also occurs, as we have seen, in relation to consumer surveillance. To understand this, the focus must shift from how people actively use their mobile devices, and even from how they might feel about the fact that their movements are traced. The focus must shift from how behaviours and exchanges become visible, or knowable, to the purposes for which they are made visible.

Seen this way, surveillance is more than a mere threat to personal privacy, or even to civil liberties, important though these are. In most countries and cultures, having access to some inviolable spaces, or controlling the circulation of information about you is important. In democratic societies, notions such as freedom of movement and the absence of the snooping, prying eye are held dear, and rightly so. But the kind of surveillance that has been burgeoning in the past couple of decades goes beyond any occasional and isolated cases of privacy infringement or limits on liberty. It is articulated with the general growth of mobilities and the emerging forms of governance – particularly those aimed at regulating the "means of movement" (Torpey 2000) – that are characteristic of social life in the early twenty-first century.

Garnering personal details without the individuals concerned knowing about it – let alone consenting – has become routine. The organizations that engage in these practices proliferate rapidly and increasingly employ networking techniques such that the growth of personal data gathering is symbiotic. Deep changes are in process. James Rule goes so far as to say that the new technologies of "perpetual contact" – such as mobile phones—represent a "significant step in the movement toward what I have called 'total surveillance' – that is, a world in which every fact and every moment of every individual's life registers with a single, centralized agency of surveillance" (Rule, 2002: 248). While there may be other ways of reading this, the point about significant social change is crucial.

A final important feature of today's surveillance, whether in law enforcement, government administration, or consumer marketing techniques, is that it usually has to do with social sorting. Questions of social divisions and of social exclusion appear in this context. Simply put, surveillance seen as social sorting is a means of management, of influence, of governance. The question is, how does it operate as such? The answer is that surveillance works in many ways, through multiple rationalities and techniques, to try to manage and manipulate behaviours. But it has some features in common across different fields of vision, different institutional areas. Increasingly, searchable databases are used to provide the means of digital discrimination. The aim is to segment populations according to certain criteria, sorting them into groups that will be treated differently. The idea is that levels of risk or of opportunity can be calculated from available data, so that relevant groups can be targeted more accurately (Henman, 2004, Lyon, 2007).

The story of surveillance in the modern world has been told elsewhere, but some brief details do help. The twentieth century saw the quickening development of "information societies" around the world; the corollary is that surveillance societies also became more evident (Lyon, 2001, Surveillance Studies Network, 2006). Bureaucratic management, developed in the early part of the century, was augmented tremendously by computerization from the 1970s onwards, with the result that systematic, routine monitoring of persons and populations for a range of purposes became commonplace in all but the poorest countries of the world by the turn of the twenty-first century. What once were fixed files became flows of personal data, first within and then between different kinds of organizations, from government departments to hospitals, schools, police, insurance brokers, credit card companies, and marketing corporations. Information technology does not *cause* but it certainly *enables* today's surveillance.

Each transaction, exchange, purchase, and interaction we make now leaves a trail of electronic footprints. These fragments of personal data tell few tales on their own, but when combined with others are a powerful means of predicting further actions, whether as consumers, offenders, claimants, travelers, or citizens. In the consumer sphere, for instance, geo-demographic marketing works with probabilities based on neighbourhood types that certain householders are good targets for specific products and so "place" as well as "past" becomes important elements of data-images. As systems such as Customer Relationship Management (CRM) were promoted in the 1990s, so deeper and richer records were created, using techniques such as data-mining to draw together even more information (Gandy and Deanna 2002). The "data-image" relating to an individual is created by combining such information. Certain well-heeled groups are targeted for special deals and privileges; others, with poorer postcodes, are passed by. As mobile lifestyles become more prevalent, so the "dead spaces" of travel time also come to be of interest to personal data agencies.

So not only do exchanges and interactions attract surveillance attention, movement does as well. The most obvious case is that of video surveillance or Closed Circuit Television (CCTV). In countries such as the UK, where CCTV systems are densely distributed in urban spaces, ordinary citizens may expect to have their images monitored, if not recorded, several hundred times a day. In cases where they are recorded, details of geographical location become available to the security and police services that install or operate them. The evidence indicates, however, that the locations of certain groups – young black males especially, but, "unofficially," young women – are disproportionately in focus (Norris, 2003). The important difference between CCTV and the surveillance capacities of mobile phones is that while CCTV is clearly about some authorities 'keeping watch," mobile phones are understood to be about ordinary people "keeping in touch." Surveillance is a side effect of mobile phone use. On the other hand, for some purposes mobile surveillance may have some thing in common with CCTV surveillance, including the fact that many (especially in the UK) assume that CCTV "works" and is a "good thing." In so far as mobile surveillance is connected with emergency services, it would not be surprising to discover that similar assumptions reign.

The surveillance data garnered from locations may be added to the data-image to inform new modes of governance. Because surveillance is ambivalent, the technologies linked with "care," such as emergency services, may also have some "control" motifs, such as targeting by police or commercial agencies. Law enforcement agencies clearly have an interest in where certain "suspects" are, and will treat different groups differently depending on their interpretation of available data. Racial profiling has become especially marked since the serious anti-terror campaigns were mounted following 9/11. Driving while black has been a cause for police interest for some time. Now flying while Arab or surfing while Muslim may also attract undue attention. But marketers also wish to target population segments so that they too can provide different levels of service or opportunity. Ideally, they would like to induce users to follow particular commercial paths, on order to target part of their individual life-time value.

Each of these techniques deserves exploration in its own right. They may have common elements but there are many variations on the digital discrimination theme. The key point is that "where you are" matters because such information about location is fed into data-images. These data images circulate, mutating as they travel, within the circuits of twenty-first century surveillance. They enjoy levels of mobility far in excess of what their human referents could experience, moving faster, further, and through a greater range of fields than them. Where the consumer may have been could inform the data-image retrieved by police investigating unrelated activities. How fast the driver was traveling could affect insurance premiums or invoices from car rental companies. All of which is a reminder that the data-image is influential in real-life situations. It is flesh-and-blood embodied, social persons who are affected for better or worse by digital discrimination.

This interpretation of mobilities does not necessarily compete with those that put the accent on how people coordinate and control *their own* activities using mobile technologies. The latter tends to be emphasized within the newer locational services using phone-and-internet technologies together. Rather, it dovetails with those focusing on action, and the ways that people are better able to cope with conflicting schedules and what Helga Nowotny (1998) calls "overlapping times" by using mobile phones. This perspective emphasizes structural constraints on action, deriving from the demands of service providers for better information, which in turn may be used by commercial, safety, and security agencies within systems of (mobile and locational) governance. The one account does not cancel the other; rather, the two accounts together provide a more nuanced picture of mobile life with inhabited machines. It must be said, however, that the trend is towards greater use of locational data for governance of all kinds. And, given inequalities of access and power mentioned earlier, mobile surveillance could well become a more influential means of exacerbating existing social divisions.

What we do not yet know much about are the empirical details and the actual consequences of such mobile monitoring of locations, over time. But the already existing systems, within which mobiles are now imbricated, are ones that contribute to digital discrimination, to the reinforcing of social division, and to social inclusion or exclusion. Some of this is unexceptional and socially benign, but other aspects are a cause for some concern, especially among civil libertarians and others who deplore the growth of digital discrimination. Many surveillance schemes that operate today tend to amplify stereotypes and to apply the most stringent and severe scrutiny to the most vulnerable – in socio-economic, ethnic, and gendered terms. It is hard to imagine how location data from mobile phones will be used differently. But it is worth finding out how they are used, and worth remembering that other ways are possible.

ACKNOWLEDGMENT

An earlier version of this paper first appeared in: Monahan, Torin, 2006 *Surveillance and Security*, London and New York: Routledge. It is reprinted with permission. Thanks to Emily Smith for research assistance.

REFERENCES

Agamben, G. (1997). *Homo Sacer: Sovereign Power and Bare Life*. Stanford, CA: Stanford University Press.

Agre, P. (2001). Changing places: contexts of awareness in computing. *Human-Computer Interaction*, *16*(2-4), 177–192. doi:10.1207/S15327051HCI16234_04

Andrejevic, M. (2004). Monitored mobility in the era of mass customization. *Space and Culture*, *6*(2), 132–150. doi:10.1177/1206331203251256

Bauman, Z. (2001). *Liquid Modernity*. Cambridge, UK: Polity Press.

Bauman, Z. (2005). *Liquid Life*. Cambridge, UK: Polity Press.

Bennett, C., & Regan, P. (2002). *What happens when you make a 911 call? Privacy and regulation of cellular technology in the USA and Canada.* Paper presented at the Canadian Political Science Association, May 31, 2002.

Black, J. (2001). No hiding from a cell phone. *Business Week Online,* 21 June. Available at http://www.businessweek.com/bwdaily/dnflash/jun2001/nf20010621_803.htm

Blumberg, A. J., & Eckersley, P. (2009). On locational privacy and how to avoid losing it. *EFF Report*. Retrieved from www.eff.org/wp/locational-privacy/

Boden, D., & Molotch, H. (1994). The compulsion to proximity. In Friedland, R., & Boden, D. (Eds.), *NoWhere: Space, Time, and Modernity*. Berkeley, CA: University of California Press.

Brand, C. (2004). EU nations set to name anti-terror czar. *The Guardian*, March19. Retrieved from http://www.guardian.co.uk/worldlatest/story/0,1280,-3880554,00.html

Clarke, R. (2003). Wireless Transmission and Mobile Technologies. Retrieved from http://www.anu.edu.au/people/Roger.Clarke/EC/WMT.html

Dong Kim, S. (2002). Personal meanings. In Katz, J. E., & Aakhus, M. (Eds.), *Perpetual Contact: Mobile Communication, Private Talk, Public Performance*. New York: Cambridge University Press.

Doward, J. (2003). Big Brother latest: now your phone can be used to track you down. *The Observer,* 7 December. Retrieved from http://observer.guardian.co.uk/libertywatch/story/0,1373,1101729,00.html

Edward, R. (2004). Lost? Help is just a mobile phone photo away. *The Scotsman, 13*(April), 5.

Eldridge, M., & Grinter, R. (2001). *Studying text messaging in teenagers*. Workshop on Mobile Technologies at CHI 2001, Seattle, WA. Available at www.cs.Colorado.edu/~palen/chi_workshop/papers/EldridgeGrinter.pdf/

Fortunati, L. (2002). The mobile phone: towards new categories and social relations. *Information Communication and Society*, *5*(4), 513–528. doi:10.1080/13691180208538803

Gandy, O., & Deanna, A. (2002). All that glitters is not gold: Digging beneath the surface of data mining. *Journal of Business Ethics*, *40*, 373–386. doi:10.1023/A:1020845814009

Gow, G., & Ihnat, M. (2004). Prepaid mobile phone service and the anonymous caller: Considering Wireless E-911 in Canada. *Surveillance & Society*, *1*(4).

Green, N. (2001). Who's watching whom? Monitoring and accountability in mobile relations. In Brown, B. (Eds.), *Wireless World: Social and Interactional Aspects of the Mobile Age* (pp. 32–45). London: Springer.

Green, N. (2002). On the move: technology, mobility, and the mediation of social time and space. *The Information Society*, *18*, 281–292. doi:10.1080/01972240290075129

Green, N., & Smith, S. (2004). A 'spy in your pocket'? The regulation of mobile phone data in the UK. *Surveillance & Society*, *1*(4).

Haddon, L., et al. (2001). *From Mobile to Mobility: The Consumption of ICTs and Mobility in Everyday Life*. In COST269 Mobility Workgroup. Retrieved from http://www.cost269.org/working%20group/cost_workgpr_mobility.htm

Haggerty, K. & Ericson, R. (2000). The surveillant assemblage. *The British Journal of Sociology*.

Harmon, A. (2003). Lost? Hiding? Your cellphone is keeping tabs. *The New York Times*. December 31.

Henman, P. (2004). Targeted! Population segmentation, electronic surveillance, and governing the unemployed in Australia. *International Sociology*, *19*(2), 173–191. doi:10.1177/0268580904042899

Honan, M. (2009). I am here: One man's experiment with the location-aware lifestyle. *Wired*, January 19. Retrieved from www.wired.com/gadgets/wireless/magazine/17-02/lp_guineapig/

Lyon, D. (1988). *The Information Society: Issues and Illusions*. Cambridge: Polity.

Lyon, D. (1994). *The Electronic Eye: The Rise of Surveillance Society*. Cambridge, UK: Polity.

Lyon, D. (2001). *Surveillance Society: Monitoring Everyday Life*. Buckingham, UK: Open University Press.

Lyon, D. (2003). *Surveillance after September 11*. Cambridge, UK: Polity Press.

Lyon, D. (2005). September 11, synopticon, and scopophilia: watching and being watched. In Haggerty, K., & Ericson, R. (Eds.), *The Politics of Surveillance and Visibility*. Toronto: University of Toronto Press.

Lyon, D. (2007). *Surveillance Studies: An Overview*. Cambridge, UK: Polity Press.

Lyon, D., Marmura, S., & Peroff, P. (2005). *Location Technologies: Mobility, Surveillance and Privacy*. Report for the Office of the Privacy Commissioner, Ottawa, Canada. Retrieved from www. Queensu.ca/sociology/Surveillance/

Markoff, J. (2008). You're leaving a digital trail. What about privacy? *New York Times*, November 29. Retrieved from www.nytimes.com/2008/11/30/business/30privacy.html?_r=1&ei=5070&emc=eta1

Mathiesen, S. A. (2001). You can ring, but you can't hide. *The Guardian*, 29 November, 2001. Retrieved from http://www.guardian.co.uk/print/0,3858,4309424-110837,00.html

McCahill, M. (2002). *The Surveillance Web: The Rise of Visual Surveillance in an English City*. Cullompton, UK: Willan Publishing.

Meyrowitz, J. (1986). *No Sense of Place: The Impact of Electronic Media on Social Behavior*. New York: Oxford University Press.

Michael, M. (2003). Between the mundane and the exotic: time for a different sociotechnical stuff. *Time & Society*, *12*(1), 127–143. doi:10.1177/0961463X03012001372

Neuman, P. R. (2004). Why nobody saw 9/11 coming. *The New York Times*, March 27.

Norris, C. (2003). From personal to digital: CCTV, the panopticon, and the technological mediation of suspicion and social control. In Lyon, D. (Ed.), *Surveillance as Social Sorting: Privacy, Risk, and Digital Discrimination*. New York: Routledge.

Norris, C., & Armstrong, G. (1999). *Maximum Security Society: The Rise of CCTV*. London: Berg.

Nowotny, H. (1998). *Time: The Modern and Postmodern Experience*. Oxford, UK: Blackwell.

O'Brian, K. J. (2008). Still searching for profit in location-based services. *New York Times*, November 9. Retrieved from www.nytimes.com/2008/11/09/technology/09iht-wireless10.1.17649240.html

O'Harrow, R. (2005). *No Place to Hide*. New York: Free Press.

Plant, S. (2001). *On the mobile: the effects of mobile telephones on social and individual life*. Retrieved from www.motorola.com/mot/documents/0,1028,333,00.pdf

Rule, J. B. (1973). *Private Lives, Public Surveillance*. London: Allen-Lane.

Rule, J. B. (2002). From mass society to perpetual contact. In Katz, J. E., & Aakhus, M. (Eds.), *Perpetual Contact: Mobile Communication, Private Talk, Public Performance*. New York: Cambridge University Press. doi:10.1017/CBO9780511489471.019

Schwartz, J. (2003). This car can talk. What it says may cause concern. *The New York Times*, December 29.

Simmel, G. (1971). The metropolis and mental life. In Levine, D. (Ed.), *George Simmel on Individuality and Social Forms*. Chicago: University of Chicago Press. [first published in German in 1903]

Surveillance Camera Players. (2003). *Ten predictions concerning cell phones*. Retrieved from http://www.notbored.org/cell-phones.html/

Surveillance Studies Network. (2006). *Report on the Surveillance Society*. London: Information Commissioner's Office. Retrieved from www.ico.gov.uk/SearchResultAsHtml.aspx?cid=zvXivWNGbIUJ&page=http://www.ico.gov.uk/upload/documents/library/data_protection/practical_application/surveillance_society_full_report_2006.pdf&keywords=report on the surveillance society

Torpey, J. (2000). *The Invention of the Passport: Surveillance, Citizenship, and the State*. New York: Cambridge University Press.

Townsend, A. (2000). Life in the real-time city: mobile telephones and urban metabolism. *Journal of Urban Technology*, 7(2), 85–104. doi:10.1080/713684114

Urry, J. (2001). Inhabiting the car. In Larreta, E. R. (Ed.), *Collective imagination: limits and beyond* (pp. 277–304). Rio de Janeiro, Brazil: UNESCO.

Wellman, B. (2001). Physical space and cyberspace: the rise of personalized networking. *International Journal of Urban and Regional Research*, 25.

Woolgar, S. (Ed.). (2002). *Virtual Society? technology, cyberbole, reality*. Oxford, UK: Oxford University Press.

Yar, M. (2003). Panoptic power and the pathlogisation of vision: critical reflections on the Foucaldian thesis. *Surveillance and Society, 1*(3), 254-271.

ENDNOTES

1. I am using the term 'mobile phone' (rather than the North American 'cell phone') because this paper was first presented in the UK.
2. I am indebted to Heidi Campbell for this observation.
3. I discuss aspects of this in Lyon 1988 and Lyon 1994.
4. The Wireless Communications and Public Safety Act 1999.
5. In Ontario, where I live, Bell Canada recently (2005) launched its "Seek and Find" system permitting parents to track children by cellphone.
6. see http://www.poptel.org.uk/cgi-bin/dbs2/statewatch?query=mobile+phones&mode=records&row_id=20049
7. http://news.bbc.co.uk/1/hi/health/3485141.stm
8. http://www.ofcom.org.uk/media_office/news_archive/nr1_20040115
9. http://www.newscientist.com/hottopics/phones/phones.jsp?id=ns99994270

Chapter 14
Casting the Ubiquitous Net of Information Control:
Internet Surveillance in China from Golden Shield to Green Dam

Zixue Tai
University of Kentucky, USA

ABSTRACT

Alongside the quick rise of the Internet as a pivotal economic and cultural force in Chinese society, the Chinese government has implemented a two-tiered strategy in coming to grips with the great potentials and underlying risks associated with the network era. This chapter offers a critical, in-depth overview of China's state-orchestrated Internet surveillance apparatus from the Great Firewall to the latest Green Dam project. It first examines the conceptual and historical evolution of the Golden Shield program, followed by an analysis of the legal framework through which official regulation is justified or rationalized. Next, the chapter looks at the prevalent practice of industry self-regulation among both Chinese and foreign companies engaged in online business in China, and it ends with the discussion of the aborted official effort of extending content control to individual computers with the Green Dam Youth Escort project.

INTRODUCTION

Three decades of explosive economic growth in China has led the country on a path of unprecedented transformation. A centerpiece behind China's quick rise as a global economic power has been the ongoing telecommunications revolution across different sectors and regions in the country (Harwit, 2008). Triggered by decades of spectacular boom in the IT sector as a direct result of state-guided development and meticulous government intervention, China unseated the United States, the long-time No. 1 in the world, to become the global leader in technology, media and telecommunications (TMT) products and services in 2007 (Morgan Stanley, 2009). In five core areas as measured by landline phones, mobile phones, cable subscriptions, Internet use, and installed PCs, China takes the lead in four while lagging only behind the United States in the remaining (i.e., installed PCs) area. In particular, the Internet, which boasts 384 million users in

DOI: 10.4018/978-1-60960-051-8.ch014

China as of June 2009 (China Internet Network Information Center, 2010) and whose staggering growth shows no signs of slowing down in the years ahead, has been a key cornerstone of China's state-orchestrated informatization strategy (Harwit, 2008; Tai, 2006).

As a vital part of the overall scheme of openness to the outside world, China has successfully incorporated the enthusiastic participation and much-sought-after contribution from global telecommunications giants such as Yahoo, Google, Cisco, Microsoft, and SunMicrosystems in its informatization strives (Cherry, 2005; Israel, 2009; MacKinnon, 2008; Santoro, 2009), and has attracted considerable global capital in financing pillar IT enterprises (Harwit, 2008; Segal, 2002; Tai, 2006). Meanwhile, it has implemented a wide array of national policies to foster a rising core of highly innovative and globally competitive Chinese high-tech enterprises encompassing major areas of IT research and development (Ning, 2009; Segal, 2002). Side by side with the increasing penetration of the Internet into every aspect of Chinese society are two simultaneous initiatives by the Chinese party-state to solidify its authoritarian control of a fast-changing society by harnessing the disruptive and freewheeling nature of information technology: one is characterized by a series of legislative acts and administrative directives to (il)legalize behaviors and prescribe content online, and the other is marked by the construction of "one of the largest and most sophisticated filtering systems in the world" (OpenNet Initiative, 2009a: 1). The latter, officially called the "Golden Shield" project and fully implemented in 2003, is more commonly known as the "Great Firewall of China." But China's online surveillance apparatus is multifaceted and multilayered in nature, encompassing many more formal and informal arrangements and approaches than the Great Firewall and co-opting a multitude of state as well as non-state actors and entities in effecting an evolving multi-dimensional regulatory and control mechanism that has few parallels in the world.

BACKGROUND: THE RISE OF SURVEILLANCE SOCIETY

The omnipresence of multiple platforms of information technologies and devices in the networked society has fundamentally transformed surveillance practices of the modern nation-state (Lyon, 2001). Ubiquitous interactivity and connectivity has led to the rise of "total surveillance society" (Parker, 2001; Rule, 2002) and "maximum security society" (Lyon, 1992; Marx, 1988) in which pervasive, perpetual, invisible, and dispersed surveillance of individuals becomes an undismissible part of everyday life. Dataveillance, or "the systematic use of personal data systems in the investigation or monitoring of the actions or communications of one or more persons" (Clarke, 1988: 499), has become a deeply ingrained ritual of today's social reality. As a result, the gathering and sorting of data has been afforded new dimensions in the "digital enclosure" (Andrejevic, 2007). Compared with the conventional state-centric scheme of social control in the industrial age, the hallmark of surveillance in the information society is the massive participation of, and indeed, oftentimes domination by, commercial interests and non-state actors in the expropriation of scattered private data that can be aggregated for a variety of monitoring schemes (Gandy, 1993; Haggerty & Ericson, 2000). Such "monitoring, observing and tracing" has nowadays expanded the "net of social control" (Cohen, 1991) to the mobile world (Lyon, Chapter 13 in this volume).

The logic of bureaucratic surveillance involving state apparatus typically hinges on justifications from two grounds: national security and crime detection/prevention (Lyon, 1992). This is applicable in democratic societies as well as authoritarian and totalitarian regimes. That the state is likely to exercise its surveillance capacity to maximize its control power is highly congruent with Levi's (1981) theory of predatory rule (although she primarily conceptualizes it in the context of wealth and revenue accumulation). In particular, sweeping changes in recent years in the expansion of government surveillance power in the global war on terror in the United States and a few other Western powers have been a cause for concern over unnecessary encroachment on civil liberties (McAdams, 2005; Winseck, 2008). Indeed, these Western practices have often been cited by Chinese authorities to justify the variety of regulations and surveillance operations they have put in place. The difference, however, is that there are institutionalized checks and balances in most democracies to keep the government's temperament within certain boundaries while little recourse exists to contain the rulers' will under authoritarian regimes.

China in the Maoist era effectively developed an all-pervasive surveillance apparatus spreading from major cities to remote corners of the rural land by incorporating elements ranging from organized state forces to neighborhood committees to individual households. In that regard, the system was very much like the "people-watching-people" (Wood, 2005) surveillance state of East Germany's *Stasiland* as accounted by Anna Funder (2004). The "total domination" of the panoptic state in Mao's China was built on "collectivization and comprehensive mutual surveillance as a strategy of social atomization" (Los, 2004: 35). Thanks to decades of economic liberalization in the reform era, the monolithic, all-powerful and all-penetrative state mechanism is no longer in place as individuals enjoy an expanding space of freedom in their day-to-day activities. To adapt to this changing socio-political environment, China has rebranded its surveillance scheme to brace for two types of perceived threats: "hostile forces" from outside and dissenting individuals from within the country. The answer by the Chinese government is a "push-and-control" strategy (Zhang, 2006) that led to the current multi-tiered and multifaceted technology-centered system of information control to reign in the unfettered and rebellious nature while at the same time to reap the full economic benefits of the network age.

INTERNET SURVEILLANCE IN CHINA FROM GOLDEN SHIELD TO GREEN DAM

Golden Shield and the Great Firewall of China

Golden Shield, the archetype of China's online surveillance scheme and often nicknamed the "Great Firewall of China," has been likened to a highly sophisticated Internet-filtering system that targets state-proscribed sites and offensive content (e.g., Banisar, 2003; OpenNet Initiative, 2009a; Santoro, 2009). To equate the Golden Shield Project to a mega-filter, however, is a misnomer and fails to capture the multi-dimensionality of this national security network. Popular media in the West have played a major role in shaping this misunderstanding.

Li Runsen, one of the chief scientists behind the Golden Shield Project, assigns six overarching goals to its architecture (Li, 2002). First, it builds a national information network infrastructure interconnecting public security forces via land-based and mobile as well as satellite-delivered multimedia communications. Second, it creates a database-oriented application platform, of which a critical component is the China Crime Information Center (CCIC) that serves the information needs of Chinese police in relation to different domains of their responsibility. Third, it promotes a national technology and terminology standard that makes inter-agency information-sharing possible across the country. Fourth, it enhances network safety and data integrity through development of its own information security systems. Fifth, it is a network management mechanism that facilitates the day-to-day performance of China's computer networks. Toward that end, it is entrusted with the task of training and certifying network professionals within China. Finally, and most importantly, it is a public network information surveillance system that monitors real-time traffic and keeps undesirable content out of China's cyberspace.

It is the last goal of the Golden Shield that has been lopsidedly propagated across the mainstream discourse in the West concerning China's Internet (Damm, 2007). China's notorious "cyber police" are a direct derivative of and operative agents for the fulfillment of this mission.

The Ministry of Public Security (MPS) is the official arm directly administering the Golden Shield. Throughout the process from conceptualization to implementation, the Chinese authorities have made a sustained effort to keep apace with the latest technological developments both in and outside of China. The immediate predecessor of the Golden Shield is the China Crime Information Center (CCIC), initially completed and fully functional in 1994. The decision to start the brand-new Golden Shield Project was made by the MPS in September 1998 – right at the time when the central government made IT a national priority to set the stage for the takeoff of the Internet in China (Tai, 2006). The project won the approval from the State Council in November 1998, and was formally enlisted as one of the key informatization initiatives by the State Planning Commission (now the National Development and Reform Commission) in January 2001. From 1998 to 2002, a total of RMB¥5.4 billion (approx. US$790 million) was invested in the Golden Shield Project across China, with the State Planning Commission injecting another RMB¥3 billion (about US$ 439 million) into the next phase of the project in 2003.

The development of the Golden Shield has gone through three key benchmarking stages thus far: initialization (1998-2001), nationalization (2001-2005), and expansion (since 2006). The initialization stage witnessed the conceptualization and initial infrastructural completion of the project. Noticeably, Golden Shield was incubated – both financially and technically – as a single-ministry (i.e., MPS) undertaking during this time. The project received a significant boost from being designated as a project of national priority by the State Planning Commission in 2001, because this recognition provided additional financial support and expanded the scope of participation to the supra-ministry, national level. Focus during the nationalization stage was on connecting all provincial cities and major metropolises throughout China via fiber optics and creating an encrypted, shared virtual private network (VPN) for law-enforcement and public security forces. The expansion stage, which started in 2006 and is still currently in progress, extends the connectivity to all county-level police as well as enhances surveillance capabilities by incorporating multimedia, electronic-eye, and mobile monitoring.

In order to strengthen the surveillance functionalities of the Golden Shield and to streamline technological development, a mega-bureau called the MPS Information Center was set up in March 2004 to be exclusively in charge of network surveillance. The Information Center was granted the status of a public institution with the following core mission: routine maintenance of the network backbones; development of key software and applications; staff training; access authorization and data protection for the MPS intranet; and information security and surveillance across all computer networks within China. Institutions in China have been traditionally classified in three ways: government agencies, public institutions, and enterprise units. Government agencies fulfill official administrative responsibilities, and enterprise units engage in profit-making endeavors and therefore pay taxes to the central and local governments. Public institutions, on the other hand, are mostly non-profit organizations that provide service to society in designated areas with no tax obligations. As a public institution, the Information Center has more leeway in hiring technical talent within specialized areas and in its daily management, as most of the employees are not professional police. The MPS, however, exercises oversight over the center's daily operations. This dual arrangement is thought to best suit the administrative needs of the center as it allows the center to hire civilian personnel to work for public security-related tasks.

The Information Center certifies surveillance workers in China through administering the Information Network Security Professional Certification (INSPC) test to network managers. Another test that network managers have to pass is the Network Management Skills Examination (NMSE) administered by the Ministry of Industry and Information Technology (MIIT), which focuses mostly on networking knowledge and skills. The MPS and MIIT work in tandem to keep an eye over the shoulders of the tens of thousands of network managers (called *wangguan* in Mandarin) dispersed in nodes of network centers throughout China. These *wangguan* are hired by respective Web sites and online content providers, but they regularly receive instructions and directives from public security officials and government offices from time to time on what to block. Lying at the center of the chain of command here is the Web Bureau of the Central Propaganda Department and its surrogates in the local governments (Wu, 2009).

A major strategy the Golden Shield utilizes in restraining online content is to territorialize China's cyberspace into a gigantic intranet by applying control at the topmost level of the network. Physical connectivity to the rest of the world is rerouted through state-sanctioned access providers for all Chinese Web sites, and therefore filtering is efficiently applied at the entry/exit point to determine what can come into/go out of China's net space (e.g., Deibert, 2002; Lacharite, 2002; Santoro, 2009). Global connectivity is controlled in a duopolistic arrangement, with China Telecom and China Unicom maintaining 59.6% and 34.5% of bandwidth at the national point of entry/exit respectively. A few other smaller Internet access providers, which are granted their own respective domains of specialization (e.g., science and technology, education, international trade, mobile communication), make up the remaining 6% of the outlets (see China Internet Network Information Center, 2010, for the latest information on bandwidth distribution).

For the limited number of state-approved gateways that interconnect China's Internet to the rest of the world, three types of filtering mechanism are in place to keep proscribed content out of Chinese cyberspace: packet dropping (or IP blocking) targets specific IP (Internet Protocol) addresses to make all content hosted there inaccessible in China, DNS (Domain Name System) poisoning renders sites using certain textual hostnames inaccessible, and IDS (Intrusion Detection System, also called TCP reset) triggers blocking of Internet traffic based on the inspection of IP packets through a constantly-updated list of banned keywords (Clayton, Murdock & Watson, 2007; OpenNet Initiative, 2009a). As a result, three broad categories of Web sites are the targets of blocking. First, Web sites, numbered in the hundreds, that are published by "international hostile forces" such as Amnesty International, Human Rights Watch, Reporters Without Borders, Falun Gong, and other blacklisted organizations and exiled Chinese dissidents are permanently banned from Chinese cyberspace (e.g., Cherry, 2005; Lacharite, 2002). Especially highlighted in the first category are many pornographic sites, although the attention to the former far outweighs that to the latter (Wu, 2009). However, it is worth noting that the Chinese authorities typically cite online pornography as driving reasons for government regulation of the Internet. Next, on-and-off games are played with popular foreign sites, most of which are run by international media organizations such as the BBC, CNN, the *New York Times*, to switch off access to these sites by Chinese netizens at sensitive times or when objectionable stories are published there (e.g., Endeshaw, 2004). This category also extends to non-news sites, among them Flickr, Blogspot, Twitter, Facebook, Youtube and Technorati, that garner a lot of visits from China. The fact that they are popular among Chinese netizens puts them top on the targets of blocking when certain proscribed content appears in their domains. Finally, there are those constantly-changing lists of individual pages that may be associated with certain types of prohibited content (e.g., Mackinnon, 2009). Such funneled access at the outmost layer works side by side with other overlapping mechanisms of control at other distributed centers of the Chinese internetworks.

Legal Framework of Internet Regulation

Multiple government agencies at the state and local levels maintain jurisdiction over different aspects of regulating Internet information and online activities. The Ministry of Industry and Information Technology (MIIT), which was founded in 2008 as part of the government institutional reform plan to streamline regulatory functions in the new millennium, has overall enhanced regulatory responsibility over the telecommunications sector. Its main mission is to make long-term planning and informatization policies, develop national standard, and promote innovativeness and competitiveness in China's telecommunications industry; it also coordinates multiple inter-ministerial agencies in the protection of information securities.[1] In addition to the MIIT and the MPS, other ministries that play major roles in managing particular areas of online content include: the Ministry of Culture, National Copyright Administration of China (NCAC), the Ministry of State Security (MSS), the Ministry of Education, and the State Administration of Radio, Film and Television (SARFT). But supervising all of these state bureaucracies from above is the Central Propaganda Department of the Chinese Communist Party (CCP), which issues overarching orientations for all ideological control and information purification in China (for a detailed discussion on the rebirth of thought control by the Central Propaganda Department in the information age, see Brady, 2006). Complementing these central government agencies are multi-layers of corresponding local offices across the country that carry out official directives at their respective regions/domains of jurisdiction.

Over the years, China has adopted a two-track strategy in Internet content control: alongside the technological implementations of Internet surveillance are a series of legislative and administrative actions to draw the legal boundaries of what can and cannot be done in cyber China.[2] Its first official policy paper, titled "Regulations for the Protection of Computer Information Systems Safety in the People's Republic of China," was issued in February 1994, one year before the Internet was commercially available in the country (Tai, 2006). This regulation delegates the overall responsibility to "supervise, inspect and guide" computer information security protection to the Ministry of Public Security. The focus of this regulation, however, is uniformly on the maintenance of computer networks and on punishing authorized intrusion into certain restricted networks; there is no mention of "harmful" content.

The most comprehensive definition of prohibited content on the Internet is offered in the "Computer Information Network and Internet Security Protection and Management Regulations," approved by the State Council and promulgated by the MPS, with an effective date of December 30, 1997. This directive criminalizes the production, circulation, and accessing of nine categories of content over the Internet ranging from subversion, defamation (to both individuals or government institutions), sabotage of national unity, disruption of social order, to superstitious, pornographic and rumoring information. Additionally, it prohibits any type of information or conduct that may endanger national security or damage "national, social, and collective interests."

Worried by rampant "unhealthy" content on the Internet, the Standing Committee of the National People's Congress, China's legislative branch, issued its "Decisions on Safeguarding Internet Safety" on December 28, 2000. These decisions, which are intended to "promote the healthy development of the Internet in China, safeguard national security and social public interests," incriminate violators for a variety of acts (e.g., spreading virus, breaking into proprietary networks or bank accounts, intercepting electronic communications), including these proscribed in a series of administrative directives issued in the previous years. In terms of publishing and circulating "unhealthy information," these decisions are rather consistent with previous government ordinances. One noticeable addition, however, is the targeting of the use of the Internet to organize activities for and contact members of "heretical religious organizations" – an umbrella term for Chinese authorities to designate what they deem as "evil" or "subversive" cult groups or religions disapproved by the government. This inclusion was apparently aligned well with the government's ongoing crackdown since the late 1990s on a couple of underground parareligous movements with Falun Gong and Zhong Gong at their lead.

Legislative and regulatory acts not only target individual netizens but also monitor institutional and corporate entities engaging in any type of online information services. The Internet Information Management Measures (passed by the State Council and publicly released on September 25, 2000) and Internet Electronic Bulletin Services Measurements (issued by the Ministry of Information Industry, the predecessor of the MIIT, on October 8, 2000) collectively stipulate that providers of any type of online content (either proprietary or user-generated material such as BBS, forums, comments, chat rooms) for commercial or non-profit purposes must obtain an official license and can only engage in the designated types of online activities; preconditions for the granting of an official license are a good business plan, technical competence, and a sound/well-thought-out network information security protection mechanism. All Internet Content Providers (ICPs) are held responsible for the publishing of any type of proscribed content available on any part of their sites from their users, and those who fail to adequately monitor their sites may incur a fine and/or have their licenses revoked. Moreover, ICPs must store user data and activities (e.g., user accounts, registration, log files showing sites visited and amount of time on each page) for at least 60 days, which must be available to government investigators upon request. Additionally, ICPs have the legal obligation to report individual offenses they know of to government authorities with supporting evidence.

As David Lyon (Chapter 13 in this volume) argues in his chapter, it is only natural that contemporary regimes of governance would extend surveillance to the mobile world to "monitor, observe, and trace" users on the move. Measures have been under consideration by the MIIT, the MPS, and the State Council Information Office to regulate the exploding field of text messaging across China by applying similar content restrictions to mobile networks. In a significant development, in January 2010, mobile carriers in three Chinese metropolises (i.e., Beijing, Shanghai, and Guangzhou) simultaneously announced that mobile customers repeatedly sending pornographic messages (including textual, graphic, and video files) will face service suspension. Understandably, this issue has become a hot issue of public denunciation in Chinese cyberspace mainly due to lack of precise definition on what constitutes pornography as well as widespread concerns over violations of privacy and civil liberties. Specific rules of enforcement, therefore, are yet to emerge.

The Interim Provisions on the Business of News Publishing on Web Sites, jointly issued by the State Council Information Office and the Ministry of Information Industry in November 2000, set the ground rules for ICPs involved in publishing any type of news-related information on their Web space. This decree was updated in September 2005 as the Provisions on the Administration of Internet News Information Services. Non-government entities and non-news organizations cannot engage in news publishing business unless they obtain an official license (which is rarely given). Internet sites can apply for a license for reprinting news stories from officially-sanctioned news outlets; all news must be clearly marked for their sources, and news translated from overseas sources can only be used by authorized ICPs. In essence, this ensures the monopolistic role of state media in disseminating news online, and it restricts most portal sites to engage in non-news types of business in attracting user bases.

The strategy to funnel the inflow of content to China's Internet is extended to audio-visual materials by the Provisions on the Administration of Audio-visual Programs on the Internet, jointly issued by the State Administration of Radio, Film and Television (SARFT) and the Ministry of Information Industry and becoming effective on January 31, 2008. According to the provisions, ICPs engaging in the publishing of audio-visual material online must obtain licenses from the SARFT. However, the eight harsh conditions of eligibility make it impossible for anyone else to qualify except existing conventional broadcast media (i.e., radio and television stations). Furthermore, Internet sites that intend to go into audio-visual news publishing must seek another license from the MIIT. In a related directive promulgated by the SARFT in December 2007, all Internet entities engaging in showing movies and teledramas are also required to be licensed.

In China's polity today, interagency bargaining and maneuvering are commonplace as each official bureaucracy tries to grab more power and promote its own spheres of influence (Lieberthal, 2003; White, 2002). Perhaps nowhere is more prominent than in the telecommunications industry, which has been developing at a break-neck speed in the past three decades in China. This partly results in the multilayered, multiplayer, and overlapped regulatory network concerning the Internet as different regulatory bodies vie for a presence in the booming Internet sector. So it is no wonder then that, similar to SARFT's regulatory hand over audio-visual content on the Internet, the General Administration of Press and Publication (GAPP) would collaborate with the Ministry of Information Industry to come forward with its Interim Provisions on Internet Publishing in 2002. The provisions stipulate that any Internet site involved in publishing "original or edited content for browsing, reading, or downloading" must operate with a license from the GAPP. Notwithstanding repeated criticism over the ambiguity of this definition of online publication, GAPP's intention here is to extend its regulatory power over conventional publications to the online world. Since late 2007, there have been numerous speculations over an imminent major update on these provisions. This update, however, has not been materialized as of the writing of this chapter.

That telecommunications regulation is tantamount to a power grab finds best support in the latest debates on who should have oversight over online video games. Three ministries all claimed primary responsibility in regulating animated games on the Internet (which has been a booming sector in recent years), and it needed the State Commission Office for Public Sector Reform, a unit under the CCP Central Committee, to intervene with an official declaration in September 2009 to delegate main regulatory responsibility to the Ministry of Culture.[3] The Ministry of Culture justifies its role in the regulatory process as it being in the best position to weed "vulgar" content out of online games.

Such a framework of having multiple government agencies exercising jurisdiction over Internet content often creates confusion and inefficiency. Moreover, statutory wording, albeit rather consistent from one government decree to another on what types of content are not permitted, only targets content in very broad strokes and lacks specificity, as many have noted (e.g., Deibert, 2002; MacKinnon, 2008; Santoro, 2009). This can certainly cause frustration for any practitioner who wants to go by the book. But just as the "regime of uncertainty" can be used effectively as an official strategy to ensure compliance from the conventional media (Hassid, 2008), this loosely-defined scheme may produce added pressure for individuals and collective entities trying to toe the official lines, and it can be used to the advantage of the state in post-hoc, whimsical persecutions of particular cases and offenders. A notorious crime under which numerous individuals have been convicted by the Chinese courts is divulging "state secret," a term that is a handy catchall excuse for Chinese authorities to retroactively pursue anyone involved in publishing a wide range of information they do not like.

Self-Discipline and the State's Willing Self-Censors

As mentioned above, ICPs and ISPs are held responsible for any "illegal" content available in the Web space of their jurisdiction, irrespective of originating sources. Self-regulation, as Weber and Lu (2007) argue, has been the "cultural logic of controlled commodification" for Chinese authorities to keep a handle on convergent media. To keep the state censors away from their doorsteps, all Internet service or content providers have developed their own patrolling systems to monitor content on their sites (e.g., MacKinnon, 2008; Shie, 2004). In fact, all ICPs, ISPs, and Web cafes have to demonstrate that they meet minimum state surveillance requirements before they are granted a license. A particularly challenging area of administration is the variety of user-generated content, ranging from user comments to the flourishing blogosphere. Because most info-space across popular Chinese Web sites typically features didactic reprints from the state-sanctioned media and boring news on a restricted number of topics, user-generated content on wide-ranging topic areas is always a big draw for Chinese netizens (Tai, 2006). As a result, all comprehensive and portal sites in China have resorted to solicit user participation in their online space as an essential strategy to direct traffic to their sites. But with increasing online traffic comes the challenge of monitoring what these users say on their sites.

The need to self-monitor real-time cyber content triggers the rise of one profession – a particular type of network managers (aka *wangguan* in Chinese) that specializes in censoring online content submitted from users. These managers, most of whom have been trained and certified by the MPS and the MIIT, work around 24-hour shifts to scour their online territory out of proscribed content. Most ICPs and ISP have implemented a three-tier filtering system in dealing with user-generated content. As the first line of blocking, user-submitted messages containing targeted keywords are automatically rejected for processing, and the users are asked to either modify the content or give up trying. However, Chinese netizens have over the years become admirably clever at inventing alternative expressions to bypass automatic filters. So messages not blocked by the spying program are placed in line for manual clearance by *wangguan* before being posted in their targeted destination. Finally, after these messages appear, most Web sites have their cybermanagers browse through published content for further checking. These sites also encourage users to help identify "unhealthy" entries for deletion through phone or email contact.

Self-discipline has been an effective protective strategy for any profession. But this has been especially true for the Internet industry in China. The Internet Society of China (ISC), a quasi-official, self-governing body of China's Internet industry made up of more than 200 members including major access, content, and service providers as well as equipment manufacturers and research institutes, is the major organization advocating self-censorship through its Public Pledge of Self-Regulation and Professional Ethics for China Internet Industry. The mission of ISC is to "promote healthy development of [the] Internet in China … [and] to be a link between different members to form self-regulation and create a good reputation of companies."[4] To accomplish that, ISC requires all its members to sign on the Public Pledge which was first drafted in March 2002 and updated in January 2005. The pledge requires all signatories, among other commitments, to refrain from "producing, posting or disseminating pernicious information that may jeopardize state security and disrupt social stability, contravene laws and regulations and spread superstition and obscenity" and obligate them to "monitor the information publicized by users on websites according to law and remove the harmful information promptly."[5]

Since 2005, the Internet Society of China has been sponsoring the annual "Contribution to the Self-discipline of China's Internet Industry Award" to select exemplar online entities that have performed well in policing their Web space.[6] From year to year, popular sites such as those run by Sohu, Sina, CCTV (China Central Television), Xinhua Net (site of the official Xinhua News Agency), People's Net (site of the official *People's Daily*) have dominated the awardees. Critical criteria for being considered for this highly-publicized annual award include purified content on the Web sites (non-porn and non-politically-harmful information), practicing real-name registration on accounts within their space, fighting against spam and malware, protecting network security, and having not received government fines or notices for (non-filtering) violations. Release of these "well-behaving" compliers undoubtedly creates public pressure for non-enforcers and laggards to comply with state demands.

This practice of subcontracting state-centric surveillance to industry self-discipline has penetrated to other areas of online services as well. In a circular dated February 22, 2008 and distributed by the SARFT (the official licensor of audio-visual services) and its regional offices, all relevant Internet services engaging in publishing audio-visual content were urged to sign the Public Pledge of Self-regulation of China's Internet Audio-Visual Programming Services. The pledge, drafted and promulgated by the SARFT, requires signatories not to publish material promoting violence, sex, pornography, gambling, and superstition or to release content that is pirated or is damaging to traditional Chinese culture.[7] Eight of the most popular sites in this business signed the pledge on February 25, 2008, and many others followed suit since then. In another development, the three leading portals in China (i.e., Sohu, Sina, and Netease) drafted and signed a similar pledge on self-discipline in 2004 in offering "honest and healthy" wireless Internet services, and called on other services to join them in this pledge.[8]

Joining the expanding list of China's willing self-censors are a number of foreign (mostly U.S.-based) companies (Israel, 2009; MacKinnon, 2008; Santoro, 2009). As early as 1997, Prodigy Inc. signed an agreement to comply with Chinese Internet laws in order to sell Internet connectivity services in China; Yahoo was the first foreign company to sign the ISC-sponsored public pledge in March 2002 (and signed on the revised version again in 2005) in order to expand its business base in China (Tai, 2006). Likewise, Microsoft-operated MSN, which signed a joint venture with Shanghai Alliance Investment Ltd. (SAIL) in 2005 to launch MSN China, has adopted a similar approach in self-censoring its online space (search engine and blog services) tailored to Chinese users. Google initially refused to filter sites sanctioned by the Chinese government to its user base in China, which triggered a punitive suspension of Google's search services within China in August 2002 for weeks. In January 2006, Google changed its strategy and launched google.cn exclusively for online searches in China that block sites forbidden by Chinese authorities. However, in the latest twist of Google's operations in China, the Internet giant astounded the world in January 2010 by going public with its frustrations over the information censorship policy imposed by the Chinese government in the wake of series of cyber attacks originating in China with its gmail server as the primary target, and it threatened to shut down its China office if it could not resolve its differences with the Chinese authorities.

The following are three high-profile cases that outraged human rights activists and raised the eyebrows of politicians in the West. At the end of December 2005, MSN deleted blog writings of Zhao Jing (also known as Michael Anti), a pro-democracy activist on the blacklist of the Chinese government, hosted on its blog pages (MacKinnon, 2008). In September 2002, Yahoo provided personal information in relation to the publication of online material targeted by government investigation in China, which led to the arrest of dissident Wang Xiaoning, and in 2005, Yahoo collaborated with Chinese authorities in revealing the identity of the owner of a Yahoo email account Chinese journalist Shi Tao used to send a document containing "state secret" to an overseas recipient (Israel, 2008). Both Wang and Shi were sentenced to 10-year prison terms respectively after a secret trial. The unfortunate reality for companies eyeing the vast Chinese market is that they either have to find ways to compromise or to face the uncertain fates of online services such as Twitter, Facebook, Flickr, Myspace or Youtube who are sporadically turned on and off at the whimsies of government censors.

Spontaneous public opinion online on hot issues of the day in Chinese cyberspace has shown to have the power to shape the course of events in Chinese society (Tai, 2006). However, there is no guarantee that individual netizens will toe the Party lines in commenting on controversial issues. Indeed, most of the online postings are negative and critical in nature, and public sentiments can quickly get out of hand. So an effective strategy to censor the Internet is to populate various forums with positive, "healthy" and uplifting opinions in line with official policy (Brady, 2004). This leads to the rise of a brand-new profession – network commentators – whose job is exclusively to post comments and messages on popular interactive sites to highjack online discourse and influence public opinion. These commentators are recruited and trained by propaganda departments at various levels of the government apparatus, and are mostly part-time in nature. Constantly in contact with propaganda officials to receive instructions on what to say on which topic, these commentators assume multiple user names, and roam popular sites and pour comments across pages to advocate Party lines on just any issue. As an indicator of its penetration in Chinese cyber life, my search for the term "Internet commentator" in October 2009 on baidu.com, China's most popular search engine, turns out 1.79 million hits! These pro-government publicists are often paid a base salary, plus bonus based on the number of postings they have contributed. As the most typical bonus payment is 50 cents in Chinese RMB, they gain the disparaging nickname of "*wumao dang*" (fifty-cent party) or "*wumao*" (fifty cents) among Chinese netizens.

As a way to mobilize mass participance in the national surveillance network, the Internet Information Service Commission of the Internet Society of China founded the China Internet Illegal Information Reporting Center (CIIRC) on June 10, 2004, under the auspices of the State Council Information Office. The CIIRC solicits information from anyone on tips concerning a wide range of "unhealthy" content over the Internet via email, phone or posting on its Web site (http://net.china.com.cn). Similar reporting centers have been established at the provincial/regional level. These local reporting centers forward tipping information to the national center at CIIRC, which then recommends actions based on the nature of the offense. The conventional people-watching-people social network of surveillance (Wood, 2005) finds an online copy on China's Internet. As of June 2009, the CIIRC reported having processed over a million tips, which generated more than 8,000 pieces of incriminating evidence and resulted in 1.33 million deletions/removals of pages, graphics or links.[9]

Green Dam Youth Escort[10]

On May 19, 2009, to the astonishment of the world, the Ministry of Industry and Information Technology (MIIT) circulated a formal notification to all computer manufacturers mandating that all personal computers sold in China be preinstalled with a government-authorized content-control program called Green Dam Youth Escort.

Response from the international media was swift and invariably critical, renewing global focus on China's scheme of Internet surveillance.

A similar directive co-sponsored by the Ministry of Education, the MIIT, the State Council Information Office, and the Ministry of Finance was issued in early April 2009 targeting computers in grade schools and Web cafes throughout China; it was anything but smooth sailing for the government as it received little attention by the overseas media and the coverage from the state-directed media was unequivocally supportive. As of late May 2009, it was reported that 2.6 million school computers and 4.7 million Web café computers were already running Green Dam, covering more than 80% of available PCs in these public facilities. MIIT officials later admitted during interviews with Chinese media that the May 19 decision to extend coverage to all computers within China was partly encouraged by their fleet success in the schools and Web cafes. But public response to the mandate quickly took on a turn beyond the wildest imagination of government bureaucrats.

The avowed goal of the Green Dam software is to block access to a variety of online content that is considered harmful to minors so as to create a "harmonious Internet environment" in the country. The software contains three layers of filtering to keep "unhealthy" material out by automatically checking visual image, semantic, and IP information; it also tracks surfing time so that users (i.e., minors) can be disconnected once the amount of online time exceeds allowed limit. Additionally, the program keeps a log of surfing record for later (supposedly parental) retrieval and scrutiny. The program will maintain a database of blacklisted sites, and will regularly update local PCs with new listing information; it has the capability to allow access to banned sites by an administrator with a password or by putting them on a white list managed by the individual user. Attempt to access blocked content will trigger a warning message and then kill the browser application on the user's computer. Essentially, Green Dam marks the latest official effort to extend content filtering from the network level to the lowest edge of the connectivity of the individual users' PC stations.

Green Dam was jointly developed by Zhenzhou Jinhui Computer Systems Engineering Corp. and Beijing Dazheng Human Language Processing Technology Co. Ltd through a public bidding conducted by the MIIT in early 2008. The MIIT disclosed that it paid RMB 41.7 million (approx. US$6.11 million) for the distribution right to allow free downloads and installations on PCs in China for the period of one year. However, an investigative story by *China PC Weekly* (CPCW) on June 15, 2009, which became a centerpiece of online debates in numerous online forums in China, reveals a long history of collaboration between the two companies and the MIIT. Since 2004, Jinhui has taken part in six state-funded projects in developing automatic visual/graphic recognition technologies on the Internet. Dazheng, on the other hand, claims to be a world leader in computer processing of human language through its proprietary technology called Hierarchical Network of Concepts (HNC), and has undertaken 13 government-sponsored research projects in a variety of Internet filtering applications from 2001 through 2007.[11] Noticeably, the CPCW story, which challenged the exorbitant price tag and raised the question of possible foul play for the bidding process, is the only piece no longer accessible at its original publication URL among all online issues.[12] Meanwhile, the CEO of Jinhui admitted that his company had received over 1,000 harassing calls and even death threats for developing Green Dam in the month after the MIIT mandatory install decision.

Separate tests by independent parties such as the OpenNet Initiative (2009b) and three computer scientists at the University of Michigan (Wolchok et al., 2009) and hundreds of user reports by the conventional media and on the Internet in China consistently reveal widespread glitches and design flaws in the software. Among other problems, the program is hard to understand and to use, and yields inconsistent performance based on different configurations; it blocks a substantial amount of legitimate content, slows down the computer, and frustrates the users by crushing the browser under unexpected circumstances. Moreover, as an application primarily designed for Window-based Internet Explorer, it does not work for Macs/Unix stations or browsers such Firefox, Chrome and Safari. Most importantly, it poses serious security vulnerabilities for the local computers and is ridden with technical errors and flaws. In another development, Solid Oak, a U.S.-based software company, received an anonymous tip that Green Dam contains 3,000 lines of proprietary code from its Cybersitter program and threatens legal actions.

The outpouring of global media coverage of the Green Dam move again puts China's Internet censorship into the spotlight. Western governments, led by the United States, strongly criticized the project as a further barrier to free flow of information on China's Internet. The U.S. government openly called on Chinese authorities to reverse this decision, and the U.S. Department of Commerce sent a protest letter to relevant Chinese ministries on June 24, 2009, followed by a similar letter addressed to Premier Wen Jiabao and co-signed by 22 trade associations dominated by U.S. and European groups that have established close business ties with China. At the same time, while major PC sellers including China's Lenovo, Taiwan's Acers and Japan's Sony had indicated their willingness to comply, U.S. companies such as Hewlett-Packard and Dell urged the Chinese authorities to reconsider this requirement.

Compared with the uniformly critical foreign media, the Chinese media adopted a much more diversified approach to covering this incident. In a highly unusual twist, state media in China reacted to Green Dam with a skepticism that is rarely seen in the coverage of major government decisions. Whereas the tone of coverage in the first few days after the official announcement was more leaned toward the supportive side, it turned more critical in late May and early June, and became dominated by questions and challenges on a number of the official claims from mid-June onward. The main controversial points of focus were the quality of the software and user test results from multiple fronts, the steep price tag, the lack of transparency/public input in official decision-making, and the implications of Green Dam for civil liberties and privacy concerns for adult netizens (which, many pointed out, are the vast majority of China's Internet population). Furthermore, many raised the question of who would foot the bill after the expiration of the one-year lease, and some argued the decision to go with Green Dam constitutes a violation of China's anti-monopoly law.

The most vehement criticism, however, originated from China's Internet, the very target of control by Green Dam. The program gained the nickname of "filter tyrant" (an ingenuous switch to two Chinese characters homophonous with the name of the software) among Chinese netizens, and became the object of ridicule in most popular online forums and in the blossoming Chinese blogosphere. Many threads started off with legitimate images or text that Green Dam blocked, and lashed at various aspects of the software and/or the government mandate. With polls after polls showing over 90% of the users opposing Green Dam, the few supportive voices were hardly conspicuous across spontaneous online discussions during this time. Ai Weiwei, a prominent activist on and off China's Internet, called on Chinese netizens to boycott the Internet for one day on July 1, 2009, with thousands of supporters spreading the message out online.

On June 30, the eve of the scheduled implementation day of Green Dam, the MIIT publicly announced that the mandate was postponed "indefinitely." The battered minister, Li Yizhong, explained to the media in early August that the official intention was "voluntary" install, and the notion that Green Dam was required on all computers was a "misunderstanding" due to poor wording in the official directive. However, Li further reiterated that making the software available was an "act for the public good," and work will continue to improve the program's performance and to fix its loopholes. The required install on computers at schools and Web cafes still stands, Li confirmed. In early 2010, officials from the Ministry of Education confirmed on numerous occasions the official policy of mandatory Green Dam install on computers at public schools.

FUTURE RESEARCH DIRECTIONS

While the debates surrounding Green Dam have died down with the demise of the official ordinance, there are no signs suggesting that the Chinese authorities will back down from or loosen their intensified attempts of Internet censorship. As the Internet revolution continues to penetrate further into everyday Chinese life, the concerns over "low-taste," "evil" and "vulgar" content will in all likelihood heat up in the coming years as the MIIT and other government agencies continue their search for more sophisticated policy and technology solutions to rise to the challenges. China certainly is not alone in its concerns over protecting minors and citizens from harmful content on the Internet; every country has invented its own mechanism of Internet control and regulation in protecting the legitimate interest of its citizens (Lyon, 2001). Indeed, Chinese officials from time to time justify their actions from the practices of their counterparts in Western nations. Unlike Western democracies, however, the Chinese regime has much more leverage in moving ahead with controversial and unpopular measures due to its highly concentrated power structure as well as lack of checks and balances in the Chinese political system. So there is no question that this trend of multilayered and multifaceted surveillance system will continue in the future. Interested scholars need to keep a watchful eye on future moves – both technological and policy ones – by the various regulatory entities concerning different dimensions of content control over the Internet. In particular, mundane mobilities (Lyon, Chapter 13 in this volume) have become major targets of today's surveillance regimes, and mobile monitoring in China is an important area worth watching for.

The burgeoning field of surveillance studies has embarked on a track of high yield of stimulating and ground-breaking scholarship in recent years through incorporating an expanding set of intellectual traditions and by crosscutting disciplinary boundaries in both its subject matter and methodological approaches (Ball & Haggerty, 2005). The growth trajectory, as Ball and Haggerty (p.129) observe, has been paralleled by the "proliferation and intensification of surveillance practices within and between societies." It is worth noting that the regional focus of most recent surveillance studies has been heavily limited to the socio-political context as manifested in a few Western countries. While this is certainly not to suggest in any way that surveillance in Western democracies should deserve any less scrutiny, expanding the scope of inquiry to include China and other authoritarian countries in surveillance studies has much to contribute to the intellectual thrust and pragmatic relevance of this fast-evolving field. This is especially so considering that the Chinese surveillance system has been a model of inspiration and emulation for many like-minded authoritarian regimes across the world. For instance, even before the dust of Green Dam has settled, the Malaysian government is reportedly contemplating a similar measure in enforcing content filtering with netizens under their jurisdiction.

The internetworked nature of the cyber era has assigned global dimensions to any move to sanction the Internet within any national context. As China continues to integrate into the global community, which finds full manifestation in the Green Dam case, the interplay among foreign governments, domestic and overseas companies, Chinese and international activists, and the Chinese regime can significantly shape the course of developments in China. The nature of these dynamics is another worthy topic of research for future scholarship.

CONCLUSION

As Eko (2001, p. 482) argues, Internet regulation reflects the "distinct cultures and socio-political and legal realities" of respective interconnecting nation-states. In less than two decades, the Internet has undeniably emerged as an earth-shattering force in Chinese society, and the accelerated nature of the Chinese Internet revolution has shown strong signs of continuation in the new millennium. Meanwhile, the Chinese government has put in place a two-tiered strategy in coming to grips with the great potentials and underlying risks associated with the unprecedented scale of transformation in China's telecommunications industry (Tai, 2006; Zhang, 2006). On the one hand, information and communication technologies (ICTs) have been afforded a prominent role in China's national economy. On the other hand, the Chinese regime has put in place a multilayered control mechanism combining a variety of technological and policy initiatives in order to harness the destabilizing and disruptive potentials of Internet-led ICTs.

At the topmost control center of China's surveillance apparatus is the Golden Shield Project, more commonly known as the "Great Firewall of China," that was started in the late 1990s and went into full effect in 2003. As a pivotal component of the Chinese national information infrastructure, the Golden Shield acts in essence as a mega-filter conduit to block "unhealthy" content out of Chinese cyberspace. All online traffic entering and leaving China's cyber border has to be rerouted through a few of the centrally-filtered national gateways administered by state-appointed censors. Below the national level, the official strategy to tame the distributed nature of the Internet is to subcontract content censoring with the growing number of thriving Internet Content Providers (ICPs) and Internet Service Providers (ISPs) covering a wide range of content and service types. Legally, companies that are engaged in Internet businesses are held responsible for any content created by any party available in their Web space. Technically, all entities involved in Internet publishing must implement particular content control systems in order to be granted a license.

At the institutional/corporate level, China's Internet industry is expanding their participation in Internet surveillance on various levels of content control through signing code of professional self-regulation. Joining in this type of self-censorship with Chinese Internet enterprises are a number of foreign (mostly U.S.-based) companies involved in different aspects of online business in China. Meanwhile, Chinese authorities at the national and local levels have also mobilized mass participation in Internet surveillance across the country by recruiting voluntary Internet commentators and through data-collecting activities at its national and regional information reporting centers. However, the government suffered a temporary blow when the latest effort to extend online surveillance to the outmost edge of the network with individual users' computers fell through with the aborted Green Dam Youth Escort project thanks to mass opposition from Chinese netizens as well as vigorous protest from foreign companies and Western governments. But this in no way marks the end of the government effort to intensify official monitoring of individual behaviors online; rather, it signifies the start of the next round of state-orchestrated control campaign in inventing new bricks and gadgets to solidify the Great Firewall.

REFERENCES

Andrejevic, M. (2007). *iSpy: Surveillance and power in the interactive era*. Lawrence, KS: University Press of Kansas.

Ball, K., & Haggerty, K. D. (2005). Editorial: Doing surveillance studies. *Surveillance & Society, 2*(2/3), 129–138.

Banisar, D. (2003). The Great Firewall of China: Cyber-policing dissent. *Media Development, 50*(3), 23–25.

Brady, A. (2006). Guiding hand: The role of the CCP Central Propaganda Department in the current era. *Westminster Papers in Communication and Culture, 3*(1), 58–77.

Cherry, S. (2005). The net effect: As China's Internet gets a much-needed makeover, will the new network promote freedom or curtail it? *IEEE Spectrum, 42*(6), 38–44. doi:10.1109/MSPEC.2005.1437036

China Internet Network Information Center (CNNIC). (2010). *The 25th statistical report on Internet development in China*. Retrieved January 29, 2010, from http://www.cnnic.org.cn/uploadfiles/pdf/2010/1/15/101600.pdf

Clarke, R. A. (1988). Information technology and dataveillance. *Communications of the ACM, 31*(5), 498–512. doi:10.1145/42411.42413

Clayton, R., Murdoch, S. J., & Watson, R. N. M. (2007). Ignoring the Great Firewall of China. *I/S: A Journal of Law and Policy for the Information Society, 3*(2), 272-296.

Cohen, S. (1992). *Visions of social control: Crime, punishment and classification*. Malden, MA: Polity.

Damm, J. (2007). The Internet and the fragmentation of Chinese society. *Critical Asian Studies, 39*(2), 273–294. doi:10.1080/14672710701339485

Deibert, R. J. (2002). Dark guests and Great Firewalls: The Internet and Chinese security policy. *The Journal of Social Issues, 58*(1), 143–159. doi:10.1111/1540-4560.00253

Eko, L. (2001). Many spiders, One Worldwide Web: Towards a typology of Internet regulation. *Communication Law and Policy, 6*(3), 445–484. doi:10.1207/S15326926CLP0603_02

Endeshaw, A. (2004). Internet regulation in China: The never-ending cat and mouse game. *Information & Communications Technology Law, 13*(1), 41–57. doi:10.1080/1360083042000190634

Funder, A. (2004). *Stasiland: True stories from behind the Berlin Wall*. London: Granta.

Gandy, O. H. Jr. (1993). *The panoptic sort: A political economy of personal information*. Boulder, CO: Westview Press.

Haggerty, K. D., & Ericson, R. V. (2000). The surveillant assemblage. *The British Journal of Sociology, 51*(4), 605–622. doi:10.1080/00071310020015280

Harwit, E. (2008). *China's telecommunications revolution*. New York: Oxford University Press. doi:10.1093/acprof:oso/9780199233748.001.0001

Hassid, J. (2008). Controlling the Chinese media: An uncertain business. *Asian Survey, 48*(3), 414–430. doi:10.1525/as.2008.48.3.414

Israel, B. R. (2009). "Make money without doing evil?": Caught between authoritarian regulations in emerging markets and a global law of human rights, U.S. ICTs face a twofold quandary. *Berkeley Technology Law Journal, 24*(1), 617–655.

Lacharite, J. (2002). Electronic decentralisation in China: A critical analysis of Internet filtering policies in the People's Republic of China. *Australian Journal of Political Science, 37*(2), 33–346. doi:10.1080/10361140220148188

Levi, M. (1981). The predatory theory of rule. *Politics & Society, 10*(4), 431–465. doi:10.1177/003232928101000403

Li, R. (2002). Strengthening police work through science and technology: An outline of the National Public Security Work Informatization Project (Golden Shield) Project. In Chinese. *Public Security Studies, 4*(90), 4-12.

Lieberthal, K. (2003). *Governing China: From revolution to reform* (2nd ed.). New York: W.W. Norton & Co.

Los, M. (2004). The technologies of total domination. *Surveillance & Society*, *2*(1), 15–38.

Lyon, D. (1992). The new surveillance: Electronic technologies and the maximum security society. *Crime, Law, and Social Change*, *18*, 159–175. doi:10.1007/BF00230629

Lyon, D. (2001). *Surveillance society: Monitoring everyday life*. Philadelphia, PA: Open University Press.

MacKinnon, R. (2008). Flatter world and thicker walls? Blogs, censorship and civic discourse in China. *Public Choice*, *134*, 31–46. doi:10.1007/s11127-007-9199-0

Marx, G. T. (1988). *Under cover: Police surveillance in America*. Berkeley, CA: University of California Press.

McAdams, A. J. (2005). Internet surveillance after September 11: Is the United States becoming Great Britain? *Comparative Politics*, *37*(4), 479–498. doi:10.2307/20072905

Morgan, S. (2009, March 20). *Economy + Internet trends*. Retrieved September 29, 2009, from http://www.slideshare.net/misteroo/economy-tech-trends-in-2009-by-mary-meeker-morgan-stanley

Ning, L. (2009). *China's rise in the world ICT industry: Industrial strategies and the catch-up development model*. New York: Routledge.

OpenNet Initiative. (2009a). *Internet filtering in China*. Retrieved September 25, 2009, from http://opennet.net/sites/opennet.net/files/ONI_China_2009.pdf

OpenNet Initiative. (2009b). *China's Green Dam: The implications of government control encroaching on the home PC*. Retrieved October 5, 2009, from http://opennet.net/sites/opennet.net/files/GreenDam_bulletin.pdf

Parker, J. (2001). *Total surveillance: Investigating the Big Brother world of e-spies, eavesdroppers and CCTV*. London: Piatkus.

Rule, J. B. (2002). From mass society to perpetual contact. In Katz, J. E., & Aakhus, M. (Eds.), *Perpetual contact: Mobile communication, private talk, public performance* (pp. 242–254). New York: Cambridge University Press. doi:10.1017/CBO9780511489471.019

Santoro, M. A. (2009). *China 2020: How Western business can – and should – influence social and political change in the coming decade*. Ithaca, NY: Cornell University Press.

Segal, A. (2002). *Digital dragon: High technology enterprises in China*. Ithaca: Cornell University Press.

Shie, T. R. (2004). The tangled Web: Does the Internet offer promise or peril for the Chinese Communist Party? *Journal of Contemporary China*, *13*(40), 523–540. doi:10.1080/1067056042000213382

Tai, Z. (2006). *The Internet in China: Cyberspace and civil society*. New York: Routledge.

Weber, I., & Lu, J. (2007). Internet and self-regulation in China: The cultural logic of controlled commodification. *Media Culture & Society*, *29*(5), 772–789. doi:10.1177/0163443707080536

White, G. (2002). *Riding the tiger: The politics of economic reform in post-Mao China*. Stanford, CA: Stanford University Press.

Winseck, D. (2008). Information operations "blowback": Communication, propaganda and surveillance in the global war on terrorism. *International Communication Gazette*, *70*(6), 419–441. doi:10.1177/1748048508096141

Wolchok, S., Yao, R., & Halderman, J. A. (2009). *Analysis of the Green Dam censorware system*. Retrieved October 8, 2009, from http://www.cse.umich.edu/~jhalderm/pub/gd/

Wood, D. (2005). Editorial: People watching people. *Surveillance & Society*, *2*(4), 474–478.

Wu, G. (2009). In the name of good governance: E-government, Internet pornography and political censorship in China. In Zhang, X., & Zheng, Y. (Eds.), *China's information and communications technology revolution: Social changes and state responses* (pp. 68–85). London: Routledge.

Zhang, L. (2006). Behind the "Great Firewall": Decoding China's Internet media policies from the inside. *Convergence: The International Journal of Research into New Media Technologies, 12*(3), 271–291. doi:10.1177/1354856506067201

ADDITIONAL READING

Abbott, J. P. (2001). Democracy@Internet. Asia? The challenges to the emancipatory potential of the Net: Lessons from China and Malaysia. *Third World Quarterly, 22*(1), 99–114. doi:10.1080/01436590020022600

Chase, S. M. (2002). *You've got dissent!: Chinese dissident use of the Internet and Beijing's counter-strategies*. Santa Monica, CA: RAND.

Chu, W. R. (2008). The dynamics of Cyber China: The characteristics of Chinese ICT use. *Knowledge. Technology & Policy, 21*(1), 29–35. doi:10.1007/s12130-008-9043-y

Deibert, R. J., Palfrey, J. G., Rohozinski, R., & Zittrain, J. (2008). *Access denied: The practice and policy of global internet filtering*. Cambridge, MA: The MIT Press.

Determann, L., & Marson, A. (2009). Internet business law in China for US companies. *The Computer & Internet Lawyers, 26*(4), 13–18.

Deva, S. (2007). Corporate complicity in Internet censorship in China: Who cares for the Global Compact or the Global Online Freedom Act? *The George Washington International Law Review, 39*(2), 255–319.

Goldsmith, J., & Wu, T. (2006). *Who controls the Internet?: Illusions of a borderless world*. New York: Oxford University Press.

Hachigian, N. (2001). China's cyber-strategy. *Foreign Affairs (Council on Foreign Relations), 80*(2), 118–133.

Healy, S. (2007). The Great Firewall of China. *Social Education, 71*(3), 158–163.

Kalathil, S. (2003). *Open network, closed regimes: The impact of the Internet on authoritarian rules*. Washington, DC: Carnegie Endowment for International Peace.

Kluver, R. (2005). US and Chinese policy expectations of the Internet. *China Information, 19*(2), 299–324. doi:10.1177/0920203X05054685

Li, S. (2010). The online public space and popular ethos in China. *Media Culture & Society, 32*(1), 63–83. doi:10.1177/0163443709350098

Mengin, F. (Ed.). (2004). *Cyber China: Reshaping national identities in the age of information*. New York: Palgrave Macmillan.

Paltemaa, L., & Vuori, J. A. (2009). Regime transition and the Chinese politics of tchnology: From mass science to the controlled Internet. *Asian Journal of Political Science, 17*(1), 1–23. doi:10.1080/02185370902767557

Qiang, C. Z. W. (2007). *China's information revolution: Managing the economic and social transformation*. Washington, DC: The World Bank. doi:10.1596/978-0-8213-6720-9

Stevenson, C. T. (2007). Breaching the Great Firewall: China's Internet censorship and the quest for freedom of expression in a connected world. *Boston College International and Comparative Law Review, 30*(2), 531–558.

Wang, S. S., & Hong, J. (2010). Discourse behind the forbidden realm: Internet surveillance and its implications on China's blogosphere. *Telematics and Informatics, 27*(1), 67–78. doi:10.1016/j.tele.2009.03.004

Weber, I. (2002). Communicating styles: Balancing specifity and diffuseness in developing China's Internet regulations. *Journal of Intercultural Studies (Melbourne, Vic.)*, *23*(3), 307–321. doi:10.1080/07256860216389

Yang, D. L. (2001). The great net of China. *Harvard International Review*, *22*(4), 64–69.

Yang, G. (2009). *The power of the Internet in China: Citizen activism online*. New York: Columbia University Press.

Yang, K. C. C. (2007). A comparative study of Internet regulatory policies in the Greater China Region: Emerging regulatory models and issues in China, Hong-Kong SAR, and Taiwan. *Telematics and Informatics*, *24*(1), 30–40. doi:10.1016/j.tele.2005.12.001

Zhang, X., & Zheng, Y. (Eds.). (2009). *China's information and communications technology revolution: Political impacts and state responses*. New York: Routledge.

Zittrain, J., & Edelman, B. (2003). Internet filtering in China. *IEEE Internet Computing*, *7*(2), 70–77. doi:10.1109/MIC.2003.1189191

KEY TERMS AND DEFINITIONS

Golden Shield: Called *jindun* in Mandarin Chinese, it is the archetype of China's Internet surveillance mechanism. Conceptualized in 1998 by China's Ministry of Public Security and fully implemented in 2003, it is a key project of China's national information infrastructure initiative. The Golden Shield interconnects all the databases for police information centers across China, enhances network security and data integrity, and ensures the day-to-day performance of China's Internet. The most important feature of Golden Shield is its content filtering mechanism that has the capability to block Web sites and online content based on a blacklist and a list of key words provided by the Chinese authorities. It also fulfills surveillance purposes based on networked multimedia and electronic-eye data.

Great Firewall of China: It is typically used as the nickname for Golden Shield for its ability to filter out unwanted content targeted by the Chinese government. This is a misunderstanding, however, because Golden Shield possesses more functionalities than just a filtering conduit. The Great Firewall can block content based on its IP address, its Domain Name System (DNS) information, and packet sniffing.

Green Dam: Called *lüba* in Chinese, this is a multi-million dollar project funded by the Chinese government, and works as a filtering program installed at the client's computer to block certain types of text and image data. It contains three layers of filters to ban Web sites and block access to certain content based on image, semantic or IP (Web addressing) information. The full name of the software is Green Dam Youth Escort, and the purported intent is to protect minors in China from harmful content on the Internet.

Internet Society of China (ISC): Chartered in 2001 with participation from more than 130 organizations, it is an industrial, quasi-official association encompassing members in a number of fields in connection to the Internet sector in China. Its more than 200 members today include major Chinese Internet businesses in the areas of network access carriers, Internet service providers, facility manufacturers and research institutes. ISC is the major organization advocating for self-regulation for all Internet-related businesses in China. It is headquartered in Beijing, and maintains a close relationship with relevant government offices regulating the Internet sector in China.

Network Commentators: This is a translation of the Chinese term *wangluo pinglun yuan*. As an emerging profession on China's Internet, it involves individuals who are recruited by propaganda officials at different levels of the Chinese government to propagate user forums and interactive online spaces with positive, uplifting and healthy postings in support of official lines and positions on issues of public interest. These individuals are typically paid a base salary, with bonus based on the number of posts they create online. They are despised by most Chinese netizens, and are also nicknamed "fifty-cent party," or just "fifty-cents" (because they are paid fifty cents of Chinese money for each online entry as a bonus).

Network Managers: It comes from the Chinese term *wangluo guanli yuan* (which is often shortened as *wangguan*). Network managers are responsible for network securities and network maintenance. In the context of China, however, some of these managers focus on patrolling the Web space under their jurisdiction to monitor online content submitted by dispersed individual users, and they timely remove sensitive and banned content from their sites. Major portal sites in China have network managers on duty around the clock.

Self-Discipline: Also called self-censorship, it is the practice of professionals voluntarily abiding by certain sets of rules in defining the boundary for themselves on what to do and what not to do. Targeted behaviors of self-discipline don't necessarily break the law, but they are deemed inappropriate or undesirable by professional standards in accordance with social norms. This is a widespread practice among Chinese Internet businesses to toe official lines in banning sensitive content from the Internet.

ENDNOTES

1 See the State Council circular available at the official site of the MIIT, at http://www.miit.gov.cn/n11293472/n11459606/11606790.html

2 China Internet Network Information Center (CNNIC) offers a comprehensive list of 50 legislations, executive directives and administrative ordinances from 1994 to 2009. The information is available at: http://www.cnnic.org.cn/index/0F/index.htm. The discussion in this section draws profusely from these official documents.

3 The full text of the document issued by the Ministry of Culture is available at: http://www.techweb.com.cn/news/2009-09-16/439915.shtml#wypl

4 The mission statement is available in English at http://www.isc.org.cn/isc_eIntroduction/index.htm. A list of current members can also be accessed on its official Web site.

5 The full text in English translation can be accessed at http://www.isc.org.cn/20020417/ca278881.htm.

6 Complete data about awardees in recent years can be found at the official Web site of the Internet Society of China at http://www.isc.org.cn/MoreArticle.php?ClassID=146.

7 The full text is available at http://www.gov.cn/gzdt/2008-02/22/content_897906.htm.

8 Public Pledge on Honesty in Wireless Internet Services, at http://www.ctws.com.cn/.

9 See the related China News Service (CNS) story at http://tech.qq.com/a/20090610/000402.htm

10 Discussion in this section has drawn from more than 100 news stories published by both Chinese and overseas media from late 2008 to July 2009.

11 This is reported on its Web site at http://hncit.com/about_us05.html

12 http://www2.shudoo.com/09/0616/10/12715966.html

This work was previously published in International Journal of Advanced Pervasive and Ubiquitous Computing (IJAPUC), edited by J. Symonds, pp. 53-70, copyright 2010 by IGI Publishing (an imprint of IGI Global).

Chapter 15
A Brief Cartography of Smart Cameras:
Proactive Surveillance and Control

Fernanda Bruno
Universidade Federal do Rio de Janeiro, Brazil

ABSTRACT

This chapter carries out a brief cartography of the so-called "intelligent" video surveillance systems. These systems are programmed to accomplish real time automated detection of situations considered irregular and/or suspicious in specific environments, in order to predict and prevent undesirable events. Three aspects of the smart cameras are focused in this cartography. First, the author explores its regime of visibility and note how it prioritizes the capture of irregularities in the body's movements in urban space. Second, the author shows how the type of monitoring and profiling of bodies and behaviors in these systems generally acts at the visible, surface and infra-individual level of human conduct. Finally, he analyzes the temporality of smart cameras, especially in its proactive dimension that intends to foresee and intervene, in real time, in future events. The analysis of these three aspects of the intelligent video surveillance identifies and highlights discourses, processes and operations that are common to the exercising of power and surveillance in contemporary societies – more specifically, those which are included in the realm of control devices.

INTRODUCTION

We care what you do, not who you are. We aim to analyze and model the behavior patterns of people and vehicles moving through the scene, rather than attempting to determine the identity of people... We are trying to automatically learn what typical activity patterns exist in the monitored area, and then have the system look for atypical patterns that may signal a person of interest—perhaps someone engaging in nefarious behavior or a person in need of help." (James W. Davis, a computer-science and engineering professor at Ohio State University, describing the construction project of smart-camera networks that automatically track suspect behavior, 2009:30)

DOI: 10.4018/978-1-60960-051-8.ch015

It is not uncommon for the more enlightened statements with regard to control mechanisms to be stated by the people who design them, rather than by social critics. Part of what we will deal with in this chapter has already been revealed, albeit in a condensed and controversial way, by the words of the inventor of a camera-based security system. This system is capable of tracking suspect or risky behavior by integrating multiple cameras which have high-resolution panoramic vision, geographic information systems (GIS), and "machine learning methods. This enables the computer to perform the kind of visual recognition that seems effortless for humans"[1]. According to the researcher:

We envision our research being applied to common urban surveillance tasks. To date, we have been focusing on the monitoring and analysis of pedestrian movement and activity... Other related applications we are considering include persistent tracking of vehicles through complex downtown environments and analyzing the traffic flows to look for atypical patterns. (Davis, 2009: 30)

Such a system is part of a new "generation" of so-called "smart" video surveillance[2] that heralds ways of monitoring behavior in an automated fashion. In most cases, the intention is for such cameras to recognize and differentiate regular patterns (which are considered to be safe) of conduct and occupation of spaces from irregular ones (which are categorized as suspect, dangerous, or simply non-functional). These "smart cameras" or "intelligent video surveillance" consist of software[3] that can be added on to cameras in order to filter or read images according to algorithms and point out individuals, objects, and/or attitudes that should be the focus of attention of the "scene". This is carried out in accordance with pre-defined applications in the system. For example, a body stopped for a certain period of time very near the safety line beside the tracks at a subway station should be automatically pointed out on the surveillance screen so that intervention can take place in time to impede the possible lethal leap of a potential suicide victim. This same device can also automatically pinpoint the following on the screen: an object that was left in the station, individuals or groups of people behaving suspiciously, bodies moving against the flow, or any situation previously categorized as needing to be highlighted in the machine's and/or camera operators' field of attention. In technical terms:

Intelligent visual surveillance systems deal with the real-time monitoring of persistent and transient objects within a specific environment. The primary aims of these systems are to provide an automatic interpretation of scenes and to understand and predict the actions and interactions of the observed objects based on the information acquired by sensors (Velastin & Remagnino, 2006: 1).

Computational vision, pattern analysis, artificial intelligence, and data management are some of the subjects and techniques involved in the construction of such systems. They rely on applications in the most varied sectors: safety, administration, transportation, commerce, and entertainment, among others. The tasks they can perform, and which are always in real time, are also varied: detection, classification, and tracking of objects, people, behavior, movements, and human activities; classification and interpretation of human behavior; detection of changes in the context or the pattern of how individuals or crowds occupy spaces; identification, etc. This broad range of functions and applications is visible in products currently on the market of smart video surveillance. ADVISOR (Annotated Digital Video for Surveillance and Optimised Retrieval), for example, which focuses on surveillance in the area of public transportation, includes automatic incident detection, content-based annotation of video recordings, and individual and crowd behavior pattern analysis. ISCAPS (Integrated Surveillance of Crowded Areas for Public Security) develops biometric techniques for identifying people in populous areas. BEHAVE, DETER, and PRISMATICA focus on the analysis and detection of suspect behavior in public places, while CAVIAR (Context Aware Vision using Image-based Active Recognition) is aimed at analyzing and recognizing objects, contexts, and situations for the purposes of urban surveillance and to allow for the planning of marketing strategies.

What is at stake? Or better yet, what is it that these smart cameras bring up for discussion? Most certainly, the question is not to simply describe this technological innovation and its effectiveness. Rather, it is a question of analyzing these devices as socio-technical systems (Latour, 1993 and 1999; Lianos, 2001) that modernize a number of aspects, discourses, and processes specific to surveillance and the control of bodies and behaviors in the produced and protected spaces of contemporary societies. In the reference chapter of this section, David Lyon (2010) discusses how our mundane, everyday mobility has become more and more transparent and traceable by way of technologies that are, themselves, mobile and locational (cell phones, GPS, RFID labels). Knowing "'where you are' matters increasingly from the point of view of contemporary regimes of governance, whether of commerce, policing or government" (Lyon, 2010: 4-5). With one single movement, the potentialities of these technologies multiply for the surveillance - "as observing, monitoring, tracing" - of citizens, consumers, employees, etc. Such potentialities do not only represent threats to the privacy of individuals; they also articulate together with ways of governing that act in fluid and virtual spaces through "coded information to monitor, predict and direct the behaviour of individuals..." (Yar, 2003: 257 apud Lyon, 2010). Intelligent video surveillance systems make up these ways of governing. Within the realm of image analysis and perception and attention automation, these systems perform functions that are similar to the technologies of observation, monitoring, and tracing mentioned by Lyon. However, they operate by inspecting and monitoring what you do or what you are doing when in a determined location, rather than simply where you are.

In this chapter, we will carry out a brief cartography of these socio-technical systems. Mimicking the devices in question, which visualize their "territories" by sweeping over surfaces – without going into greater depth, we will map their most prominent traits in three domains. Initially, we will deal with the regime of visibility present in these surveillance devices, as well as their policies and orderings of that which is visible, especially with regard to perception and attention. We will note that such a regime focuses on picking up irregularities in the algorithmic visualization of the movements of bodies and their general patterns of conduct. Next, we will attempt to show that this regime of visibility and surveillance goes hand in hand with a specific type of power and knowledge over individuals' bodies that generally acts at the infra-individual, visible, and surface level of the action and the conduct in order to incite, guide, or contain these actions and conducts. Finally, we will focus on the device's temporality, demonstrating that there is surveillance in force in this device that is intended to be proactive and which ideally coordinates the real time of the vision and the action in the present with a memory or archive of indexes and patterns of conduct that project a future needing to be controlled.

The perspective that guides the overview of these three aspects of smart video surveillance systems identifies and highlights discourses, processes, and operations that are characteristic of the way power and surveillance are exercised in contemporary societies – more specifically, those which are included in the realm of control devices (Deleuze, 1992; Lianos, 2001; Rose, 2000). As a strategy of analysis, we will compare two models of power in which surveillance and visibility play a central role: discipline, as Foucault (1995) understood and analyzed it; and control, for which Deleuze (1992) traces more general lines and to which other analyses are added that have greater or lesser affinities (Rose, 2000; Lianos, 2001) with this author. Such a comparison should not be understood according to principles of exclusion or historic overcoming. Although we recognize the strong implications of each of these models for their eras, there are currently zones of commonality between them. Discipline is not lodged in a past that has been completely left behind, just as control is not the current, exclusive model of power. However, the zones of commonality do not minimize the strong transformational process taking place, which involves the emergence of new surveillance processes. In the analysis of intelligent video surveillance, we will privilege the aspects that attest to its affinities with control and contrasts with discipline. We will note that elements which were already indispensable to disciplinary power – such as the knowledge of interiority and the processes of interiorization, the detailed analysis of each individual, and the careful production of their identities – certainly do not disappear. However, these elements are no longer at the forefront of the operations of power and knowledge in most of these devices.

It should be noted that the cartography traced out here is as brief as it is incomplete. We not only leave out a series of aspects, but also remain on the surface of the processes analyzed. We do not go into the necessary depth that such topics deserve in order to be understood in their complexity. However, the device in question is well-suited for the type of analysis that is intended to be carried out, considering the fact that tasks which humans are not able to fully accomplish are intended to be delegated to the device. It thus embodies part of the ideals of surveillance and control that are present in the socio-technical systems of our time. Moreover, these ideals are made especially explicit because they deal with automated systems that need to be programmed. Hence, our map serves as a first reading guide of these automated and "intelligent" surveillance devices.

VISIBILITY, PERCEPTION, AND ATTENTION

What does a smart camera see or perceive? Or better yet, what regime of visibility is put to work by this video surveillance that claims to be intelligent? One of the most recurring arguments in research and industries that design such artifacts is that they surpass the perceptive and attentional limitations present in monitoring carried out by conventional video surveillance systems. Human attention is excessively limited when dealing with the volume and monotony of surveillance images. After only 20 minutes, the attention of most individuals falls to a level below that which is acceptable for an efficient monitoring activity (Hampapur et alli, 2003 apud Gouaillier & Fleurant, 2009). A guard is not capable of attentively observing from nine to twelve cameras for more than fifteen minutes. Some studies show that the proportion of the number of guards in relation to the number of screens in some cases can actually vary from 1:4 to 1:78 (Hearing et alli, 2008 apud Gouaillier & Fleurant, 2009).

Moreover, according to such research and industries, this is one of the main reasons for the inefficiency of video surveillance in providing safety – cameras are more effective at producing after-the-fact proof than at preventing incidents or crimes. Therefore, adding an "intelligent" or cognitive layer to the cameras has the intention of automating perception and attention in a way that points out only the indexes of threat or danger or any other situation that is worth highlighting in the images, in accordance with the defined purpose. The system should automatically differentiate and recognize that which is meaningful in a scene and that which is irrelevant, that which is irregular and that which is regular. Herein lies its "intelligence". In other words, it not only deals with seeing or capturing, transmitting, and archiving images, but also with "interpreting", in accordance with pre-defined categories, that which is "viewed" in a scene. The system thus incorporates cognitive functions – more specifically perceptive and attentional functions – in an automated and pre-programmed way.

Let us take DETER (Detection of Events for Threat Evaluation and Recognition) as an example. Its focus is to detect and report unusual patterns of pedestrian and vehicle movement in external areas. For this system to work, it must recognize and differentiate the objects in the scene (pedestrians and vehicles), as well as the usual and unusual patterns of movement of each object, in order to recognize threats. According to a research report (Morellas; Pavlidis; Tsiamyrtzis, 2003), DETER has been successful in, for example, detecting the following patterns of movement that the system considered to be potentially alarming in certain external areas, such as parking lots: overspeeding vehicles, overrun of pedestrian pavement, running pedestrians, multi-vehicle attack (vehicles entering simultaneously from different entries in the parking lot and converging on a common parking lot lane) and M pattern (this refers to pedestrians following a serpentine course. It is more often than not a suspicious pattern associated with vehicle break-ins). Upon detecting such potential threats, the system sounds an alarm in the guard's attentional field, thus allowing for intervention at the moment of or before the predicted incident.

Through this delegation of perception and attention (Latour, 1994), not only are technical and administrative parameters of efficiency defined and reiterated; regimes of visibility, surveillance, and control of the space and of human behavior are as well. A regime of visibility does not consist so much of what is seen. Rather, it consists of that which makes what is seen possible. Machines, practices, discourses, and rules that are linked to the formation of knowledge and games of power (Foucault, 1995) participate in these conditions of visibility (Deleuze, 1992). Intelligent video surveillance systems make evident that which is currently defined as needing to be visible and noteworthy in the field of surveillance. In the context of an excess of images and a lack of attention, which is the case of video surveillance operators as well as contemporary societies in general, there is a need to filter out that which is relevant. In these systems, only that which is irregular or unusual is worth seeing. The flowing regularity of bodies in movement remains in the attentional and perceptual background. However, it should be added that irregularity is an index of threat or suspicion – and that is why it should occupy the foreground. Moreover, the irregularity in question is no longer confused with the focal points of the disciplinary regimes of visibility, which read an abnormal soul through behavioral deviation. Here, behavioral deviation is an index of imminent risk and undesired or threatening action. The psychological motives or traits that underlie the action are of little importance.

This task of catching irregularities or even foreseeing them is already present in conventional video surveillance and in many other forms of human or mechanical inspection. In this case, however, paying attention to that which is irregular is already incorporated or programmed into the viewing device itself. Thus, the type of ordering of that which is visible becomes more explicit in this model of surveillance. In this ordering, there is a particular way of observing everyday activities. We know to what extent we can make surveillance models correspond to regimes of visibility of everyday activities. We also know that disciplinary technologies make an entire field of everyday gestures and actions, which used to remain far from the investments of power, visible: activities; gestures; exercises; the following of rules, regulations, and schedules. The panoptic scale of disciplinary surveillance is spoken of a great deal. A whole political anatomy of detail, which extends to the lay world and the ordinary individual that which was already important to theology and asceticism, is relegated to a second level:

The mystique of the everyday is joined here with the discipline of the minute... The meticulousness of the regulations, the fussiness of the inspections, the supervision of the smallest fragment of life and of the body will soon provide, in the context of the school, the barracks, the hospital or the workshop, a laicized content, an economic or technical rationality for this mystical calculus of the infinitesimal and the infinite (Foucault, 1995: 140).

The meticulous observation of detail makes a series of small things, which used to be ignored by the great moral and judicial systems because of their relative indifference, noticeable in the sense of becoming meaningful and visible: delays, absences, interruption of tasks, negligence, rude gestures, immodest gestures, indecencies. This optic scale, which was at the same time both very detailed and all-encompassing, also depended on the constitution of meticulous files for each individual and the sharp observation of exams, in which the overlapping of the relations of power and knowledge assumed "all its visible brilliance" (Idem, p.190). The daily exam rituals in disciplinary institutions correspond to the individual entering the field of human and "clinical" sciences, through which he or she "may be described, judged, measured, compared with others, in his very individuality" (Idem, p.191).

The Intelligent video surveillance systems of today differ from this disciplinary optic scale. They deal with an observation that tracks bodies and spaces with a sweeping motion. This observation is not really concerned with the minutiae of everyday activities. It also does not concern itself with an inventory and objectivization of the individual differences that allow one to see an interiority – through gestures, activities, and performances – that is no less rich in details. These systems deal with an algorithmic view that pays less attention to details and depth than to superficial patterns and movements of bodies, which are understood more in their general contours than in their individuality. Some software even uses the term "silhouette" in order to designate the patterns that correspond to certain body movements.

This scrutinization of that which is visible is intimately linked to its normative effects. Such cameras are not so much for introducing or establishing normality in the heart of deviant populations (as in the case of some panoptic institutions). Rather, they are for capturing or catching a break in the flowing order. It is worth pointing out that order and regularity are maintained. However, their occurrence is not because of an internalization of values that guide an identity or biographical project, as was predicted by normalizing, disciplinary jurisdictions and their regimes of visibility. These cameras have a "formal," "pragmatic," and "utilitarian" normative effect in which "seeming normal" is more decisive than "being normal." Normality is, above all, a surface effect, an adherence to protocols of action and the use of managed spaces, and a belonging to a particular "ethos" – the supermarket or bank customer, the airline passenger, the subway user, etc. (Cf. Lianos, op. cit., p.126). Deviance, as we have already stated, is an index of threat or suspicion. However, the focus is on the action more than on the agent. What is being dealt with here is not seeing specifically or even seeing through. Rather, it has to do with recognizing in an automated way and seeing into the future (making behavioral patterns correspond to patterns of pixels in the image). It is a view that has foresight and also allows for action in real time, thus frustrating or averting that which was predicted. In the following topics we will explore the emphasis given to the surface of the bodies and their correlated categorization of monitored behaviors in greater detail, as well as the temporality of this proactive surveillance.

MOBILE BODIES, ACTION, AND INFORMATION

The body has always been of interest to power. As a vast tradition of studies on the topic reveals, there are many ways for power to be interested by bodies: the body of habits and customs (Elias, 1969); of sexuality (Brown, 1988; Foucault, 1976); of life, health, and illness (Canguilhem, 2009; Foucault, 1963; Rose, 2006); of work; of care with daily cleanliness and beauty (Vigarello, 1987 and 2004), among others. As was seen in the previous topic, there are also many ways for power to "gaze upon" the body, to make it available for visibility, and to make it an object of perception, attention, description, knowledge, classification, record (Crary, 1992 and 2001; Sekula, 1986).

We have recently seen a recurring diagnosis arise in post-industrial societies with regard to the investments of power over the body. On the one hand, we are living an intensification of the most varied forms of biopower (Foucault, 2004; Agamben, 1998) – in other words, of the different entries of the body and of life into the dominion of the explicit calculations of power, from bio-technologies to biosocialities (Rabinow, 1992) and to the penetration of power in multiple spheres of social, cognitive, affective, genetic life, etc. (Negri & Hardt, 2000; Lazzarato, 2004). At the same time, it has been certified that the body, in its materiality and physical force, interests power less and less. Power is more interested in the body's dimensions that are informational, immaterial, cognitive, etc. (Lazzarato, 2004). Indeed, we see distinct forms of relationship between body and power that coexist in contemporary societies. This can also be seen in surveillance technologies, which invest in biometric and genetic data, as well as in various ways of monitoring bodies and their activities from a distance – be it in physical space or in informational space. Social and affective dimensions are not left out of these investments, given that more and more of these surveillance devices exist, not only in control and security circuits, but also in entertainment, sociability, show circuits, and, above all, in communication technologies and networks.

In intelligent video surveillance, the monitoring of bodies in spaces reflects some important aspects of the current forms of distance control and surveillance (Lianos & Douglas, 2000). As has been noted, bodies are inspected in their daily mobility and movement without interrupting the flow of displacement in urban spaces, except in the event of suspicion. Disciplinary devices needed to stop and confine the bodies or register them in a predefined system of activities in order to observe them, know them, and normalize them. Video surveillance systems, however, are interested in the flow of moving bodies within the course of their lives and daily actions. In this sense, they are part of a set of contemporary technologies that makes it possible to track the everyday mobility and displacement of individuals in physical space (Wood and Graham, 2006; Lyon, 2010) and in cyberspace (Andrejevic, 2004). As Lyon states in the reference chapter of this section, "tracing parolees by satellite would have sounded like science fiction, and posting invitations by text message to potential customers passing near to Starbucks like a marketer's fantasy. All these things now happen." (Lyon, op.cit., p.2-3).

Nevertheless, the monitoring of mobility is not recent. The demarcation of borders and territorial protections, the control of migrations, and the circulation of people, goods, diseases, etc., remind us of just how old the crossovers are between surveillance and mobility (Salter & Zureik, 2005; Foucault, 2007). On the one hand, surveillance practices and techniques have historically acted as mobility containment. On the other hand, and especially since the constitution of modern cities and states, surveillance devices do not simply run counter to mobility. Rather, these devices accompany the different forms of mobility and order them, not only in the sense of containing or immobilizing them, but also in the sense of capitalizing on them and potentializing them for their service. This is especially apparent in the urbanization processes that began in the 18th century, in which surveillance and security devices (the constitution of police forces, health and population administration policies, etc.)

sought not only to establish limits, borders, and localizations, but also to permit and guarantee the circulation of people, goods, etc. (Foucault, 2007).

This dual relationship between surveillance and mobility has become more acute and more complex in the contemporary world (Lyon, 2002 and 2009). As has already been seen, the observation of mobile bodies by smart cameras is not simply to know where you are (Lyon, 2010), but rather to know what you are doing when in a determined place. As researcher James W. Davis pointed out at the beginning of this chapter, it is not always "you" that is important. Although some systems potentialize identification procedures, the first observational focus of many of them is not on the identity or the identification of the individuals but on their actions and behavior. It remains to be understood in what way this automated and "intelligent" visual monitoring of bodies and behaviors is associated with the formation of knowledge and power over individuals.

Disciplinary systems certainly made use of careful analyses of behaviors, actions, and performances. However, all of this was to be accompanied by a technology of the soul (which was correlated to the political investments in the body) where knowing and producing, examining and normalizing, measuring and reforming were sought in one single movement. This incorporeal but very real subjectivity was, as we know, decisive in circulating and articulating the effects of a certain type of power and knowledge that made up the disciplinary apparatus and its regime of visibility. According to Lianos (2001), in a highly institutionalized and media-influenced world, the mechanisms of control organize themselves around the action itself, instead of focusing on the supports of a socially-filtered conscience that sustains the action. In a model of control and government that uses simulation and incitation more than interdiction and coercion in order to accomplish and obtain results, the investments and calculations of power grant privilege to autonomy, initiative, surpassing, and continual choice (Rose, 199). The active user and consumer are the privileged subjects of contemporary control. In such a scenario, control is often carried out by being mixed with the very contexts of consumption and use of goods and services and with the very systems and technologies of training and coordinating of individual choices, thus providing protocols for action and contexts for interaction. In a word, technologies of empowerment of individual choice and technologies of control blend more and more into contemporary managed spaces (Rose, 2000; Lianos & Douglas, 2000).

In a parallel manner, a whole culture and rhetoric of risk and security (Garland, 2001) permeates the ordering of contemporary socio-technical spaces, bodies, and environments. It is not enough to just incite the action. It is also necessary to foresee and avoid all behavior that represents risk or danger. This focus on the action and behavioral patterns in order to construct algorithms capable of foreseeing events is recurrent in other control devices in the fields of health, crime, and labor. Such devices act more on the illness than on those who are ill (Rose, 2006), on the crime rather than the criminal (Garland, 2001), on the performance rather than the training (Ehrenberg, 1999).

Thus, the functions of management, control, and security overlap more and more in contemporary socio-technical environments. From shopping centers to subways and electronic Internet sites, comfortable and safe conditions for actions and choices are created, as are mechanisms for predicting and preventing actions considered to be suspicious or risky.

All of these elements are in some way present in intelligent video surveillance systems. They also aim to be diverse in their application by monitoring and intervening in behaviors and ways of occupying spaces with the most varied ends: consumption, commerce, management, security. Among their various applications are: counting clients; analyzing consumption habits, patterns of movement, and transportation; identifying intrusions in controlled or prohibited zones or areas of risk; detecting abandoned objects and suspicious behavior; monitoring and analyzing populational or crowd flows (crowd density estimation, face detection and recognition in crowds, and crowd behavior monitoring). The diverse nature of smart cameras is explicit in the advertising materials of certain manufacturers: "Whether the need is real-time security and surveillance or gathering business intelligence, ObjectVideo is the key to enabling truly intelligent solutions" (http://www.objectvideo.com/solutions/).

In the great majority of cases, what is being dealt with is the monitoring of routine behaviors in order to extract patterns with regard to the daily gestures of bodies located in their ordinary environments so as to incite the bodies to act in a certain way (consumption, movement, attention) or to recognize and impede irregular and/or suspect patterns of conduct. With its differing visual and algorithmic layers, a single system monitors, analyzes, categorizes, and intervenes in the behaviors. This process of categorization of bodies, movements, and routine gestures is intimately linked to the ordering and codifying of urban spaces, which in turn are converted into "automated socio-technical environments" (Lianos & Douglas, 2000).

Smart cameras and their sensors possess a type of power and knowledge over bodies that transforms their actions within a physical space into information (Manovich, 2006). This information permits the extraction of regular and irregular conduct patterns and thus makes interventions, planning, and calculations on the ordering of bodies and their flows possible. Intelligent video surveillance, in a way, goes hand in hand with the so-called intelligent environments that add informational layers to spaces. This therefore broadens the possibilities of interacting with the bodies present and allows them to be called upon in a contextual manner by the surrounding environment itself. In the words of Manovich,

By tracking the users – their mood, pattern of work, focus of attention, interests, and so on – these interfaces acquire information about the users, which they then use to automatically perform the tasks for them. The close connection between surveillance/monitoring and assistance/augmentation is one of the key characteristics of the high-tech society (Manovich, 2006: 222).

In this way, intelligent video surveillance produces a typology or taxonomy of the daily movement of bodies in spaces, codifying their patterns of conduct and allowing for the calculating and planning of actions on these bodies. It is part of the capture model proposed by Agre (1994) and revisited by Kitchin & Dodge (2006):

The capture model acknowledges that the mechanisms by which information is gathered is increasingly an integral part of the same system that they seek to monitor and regulate (e.g., a computer operation system logs its own use by an individual) and that these mechanisms in turn re–define and re–configure that system (e.g. change workplace practices), quite often in real–time. Agre (1994) argues that these modes of informational capture is possible because a grammar of action (formalized rules) has been imposed on a system. A grammar of action is a means of systematically representing aspects of the world, an organized language for modeling human behaviors (Kitchin & Dodge, 2006: 6).

But of what does this typology consist? In what way is it similar to or different from the modern techniques of categorizing corporal data? If we compare this typology to the known historical methods of classifying corporal characteristics that also used vision technologies, such as photography, we notice that modernity's inventories of corporal patterns were focused on specific traits and details. We need only remember the catalogs of ear types designed by Bertillon (Sekula, 1986). As in that time, we are now dealing with the exercise of political and scientific power over bodies through a classification and recording system that converts the image into convincing information and permits the analysis of indications and the recognition of corporal patterns, their norms, and their deviances. However, in the place of the rows of ears, little fingers, and forearms, the taxonomies of intelligent video surveillance depend on algorithms that "represent" patterns of conduct and movement of bodies in a given context. Instead of categorizing specific traits and fragmented corporal details, the emphasis is on contexts of the broadest gestures and action of the bodies. These contexts are then converted into information and detected by smart camera sensors and algorithms.

Modern taxonomies were also focused on the erudite and meticulous eyes of specialists and authorities who were to combine instruments and knowledge, such as photography, physiognomic description, anthropometry, and statistics. The categorizations of smart cameras, in their turn, are to be recognized in an automated fashion by the machine itself, which depends on computational vision, pattern analysis, artificial intelligence, and data management. Another significant difference is the main purpose of each of the systems. The visual diagnosis of a criminal personality hidden within bodily details and measurements (present, above all, in the composite portraits of Galton) and the identification and recognition of specific criminals (the first objective of Bertillon's records) in the heart of an anonymous mass that suddenly appeared in the confused territory of cities occupied the forefront of concerns and purposes of the modern typology of bodies, their measurements, and images. In the typologies with which we are dealing here, as has already been seen, we are no longer dealing with diagnosing a criminal personality through bodily images and details. Rather, we are concerned with foreseeing – on the surface of the image and in the movements of the bodies in a given context – a possible crime or incident that is about to happen. In one case, the body-image is the index of something that lies beneath or that comes before; in the other, it is an index of an action that is yet to come.

The differences between these indexing models and their respective temporalities are better understood if we consider the proactive nature of intelligent video surveillance, as will be discussed in the next topic.

REAL TIME, PREDICTION, AND PROACTIVITY

The last trait in relief in our cartography is the temporality of smart cameras. In the descriptions and advertisements of these devices, the main emphasis is given to the "real time" of the monitoring, detecting, and intervening in the contexts under surveillance. In other words, in addition to transmitting and observing the image in real time, which is already present in video surveillance controlled by human operators, the intelligent systems operate an automated and "instant" analysis of the scene under observation. This allows for any intervention to occur at the very moment in which the incident is taking place. In theory, possible delays or lapses are eliminated, be they because of human perception or attention or because of action at the opportune moment. It should be noted that real time here is not that of the observation, detection, or action taken as isolated elements. Rather, it is that of the almost immediate or instantaneous connection between these three normally diachronic, separate "moments," with the interval between them being reduced to the extreme. The image, which already has a real time of observation, now has a real time of reaction as well. In order to understand the reach or extent of this continuously alert and active present, it is necessary to understand the past or the memory, which serves as a parameter, as well as the future, which is projected in the present.

The memory of the device is not simply, as in "conventional" video surveillance, its ability to register. Smart cameras are equipped with an algorithmic memory, which consists of a repertoire of patterns that the camera should recognize as regular – and thus remain indifferent – or as irregular – and therefore intervene. In this way, the memory serves as a parameter or a framework for the analysis of the scene being monitored. If we consider the device's whole sequence of elaboration, this "intelligent" memory, which serves as a guide for the camera's "glance" and its perceptive and attentional filters, is constituted through the observation and archiving of an immense mass of images submitted for analysis in order to extract patterns. These archives can be elaborated in order to build an intelligent system, or they can be put together by reusing and analyzing previous records, which in large part do not have any use or end. The gigantic and humanly unsearchable archives of video surveillance images become a useful memory, according to the creators of intelligent video surveillance. As researchers and manufacturers Frost & Sullivan state, video analytics "is the next step to video surveillance where the intelligence of the system is utilized to enable the end user to identify key trends and significant changes in recorded images. The end user will be alerted when there is an unusual event. Video analytics is the key to help end users with the abundance of recorded information." (http://www.frost.com/prod/servlet/svcg.pag/AEID)

The greatest promise of this memory or of these intelligent archives, as can already be noted, is not to save and recover the past. Rather, it is to anticipate and avoid undesirable future events, above all when surveillance is for the purpose of security. We are talking about a record of patterns that is to serve as an index of the future. Intervention in real time is, in this case, an action in the present in order to avoid the occurrence of another action in the future. It is for this reason that we suggest discussing proactive video surveillance here, which should come before the foreseen action and, in this case, avert it. We now return to the type of indexing present in this model of surveillance. It does not have to do with the index of the past, nor is it solely the index of the present and the force of evidence that is characteristic of the real time of the transmission and observation of the image. It also mainly deals with the index of an occurrence which is yet to come. An extreme example of this proactivity is provided by the FAST (Future Attributable Screening Technology[4]) software, which uses sensors and starts at a distance of around two meters in order to capture a series of body signals of individuals, such as skin temperature, blood-flow patterns, perspiration, and heart and breathing rates, which serve as indications of a hostile act yet to come.

This index and this "yet to come" have a curious, paradoxical, disturbing meaning, however. The index of the past has the facticity and relative stability of "something happened" (Barthes, 2006), and the index of the present has the supposed live referential that "something is" or "something is happening." The index of the future, however, is uncertain by nature. In this case, it is also "unverifiable", given that the proactive aspect should impede or avert that which the body-image indicates is about to happen. The uncertainty and the many possible ramifications of what could happen in the course of time are therefore reduced. However, this reduction does not take place because of accuracy in the prediction. Rather, it occurs through the effectiveness or performance of the anticipation. We will never know if the body that stops for too long at the edge of the subway tracks would have jumped to its death or not because the future is anticipated. In this case, the future is anticipated in order to be averted. Even though it is uncertain by nature, it becomes certain at the moment that it is foreseen, and yet it cannot be carried out. The same is true for the repertoire of suspicious behaviors that serves as an index of crimes or infractions that are yet to occur or that perhaps will not be carried out. They become suspect at the moment they are predicted, thus transforming the body-images into potential criminals.

The future projects itself onto the present and thus limits the stock of possibilities that belong to the present. When smart cameras are focused on optimizing the use of space, consumption, or the efficiency of services, this colonization of the present by anticipating the future is less ostensible. Instead of averting an undesired action, there is an attempt to incite desirable behavior in specific contexts. At any rate, and above all in the case of proactive surveillance with the purpose of security, the "birth of the management of probability as a possible reality as valid as the present reality places the problematic of power in a qualitatively different context; it frees power from the limit of a reference to the occurrence and allows it to make that which has yet to exist (and which will perhaps never exist) into a 'happening of power'"[5] (Lianos, 2001: 135).

Smart cameras, through the combining of real time, foresight, and proactivity, produce a type of power over bodies, images, and times that is guided by an indexing of suspicion and the proactivity of surveillance. They therefore come to augment the already abundant assortment of predictive and proactive surveillance devices, such as data monitoring and profiling, in the most diverse fields: consumption, health, security, efficiency, etc. Video surveillance surpasses the dominion of the proof of that which happened and promises to proactively intervene in that which has not yet occurred.

REFERENCES

Agamben, G. (1998). *Homo Sacer: Sovereign Power and Bare Life*. Stanford, CA: Stanford University Press.

Agre, P. E. (1994). Surveillance and capture: two models of privacy. *The Information Society*, *10*(2), 101–127. doi:10.1080/01972243.1994.9960162

Andrejevic, M. (2004). Monitored mobility in the era of mass customization. *Space and Culture*, *6*(2), 132–150. doi:10.1177/1206331203251256

Barthes, R. (2006). *La Chambre Claire: Note Sur LA Photographie*. Paris: Gallimard.

Brown, P. (1988). *The Body and Society*. New York: Columbia University Press.

Canguilhem, G. (2009). *Le normal et le pathologique*. Paris: PUF.

Crary, J. (1992). *Techniques of the observer*. Cambridge, MA: MIT Press.

Crary, J. (2001). *Suspensions of Perception*. Cambridge, MA: MIT Press.

Davis, J. W. (2009). Research Report Article: Eye in the Sky. OSU. *The Alumni Magazine*, (May/June): 30.

Davis, J. W. (n.d.). *James W. Davis Home Page*, from http://www.cse.ohio-state.edu/~jwdavis/

Deleuze, G. (1992). Postscript on the Societies of Control. *October*, 59, Winter, 3-7.

Ehrenberg, A. (1999). *Le culte de la performance*. Paris: Hachette.

Elias, N. (1969). The Civilizing Process: *Vol. I. The History of Manners*. Oxford: Blackwell.

Eye in the Sky. (2009). *Research Report Article, May/June*, 30. Retrieved from www.ohiostatealumni.org

Foucault, M. (1963). *Naissance de la clinique*. Paris: PUF.

Foucault, M. (1976). *Histoire de la sexualité I - La Volonté de savoir*. Paris: Gallimard.

Foucault, M. (1995). *Discipline & Punish: The Birth of the Prison*. New York: Vintage Books.

Foucault, M. (2004). *Naissance de la biopolitique*. Paris: Gallimard/Seuil.

Foucault, M. (2007). *Security, Territory, Population: Lectures at the Collège de France 1977-78. London: Palgrave Macmillan. Garland, D. (2001). The Culture of Control.* Chicago: University of Chicago Press.

Gouaillier, V., & Fleurant, A.-E. (2009). *La vidéosurveillance intelligente: promesses et défis: rapport de veille technologique et commerciale*. Montréal: Centre de recherche informatique de Montreal (CRIM)/ Technopôle Défense et Sécurité, 2009.

Hampapur, A., Brown, L., Connell, J., Pankanti, S., Senior, A., & Tian, Y. (2003). Smart Surveillance: Applications, Technologies and Implications. In *Joint Conference of the Fourth International Conference on Information, Communications & Signal Processing and Fourth Pacific-Rim Conference on Multimedia, 2* (pp. 1133- 1138). New York: December.

Hardt, M., & Negri, A. (2000). *Empire*. Cambridge, MA: Harvard University Press.

Hearing, N., Venetianer, P. L., & Lipton, A. (2008). The evolution of video surveillance: an overview. *Machine Vision and Applications*, *19*(5-6), 279–290. doi:10.1007/s00138-008-0152-0

Kitchin, R., & Dodge, M. (2006). Software and the mundane management of air travel. *First Monday*, *11*(Nr. SI-7).

Latour, B. (1993). *We Have Never Been Modern*. Cambridge, MA: Harvard University Press.

Latour, B. (1994). On technical mediation: philosophy, sociology, genealogy. *Common Knowledge*, *2*(3).

Latour, B. (1999). On recalling ANT. In Law, J., & Hassard, J. (Eds.), *Actor Network Theory and After*. Oxford: Blackwell.

Lazzarato, M. (2004). *Les revolutions du capitalisme*. Paris: Les Empêcheurs de Penser en Rond.

Lianos, M. (2001). *Le nouveau contrôle social*. Paris: L'Harmattan.

Lianos, M., & Douglas, M. (2000). Dangerization and the end of deviance. *The British Journal of Criminology*, *40*, 261–278.

Lyon, D. (2002). Surveillance Studies: understanding visibility, mobility and the phenetic fix. *Surveillance & Society*, *1*(1), 1–7.

Lyon, D. (2010). Why where you are matters: mundane mobilities, transparent technologies, and digital discrimination. In Firmino, R., Duarte, F., & Ultramari, C. (Eds.), *ICTs for Mobile and Ubiquitous Urban Infrastructures: Surveillance, Locative Media and Global Networks*. Hershey, PA: IGI Global.

Manovich, L. (2006). The poetics of augmented space. *Visual Communication*, *5*(2), 219–240. doi:10.1177/1470357206065527

Morellas, V., Pavlidis, I., & Tsiamyrtzis, P. (2003). DETER: Detection of events for threat evaluation and recognition. *Machine Vision and Applications*, *15*(1), 29–45. doi:10.1007/s00138-003-0121-6

Rabinow, P. (1992). Artificiality and enlightenment: from sociobiology to biosociality. In Crary, J., & Kwinter, S. (Eds.), *Incorporations* (pp. 234–252). New York: Zone Books.

Rose, N. (2000). *Power of Freedom: Reframing Political Thought*. Cambridge, UK: Cambridge University Press.

Rose, N. (2006). *Politics of life itself: biomedicine, power and subjectivity in the twenty-first century*. Princeton, NJ: Princeton University Press.

Sekula, A. (1986).The Body and the Archive. *October, 39*, 3-64.

Velastin, S. A., & Remagnino, P. (Eds.). (2006). *Intelligent distributed video surveillance systems*. London: Institution of Engineering and Technology.

Vigarello, G. (1987). *Le Propre et le Sale. L'hygiène du corps depuis le Moyen Age*. Paris: Seuil.

Vigarello, G. (2004). *Histoire de la beauté, le corps et l'art d'embellir de la renaissance à nos jours*. Paris: Seuil.

Wood, D., & Graham, S. (2006). Permeable boundaries in the software-sorted society: surveillance and the differentiation of mobility. In Sheller, M., & Urry, J. (Eds.), *Mobile Technologies of the City* (pp. 177–191). London: Routledge.

ADDITIONAL READING

Agre, P. E. (2001). Changing Places: Contexts of Awareness in Computing. *Human-Computer Interaction*, *16*, 177–192. doi:10.1207/S15327051HCI16234_04

Andrejevic, M. (2003). Tracing space: monitored mobility in the era of mass customization. *Space and Culture*, *6*(2), 132–150. doi:10.1177/1206331203251256

Andrejevic, M. (2005). Nothing comes between me and my CPU: smart clothes and "ubiquitous" computing. *Theory, Culture & Society*, *22*(3), 101–119. doi:10.1177/0263276405053723

Beer, D. (2007). Thoughtful territories: imagining the thinking power of things and spaces. *City*, *11*(2), 229–238. doi:10.1080/13604810701395845

Bogard, W. (1996). *The Simulation of Surveillance: Hypercontrol in Telematic Societies*. New York, NY: Cambridge University Press.

Cole, S. A. (2001). *Suspect Identities: A History of Fingerprinting and Criminal Identification*. Cambridge: Harvard University Press.

Crang, M., & Graham, S. (2007). Sentient cities ambient intelligence and the politics of urban space. *Information Communication and Society*, *10*(6), 789–817. doi:10.1080/13691180701750991

Dodge, M., & Kitchin, R. (2005). Code and the transduction of space. *Annals of the Association of American Geographers. Association of American Geographers*, *95*(1), 162–180. doi:10.1111/j.1467-8306.2005.00454.x

Dodge, M., & Kitchin, R. (2005). Codes of life: Identification codes and the machine-readable world. *Environment and Planning. D, Society & Space*, *23*(6), 851–881. doi:10.1068/d378t

Dodge, M., & Kitchin, R. (2007). Outlines of a world coming into existence: pervasive computing and the ethics of forgetting. *Environment and Planning. B, Planning & Design*, *34*(3), 431–445. doi:10.1068/b32041t

Dodge, M., & Kitchin, R. (2009). Software, objects and home space. *Environment & Planning A*, *41*(6), 1344–1365. doi:10.1068/a4138

Galloway, A. (2004). Intimations of everyday life: Ubiquitous computing and the city. *Cultural Studies*, *18*(2), 384–408. doi:10.1080/0950238042000201572

Graham, S. (2005). Software-sorted geographies. *Progress in Human Geography*, *29*(5), 562–580. doi:10.1191/0309132505ph568oa

Greenfield, A. (2006). *Everyware: The Dawning Age of Ubiquitous Computing*. Berkeley, CA: Peachpit Press.

Law, J., & Hassard, J. (Eds.). (1999). *Actor-Network Theory and After*. Oxford: Blackwell.

Lessig, L. (1999). *Code*. New York: Basic Books.

Lovink, G., & Gerritzen, M. (Eds.). (2002). *Mobile Minded*. Corte Madera, CA: Gingko Press.

Lyon, D. (Ed.). (2003). *Surveillance as social sorting: Privacy, risk, and digital discrimination*. London: Routledge.

Lyon, D. (2003). *Surveillance After September 11*. Cambridge, UK: Polity Press.

McCue, C. (2005). Datamining and predictive analytics: battlespace awareness for the war on terror. *Defense Intelligence Journal*, *13*(1/2), 47–63.

McCullough, M. (2004). *Digital Ground: Architecture, Pervasive Computing and Environmental Knowing*. Boston, MA: MIT Press.

Mitchell, W. (2004). *ME++: The Cyborg Self and the Networked City*. Cambridge, MA: MIT Press.

Monahan, T. (forthcoming). Dreams of control at a distance: Gender, surveillance, and social control. *Cultural Studies - Critical Methodologies*, 8(4).

Shields, R. (2004). Visualicity. *Visual Culture in Britain*, *5*(1), 23–36.

Virilio, P. (1994). *The Vision Machine*. Bloomington: Indiana University Press.

Wright, D., Gutwirth, S., Friedewald, M., Vildjiounaite, E., & Punie, Y. (Eds.). (2008). *Safeguards in a World of Ambient Intelligence*. London: Springer.

KEY TERMS AND DEFINITIONS

Control: In this paper, the term control is used in the sense proposed by Gilles Deleuze: a system of power characteristic of contemporary societies, which differs from the system of disciplinary power, as conceived by Michel Foucault in modern societies. In addition to Gilles Deleuze, this text uses the contributions of Michalis Lianos on social control in Automated Socio-Technical Environments.

Human Behaviour Monitoring: Regular, systematic and focused monitoring of human behavior in order to control, influence or prevent specific actions and/or events.

Intelligent Video Surveillance: Intelligent visual surveillance systems are defined as real-time monitoring of persistent and transient objects within a specific environment. The main objectives of these systems are to provide an automatic interpretation of scenes and to understand and predict the actions and interactions of the observed objects based on the information acquired by sensors (Reference: Velastin & Remagnino, 2006: 1).

Proactive Surveillance: Procedures and/or technologies that seek to anticipate danger or risk in order to act preventively to avoid the events anticipated to take effect.

ENDNOTES

1. For a technical description of the project, Cf. Karthik Sankaranarayanan; James W. Davis A Fast Linear Registration Framework for Multi-Camera GIS Coordination. IEEE International Conference on Advanced Video and Signal Based Surveillance, September 2008.
2. Video surveillance systems are usually divided into three categories or generations: operator-controlled video surveillance, basic automated video surveillance, and smart video surveillance.
3. Such software, usually called video analytics, seeks to automatically analyze and identify specific objects, behavior or attitudes in the video sequences. The software transforms the video into data that will be transmitted or archived to allow the video surveillance system to act, be it by activating a mobile camera in order to obtain more precise data of the scene or by simply sending an alert signal to the system's operators.
4. Software that is part of the Project Hostile Intent, developed by The Human Factors Division of America's Department of Homeland Security (DHS). Cited in the article "If looks could kill", *The Economist* print edition, Oct 23rd 2008.
5. In the original, in French, "événement de pouvoir" (Lianos, 2001, p. 135).

Chapter 16

Recording and Reporting: Camera Phones, User-Generated Images and Surveillance

Bilge Yesil
City University of New York - College of Staten Island, USA

ABSTRACT

This chapter addresses the changing nature of surveillance by way of user-generated images, especially caught-on-tape style photographs and videos captured on mobile phones. Through a discussion of examples from Turkey (as well as from around the world), this chapter discusses the emergent function of the camera phone as a tool of surveillance used to document the misconduct of other individuals or authority figures. Aligned with the complex, decentralized networks of the synoptic paradigm rather than the more static, closed model of the Panopticon, camera phones intensify the visibility of anyone, anytime, anywhere. They facilitate lateral surveillance and sousveillance practices, enabling ordinary individuals to watch social peers or those in power positions, albeit in non-systematic, non-continuous and spontaneous ways. One could assume that camera phones and these new socio-technological practices they permit are empowering the individuals. However, by engaging in sousveillance, individuals become implicit partners in surveillance society.

INTRODUCTION

On October 17, 2006, Turkish Prime Minister Recep Tayyip Erdogan was in his armored limousine riding from his private residence to the Parliament in Ankara. Just as he arrived at the Parliament, he suffered a sudden drop in blood sugar and passed out momentarily. The Prime Minister's chief security guard and a member of the Parliament riding with him that morning asked the driver to make a quick turn to the nearest hospital. As they arrived, the security guard and the driver jumped out of the car at the same time, with the panic-stricken driver forgetting the keys in the ignition. The doors of the armored vehicle locked automatically because of the special security system, trapping the unconscious Erdogan inside. As the guard and the driver tried helplessly to unlock the doors,

DOI: 10.4018/978-1-60960-051-8.ch016

the alarm system was activated, making matters worse. After ten long minutes, they were able to open the door and rushed the Prime Minister into the hospital, only by smashing the front window of the vehicle with a sledgehammer they grabbed from a nearby construction site. The Prime Minister was hospitalized for about nine hours and later his condition was stable.[1]

The next day the unfortunate event was dubbed a "security scandal" by the Turkish media with reports primarily based on an amateur video of the incident captured by a bystander on his camera phone and photographs taken by a reporter. It was perhaps the raw, unedited nature of the video footage, showing the panic, alarm and incompetence of the security personnel in full view that made the whole incident even more shocking. Were it not for this camera phone footage, perhaps the newspaper columnists and media pundits would not have called the qualifications of the Prime Minister's security team into question, and more significantly, raised doubts about his health.

A reporter from the *Milliyet* newspaper who happened to be in the vicinity of the hospital and took photographs of the incident claimed that the Prime Minister's press secretary asked him not to give the photographs to his editors and "keep them to himself."[2] Surely, the press secretary did not want the media splashing these unflattering images across the country, but the amateur footage, on the other hand, made its way to local news sites and programs in any case, within hours.

In recent years, Turkish media has been feeding its own and the public's appetite for such scandalous stories, aided in no small measure by the availability of amateur videos and photographs, most commonly captured on mobile phones. This chapter will take a close look at these caught-on-tape style images, and the new ways of watching they engender—especially ways of watching other individuals and authorities, public figures and those in power positions. In contemporary media landscape, mobile phones and the images captured on them have come to occupy a key position in the visual matrix of information. In Turkey, for example these images have significantly shaped the public discourse pertaining to certain, highly-charged events such as children physically abused in a public orphanage, police beatings, a school principal harassing female students, and other such raw and shocking data now available in the public sphere in a way never possible before the ubiquity of personal image-capture devices.[3]

USER-GENERATED IMAGES

Before moving on to a more detailed discussion of how the increasing prevalence of images captured on mobile phones shapes and alters ways of watching and being watched, it is necessary to give a general overview of the uses and implications of user-generated images.

User-generated images captured on digital cameras or mobile phones have been the subject of much conversation in recent years. Wide availability and lower prices for these devices, together with video-sharing websites, as well as advanced broadband and bit torrent technologies, have made it possible for users to generate and distribute visual content. User-generated content varies from popular entertainment videos to those of "real" events caught on tape for purposes of documentation. Some of these now well-known images are of celebrities snorting cocaine, politicians making racist comments, or citizens rallying in political demonstrations. Stealthily captured photographs of Prince Harry's Nazi costume or Kate Moss's cocaine sessions provide the entertainment media with "good" visuals and spur sensational news coverage, while images of snowstorms or wildfires feed websites and airwaves with mini-spectacles. In another category, one can find disturbing images such as those of Saddam Hussein's execution or Al Qaeda's beheading of American soldiers. There are also photographs or videos of national or personal calamity such as those from the Southeast Asian tsunami in December 2004 or the London subway bombings in July 2005 that provide audiences with eyewitness reports and shape media coverage in significant ways. To these, we can add user-generated images of political events which circumvent official sources of information, censorship or news blackouts, and make claims to "truth" by way of their unfiltered, unedited nature. For example, when foreign and local journalists were banned from reporting the political protests in Iran in the summer of 2009, citizens on the streets were able to capture photographs and videos on their mobile phones and then disseminate them online, as well as "tweet" their eyewitness reports.[4]

Mainstream media has come to rely on user-generated images to fill web pages and airwaves with free visual content, taking advantage of users' free labor yet labeling it as the power of the user. For example, CNN has a special online section and a weekly TV program, *iReport*, which is devoted to user-generated stories, videos and photographs.[5] On its website, one can also find the *iReport* toolkit, the "handy guide" that instructs users on how to "shoot great videos," "take better photos" and trains them on journalistic elements such as the "ingredients of a story" and the "art of sound."[6] Meanwhile, MSNBC promotes its *First Person* section, which features user stories, photos and videos "both serious and light-hearted."[7] Fox News also encourages users to pitch in via its *U-Report*, "wherever you are," and showcases user videos on its website and on TV that range from catnaps to hotel bombings.[8] The Weather Channel posts *iWitness Weather* videos displaying footage of floods, storms, and hurricanes.[9] Celebrity gossip and entertainment news sites such as TMZ, Gawker, and Radar Online invite audiences to call or email should they have "news" or "hot tips" about celebrities.[10]

Attracting viewers online (sometimes in the millions), user-generated images make their way into the mainstream media, eventually re-doubling as content on television. User-generated visual content is either integrated into existing news or news magazine shows or forms the basis for shows exclusively devoted to user videos. Examples of the latter include CNN's weekly *iReport*, ABC's *i-CAUGHT*, and Headline News' *News to Me*.[11]

CAMERA PHONES

User-generated images (both still and moving) are captured on mobile cameras, an umbrella term that includes digital cameras, digital video cameras and camera phones. This chapter focuses on camera phones and does not place other mobile cameras in the same category, since each visual reproduction technology has different functionalities, operates in different contexts, produces different social, cultural implications, and therefore has different meanings.

The primary use of mobile phones is for personal communication. Yet technological innovations have transformed the mobile phone from a mere communication device into an appliance that enables users to listen to music, shoot moving and still images, surf the Web, send and receive email and text messages, and play games.

As Gerard Goggin (2006) shows, from the early 1990s onward, digital technology in mobile phones extended the range of telephony features and made possible communication through text, image, and sound. Goggin notes that the widespread adoption of text messaging and multimedia applications (such as receiving and sending images or short videos, or downloading music) and more recently the introduction of 3G mobile networks and phones that offer the possibility of interactive video communications, have made the social and the technical system of the telephone "absolutely pivotal by the close of the twentieth century" (p. 33).

Mobile phones equipped with cameras (camera phones) are primarily thought of as communication rather than imaging devices. However, in recent years, especially with the general improvement in pixel quality, the use of camera phones as imaging devices has substantially increased. They have become "much more than a 'poor relation' to digital and conventional cameras" (Kindberg, Spasojevic, Fleck, and Sellen 2005, Spasojevic 2005). According to a 2008 study by InfoTrends, worldwide sales of camera phones will jump from 700 million in 2007 to 1.3 billion in 2012, with much of this growth coming from Eastern Europe, Middle East and Africa.[12] The availability of higher resolution phones will also boost mobile phone photographic behaviors such as taking, sharing, printing, and storing photos. With increased resolution and optical quality, worldwide camera phone sales have indeed vastly outstripped digital camera sales; in 2007 global digital camera sales were below the 100-million-unit mark (Rasnake, 2008).

Apart from the original accessory function intended by their inventors, what are camera phones actually used for? In a 2005 study, Kindberg et al. organized motivations for image capture along two dimensions: affective reasons (was the image taken for sentimental, emotional, or jocular purpose?) and functional reasons (was the image taken for an individual or a shared social purpose?). Subjects who participated in the study used their camera phone as a "spontaneous capture device, for spur-of-the-moment capture, for capturing funny moments, interesting objects or events, or because the camera phone was handy" (Kindberg et al., 2005, pp. 5, 6). A majority of images (two-thirds) were taken for affective reasons, that is, to enrich a shared, co-present experience, for personal reminiscing or communicating with absent friends or family. Meanwhile, images taken for functional purposes were used as part of an identifiable task, to serve as a shared record required to discuss something or to record information for later reference (ibid.).

Although there are similarities between the uses of camera phones and other photographic devices—both are used for constructing personal and group memory, creating and maintaining social relationships, and for self-expression and self-presentation—there are also differences (Gye, 2007). The preferred devices at significant events such as weddings and births are digital or other imaging devices, not camera phones, mostly because of image and print quality. It is also argued that camera phones do not facilitate shared conversations and storytelling because people find it difficult to show photos to others on their mobile phones (ibid). Yet camera phones are increasingly used as "digital wallets," enabling users to carry their images with them at all times with an emphasis on casual image reviewing and sharing (Spasojevic, 2005). It is also noteworthy to mention that users can send their images to a number of contacts from their mobile phones or to online photo sharing websites, such as Flickr, Multiply, Photobucket, Picasa, Kodak Easy Share Gallery and Snapfish, among several others. Such sharing may not necessarily start a two-way, in-person conversation like the photo album does, but it undoubtedly creates novel forms of conversation, such as text messaging, posting online comments to these websites and so forth.

In terms of size, portability and convenience, the camera phone is very different from handheld analog or digital cameras. Unlike the traditional camera, which is associated with photography as a specific practice "reserved for certain occasions, for specific events," (Riviere, 2005, p. 171), the camera phone is not a stand-alone camera, nor a specific object. Indeed, it is barely discerned as a camera. Since we carry our mobile phones with us all the time, we also end up carrying cameras all the time, and this stands in stark contrast to the "traditional camera, which gets trotted out for special excursions and events—noteworthy moments bracketed off from the mundane," (Daisuke and Ito, 2003). In cases where you forget your camera at home, you can still rely on your camera phone to shoot photos or videos. The increasing megapixel quality has almost put the camera phones on a par with regular digital cameras, enabling users not to have to rely on carrying their traditional cameras with them.

Role of Camera Phones in the Public Sphere

Thanks to its convergent nature and ability to connect to networks, the camera phone has implications not only for personal communications but also the public sphere. As Levinson (2004) notes, the compact, live and interactive nature of the mobile phone enables immediate and fast-moving coverage on the part of journalists. Through examples of the coverage of the 2003 Iraqi War, Levinson argues that the mobile phone together with the video phone made it possible for journalists to televise live events without having to carry cumbersome equipment and therefore enabled them to report unexpected, unscripted events live (ibid, p. 149).

Not only journalists but users also rely on camera phones to take photographs and short films of events and transmit them to their personal contacts or media outlets. Gordon (2007b) shows, for example, how mobile phones alongside other mobile devices can be used to enhance public communication, contribute to or even shape media coverage of first-person accounts and images of natural disasters or other calamitous events.

Especially in times of national or personal calamity, the camera phone becomes an important tool providing eyewitness perspective. Gordon (2007) notes that camera phones provided valuable images and reports and helped to set the news agenda during the Chinese SARS outbreak, the Southeast Asian tsunami and the London subway bombings, but she also reminds us that once these images and reports were submitted to mainstream media they were subject to gatekeeping and the usual editorial processes.

In their analysis of the role mobile communication devices play in user-generated content, Robinson and Robison (2007) note that during the Southeast Asian tsunami, average people carrying ordinary portable electronic equipment were able to cover news stories before, alongside and after the professionals (pp. 86-87). Robinson and Robison argue that mobile and wireless devices, and on-the-go electronic and networked access, have changed the practices of gathering, reporting and dissemination of news and information during a crisis. The tsunami story was told, not by mainstream media, but by an "army of citizen journalists" who simply grabbed a mobile phone instead of a landline phone, used a PDA or wireless access instead of email from a desktop computer, and told the story from their point of view (p. 92-93).

Implications of Camera Phones on Visual Documentation

Due to their portability and connectivity to telecommunications networks, camera phones alter existing imaging practices and create new ones. First and foremost, they enable users to capture and share with others the ordinary moments of everyday life. Some scholars argue that photos taken by camera phones reinforce the user's individuality rather than their ties to other groups (Gye, 2007); that they are more personal, fleeting and short-lived (Okabe and Ito, 2006); and that they tend to focus on the mundane, trivial aspects of everyday life (Koskinen, 2005). Okabe and Ito (2006) argue that because of its ubiquitous and lightweight presence and its less objectified viewpoint, the camera phone tends to be "used more frequently as a kind of archive of a personal trajectory, a collection of fragments of everyday life" (p. 81). According to Koskinen (2005), images captured on camera phones participate in the aesthetics of banality, elevating ordinary things in everyday life to a higher status, thus creating "monadic clusters" of friends and acquaintances that "become even more emotionally and relationally more self-reliant than before" (p. 15). As Kindberg et al.'s (2005) study shows, most images captured on camera phones do indeed fall into this category of the personal and the affective. However, we must also keep in mind that even though the majority of images captured on camera phones and shared through online services are individualized and mundane, camera phone images are also the site of "potential news and visual archiving" (Okabe and Ito, 2003). As mentioned above, camera phone images taken during the London subway bombings, the Southeast Asian tsunami, or more recently, the anti-government protests in Iran, should attract our attention to the ways in which users capture and send images to news outlets and engage in moblogging and everyday photojournalism via their camera phones.

Moblogging (mobile blogging)—posting text, photographs or videos to blogs from a mobile phone—heralds the convergence of mobile communication technologies with the broadcasting powers of the Internet. Thanks to this convergence, camera phone users can easily and immediately share their images and make them public, either by way of posting them to blogs or sending them to news websites by email or MMS (Multimedia Messaging Service), even in situations where they lack access to a computer with an Internet connection. Most commonly, users post images of the personal and the affective kind to maintain social relationships or to archive images for their own use. This chapter is interested in the moblogging of functional images, such as eyewitness videos or on-the-scene reportage which are specifically meant to be shared and published. Functional images, from the moment of capture to the moment of distribution, are intended for the public sphere. Posting or sending images of bombings, national disasters, political protests or scandalous events to news outlets gives users a sense of participation and creativity. It also profoundly changes the meaning of the recorded image from something to be decided by newsmakers and gatekeepers to something to be "captured" from reality. Moreover, by traversing the boundaries between the public and the private, the journalist and the user, camera phone images modify established ways of transmitting collective knowledge and everyday memory (Reading, 2009). These images transform the conventional boundaries between the "ordinary" and the "event" as they enable users to record, commemorate, share and store mundane moments and elevate them to the level of picture-worthy (Rubinstein, 2005).

Examples from Turkey illustrate the potential of the camera phone as a documentation tool that contributes to the public sphere. According to 2008 statistics by the International Communication Union, the number of mobile phone subscribers in Turkey is 65.8 million (Turkey's population is 71 million). Mobile phones equipped with cameras are commonplace among the Turkish population and have been on the market since 2000. According to a 2007 global mobile phone survey conducted by Gartner Dataquest, every other mobile phone sold in Turkish market has a built-in camera.[13] Turkish users have embraced camera phones to photograph family and friends, and document personal lives. In recent years, however, a distinct and more ulterior function of the camera phone has also emerged: photographing the misconduct of those in power positions. Ordinary individuals have exposed incidents such as the sexual harassment of a female student by an assistant principal, physical abuse of the elderly at a nursing home, beating of a female suspect at a police station, and the like. These user videos are generally sent directly to television news programs, which are hungry for ever more scandalous stories and graphic imagery.

Turkish media outlets from online editions of newspapers to television shows now invite audiences to send images of illegal or wrongful behavior and help them to bring to daylight incidents of corruption, injustice and misconduct. Most online editions of mainstream newspapers have photo and video galleries, complete with lists of most viewed and most popular videos. Online editions of *Hurriyet* and *Vatan* ask readers to post their own videos, whereas some TV stations and investigative journalism shows in particular ask audiences to report stories or send their videos to producers. Among these, *Desifre* (Deciphered) calls on audiences to send tips to their 24/7 hotline reminding them that "being a perceptive human being and helping to voice our country's problems is one of the fundamental duties of a citizen."[14]

Desifre has been on air since 2001 and is known for breaking scandalous stories about corruption, deviant religious sects, mismanaged public hospitals and other stalwarts of tabloid journalism. Among *Desifre*'s most sensational stories is one about the beating and physical abuse of young children at a public orphanage at the hands of an agency worker and three other personnel in October 2005.[15] The camera phone video, captured by a horror-struck employee, showed graphic images of beatings and caused great uproar, rage and sorrow among the Turkish population, and ultimately resulted in the arrest and conviction of the abusers.

A more recent example of camera phone images that supply the visual material for breaking news is the brutal beating of a youth by police officers in Istanbul in 2009. On May 1 of that year, as labor union members and activists marched towards Taksim Square in Istanbul to celebrate Labor Day, the police were trying to block them from reaching the square. When a demonstrator tried to hide from the police by taking cover in the entrance of an apartment building, he was pulled out to the street by five police officers and beaten viciously. The incident was captured by an onlooker on his camera phone and once the video made its way to mainstream media, it further fuelled the criticism aimed at Istanbul police and their harsh techniques (Tekten, 2009).

What can we glean from these and other examples involving the use of camera phones and caught-on-tape style footage? There are three points to note about: the role camera phones play in breaking stories, in changing the definition of who is a photographer/observer, and in functioning as tools of surveillance.

First, camera phone images play a significant role in breaking scandalous news stories. One key factor has to do with the fact that these images make stronger the claims to truth and reality than professionally recorded (and edited) footage. The raw, out-of-focus and wobbly nature of the amateur camera phone images make them credible and appealing—both to news producers and audiences. As Rubinstein (2005) notes,

> *The camera phone image has a unique status among digital images insofar as it is perceived as a direct imprint from the real... At the hands of the people who happen to be at the right place at the right time, their phone becomes a part of an alternative network to the police surveillance cameras. This special status of the camera phone image as non-manipulated and therefore evidential is due to the way the image is being stored in the memory of the phone and not on a computer equipped with image editing software. The immediacy with which the image can be sent and received (with a date and time stamp attached) adds to the notion that every person with a phone is a witness (p. 10).*

Camera phones are now commonly recognized as an eyewitness device to provide an audio-visual record of events. They are considered highly effective to challenge the established conventions of documentation and authenticity, enabling users to play a significant role in setting the news agenda, as has been the case in South Asian tsunami, London subway bombings or political protests in Iran.

Second, camera phones enable anyone and everyone to become a photographer, and offer greater latitude for what or who can be photographed. While the photographic or video camera declares the intention to photograph and establishes one's identity as a photographer, the camera phone is not bound by such meanings. It is not a stand-alone camera, but is integrated into the mobile phone which frees it from the anchors of a priori meanings of the traditional camera. A consequence of this is the destabilization of the certainty of the photographer and the photographed, the observer and the observed.

The photographic camera and the photographer are part of an explicit structure in the visual space, but with camera phones this structured space is transformed into a flexible one. Similar to the blurring of boundaries between the author, reader and the text that Barthes discusses in "Death of the Author" (1978), the boundaries between the photographer, photographed and the image are also blurred. In his discussion of the separation of the author's identity from the text, Barthes argues that the modern "scriptor" does not precede or exceed the text but is born simultaneously with it: "There is no other time than that of the enunciation and every text is eternally written here and now" (p.146). In the context of camera phone practices, it can be argued that the process of imaging has become more spontaneous than planned, similar to the simultaneity of the utterance Barthes mentions. Equipped with the camera phone, the user can turn into a "roaming photographer" (Gye, 2007, p. 286) in an instant, able to photograph whenever, wherever. The identity of the user/photographer does not predicate the image. His identity is ephemeral because he continuously traverses the boundaries between being a photographer and not. He does not necessarily contemplate what to photograph and how to photograph it, but acts without any prior intention to photograph. The instantaneous decision to capture an image, especially when "gotcha moments" present themselves further contributes to the blurring of the boundaries between the photographer and the photographed, the photographer and the image.

The third point to note regarding the above examples from the Turkish context has to do with how camera phones function as tools of surveillance, especially in consideration of their role in exposing any wrongdoing. The following section reviews some key issues about surveillance, and explores in detail how individuals use camera phones to document the misconduct of other individuals or those who occupy higher segments in the social hierarchy.

CAMERA PHONES, SURVEILLANCE AND SOUSVEILLANCE

Although the primary function of mobile communication systems is to allow individuals to communicate, these very same technical systems also allow them to be monitored. Aside from their image capture capabilities, mobile phones are used to locate the geographical position of users. As Lyon (2010) notes in the reference chapter, the need to know the whereabouts of people have played a significant role in the rapid development and use of tracking and mobile technologies, especially the mobile phone (p.2). Used in conjunction with other technologies such as GPS, mobile phones enable marketers, employers, law enforcement and emergency services to "monitor, observe and trace their users continuously, and in real time" (p.5). For example, institutions that give mobile phones to their employees can track their whereabouts and hold them accountable for their day-to-day activities. In the meantime, individuals can also use location-based services to locate the whereabouts of other individuals, such as friends or family. Clearly, the introduction of location-based and satellite services has extended the surveillance capacity of mobile communication systems beyond the surveillance of individuals by institutions to the mutual surveillance of individuals by individuals (Green, 2002, p. 36), a phenomenon Andrejevic (2005) calls "lateral" or "peer-to-peer" surveillance. Lateral surveillance refers to individuals surveilling other individuals (family, friends, babysitters, suspicious persons in the neighborhood, etc). Extending the reach of surveillance beyond institutional boundaries, lateral surveillance is facilitated by the "democratization of access to the technologies and strategies for cultivating investigatory expertise and the need to enlist monitoring strategies as a means of taking responsibility for one's own security in networked communication environment in which people are not always what they seem" (p. 482).

In addition to lateral surveillance, another development in contemporary surveillance is sousveillance. Coined by Mann, the term sousveillance refers to "watchful vigilance from underneath" or the monitoring/observation of authority figures by watchful citizens (Mann 1998, Mann et al., 2004). Sousveillance is inverse surveillance, a counter dynamic to organizational surveillance, and is carried out by individuals to "observe the organizational observer." It focuses on "enhancing the ability of people to access and collect data about their surveillance and to neutralize surveillance" (Mann et al., 2004, p. 333).

Sousveillance is perhaps best exemplified by the 1992 Rodney King tape—an amateur video showing the beating of Rodney King by Los Angeles Police Department officers. The video was captured by a bystander on his handheld recorder, and since then has served as one of the first and most widely-viewed examples of the power of the mobile recorded image (Kingsley, 2008). The message of the Rodney King tape was that no person, institution or organization was immune from being monitored. The tape's wide dissemination and unprecedented public awareness and reaction were influential in the founding of the Witness Project. Aiming to "open the eyes of the world to human rights violations," this international activist organization can be thought of as engaged in sousveillance: it uses video and online technologies, and provides video cameras, editing equipment, training and support to local groups around the world to expose human rights violations and therefore to act as digital witnesses.[16] Another group engaged in sousveillance is Copwatch, a network of volunteer organizations in about a dozen U.S. cities that monitors police conduct and aims to "reduce police violence by directly observing the police on the street, documenting incidents and keeping police accountable" by using video cameras.[17]

Aside from sousveillance undertaken by organizations, individuals are also engaged in monitoring/observing those in power. Recent examples of sousveillance by individuals include the video of a New York City police officer shoving a bicyclist who was riding in Times Square as part of a demonstration. The video, which was shot by a bystander on his camera phone and uploaded on YouTube, was picked up by mainstream media and eventually resulted in the police officer being stripped of his badge (El Ghobashy, 2008). In another example in New York City, a passerby took photographs of two security guards at the George Washington Bridge who were napping while on duty (NY1 News, 2009). The photographs were published on a website (cliffviewpilot.com) and then picked up by local and national news media, resulting in the firing of the guards by the Port Authority.

To make sense of these examples and the role mobile communications and imaging technologies play in the emergence of lateral surveillance and sousveillance practices, we must first look at the transformation surveillance has gone through lately.

As Lyon (2010) notes in the reference chapter, surveillance systems are part of larger entities, closely aligned with modern bureaucratic organizations, information systems, computerized systems and searchable databases to govern the population (p. 21). Lyon also reminds us that since the 1970s, the state's role in surveillance systems has been downplayed in favor of private corporations, market agencies, civil society and transnational organizations creating "flows of personal data first within and then between different kinds of organizations, from government departments to hospitals, schools, police, insurance brokers, credit card companies, and marketing corporations (ibid.) In other words, surveillance is no longer the birthright of any one institution, but is now undertaken by diverse entities, government and non-government alike, and in diverse locations for diverse purposes (see also Lyon, 2004, p.133).

Another shift in contemporary surveillance is that surveillance technologies and practices are no longer the exclusive domain of institutions (public or private), but are also undertaken by ordinary individuals—individuals who do background checks on potential dates, use nannycams to monitor their babysitters in their homes or post camera phone images of sexual harassers on websites. As a result of these shifts, contemporary surveillance society can no longer be thought of as "practices of watching specific persons for specific purposes in specific, usually bounded places (such as the "Panopticon" prison)" but it is rather "generalized across populations, for numerous, overlapping purposes, and in virtual and fluid spaces" due to its reliance on electronic technologies (Lyon, 2010, p. 6).

Surveillance is no longer about top-down, hierarchical, institutional forms and practices but also lateral, mutual or even bottom-up ones. These forms and practices are non-systematic, non-continuous and carried out by ordinary individuals, and therefore they fall outside the theoretical model of Panopticon. They are more closely aligned with distributed, decentralized networks of lateral surveillance and sousveillance. Prior to discussing these more complex networks, it is necessary to explicate the Panoptic model.

Since Michel Foucault's introduction in *Discipline and Punish* (1977), the Panopticon has been widely used by surveillance and privacy studies scholars to understand the driving forces behind, and the implications of, surveillance. This theoretical model is inspired by Jeremy Bentham's prison design that dates back to the 19th century. In *An Introduction to the Principles of Morals and Legislation* (1823), Bentham, a utilitarian British philosopher, called for a new form of punishment that was not to cause pain or suffering, but to set an example and bring about reform. Bentham recognized that in order to deter others by force of example, punishment had to be made as rational as possible so that it would be supported by the public (p. 412). Punishment should no longer be an act of wrath or vengeance, but of calculation and discipline. This idea of rational punishment was also the core concept of the Panopticon—a prison run like a factory, as a capitalist enterprise. The Panopticon was a rotunda-form circular building with cells on the circumference. Its center went all the way up to the inspection tower where the inspector was concealed from observation of prisoners by blinds, but could survey the whole building (Mack, 1969, pp. 194-97).

To deter prisoners from transgressing, the Panopticon relied on the "apparent omnipresence of the inspector" (Bozovic, 1995, p. 4-5), but not his real presence. This was how the Panopticon differed from ordinary prisons: the inspector's power derived from his invisibility. The important element of the Panopticon was this "desubjectivized" gaze that could not be pinned down to any particular bearer. A prisoner could not see who saw him, or who talked to him (p. 8-11).

The key element of the Panopticon was omnipresent observation, visible but unverifiable. The power of observation had to be visible in the sense that the prisoner would assume the inspector in the central watchtower was always watching him; unverifiable in the sense that the prisoner did not know if or when he was being watched. He would therefore assume that observation was constant and would exert self-control over his behaviors.[18]

The idea of the Panopticon was taken up by Foucault (1977) to introduce and illustrate a new theory of power. Foucault argues that the panoptic principle of self-governance renders superfluous the visible devices of surveillance by generating "disciplinary society," which he describes as one that observes, retrains and renders obedient the individual instead of punishing him. The Panoptic modality of control focuses its gaze particularly on this population, for it is the deviants that are thought to need self-discipline most and therefore are made subject to systematic surveillance in prisons, hospitals, schools, mental institutions, poorhouses, etc.

For surveillance studies, the Panoptic model is appealing, and has indeed become the dominant theoretical model. However, as Haggerty (2006) shows, the Panopticon directs attention only to specific attributes of surveillance and neglects contemporary developments (pp. 23-26). It primarily focuses on 18th and 19th century institutions and forms of surveillance carried out by the state to rationalize and regulate the population, but excludes contemporary dynamics such as the proliferation of surveillance to "people at home, work or leisure…constituted as viewers…both watching others and exposing [themselves]… as pleasant entertainment activities" (p. 28). Moreover, the Panoptic model accentuates the surveillance of dangerous or marginalized groups by the unidirectional gaze of the powerful, but does not apply to new forms of surveillance whereby people from all segments of social hierarchy are subject to observation and even the powerful come under greater visual and documentary scrutiny (p. 29).

These contemporary developments can be best understood within the conceptual framework of the "surveillant assemblage," a term Ericson and Haggerty (2000) use to argue that contemporary surveillance is not hierarchical, whereby a few powerful institutions watch the many; it is rather rhizomatic. Like a rhizome, a plant that grows in surface extensions through interconnected vertical root systems, contemporary surveillance is undertaken by diverse agencies and organizations, and therefore operates by variation and disjunction, and grows by expanding its uses in different realms, and by targeting new populations.

Ericson and Haggerty argue that contemporary surveillance by way of its rhizomatic nature has a leveling effect on hierarchies. Unlike top-down surveillance where a few powerful individuals or groups watch the many, surveillance has "transformed hierarchies of observation, and allows for the scrutiny of the powerful by both institutions and the general population" (p. 617). For example, the poor come into contact with social assistance or the criminal justice system, and become targets of surveillance. Meanwhile, the middle and upper classes come into contact with a greater number of institutions, and are thus subject to more scrutiny in terms of their consumption habits, communication patterns, financial transactions, Internet use, credit history, transportation patterns, health profile, etc. Moreover, people can scrutinize their leaders through mass media. Television in particular enables the many to focus on, observe and monitor the few. Handheld cameras help people to tape instances of police brutality and thus level the hierarchy of surveillance. Cumulatively, these various developments point to a "fractured criss-crossing of the gaze such that no major population groups stand irrefutably above or outside of the surveillant assemblage" (p. 618), which Ericson and Haggerty use to argue that rhizomatic surveillance partially neutralizes surveillance hierarchies.

Although Ericson and Haggerty do not discuss mobile communication or imaging technologies in detail, it is nonetheless warranted to explore the role of these technologies in the decentralized, distributed networks of lateral surveillance and sousveillance. More specifically and in line with the focus of this chapter, it is important to consider the role of camera phones in the intensification of the visibility of anyone, anytime, anywhere and in the proliferation of sousveillance.

Sousveillance: Empowering Individuals?

It is appealing to portray camera phones as empowering on the part of ordinary people especially in light of their sousveillance potential. They can be considered to be the ideal apparatus to expose government corruption, police beatings and any other misuse of authority, and as an emancipatory tool to challenge the official discourse or intervene in the actions of the authority they are supposed to obey. Following Ericson and Haggerty, one could argue that camera phones help to level the hierarchy of surveillance because they enable ordinary people to surveil the actions of those in power positions, become surveillers themselves and thus share the power to observe and control. But do camera phones and attendant sousveillance practices really have a democratizing effect on surveillance society? Does a decentralized system where individuals can share the power to surveil necessarily mean that camera phones and sousveillance practices they facilitate equalize the playing field?

According to Kingsley (2008), the camera phone is a "miniaturized and mobilized surveillance device" which facilitates the mutual surveillance at the micro-level of everyday life, aiding in the creation of the participatory Panopticon—a term used to describe the constant surveillance undertaken by citizens themselves and by choice, as opposed to imposed by institutions (Cascio, 2005). Bearing similarities to lateral surveillance and sousveillance (discussed above), Kingsley's and Cascio's characterizations direct our attention once again to the shifting dynamics in contemporary surveillance, that is ordinary individuals partaking in the surveillance/sousveillance matrix thanks to mobile and online communication technologies.

In as much as sousveillance shifts the position of the watched from object to subject, from target to agent, it does not necessarily mean that it displaces top-down forms of surveillance and acts as an equalizer between the watchers and the watched. Compared to systematic, institutionalized forms of surveillance, which are firmly established, ubiquitous and have extended into all areas of everyday life, sousveillance is more random. With the exception of the Witness Project, Copwatch and perhaps other similar activist organizations, sousveillance is rather individualized. Unlike hierarchical forms of surveillance, such as surveillance camera systems trained on individuals on city streets, airports, schools, shopping malls, and offices on a permanent basis and operate within a network of police officers, security personnel, administrators and technicians, mobile imaging devices are instead used by individuals and on a non-systematic basis. Sousveillance practices are not planned; they are rather products of being at the right place at the right time. They are the outcome of spontaneous decisions made by individuals who happen to witness an incident and take opportunity of that "gotcha" moment.

Moreover, engagement in sousveillance is not simply an act of watching other individuals or those in power; more importantly, it is the internalization of the already existing notions of surveillance. We become increasingly aware of our surroundings, pay attention to which behaviors are inappropriate, unwanted or unreasonable, and make decisions as to which ones warrant recording and reporting. We become more reflexive about institutionally established norms of appropriate behavior, and apply them not only to others but to ourselves as well.

In this context, Kingsley (2008) rightly directs our attention to a significant reference to self-control in Mann's discussion of sousveillance, that is, sousveillance does not simply invert surveillance; it instills self-reflective responsibility and encourages social responsibility:

It requires that surveillance is enacted as a form of self-control, as self-maintenance. It is the discipline of being inwardly secure; firstly vigilant towards the self; secondly towards other people/selves. This form of discipline seems to suggest that there is little room for negligence when watchfulness is the order of the day. Yet it also prompts the 'user' of sousveillance to be active and participate in the surrounding environment (p. 349).

Lately watchfulness and participation in the surrounding environment have emerged as dominant premises utilized by government and law enforcement agencies to enlist individuals in the surveillance apparatus. Lyon (2004) discusses the active engagement of individuals in surveillance programs, and notes that people have come to view surveillance systems as necessary and beneficial, and even handed over personal information to government agencies on a voluntary basis as fear and suspicion have become dominant motifs in 9/11-era (p. 135). Writing on the symbiotic relationship between culture of fear and proliferation of surveillance, Lyon cautions us to consider how individuals have been encouraged to participate in the surveillance system:

One can buy peace of mind, apparently, by purchasing items such as 'nanny-cams' with which children in daycare may be watched from a 'window' in the corner of the parental workplace computer screen....On a societal level, fear has become a dominant motif since 9/11...Fears have been fanned, no doubt unintentionally, by the establishment of upgraded security arrangements, the relentless references to orange and red alerts, and by the constant admonitions to ordinary citizens to become the eyes and ears of the agencies of policing and law enforcement. Such 'eyes and ears' are intended to work in conjunction with the fully fledged systems of intelligence and surveillance whose budgets have burgeoned since the fateful events of 9/11 (p. 134).

The extension of existing forms of surveillance as well as development of new ones and the imperative to enlist individuals as "eyes and ears" of government and law enforcement agencies, all fuelled by fear and suspicion, can also shed light on the use of camera phones as crime-fighting tools.

As fear becomes the dominant cultural theme, and public safety turns into the perennial concern of not just the government but of everyone, individuals not only support surveillance, they also enter into both real and symbolic partnerships with law enforcement. Programs implemented in New York City, Manchester, and in several Mexican cities that enable individuals to submit their camera phone images of wrongdoing to law enforcement exemplify this process. In January, 2007, New York City Mayor Michael Bloomberg outlined a new project to encourage citizens to send in camera phone shots of any wrongdoing: "If you see a crime in progress or a dangerous building condition, you'll be able to transmit images to 911 or online to nyc.gov," Bloomberg said. "It's basically technology that exists that matches words with pictures. It could be done through a web site or it could be done through text messaging," he added. By September, 2008, New York City's 911 emergency system was upgraded to accept photos and videos sent from mobile phones, PDAs and computers (Musil, 2008). In the U.K., the Manchester police department implemented a multi-media program in November, 2007, to enable citizens upload photographs and videos of suspicious activity or evidence of a crime. Commenting on the new program, which was initially brought in as part of the fight against terrorism, the Chief Inspector said, "Nowadays people get so much evidence by using their phones and cameras and recording videos. It's like an extra set of eyes and ears for us" (Keaveny, 2007). In several Mexican cities, the government implemented a new crime-fighting program called the *Taxista Vigilante*, enlisting taxi drivers to report criminal activity and monitor infrastructure and public services. Starting in early 2009, taxi drivers were given free 3G phones enabling them to send pictures and messages to the local police when they see incidents such as water leaks, car accidents, street fights and even kidnappings and assault (Cellular News, 2009).

These examples shed light on how law enforcement and government agencies encourage individuals to become their "eyes and ears" and throw off at least some of the responsibility for crime control to them. Individuals are called to take responsibility for their surroundings, watch their surroundings and others for suspicious activity, and thus participate in the existing surveillance apparatus. We must keep in mind that individuals are also watching themselves assuming a self-reflective responsibility whereby they monitor their own behaviors, shun inappropriate, unwanted, unreasonable acts, and take responsibility for themselves, their loved ones and communities (see Mann, Kingsley above). In this sense, these new forms and practices of surveillance/sousveillance can hardly be celebrated as practices that empower the individuals or equalize the power relations between institutions and individuals.

CONCLUSION

In the reference chapter, Lyon (2010) examines mobile phones within the context of locational surveillance noting that they are increasingly likely to be "used for tracking purposes, in relation to both public and private services" (p. 16). Mobile phones enable schools, government departments, marketers, law enforcement and emergency services to track geographical location of people, and permit a greater "visibility – as traceability – of [people]...with public interest and personal safety or profitability or personnel coordination in mind" (p. 2).

While Lyon explores how and in what ways mobile phones are used to track and trace people, this chapter has focused on another dimension of mobile phones as surveillance technology, that is how they can be used for sousveillance purposes by ordinary individuals.

As discussed earlier, mobile phones equipped with cameras (camera phones) have implications for both personal communications and the public sphere. Thanks to better optical quality and the convergence of mobile communication technologies with networks, users can forgo photographic cameras (digital or not) and instead use their camera phones to capture images, and email them to personal contacts, publish them on blogs, websites, etc. Camera phones thus play a significant role in breaking stories, documenting the misconduct of others, and functioning as tools of surveillance. They reorganize visual documentation and the construction of truth and reality, especially through the emphasis placed on users, and raw, unedited footage. They are generally conceptualized as instruments that we can believe in as neutral recorders of truth and reality, and stand as symbols of neutral vision and transparency mostly because they serve as "nonhuman witnesses" in the sense that human capacities are irrelevant to their operation. As such these devices have begun to occupy a central position within the matrix of visual documentation and the construction of truth and reality.

In addition, with the rising popularity of user-generated images online and on television, camera phones have come to be considered as instruments of activism, emancipation, and meaningful media participation. Individuals use their camera phones not only for personal communication but also for documenting the misconduct of others, which leads to the description of such socio-technological practices as enablers of inverse surveillance that empower ordinary individuals to watch the authorities from below.

Mathiesen's (1997) conceptual framework of the synopticon is useful here to remain skeptical about the use of camera phones as an empowering practice. Mathiesen argues that while the Foucaldian panoptic paradigm focuses on the few watching the many through a hierarchical system, it overlooks the opposite force of synopticism. Synopticism refers to the ability of a large number of people to "see and contemplate" the actions of a few individuals (celebrities, politicians, stars, VIPs) through mass media (p. 219) and is therefore described as an opposing force. However, Mathiesen also notes that synopticism does not simply reverse panopticism. Rather panoptic and synoptic mechanisms mutually reinforce each other because they both promote visibility as a desirable aim. The end result is the "viewer society" where individuals are not only subject to surveillance by government agencies, state institutions, corporations, etc. but also become surveillers themselves as they "watch" the few and scrutinize them through mass media and television (ibid.).

Mathiesen focuses on mass media and television, yet his argument can be extended to online and mobile communication technologies, which he does not discuss because they were not widely used at the time of his writing. Within the context of camera phones and sousveillance, it is tempting to argue that ordinary individuals' access to information and communication technologies, and ability to capture and broadcast images of wrongdoing (police brutality, for example) can be portrayed as synoptic forces offsetting the panoptic hierarchies.

However, we must remember that Mathiesen emphasizes the mutual operation of synoptic and panoptic forces, not the dissolution of the latter. Along these lines, this chapter has also argued that sousveillance does not lead to the diminution of top-down surveillance or its democratization, but rather to its intensification. Camera phones enable ordinary individuals (the many) to surveil those in higher social positions (the few), but in doing so they also reinforce the existing surveillance culture. Individuals become voluntary participants surveilling others, recording and reporting their actions, and therefore become acculturated to networks of surveillance. Even as they watch those in power positions and expose their misconduct, they take on active roles in the larger surveillance culture and become acclimated to observing and being observed. They internalize a social and self-reflective responsibility that encourages them to evaluate others' and their own behaviors within institutionally established norms. Therefore, we must be cautious not to position bottom-up sousveillance as a force that offsets top-down surveillance, but remember that both sousveillance and surveillance are tied to the same aim, that is the intensification of visibility, observation and control.

REFERENCES

Allan, S. (2007). Citizen journalism and the rise of 'mass self communication': Reporting the London bombings. *Global Media Journal*, *1*(1), 1–20.

Andrejevic, M. (2005). The work of watching one another: Lateral surveillance, risk and governance. *Surveillance & Society*, *2*(4), 479–497.

Andrejevic, M. (2007). *I-Spy: Surveillance and power in the interactive era*. Lawrence, KS: University of Kansas Press.

Barthes, R. (1978). *The death of the author. Image-music-text* (pp. 142–148). New York: Hill and Wang.

Beck, U. (1992). *Risk society: Toward a new modernity*. London: Sage.

Belgiorno, K. (2006, April 18). The 21st century peep show. *Village Voice*. Retrieved November 1, 2009, from http://www.villagevoice.com/2006-04-18/news/the-21st-century-peep-show

Bentham, J. (1823). *An introduction to the principles of morals and legislation*. London: E. Wilson.

Bozovic, M. (1995). *The Panopticon writings: Jeremy Bentham*. New York: Verso.

Cascio, J. (2005). *The rise of the participatory Panopticon*. Retrieved October 23, 2009, from http://www.worldchanging.com/archives/002651.html

Cellular News. (2009). *Vigilante taxi drivers reporting crimes over 3G phones*, September 22, 2009. Retrieved November 1, 2009, from http://www.cellular-news.com /story/39715.php

Citizens take to streets protesting beating, torture at daycare. (2005, October 26). *Hurriyet*. Retrieved November 12, 2009, from <http://hurarsiv.hurriyet.com.tr /goster /haber.aspx?id=3441525>

Dinc, S. (2006, September 5). Congregation says it's lynching. *Hurriyet*. Retrieved November 12, 2009, from <http://hurarsiv.hurriyet.com.tr/goster/haber.aspx?id=5033063&tarih=2006-09-05>

El Ghobashy, T. (2008, July 28). Video shows NYPD cop assaulting cyclist. *Daily News*. Retrieved October 19, 2009, from < http://www.nydailynews.com/news/ny_crime /2008/07/28/2008-07-28_video_shows_nypd_cop_assaulting_cyclist.html>

Ericson, R. V., & Haggerty, K. D. (2000). The surveillant assemblage. *The British Journal of Sociology*, *51*(4), 605–622. doi:10.1080/00071310020015280

Facebook and freedom: New technologies are encouraging the change in Iran that U.S. desires. (2009, June 18). *Newsday*, A38.

Foucault, M. (1972). Prison talk. In Gordon, C. (Ed.), *Power/Knowledge: Selected interviews and other writings, 1972-1977* (pp. 37–54). New York: Pantheon.

Foucault, M. (1977). *Discipline and punish: The birth of the prison*. New York: Vintage Books.

Gordon, J. (2007). The mobile phone and the public sphere: Mobile phone usage in three critical situations. *Convergence*, *13*(3), 307–319.

Gordon, J. (2007b). The cell phone: An artifact of popular culture and a tool of the public sphere. In Kavoori, A., & Arceneaux, N. (Eds.), *The cell phone reader: Essays in social transformation* (pp. 45–60). New York: Peter Lang.

Green, N. (2002). Who's watching whom? Monitoring and accountability in mobile relations. In Brown, B., Green, N., & Harper, R. (Eds.), *Wireless world: social and interactional aspects of the mobile age* (pp. 31–45). London: Springer.

Gye, L. (2007). Picture this: The impact of mobile camera phones on personal photographic practices. *Continuum*, *21*(2), 279–288. doi:10.1080/10304310701269107

Haber Vitrini. (2007). 1 out of every 100 camera phones is in the hands of a Turkish consumer. Retrieved November 12, 2009, from <http://www.habervitrini. com /haber. aspx?id =266906>

Haggerty, K. D. (2006). Tear down the walls: On demolishing the Panopticon. In Lyon, D. (Ed.). *Theorizing surveillance: The Panopticon and beyond*. (23-45). Devon, UK: Willan Publishing.

Ignatieff, M. (1978). *A just measure of pain: The penitentiary in the Industrial Revolution, 1750-1850*. Macmillan.

InfoTrends. (2007). InfoTrends study shows increased use of camera phones among GenZers. Retrieved January 5, 2010 from <http://www.infotrends.com/public/Content /Press/2007 /10.23.07.html

International Communication Union. (2008). *Mobile cellular subscriptions*. Retrieved October 19, 2009 from <http://www.itu.int/ITU-/icteye/Reporting/ShowReportFrame.aspx?ReportName=/WTI/CellularSubscribersPublic&RP_intYear=2008&RP_intLanguageID=1>

Keaveny, P. (2007, November 28). Caught a criminal on your phone? *The Bolton News*. Retrieved from October 9, 2009 from < http://www.theboltonnews.co.uk /news/1863234.caught_a_criminal_on_your_phone/>

Kindberg, T., Spasojevic, M., Fleck, R., & Sellen, A. (2005). The ubiquitous camera: An in-depth study of camera phone use. *IEEE Pervasive Computing / IEEE Computer Society [and] IEEE Communications Society*, *4*(2), 42–50. doi:10.1109/MPRV.2005.42

Kingsley, D. (2008). Keeping a close watch: The rise of self-surveillance and the threat of digital exposure. *The Sociological Review*, *56*(3), 347–357. doi:10.1111/j.1467-954X.2008.00793.x

Koskinen, (2005). Seeing with mobile images: Towards perpetual visual contact. In Nyiri, K. (Ed.), *A Sense of place: The global and the local in mobile communication*. Vienna: Passagen Verlag.

Levinson, P. (2004). *Cell phone: The story of the world's most mobile medium and how it has transformed everything*. New York: Palgrave MacMillan.

Luckhurst, T. (2007, January 7). Now we can all set the news agenda. *The Independent.* Retrieved October 15, 2009 from <http://www.independent.co.uk/news/media/now-we-can-all-set-the-news-agenda-431038.html>

Lyon, D. (2001). *Surveillance society: Monitoring everyday life*. Buckhingham, UK: Open University Press.

Lyon, D. (2004). Surveillance technologies: Trends and social implications. In Stevens, B. (Ed.), *The security economy* (127-148). Paris: OECD.

Lyon, D. (2010). Why where you are matters: Mundane mobilities, transparent technologies, and digital discrimination. In Firmino, R., Duarte, F., & Ultramari, C. (Eds.), *ICTs for Mobile and Ubiquitous Urban Infrastructures: Surveillance, Locative Media and Global Networks*. Hershey, PA: IGI Global.

Mack, M. P. (1969). *A Bentham reader*. New York: Pegasus.

Mann, S. (1998). Reflectionism and diffusionism: New tactics for deconstructing the video surveillance superhighway. *Leonardo*, *31*(2), 93–102. doi:10.2307/1576511

Mann, S. (2004). Sousveillance: Inverse surveillance in multimedia imaging. In *Proceedings of the 12th Annual ACM International Conference on Multimedia*, (pp. 620-627). New York: ACM.

Mathiesen, T. (1997). The viewer society: Michel Foucault's Panopticon revisited. *Theoretical Criminology*, *1*(2), 215–234. doi:10.1177/1362480697001002003

Mokey, N. (2009, January 28). Bill would ban silent camera phones. *Digital Trends.* Retrieved October 15, 2009 from <http://www.digitaltrends.com/photography/bill-would-ban-silent-camera-phones/>

Musil, S. (2008, September 9). NYC's 911 system upgraded to accept photos, video. *CNET News*. Retrieved October 20, 2009 from < http://news.cnet.com/8301-1035_3-10037418-94.html?tag=newsEditorsPicksArea.0>

NY1 News. (2009, September 1). *Port Authority fires bridge guards caught napping*. Retrieved October 20, 2009, from < http://ny1.com/1-all-boroughs-news-content/top_stories/105052/port-authority-fires-bridge-guards-caught-napping/?ap=1&=Flash

News, A. B. C. (n.d.). Retrieved from http://abcnews.go.com/video/playerIndex?id=3448815

Okabe, D., & Ito, M. (2003, 28 August). Camera phones changing the definition of picture-worthy. *Japan Media Review*. Retrieved October 12, 2009 from http://www.ojr.org/japan/wireless/1062208524.php

Okabe, D., & Ito, M. (2006). Everyday contexts of camera phone use: steps toward technosocial ethnographic frameworks. In Hoflich, J., & Hartmann, M. (Eds.), *Mobile communication in everyday life: An ethnographic view* (pp. 79–102). Berlin: Frank and Timme.

Palser, B. (2007, Oct/Nov). Mining the Web. *American Journalism Review*, *29*(5), 70.

Panic about Erdogan. (n.d.). *Milliyet*, October 18, 2006. Retrieved on November 12, 2009, from http://www.milliyet.com.tr/2006/10/18/guncel/agun.html

Rasnake, D. (2008, August 6). Camera phone sales to double by 2012. *DigitalCameraReview.com*. Retrieved November 12, 2009, from <http://www.digitalcamerareview.com/default.asp?newsID=3612>

Reading, A. (2009). Mobile witnessing: Ethics and the camera phone in the 'war on terror.'. *Globalizations*, *6*(1), 61–76. doi:10.1080/14747730802692435

Riviere, C. (2005). Mobile camera phones: a new form of being together in daily interpersonal communication. In Ling, R., & Pederson, P. E. (Eds.), *Mobile communications: Re-negotiation of the social sphere* (pp. 167–185). London: Springer.

Robinson, W., & Robison, D. (2007). Tsunami mobilizations: Considering the role of mobile and digital communication devices. In Kavoori, A., & Arceneaux, N. (Eds.), *The cell phone reader: Essays in social transformation* (pp. 85–104). New York: Peter Lang.

Rubinstein, D. (2005). Cellphone photography; The death of the camera and the arrival of visible speech. Retrieved October 28, 2009 from < http://lsbu.academia.edu /DanielRubinstein/Papers/98273/Cellphone-photography--The-death-of-the-camera-and-the-arrival-of-visible-speech>

Schleifer, Y. (2009, June 19). Why Iran's Twitter revolution is unique. *Christian Science Monitor, 6*.

Security scandal, (2006, October 18). *Hurriyet*. Retrieved on November 12, 2009, from <http://hurarsiv.hurriyet.com.tr/goster/haber.aspx?id=5277220>

Shankland, S. (2007). Camera market to peak in 2010, IDC says. *Cnet News.* Retrieved January 5, 2010 from <http://news.cnet.com/Camera-market-to-peak-in-2010,-IDC-says/2100-1041_3-6178950.html>

Sirt, T. (2007). Mobile phone sales reach 10 million in 10 months. *Sabah,* December 31, 2007. Retrieved on January 5, 2010, from <http://arsiv.sabah.com.tr/2007/12/31/haber218ACE9477514AA18D986F-B64C1E300D.html>?>

Spasojevic, M. (2005). *Camera phone use and its implications*. Retrieved October 19, 2009, from <http://www.spasojevic.org/pics/papers.htm>

Stone, B., & Cohen, N. (2009, June 16). Networks spread defiance online. *The New York Times, 11*.

Tatsuno, K. (2006). Current trends in digital cameras and camera phones. *The Quarterly Review, 18*, 35–44.

Tekten, E. (2009, May 2). May 1 beatings by police. *Hurriyet.* Retrieved November 1, 2009, from <http://arama.hurriyet.com.tr/arsivnews.aspx?id=11564286>

Thamel, P., & Evans, T. (2009, September 16). College stars run for cover from fans' cameras. *The New York Times*. Retrieved October 19, 2009 from <http://www.nytimes.com/2009/09/17/sports/ncaafootball/17colleges.html?_r=2&hpw>

Vigilante taxi drivers reporting crimes over 3G phones. (2009, September 22). *Cellular News.* Retrieved November 1, 2009, from http://www.cellular-news.com /story/39715.php

What did Akif Beki do to stop Milliyet reporter? *Medya Faresi.* (2006, October 19). Retrieved November 12, 2009, from <http://www.medya-faresi.com/haber/1545 /medya-akif-beki-balyoz-skandalini-goruntuleyen-milliyet-muhabirini-engellemek-icin-ne-yapti.html>

Wood, D. (2005). People watching people. *Surveillance & Society, 2*(4), 474–478.

World's favorite cell phones. (n.d.). *Telekom-Haber.com.* Retrieved November 12, 2009, from <http://www.telekomhaber.com/haber.asp?haber_id=20404>

ADDITIONAL READING

Aas, K., Oppen Gundhus, H., & Mork Lomell, H. (Eds.). (2008). *Technologies of insecurity: The surveillance of everyday life*. New York: Routledge-Cavendish.

Barry, A., Osborne, T., & Rose, N. (Eds.). (1996). *Foucault and political reason: Liberalism, neo-liberalism, and rationalities of government.* Chicago: University of Chicago Press.

Burchell, G., Gordon, C., & Miller, P. (Eds.). (1991). *The Foucault effect: Studies in governmentality*. Chicago: University of Chicago Press.

Castel, R. (1991). From dangerousness to risk. In Burchell, G., Gordon, C., & Miller, P. (Eds.). *The Foucault effect: Studies in governmentality* (281-298). Chicago: The University of Chicago Press.

Cohen, S. (1979). The punitive city: Notes on the dispersal of social control. *Contemporary Crises, 3*, 339–363. doi:10.1007/BF00729115

Cohen, S. (1985). *Visions of social control: Crime, punishment and classification*. Cambridge: Polity Press.

Dandeker, C. (1990). *Surveillance, power and modernity: Bureaucracy and discipline from 1700 to the present day*. New York: St. Martin's Press.

Deleuze, G. (1992). Postscript on the societies of control. *October.* 59, 3-7.

Doyle, A. (2006). An alternative current in surveillance and control: Broadcasting surveillance footage of crimes." In Haggerty, K.D & Ericson, R.V. (Eds.) *The new politics of surveillance and visibility* (199-224). Toronto: University of Toronto Press.

Ericson, R. V., & Haggerty, K. D. (1997). *Policing the risk society*. Toronto: The University of Toronto Press.

Ericson, R. V., & Haggerty, K. D. (Eds.). (2006). *The new politics of surveillance and visibility*. Toronto: University of Toronto Press.

Fiske, J. (2002). Videotech. In Mirzoeff, N. (Ed.), *The visual culture reader*. New York: Routledge.

Foucault, M. (1972). "Prison talk." In Gordon, C. (Ed.). *Power/Knowledge: Selected interviews and other writings, 1972-1977.* (37-54). New York: Pantheon.

Foucault, M. (1983). Afterword: The subject and power." In Dreyfus, R., Rabinow, P. (Eds.). *Michel Foucault: Beyond structuralism and hermeneutics* (208-226). Chicago: The University of Chicago Press.

Foucault, M. (1991). Governmentality. In Burchell, G., Gordon, C., & Miller, P. (Eds.). *The Foucault effect: Studies in governmentality* (87-104). Chicago: The University of Chicago Press.

Fyfe, N., & Bannister, J. (1998). The eyes upon the street: Closed-circuit television surveillance and the city. In Fyfe, N. (Ed.), *Images of the street: Planning, identity and control in public space*. London, New York: Routledge.

Gandy, O. H. (1989). The Surveillance Society: Information Technology and Bureaucratic Social Control. *The Journal of Communication, 39*(3), 61–76. doi:10.1111/j.1460-2466.1989.tb01040.x

Gandy, O. H. (1993). *The Panoptic sort: A political economy of personal information*. Boulder: Westview Press.

Garland, D. (2001). *The culture of control: crime and social order in contemporary society*. Chicago: University of Chicago Press.

Gates, K. (2006). Identifying the 9/11 'faces of terror': The promise and problem of facial recognition technology. *Cultural Studies, 20*(4/5), 417–440. doi:10.1080/09502380600708820

Gilliom, J. (2001). *Overseers of the poor: Surveillance, resistance, and the limits of privacy*. Chicago: The University of Chicago Press.

Graham, S. (1998). Towards the fifth utility? On the extension and normalization of public CCTV. In Norris, C., Moran, J. & Armstrong, G. (Eds.). *Surveillance, closed circuit television and social control.* (89-112). Aldershot, England: Ashgate Publishing.

Haggerty, K. D. (2006). Tear down the walls: On demolishing the Panopticon. In Lyon, D. (Ed.), *Theorizing surveillance: Panopticon and beyond*. UK: Willan Publishing.

Hier, S., & Greenberg, J. (Eds.). (2007). *The surveillance studies reader*. McGraw-Hill.

Koskela, H. (2006). The other side of surveillance: webcams, power and agency. In Lyon, D. (Ed.). *Theorizing surveillance: The Panopticon and beyond*. (163-181). Devon, UK: Willan Publishing.

Levin, T., Frohne, U., & Weibel, P. (Eds.). (2002). *CTRL[SPACE]: Rhetorics of surveillance from Bentham to Big Brother*. Cambridge, MA: The MIT Press.

Lyon, D. (1994). *The electronic eye: The rise of surveillance society*. Cambridge, UK: Polity Press.

Lyon, D. (2003). *Surveillance after September 11*. Cambridge, UK: Polity Press.

Lyon, D. (Ed.). (2006). *Theorizing surveillance: The Panopticon and beyond*. Portland, OR: Willan Publishing.

Lyon, D. (2007). *Surveillance studies: An overview*. Malden, MA: Polity Press.

McCahill, M. (2002). *The surveillance web: The rise of visual surveillance in an English city*. Cullompton, UK: Willan Publishers.

McGrath, J. E. (2004). *Loving Big Brother: Performance, privacy and surveillance space*. New York: Routledge.

Monahan, T. (Ed.). (2006). *Surveillance and security: Technological politics and power in everyday life*. New York: Routledge.

Norris, C., & Armstrong, G. (1999). *The Maximum Surveillance Society: The Rise of CCTV*. Oxford, New York: Berg.

Norris, C., Moran, J., & Armstrong, G. (Eds.). (1998). *Surveillance, closed circuit television and social control*. Aldershot, UK: Ashgate Publishing.

O'Malley, P. (1996). Risk and responsibility. In Barry, A., Osborne, T., & Rose, N. (Eds.). *Foucault and political reason: Liberalism, neo-liberalism, and rationalities of government* (189-208). Chicago: The University of Chicago Press.

Parenti, C. (2003). *The soft cage: Surveillance in America from slavery to the war on terror*. New York: Basic Books.

Rentschler, C. A. (2003). Designing fear: How environmental security protects property at the expense of people. In Bratich, J.Z., Packer, J. and Cameron McCarthy (Eds.). *Foucault, Cultural Studies, and governmentality*. Albany: State University of New York Press.

Rose, N. (1996). Governing 'advanced' liberal democracies. In Barry, A., Osborne, T., & Rose, N. (Eds.). (1996). *Foucault and political reason: Liberalism, neo-liberalism, and rationalities of government* (37-64). Chicago: The University of Chicago Press.

Rosen, J. (2001). *The unwanted gaze: the destruction of privacy in America*. New York: Vintage Books.

Schlosberg, M., & Ozer, N. (2007). *Under the watchful eye: The proliferation of video surveillance systems in California*. http://www.aclunc.org/docs/criminal_justice/police_practices/under_the_watchful_eye_the_proliferation_of_video_surveillance_systems_in_california.pdf

Simon, J. (1987). The emergence of a risk society: insurance, law and the state. *Socialist Review, 95*, 61–89.

Staples, W. (2000). *Everyday surveillance: Vigilance and visibility in postmodern life*. Lanham, MD: Rowman and Littlefield Publishers, Inc.

Yesil, B. (2006). Watching ourselves: video surveillance, urban space, and self- responsibilization. *Cultural Studies*, *20*(4-5), 400–416. doi:10.1080/09502380600708770

Yesil, B. (2009). *Video surveillance: Power and privacy in everyday life*. El Paso, TX: LFB Scholarly Publishing.

KEYWORDS AND DEFINITIONS

Camera Phone: Mobile phone quipped with a built-in camera to capture still or moving images.

User-Generated Images: Images captured by users on photographic or video cameras and mobile phones, and then distributed online or through mobile communication devices to networks of contacts, blogs, news sites.

Moblogging: Mobile blogging—posting text, photographs or videos to blogs from a mobile phone.

Surveillance: Systematic monitoring of one or more persons by public or private institutions in order to collect information, investigate or record their actions or communications in administrative, commercial, law enforcement, security contexts.

Sousveillance: Monitoring of authority figures by individuals in order to collect information, investigate or record their actions or communications to expose wrongful behavior or misconduct.

Panopticon: Prison building designed by Jeremy Bentham; used in surveillance studies as a theoretical model to refer to top-down forms of monitoring by social institutions.

Synopticon: Coined by Thomas Mathiesen to refer to bottom-up forms of monitoring by ordinary individuals.

ENDNOTES

1. Panic about Erdogan. *Milliyet*, October 18, 2006. Retrieved on November 12, 2009, from http://www.milliyet.com.tr/2006/10/18/guncel/agun.html, Security scandal. *Hurriyet*, October 18, 2006. Retrieved on November 12, 2009, from <http://hurarsiv.hurriyet.com.tr /goster /haber.aspx?id=5277220>
2. What did Akif Beki do to stop Milliyet reporter? *Medya Faresi*. (2006, October 19). Retrieved November 12, 2009, from http://www.medyafaresi.com/haber/1545 /medya-akif-beki-balyoz-skandalini-goruntuleyen-milliyet-muhabirini-engellemek-icin-ne-yapti.html
3. For information on the ubiquity of personal imaging devices around the world, see InfoTrends (2007), Shankland (2007), Tatsuno (2006). For statistics from Turkey, see Haber Vitrini (2007), Sirt (2007).
4. Although mobile phones, social networking and video-sharing sites do play a role in contributing to the public sphere and in some instances help citizen movements confront repressive governments, we must be cautious not to credit the technology alone and unduly call it a "Twitter revolution" as some pundits have done to describe the anti-government movement in Iran in June 2009. See, Facebook and freedom: New technologies are encouraging the change in Iran that U.S. desires. *Newsday*, June 18, 2009, p. A38, Schleifer, Y. (2009, June 19). Why Iran's Twitter revolution is unique. *Christian Science Monitor*, p. 6, Stone, B. and Cohen, N. (2009, June 16). Networks spread defiance online. *The New York Times*, p. 11.
5. http://www.ireport.com/?cnn=yes
6. http://edition.cnn.com/exchange/ireports/toolkit/
7. http://www.msnbc.msn.com/id/16712587/ns/community-firstperson
8. http://ureport.foxnews.com/snc/groupsearch.aspx?pguid=7FBF4CC0-49AE-455C-8E55-7EECB46B5E30

9 http://www.weather.com/photos/index.html?role=&from=hp_dwp

10 http://www.tmz.com/tips, http://www.gawker.com, http://www.radaronline.com/got-news

11 See http://www.ireport.com/?cnn=yes, http://abcnews.go.com/icaught/iCaught/ News to Me site is no longer available, but Headline News provides a direct link to CNN's *iReport*.

12 World's favorite cell phones. (n.d.). *Telekom-Haber.com.* Retrieved November 12, 2009, from <http://www.telekomhaber.com/haber.asp?haber_id=20404>

13 1 out of every 100 camera phones is in the hands of a Turkish consumer. (2007, March 11). *Haber Vitrini.* Retrieved November 12, 2009, from <http://www.habervitrini.com / haber.aspx?id=266906>

14 http://www.desifrehaber.com/ihbar.aspx

15 Citizens take to streets protesting beating, torture at daycare. (2005, October 26). *Hurriyet*. Retrieved November 12, 2009, from <http://hurarsiv.hurriyet.com.tr /goster / haber.aspx ?id=3441525>

16 http://www.witness.org

17 http://www.berkeleycopwatch.org

18 Despite Bentham's twenty-year campaign to see its construction, the Panopticon was rejected by the British government, based on the argument that Bentham placed far too much importance on the exploitation of prison labor at the expense of religious reformation (Ignatieff, 1978, pp. 109-113). Although the Panopticon never materialized, English penitentiaries in the 19th century did rely on panoptic principles. For example, a regimen of hard labor was institutionalized as a replacement for idleness, which previously reigned in English penitentiaries. Uniforms, walls and bars secured the social distance between the criminals and the outside world. According to Michael Ignatieff (1978) these were panoptic principles that resonated with the "impartial, humane and vigilant eye of the state, holding the 'deviant' in the thrall of its omniscient gaze" at all times (p. 113).

Chapter 17
Mobile and Locative Media:
In between Thanatos and Eros

Lucia Santaella
Pontifícia Universidade Católica de São Paulo, Brazil

ABSTRACT

Mobile and locative media are, inescapably, surveillance media. Surveillance is a feature which has not been decreasing by the use of these media, but instead it has been increasing with ever growing levels of subtlety. These media are introducing a new regime of surveillance, one which I have been calling tracking surveillance, a regime that is distinct from panoptic and scopic surveillance. Tracking surveillance's omnipresence should not mislead us to assume that these other two modes of surveillance have disappeared. Much on the contrary, these three regimes operate simultaneously, since the appearance of a new mode of surveillance does not lead to the demise of another. Due to the capillarity which characterizes surveillance in this era of connectedness and mobility, surveillance as an issue stands as a privileged standpoint for examining the ambivalent character, in between Thanatos and Eros, with which mobile and locative media have been operating in societies nowadays.

INTRODUCTION

The acceleration in the development of new digital technologies and the expansion of its apparatus are disconcerting to say the least, and these are showing no signs of reduction or of stoppage. At the current state of the art, there are many fronts: Web 3.0, the era of terabytes and petabytes, cloud computing, the era of omnipresent connection and continued mobility, of pervasive, sentient and ubiquitous computing, of augmented and mixed reality.

Amongst all these fronts, this work gives special attention to mobile media and the complex structure of its implications: connection, mobility, ubiquity and sentience. Our goal is, however, to go beyond a mere presentation of such structure. At a previous work (Santaella, 2008), I affirmed that the extensive and intense operational field of mobile and locative media works as a kind of liv-

DOI: 10.4018/978-1-60960-051-8.ch017

ing map of the paradoxes and contradictions that plague turbo capitalist societies. At one extreme, they are technologies utilized for tracking and for military and governmental control, opening doors to an era of ubiquitous, incredibly subtle, invisible forms of monitoring and surveillance. That is why there is, in such technologies, a latent potential for evil, even sinister, purposes. At another extreme, these same technologies are being appropriated by art practices, in the field of locative media, which counterbalance any evil tendencies, by pressing hard on the keys of freedom, playfulness, joy and pleasure as intrinsic aspirations of human condition.

These two extremes appear in the title of this paper: mobile and locative media in between Thanatos, the tendency towards destruction, and Eros, the affirming strength of the power of life. Mobile media have turned Thanatos even more powerful. These apparatuses have brought ammunition to the malign side of human beings and social forces which are now always lying in wait for potential menaces ranging from fraud and terrorism to organized crime. Eros, on the opposite side, gains energy in artistic practices with locative media to which more attention will be given at the end of this article.

However, in the majority of cases, the uses allowed by mobile media are ambivalent and range among gradations between those two extremes. In this paper I will explore these ambivalences to avoid a dichotomist view of the two opposing poles. The aim is to highlight the complexities and subtleties of what happens in between them. Surveillance's capillarity in this era of connection and mobility makes it a privileged standpoint for the examining of the ambivalent character of mobile and locative media operating in societies nowadays. Lyon's works on the subject, which will be cited extensively in this paper, in particular the one where he discusses "mundane mobilities, transparent technologies, and digital discrimination" (Lyon, 2010), have been very useful in the task of avoiding the dangers of falling into Manichaeism. But let us begin the discussion by the complex structure of mobile media implications.

MOBILE AND LOCATIVE MEDIA: IMPLICATIONS

Clark (2003) gives four distinct meanings to mobile technologies:

a. devices may be, at any given time, at different locations "from that in which they were at one or more previous times" (§ 3);
b. devices are mobile in the sense that they are at any location that allows transmission for another device;
c. they are mobile in relation to the surface of the Earth, for example, when a user is on a plane;
d. lastly, devices are designed to be easily and conveniently portable and independent from wire transmission.

Mobile media and locative media are terms that have been used widely as synonyms. Therefore, it might sound redundant to use them juxtaposed. I have made this decision deliberately in order to make explicit that, when talking about locative media, we are necessarily talking about mobile media with geographical positioning and context sensitivity. They are, therefore, mobile and locative at the same time, despite the fact that this may seem a paradox.

In this manner, mobile media and locative media refer to a group of technologies that constitute open and dynamic systems portraying all the characteristics of complex systems: chaotic flux, turbulence, instability, but also emergence, adaptation and self-organization. These media are palmtops and third generation multifunctional cell phones which, according to Lemos (2004), have become a *mobile everything* allowing daily life's management, very much like portable remote controls commanding our routines.

Connected to the net via wireless networks (Wi-Fi, Wi-Max and *Bluetooth*), to satellite networks via GPS and radio frequency identification (RFID) tags and sensors, cell phones have become, in reality, in Lemos words (2007: 25-26) "hybrid mobile gadgets of multi network connection". They put together "communicative potency (voice, text, images, videos), network connection, mobility across informational territories", areas of informational flux control in between cyberspace and urban space, "reconfiguring social practices of informational mobility across urban physical spaces". Moreover, amongst the great many functions making of cell phones a kind of *metagadget,* some of them resemble human cognitive features, what also makes of cell phones objective versions of many human cognitive abilities integrated in one single device (Kövecses, 2008: 32).

This dynamic system gave origin to the era of nothing less than omnipresent connection, "perpetual contact" (Rule, 2002), continuous mobility and augmented and mixed reality, of ubiquitous, pervasive and sentient computing. Connection is omnipresent because, even when users are distracted, tired or asleep, connection remains active. Mobility is continuous because it is in a state of permanent availability. Even when the device is off, invisible clouds of bytes are moving without interruption. Reality is mixed, since it is an inextricable mix of virtual worlds made of informational bits and the world of physical matter. It is also an augmented reality; since day-to-day objects and places are being augmented through information processing that expands its affordance.

Ubiquitous computing means that computers, of which computational nature is getting less and less perceptible, are to be found everywhere. From this comes the word pervasive, meaning that, by the proliferating number of chips, computation pervades all things, especially when these, sentient and equipped with sensors or RFID tags, exchange information with computers.

If, at the first stage of cyberspace and cyber culture, the stage of fixed access points, infinite layers of information bytes seemed to come from some cyber place above our heads (one must only mention the word *download,* as an example), now cyberspace has descended upon us and at the same time in which data clouds do not stop growing and multiplying, they embrace us all around, accessible from any point in space and, soon enough, from any object at all, within the context of the internet of things (Kranenburg, 2008).

The spread of information and communication technologies embedded in objects turns obsolete the idea of computers as boxes on top of tables or computer rooms. Computers are now everywhere without being noticed because technologies, starting from 3G cell phones, soon to become 4G (enhanced with broad bandwidth), are getting inside things. Computers got rid of boxes and are starting to become a feature of our environment. As integral parts of products, services and artifacts they will add and spread intelligence over our surroundings, furthering ambient intelligence with their multiple smart information surfaces, giving texture and width to day-to-day life (Kidd, 2007: 55).

While satellites create connectivity from above, RFID tags create it from below. In environments in which connectivity is everywhere, it is resonance, not interactivity, the guiding principle of design, and, when computers become even more invisible than they are today, the environment will be the interface and intelligence will be "extelligence" (Kranenburg, 2008: 16). All of that remains, however, on just one flip side of the coin. The other side is that mobile and locative media are inescapably surveillance media. Besides being their hidden side (Lyon, 2010), the surveillance aspects, far from decreasing, will increase with ever growing levels of subtlety. We shall explore this issue further here.

THREE REGIMES OF SURVEILLANCE: PANOPTIC, SCOPIC AND TRACKING

The word surveillance and its concept are widely used. Everyone seems to intuitively know what surveillance means. In a research context, however, we must follow an ethics of terminology, by defining our sources and the meaning implied in the terms being used. A simple definition is given by Bennet & Regan (2004: 452): "surveillance is a way of determining who is where and what s/he is doing in the physical or virtual world, on a given moment in time." Bruno (2008b) mentions a functional definition of surveillance given by Wood et al. (2006: 9): "Wherever we may find purposeful, routine oriented, systematic and focused attention given to personal details, with the objective of control, authorization, management, influence or protection, we are facing surveillance." For Lyon (2004: 129), serious and systemic attention to personal details for purposes of influence, administration and control is defined as surveillance. More recently Lyon (2010: 6) added to the definition that "in part due to its reliance on electronic technologies, surveillance is generalized across populations, for numerous, overlapping purposes, and in virtual and fluid spaces."

Lemos (2010: 8) cites Grow (2005a), according to whom surveillance "implies something very specific such as the observation of someone's actions or the gathering of personal information in order to monitor actions taken in the past or in the future." Lemos questions this definition by pointing out that "not every form of control and/or monitoring might be called surveillance", since surveillance requires the presence of two elements: "intentionality, aimed at avoiding or causing something, and a nominal identification of individuals and groups". Lemos finds anonymous surveillance a difficult concept to grasp without preventive intention, which aims to avoid something, and the identification of the one being surveilled.

According to Lyon (2002: 4), the key method for the study of surveillance is to gather historical and comparative instances. Surveillance models and paradigms are valid only for a given period of time. A current example, in my view, is the blatant inappropriateness of the generalized application of Bentham's panoptic model to digital media, despite all the undergoing transformations that the digital world has been causing, continuously, to surveillance modes. In order to keep that in mind, and better comprehending the various surveillance profiles introduced by mobile media, we must establish comparisons and distinctions between what I will call three surveillance regimes: the panoptic, the scopic and the tracking regime. The first refers to the disciplinary surveillance that is exerted in circumscribed environments. The scopic regime corresponds to the proliferating distribution, for various purposes, of recording cameras and image visualization, in strategic places both indoors and outdoors. The third regime has sprouted directly from the digital universe, and the complex pattern of its weaving becomes ever more subtle.

In order to grasp some of the main nodes of such weaving, as we will address further below, mobile digital surveillance, based fundamentally on data tagging, must be taken from various angles and multiple dimensions, such as: who and what is being surveilled, according to which technology and media surveillance operates from? What is the extension of its operations? What are the procedures and processes executed on the data being tagged, for what purposes is surveillance enacted? What is the destination of all data collected?

Digital surveillance's omnipresence should not mislead us into the mistake of believing that the two other modes of surveillance have disappeared. Much on the contrary, the three regimes operate simultaneously, in the constitution of a mixed paradigm, since the appearance of a new regime does not entail the disappearance of previous ones. Preserving discipline is still a goal being pursued by means of panoptic surveillance. Cities, in their diverse environments, public and even private, have not ceased to install hidden or explicit cameras capturing gestures, steps, regards, profiles and shadows. It is precisely the simultaneity of these regimes that explains the intricate weaving of surveillance's functioning in societies nowadays, a weaving that has resulted in the transformation of our societies in surveillance societies *tout court*. Societies in which "routine, systematic, and ubiquitous identifying, checking, monitoring, tracking and recording of everyday activities, communication, and exchanges have become a commonplace, unremarkable experience" (Lyon, 2004: 130). Not surprisingly, the scenario of present surveillance, not always visible, is "extremely multiple and complex, not only because of the myriad of surveillance artifacts scattered around towns, but also due to the multiplicity of functions, purposes and affections that per pass them" (Bruno, 2008b: 46). To illustrate the enormous amount of artifacts, Bruno lists some of them:

Surveillance cameras at public, semi-public and private places, personal or institutional webcams, traffic control systems (cameras, radars, road sensors), geotracking systems (GPS, GIS, RFID), electronic borders and gates (passwords and access cards, scanners for people and products), identification and authenticity control (identity cards and gadgets for biometric identification), information and communication technologies (computers, cell phones), data monitoring and connection networks, data archives, mining, analysis and retrieval systems (databases, computational profiles), among others. Some of these artifacts operate together, making explicit, in the field of surveillance, the tendency of technological convergence that exists in other sectors, such as telecommunications. (Bruno, 2008b: 46)

Marx (2002: 9) confirms Bruno's conclusion, acknowledging the significant rise in the use of technologies for the gathering of personal information and calling attention to the multimedia, multisensory, and semiotic and intersemiotic nature of devices and surveillance modes such as video and audio surveillance, heat sensors, light, movement, sound and smell (tact and taste being the only two senses that are still out), night vision eyewear, electronic tags, biometric access gadgets, drug tests, DNA analysis, computational monitoring, as well as smart systems, comparison and profiling, data mining, mapping, network analysis and simulation. In sum: control techniques today, manage to go beyond the dystopic imagination of science-fiction, replacing Weber's iron cage with a flexible glass cage.

If this was the scenario in 2002, when Mark wrote his article, imagine what it is today, at the peak of mobile technology accelerated growth, which the author had no time to evaluate, only seven years ago. In fact, the new characteristics that the regime of surveillance is acquiring in the era of connection and mobility are exactly one of its facets which this paper intends to look upon.

A NEW SURVEILLANCE REGIME AT THE ERA OF MOBILITY

Lyon (2010) calls "mobile surveillance" the new fluid and liquid forms of digital surveillance. I prefer to name it a *tracking* regime, because, amongst a profusion of media, processes, procedures and purposes implied in digital surveillance, tracking – in its connotations of trace, trail, clue, and vestige – is at the core of the enhanced potential for data retrieval by digital media. Furthermore, its indexical and symbolic nature, in the sense given by Peirce to these two processes of semiosis (Santaella, 2002: 12-28), differs from the indexical and iconic nature of the scopic surveillance regime. This difference has many and significant consequences to the comprehension, treatment and goals of what surveillance apparatuses are, each on its own way, capable of capturing data. While a scopic regime leads us into seeing, a tracking regime leads us into *seeing through*. This happens thanks to the symbolic systems of coding that are embedded in the devices themselves and that become even more complex given the treatment applied to data retrieved by such gadgets.

Although the scopic regime is also indexical, since that what is captured by cameras is, in fact, there – pointing to Barthes' factor of reality assurance in his *Camera Lucida* (Barthes, 1981) – the result of this capturing feature are images that imply slower processes of observation, comparison, analysis and judgment. Data retrieval, monitoring and treatment, enabled through digital media, are executed at the vertiginous combinatory instantaneous speed of pentabytes. Only such velocity could make surveillance omnipresent, tracking even our most insignificant steps and gestures. As Stalder (2002: 120) points out, every time we sign in a supermarket's fidelity card, or at a store or check in, our names are tagged to purchase lists and destinations, getting inserted, immediately, into gigantic databases. Every time we pay a toll on a highway, every time we use the cell phone or the credit card, our locations are being tagged, analyzed and stored. Every time we submit our health insurance card to a doctor or hospital, pay our bills, send in our tax declaration or get into cyberspace, the mapping of our actions becomes wider and finer.

No researcher who has investigated this issue could doubt for a second that something very new is emerging, new in quantity, degree and quality. Lemos (2010: 6) states that portable gadgets, mobile and wired – cell phones, Wi-Fi networks, Bluetooth, GPS, sensors and RFID tags – "increase the different forms of control, monitoring and surveillance", making them more "more diffuse, more performative (electronic database) and invisible". This includes a second incremented generation of scopic regime which is now incorporated to the digital, such as in "IP cameras that combine the use of digital wireless networks to communicate with control, monitoring and mobile surveillance systems (police cars, for example) with localization by GPS." Moreover, the widespread use of cell phone cameras, allowing for recorded testimony of events, voyeurism, and invasion of privacy and of anonymity, places "the power of surveillance into everybody's hands". Finally, "everything is undoubtedly less visible and more diffuse, making this watchful invisibility more performative and the control of movements more effective" (Lemos, 2010: 7). In sum: a kind of surveillance that lets movement flow, very distinct from the rigid and static mechanisms of the panoptic, which need "enclosing and immobilizing in order to place under surveillance".

While the panoptic regime was aligned with old and heavy top-down bureaucracies – and are still aligned to those which have remained in place – the scopic regime emerged on the period of the explosion of image technologies (photos, cinema, video), representing a multiplicity of regards. Scattered around public, semi-public and private places, surveillance cameras, with various functionalities and for diverse purposes, capture, most of the time on a deadly silent atmosphere, a myriad of spaces, locations, scenes and people, uncovering the city and the bodies passing by. Although they always represent an instance of observation, they can "act according to a symbolic efficiency, working as signs that dissuade the realization of undesirable behaviors, and also as an eye that captures efficiently the action" (Bruno, 2008b: 47). However, just as the movie *Blow Up* has shown us, if there is no record there is no crime; in the scopic regime, if there is no camera there is no record, that is, although cameras are plenty, they do not cover the entire surface of territories, in spite of the feasibility of such all encompassing paranoia.

From the pulverized, ubiquitous tracking by mobile media there is practically nowhere to hide. Urban spaces, work places, leisure, stores and home are not separate places from which people are watched, but instead they are points of a continuous flux of surveillance, in which spaces are connected to one another, "providing a more completely textured rendition of one's everyday life" (Bennet & Regan, 2004: 453). All our steps go under scrutiny and the objects that we use (cars, phones, computers, electricity) become surveillance tools. Movement is not a way out of surveillance, but on the contrary it has become the very subject of surveillance, with an ease never imagined by Max Weber, Franz Kafka or George Orwell. In as much as we still have things to learn from these authors, their ideas are not entirely applicable to present conditions. Far from resembling "the old top-down pyramidal structure of totalitarian states – or some neat new technological mega-machine", tracking surveillance is a fabric weaved in a free, "loose-knit, fluctuating, fragmentary and contested arena of control" (Lyon, 2004: 133).

Bennet & Regan (2004) have sketched a typology of mobility in its relation to surveillance. Concerning the dimension which seeks to demonstrate the objects of any surveillance, they suggest a tripartite categorization of "body (the person), transactions (things the person does either as physical actions or as captured in data), and artifacts (things associated with the individual)" (Bennet & Regan, 2004: 451). To apprehend the degree or level of mobility and the depth of surveillance, the second dimension aims at capturing movement in itself, a more complicated concept when trying to capture that which is moving from a place to another, and also from a moment to the next, in relation to the movement of the Earth. As a consequence, the authors propose that mobility should be seen not as a static category, but as a continuum: "movement occurs both within certain fixed spaces and across a range of spaces. Boundaries of spaces may be more or less fixed or, as is increasingly the case, malleable" (Bennet & Regan, 2004: 451). This classification opens the way for a better detailed description of mobile surveillance's operation conditions.

Digital Surveillance: What, How, to Whom, What For?

The easiest conclusion to be found is that digital surveillance captures personal data. Scrutiny has as its targets people and populations, systems and categories of persons, their identities and traces of their behavior. Many dictionaries define surveillance as the careful observation of suspect individuals. This is a narrow definition, given that, in digital environments, surveillance goes beyond suspicion and also of people, encompassing contexts, places and geographical spots, time periods, networks.

There are multiple retrieval technologies at stage. Marx (2002: 28-29) enumerated 28 useful dimensions for the characterization of new media surveillance as opposed to traditional ones. From these dimensions we must stress the fact that these new media are invisible and transcend from afar the physical limitations of pre-digital media, since they gather evidence in a much deeper, wide and subtle way transcending distance, darkness, skin, time and microscopes, surpassing walls and closed envelopes that used to protect individual privacy. We are talking about a surveillance that, by making use of network technologies, has replaced the top-down apparatus with a flexible group of pulsating, waving observations (Ericson & Haggerly, 2001*apud*Lyon, 2002: 3).

Biometric techniques, that is, procedures to identify or authenticate individuals, appeared in the 20th century, especially under the form of finger print. At the end of the century, a stronger biometric movement emerged with the recognition of face, iris, ears, and most importantly, the DNA test. Besides these the sophistication of the apparatuses that are used can be exemplified by the thermal detection of lies, ID new intelligent systems, CCTV (closed circuit TV) with facial recognition and developed techniques to intercept communication. According to Didier (2004: 46), the next hundred years will be the "biometric century."

Data retrieval is a routine activity, automated and machine-like, mediated by remote media. Data is continuous; remains available in real time, information can be made available not only about the past and present, but also about the future thanks to statistics based-predictions. Data is not confined to direct representation, but reach further into simulation. The treatment of collected data encompasses a wide range of procedures, enhanced by digitalization, and which are distributed by recordings, archival, monitoring, transmission, recovery, processing, verification, comparison, analysis, categorization and use, always involving a higher level of manipulation than coercion.

In a society of flux, surveillance is itself part of the flux. It is invisible, but renders all visible. It is anonymous and omnipresent, but that does not mean it is devoid of purpose. It fulfills many functions and has many purposes, as multifaceted as dictated by the nature of digital surveillance itself. Citing Wood et al. (2006), Bruno (2008b: 45) states that, concerning urban environments, "contemporary surveillance is, in part, an heir to the 'desire for efficiency, speed, control and coordination' of modern management". The author adds, however, that "in contemporary societies a series of transformations distance us from modern models of surveillance, both in the realm of gadgets, as in the realms of social meaning and control procedures." For Lyon (2002), if the modern world purveyed urgency for classification, now such urgency became endemic. Classifying and categorizing are now the keys to comprehend contemporary surveillance.

Determining who is where, when, and doing what is a common purpose of surveillance at anytime and anyplace. Within a culture of mobility, movement tracking is a target for the monitoring of physical and virtual activities of consumers, travelers, phone users, children, etc. But within complex and hybrid societies, this information is not enough. So security systems operate according to multiple purposes. Data is retrieved from physical bodies and the resulting abstractions are used at least in four destinations: government administration, organizational and labor management, marketing and safety.

Marx (2002: 18) reminds us that the expansion of bureaucracy, from the 19th to the 20th century in ruled States, has led also to the expansion of surveillance with the purpose of establishing popular conformity to a series of laws and eligibility to various programs of intervention, from social security to animal rights. "A state bureaucratically organized around the certification of identity, experience and competence is dependent on the collection of personal information. Risk assessment, prediction, prevention and rational planning also require such information".

Monitoring behavior and performance of members of an organization, especially work related, is an essential feature of the modern world. Control of employees database, managerial access to emails and phone calls by employees have become legit routines due to the conviction that any and all resources are at the service of organizational good.

Market societies are unconceivable without massive personal data retrieval, demographics, communications, consumption and movement transactions, in order to rank people according to new social strata that are anchored at income levels, attributes, habits, preferences, for influencing, persuading and manipulating desires. Lyon (2010) foresees that marketing will be the most flourishing area for surveillance.

Another tendency of surveillance is directed toward risk reduction, among which the most obvious is crime control, which has become a task that is not restricted to internal police work but that is now spread over innumerable social spaces. Less obvious is child monitoring, which is orchestrated by parents.

A type of surveillance that is not always remembered, but ever more present, is self-surveillance and self-monitoring according to the rules that are given to people about their own health management, a responsibility now transferred to individuals. People are drowning in health devices and resources to monitor their own health. Wristwatches for the monitoring of heart rates during exercise or the amount of calories lost during a run, blood pressure devices, etc. are now fully integrated to our daily lives and biometric tests for measuring blood properties, pregnancies, etc. are available at every corner. There is intelligent biometric clothing that is already capable of sending continuous information for monitoring by a doctor (Dittmar, 2007). What we have here is what Bruno (2008a: 15) calls "normative pluralism, in which the individual is more and more the owner of his own self."

Across all these prospects, the keyword is control. More rationalizing, more operability, higher precision for intensifying control. Even when such control is directed at providing care and safety, it is not very reassuring to the individual to know that he is under scrutiny, that his movements are being tracked and stored in memories that do not sleep, rest or go off and that data mining is capable of constructing fine narratives which are prone to profiling toward unknown purposes. That is why Lyon (2010: 5) states that "surveillance – as monitoring, observing, tracing – is not necessarily negative, but power relations are always present, for better or for worse."

As dark as these clouds may seem, we must place emphasis on the ambivalences of contemporary vigilance so as not to fall prey of an Orwellian paranoia, as if there were ghosts pursuing us in our sleep. What we should keep in mind is that just like Jano surveillance always has two faces, no matter from how many angles we can or want to see them. Furthermore, as stated by Lyon (2004: 143), "we must go beyond Orwell – and some Orwellian clichés such as Big Brother – if we are to grasp the elements of a 21st century surveillance dystopia."

THE AMBIVALENCES OF MOBILE SURVEILLANCE

First of all we must stress, like Bruno (2008b: 46), that many of the devices which might be used for digital surveillance are not surveillance devices *per se*. Not all of them are "directly or intentionally geared towards the exercise of surveillance; which is, in many instances, an effect or secondary feature of a device of which primary function is another – a cell phone with a camera, for example, has a primary function of communication and image taking, but could be utilized as a surveillance camera in certain occasions."

Mentioning Rose (1999: 325), Bruno (2008a: 15) also calls attention to the fact that one of the main characteristics of present day technologies is its pulverization across non hierarchical networks, "in which citizens behavior is continuously modulated by a logic which is immanent to the group of social practices 'according to principles of optimizing benign impulses and minimizing malign ones'. Control is exerted in a partnership regime by diverse social agents, obeying a sharing ethics of responsibilities and risks, self-control and self-management."

Indeed, unresolved ambiguities surround current modes of surveillance. At the same time that they are feared given their invasive power over personal lives, meaning threat, they are also there to protect, safeguard life, and promote justice in relations of property or political participation. Lyon (2002: 4) is right in saying that surveillance always shows these two faces. That is why, still following Lyon (2004: 130), surveillance societies do not have to be equated with totalitarianism, neither do we have to argue that "it is necessarily sinister or malign. It is an aspect of the early 21st century world that has, in its present forms, been under construction for less than 20 years. Surveillance devices are installed to ensure convenience, comfort, efficiency, productivity, speed and security."

Besides, there are cases in which people need and want their data to be archived and made available, because not having them is undesirable, like in emergency situations. Strictly, speaking of two faces – beneficial and harmful – is a way of simplifying a field in which the major figure is, often, a disconcerting ambiguity. For example, it is not sharp the dividing line between direct political surveillance and modern, benign or at least neutral management and governance. Information is necessary for taxation, law enforcement and immigration control. It also determines citizenship, democratic participation, eligibility and social planning. In short, it is an integral part of the new landscapes of social power, not necessarily arbitrary and nefarious.

Likewise, there are negotiation spaces that are many times ruled by law. The concepts of virtual bubbles and walls are paramount to understanding these negotiations. Lemos (2010) has dedicated special attention to these concepts that, referring to the permeability levels of borders, fit perfectly within his theory of informational territories. As a general definition, a bubble is a temporary space, well defined, that works to gather all interfaces, formats and concordances for the management of personal data, groups, audiences, and informational interactions (Besley & Hakala, 2007: 71). The bubble is an activity based on privacy, custom-made practices, priority, location, circumstances and time. It can be described as a "semi-transparent membrane that can be tuned to work in different ways depending on data movement and direction" (Besley et al.: 72). When it filters outwards, people, inside the bubble, decide what they wish to send others outside the bubble. Inwards bubble informational flux is based on requirements and informational needs. Bubbles can be created whenever they are needed for a community or for global use.

In the future, authors predict that RFID tags (extremely tiny gadgets that can store data about the object to which they are tagged and that can communicate with the outer world) will be embedded in a multitude of everyday objects. Because of that, people will be better informed about their surroundings. Nevertheless, if precautions are not taken, a lot of sensitive personal information will also be transmitted. In this case, implementing bubbles becomes a priority in order to control data flow across tags.

Bubbles presuppose bridges between physical and digital environments. Emerging technologies, such as services based on location, 4G cell phones, biometrics, etc., have a tendency to fill a gap between specific places and digital knowledge and information. Here again it is possible to see the ambivalence of surveillance: additional value to the user is undeniable, but there are also potential threats (Lemos, 2010).

In addition to bubbles and bridges, there are interstitial spaces, in which one can find flows between virtual and physical, including walls. When the concepts of bubbles, bridges and walls get on stage, the correctness of Lemos' theory of informational borders and territories (2008a; 2008b; 2010) shows all of its strength. Users that navigate through intelligent environments, endowed with sensors and locative gadgets, leave digital footprints behind. Similar to the concept of bubble, the concept of wall, according to Lemos (2010: 15), refers to:

interface systems (a GUI or graphical user interface), must allow users to control their digital footprints (generation, storage and distribution). These virtual walls, like digital bubbles, show the new territoriality of places in the form of an informational control zone. By controlling the electronic boundaries that make up spaces, privacy, anonymity and freedom should be guaranteed in ubiquitous environments.

Additional perceptions of mobile digital surveillance's ambiguity refer to the existence of laws that seek to determine the limits of what is allowed. Working from the premise that locative information is not personal information *per se*, but that it becomes as such only when it is connected to other types of information, Gow (2005b: 140) debates the issue of consentience situations, that is, "the terms and conditions over which locative information may be collected and combined with other details in order to produce personal profiles for public safety and commercial purposes."

Locative tracking is not enough to satisfy mobile marketing and mobility based service's requirements, as both depend on the establishing of connections between multiple databases relative to users in different domains. The legal terms and conditions of these connections depend on the user consentience, an issue that is far more complicated than it may seem.

Media and uninformed scholarship usually wreck sensationalism with the idea that it is enough to have a cell phone for having your privacy threatened. In reference to White (2003), Gow (2005b), raises three necessary operations to distinguish locative privacy from information privacy: the first refers to the initial locative data retrieval, the second to the use of data processing mechanisms that are applied to the information to render it useful, and the third is the application of results for expanding public safety and commercial services.

For a better understanding of these operations we must combine them with regulations, which vary from country to country, for processing and use of personal information, given that the simple act of collecting personal data is not equivalent to its retrieval for further recombination. The larger the ratio of knowledge about a person's identity, the greater the capacity of generating detailed personal profiles in connection with locative information. However that depends on consentience that is described as *con-inwards* and *con-outwards*, on individual choices in some cases, and not on others, such as, for instance, bank registries. In commercial cases, in order to get detailed data, there are strategies of incentive, rewards, etc.

The guiding line of surveillance debates goes always in the direction of its effects related to outbreak, invasion and threats to privacy. As a consequence, a more careful observation of privacy and anonymity is required.

SURVEILLANCE VS PRIVACY

Many authors converge on acknowledging that privacy has become a concept that is difficult to define. Taylor (2002: 67) states that, notwithstanding all the literature available on the subject, privacy has become a somewhat nebulous concept. Wacks (1980a) also states that searching for a definition of the term has produced a continuous debate that is always sterile and, finally, useless, despite the fact that privacy rights are now part of international agreements and national constitutions.

For Lyon (2002: 2), privacy is a relative term. Home has been considered to be a realm of privacy *par excellence*, a place safe from intruders. Now, however, surveillance media pervades domestic spaces in our cell phones, TVs, computers. In a mega polis such as São Paulo, houses and apartments are connected to internal video circuits of security. Still, at the age of mobility, one looks for privacy in public spaces, on the streets, not only when we walk by with our *ipods* plugged on to our ears, but also as we hide from cameras around us. What is more significant is that privacy is needed for communication and transactions, many of which take place while we move from here to there. That is exactly why privacy is not reserved to fixed spaces. Both privacy and surveillance participate in the world of flux.

Stalder (2002: 121) confirms that privacy is notoriously a vague term and suggests that different cultures conceive of it differently. For Europeans, for example, protection to privacy is grounded on a wide principle of respect to human dignity (Marx, 2002: 10) and privacy is understood as informational self-determining, that is, the individual should be capable of establishing the extension according to which data about himself is collected within a given context.

The metaphor of the bubble encapsulating a person with dimensions proportional to each person's ability to control what gets in and out comes back here. In as much as this concept may seem attractive and intuitive, it does not really work. Our privacy is being consistently eroded and our walls are becoming ever more porous. Stalter then asks us to imagine the situation where our fridge communicates with our smart phone, updating supermarket listings because there is no milk, or even sending a message to the supermarket asking for home delivery! Outside our homes, situations of personal data extraction are difficult to avoid.

Even more difficult will be to imagine privacy within pervasive ambient intelligence. Intelligent environments, according to Berley & Hakala (2007: 71), are spaces populated by a collection of technologies, infra-structures, applications and services, composing different smart systems in environments. These aim at facilitating and widening people's daily life experiences by retrieving and analyzing a tremendous amount of data for the creation of an environment better adapted to its occupants. Information and data necessary to social and business transactions will follow people and will be accessible from anywhere. It is not hard to notice how all these charming features might become a nightmare, if design does not entail personal control over the environment.

The great paradox of contemporary surveillance, however, is found at the ever more frequent situations in which youth, and also the not so youthful, instead of striving to maintain privacy, strive to increase self-exposure, which does often become almost obscene. This paradox was addressed brightly by Bruno (2008b). According to the author, the relation between surveillance and spectacle is getting closer and the differences are getting slighter. This is illustrated by the proliferation of reality shows in which confinement and surveillance apparatuses are set up for entertainment. Or by the many amateur pictures and videos that circulate over the internet or in mass media, making evident how a surveilling regard becomes common place and natural in contemporary culture, taking many shapes. Even more acute is the author's finding that movement, as much as surveillance and spectacle, are now transformed. The latter does not fit in anymore most of Debord's meanings (Debord, 1967) and their more or less faithful derivatives. Such transformations can only be well understood when the axis of analysis is displaced from control circuits to pleasure, entertainment and voyeurism circuits.

Over the course of this work, I first called attention to the potential usage of mobile media for malign ends. This is one of their extreme sides, the one under the command of Thanatos, master of destruction, crime, and arbitrary power. It is this side that is responsible for the constitution of a culture of fear, suspicion and secrecy (see Lyon, 2004: 135-137). Proof that Thanatos is at least potentially omnipresent in surveillance societies can be found in the new industries and new economy of security to which these societies have given rise, "a kaleidoscope cluster of activities concerned with preventing or reducing risk of deliberate harm to life and property" (Stevens, 2004: 8). Surveillance society under the command of Thanatos and the new economy of security are to a certain extent the two faces of the same coin.

However – to recall what was stated before – exclusive attention to the malign side of surveillance is partial and not representative of its real complexity. That is why I gradually left the dark clouds of surveillance, passing through its paradoxes and ambivalences in order to reach its other sides, the beneficial ones. Now, it is time to lead out attention to the extreme opposite of Thanatos, which can be found in a large number of mobile and locative art practices all over the world. It is on the opposite side of control and power that the artists load their side of the scales, when they creatively explore mobile devices in varied and always surprising re-contextualizations, which are sometimes critical, politically active, other times full of humor and pleasure. Let us dive into that.

THE POWER OF EROS AGAINST THANATOS

It is a truism to say that digital technologies, now mobile, have emerged and were developed by pure military necessities. The motivation behind technology, and also military technology, determines the direction of its development. Nevertheless, the fact that usually technological applications deviate radically from their intended purposes has become a rule. Users are, in fact, creators of new functionalities and domains of application through the discovery and creation of unsuspected needs and practices. There are no pre-determined sets of usages for technologies: user guides from Nokia, Motorola or Siemens do not have a section teaching users how to organize smart mobs (Rheingold, 2002) for political activism in less than an hour. The history of digital revolution is only a few decades old, but it is ripe with examples of healthy anarchy through network activism, open system cooperatives, or of what Lemos (2010) has been calling the power for creating lines of escape.

One can not deny, therefore, that an ethics of curiosity and liberation from the chains of what is pre-determined actively exists. It is precisely from this ethics that artists nourish their action. That is also why it comes from them the magna contribution to the continuity of the human project that, for Karl Marx, represents making what is human ever more human. It is not a coincidence that the creation of new modes of imagination, perception and feeling for these new technological extensions and hybrids comes from artists. They project re-contextualizations that determine cultural appropriation. In the field of mobile technologies, some prime examples of such re-contextualizations are art practices based on locative media.

The digital "*Mciclopedia*" describes locative media as technologies based on locations, that is, wireless technologies, surveillance technologies of tracking and positioning that enable information to be tagged to geographical spaces. The Global Positioning System (GPS) is the most familiar technology making use of location sensitive computation. Two dozen satellites orbiting at 12.000 miles from the surface of the Earth help drivers and wanderers to find their ways virtually from anywhere in the globe. In addition to GPS, other devices weaving the fabric of locative media are: cell phones, wireless palms and laptops, bluetooths, RFID tags, etc. These are devices that allow people to locate themselves and one another across geographical space and also to connect information to geographical locations. These technologies of mobility, location sensitive, are increasingly enabling access to the net, allowing for information retrieval and recovery from remote databases.

Practices of mapping, geolocation and tagging allowed by such technologies are innumerable and are on the rise, expanding our concepts of displacement, both of the devices mediating it, and of the information circulating incessantly across interstitial spaces, in between the physical and the virtual. Locative media is being increasingly used by industries and commerce as location based services. As first generation applications, they are still not more than variations on the way we search for a restaurant, a building, etc. Car navigation systems mostly still belong to this generation. However, new applications are emerging that are even more complex. Engineers, for example, are working toward the detection of our own location, of what objects and places are near us, devices that are capable of talking to other devices via new protocols, in such manner that location becomes a new kind of data applied to the net.

Moreover, re-appropriation, from the public in general, of functions inherent to mobile gadgets, such as Bluetooth and SMS, functions that are cheap or even free, enables new ways of spontaneous self-organization that would not be possible without them. By turning its constructive collectivism into action, locative media denounce the power and also the limits of new modes of surveillance, deconstructing technological operations of political control by introducing moments of distortion or uncertainty, or by constructing open platforms that offer the possibility of reverting, multiplying or refracting our gaze. From there, comes the potential to change the way in which we perceive and interact with space, time and one another, in decentralized activities which defy society's hierarchal structures.

Locative media art practices are prime examples of that, at the opposite extreme of traditional modes of power and control. It has been a while that artists have demonstrated their concern about locations. But the present plethora of mobile devices endowed with positioning technologies is opening infinite different ways of finding and designing geographical space, framing a wide variety of spatial practices.

There is no doubt about the fact that plurality is the most important characteristic of locative media. From what I am aware of, it was Ronald Lenz (2007) who brought to life the most comprehensive research on the different kinds of projects and practices under the huge umbrella of locative media, not to mention the many subcategories established by Lenz. Nineteen kinds of practices are presented, including the listing and description of a great number of works. Some categories follow here: art, story telling, geolocative blogs incorporating semantic locative information, hybrid or pervasive games connecting virtual to physical spaces, mobile social software, spatial annotation and geodesigns, services, metadata, mobility devices, such as movement detection phones and control via sensors, location sensitive computation, mobile net, RFID tags, wireless networks, semacoding for fast access to a website, geocoding, etc.

From all these possibilities, emerge projects that, for example, explore the edges of urban geopolitical spaces by allowing common people to add their own social knowledge to urban landscapes via geotagging. Other projects assume a documental purpose, trying to connect hidden meanings to their locations, rescuing social memory from its imminent loss. Widely known are the urban annotation projects that encourage people to post, on geographical locations, personal history events, thoughts, any information, calls to action, users exchanges. Annotation is posted virtually at a geographical space using GPS coordinates so it may be asynchronously reached by other users. In this manner, urban space gets filled with stories that might be accessed by an enormous variety of people – tourists, newcomers or old dwellers looking to find new spaces on familiar surroundings.

These are projects that find the invisible threads of their own cohesion in rescuing the human experience of story telling, of recovering collective memory that lie outside official history, in the ever more encompassing availability of devices traditionally marked by the insignia of power for critical, or even naïve, uses. Finally, these are projects that enable collective processes of socialization based on networks of reciprocity and trust, in collaborative communication and the collective construction of knowledge.

It is important to point out how precise were the prognostics of Ben Russell's *Headmap Manifesto*, from 1999, that is now considered the urtext of locative media, even before such expression existed. Built around the idea that the internet was starting to "drop in the real world", the manifesto alerted to the enriching of our spatial experience by the superposition of information layers – pictures, texts, sounds – made available by mobile devices and GPS wireless computation, nourished by an intense community spirit. Furthermore, it proposed a series of tactics for applying web semantics ontologies to mobile sensitive technologies, transforming the latter in a gateway for access to locative content as the basis for a new kind of mobile presence on the web. What is truly remarkable about this manifesto, ten years after it was written, is the intense community spirit it purveys as a fundamental aspect of locative practices. This same community spirit lies under the logic of web 2.0 and 3.0, in which the new mottos are: expose yourself, share, and collaborate in interactive activities that are based on principles of trust and exchange.

By so doing, besides working as the most legitimate examples of what I call a pluralist ecology of communication and culture (Santaella, 2007; 2008; forthcoming), locative media also works as a precise index of the double sided aspects of human psyche that were studied by Freud. From one extreme, the destructive side of death wish, and from another extreme, a constructive side under the influence of Eros. It is this extreme side which struggles for life and creativity that locative media aesthetic projects try to explore, by counterbalancing the contrary forces exerted by the dissimulated power of ubiquitous tracking and surveillance.

REFERENCES

Barthes, R. (1981). *A câmara clara*, (M. Torres, Trans.). Lisboa: Edições 70.

Bennet, C. J., & Regan, P. M. (2004). Editorial: Surveillance and mobilities. *Surveillance & Society*, *1*(4), 449–455.

Beslay, L., & Hakala, H. (2007). Digital territory: Bubbles. In Kidd, P. T. (Ed.), *European visions for the knowledge age* (pp. 69–78). Macclesfield, UK: Cheshire Henbury.

Bruno, F. (2008a). Monitoramento, classificação e controle nos dispositivos de vigilância digital. *Revista Famecos*, *36*, 10–16.

Bruno, F. (2008b). Controle, flagrante e prazer: Regimes escópicos e atencionais da vigilância nas cidades. *Revista Famecos*, *37*, 45–53.

Clark, R. (2003). *Wireless transmission and mobile technologies*. Roger Clark Website. Retrieved July 03, 2009 from http://www.anu.edu.au/people/Roger.Clarke/EC/WMT.html

Dittmar, A. (2007). myHealth. In P. T. Kidd (Ed.), *European visions for the knowledge age* (pp. 105-114). Macclesfield, UK: Cheshire Henbury.

Eericson, R. V., & Haggerty, K. D. (2001). The surveillant assemblage. *The British Journal of Sociology*, *51*(4), 605–622.

Gow, G. A. (2005a). *Privacy and Ubiquitous Network Societies*. Paper presented at the International Telecommunication Union Workshop on Ubiquitous Network Societies. Geneva, 6-8 April 2005 (Document: UNS/10 11 April 2005). Retrieved July 03, 2009 from http://www.itu.int/osg/spu/ni/ubiquitous/UNSChairReport.pdf.

Gow, G. A. (2005b). Pinpointing consent. Locative privacy and mobile phones. In Nyíri, K. (Ed.), *A sense of place. The global and the local in mobile communication* (pp. 139–150). Vienna: Passagen Verlag.

Kidd, P. T. (2007). Human centered ambient intelligence: Human-computer relationships for the knowledge age. In Kidd, P. T. (Ed.), *European visions for the knowledge age* (pp. 55–68). Macclesfield, UK: Cheshire Henbury.

Kövecses, Z. (2008). The cellphone as a conceptual category. In Nyíri, K. (Ed.), *Integration and ubiquity. Towards a philosophy of telecommunications convergence* (pp. 29–44). Vienna: Passagen Verlag.

Lemos, A. (2004). Cibercultura e mobilidade: a era da conexão. *Razón y Palabra*, Oct./Nov. 2004. Retrieved July 16, 2009 from http://www.razonypalabra.org.mx/anteriores/n41/alemos.html.

Lemos, A. (2007). Comunicação e práticas sociais no espaço urbano: As características dos dispositivos híbridos móveis de conexão multirredes (DHMCM). *Comunicação. Mídia e Consumo*, *4*(10), 23–40.

Lemos, A. (2008a). Mídias locativas e territórios informacionais. In Santaella, L., & Arantes, P. (Eds.), *Estéticas tecnológicas. Novos modos de sentir* (pp. 207–230). São Paulo, Brazil: Educ.

Lemos, A. (2008b). Mobile communication and new sense of places: a critique of spatialization in cyberculture. *Revista Galáxia, 16*, 91–108.

Lemos, A. (2010). Locative media and surveillance at the boundaries of informational territories. In R. Firmino, F. Duarte, & C. Ultramari, C. (Eds.). *ICTs for mobile and ubiquitous urban infrastructures: surveillance, locative media and global networks*. Hershey, PA: IGI Global.

Lenz, R. (2007). Locative media. Retrived January 8, 2008, from http://spresearch.waag.org/images/LocativeMedia.pdf.

Lyon, D. (2002). Surveillance studies: Understanding visibility, mobility, and the phenetic fix. *Surveillance & Society, 1*(1), 1–7.

Lyon, D. (2004). Surveillance technologies: Trends and social implications. In Barrie, S. (Ed.), *The security economy* (pp. 127–148). Paris: OECD Publishing.

Lyon, D. (2010). Why where you are matters: Mundane mobilities, transparent technologies, and digital discrimination. In Firmino, R., Duarte, F., & Ultramari, C. (Eds.), *ICTs for mobile and ubiquitous urban infrastructures: Surveillance, locative media and global networks*. Hershey, PA: IGI Global.

Marx, G. T. (2002). What is new about the new surveillance? Classifying for change and continuity. *Surveillance & Society, 1*(1), 9–29.

Rheingold, H. (2002). *Smart mobs: The next social revolution*. New York: Basic Books.

Rose, N. (1999). *Powers of freedom. Reframing political thought*. Cambridge, UK: Cambridge University Press. doi:10.1017/CBO9780511488856

Rule, J. B. (2002). From mass society to perpetual contact. In Katz, J. E., & Aakhus, M. (Eds.), *Perpetual contact: Mobile communication, private talk, public performance*. Cambridge: Cambridge University Press. doi:10.1017/CBO9780511489471.019

Santaella, L. (2002). *Semiótica aplicada*. São Paulo, Brazil: Thomson.

Santaella, L. (2007). A ecologia pluralista. In Oliva, F., & Rezende, M. (Eds.), *Comunismo da forma. Som, imagem e política da arte*. São Paulo, Brazil: Alameda Situações.

Santaella, L. (2008). A ecologia pluralista das mídias locativas. *Revista Famecos, 37*, 20–24.

Santaella, L. (in press). *A ecologia pluralista da comunicação. Conectividade, mobilidade, ubiqüidade*. São Paulo, Brazil: Paulus. Stalder, F. Opinion. Privacy is not the antidote to surveillance. *Surveillance & Society, 1*(1), 120-124.

Stevens, B. (2004). The emerging security economy. An introduction. In Stevens, B. (Ed.), *The security economy* (pp. 7–16). Paris: OECD Publishing.

Taylor, N. (2002). State surveillance and the right of privacy. *Surveillance & Society, 1*(1), 66–85.

Van Kranenburg, R. (2008). *The internet of things. A critique of ambient technology and the all-seeing network of RFID*. Amsterdam: Network Notebooks.

Wacks, R. (1980). *The protection of privacy*. London: Sweet & Maxwell.

White, J. G. (2003). *People, not places: A police framework for analysing location privacy issues. Masters memo prepared for the Electronic Privacy Information Center*. Terry Sanford Institute of Public Policy, Duke University.

Wood, D. M. (Ed.). (2006). A report on the surveillance society. *Information commissioner by the surveillance studies*, September-2006.

ADDITIONAL READING

Anders, P. (1999). The cybrid condition: Implementing hybrids of electronic and physical space. In Ascott, R. (Ed.), *Reframing consciousness. Exeter & Portland: Intellect*.

Bambozzi, L. (2006). *Public life and pervasive systems. A critical practice.* Master of Philosophy Dissertation. Institute of Digital Art and Technology. School of Computing, Communications and Electronics, University of Plymouth, UK.

Beiguelman, G., Bambozzi, L., Bastos, M., & Minelli, R. (2009). *Apropriações do (in)comum. Espaço público e privado em tempos de mobilidade*. São Paulo: Instituto Sérgio Motta.

Bennett, C., & Raab, C. (2003). *The governance of privacy: Policy instruments in global perspective*. Aldershot: Ashgate.

Blicker, J. (2006). Locative media: A brief bibliography and taxonomy of Gps-enabled locative media. Retrived December/05, 2007 from http://leoalmanac.org/journal/Vol_14/lea_v14_n03-04/jbleecker.asp.

Castells, M. (1996). *The rise of the network society*. New York: Blackwell.

Dandeker, C. (1990). *Surveillance, power and modernity*. Cambridge: Polity Press.

Eberle, G. (1994). *The geography of nowhere: Finding one's self in the postmodern world*. Kansas City, MO: Sheed & Ward.

Ericson, R., & Haggerty, K. (1997). *Policing the Risk Society*. Toronto: University of Toronto Press.

Flaherty, D. (1989). *Protecting privacy in surveillance societies*. Chapel Hill, NC: University of North Carolina Press.

Furedi, F. (1997). *Culture of fear: Risk-taking and the morality of low expectation*. London: Cassell.

Garland, D. (2001). *The culture of control*. Chicago, IL: University of Chicago Press.

Glassner, B. (1999). *The culture of fear: Why Americans are afraid of the wrong things*. New York: Basic Books.

Lessig, L. (1999). *Code and other laws of cyberspace*. New York: Basic Books.

Lyon, D. (1994). *The electronic eye. The rise of surveillance society*. Minneapolis: University of Minneapolis Press.

Lyon, D. (2001). *Surveillance society. Monitoring everyday life*. Buckingham: Open University Press.

Lyon, D. (Ed.). (2003). *Surveillance as social sorting: Privacy, risk, and digital Discrimination*. London: Routledge.

Norris, C., & Armstrong, G. (1999). *Towards the maximum security society*. London: Berg.

Nyíri, K. (Ed.). (2005). *A sense of place. The global and the local in mobile communication*. Vienna: Passagen Verlag.

Nyíri, K. (Ed.). (2006). *Mobile understanding. The epistemology of ubiquitous communication*. Vienna: Passagen Verlag.

Nyíri, K. (Ed.). (2007). *Mobile studies. Paradigms and perspectives*. Vienna: Passagen Verlag.

Nyíri, K. (Ed.). (2008). *Integration and ubiquity. Towards a philosophy of telecommunications convergence*. Vienna: Passagen Verlag.

Regan, P. (1995). *Legislating privacy*. Chapel Hill, NC: University of North Carolina Press.

Rose, N. (2000). Government and conduct. In Garland, E., & Sparks, R. (Eds.), *Criminology and Social Theory* (pp. 183–208). Oxford: Oxford University Press.

Slater, I. (2003). *Orwell: The road to Airstrip One*. New York: Norton.

Wright, S. (1998). *An appraisal of the technologies of political control*. Luxembourg: European Parliament/STOA Publications.

KEY TERMS AND DEFINITIONS

Ambivalence: Psychologically, ambivalence is a concept referring to someone divided between opposing feelings. In this article, the use of the word refers to a specific phenomenon: mobile media. By ambivalence I intended to refer to the uncertainty or fluctuation of mobile media between two opposite or conflicting situations: negative and positive, that is, the coexistence of opposite directions within the uses of mobile media.

Eros: In Greek mythology, Eros is the god of love. In Plato, if goodness, beauty, and justice are our destiny, then love inspires us toward them. That is why Eros is sometimes defined as an attraction toward perfection or integration. In his tendency to make use of mythological figures to describe human psychic forces, Freud chose Eros to represent life drives, those drives which try to unify organic life, those impulses that guide us both in the search for contact with the other and in our fight for the preservation of life. That is why Eros is in opposition to Thanatos, the personification of death.

Internet of Things: Some forms of ubiquitous information and communication networks are already evident in the widespread use of cell phones, which have become an integral and intimate part of our everyday life. New developments are now in course to lead us a step further when short-range mobile transceivers will be embedded into a wide array of additional gadgets and everyday items, enabling new forms of communication between people and things, and between things themselves. This is called the internet of things.

Interstitial Spaces: Interstitial spaces combine the physical and the digital spaces in a new environment which is created by the mobility of users connected via mobile communication devices. Hence the borders between the physical and the digital spaces become blurred and not completely distinguishable. Although both spaces continue to exist, a third entirely new type of space is created. This is a consequence of the emergence of mobile apparatuses which allow our being constantly connected to digital spaces, literally carrying the internet wherever we go.

Mobility: Mobility is defined in opposition to fixity which is commonly associated with place. Evidently, mobility means movement. This is understood by the idea of an act of displacement which allows objects, people, things, and even ideas to circulate between localizations. There is also a virtual mobility which is allowed by tele-media, from the telephone to the Internet. With the advent of mobile media, the idea of mobility became omnipresent since these media produce the intersection of two types of mobility: the physical and the virtual.

Scopic Regime: This expression was coined by the French film critic Christian Metz. The substitution of expressions such as visual regime or image regime by scopic regime indicates that the expected definition of vision as a universal and natural phenomenon is now replaced by culturally specific ways of seeing. The complex definition of the scopic drive in psychoanalysis implies that there is a hidden relation of power between the gaze and the object aimed by the gaze. This idea is also adequate to characterize the scopic regime where the screen image does not correspond exactly to the image that is seen. There is something beyond it, that is, suspicion.

Thanatos: In Greek mythology, the role performed by Thanatos is small since it was eclipsed by Hades who reigned upon death. Thanatos was considered to be an enemy of humankind. That must be the reason why Freud chose this figure to be the opposite of Eros. According to Freud human beings oscillate between two great drives: the drive for life (Eros) and the drive for death, destruction and war (Thanatos).

Chapter 18
Notes about Vehicle Monitoring in Brazil and Europe from a Data Protection Perspective

Danilo Doneda
Fundação Getúlio Vargas, Brazil

Mario Viola de Azevedo Cunha
European University Institute, Italy

ABSTRACT

The Brazilian National Traffic Council, in a Resolution adopted in 2006, stated that every vehicle to be sold in the country should have an RFId chip. The nature of the whole project, named SINIAV, is to assemble an infrastructure all over public roads and streets capable of recognizing and identifying vehicles. A surveillance system such as SINIAV, presented as a cutting-edge system capable of bringing security to Brazilian's streets by reducing car's theft, has a crucial (and political) aspect which addresses the level of security that should be developed in the IT system for the use of such database, especially in a country which does not have a specific data protection legislation. The regulation of databases of personal information is an unavoidable step to be done, as the real danger to personal liberties in an automatic surveillance system, such as this one, is not based in personal surveillance, but is related to the use of this personal data. It is not by chance that the European Union is currently discussing a new Action Plan for the Deployment of Intelligent Transport Systems in Europe. Taking into account this scenario, the current chapter analyses the SINIAV regulation from a data protection perspective.

INTRODUCTION

Personal data has been widely used as it became a fundamental tool for the development of various activities in the public and private domain. The automation of information processing has become indispensable due to increasing demands from a mass society, to the point that today, in many circumstances, it would be unthinkable not to take advantage of this resource[1]. The technology applied to information processing, on the other hand, increases the risk of invasion of privacy and control over individuals through the misuse of personal information, what encouraged the emergence of legal institutes capable of counterbalancing this

DOI: 10.4018/978-1-60960-051-8.ch018

trend and of providing citizens with control over their own personal data.

Such institutes have developed to an enormous extent in recent decades. Without going into details about the complex legislative development, it can be said that its features are rooted in principles of personal data protection that started to be elaborated at the beginning of the 1970s. These principles, which are often referred to as Fair Information Principles[2], have their roots in various laws about data protection and have formed the backbone of the first international documents which deal with the theme from a broader perspective, the Convention 108 from the Council of Europe[3] and the OECD (Organization for Economic Co-operation and Development) Guidelines[4], both at the beginning of the 1980s.

Brazil, unlike other countries (even neighboring countries like Argentina and Uruguay)[5], does not have a general norm that tackles the protection of personal data[6], having only constitutional provisions of general character and some norms about data protection restricted to specific sectors (Bessa, 2003). In the lack of a mature legal data protection framework, some projects that include heavy treatment of personal data are being developed in Brazil without the proper measures to ensure the protection of citizens against the misuse of their data. Taking into account this scenario, this chapter will analyze a 'new' regulation from the Brazilian National Traffic Council regarding the monitoring of vehicles in roads and streets all over the country, which poses many threats to individual privacy and data protection.

BACKGROUND: THE SINIAV PROJECT

In 2006 the Brazilian National Traffic Council adopted a regulation (CONTRAN Resolution 212/2006)[7] requiring that every licensed Brazilian vehicle shall have an RFId chip and that all the major highways and urban areas will be covered by an extensive array of RFId sensors. In order to make use of these chips, this regulation also creates a nationwide automated system for identifying vehicles (SINIAV), which includes a centralized database of every monitored vehicle's wanderings.

Such a regulation is not unique in the sense that it is part of a group of regulatory initiatives which, in the recent past, made Brazil one of the most willing countries to make use of the technological measures available to control its population and to provide as much as possible data for administrative purposes. The measure, however, does not seem to consider a series of probable pitfalls related to privacy and data protection issues.

Organizing a rather large population in one of the largest countries in the world has always been one of the main challenges of the Brazilian public administration. To make goods and services, either public or private, arrive in Brazil's most inner locations is a rather usual problem and a fact of life for many people living in most remote areas. That has also probably been a cause for the concentration of both population and capital in southeastern Brazil.

So, with the 'arrival' of technologies capable to keep track of the actions and whereabouts of people, the enforcement of those technologies started to be seen by many policy-makers as the next logical step. Thus, several projects in this sense are already being implemented, such as the biometrical authentication of voters by the electronic voting machine in all Brazilian's elections; the unique ID for civil identification that comes with an all-new plastic-made and chip-powered ID card and a central database, according to the RIC project[8]; as well as the SINIAV project.

As pointed out by David Lyon:

Keeping track of where people are has always been important for families, employers, authorities. They want to know that children are safe, workers are busy, and that citizens are living lawfully. In the modern era, with its bureaucratic organizations and high mobility rates, schools, govern-

ment departments, marketers, law enforcement and emergency services also want to know where people are – as students, claimants, consumers, offenders and accident victims. (Lyon, 2010: 2)

The technocratic logic behind this project supports the arguments presented in its favor: the benefits for urban planning, the reduction of car theft, the identification of bad taxpayers and so on. This and the fact that the regulation in the very base of SINIAV is only an administrative regulation reveals undoubtedly how the whole question is being treated as mainly a bureaucratic side issue, without taking into account its collateral effects and implications for citizenship.

DATA PROTECTION AND SURVEILLANCE

The growing presence of things as information subjects in the networked environment, in a phenomenon that was named the Internet of things,[9] has not passed unnoticed. Things and objects, connected to networks, create intelligent environments that can be reactive to the presence of man, with its steps and moves, adding to the new concepts of Ubiquitous computing[10] or even Ambient Intelligence.[11]

Nonetheless, monitoring things is often a way to monitor people. Not surprisingly, Mark Weiser, in one article that contributed to shape the notion of Ambient Intelligence, mentioned that an array of networked sensors could behave as a kind of diary capable of self-writing – there is no need of writing a diary when machines will sense your every move and write it down (Weiser, 1991).

Apart from only registering moves, modern technologies can also contribute directly to limit, prohibit or condition movement or even liberty. In this sense, machines - and the idea of a 'inhabited machine', such as a vehicle, can be mentioned here (Lyon, 2010) - by revealing locational data about someone, it can also, increasingly, limit his movements, and thus cause a concrete misbalance of power.

As stated by David Lyon, relations of power are very often linked with surveillance (Lyon, 2010) and the imbalance of power it generates can be taken as a sign that there is more than the purely individual interest to be taken into account in this case - as would be the case if these situations were evaluated through the privacy filter.

The very emergence of data protection as a value and a right per se, related to, but in its core different from, the protection of privacy, indicates that there is room for other values apart from the traditional privacy values - secrecy, intimacy, isolation, among others - to be evaluated. These other values can point to a new collective dimension of the privacy problem, as pointed out by Stefano Rodotà:

(...) the evocation of privacy goes beyond the traditional individualistic frame and mixes in a collective dimension from the moment the interest of the individual is not taken as itself, but as the interest of someone belonging to a certain social group. (RODOTÀ, 1995: 27)

But, even when this collective approach is accepted and considered as part of data protection, there is a limit on the effectiveness of these laws that lies on their very nature, instruments and principles they are based on. As David Lyon observes:

As applications and services are 'personalized' (involving some forms of identification verification protocols) and as data are collected, stored and processed in increasingly invisible and imperceptible ways, with profiles mutating and recombinating constantly, or merely the opportunities for but the reality of vastly expanded surveillance capacities will demand radically new approaches for familiar requirements such as consent and accountability. At present, the kinds of proposal made lean towards 'giving individuals more control', but generally presupposes - optimistically – high levels of knowledgeability among such users. (Lyon, 2009: 105)

DATA PROTECTION IN THE BRAZILIAN LEGAL SYSTEM[12]

The Brazilian Constitution recognizes in its Article 5, section X, privacy, intimacy, honor and image as fundamental rights. The same Article, in its sections XI, XII and XIV, provides protection to other aspects of privacy. Moreover, the same item LXXII of the same Article 5 refers to a constitutional remedy with regard to the protection of personal data, which is the action of habeas data. Similarly, the Civil Code included in its Article 21, the right to privacy in the list of personality rights.

However, the only statute that specifically addresses the protection of personal data, with the exception of the rule that governs the action of habeas data, is the Consumer Protection and Defense Code (CDC), which, in its Articles 43 and 44, regulates the maintenance of databases and records of consumers, establishing a series of guarantees for the latter. It is possible to notice in this text, even if in a subtle way, the influence of more modern standards related to the protection of personal data, with reference to some of the principles of data protection mentioned previously.

The first guarantee in this regard is the right for consumers to be informed that data about themselves is being processed (Article 43, § 2). This communication shall be done before the data is actually used, in order to enable the consumer to exercise other rights conferred by the CDC, that also enables for compensation of material and moral damages in the cases of absence or delay of this communication. However, it is enough for the controller of the database to prove that he has sent the consumer the notification about the inclusion of his/her data in the registry or database, without needing to prove that the consumer received such a statement.

The other rights of consumers established by the CDC concerning the protection of their personal data are the rights of access and rectification, which enable them to consult any personal information about them stored "in databases, reference lists, records, personal data and consumption-related files" and, in the event of finding any inaccuracies, to request rectification of data (Article 43, caput and § 3). If the exercise of such rights is denied, consumers may make use of the legal ordinary proceedings (Article 43, § 4) or the aforementioned action of habeas data.

Furthermore, Article 43, in its §§ 1 and 5, establishes that any negative information about consumers, that restricts their access to credit, cannot be stored for more than five years. Here again, consumers can make use of legal mechanisms to enforce their right and request compensation, both for material and moral damages, if the controller of the database fails to fulfill his duty.

VEHICLE MONITORING IN THE EUROPEAN UNION

In recent years many projects involving the monitoring of transport have been started in the European Union, in what they call 'Intelligent Transport Systems' (ITS). The SESAR (Single European Sky Air Traffic Management Research) for air transport, the RIS (River Information Services) for water ways, the ERTMS (European Rail Traffic Management System) for railways, and the TAF-TSI (Telematics Applications for Freight), the SafeSeaNet and the VTMIS (Vessel Traffic Monitoring and Information Systems) for shipping are just few examples of European initiatives in this field (EU Commission COM[2008] 886 final).[13]

Currently, it is under discussion at the EU level an "Action Plan for the Deployment of Intelligent Transport Systems in Europe" and a "Proposal for a Directive of the European Parliament and of the Council laying down the framework for the deployment of Intelligent Transport Systems in the field of road transport and for interfaces with other transport modes." The Action Plan (and the respective Directive Proposal) "aims to accelerate and coordinate the deployment of Intelligent Transport Systems (ITS) in road transport [both in passenger and freight transport], including interfaces with other transport modes" (EU Commission COM[2008] 886 final).[14]

Recital 3 of the Proposal for a Directive advocates that,

The application of information and communication technologies to the road transport sector and its interfaces with other transport modes (ITS) will make a significant contribution to improving environmental performance, efficiency, including energy efficiency, safety and security of road transport and passenger and freight mobility whilst at the same time ensuring the functioning of the internal market and increased levels of competitiveness and employment.[15]

In the implementation of this ITS, navigation, tracking and tracing systems will be used, including not only RFID technology (Radio Frequency Identification Devices) but also GPS (Global Positioning System) and Satellite-based infrastructures (such as Galileo and EGNOS),[16] making possible (or even necessary) the identification and surveillance of individuals.

It is not by hazard that the European Commission has recognized as some of the "Main problem drivers" for the implementation of the ITS "unsolved data privacy and liability issues",[17] and that all parties involved in the European law-making process have highlighted the need to comply with data protection rules in the context of the operation of ITS.

In that sense Recital 9 and Article 6 of the Proposal for a Directive are:

(9) The deployment and use of ITS applications and services will entail the processing of personal data. Such processing should be carried out in accordance with Community rules, as set out, inter alia, in Directive 95/46/EC of the European Parliament and of the Council of 24 October 1995 on the protection of individuals with regard to the processing of personal data and on the free movement of such data and in Directive 2002/58/EC of the European Parliament and of the Council of 12 July 2002 concerning the processing of personal data and the protection of privacy in the electronic communications sector.

Article 6

Rules on privacy, security and re-use of information

1. Member States shall ensure that the processing of personal data in the context of the operation of ITS is carried out in accordance with the Community rules protecting the freedoms and fundamental rights of individuals, in particular Directives 95/46/EC and 2002/58/EC.

2. In particular, Member States shall ensure that ITS data and records are protected against misuse, including unlawful access, alteration or loss.

3. Directive 2003/98/EC shall apply.

In Europe, different from Brazil, there is a well developed legal framework of data protection, which includes the Convention 108/81 of the Council of Europe (CoE) and its additional protocol of 2001, applying not only to European Union Member States but also to the other CoE Member States; the Directive 95/46/EC (General Data Protection Directive),[18] Directive 2002/58/EC (Directive on privacy and electronic communications),[19] and Directive 2006/24/EC (Data Retention Directive),[20] having application to EU and EEA Member States and focusing on the harmonization of data protection rules within the former EU first pillar;[21] the Regulation (EC) n°

45/2001[22] regarding the processing of personal data by Community institutions and bodies and, more recently the Council Framework Decision 2008/977/JHA of 27 November 2008 on the protection of personal data processed in the framework of police and judicial cooperation in criminal matters.[23] There are also other legal instruments dealing with data protection within the former third pillar (Police and Judicial co-operation in criminal matters), such as the Schengen Agreements, Europol and Eurojust, but they do not provide for general rules, as the Council Framework Decision 2008/977/JHA does.

The adoption of Intelligent Transport Systems, due to the need of collecting personal information both from public and private sectors, and to access databases implemented for completely different purposes, tends to involve processing operations that fall under more than one legal regime. In this regard, the opinion of the European Data Protection Supervisor about the Action Plan for the Deployment of Intelligent Transport Systems in Europe and the respective Proposal for a Directive (p.3), points out the different sources of data used by ITS:

Intelligent Transport Systems are based on the collection, processing and exchange of a wide variety of data, from public and private sources; they therefore constitute a data-intensive area. The deployment of ITS will rely to a large extent on geolocalisation technologies, such as satellite-positioning and contact-less technologies, such as RFID, which will facilitate the provision of a variety of public and/or commercial location-based services (e.g. real-time traffic information, eFreight, eCall, eToll, parking reservation, etc.).

Such a variety of data and of navigation, tracking and tracing systems opens the possibility for a wide range of uses not directly related to make transport and travel cleaner, more efficient, safer and more secure, which are the main goals the Action Plan intends to achieve.[24] Invoicing vehicles, monitoring drivers for enforcement purposes and imposing sanctions are just few examples of the possible uses of those technologies and information processed (EDPS Opinion, p.12).

The EDPS also presented some concerns about the need for 'privacy by design' in the development of ITS and some other privacy considerations regarding data minimization and anonymity; interoperability, data quality and purpose limitation; and security of data, which "must be further addressed for the proper deployment of ITS" (EDPS Opinion, p.4).

The debate about vehicle monitoring in Europe, where, as said before, there is a well developed data protection legal framework, shows the importance of discussing this issue in Brazil, where a national system of vehicle surveillance was created by an administrative act enacted by the Brazilian National Traffic Department, without the necessary legislative debate, and without the necessary data protection legal framework, putting into risk the privacy of the individuals, which is a fundamental right recognized by the Brazilian Constitution.

In the words of the European Data Protection Supervisor:

In a democratic society, decisions on essential principles and modalities that impact fundamental rights should be taken within a full legislative procedure, which includes the appropriate checks and balances. In this case, this means that decisions that have a major impact on the privacy and data protection of individuals, such as purposes and modalities of mandatory data processing activities and the definition of modalities for the deployment of ITS in new areas should be decided by European Parliament and Council and not through comitology procedure. (EDPS Opinion, p.7).

VEHICLE MONITORING IN BRAZIL FROM A DATA PROTECTION PERSPECTIVE

Besides the SINIAV, which will be analyzed below, there is another nationwide vehicle monitoring initiative being implemented, created and regulated initially by a Brazilian National Traffic Council Resolution (245/2007) and by a Brazilian National Traffic Department Decision (47/2007), which made compulsory the implementation of geolocalization technologies in all new vehicles produced in or imported to Brazil, with the aim of fighting the robbery of vehicles. In this case, the systems would be compulsorily implemented together with anti-robbery systems in the vehicles and their owners would decide whether to activate or not the geolocalization system.

These administrative acts were suspended by a federal judge decision, on the grounds of consumer protection, because according to the judge this practice of putting together in a same equipment both the gelocalizator and the anti-robbery system violates consumer protection legislation (Article 39, I of the Consumer Code)[25]. As a consequence of such decision, both the Brazilian National Traffic Council and the Brazilian National Traffic Department, enacted other administrative rules (Resolution CONTRAN 329/2009 and Decision DENATRAN 253/2009), amending the former ones, in order to 'comply with' consumer protection legislation. However, these new regulations were challenged again and, finally, suspended by another federal judge decision (Case 2009.61.00.007033-0, Federal Jurisdiction of São Paulo), which, in recognizing that even if the geolocalization system is not activate, it is still possible to 'monitor' the vehicle and to store information concerning its last two hundred locations, declared incidentally the administrative acts illegal and unconstitutional, since they violate not only the consumer protection legislation, but also the fundamental right of privacy.

This decision, which was later cancelled by the same judge after the pronouncement of the Brazilian National Traffic Department in the sense that the necessary technological changes were introduced in the system in order to ensure the protection of individual privacy,, is a very important one, because the judge recognized not only the traditional dimension of the right to privacy ("the right to be let alone") but also the informational aspect of privacy ("the ability of people to control information about themselves") and the right to self determination (the individuals should have the capacity to decide about circumstances that affect them).[26]

The case of SINIAV is different. Although both 'systems' deal with vehicle monitoring, the former creates the possibility of surveillance by the private sector (geolocalization service providers) and the latter by the public sector (Local Traffic Authorities and the National Traffic Department). The second difference is that with the 'first' system a vehicle can eventually be monitored, while in the SINIAV monitoring is the rule. This wide option for monitoring by default can be found in Resolution 212/2006 when it states that "the SINIAV shall be implemented in all national territory" and the ones in charge of the implementation and management of this system are the states traffic authorities, thus creating a huge centralized database with information of "identified or identifiable persons" with no possible opt-out.

One could argue that since the SINIAV uses only RFId technologies it is less effective (and less dangerous) in terms of "mobile surveillance" than the systems which use other geolocalization technologies, as recognized by David Lyon (Lyon, 2009: 13). Nonetheless, through the interconnection of the information processed by SINIAV with other governmental databases already under control of the Brazilian National Traffic Department, it will be possible to use the system not only for geolocalization purposes but also for law enforcement purposes, for imposing sanctions to drivers or even to collect taxes. David Lyon presents two interesting examples which show how locational information of vehicles can be used for law enforcement:

On-board navigation systems for cars, transponders for electronic tolls at bridges or tunnels or on private highways, and the increasing use of 'black box' sensors in cars offer multiple possibilities for generation mobile data. California resident Scott Knight, for example, was convicted in 2001 after a hit-and-run death when his OnStar system reported an airbag inflation. And Acme Rent-a-Car in New Haven fined drivers $150 when their GPS system showed they had been consistently speeding (Schawartz 2003). (Lyon, 2009: 17)

There is also the possibility that information processed under the SINIAV framework is transferred to private parties, as has been the case with other databases managed by the Brazilian National Traffic Department,[27] since this kind of information is very useful for some industries. For example, "How fast the driver was traveling could affect insurance premiums or invoices from car rental companies" (Lyon, 2009: 24).

Despite all the concerns about privacy and data protection that arose when analyzing the SINIAV, no judicial action against it or the regulation which established the system has been brought in Brazilian courts but probably it is due to the fact that SINIAV has not been implemented yet.

Nonetheless, taking into account the lack of a general legal data protection framework and the potential risks to privacy and data protection imposed by SINIAV, the debate over the development of a Brazilian legal framework on data protection and over the legitimacy of SINIAV should be pushed to the political arena.

CONCLUSION

The implementation of vehicle monitoring in Brazil is not an isolated phenomenon in terms of government projects that deal with large amounts of personal data, as the above-mentioned unique ID for all citizens or the biometric identification of all voters. In spite of the fact that each of these initiatives has a specific background and justification, they all share the fact that they can originate gigantic databases with personal data.

These new databases are being drawn in a scenario without a developed framework of data protection laws. In such a case, the potential danger in every single treatment of personal data is concrete, and a initiative of a major scale as SINIAV present an even greater risk. The technocratic argument behind the vehicle monitoring leaves little room (if any) to privacy concerns. As we have mentioned, until this moment no specific public concern about surveillance and monitoring has leveled up the debate about liberty and control and the use of new monitoring technologies.

The first signs of what is happening with vehicle monitoring in Brazil indicate that citizens are probably not as passive to surveillance as this set of public policies tends to point out. The very possibility of being monitored inside a car and with an obligatory tool paid by the car's owner seems to have surpassed a maximum limit and raised some real counter-arguments which are already included in the judiciary discussions about these monitoring initiatives.

Such discussions, although, are less based on considerations about the complex situation that rounds the monitoring systems than in particular considerations about the cost and the details of the system itself. Such arguments tend to disappear if the project tries to evade these concerns, while continuing to affect directly the privacy of citizens.

The real point and the real concern about monitoring systems, such as those described here, are in fact the ones about personal databases that they create. Their management is complex and risky, and the lack of specific regulation about data protection is surely an indication that problems tend to happen. The generic data protection provisions in Brazilian law are not able to deal with specific problems regarding data protection, and the development of such a regulation must be the first obligatory step to make debatable the vehicle monitoring systems envisaged.[28] Such discussion about privacy, data protection and vehicle monitoring, as said before, has to be brought to the political arena, which is the only adequate forum.

REFERENCES

Bessa, L. R. (2003). O Consumidor e os Limites dos Bancos de Dados de Crédito. São Paulo, Brazil: Revista dos Tribunais.

Doneda, D. (2006). *Da privacidade à proteção de dados pessoais*. Rio de Janeiro: Renovar.

Doneda, D., & Viola, M. (2009). *Risk and Personal Information: The Finality Principle and Data Protection in the Brazilian Legal System. RBRS International (RBRSi)* (pp. 133–149). Rio de Janeiro: Funenseg.

Ducatel, K., Bogdanowicz, M., Scapolo, F., Leijten, J., & Burgelman, J.-C. (2001). European Commission. Scenarios for Ambient Intelligence in 2010. Final Report. Retrieved February 4, 2010, from http://jbr.org/articles.html http://www.ist.hu/doctar/fp5/istagscenarios2010.pdf

Ley, D. (2007). Ubiquitous Computing. Emerging Technologies for Learning, (Vol. 2). Retrieved February 4, 2010, from http://schools.becta.org.uk/upload-dir/downloads/page_documents/research/emerging_technologies07_chapter6.pdf

Lyon, D. (2009). *Identifying citizens*. Cambridge, UK: Polity Press.

Lyon, D. (2010). Why where you are matters: mundane mobilities, transparent technologies, and digital discrimination. In Firmino, R., Duarte, F., & Ultramari, C. (Eds.), *ICTs for Mobile and Ubiquitous Urban Infrastructures: Surveillance, Locative Media and Global Networks*. Hershey, PA: IGI Global.

Rodotà, S. (1995). *Tecnologie e diritti*. Bologna, Italy: Il Mulino.

Rodotà, S. (2008). *A vida na sociedade da vigilância. Privacidade hoje*. Rio de Janeiro, Brazil: Renovar.

Saint-Exupery, A. (2009). Internet of Things – Strategic Research Roadmap. Retrieved February 4, 2010, from http://www.sintef.no/upload/IKT/9022/CERP-IoT%20SRA_IoT_v11_pdf.pdf

Solove, D. (2008). *Understanding Privacy*. Cambridge, MA: Harvard University Press.

Weiser, M. (1991). The computer for the 21st century. Scientific American. Retrieved February 4, 2010, from http://www.ubiq.com/hypertext/weiser/SciAmDraft3.html

Westin, A. F., & Baker, M. A. (1972). *Databanks in a Free Society – Computers, Record-Keeping and Privacy. Report of the Project on Computer Databanks of the United States National Academy of Sciences*. New York: Quadrangle Books.

ADDITIONAL READING

al Bisso, G. (Ed.). (2000). *Dati Sensibili e Soggetti Pubblici: Commento Sistematico al D.Lgs. 135/1999: Comment e Casi Pratici*. Milan, Italy: Giuffrè Editore.

Arteaga Botello, N. (2009). Sociedad de la vigilancia en el Sur-Global. Ciudad de Mexico: Porrúa.

Bénédicte, H., & Lacoste, A. (2001). Les flux transfrontaliers de données à caractère personnel en droit européen. Journal des Tribunaux. *Droit Européen*, *9*(84), 241–248.

Bennett, C. (2008). *The privacy advocates*. Cambridge: MIT Press.

Bennett, C., & Lyon, D. (Eds.). (2008). *Playing the identity card*. London: Routledge.

Hijmans, H., & Scirocco, A. (2009). *Shortcomings in EU Data Protection in the Third and the Second Pillars. Can the Lisbon Treaty be Expected to Help? Common Market Law Review 46* (pp. 1485–1525). Netherlands: Kluwer Law.

Lyon, D. (2001). *Surveillance society: Monitoring everyday life*. Buckingham: Open Univ. Press.

Lyon, D. (Ed.). (2003). *Surveillance as a social sorting: Privacy, risk and digital discrimination*. New York: Routledge.

Lyon, D. (2007). *Surveillance studies: An overview*. Cambridge: Polity Press.

Mumford, L. (1934). *Technics and civilization*. New York: Harcourt.

Mumford, L. (1998). *A cidade na história: suas origens, transformações e perspectivas*. São Paulo: Companhia das Letras.

Poullet, Y; Peres Asinan, M. V. (2004). Données des voyageurs aériens: le débat Europe - États-Unis. Journal des Tribunaux, Droit Européen. N° 113 - 12e année.

Sarmento e Castro, C. (2005). *Direito da informática, privacidade e dados pessoais*. Coimbra: Almedina.

Solove, D. (2007). *The future of reputation*. New Haven: Yale Univ. Press.

Vagelis, P., & De Hert, P. (2009). *The PNR Agreement and transatlantic anti-terrorism co-operation: no firm human rights framework on either side of the Atlantic. Common Market Law Review 46* (pp. 885–919). Netherlands: Kluwer Law.

Viola, M. (2009). *Privacidade e seguro: a coleta e utilização de dados nos ramos de pessoas e de saúde*. Rio de Janeiro: Funenseg.

Viola, M. (2010). Data Protection and Insurance: The Limits on the Collection and Use of Personal Data on Insurance Contracts in EU Law. Global Jurist: Vol. 10: Iss. 1 (Topics), Article 6.

ENDNOTES

1 In order to illustrate the indispensability of automated data processing, it is worth mentioning an experience also linked to the automotive sector: in 1970, the New York Department of Motor Vehicles managed information about 8.3 million drivers and 7.2 million vehicles (including information about licensing, insurance and fines) in a manual archiving structure that has been impossible to deal with due to the annual increase of 5% to 6% in the New York City fleet. Before the computerization of the service, the annual licensing of a new car used to take months (see WESTIN and BAKER, 1972).

2 In the United States, the Secretary for Health, Education and Welfare conducted a study very influential in the area, which found a direct relationship between privacy and the treament of personal data, and the need to establish the rule of individual control over his/her own information. This control would be accomplished through collaterals, such as that:"- There should not be a system for storage of personal information with its existence being kept secret. - There should be a way for an individual to discover what information about him/her is contained in a record and which way it is used. - There should be a way for an individual to protect the information about him/her from being collected for a particular purpose and used or made available for other purposes without his/her knowledge. - There should be a way for an individual to correct or amend a record of information about him/her.- Every organization that structures, maintains, uses or disclosures records containing personal data must assure the reliability of the data for the intended purposes, and should take precautions to prevent the misuse of such data. See Records, computers and the rights

of citizens. Report of the Secretary's Advisory Committee on Automated Personal Data Systems (1973) available at: http://aspe.hhs.gov/DATACNCL/1973privacy/tocprefacemembers.htm.

3 Convention 108 of the Council of Europe - Convention for the Protection of Individuals with regard to automatic treatment of personal data.

4 Guidelines on the Protection of Privacy and Transborder Flows of Personal Data. Available at http://www.oecd.org/document/18/0,2340,en_2649_34255_1815186_1_1_1_1,00.html.

5 In Argentina, there is Law 25326, and Uruguay has recently enacted the Law 18331, a norm of data protection similar to the one in Argentina.

6 The words of Maria Celina Bodin de Moraes in the introduction to the Portuguese version of Stefano Rodota's (2008: 12) A Vida na Sociedade da Vigilância have a similar tone: "The Brazilian choice, however, has not yet been made. It is expected that the same respect for human dignity, ratified in Article 1, III of our Constitution and the civilian tradition existent in our legal system, combined with the so-called globalization through rights, may allow the proximity to the European model through a legislation based on principles."

7 Resolution 212/2006 – CONTRAN. Available at http://www.denatran.gov.br/download/Resolucoes/RESOLUCAO_212.rtf.

8 Registro único de identidade civil.

9 "The term 'Internet of Things' could be defined as a dynamic global network infrastructure with self configuring capabilities based on standard and interoperable communication protocols where physical and virtual "things" have identities, physical attributes, and virtual personalities and use intelligent interfaces, and are seamlessly integrated into the information network" (Saint-Exupery, 2009).

10 "Ubiquitous computing is a vision of computing power 'invisibly' embedded in the world around us and accessed through intelligent interfaces: 'Its highest ideal is to make a computer so embedded, so fitting, so natural, that we use it without even thinking about it'" (Ley, 2007). See also Weiser (1991).

11 "Ambient Intelligence (AmI) stems from the convergence of three key technologies: Ubiquitous Computing, Ubiquitous Communication, and Intelligent User Friendly Interfaces. According to the vision statement, on convergence humans will be surrounded by intelligent interfaces supported by computing and networking technology which is everywhere, embedded in everyday objects such as furniture, clothes, vehicles, roads and smart materials even particles of decorative substances like paint. AmI implies a seamless environment of computing, advanced networking technology and specific interfaces. It is aware of the specific characteristics of human presence and personalities, takes care of needs and is capable of responding intelligently to spoken or gestured indications of desire, and even can engage in intelligent dialogue" (Ducatel et al., 2001).

12 A preliminary version of this session of the chapter was published in Doneda, D.; Viola, M. Risk and Personal Information: The Finality Principle and Data Protection in the Brazilian Legal System. (2009). RBRS International (RBRSi). Rio de Janeiro: Funenseg.

13 Communication from the Commission (CommissionCOM[2008] 886 final) – Action Plan for the Deployment of Intelligent Transport Systems in Europe, p.3.

14 Communication from the Commission (COM[2008] 886 final) – Action Plan for the Deployment of Intelligent Transport Systems in Europe, p.3.

15 Recital 3 of the Proposal for a Directive of the European Parliament and of the Council laying down the framework for the deployment of Intelligent Transport Systems in the field of road transport and for interfaces with other transport modes (2008/0263 [COD]).

16 Annex II of the Proposal for a Directive of the European Parliament and of the Council laying down the framework for the deployment of Intelligent Transport Systems in the field of road transport and for interfaces with other transport modes (2008/0263 [COD]). P. 22. "(b) The definition of the necessary measures to use innovative ITS technologies (Radio Frequency Identification Devices (RFID) or Galileo/Egnos) in the realisation of ITS applications (notably the tracking and tracing or freight along its journey and across modes) for freight transport logistics (eFreight) (…)".

17 Commission Staff Working Document accompanying document to the Communication from the Commission: Action Plan for the Deployment of Intelligent Transport Systems in Europe and the Proposal for a Directive of the European Parliament and of the Council laying down the framework for the deployment of Intelligent Transport Systems in the field of road transport and their interfaces with other transport modes – Summary of the Impact Assessment {COM(2008) 886 final}; {COM(2008) 887 final}; {SEC(2008) 3083}. P. 2.

18 Directive 95/46/EC of the European Parliament and of the Council of 24 October 1995 on the protection of individuals with regard to the processing of personal data and on the free movement of such data.

19 Directive 2002/58/EC of the European Parliament and of the Council of 12 July 2002 concerning the processing of personal data and the protection of privacy in the electronic communications sector.

20 Directive 2006/24/EC of the European Parliament and of the Council of 15 March 2006 on the retention of data generated or processed in connection with the provision of publicly available electronic communications services or of public communications networks and amending Directive 2002/58/EC

21 The three former pillars of the European Union were: 1) Community; 2) Common Foreign and Security Policy (CFSP); and, 3) Police and Judicial Co-operation in Criminal Matters (PJCC).

22 Regulation (EC) n° 45/2001 of the European Parliament and of the Council of 18 December 2000 on the protection of individuals with regard to the processing of personal data by the Community institutions and bodies and on the free movement of such data

23 Council Framework Decision 2008/977/JHA of 27 November 2008 on the protection of personal data processed in the framework of police and judicial cooperation in criminal matters.

24 Communication from the Commission (COM[2008] 886 final) – Action Plan for the Deployment of Intelligent Transport Systems in Europe, p.2.

25 Ação Civil Pública n° 2009.61.00.007033-0. 7ª Vara Federal, SP, j. 16.04.2009.

26 For an analysis of the different facets of the right to privacy see SOLOVE, D. (2008).

27 INSTRUÇÃO NORMATIVA DENATRAN N° 01, of 9 December 2003.

28 The Brazilian Ministry of Justice announced during the International Seminar "Desafios e Perspectivas para a Proteção de Dados no Brasil" in August 2010, that it would open to public consultation a draft bill of a general data protection law.

Chapter 19
Urban Surveillance in Mexico

Nelson Arteaga-Botello
Universidad Autónoma del Estado de México, Mexico

ABSTRACT

In this chapter, the symbolic cultural dimension of technology and surveillance technologies in two cities and two commercial centers in central Mexico will be explored, especially the various Closed Circuit Television Systems (CCTV). This will allow the analysis of the way in which these technologies have made viable specific ways of sorting and governance of public and private spaces in the country. This document then examines the relationship established between the symbolic meanings given to these surveillance technologies in said urban spaces. Included is a series of observations and interviews of those in charge of these systems.

INTRODUCTION

During the last 10 years, an important increase in the installation of closed-circuit television (CCTV) in Mexico has been observed, both in public and private spaces. This is a response from government authorities, as well as from private administration instances, to the growing feeling of insecurity dealing with crime and delinquency experienced by the population. Although this can be seen in some spaces of Mexico (Arteaga Botello, 2007), it does not turn out to be a generalized rule as yet. In the case of the municipalities analyzed in this document, Tlalnepantla and Toluca (located in the state of Mexico), CCTV has been used, initially, as a tool for urban management, the organization of transit ways, as well as the supervision of public services (such as potable water, drainage and electricity). Subsequently, the usage of surveillance systems has been modified, being directed toward the supposed prevention of offenses and crime. Another transformation in the utilization of CCTV can be observed in the case of commercial centers – which are also examined in this paper. Being installed for the maintaining and securing of these spaces, surveillance systems

DOI: 10.4018/978-1-60960-051-8.ch019

were directed towards the supervision of daily activities of employees, the social classification of their visitors, as well as the harmonization with other systems of public management of the municipalities.

Traditionally, this shift in the routine applied to CCTVs has been attributed by the system´s operators as a natural consequence, on one side, to the viewing capacity given by the cameras and on the other, to the information and data offered. In a certain way, the metamorphoses can be explained as driven by the technological capacity that surveillance systems have on their own. In this document a critique of this vision is given, highlighting the fact that such metamorphosis responds to the symbolic weight given to the video cameras instead of their actual capacity to see.

In the same way as what happened with the introduction of computers after the Second World War (Alexander, 2006), CCTVs perform a speech on which they are considered salvation as far as they allow the apparent organization of social life, the rationalization of public and private spaces, apart from guaranteeing the reduction to a minimum of crime and disruptive acts. Its usage, in this way, is framed on the notion of technology as a sacred object. This analysis proposes, following the developments of cultural sociology by Jeffrey C. Alexander (2000), that surveillance put in place through the use of CCTV, in the cases outlined here, respond more to the logic of a symbolic network, than to its "technological capacities". In this sense, videosurveillance cameras are signs of a cultural framework; and the cameras operators, determined by this framework, give a special meaning to this technology. This explanation attempts to distance itself from the idea that social transformation is based on technological development and the utilitarian approach, which considers CCTV as the only logical answer to the problems of public insecurity. The camera operator works from the basis of a symbolic social framework and not from the logic of the rationalization of space in the urban and commercial environment.

A PERSPECTIVE ANALYSIS

Technology is inserted in the cultural narratives as an element that guarantees the organization and the rationality of social relations –transforming ordinary language of complex systems into a numeric meaning–, taking for granted that which responds to a certain objective materiality. In this way, concerns such as risk, security, well-being, social classification, as well as its legitimacy or illegitimacy, can be revised from specific cultural structures, who have inserted the use of technologies (Alexander & Smith, 2000), in particular those oriented to surveillance –such as CCTV, although not exclusively.

CCTV is found immersed –as technological instruments– in the logic of meaning that opposes the world of negative and positive signs. As stated by Alexander (2000), in the case of the use of computers after the Second World War, these were considered both as a salvation (its role would be important to human development), as well as an element of destruction: simultaneously, they were conceived as gods and demons. The computer represented, therefore, a sacred and mysterious object, which contributed to the fact that it was outside the contact of ordinary people, and its use reserved for a group of experts. But also, the computer, as stated by Alexander (2000), produced much fear, and generated the idea of the alienation of people, generating the feeling of slavery, as though its presence will destroy the foundations of society. This eschatological vindication certainly has changed much with the introduction of the personal computer, turning this technological development into a routine object, and each time more divested of the positive and negative characteristics of which were provided in the beginning.

Electronic technologies, in this sense, would not be in and of themselves regarded as empirical, objects and rational references, but the transference from a myth to scientific forms. In this way, CCTV's, as well as computers during the middle of the last century, are symbolic representations of mysterious powers of good and evil (Alexander & Smith, 2000). Therefore, surveillance technologies would not be activated thanks to the logic of a rational organization, tending to order and administer quantitatively the public and private spaces, but which are registered within a deep network of cultural significations. The rationalization, in any case, should be understood as the result of an emission of symbolic networks more than an explanation in itself.

According to Alexander (2000), we could define that symbolic network as culture: an organized placement of symbolic parameters significantly understood and institutionalized. Culture will be made up by solid relationship structures, independent of any voluntary act of any particular actor. Parting from this, CCTV's–like other surveillance technologies– are, paraphrasing Alexander (2000), objects charged with meanings linked to others; but, above all, are significant, cultural codes. Its structure is found marked in the distinction between the sacred and the profane. The sacred remains, by its nature, isolated permanently from society. Society maintains its separation with respect to the understanding of how CCTV functions, how it is administered and in what manner cities are administered with them. In some way, this separation guarantees the conservation of that which is sacred of CCTV, keeping it away from the world of the profane.

To this idea, the operators of these systems contribute, avoiding, as much as possible, the contamination, which could produce a characterization of the profane. By keeping CCTV as a symbolic sacred reference, it lends itself to a meaning of good, consolidating in both symbolic references signs that reestablish or guarantee the linking of communities and the protection of the group. On the other side, the profane shows the image of evil, drawing the borders of a place where social relationships should be restored after its decomposition, manifesting itself in crime and delinquency. In this sense, for those who encourage the installation of CCTV and, of course, for those who support these measures, surveillance technologies are the mechanism for avoiding social collapse.

The constructions of networks of meaning around CCTV have effects in the real world. As will be shown in this document, videosurveillance systems enable the specific organization of public and private space, even though it doesn't necessarily respond to the rational organizational criteria, which are supposed to stem from technology in a natural way (particularly from its capacity to obtain clearer images of people in social groups). In the cases analyzed here, when the operators say "to be surprised" at the capacity obtained from CCTV's, its meaning results from their own feelings that the cameras expand their view when considering that they can observe almost anything both in public and private spaces. In this way, the exploration of new fields for the utilization of video cameras is not only determined by its technical capacity, but by a network of cultural meanings in which they are immersed, and there are facts that can be foreseen in organizational forms of different social spaces.

In the cases we refer to, CCTV's are not only mere mechanisms of support to other devices – *dispositif,* in terms of Foucault (1980)– of spatial organization, and become themselves symbolic objects, affecting the arrangement of spaces and establishing forms of social classification. This transformation responds to the acquired meaning of CCTV, as devices referred with a capacity for amplification of vision, for both public and private administrations. Additionally, this may seem to typify social behaviors tending to facilitate social sorting. In this way, the symbolic meaning results in a motor that transforms the use of CCTV: above this irrational base of social sorting where the pretend rationalization of social spaces analyzed here is constructed.

It's important to point out that surveillance as a form of social sorting becomes relevant in modern societies. In this sense, the formation of surveillance societies can be observed. This concept can refer to those societies in which "routine, systematic ubiquitous, identifying, checking, monitoring, tracking and recording of everyday activities, communications and exchanges have become commonplace" (Lyon, 2004: 130). This is carried out by specific institutions, which utilize certain technologies in accordance to specific protocol, justifying ways of governance and management. In surveillance societies, the installation of observation and data gathering technologies had as a goal to ensure convenience, comfort, efficiency, productivity, speed and security (Lyon, 2010). In this way, surveillance technology mediation appears to be based on the legitimacy of the significant discourses.

In this sense, says Alexander (2000), the cultural signs turn themselves into the medium for social meaning. In the same way, surveillance technologies are mediated by technologies with the highest symbolic meaning within themselves (Lyon, 2004). Culturally, then, during the last century, surveillance societies have legitimized the automation of "watching", based on the trust of these technologies, supposing a "logic of technology" (Lyon, 2010: 3). The cultural consequences of surveillance societies, according to David Lyon (2004), may be observed in three areas: fear, suspicion, and secrecy. In this way, there would be a "culture of fear", "culture of suspicion", and "culture of secrecy" –each with particular social meaning. These three cultures have recently been extended and deepened with the expansion of surveillance technologies, both by public and private entities, allowing a social sorting and categorization, based on cultural stereotypes. Within the cities, financial or commercial centers, the sign of instability is that which is "out of place": young people, the underclass, migrants, and political activists.

In the following analysis, this interpretation becomes relevant, since it permits, thanks to these circles of inclusion/exclusion, by surveillance technologies mediated as cultural marks dividing society in two worlds, legitimized by a mythology: the sacred (security, well-being, efficiency, order, legitimacy, rationality) and the profane (fear, suspicion, and deviants). At the same time, the symbolic borders of space are drawn: "safe" or "unsafe" places. To demonstrate this, in the following, it will be shown how these cultural meanings allow the justification and the utilization of surveillance technologies in the case of the two cities and two shopping centers in Mexico.

TRAFFIC LIGHTS, CRIME AND POLITICS: A GENEALOGY OF CCTV

The initial purpose of the CCTV's installed in the case of the municipality of Tlalnepantla and Toluca (two municipalities located in the center of Mexico, the first of these is actually part of the Mexico City metropolitan area and the second is about 70 km from it), is situated in monitoring the flow of traffic in its streets and avenues. However, little by little they were used in an attempt to slow down public insecurity, and even as devices which help social sorting.

In Tlalnepantla, the surveillance of urban space began with the installation of a traffic light control system. Based on a traffic study, public organizations, supported by private ones, determined the rate of vehicle affluence to specific hours of the day in streets considered problematic, allowing, with this, the programming of traffic lights, which, at the same time, allow the design of a general transit plan for the municipality. As stated by one of the operators, the system begins to work automatically, giving "… a way out to the south to all roads […]. It is the same in the afternoon, the plan automatically changes to give a way out or back in to all of the avenues" (Operator, Centro de Semaforización (Traffic Light Center) and Tlalnepantla call center, State of Mexico, 2 June 2009). This system is designed to send a program signal to a specific traffic light, executing a change of color according to the necessities of the automobile traffic flow.

According to the operators of the automatic traffic light system, the above results in a great advance in the organizational traffic flow in the municipality, since street officers do not control the functioning or the lights nor can modify at their own will the timings of the them, since they lack a complete vision of traffic arrangements. In addition to this, the automatic traffic light system can be adapted to the necessities and future demands, since, as the operators mention, when they began to observe that the timings in the traffic lights are insufficient to relieve the flow of automobiles, the company who designed the system is requested to complete a new study of vehicle capacity, based on which the person in charge of the traffic lights, indicates new necessities: "change the timings of this traffic light or […] put a traffic light with an extra turn" (Operator, Centro de Semaforización (Traffic Light Center) and Tlalnepantla call center, State of Mexico, 4 June 2009).

On the other hand, the automatic traffic light system, working by codes and cartographic references, indicate the situation of traffic in real time, in Abstract Type Data (TAD, Spanish acronym) observation of that which in reality is causing the traffic jams. That is why it was decided to install CCTV, set up as a tool to support the work of the traffic light system, even though little by little it has been doing other activities especially in the manner of public security. In effect, by principle, fourteen cameras were installed at points where a recurrence of traffic flow conflicts was detected, for which a majority of the devices remain in the largest and busiest avenues and streets in the municipality. However, as stated by the operators, as time went by the amplitude of the use of CCTV was evident, since it allowed, among other things, the ability to give support to emergency units (ambulances and civil protection units) and public security (patrols, especially), directing them to the needed places. In fact, the coordination between the automatic traffic light system and CCTV had been guaranteed when, for example:

[…] [if] we have the position of a vehicle with the intention of escaping [for having committed a crime], a police officer tells us: you know what, the vehicle is going on Mario Colin towards Gustavo Baz. We confirmed with the camera and we put [the traffic lights] in red and not green. Why in red? Because the natural flow will stop the vehicle and will allow our units to arrive on adjacent streets, to capture him. We would be monitoring this constantly with the camera (Operator, Centro de Semaforización (Traffic Light Center) and Tlalnepantla call center, State of Mexico, 1 June 2009).

On the other hand, CCTV also functions as a mechanism to watch social protests heading toward government buildings, which allows the establishment of transit police operations, reorganizing the sequence of traffic lights and, of course, monitoring the necessities, and keeping an eye on their organization and the direction they are taking, as well as identifying leaders and certain protesters, preventing any eventuality. In the future, the installation of more video cameras is planned depending on the results which are shown by traffic circulation statistics and automobile accidents, as well as rates of delinquency generated in the different areas of the municipality.

Despite all of this, it must be stated, that the CCTV in Tlalnepantla presents a technical difficulty, consisting of the recording, which is analog (VHS) and not digital (in a hard-drive, for example). Therefore when an incident or anomaly considered relevant is reported or noted – an apparent robbery or a report of an automobile driving in a suspicious manner–, the recording is immediately activated and only if it turns out to be something classified as important the recording is saved; otherwise, it is erased, since the capacity to save video is very reduced. This, however, is not considered by the people in charge as a large problem, considering that video surveillance systems do not guarantee, according to them, the decrease in delinquency, but only, the administration of risk in determined spaces. In other words, the lack of a digital CCTV system does not represent for them an obstacle, since such devices have, from their perspective, a very short reach in the reduction of crime. As the operators of CCTV in Tlalnepantla state:

[...] [delinquency] is measurable but not approachable: if I do this then this happens. Remember that delinquency is a product of a social condition of the country, so several times it can be maintained in average but not decreased. He has been able to be deterred. Someway security fences are created (with the support of video cameras), so we know that in this zone where we have operations, where we have that camera, etc., people can walk peacefully (Operator, Centro de Semaforización (Traffic Light Center) and Tlalnepantla call center, State of Mexico, 6 June 2009).

The CCTV, therefore, is conceived as a tool to support public security, but not the only one or the most effective. Because of this, the municipality has figured out other types of mechanisms, specifically a call center, with the objective of responding to the demands of public security and emergencies, in addition to guaranteeing the satisfaction of public services, such as water supply, the malfunctioning of drainage, the problems of public wiring, paving or potholes. For that, the call center is joined to the CCTV, so, if a call is received to notify the presence of a person or of some suspicious vehicle on an avenue or street, and the place stated is in the individual reach of the cameras, it is monitored –in the case of a vehicle, license plates are checked –and at the same time, a police patrol is sent and any movement is supervised.

Furthermore, joined to traffic lights and CCTV devices, the municipality developed a database with information obtained from the call center. In this way, when someone uses the center, the telephone number is identified as well as the type of line, the name of the owner of the line, its location and the number of the citizen with which they can be identified; in fact, if that caller has called the center before, a history will be registered of these calls. This generates a search, by the operators, of the articulation of one of the different forms of surveillance (automated traffic light system, CCTV, call center) in a large data base which would have as an aim to interconnect and manipulate information, in order to increase the rate of the prevention of delinquency, to detect the zones considered to be of high traffic risk, to control the services provided by the municipality and to provide a statistic of the people who request attention in the matters of emergencies or complaints of different types.

In this way, when linking these different technologies, the aim is the harmonization of surveillance, connecting information, databases and networks of communication from the observation of spaces, social groups and even including individuals, and with it, forms of organization of police activity itself, tending to prevent probable risky situations or reacting previous to dangerous situations. For its part, these links create governing mechanisms of spaces and populations, sorting, administrating and controlling spaces and populations, whose behavior, attitudes, faces and aspects can potentially be analyzed to prevent apparent risks, which could be related to traffic saturation, robberies on the street, and movements of social protest; risks to which, to begin with, are either dealt with individually by a surveillance technology which, later on, is added to another one, articulating and connecting between them.

In the case of Toluca, as in Tlalnepantla, CCTV started with the intention of controlling vehicle transit and avenue organization. In 2005 a computerized traffic light system was installed, a project which considered the centralization of traffic light control located in one hundred thirty nine traffic intersections, grew in parallel with sixty nine devices that interconnect them, which allows this sequencing of traffic control devices. However, the system installed in the city has the same problem as the one in Tlalnepantla: it's impossible to know with precision what causes traffic jams, since it could be an automobile parked over a detector, generating information which indicates a traffic problem when in reality none exist.

In order to overcome this problem, a CCTV system was used since the images obtained by cameras can prove if there is a real traffic problem or simply a vehicle sending distorted data. In this way, the program of installing automatic traffic lights was carried out along with the setting up of seven cameras connected to a main center through a digital quality radio communication system. The connection includes the generation of images, their transmission and processing. Of the seven cameras, six were positioned in the first quarter of the city, with the objective of improving vehicle control and guaranteeing to decongest the avenues in this zone: the leftover camera was set up outside the first quarter of the city, right across from the most important market, to support, this way, the analysis of traffic flow in this area of the city.

On the other hand, with time, CCTV was attributed the ability to see "almost everything", which led to their programming in order to make a visual tour not only in the traffic light intersections, but also to direct them towards nearby businesses or difficult traffic intersections. This permitted, with time to use them, as a tool to reconstruct automobile accidents –even though the images captured by the CCTV are only available if there is a legal order for information on behalf of the Ministerio Público (Attorney General). This took place, as stated by the operators, when there was an overturned car in front of the city government palace. The accident occurred in the morning, when a car went through a red light and collided with another, which had the green light. The interesting point is that those who operate the system did not see the accident, but a camera recorded the event, since at that moment it was focused on the intersection. Once the legal order from the attorney general arrived, the digital database of the CCTV was checked to establish who was responsible for causing the event.

All in all, the CCTV is not only linked to these functions: from its reprogramming, it has also been utilized in the matter of public security. The cameras, programmed to perform inspection tours, had been orientated on several occasions by the operators towards small groups of people, for example, in front of commercial storefronts. From that point on, there began the monitoring of the actions of certain types of thieves, in particular muggers. If such behaviors are detected, the police are notified so they can send the personnel necessary and stop the presumed delinquent. When an operation of this type takes place, it is recorded in order to gather evidence of the facts. However this type of information is only used in the jurisdiction of the municipality. That is the reason why, if a crime is committed in a state jurisdiction, the information doesn't flow in an immediate manner, but it is transmitted slowly to the interior of the communication structures by means of the hierarchy and governmental organization.

The CCTV system is utilized, also to observe and follow social and political protests in the municipality. On one hand, the surveillance of these movements pretends to notify about the way that traffic is affected by these movements: the data is transmitted to local radio stations so that they can inform the population about the options for circulating with less difficulty, communicating the location and direction of protesters, as well as the state of the avenues and alternative routes to those which are found affected. On the other hand, when social and political movements arrive to the center of the city, in particular to the government palace, they are watched: if demonstrators are observed, as well as their leaders, and measures are taken to avoid incidents which put in risk the "public peace", a procedure that, is not carried out when social protests are heading towards other governmental buildings other than those of the municipality, such as the state government palace or the chamber of deputies. When this happens, a constant surveillance is not carried out,

[...] [suddenly] it is seen what they are doing, and if they are tranquil, the Avenue keeps being monitored. Then the place of the protest is focused on again. The camera is not left focused on that spot permanently, because any other situation that may require attention could take place at any moment in the surroundings (Operator, Centro de Semaforización (Traffic Light Center) and Toluca call center, State of Mexico, 6 August 1, 2009).

On a majority of occasions, what is done is to follow the whole manifestation or social protest along the avenues, which allows the defining of organizational strategies for vehicle transit: "[...] here we have to keep an eye on where they go" (Operator, Centro de Semaforización (Traffic Light Center) and Toluca call center, State of Mexico, August 15, 2009). It should be noted, for example, the importance obtained by the CCTV when the planning out of the evacuation of three thousand business people located in the esplanade of an important market located behind the central bus terminal that connects Toluca with the rest of the country. As mentioned previously, in the original CCTV system plan, the installation of a video camera there was considered in order to have a clear view of the traffic problems in this zone, which became much worse on Fridays, a day in which, since 1972, a large number of business people gathered, but at the same time, to detect robberies in this place, because of the high number of clients and vendors.

So then, when the decision to evict the street vendors as an only solution for traffic congestion in the zone was carried out, and to guarantee with that the proper functioning of avenues as well as the bus station itself, a camera installed in the area was used in order to define the strategy for police activities, and in that way ensure tactical support for the unavoidable confrontation between the police and the people who would be displaced. The camera installed in the place, therefore, allowed the observation in real time, day and night. It kept track of what happened during the eviction, making it possible to coordinate the different police forces –municipal and state– since an adequate communication system was needed between the municipal and state governments, given the magnitude of the action taking place. In fact, at the moment of the eviction, the camera detected from above the gathering of different groups of street vendors at the market esplanade, which allowed the participating policemen to define a strategy in order to isolate them, break them up and that way reduce their strength and their resources to confront or resist the police.

Moreover, the cameras located in the different avenue intersections of the city, made it possible to monitor the mobilization towards the city center by the street vendors after the evacuation as a protest, and whose destination was the municipal and state government buildings. By means of the surveillance cameras, it was possible to observe the street vendors leaving the area and their mobilization through the different streets of the city, noticing also that a smaller group was heading towards the CCTV control center with the intention of sabotaging it, since they knew of the existence of cameras and assumed the protest was being recorded to identify alleged leaders as well as active participants in the movement, and that way carry out a judicial order against them.

In addition, the installation of twenty security cameras in different city points considered as "strategic" was announced in 2008. The objective of having such cameras would be,

[...] [to] virtually fence in the municipality, and in this way offer more security to the public, and know who goes in and out of the territory [...] [in addition to] to inform more immediately [sic] about traffic jams in the city, in order to promote traffic flow as well as to verify the performance of traffic officers and of course, to detect any illicit

acts. [...] the usefulness of these cameras can be greater, since it is possible to clearly identify car license numbers, or verify any other information related to the vehicle such as the fact that it may be stolen (Operator, Centro de Semaforización (Traffic Light Center) and Toluca call center, State of Mexico, 5 August 1, 2009)

In this sense, the CCTV in Toluca –contrary to the one in Tlalnepantla– has a different configuration, based more in the organization of the urban space, directed toward the handling and administration of the flow of the population and transport, at the same time that the surveillance of the development and mobilization of social protests, while in Tlalnepantla, everything indicates that the CCTV is located outside of a wider system of surveillance devices.

In a sense, it can be said that the CCTV analyzed here had been directed, initially, to help support the Intelligent Transport System (SIT, Spanish acronym), which, when providing coded information, are not able to give an account of that which is making vehicular traffic flow difficult, which is the reason why a strengthening of the functioning of the video cameras was needed. This clearly allows the observation that the CCTV had not been installed, at least in these two cases, as an answer to a feeling of insecurity, fear and paranoia with respect to crime, as has happened, for example, in Europe and the United States (Carroll-Mayer, Fairweather, & Carsten Stahl, 2008). However, in Toluca and Tlalnepantla, slowly, these devices have been included in the functioning of public security and traffic, which has generated information that allows the definition of strategies and police tactics, as well as mechanisms of political control.

It must be stated, despite all that, that in the two municipalities, the evolution of CCTV has followed different paths: in the case of Tlalnepantla, a wider group of surveillance technologies, databases, and systems for collecting social and personal information have been connected together. In the case of Toluca, it has more likely adopted a greater independence and an orientation directed above all to the problems of public security. In the first municipality, government authorities search for the perfection of mechanisms and database backup, while in the second, there is a continued expansion of a system in the city under the view of the video cameras.

WATCHING OVER CONSUMERS AND EMPLOYEES: CCTV IN COMMERCIAL CENTERS

The CCTV installed in the commercial centers analyzed here, Mundo E and Galerías Metepec, had started to operate with the objective of preventing crime in their businesses and securing their spaces. With this, they can evolve little by little as devices directed to confronting other types of emergencies: in the case of Mundo E, the surveillance of customers; while in Galerías Metepec, the surveillance of its employees.

Mundo E, as almost any other commercial center, is designed as a consumption area, especially for medium and medium-high social sectors. This implies the circulation of a high number of the population, money and automobiles, which, for those in charge of administering this commercial Plaza implies a challenge. Mundo E also contains some casinos that generate a large circulation of money, all of which explains why in such a center the most important thing is, according to those in charge of its administration, to maintain it as a safe place. In the corporate information of the commercial Plaza, in fact it is defined as one of the installations with the most complete security system, controlled by CCTV and highly qualified personnel.[1]

On the other hand, after carrying out interviews of those in charge of security in the Plaza, two types of risk were established: one towards the users of the Plaza and another towards the functioning and integrity of the facilities. The first type is related with the possible robbery of clients (either to their person or their automobiles), missing persons (and particularly minors), accidents (falls, in general), missing personal objects (specifically handbags or briefcases) and the detection of behavior considered suspicious (in regards to clothing or not having a normal behavior, appropriate for a consumer). This second type of risk refers to the avoidance of payment for certain services provided by the Plaza (such as parking tariffs), damage to building property (graffiti, accidents in the parking lot or the maltreatment of green areas), erratic behavior of people in the parking lot (staying more than 10 minutes inside their automobile), or simply being there for no reason, which in a way he means "not consuming".

It is precisely in regards to these risks that surveillance inside the commercial Plaza is organized. In regards to the first type of risk, the robbing of clients, is controlled through the use of the CCTV and security personnel consisting of private police making rounds, in coordination with video camera operators. In the first two years of the existence of the Plaza, surveillance was done only with the use of private police contracted by the administration, but the installation of the first circuit camera permitted the establishment of a monitoring device which records–even for a short time– possible criminal acts, as well as providing a practical mechanism of deterrence, creating fear among possible delinquents[2].

At the same time, the installation of CCTV in Mundo E had other advantages: it could keep an eye on accidents or medical crisis affecting clients, in addition to being able to follow up the work done by paramedics in the field. The video cameras have also assisted in the search for lost minors, directing security personnel to them, and the location of lost or forgotten objects: with the information provided by the owner, their steps can be reconstructed to determine the moment and location of the lost item or person who may have found the objects in question.

The most important task of these systems, however, is the detection of people who may represent in any moment a danger to the rest of the users of the Plaza. The operators can reference, in this case, people who enter Mundo E, for example, with clothing that does not match the season of the year: "quite loose or large jackets in the summer" (CCTV operator, Mundo E shopping mall, Tlalnepantla, State of Mexico, 1 September, 2009). There are also other criteria for considering who may be suspect: a person who may be stationary for a long time, "[...] let's say, standing in front of a business turning and looking to all sides, and not buying anything" (CCTV operator, Mundo E shopping mall, Tlalnepantla, State of Mexico, 20 September 2009), he is approached and questioned if he is waiting for someone or if he can be helped with something. A similar situation occurs with those people who enter the commercial center with garments identified with certain urban subcultures such as followers of the punk or heavy metal movement, who when crossing any of the commercial Plaza entrances, are immediately identified and followed from one side to the other until they exit the Plaza:

Since it may not be very common for example that a gang member who comes in with torn pants, in other words sloppy, his access is not denied, since it is public, he is followed up on, where he is, where he settles down, recording if he has a suspicious attitude. If not, then, he is left alone, and a report is issued. (CCTV operator, Mundo E shopping mall, Tlalnepantla, State of Mexico, 2 September, 2009).

In fact, when a client matching this accentuated stereotype according to the operators of the CCTV (called "monitoristas" [monitors]) a private guard is immediately sent to "invite" this person to leave the Plaza. However, the monitors don't constantly keep an eye on who enters the commercial Plaza, nor frequently check the behavior of each one of the clients in the Plaza, but in general, direct their view towards sections which represent, according to them a greater risk for the consumer and entertainment: the food court area, escalators and elevators. These three spaces are considered the highest risk, since it's there were more things get lost (the food court, for instance). Also in those areas young people and children present behavior that may put at risk their security (such as playing on the escalators and elevators).

Galerías Metepec shopping center has a surveillance center which handles risk, both in the parking lot and in the interior of the building. From the moment one enters, everyone is subject to the view of the video cameras. Without going too far, when approaching to the machine, which provides the ticket for entering the parking lot, the camera registers the license plate and a frontal view of the automobile; then when taking the ticket, another camera focuses on the face of the driver. In this way, the characteristics of the automobile, (color, make and model), the license plates and the driver are registered, establishing an exact record of the time of entrance thanks to a timer access control. In this way, the six entrances to the parking lot consist –as part of the one hundred ninety video cameras that the shopping center has–the first line of digital video recording, in color, with movement sensors and night vision. That is why Galerías is advertised as a place which, is thinking about "… your security, and has […] with 24 hour closed circuit surveillance and patrols that monitor all day long"[3]. The importance of this resides in the fact that, on one given day during the weekend, for instance, between six and eight at night approximately two thousand four hundred people enter the main entrances of the Plaza.

When this Plaza first opened, there were no types of CCTV, as surveillance was done by means of private police contracted by the administration. However, after three years, the administration installed the first of these circuits with thirty-six video cameras giving them the same level of security as eight other commercial plazas constructed by a large chain of department stores. Nowadays, however, the cameras in this shopping center cover the parking lot, the commercial area and the passages, which connect the warehouses, located at the back of each store. So, there are three risky places in the Plaza where incidents are probable that need to be watched: the parking lot, the commercial area, and passages behind the stores.

In regards to the first of these spaces, the most important responsibility is linked to the loss of tickets, to the people who stay in their automobiles longer then the "reasonable" time and a system for taking care of emergencies distributed within the parking lot, which consists of columns with panic buttons which, when activated, establish an immediate communication with the security body of the establishment, and at the same time automatically focus one of the video cameras towards the alarm. Also, there exist private policeman, which make rounds within the parking lot, according to a preset schedule. In the case of this commercial center, although there haven't been problems with auto parts theft or automobile theft, some people have tried to leave without paying the set fare, attempting even, to break the barriers, which on every occasion, has been registered in a video database allowing the sanctioning, in a majority of the cases, those responsible.

In regards to the risks in the commercial area, the most common are lost objects and children. Just as in Mundo E, in this other Plaza the video cameras can work as the vice is for finding people and objects (handbags, cell phones, wallets, merchandise) or as witness that point out who has picked them up. However though, there are also other risks related to the behavior or the "look" of customers or people who enter the commercial center. Even though it's considered a public place with everyone having access, extra care is taken in regards to those people with some kind of behavior considered abnormal as stated by the operators of the CCTV. People dressed in such a way as to have links with teenage groups, have a particular follow-up, although in the experience of those in charge of monitoring the video cameras, the most problematic are, dealing with certain stereotypes, the so-called *juniors* (middle to upper class youngsters, according to their income, and at times even looked after by bodyguards), since often, they create disorder in the areas next to the cinema and food court (the Plaza has, a bar with billiards and bowling), throwing for instance "stink bombs" in the elevators, which affect the other users of the facilities. To understand this, it must be taken into account that this Plaza is located in the municipality of Metepec, which has one of the largest populations in the region gated communities, which is the reason why the behavior of juniors is something that has to be dealt with constantly.

Additionally, through the monitoring system, shop-lifters have been detected and prosecuted. The third risk area are the passageways behind the stores within the Plaza, where CCTV allows the detection of objects that may block the passage of merchandise or people, and at the same time look after people in case of fire or earthquake, facilitating a rapid exit. Additionally, with the video recordings in this zone, any robbery by employees can be investigated and made evident if necessary. With all, perhaps the most outstanding is that these cameras allow the daily and systematized monitoring of workers in the commercial center, not only observing the hour in which they begin their shifts or the hour in which they leave the establishment, but also, to learn about personal conversations of the employees, confirmed by many of the CCTV operators who have learned to read lips.

The surveillance of these passageways, in addition, has allowed the recording of intimate contact between workers of the stores and even has filmed when couples have had encounters of a sexual nature; information which, later has been given to the owners of the commercial businesses, with the intention of informing them of the activities taking place during the workday, which in some cases, has resulted in the people involved losing their job. In this way, the observation of the passageways not only has the function of security; but also allows the monitoring of the employees, a fact which not even CCTV operators can escape from. There exists a camera that keeps an eye on them, without them knowing the location of this other observer, which could be installed inside the complex's administration offices or in the central control of the corporation on a national level, with offices located in Mexico City.

However, in the particular case of Galerías Metepec, CCTV goes beyond the management of risks within the limits of the space from the entrance to the parking lot to the passageways behind the stores. The Federal Preventive Police, the Federal Agency of Investigation and the State Security Agency of the state of Mexico have entered a contract with those in charge of security in the commercial Plaza, relying on their support to detect people linked to credit and debit card fraud, as well as store robberies in the commercial centers: these different agencies provide photos of people considered suspects of committing illicit acts, alerting the CCTV operators and hoping that during a routine surveillance they may be located.

As described here up to this point, CCTV in shopping centers is established, after their construction and opening, with the objective of guaranteeing, above all, that people can consume with the least number of complications. In the two cases described, the inability of CCTV to halt an illicit act when it's happening is acknowledged; however they allow the keeping of a record of the moment in which the act occurs. In the same way, those who handle such technology, consider that, despite such limitations, CCTV still allows the discouragement of some criminal acts. In the shopping centers, therefore, the fear of possible criminal act in the space designated for buying and selling, has pushed the installation of CCTV, which establishes a clear difference with respect to the cases analyzed by municipal police, were such devices are installed as support for the management of traffic in the streets of the city and are used as instruments to record evidence of criminal acts.

Even though Mundo E and Galerías Metepec are similar spaces, where the use of CCTV would allow the optimization of consumption, they represent noticeable differences in the definition of spaces of risk, which means, those that are considered for surveillance. More over –and this is relevant–, in the last shopping center, surveillance through the use of CCTV goes beyond the mere space for clients and to safeguarding of the conditions for the functioning of the building, since it involves a systematic and everyday observation of the activities of its employees in the passages which are found behind the stores where they work, while allowing, if necessary, the transmission of information obtained to their employers.

There exist, then, in these spaces of consumption, two different ways of management. In the case of Galerías Metepec, a monitoring and control of employees is also carried out, which is different from the other shopping center. However, another difference between the two, is the larger connection that Galerías Metepec has with companies external to the administration environment, such as the collaboration with municipal, state and federal police, who rely on CCTV for the detection of people who have committed fraud and also to keep a follow-up on those suspected of committing other types of illicit acts outside the commercial center. Even though they are not obligated to, such connections to private surveillance companies with public bodies of security and justice represent the management of the population: now the public space has to turn to private population management companies to expand their capacity, in this case, for the detention of presumed delinquents.

In this way, even when CCTV, as a surveillance technology, allows the regularization of the capacity to observe, the crystallization of the differences of risks, in this case, for each of the commercial centers, is not the same, but fluctuates. The execution of power by the administrators of the commercial centers is put in practice at the moment in which a person considered suspicious is observed: their movements are inspected, where they're heading to, activities, consumption, there looks, their gestures and what can be read from their lips. If the decision is that they cannot leave, they are "invited" to change their behavior, to a more normal way, and if they don't, they are "invited" to leave, to abandon the place where their behavior has given them away: they don't want to consume and they are not doing things in a normal way as expected.

CHANGES IN THE USE OF CCTV

In general, what is presented here shows two forms of management of the population. The surveillance systems above mentioned, can remit a particular sphere of every day life (law and order of the city and public security, for example), for vehicle transit and the flow of people. These devices establish, as a consequence, a space for management, representing signs of the undesirable and risky: that which can get out of control. Determining that which can be considered as a possible dangerous event, and which has to be feared, depends as much on the sphere of intervention (traffic, public avenues), as the connection of different surveillance technologies.

Those who make use of surveillance technology in these spaces, however, give the CCTV the capacity which allows it to see further than originally established. This permit the video cameras to be equipped with a certain expressiveness: the surveillance devices are used not only for the emergence of new problems, but for their apparent visual faculty to make out the most remote social relations in concrete spaces. In the case of the two municipalities analyzed here, CCTV is used to reinforce traffic light systems. In this sense, these surveillance technologies were secondary systems. However, little by little, the volume of images on the screen's were interpreted as a wider window of observation that would, apparently, positioned CCTV's as cultural signs of security, well-being and consumption (Shields, 1992; Christopherson, 2000; Newburn & Hayman, 2002; Goold, 2009).

In the case of CCTV in shopping centers a similar transformation took place. In the case of Mundo E and Galerías Metepec, the installation of CCTV was directed to avoid delinquency and criminal acts in their interiors. As time went by, and the vital information that could be obtained with such systems provided them with a wider cultural sense: in both cases, to be the guarantee to tell apart the good consumers from who are not, and with that, apparently, guaranteeing the reduction of possible behaviors considered inadequate in a shopping center. But in the particular case of Galerías Metepec, it has gone farther: not only observing the customer but also the behavior of its own employees.

In the four cases analyzed, CCTV in and of themselves are charged with a cultural meaning, condensed in the signs of efficiency, order, profound gaze, visibility, and transparency (Lyon, 2010). This may seem to provide with confidence to these monitoring devices, in the way in which they can apparently guarantee, in the most exact way, government and administration tasks than those traditional, non-technical and more related. It covers them with a particular sense: they are formed, both by users as well as by operators, into a form of sacred object, in other words, legitimate. As a result of this cultural definition, CCTV and other surveillance devices have permitted their restructuring in the administration of certain spaces. In the cases stated here, the efficient symbolic use of these technologies allows the restructuring of their purposes. First, in the urban space, of the uses for the administration of municipal resources, the assurance and stigmatize social movements of the city, and secondly, in the shopping centers, the security and guaranteeing of consumption, the monitoring of everyday activities of those who go to the shopping centers, as well as supplemental support of security to government organizations.

CONCLUSION

The above, has tried to analyze the use of surveillance technologies, such as CCTV, to solve in Mexico the growing problem of crime, violence, and the insecurity in urban commercial spaces. However, these technologies may seem to fit in a wider mythological discourse, which complements them with a specific cultural meaning, legitimizing emergent forms of governance. Such discourse, have been empowered both by governments and those governed, by administrators, operators and users. From this point of view, technological determinism does not exist; the surveillance technologies are cultural signs in themselves.

In the previous analysis cultural signs sustained by the use of CCTV in urban and commercial spaces were enhanced. The cultural meaning that shapes the social perceptions around the technology in general, and of the surveillance technologies in particular, allows the observation of the expansion in the use of this equipment, in the way in which they serve as a means to establish a distinction between sacred and profane spaces: they are used to allegedly distance social actors from insecurity, violence and crime. In this sense, the mythological discourse in which these surveillance technologies are inscribed, legitimize specific uses of governance, interacting public and private entities. In the Mexican case, the use of CCTV and other surveillance systems has naturalized, suggesting, both in a political and civil spheres, that given a certain dependence on technology, and the most effective way to face social problems resides in classifying and monitoring social actors, having as a consequence the intention of reorganizing certain spaces and the social relations that occur.

This refers back to two issues: the problem of governance and the matter of privacy. Given the fact that surveillance technologies are founded in cultural meaning, its revision and criticism would fall back in that area. For this, an investigation of the conditions of the possibility of these technologies in the Mexican context is recommended, including a reconsideration of its global and regional references. In this sense, the use of surveillance devices as they're concerned in the relation with privacy, has been studied little in this country (Arteaga, 2010). As a consequence, the analysis of the relationship between these two issues should be analyzed, at the light of the cultural meanings of the democratic state, the transparency and protection of personal data.

Towards the future, it is expected to be put on the table of discussion the problems of governance and privacy resulting by the use of surveillance systems in Mexico and Latin America. In this context, little has been analyzed. That is why, it would be of great importance to revise these themes, through an analysis that goes farther from the problems of public security, acknowledging that surveillance in itself is a problem in the region, since it may seem naturalized through discourses that support its use with the purpose of combating crime and violence, and generating a kind of blindness before the perverse effects of these technologies. So, in the future, an analysis of the symbolic constitution given to CCTV in Latin America, the users, administrators and operators, could be carried out, establishing its analysis from the symbolic constitution of the technology just as Alexander theorized.

REFERENCES

Alexander, J. (2000). La promesa de una sociología cultural. Discurso tecnológico y la máquina de información sagrada y profana. En J. Alexander, *Sociología cultural. Formas de clasificación en las sociedades* (pp. 165-201). Barcelona: Anthropos/FLACSO.

Alexander, J. C., & Smith, P. (2000). *Ciencia social y salvación: sociedad del riesgo como discurso mítico. En J. C. Alexander, Sociología cultural. Formas de clasificación en las sociedades complejas* (pp. 1–29). Barcelona: Anthropos-FLACSO.

Arteaga Botello, N. (2007). An orchestration of electronic surveillance. *International Criminal Justice Review*, *17*(4), 325–335. doi:10.1177/1057567707311566

Arteaga Botello, N. (2010). Privacy and Surveillance in Mexico and Brazil. En Elia Zureik, L. Lynda Harling Stalker, Emily Smith, David Lyon, y Yolan de E. Chan (Ed.), *Privacy, Surveillance and the Globalization of Personal Information: International Comparisons*, Montreal, Kingston: McGill-Queen's University Press (Forthcoming).

Carroll-Mayer, M., Fairweather, B., & Carsten Stahl, B. (2008). CCTV Identity Management and Implications for Criminal Justice: some considerations. *Surveillance & Society*, *5*(1), 33–50.

Christopherson, S. (2000). The Fortress City: Privatized Spaces, Consumer Citizenship. In Amin, A. (Ed.), *Post-Fordism. A reader* (pp. 409–427). Oxford: Blackwell.

Foucault, M. (1980). Le jeu de Michel Foucault. [The confession of the flesh] In Gordon, C. (Ed.), *Power/Knowledge: Selected interviews and other writings 1972-1977* (pp. 194–228). New York: Pantheon.

Goold, B. (2009). Technologies of surveillance and the erosion of institutional trust. In Franko, A., Oppen Gundhus, H., & Mork Lomell, H. (Eds.), *Technologies of (In)Security: The Surveillance of Everyday Life* (pp. 207–218). New York: Routledge-Cavendish.

Lyon, D. (2004). *Surveillance Technologies: Trends and Social Implications. En O. f.-O. Development, The Security Economy* (pp. 127–148). Paris: OECD Publications.

Lyon, D. (2010). Why where you are matters: mundane mobilities, transparent technologies, and digital discrimination. In Firmino, R., Duarte, F., & Ultramari, C. (Eds.), *ICTs for Mobile and Ubiquitous Urban Infrastructures: Surveillance, Locative Media and Global Networks*. Hershey, PA: IGI Global.

Newburn, T., & Hayman, S. (2002). *Policing, surveillance and social control: CCTV and police monitoring of suspects*. Cullompton, UK: Willan Publishing.

Shields, R. (1992). *Lifestyle shopping: The subject of consumption*. London: Routledge.

ADDITIONAL READING

Arteaga Botello, N. (2009). *Vigilancia al Sur Global. Mirando América Latina.* Toluca: Miguel Ángel Porrúa.

Ball, K. (2001). Situating surveillance: representation, meaning, movement, and manipulation. *Birmingham Business School Working Paper Series* (2000-7).

Ballucci, D. (2008). Risk in Action: the Practical Effects of the Youth Management Assessment. *Social & Legal Studies*, *17*, 175–197. doi:10.1177/0964663908089610

Coleman, R. (2004). *Replanning the streets: surveillance, social control and the city.* Culompton: William.

Ericson, R. V., Dean, B., & Doyle, A. (2000). The moral hazards of neoliberalism: lessons from the private insurance industry. *Economy and Society*, *29*, 532–558. doi:10.1080/03085140050174778

Ericson, R. V., & Haggerty, K. (1997). *Policing risk society*. Toronto: University of Toronto Press.

Flichy, P. (1995). *L'innovation technique*. Paris: La Découverte.

Flint, J. (2006). Surveillance and exclusion practices in governance af access to shopping centers on periphery estates. *Surveillance & Society*, *4*(1), 52–68.

Graham, S. (2005). Sofware-sorter geographies. *Progress in Human Geography*, *29*(5), 562–580. doi:10.1191/0309132505ph568oa

Heilmann, E. (2003). La videosurveillance, un résponse à la criminalité. *Criminologie*, *1*(1), 89–102.

Heilmann, E. (2008). *La vidéosurveilllance, un mirage technologique et politique. En L. Mucchielli, La frésésie sécuritaire* (pp. 114–124). Paris: La Découverte.

Hier, S. P. (2004). Risky Spaces and Dangerous Faces: Urban Surveillance, Social Disorder and CCTV. *Social & Legal Studies*, *13*, 541–554. doi:10.1177/0964663904047333

Hier, S. P., & Lyon, D. (2004). Surveillance, Technology, and the Management of Risk. *International Sociology*, *19*(2), 131–134. doi:10.1177/0268580904042895

Hier, S. P., Walby, K., & Greenberg, J. (2006). Supplementing the panoptic paradigm: surveillance, moral governance and CCTV. In D. Lyon, *Theorizing Surveillance: The panopticon and Beyond* (págs. 230-244). Cullompton: Willan Publishing.

Klauser, F. R. (2007). Difficulties in Revitalizing Public Space By CCTV. *European Urban and Regional Studies*, *14*(4), 337–348. doi:10.1177/0969776407081166

Koskela, H. (2000). 'The gaze without eyes': video-surveillance and the changing nature of urban space. *Progress in Human Geography*, *24*(2), 243–265. doi:10.1191/030913200668791096

Langman, L. (1992). *Neoncages: shopping for subjectivity. En R. Shields, Life-style shopping: the subject of consumption*. London: Routledge.

Lippert, R. (2009). Signs of the Surveillant Assemblage: Privacy Regulation, Urban CCTV, and Governmentality. *Social & Legal Studies*, *18*(4), 505–522. doi:10.1177/0964663909345096

Lyon, D. (2006). Why where you Matters: Mundane Mobilities, transparent Technologies, and Digital Discrimination. In Monahan, T. (Ed.), *Surveillance and security: Technological poltics and power in everyday life* (pp. 209–224). London: Routledge.

Marquis, G. (2003). Private security and surveillance: from the 'dossier society' to 'database'. En D. Lyon, *Surveillance as social sorting: privacy, risk and digital discrimination* (págs. 226-248). London: Routledge.

Miller, P., & Rose, N. (2009). *Governing the Present. Administering economic, social, adn personal life*. Cambridge: Polity Press.

Mourâo Kanashiro, M. (2008). Surveillance Cameras in Brazil: exclusion, mobility regulation, and the new meanings of security. *Surveillance & Society*, *5*(3), 270–289.

Norris, C. (2003). From Personal to digital: CCTV, the panopticon, and the technological medaition of suspicion and social control. In Lyon, D. (Ed.), *Surveillance as social sorting: privacy, risk and digital discrimination* (pp. 249–281). London: Routledge.

Reeve, A. (1998). *The Panopticisation of Shopping: CCTV and Leisure Consumption. En C. Norris, J. Morran, & G. Armstrong, Surveillance, CCTV and Social Control* (pp. 69–88). Aldershot: Ashgate.

Samatas, M. (2004). *Surveillance in Greece: from anti-communist to consumer surveilllance*. New York: Pella Publishing Company.

Smith, G. (2004). Behind the screens: exmining constructions of deviance and informal practices among CCTV control room operators in the UK. *Surveillance & Society*, *2*(2-3), 376–395.

Thompson, K. (2009). *Moral regulation: beyond Janet Jackson and the Passion. En I. Reed, & J. C. Alexander, Meaning and Method. The cultural approach to sociology* (pp. 63–76). Boulder: Paradigm Publishers.

Tremblay, P., & Grandmaison, R. (1997). Évaluation des effects de la télésurveillance sur la criminalité commise dans treize stations du métro de Montréal. *Criminologie*, *1*(3), 97–110.

Yesin, B. (2006). Watching ourselves: video surveillance, urban space, and self-responsabilization. *Cultural Studies*, *20*(4-5), 400–416.

ENDNOTES

1. www.mundoe.com.mx
2. The first monitors were black and white, and included a recording system on VHS tape, which was later substituted for color monitors and digital recording systems.
3. www.galeriasmetepec.com.mx

Compilation of References

Abele, J. et al. (2005). *Exploratory study on the potential socio-economic impact of the introduction of intelligent safety systems in road vehicles.* SEiSS Final Report, eSafety Forum.

Abler, R. (1974). The geography of communications. In Hurst, M. E. (Ed.), *Transportation Geography* (pp. 327–346). New York: McGraw Hill.

Adams, P. (1997). Cyberspace and Virtual Places. *Geographical Review*, *87*, 155–171. doi:10.2307/216003

Agamben, G. (1997). *Homo Sacer: Sovereign Power and Bare Life*. Stanford, CA: Stanford University Press.

Agre, P. (2001). Changing places: contexts of awareness in computing. *Human-Computer Interaction*, *16*(2-4), 177–192. doi:10.1207/S15327051HCI16234_04

Agre, P. E. (1994). Surveillance and capture: two models of privacy. *The Information Society*, *10*(2), 101–127. doi:10.1080/01972243.1994.9960162

Aijaz, A., Bochow, B., Dotze, F., Festag, A., Gerlach, M., Kroh, R., & Leinmuller, T. (2005). Attacks on Inter Vehicle Communication Systems - an Analysis. In *Proceedings of the 3rd International Workshop on Intelligent Transportation (WIT 2006).*

Albrescht, K., & Mcintyre, L. (2006). *Spychips: How Majors Corporations and Government Plan to Track Your Every Purchase and Watch Your Every Move*. New York: Plume Book.

Alexander, C. (1977). *Pattern Language: Towns, Buildings, Construction*. New York: Oxford University Press.

Alexander, J. (2000). La promesa de una sociología cultural. Discurso tecnológico y la máquina de información sagrada y profana. En J. Alexander, *Sociología cultural. Formas de clasificación en las sociedades* (pp. 165-201). Barcelona: Anthropos/FLACSO.

Alexander, J. C., & Smith, P. (2000). *Ciencia social y salvación: sociedad del riesgo como discurso mítico. En J. C. Alexander, Sociología cultural. Formas de clasificación en las sociedades complejas* (pp. 1–29). Barcelona: Anthropos-FLACSO.

Allan, S. (2007). Citizen journalism and the rise of 'mass self communication': Reporting the London bombings. *Global Media Journal*, *1*(1), 1–20.

Allen, E. (2001). INDEX: software for community indicators. In Brail, R., & Klosterman, R. (Eds.), *Planning Support Systems* (pp. 229–261). Redlands, CA: ESRI Press.

American National Standards Institute (ANSI). (1998). *Network and Customer Installation Interfaces: Asymmetric Digital Subscriber Line (ADSL)*. Metallic Interface.

Anders, P. (2001). Anthropic Cyberspace, Defining Electronic Space from First Principles. *Leonardo*, *34*(5), 409–416. doi:10.1162/002409401753521520

Andrejevic, M. (2004). Monitored mobility in the era of mass customization. *Space and Culture*, *6*(2), 132–150. doi:10.1177/1206331203251256

Andrejevic, M. (2005). The work of watching one another: Lateral surveillance, risk and governance. *Surveillance & Society*, *2*(4), 479–497.

Andrejevic, M. (2007). *I-Spy: Surveillance and power in the interactive era*. Lawrence, KS: University of Kansas Press.

Antoun, H. (2001). *Jornalismo e ativismo na hipermídia: Em que se pode reconhecer a nova mídia*. Porto Alegre, Brazil: EDIPUCRS.

Arseni, P., Boggia, G., & Camarda, P. (2001). Modeling telecommunication infrastructures integrating wideband wireless and wired networks. *Simulation*, *78*(3), 173–184. doi:10.1177/0037549702078003528

Arteaga Botello, N. (2007). An orchestration of electronic surveillance. *International Criminal Justice Review*, *17*(4), 325–335. doi:10.1177/1057567707311566

Arteaga Botello, N. (2010). Privacy and Surveillance in Mexico and Brazil. En Elia Zureik, L. Lynda Harling Stalker, Emily Smith, David Lyon, y Yolan de E. Chan (Ed.), *Privacy, Surveillance and the Globalization of Personal Information: International Comparisons*, Montreal, Kingston: McGill-Queen's University Press (Forthcoming).

Askew, J., Sheppard, A., Dalton, A., Baker, N., Appleby, T., & Peel, D. (2009). *Research Project for a Review of Mobile Phone Operators Permitted Development Rights*. Cardiff, UK: The Wales Planning Policy Development Programme Cardiff, Welsh Assembly Government.

Augè, M. (2006). *Sobremodernidade: Do mundo tecnológico de hoje ao desafio essencial do amanhã*. Rio de Janeiro, Brazil: Mauad.

Aurigi, A. (2006). New Technologies, yet same dilemmas? Policy and design issues for the augmented city. *Journal of Urban Technology*, *13*(3), 5–28. doi:10.1080/10630730601145989

Aurigi, A., & De Cindio, F. (2008). Introduction. In Aurigi, A., & De Cindio, F. (Eds.), *Augmented Urban Spaces* (pp. 1–4). London: Ashgate Publishers.

Aurigi, A., & De Cindio, F. (Eds.). (2008). *Augmented urban spaces*. Hampshire, UK: Ashgate.

Babe, R. E. (2006). Innis and the News. *Javnost—The Public, 13*(3), 43-56.

Baldwin, R., & Cave, M. (1999). *Understanding Regulation: Theory, Strategy, and Practice*. Oxford, UK: Oxford University Press.

Ball, K., & Haggerty, K. D. (2005). Editorial: Doing surveillance studies. *Surveillance & Society*, *2*(2/3), 129–138.

Banisar, D. (2003). The Great Firewall of China: Cyberpolicing dissent. *Media Development*, *50*(3), 23–25.

Barnes, S. B. (2001). *Online Connections: Internet Interpersonal Relationships*. Cresskill, NJ: Hampton Press.

Barthes, R. (1978). *The death of the author. Image-music-text* (pp. 142–148). New York: Hill and Wang.

Barthes, R. (1981). *A câmara clara*, (M. Torres, Trans.). Lisboa: Edições 70.

Barthes, R. (2006). *La Chambre Claire: Note Sur LA Photographie*. Paris: Gallimard.

Bauman, Z. (1999). *Comunidades: A busca por segurança no mundo atual*. Rio de Janeiro, Brazil: J. Zahar Editor.

Bauman, Z. (2001). *Liquid Modernity*. Cambridge, UK: Polity Press.

Bauman, Z. (2002). L'Etat face à la demande de sécurité. *Esprit (Paris, France)*, (décembre): 59–69.

Bauman, Z. (2005). *Identidade: Entrevista à Benedetto Vecchi*. Rio de Janeiro, Brazil: J. Zahar Editor.

Bauman, Z. (2005). *Liquid Life*. Cambridge, UK: Polity Press.

Baumgartner, J. (2005). Cable consortium mobilizes quad-play with Sprint. *CedMagazine.com*, November 02.

Beaverstock, J. V., Smith, R. G., & Taylor, P. J. (1999). A roster of world cities. *Cities (London, England)*, *16*, 445–458. doi:10.1016/S0264-2751(99)00042-6

Beaverstock, J., Smith, R., Taylor, P., Walker, D., & Lorimer, H. (2000). Globalization and world cities: some measurement methodologies. *Applied Geography (Sevenoaks, England)*, *20*(1), 43–63. doi:10.1016/S0143-6228(99)00016-8

Beck, U. (1992). *Risk society: Toward a new modernity*. London: Sage.

Belgiorno, K. (2006, April 18). The 21st century peep show. *Village Voice*. Retrieved November 1, 2009, from http://www.villagevoice.com/2006-04-18/news/the-21st-century-peep-show

Benford, S. (2005). Future Location-Based Experiences. *JISC Tech Report (TSW0501)*.

Benford, S., Flintham, M., & Drodz, A. (2006). The Design And Experience of The Location-Based Performance Uncle Roy All Around You. *Leornardo, 14*(3). Retrieved May 10th 2008, from http://leoalmanac.org/journal/ Vol_14/lea_v14_n03-04/roy.asp

Bennet, C. J., & Regan, P. M. (2004). Editorial: Surveillance and mobilities. *Surveillance & Society*, *1*(4), 449–455.

Bennett, C., & Regan, P. (2002). *What happens when you make a 911 call? Privacy and regulation of cellular technology in the USA and Canada*. Paper presented at the Canadian Political Science Association, May 31, 2002.

Bentham, J. (1823). *An introduction to the principles of morals and legislation*. London: E. Wilson.

Beslay, L., & Hakala, H. (2005). *Digital territory: Bubbles*. Draft Publication, European Community. Retrieved 10th May 2008 from http://cybersecurity.jrc.es/ docs/DigitalTerritoryBubbles.pdf

Beslay, L., & Hakala, H. (2007). Digital territory: Bubbles. In Kidd, P. T. (Ed.), *European visions for the knowledge age* (pp. 69–78). Macclesfield, UK: Cheshire Henbury.

Bessa, L. R. (2003). O Consumidor e os Limites dos Bancos de Dados de Crédito. São Paulo, Brazil: Revista dos Tribunais.

Bicalho, L. M., & Oliveira, M. (2005) *Transdisciplinaridade nas ciências: o lugar da Ciência da Informação*. I EBEC - Encontro Brasileiro de Estudos da Complexidade – Curitiba, Brasil, July 11th to 13th, 2005.

Biocca, F. (1997). The cyborg's dilemma: Progressive embodiment in virtual environments. *Journal of Computer-Mediated Communication, 3*(2). Retrieved from www.ascusc.org/jcmc/vol3/issue2/biocca2.html accessed Sept. 12, 2009.

Biswas, S., Tatchikou, R., & Dion, F. (2006). Vehicle-to-vehicle wireless communication protocols for enhancing highway traffic safety. *IEEE Communications Magazine*, *44*(1), 74–82. doi:10.1109/MCOM.2006.1580935

Bjork, S. (2002). Designing ubiquitous computing games. *Personal and Ubiquitous Computing*, *6*, 442–458.

Black, J. (2001). No hiding from a cell phone. *Business Week Online,* 21 June. Available at http://www.businessweek.com/bwdaily/dnflash/jun2001/nf20010621_803.htm

Blascovich, J. (2002). Social influence within immersive virtual environments. In Schroeder, R. (Ed.), *The Social Life of Avatars* (pp. 127–145). Berlin: Springer-Verlag.

Blumberg, A. J., & Eckersley, P. (2009). On locational privacy and how to avoid losing it. *EFF Report*. Retrieved from www.eff.org/wp/locational-privacy/

Boden, D., & Molotch, H. (1994). The compulsion to proximity. In Friedland, R., & Boden, D. (Eds.), *NoWhere: Space, Time, and Modernity*. Berkeley, CA: University of California Press.

Boertien, N. (2002). Location based services: services and technologies, *Virtuele Haven report series T3.D9, Telematica Instituut*. Retrieved March 5, 2006, from https://doc.telin.nl/dscgi/ds.py/Get/File-19920

Boler, M. (2008). *Digital Media and Democracy Tactics in Hard Times*. Boston: MIT Press.

Borja, J., & Castells, M. (1997). *Local and global: management of cities in the information age*. London: Earthscan.

Boxill, S. A., & Yu, L. (2000). *An Evaluation of Traffic Simulator Models for Supporting ITS*. Houston, TX: Development Centre for Transportation Training and Research, Texas Southern University.

Bozovic, M. (1995). *The Panopticon writings: Jeremy Bentham*. New York: Verso.

Bradwell, P. Johar. I., Maguire, C. & Miner, P. (2007). *Future Planners: Propositions for the Next Age of Planning*. London: Demos.

Brady, A. (2006). Guiding hand: The role of the CCP Central Propaganda Department in the current era. *Westminster Papers in Communication and Culture*, *3*(1), 58–77.

Brand, C. (2004). EU nations set to name anti-terror czar. *The Guardian*, March19. Retrieved from http://www.guardian.co.uk/worldlatest/story/0,1280,-3880554,00.html

Breitman, K. K. (2005). *Web semântica: a Internet do futuro*. Rio de Janeiro, Brazil: LTC.

Brenner, N. (2009). Restructuring, Rescaling, and the Urban Question. *Critical Planning*, *16*(Summer), 61–79.

Brenner, N., & Elden, S. (2009). Henri Lefebvre on State, Space, Territory. *International Political Sociology*, *3*, 353–377. doi:10.1111/j.1749-5687.2009.00081.x

Britchie, J., Hall, P., & Newton, J. (1987). The Transition to an Information Society. In Brotchie, (Eds.), *The Spatial Impact of Technological Change*. London: Croom Helm.

Brown, B. B., & Altman, I. (1983). Territoriality, defensible space, and residential burglary: An environmental analysis. *Journal of Environmental Psychology*, *3*, 203–220. doi:10.1016/S0272-4944(83)80001-2

Brown, B. B., & Perkins, D. D. (1992). Disruptions in place attachment. In I. Altman, & &S. Low (Eds.), *Place attachment*, (pp. 279–304). New York: Plenum.

Brown, B., Perkins, D., & Brown, G. (2004). Incivilities, place attachment and crime: Block and individual effects. *Journal of Environmental Psychology*, *24*, 359–371. Retrieved from http://www.observatoriodeseguranca.org/files/sdarticle.pdf accessed August 30, 2009. doi:10.1016/j.jenvp.2004.01.001

Brown, P. (1988). *The Body and Society*. New York: Columbia University Press.

Brugman, J. (2009, May 5). *Living on Urban Planet Forbes.com*. Retrieved September12, 2009 from http://www.forbes.com/2009/05/05/state-of-the-city-opinions-contributors-urban-planet.html

Brunn, S. (2003). A note on the hyperlinks of major Eurasian cities. *Eurasian Geography and Economics*, *44*(4), 321–324. doi:10.2747/1538-7216.44.4.321

Brunn, S. (2004). An e-classification of the world's capital cities: URL references to websites. In Kehal, H. (Ed.), *Digital Economy: Impacts, Influences and Challenges* (pp. 200–216). Hershey, PA: Idea Group, Inc.

Brunn, S., & Williams, J. (2005). Cybercities of Asia: measuring globalization using hyperlinks. *Asian Geographer*, *23*(1/2), 121–147.

Bruno, F. (2008a). Monitoramento, classificação e controle nos dispositivos de vigilância digital. *Revista Famecos*, *36*, 10–16.

Bruno, F. (2008b). Controle, flagrante e prazer: Regimes escópicos e atencionais da vigilância nas cidades. *Revista Famecos*, *37*, 45–53.

Bulik, L. (1990). *Doutrinas da informação: No mundo de hoje*. São Paulo, Brazil: Loyola.

Burd, G., Drucker, S. J., & Gumpert, G. (Eds.). (2007). *The Urban Communication Reader*. Cresskill, NJ: Hampton Press.

Caballero, E. G. *Pluralidad teórica, metodológica y técnica en el abordaje delas redes sociales: hacia la "hibridación" disciplinaria*. REDES - Revista hispana para el análisis de redes sociales Vol.9#1, Dic.2005. Avaiable at: http://revista-redes.rediris.es.

Caillois, R. (1961). *Man, Play and Games*. Chicago: University of Illinois Press.

Caliskan, M., Graupner, D., & Mauve, M. (2006). Decentralized discovery of free parking places. In *VANET - Proceedings of the Third ACM International Workshop on Vehicular Ad Hoc Networks*, (pp. 30-39).

Campbell, H., & Marshall, R. (2002). Utilitarianism's bad breath? A re-evaluation of the public interest justification for planning. *Planning Theory*, *1*, 163–187. doi:10.1177/147309520200100205

Canguilhem, G. (2009). *Le normal et le pathologique*. Paris: PUF.

Canter, D. V. (1977). *The Psychology of Place*. New York: Architectural Press.

Carey, J. (1985). *Communication as Culture: Essays on Media and Society*. Boston: Unwin Hyman.

Carey, J. W. (2005). Historical Pragmatism and the Internet. Retrieved September 1 5, 2009 from http://nms.sagepub.com/cgi/content/abstract/7/4/443

Carmona, M., & Burgess, R. (2001). *Strategic Planning and Urban Projects*. Delft, The Netherlands: Delft University Press.

Carroll-Mayer, M., Fairweather, B., & Carsten Stahl, B. (2008). CCTV Identity Management and Implications for Criminal Justice: some considerations. *Surveillance & Society*, *5*(1), 33–50.

Cascio, J. (2005). *The rise of the participatory Panopticon*. Retrieved October 23, 2009, from http://www.worldchanging.com/archives/002651.html

Casey, E. (1997). *The fate of place*. Berkeley, CA: University of California.

Castells, M. (1989). *The Informational City: Information Technology, Economic Restructuring, and the Urban-Regional Process*. Oxford, UK: Blackwell.

Castells, M. (1996). *The Rise of the Network Society, The Information Age: Economy, Society and Culture* (*Vol. I*). Oxford, UK: Blackwell.

Castells, M. (1996). *The Rise of the Network Society*. Oxford: Blackwell.

Castells, M. (1999). A sociedade em rede. In *A era da informação: economia, sociedade e cultura*, (Vol. I). São Paulo: Editora paz e Terra.

Castells, M. (2000). *The Rise of the Network Society* (2nd ed.). New York: Blackwell Publishing.

Castells, M. (2002) *A sociedade em rede*. (6ª Ed.). São Paulo, Brazil: Paz e Terra.

Castells, M. (2003). *A galáxia da internet: Reflexões sobre a internet, os negócios e a sociedade*. Rio de Janeiro, Brazil: J. Zahar Editor.

Castells, M. (2008). The New Public Sphere: Global Civil Society, Communication Networks, and Global Governance. *The Annals of the American Academy of Political and Social Science*, *616*(1), 78–93. doi:10.1177/0002716207311877

Castells, M., Fernandez-Ardevol, M., Qui, J. L., & Sey, A. (2004). *The mobile communication society: A cross-cultural analysis of available evidence on the social uses of wireless communication technology.* Research Report. Retrieved July 08, 2009, from http://arnic.info/WirelessWorkshop/MCS.pdf

Cellular News. (2009). *Vigilante taxi drivers reporting crimes over 3G phones*, September 22, 2009. Retrieved November 1, 2009, from http://www.cellular-news.com/story/39715.php

Chandler, A. D., & Cortada, J. W. (Eds.). (2000). *A Nation Transformed by Information. How Information Has Shaped the United States from Colonial times to the Present*. New York: Oxford University Press.

Chang, B. R., Tsai, H. F., & Young, C.-P. (2009). (Article in Press). Intelligent data fusion system for predicting vehicle collision warning using vision/GPS sensing. *Expert Systems with Applications*.

Cherry, S. (2005). The net effect: As China's Internet gets a much-needed makeover, will the new network promote freedom or curtail it? *IEEE Spectrum*, *42*(6), 38–44. doi:10.1109/MSPEC.2005.1437036

Cheskin Research (2002). *Designing Digital Experiences for Youth*, (Market Insights Series, Fall).

China Internet Network Information Center (CNNIC). (2010). *The 25th statistical report on Internet development in China*. Retrieved January 29, 2010, from http://www.cnnic.org.cn/uploadfiles/pdf/2010/1/15/101600.pdf

Christopherson, S. (2000). The Fortress City: Privatized Spaces, Consumer Citizenship. In Amin, A. (Ed.), *Post-Fordism. A reader* (pp. 409–427). Oxford: Blackwell.

Cicognani, A. (1998). On the linguistic nature of cyberspace and virtual communities. *Virtual Reality (Waltham Cross)*, *3*, 16–24. doi:10.1007/BF01409794

Citizens take to streets protesting beating, torture at daycare. (2005, October 26). *Hurriyet*. Retrieved November 12, 2009, from <http://hurarsiv.hurriyet.com.tr /goster / haber.aspx?id=3441525>

Clark, R. (2003). *Wireless transmission and mobile technologies*. Roger Clark Website. Retrieved July 03, 2009 from http://www.anu.edu.au/people/Roger.Clarke/EC/WMT.html

Clarke, R. A. (1988). Information technology and dataveillance. *Communications of the ACM*, *31*(5), 498–512. doi:10.1145/42411.42413

Clayton, R., Murdoch, S. J., & Watson, R. N. M. (2007). Ignoring the Great Firewall of China. *I/S: A Journal of Law and Policy for the Information Society, 3*(2), 272-296.

Cohen, S. (1992). *Visions of social control: Crime, punishment and classification*. Malden, MA: Polity.

Coursey, D. (2009). Spy on Your Workers With Google Latitude. *PC World*, Business Center, 5th February 2009. Retrieved 5th February 2009 from http://www.pcworld.com/businesscenter/article/158975/spy_on_your_workers_with_google_latitude.html

Coutard, O., Hanley, R., & Zimmerman, R. (Eds.). (2005). *Sustaining urban networks*. New York: Routledge.

Crary, J. (1992). *Techniques of the observer*. Cambridge, MA: MIT Press.

Crary, J. (2001). *Suspensions of Perception*. Cambridge, MA: MIT Press.

Croswell, T. (1996). *In Place/Out Place: Geography, Ideology, and Transgression*. Minneapolis: University of Minnesota.

Crutcher, M., & Zook, M. (2009). (in press). Placemarks and waterlines: racialized cyberscapes in post-Katrina Google Earth. *Geoforum*. doi:10.1016/j.geoforum.2009.01.003

Cuff, D. (2003). Immanent Domain Pervasive Computing and the Public Realm. *Journal of Architectural Education, 57*(1), 43–49. doi:10.1162/104648803322336575

Cunningham, C., & Turner, G. (2005). The Media and Communications in Australia. In Flew, T. (Ed.), *New Media: an Introduction* (2nd ed.). Sydney: Allen & Unwin.

Curtin, J. (2001). *A digital divide in rural and regional Australia? Current issues brief 1*. Australia: Information and Research Services, Department of the Parliament Library.

Damm, J. (2007). The Internet and the fragmentation of Chinese society. *Critical Asian Studies*, *39*(2), 273–294. doi:10.1080/14672710701339485

Davey, K. (1993). *Elements of urban management*. New York: World Bank. doi:10.1596/0-8213-2424-1

Davis, J. W. (2009). Research Report Article: Eye in the Sky. OSU. *The Alumni Magazine*, (May/June): 30.

Davis, J. W. (n.d.). *James W. Davis Home Page*, from http://www.cse.ohio-state.edu/~jwdavis/

Davis, K. (1959). *The World's Metropolitan Areas*. Berkeley, CA: University of California Press.

De Sá, S. (2004). Telefones Móveis e Formas de Escuta na Contemporaneidade. *Razón y Palabra*. n.41. October-November. Retrieved January 16, 2006, from http://www.cem.itesm.mx/dacs/publicaciones/logos/anteriores/n41/spereira.html.

De Souza e Silva, A. (2004). *From multiuser environments as (virtual) spaces to (hybrid) spaces as multiuser environments: Nomadic technology devices and hybrid communication places. Tese de Doutorado*. Rio de Janeiro, Brazil: UFRJ/CFCH/ECO.

De Souza e Silva, A. (2006a). From cyber to hybrid: mobile technologies as interfaces of hybrid spaces. *Space and Culture*, *9*(3), 261–278. doi:10.1177/1206331206289022

De Souza E Silva, A. (2006b). Re-conceptualizing the mobile phone: From Telephone to collective interfaces. *Australian journal of emerging technologies and society*, *4*(2), 108-127.

De Souza e Silva, A., & Sutko, D. M. (2009). *Digital Cityscapes: Merging Digital and Urban Playspaces*. New York: Peter Lang Publishing.

De Souza Santos, B. (2008). The World Social Forum and the Global Left. *Politics & Society*, *36*(2), 247–270. doi:10.1177/0032329208316571

Debray, R. (1995). *Manifestos Midiológicos* (Teixeira, J. F., Trans.). Petrópolis, Brazil: Vozes.

Deibert, R. J. (2002). Dark guests and Great Firewalls: The Internet and Chinese security policy. *The Journal of Social Issues*, *58*(1), 143–159. doi:10.1111/1540-4560.00253

Dekker, A. *Conceptual Distance in Social Network Analysis*. Journal of social structure, vol. 6. Available at: http://www.cmu.edu/joss/content/articles/volume6/dekker/, Accessed July 5th, 2009.

Deleuze, G. (1992). *Post-Scriptum sobre as Sociedades de controle*. In Deleuze, G., (Ed.), *Conversações: 1972-1990*, (Ed. 34, pp. 219-226). Retrieved 21st April 2008, from http://netart.incubadora.fapesp.br/ portal/midias/controle.pdf

Deleuze, G., & Guatari, F. (1980). *Mille Plateaux. Capitalisme et Schizophrénie*. Paris: Les Editions de Minuit.

Deloitte & Touche. (2003). *Implementation Review of the Ten Commitments to Best Siting Practice for the UK Mobile Industry, September*. London: Deloitte & Touche.

Deloitte & Touche. (2005). *Implementation of the Ten Commitments to Best Siting Practice for the UK Mobile Industry, January*. London: Deloitte & Touche.

Demographia. (2008). *Largest Urban Areas in the World*. Retrieved October 4, 2009, from http://www.demographia.com/db-wlargestua.pdf

Dena, C. (2007). Creating Alternate realities. In Borries, F., Walz, S., & Bottger, M. (Eds.), *Space Time Play: Computer Games, Architecture and Urbanism: the Next Level*. Basel, Switzerland: Birkhauser Verlag AG.

Denstadli, J., & Gripsrund, M. (2010). Face-to-face by travel or picture: the relationship between travelling and video communication in business settings. In Beaverstock, J., Derudder, B., Faulconbridge, J., & Witlox, F. (Eds.), *International Business Travel and the Global Economy*. London: Ashgate.

Department of Trade & Industry. (2001, March). *Communications Liberalisation in the UK. Key Elements, History & Benefits*. London: DTI.

Department of Trade and Industry. (1991). *Competition and Choice: Telecommunications Policy for the 1990s. Cm 1461*. London: HMSO.

Derrida, J. (1995). *On the name*. Standord, CA: Stanford University.

Derudder, B. (2006). On conceptual confusion in empirical analyses of a transnational urban network. *Urban Studies (Edinburgh, Scotland)*, *43*(11), 2027–2046. doi:10.1080/00420980600897842

Derudder, B., Devriendt, L., & Witlox, F. (2007). Flying where you don't want to go: an empirical analysis of hubs in the global airline network. *Tijdschrift voor Economische en Sociale Geografie*, *98*(3), 307–324. doi:10.1111/j.1467-9663.2007.00399.x

Derudder, B., Taylor, P. J., Ni, P., De Vos, A., Hoyler, M., & Hanssens, H. (2010). Pathways of growth and Decline: connectivity changes in the world city network, 2000-2008. *Urban Studies (Edinburgh, Scotland)*, 47.

Devriendt, L., Boulton, A., Brunn, S., Derudder, B., & Witlox, F. (2009). *Major Cities in the Information World: Monitoring Cyberspace in Real-Time*. GaWC Research Bulletin 308. Retrieved from www.lboro.ac.uk/gawc/rb/rb308.html

Devriendt, L., Boulton, A., Brunn, S., Derudder, B., & Witlox, F. (2009). Major cities in the Information World: monitoring cyberspace in real-time. *GaWC Research Bulletin 308*. Retrieved June 23, 2009 from http://www.lboro.ac.uk/gawc/rb/rb308.html.

Devriendt, L., Derudder, B., & Witlox, F. (2008). Cyberplace and Cyberspace: two approaches to analyzing digital intercity linkages. *Journal of Urban Technology*, *15*(2), 5–32. doi:10.1080/10630730802401926

DEWHA. (2009). *Environmental Management System Tool. Department of the Environment, Water, Heritage and the Arts*. Sydney, Australia: DEWHA.

Dinc, S. (2006, September 5). Congregation says it's lynching. *Hurriyet*. Retrieved November 12, 2009, from <http://hurarsiv.hurriyet.com.tr/goster/haber.aspx?id=5033063&tarih=2006-09-05>

Dittmar, A. (2007). myHealth. In P. T. Kidd (Ed.), *European visions for the knowledge age* (pp. 105-114). Macclesfield, UK: Cheshire Henbury.

Dobson, K. (2002). *AgoraPhone*. Retrieved April 08, 2008, from http://web.media.mit.edu/~monster/AgoraPhone/webcam/index.html

Dodge, M., & Kitchim, R. (2007). Outlines of a world coming into existence: pervasive computing and the ethics of forgetting. *Environment and Planning. B, Planning & Design*, *34*, 431–445. doi:10.1068/b32041t

Dolozel, L. (1998). *Heterocosmica. Fiction and Possible Worlds*. Baltimore: Johns Hopkins University Press.

Doneda, D. (2006). *Da privacidade à proteção de dados pessoais*. Rio de Janeiro: Renovar.

Doneda, D., & Viola, M. (2009). *Risk and Personal Information: The Finality Principle and Data Protection in the Brazilian Legal System. RBRS International (RBRSi)* (pp. 133–149). Rio de Janeiro: Funenseg.

Dong Kim, S. (2002). Personal meanings. In Katz, J. E., & Aakhus, M. (Eds.), *Perpetual Contact: Mobile Communication, Private Talk, Public Performance*. New York: Cambridge University Press.

Dourish, P. (2004). What we talk about when we talk about context. *Personal and Ubiquitous Computing*, *8*(1), 19–30. doi:10.1007/s00779-003-0253-8

Dourish, P. (2006). Re-Shape-ing Place: "Place" and "Space" Ten Years On. In [Banff, Alberta, Canada.]. *Proceedings of CSCW*, *06*(November), 4–8.

Dourish, P., & Harrison, S. (1996). Re-Place-ing Space: The Roles of Place and Space in Collaborative Systems. In *Proceedings of CSCW*. New York: ACM.

Doward, J. (2003). Big Brother latest: now your phone can be used to track you down. *The Observer*, 7 December. Retrieved from http://observer.guardian.co.uk/libertywatch/story/0,1373,1101729,00.html

Duany Plater-Zyberk. (2003). Retrieved from http://www.smartcodecentral.org/smartfilesv9.html, accessed 16 April 2007.

Duarte, F. (2002). *Crise das matrizes espaciais*. São Paulo, Brazil: Perspectiva.

Duarte, F., & Firmino, R. (2009). Infiltrated city, augmented space: information and communication technologies, and representations of contemporary spatialities. *Journal of Architecture*, *14*, 545–565. doi:10.1080/13602360903187493

Ducatel, K., Bogdanowicz, M., Scapolo, F., Leijten, J., & Burgelman, J.-C. (2001). European Commission. Scenarios for Ambient Intelligence in 2010. Final Report. Retrieved February 4, 2010, from http://jbr.org/articles.html http://www.ist.hu/doctar/fp5/istagscenarios2010.pdf

Dutton, W., & Kraemer, K. (1977). Technology and urban management: the power payoffs of computing. *Administration & Society*, *9*(3), 305–340. doi:10.1177/009539977700900303

Dwyre, D. (1998). Newsatellite services to bridge the gap. *Telecommunications*, *32*(12), 47–49.

Edward, R. (2004). Lost? Help is just a mobile phone photo away. *The Scotsman*, *13*(April), 5.

Eericson, R. V., & Haggerty, K. D. (2001). The surveillant assemblage. *The British Journal of Sociology*, *51*(4), 605–622.

Ehrenberg, A. (1999). *Le culte de la performance*. Paris: Hachette.

Eko, L. (2001). Many spiders, One Worldwide Web: Towards a typology of Internet regulation. *Communication Law and Policy*, *6*(3), 445–484. doi:10.1207/S15326926CLP0603_02

El Ghobashy, T. (2008, July 28). Video shows NYPD cop assaulting cyclist. *Daily News.* Retrieved October 19, 2009, from < http://www.nydailynews.com/news/ny_crime/2008/07/28/2008-07-28_video_shows_nypd_cop_assaulting_cyclist.html>

Eldridge, M., & Grinter, R. (2001). *Studying text messaging in teenagers*. Workshop on Mobile Technologies at CHI 2001, Seattle, WA. Available at www.cs.Colorado.edu/~palen/chi_workshop/papers/EldridgeGrinter.pdf/

Elias, N. (1969). The Civilizing Process: *Vol. 1. The History of Manners*. Oxford: Blackwell.

Endeshaw, A. (2004). Internet regulation in China: The never-ending cat and mouse game. *Information & Communications Technology Law*, *13*(1), 41–57. doi:10.1080/1360083042000190634

Ericson, R. V., & Haggerty, K. D. (2000). The surveillant assemblage. *The British Journal of Sociology*, *51*(4), 605–622. doi:10.1080/00071310020015280

European Commission. (2006). *Communication from the Commission to the Council, the European Parliament, the European Economic and Social committee and the Committee of the Regions On the Intelligent Car Initiative - "Raising Awareness of ICT for Smarter, Safer and Cleaner Vehicles" COM/2006/0059final*. Retrieved July 17, 2006, from http://eur-lex.europa.eu/LexUriServ/LexUriServ.do?uri=COM:2006:0059:FIN:EN:HTML

Eye in the Sky. (2009). *Research Report Article, May/June*, 30. Retrieved from www.ohiostatealumni.org

Facebook and freedom: New technologies are encouraging the change in Iran that U.S. desires. (2009, June 18). *Newsday*, A38.

Feitosa, A. (2006). *Organização da informação na Web: das tags à web semântica*. Brasília: Thesaurus.

Fels, S. (2002). *PlesioPhone series.* Retrieved April 08, 2008, from http://hct.ece.ubc.ca/research/plesiophone/plesiophone.pdf

Felson, M. (1987). Routine activities and crime prevention in the developing metropolis. *Criminology*, *25*, 911–931. doi:10.1111/j.1745-9125.1987.tb00825.x

Ferrara, L. (2008). *Comunicação, espaço, cultura.* São Paulo, Brazil: Annablume.

Ferreira, E., & Falcão, T. (2009). Through the Looking Glass: Weavings Between the Magic Circle and the Immersive Processes in Video Games. In *Digital Games Research Association 2009 Conference Proceedings*, London, September 2009.

Firmino, R. (2003). "Not Just a Portal" - Virtual Cities as a Complex Sociotechnical Phenomenon. *Journal of Urban Technology*, *10*(2).

Firmino, R., Duarte, F., & Moreira, T. (2008). Pervasive Technologies and Urban Planning in the Augmented City. *Journal of Urban Technology*, *15*(1), 77–93. doi:10.1080/10630730802401983

Fisher, J., & Monahan, T. (2008). Tracking the social dimensions of RFID systems in hospitals. *International Journal of Medical Informatics*, *77*(1), 176–183. doi:10.1016/j.ijmedinf.2007.04.010

Fitzgibbons, B., Fujimoto, R., Guensler, R., Hunter, M., Park, A., & Wu, H. (2004). Simulation-Based Operations Planning For Regional Transportation Systems. In *Proceedings of the 5th Annual Nat. Conf. on Digital Government Research: New Challenges and Opportunities*, Seattle.

Flew, T. (2008). *New Media: An Introduction* (3rd ed.). Melbourne, Australia: Oxford University Press.

Foot, K. (2006). Web Sphere Analysis and Cybercultural Studies. In Silver, D., Massanari, A., & Steve, J. (Eds.), *Critical Cyberculture Studies* (pp. 88–96). New York: New York University.

Fortunati, L. (2002). The mobile phone: towards new categories and social relations. *Information Communication and Society*, *5*(4), 513–528. doi:10.1080/13691180208538803

Foucault, M. (1963). *Naissance de la clinique*. Paris: PUF.

Foucault, M. (1972). Prison talk. In Gordon, C. (Ed.), *Power/Knowledge: Selected interviews and other writings, 1972-1977* (pp. 37–54). New York: Pantheon.

Foucault, M. (1976). *Histoire de la sexualité I - La Volonté de savoir*. Paris: Gallimard.

Foucault, M. (1977). *Discipline and Punish: The Birth of the Prison*. Harmondsworth, UK: Penguin.

Foucault, M. (1980). Le jeu de Michel Foucault. [The confession of the flesh] In Gordon, C. (Ed.), *Power/Knowledge: Selected interviews and other writings 1972-1977* (pp. 194–228). New York: Pantheon.

Foucault, M. (1984). De Outros Espaços. In *Architecture, Mouvement, Continuité*. Retrieved August 2009, from http://www.rizoma.net/interna.php?id=169secao=anarquitextura

Foucault, M. (1984). Des espaces autres (conférence au Cercle d'études architecturales, 14 mars 1967). *Architecture, Mouvement, Continuité*, (5, octobre), 46-49. Retrieved 21st April 2008, from <http://foucault.info/documents/heteroTopia/ foucault.heteroTopia.fr.html

Foucault, M. (1995). *Discipline & Punish: The Birth of the Prison*. New York: Vintage Books.

Foucault, M. (2004). *Naissance de la biopolitique*. Paris: Gallimard/Seuil.

Foucault, M. (2007). *Security, Territory, Population: Lectures at the Collège de France 1977-78. London: Palgrave Macmillan. Garland, D. (2001). The Culture of Control*. Chicago: University of Chicago Press.

Fox, W., & Porca, S. (2001). Investing in Rural Infrastructure. *International Regional Science Review*, *24*(1), 103–133. doi:10.1177/016001701761012971

Fraser, N. (2007). Transnational Public Sphere: Transnationalizing the Public Sphere: On the Legitimacy and Efficacy of Public Opinion in a Post-Westphalian World. *Theory, Culture & Society*, *24*(4), 7–30. doi:10.1177/0263276407080090

Frey, K., & Procopiuck, M. (2007). *Policy Websphere Analysis: Uma abordagem para se (re)pensar a transformação estrutural da esfera pública na era da Internet. Revista Brasileira de Ciências Sociais*. Artigo Submetido.

Friedmann, J. (1986). The world city hypothesis. *Development and Change*, *17*(1), 69–83. doi:10.1111/j.1467-7660.1986.tb00231.x

Friedmann, J. (2001). World Cities Revisited: A Comment. *Urban Studies (Edinburgh, Scotland)*, *38*(13), 2535–2536. doi:10.1080/00420980120094641

Funder, A. (2004). *Stasiland: True stories from behind the Berlin Wall*. London: Granta.

Gallagher, B., Akatsuka, H. & Suzuki, H. (2006). Wireless communications for vehicle safety: Radio link performance & wireless connectivity methods. *IEEE Vehicular Technology Magazine*, *1*(4), 4-16+24.

Gallent, N., Juntti, M., Kidd, S., & Shaw, D. (2008). *Introduction to Rural Planning*. London: Routledge.

Galloway, A. (2003). *Resonances and everyday life: ubiquitous computing and the city*. Accessed on 6 Oct 2003 from www.purselipsquarejaw.org/mobile/cult_studies_draft.pdf

Gandy, O. H. Jr. (1993). *The panoptic sort: A political economy of personal information*. Boulder, CO: Westview Press.

Gandy, O., & Deanna, A. (2002). All that glitters is not gold: Digging beneath the surface of data mining. *Journal of Business Ethics*, *40*, 373–386. doi:10.1023/A:1020845814009

Garton, L. (n.d.). Studying Online. *Social Networks*. Available at http://jcmc.indiana.edu/vol3/issue1/garton.html#References Accessed on July 5th, 2009.

Geertman, S., & Stillwell, J. (2003). Planning support systems: an introduction. In Geertman, S., & Stillwell, J. (Eds.), *Planning Support Systems in Practice* (pp. 3–22). Berlin: Springer.

Gergen, K. J. (2002). The challenge of absent presence. In Grant, C. A., & Ladson Billings, G. (Eds.), *Dictionary of multicutural education* (pp. 227–241). New York: Oryx Press.

Geuting, E. (2007). Proprietary governance and property development: using changes in a property-rights regime as a market based policy tool. *The Town Planning Review*, *78*(1), 23–40. doi:10.3828/tpr.78.1.3

Giaoutzi, M., & Vescoukis, V. (2006). The Context of IST Impacts on Urban Policy-Making: the Case of Integrated Mobile Spatial Information Systems. In Giaoutzi, M., & Nijkamp, P. (Eds.), *Transport and Information Strategies for Emerging European Networks*. London: Ashgate.

Giaoutzi, M., & Vescoukis, V. (2008). Integrated Mobile Spatial Information Systems and Urban Services. In In Giaoutzi, M., & Nijkamp, P. (Eds.), *Network Strategies in Europe, Developing the Future for Transport and ICT*. London: Ashgate.

Gibson, T. A., & Lowes, M. A. (2006). *Urban Communication: Production, Text, Context*. New York: Rowman & Littlefield Publishers.

Giddens, A. (1984). *The constitution of society: outline of the theory of structuration*. Cambridge, UK: Polity Press.

Ginsberg, J., Mohebbi, M., Patel, R., Brammer, M., & Brilliant, L. (2009). Letter: Detecting influenza epidemics using search query data. *Nature*, *457*, 1012–1014. doi:10.1038/nature07634

Goffman, E. (1967). *Interaction ritual, Essays on face-to-face behaviour*. New York: Pantheon Books.

Goldberger, P. (n.d.). *Cities, Place and Cyberspace*. Retrieved March 21, 2005, from http://www.paulgoldberger.com/speeches.php?speech=berkeley#articlestart

Goldsmith, J., & Wu, T. (2006). *Who Controls the Internet? Illusions of a Borderless World*. Oxford, UK: Oxford University Press.

Goold, B. (2009). Technologies of surveillance and the erosion of institutional trust. In Franko, A., Oppen Gundhus, H., & Mork Lomell, H. (Eds.), *Technologies of (In)Security: The Surveillance of Everyday Life* (pp. 207–218). New York: Routledge-Cavendish.

Gordon, E. (2010). *The Urban Spectator: American Concept-Cities from Kodak to Google*. Dartmouth, MA: Dartmouth.

Gordon, J. (2007). The mobile phone and the public sphere: Mobile phone usage in three critical situations. *Convergence*, *13*(3), 307–319.

Gordon, J. (2007b). The cell phone: An artifact of popular culture and a tool of the public sphere. In Kavoori, A., & Arceneaux, N. (Eds.), *The cell phone reader: Essays in social transformation* (pp. 45–60). New York: Peter Lang.

Gorman, S., & Malecki, J. (2000). The networks of the Internet: an analysis of provider networks in the USA. *Telecommunications Policy*, *24*(2), 113–134. doi:10.1016/S0308-5961(00)00005-7

Gottmann, J. (1973). *The Significance of Territory*. Charlottesville, VA: University Press of Virginia.

Gouaillier, V., & Fleurant, A.-E. (2009). *La vidéosurveillance intelligente: promesses et défis: rapport de veille technologique et commerciale*. Montréal: Centre de recherche informatique de Montreal (CRIM)/ Technopôle Défense et Sécurité, 2009.

Gow, G. A. (2005a). *Privacy and Ubiquitous Network Societies*. Paper presented at the International Telecommunication Union Workshop on Ubiquitous Network Societies. Geneva, 6-8 April 2005 (Document: UNS/10 11 April 2005). Retrieved July 03, 2009 from http://www.itu.int/osg/spu/ni/ubiquitous/UNSChairReport.pdf.

Gow, G. A. (2005b). Pinpointing consent. Locative privacy and mobile phones. In Nyíri, K. (Ed.), *A sense of place. The global and the local in mobile communication* (pp. 139–150). Vienna: Passagen Verlag.

Gow, G., & Ihnat, M. (2004). Prepaid mobile phone service and the anonymous caller: Considering Wireless E-911 in Canada. *Surveillance & Society*, *1*(4).

Graham, S. (1999). Global grids of glass: on global cities, telecommunications and planetary urban networks. *Urban Studies (Edinburgh, Scotland)*, *36*(5-6), 929–949. doi:10.1080/0042098993286

Graham, S. (Ed.). (2004). *The Cybercities Reader*. New York: Routledge.

Graham, S., & Marvin, S. (1995). More than Ducts and Wires: Post-Fordism, Cities and Utility Networks. In Healey, P., Cameron, S., Davoudi, S., Graham, S., & Madani-Pour, A. (Eds.), *Managing Cities: The New Urban Context* (pp. 169–189). London: John Wiley.

Graham, S., & Marvin, S. (1996). *Telecommunications and the city*. New York: Routledge. doi:10.4324/9780203430453

Graham, S., & Marvin, S. (1996). *Telecommunications and the City*. London: Routledge. doi:10.4324/9780203430453

Green, N. (2001). Who's watching whom? Monitoring and accountability in mobile relations. In Brown, B. (Eds.), *Wireless World: Social and Interactional Aspects of the Mobile Age* (pp. 32–45). London: Springer.

Green, N. (2002). On the move: technology, mobility, and the mediation of social time and space. *The Information Society*, *18*, 281–292. doi:10.1080/01972240290075129

Green, N., & Smith, S. (2004). A 'spy in your pocket'? The regulation of mobile phone data in the UK. *Surveillance & Society*, *1*(4).

Greenfield, A. (2006). *Everyware: The dawning age of ubiquitous computing. Berkeley, CA: New Riders Press. De Kerckhove, D. (1997). Connected Intelligence: the arrival of the Web society*. Toronto: Somerville House Publishing.

Guild, R. (2000). Infrastructure Investment and Interregional Development: Theory, Evidence, and Implications for planning. *Public Works Management Policy*, *4*(4), 274–285. doi:10.1177/1087724X0044002

Gumpert, G., & Drucker, S. (2001). A Plea for Chaos. *Qualitative Research Reports in Communication, 2* (2, Spring), 25-32.

Gumpert, G., & Drucker, S. (2004). The Perfections of Sustainability and Imperfections in the Digital Community: Paradoxes of Connection and Disconnection. In Tanabe, M., Van den Besselaar, P., & Ishida, T. (Eds.), *Digital Cities III* (pp. 369–379). Berlin: Springer-Verlag.

Gumpert, G., & Drucker, S. (2008). Communicative Cities. *The International Communication Gazette, 70* (3-4, June), 195-208.

Gumpert, G., & Drucker, S. (2008). The City and the Two Sides of Reciprocity. In Aurigi, A., & De Cindio, F. (Eds.), *Digital Cities: the Augmented Public Space*.

Gye, L. (2007). Picture this: The impact of mobile camera phones on personal photographic practices. *Continuum*, *21*(2), 279–288. doi:10.1080/10304310701269107

Haber Vitrini. (2007). 1 out of every 100 camera phones is in the hands of a Turkish consumer. Retrieved November 12, 2009, from <http://www.habervitrini. com /haber. aspx?id =266906>

Hackler, D. (2003a). High-tech growth and telecommunications infrastructure in cities. *Urban Affairs Review*, *39*(1), 59–86. doi:10.1177/1078087403253054

Hackler, D. (2003b). Invisible infrastructure and the city: the role of telecommunications in economic development. *The American Behavioral Scientist*, *46*(8), 1034–1055. doi:10.1177/0002764202250493

Haddon, L., et al. (2001). *From Mobile to Mobility: The Consumption of ICTs and Mobility in Everyday Life*. In COST269 Mobility Workgroup. Retrieved from http://www.cost269.org/working%20group/cost_workgpr_mobility.htm

Haggerty, K. D. (2006). Tear down the walls: On demolishing the Panopticon. In Lyon, D. (Ed.). *Theorizing surveillance: The Panopticon and beyond.* (23-45). Devon, UK: Willan Publishing.

Haggerty, K. D., & Ericson, R. V. (2000). The surveillant assemblage. *The British Journal of Sociology*, *51*(4), 605–622. doi:10.1080/00071310020015280

Hall, A. (2009). "I am Trying to Believe": Dystopia as Utopia in the Year Zero Alternate Reality Game. *Eludamos. Journal for Computer Game Culture*, *3*(1), 69–82.

Hall, E. T. (1982). *The hidden dimension* (2nd ed.). Garden City, New York: Anchor Books Editions.

Hall, P. (1966). *The World Cities*. New York: McGraw-Hill.

Hampapur, A., Brown, L., Connell, J., Pankanti, S., Senior, A., & Tian, Y. (2003). Smart Surveillance: Applications, Technologies and Implications. In *Joint Conference of the Fourth International Conference on Information, Communications & Signal Processing and Fourth Pacific-Rim Conference on Multimedia, 2* (pp. 1133- 1138). New York: December.

Hanafizadeh, M., Saghaei, A., & Hanafizadeh, P. (2009). An index for cross-country analysis of ICT infrastructure and access. *Telecommunications Policy*, *33*(1), 385–405. doi:10.1016/j.telpol.2009.03.008

Handy, C. (1994). *The Empty Raincoat: Making Sense of the Future*. London: Hutchinson.

Hanneman, R. (n.d.). *Introduction to social network methods*. Available at: http://wizard.ucr.edu/~rhannema/index.html#news. Accessed on May 1st, 2008.

Hardt, M., & Negri, A. (2000). *Empire*. Cambridge, MA: Harvard University Press.

Harmon, A. (2003). Lost? Hiding? Your cellphone is keeping tabs. *The New York Times.* December 31.

Harris, P. B., & Brown, B. B. (1996). The home and identity display: Interpreting resident territoriality from home exteriors. *Journal of Environmental Psychology*, *16*, 187–203. doi:10.1006/jevp.1996.0016

Harwit, E. (2008). *China's telecommunications revolution*. New York: Oxford University Press. doi:10.1093/acprof:oso/9780199233748.001.0001

Hassid, J. (2008). Controlling the Chinese media: An uncertain business. *Asian Survey*, *48*(3), 414–430. doi:10.1525/as.2008.48.3.414

Hayles, K. (1999). *How we became posthuman—virtual bodies in cybernetics, literature, and informatics*. Chicago: The University of Chicago Press.

Healey, P. (2002). On creating the city as a collective resource. *Urban Studies (Edinburgh, Scotland)*, *39*(10), 1777–1792. doi:10.1080/0042098022000002957

Hearing, N., Venetianer, P. L., & Lipton, A. (2008). The evolution of video surveillance: an overview. *Machine Vision and Applications*, *19*(5-6), 279–290. doi:10.1007/s00138-008-0152-0

Henman, P. (2004). Targeted! Population segmentation, electronic surveillance, and governing the unemployed in Australia. *International Sociology*, *19*(2), 173–191. doi:10.1177/0268580904042899

Hodson, M., & Marvin, S. (2009b). Cities mediating technological transitions: understanding visions, intermediation and consequences. *Technology Analysis and Strategic Management*, *21*(4), 515–534. doi:10.1080/09537320902819213

Hodson, M., & Marvin, S. (2009b). Urban Ecological Security': A New Urban Paradigm? *International Journal of Urban and Regional Research*, *33*(1), 193–215. doi:10.1111/j.1468-2427.2009.00832.x

Holden, J. (2006). *Cultural Value and the Crisis of Legitimacy: Why culture needs a democratic mandate*. London: Demos.

Honan, M. (2009). I am here: One man's experiment with the location-aware lifestyle. *Wired*, January 19. Retrieved from www.wired.com/gadgets/wireless/magazine/17-02/lp_guineapig/

Horner, L., Lekhi, R., & Blaug, R. (2006). *Deliberative Democracy and the Role of Public Managers*. London: The Work Foundation.

Hoskote, R. (2008). Versions of a postcolonial metropolis: competing discourses on Bombay's image. In Segbers, K. (Ed.), *The Making of Global City Regions: Johannesburg, Mumbai/Bombay, Sao Paulo, and Shanghai* (pp. 258–287). Baltimore, MD: JHU Press.

Hudson-Smith, A., & Milton, R. Dearden, J. & Batty, M. (2007). Virtual cities: digital mirrors into a recursive world. *UCL Working Papers Series, 125*(December 2007), 1-24.

Huizinga, J. (1950). *Homo Ludens: A Study of the Play-Element in Culture*. Boston: Beacon Press.

IGDA. (2006). *Alternate Reality Games White Paper*. IGDA ARG SIG.

Ignatieff, M. (1978). *A just measure of pain: The penitentiary in the Industrial Revolution, 1750-1850*. Macmillan.

Independent Expert Group on Mobile Phones [IEGMP]. (2000). *Mobile Phones and Health*. Didcot, UK: Oxon.

InfoTrends. (2007). InfoTrends study shows increased use of camera phones among GenZers. Retrieved January 5, 2010 from <http://www.infotrends.com/public/Content/Press/2007 /10.23.07.html

Ingallina, P. (2001). *Le Projet Urbain. Presses*. Paris: Universitaires de France.

Innis, H. A. (1950). *Empire and Communications*. Oxford, UK: Oxford University Press.

Innis, H. A. (1951). *The Bias of Communication*. Toronto: University of Toronto Press.

Innis, H. A. (1971). *The Bias of Communication. Introduction by Marshall McLuhan*. Toronto: University of Toronto Press.

International Communication Union. (2008). *Mobile cellular subscriptions*. Retrieved October 19, 2009 from <http://www.itu.int/ITU-/icteye/Reporting/ShowReportFrame.aspx?ReportName=/WTI/CellularSubscribersPublic&RP_intYear=2008&RP_intLanguageID=1>

Israel, B. R. (2009). "Make money without doing evil?": Caught between authoritarian regulations in emerging markets and a global law of human rights, U.S. ICTs face a twofold quandary. *Berkeley Technology Law Journal, 24*(1), 617–655.

Jacobs, J. (1960). *The Death and Life of Great American Cities*. New York: Vintage Books.

Jassem, H. (2007). Municipal Wi-Fi-ing of the United States. In Burd, G., Drucker, S., & Gumpert, G. (Eds.), *The Urban Communication Reader* (pp. 219–235). Cresskill, NJ: Hampton Press.

Jefferson, M. (1939). The law of the primate city. *Geographical Review, 29*, 226–232. doi:10.2307/209944

Jeffres, L., Lee, J., & Jian, G. (2010). Modeling Neighborhood Attachment Influence. In Jassem, H., Drucker, S., & Burd, G. (Eds.), *Urban Reader II* (pp. 103–131). Cresskill, N.J.: Hampton Press.

Jenkins, H. (2006). *Convergence Culture: Where Old and New Media Collide*. New York: New York University Press.

Joerin, F., Rey, M., Nembrini, A., & Desthieux, G. (2001). Information et participation pour l'am'enagement du territoire. *Revue Internationale de Geomatique, 11*(3/4), 309–332.

Johnston, B. (2001). Mobile firms act on message. *Planning, 1432*, (17 August), 12-13.

Jones, P., Tauleelo, T., & Kohlhase, J. (2002). Growing pacific town and cities: Samoa's new planning and urban management system. *Australian Planner, 39*(4), 186–193.

Juul, J. (2005). *Half-Real: Video Games between Real Rules and Fictional Worlds*. Cambridge, MA: The MIT Press.

Juul, J. (2008). The Magic Circle and the Puzzle Piece. In S. Günzel, et al (eds.), *Conference Proceedings of the Philosophy of Computer Games*. Potsdam, The Netherlands: Potsdam University Press.

Kaba, S. (1996). Building the future: an architectural manifesto for the next Millennium. *Web Architecture Magazine, April*.

Kanafani, A., Khattak, A., Crotty, M., & Dahlgren, J. (1993). *A planning methodology for intelligent urban transportation systems.* California Partners for Advanced Transit and Highways (PATH). Research Reports: Paper UCB-ITS-PRR-93-14.

Kapadia, A., Henderson, T., Fielding, J., & Kotz, D. (2007). Virtual Walls: Protecting Digital Privacy in Pervasive Environments. In *Proceedings International Conference on Pervasive Computing 2007,* (pp. 162-179). Berlin: Springer-Verlag.

Kärrholm, M. (2007). The Materiality of Territorial Production: A Conceptual Discussion of Territoriality, Materiality, and the Everyday Life of Public Space. *Space and Culture*, *10*(4), 437–453. doi:10.1177/1206331207304356

Keaveny, P. (2007, November 28). Caught a criminal on your phone? *The Bolton News*. Retrieved from October 9, 2009 from < http://www.theboltonnews.co.uk / news/1863234.caught_a_criminal_on_your_phone/>

Keck, M. E., & Sikkink, K. (1998). *Activists beyond borders: Advocacy networks in international politics*. Ithaca, NY: Cornell University Press.

Kellerman, A. (2002). *The Internet on Earth. A Geography of Information*. West Sussex, UK: John Wiley & Sons, Ltd.

Kellerman, A. (2006). *Personal Mobilities*. New York: Routledge.

Kenis, P., & Schneider, V. (1991). Policy networks and policy analysis: Scrutinizing a new analytical toolbox. In Marin, B., & Mayntz, R. (Eds.), *Policy Networks. Empirical Evidence and Theoretical Considerations* (pp. 25–59). Frankfurt: Campus.

Kidd, P. T. (2007). Human centered ambient intelligence: Human-computer relationships for the knowledge age. In Kidd, P. T. (Ed.), *European visions for the knowledge age* (pp. 55–68). Macclesfield, UK: Cheshire Henbury.

Kim, T. (2008). Planning for knowledge cities in ubiquitous technology spaces. In Yigitcanlar, T., Velibeyoglu, K., & Baum, S. (Eds.), *Creative Urban Regions: Harnessing Urban Technologies to Support Knowledge City Initiatives* (pp. 218–230). Hershey, PA: Information Science Reference.

Kindberg, T., Spasojevic, M., Fleck, R., & Sellen, A. (2005). The ubiquitous camera: An in-depth study of camera phone use. *IEEE Pervasive Computing / IEEE Computer Society [and] IEEE Communications Society*, *4*(2), 42–50. doi:10.1109/MPRV.2005.42

Kingsley, D. (2008). Keeping a close watch: The rise of self-surveillance and the threat of digital exposure. *The Sociological Review*, *56*(3), 347–357. doi:10.1111/j.1467-954X.2008.00793.x

Kirkwood, N. (2008). *Research on U-eco city. Final consultancy report*. Boston, MA: Centre for Technology and Environment, Harvard University.

Kitchin, R., & Dodge, M. (2006). Software and the mundane management of air travel. *First Monday*, *11*(Nr. SI-7).

Kleinrock, L. (2000). On some principles of nomadic computing and multi-access communications. *IEEE Communications Magazine*, (July), 46–50. Retrieved April 08, 2006, from http://www.comsoc.org/~ci/public/2000/jul/index.html

Klijn, E.-H., & Koppenjan, J. F. M. (2000). Public management and policy networks: Foundations of a network approach to governance. *Public Management: an international journal of research and theory, 2*(2), 135-158.

Kline, E. (2000). Planning and creating eco-cities: indicators as a tool for shaping development and measuring progress. *Local Environment*, *5*(3), 343–350. doi:10.1080/13549830050134275

Knoke, D., & Kuklinski, J. H. (1982). *Network Analysis*. Beverly Hills, CA: Sage.

Knox, P. (1994). *Urbanization: An Introduction to Urban Geography*. Englewood Cliffs, NJ: Prentice Hall.

Koskinen, (2005). Seeing with mobile images: Towards perpetual visual contact. In Nyiri, K. (Ed.), *A Sense of place: The global and the local in mobile communication*. Vienna: Passagen Verlag.

Kövecses, Z. (2008). The cellphone as a conceptual category. In Nyíri, K. (Ed.), *Integration and ubiquity. Towards a philosophy of telecommunications convergence* (pp. 29–44). Vienna: Passagen Verlag.

Kratke, S. (2000). Berlin: the metropolis as a production space. *European Planning Studies*, *8*, 7–27. doi:10.1080/096543100110901

Kuitenbrower, K. (2006). The Cultural and Social Possibilities of RFID. *Open, 11*. Retrieved 21st April 2008, from http://www.skor.nl/id.php/ KUITENBROUWERENGELSOPEN11

Lacharite, J. (2002). Electronic decentralisation in China: A critical analysis of Internet filtering policies in the People's Republic of China. *Australian Journal of Political Science*, *37*(2), 33–346. doi:10.1080/10361140220148188

Lacy, I., Quarles, A., Stokes, T., & Tabuchi, L. (2001). *Location, Location, Location. Will Location – Based Services be the Next Golden Child? Technical report*. Kellogg Tech Venture.

Lai, K. (2009). Global Cities in Competition? A Qualitative Analysis of Shanghai, Beijing and Hong Kong as Financial Centres'. *GaWC Research Bulletin,* 313. Retrieved October 4, 2009 from http://www.lboro.ac.uk/gawc/rb/rb313.html.

Latour, B. (1993). *We Have Never Been Modern*. Cambridge, MA: Harvard University Press.

Latour, B. (1994). On technical mediation: philosophy, sociology, genealogy. *Common Knowledge*, *2*(3).

Latour, B. (1999). On recalling ANT. In Law, J., & Hassard, J. (Eds.), *Actor Network Theory and After*. Oxford: Blackwell.

Lawless, P., & Gore, T. (1999). Urban regeneration and transport investment: a case study of Sheffield 1992-96. *Urban Studies (Edinburgh, Scotland)*, *36*(1), 527–545. doi:10.1080/0042098993510

Lazega, E. (2007). *Réseau sociaux et strutures relationnelles*. Paris: PUF.

Lazzarato, M. (2004). *Les revolutions du capitalisme*. Paris: Les Empêcheurs de Penser en Rond.

Le Gales, P. (1998). Regulation, territory and governance. *International Journal of Urban and Regional Research*, *22*(3), 482–506. doi:10.1111/1468-2427.00153

Lee, S., & Leem, Y. (2009). *Philosophical and Conceptual Characteristics of Ubiquitous City Strategies and Projects*. CUPUM'09, Hong Kong, 16-19 June 2009.

Lee, S.-H., Yigitcanlar, T., Han, J.-H., & Leem, Y. T. (2008). Ubiquitous Urban Infrastructure: Infrastructure Planning and Development in Korea. *Innovation: Management. Policy & Practice*, *10*(2/3), 282–292.

Lee, T. Berners, Hendler, J. & Lassila, O. (2001). The Semantic Web. *Scientific American*, May.

Lefebvre, H. (1991). *The Production of Space*. London: Blackwell.

Lefevbre, H. (1991). *The Production of space*. Oxford, UK: Blackwell Publishers.

Lemos, A. (2004). Cibercultura e mobilidade: a era da conexão. *Razón y Palabra*, Oct./Nov. 2004. Retrieved July 16, 2009 from http://www.razonypalabra.org.mx/anteriores/n41/alemos.html.

Lemos, A. (2007). Cidade e Mobilidade. Telefones Celulares, funções pós-massivas e territórios informacionais. *Matrizes. Revista do Programa de Pós-Graduação em Ciências da Comunicação*, *1*(1), 121–137.

Lemos, A. (2007). Comunicação e práticas sociais no espaço urbano: as características dos Dispositivos Híbridos Móveis de Conexão Multirredes (DHMCM). *Revista Comunicação. Mídia e Consumo*, *4*(10), 23–40.

Lemos, A. (2008). *Ciberespaço e Tecnologias Móveis: Processos de Territorialização e Desterritorialização na Cibercultura*. COMPÓs, 2008. Available September 2008, at [http://www.facom.ufba.br/ciberpesquisa/andrelemos/territorio.pdf

Lemos, A. (2008). Mídias Locativas e Territórios Informacionais. In Santaella, L., & Arantes, P. (Eds.), *Estéticas Tecnológicas: Novos Modos de Sentir* (pp. 207–230). São Paulo, Brazil: EDUC.

Lemos, A. (2008a). Mídias Locativas e Territórios Informacionais. In Santaella, L., & Arantes, P. (Eds.), *Estéticas Tecnológicas: Novos Modos de Sentir* (pp. 207–230). São Paulo: EDUC.

Lemos, A. (2008a). Mídias locativas e territórios informacionais. In Santaella, L., & Arantes, P. (Eds.), *Estéticas tecnológicas. Novos modos de sentir* (pp. 207–230). São Paulo, Brazil: Educ.

Lemos, A. (2008b). Mobile Communication and new sense of places: a critique of spatialization in cyberculture. [PUCSP]. *Galáxia, 16*, 91–108.

Lemos, A. (2009). Pervasive Games and Processes of Spacialization Communication, Informational Territories and Mobile Technologies. In *Canadian Journal of Communication*.

Lemos, A. (2010). Locative media and surveillance at the boundaries of informational territories. In R. Firmino, F. Duarte, & C. Ultramari, C. (Eds.). *ICTs for mobile and ubiquitous urban infrastructures: surveillance, locative media and global networks*. Hershey, PA: IGI Global.

Lemos, A. (2011). Locative media and surveillance at the boundaries of informational territories. In Firmino, R., Duarte, F., & Ultramari, C. (Eds.), *ICTs for Mobile and Ubiquitous Urban Infrastructures: Surveillance, Locative Media and Global Networks*. Hershey, PA: IGI Global.

Lenz, R. (2007). Locative media. Retrived January 8, 2008, from http://spresearch.waag.org/images/LocativeMedia.pdf.

Levi, M. (1981). The predatory theory of rule. *Politics & Society, 10*(4), 431–465. doi:10.1177/003232928101000403

Levinson, P. (2004). *Cell phone: The story of the world's most mobile medium and how it has transformed everything*. New York: Palgrave MacMillan.

Lévy, P. (1993). *As tecnologias da Inteligência: o futuro do pensamento na era da informática,* (pp. 34). Rio de Janeiro, Brazil, Ed.

Ley, D. (2007). Ubiquitous Computing. Emerging Technologies for Learning, (Vol. 2). Retrieved February 4, 2010, from http://schools.becta.org.uk/upload-dir/downloads/page_documents/research/emerging_technologies07_chapter6.pdf

Li, R. (2002). Strengthening police work through science and technology: An outline of the National Public Security Work Informatization Project (Golden Shield) Project. In Chinese. *Public Security Studies, 4*(90), 4-12.

Lianos, M. (2001). *Le nouveau contrôle social*. Paris: L'Harmattan.

Lianos, M., & Douglas, M. (2000). Dangerization and the end of deviance. *The British Journal of Criminology, 40*, 261–278.

Licoppe, C. (2003). Two modes of maintaining interpersonal relations through telephone: from the domestic to the mobile phone. In Katz, J. (Ed.), *Machines that become us: the social context of personal communication technology* (pp. 171–185). New Brunswick, New Jersey: Transaction Publishers.

Lieberthal, K. (2003). *Governing China: From revolution to reform* (2nd ed.). New York: W.W. Norton & Co.

Ling, R. (2000). Direct and mediated interaction in the maintenance of social relationships. In Sloane, A., & Van Rijn, F. (Eds.), *Home informatics and telematics: Information, technology and society* (pp. 61–86). Boston: Kluwer.

Ling, R. (2002). *The social juxtaposition of mobile telephone conversations and public spaces*. Chunchon, Korea, July. Retrieved May 15, 2008, from http://www.richardling.com/publications.php.

Ling, R. (2004a). Where is mobile communication causing social change? In Lim, S.D., (ed.), *Mobile communication and social change.* Seoul, South Korea. Retrieved June 17, 2006, from http://www.rheingold.com/texts/Ling_2004_Socialchange.htm#_ftn9

Ling, R. (2004b). *The mobile connection: the cell phone's impact on society*. San Francisco: Elsevier; Morgan Kaufmann Publishers.

Ling, R. (2008). *New tech, new ties: how mobile communication is reshaping social cohesion*. Cambridge, MA: The MIT Press.

Lloyd, M. G., Peel, D., Roberts, P. M., & Riley, J. (2004). *An Evaluation of Revised Planning Controls over Telecommunications Development*. Edinburgh, UK: Scottish Executive Social Research.

Los, M. (2004). The technologies of total domination. *Surveillance & Society*, *2*(1), 15–38.

Luckhurst, T. (2007, January 7). Now we can all set the news agenda. *The Independent.* Retrieved October 15, 2009 from <http://www.independent.co.uk/news/media/now-we-can-all-set-the-news-agenda-431038.html>

Lyon, D. (1988). *The Information Society: Issues and Illusions*. Cambridge: Polity.

Lyon, D. (1992). The new surveillance: Electronic technologies and the maximum security society. *Crime, Law, and Social Change*, *18*, 159–175. doi:10.1007/BF00230629

Lyon, D. (1994). *The Electronic Eye: The Rise of Surveillance Society*. Cambridge, UK: Polity.

Lyon, D. (2001). Facing the future: Seeking ethics for everyday surveillance. [from http://csalt.education.ecu.edu.au/projects/ cyberspace/lyon/ethics_surveillance.pdf]. *Ethics and Information Technology*, *3*, 171–181. Retrieved May 10th, 2008. doi:10.1023/A:1012227629496

Lyon, D. (2001). *Surveillance Society: Monitoring Everyday Life*. Buckingham, UK: Open University Press.

Lyon, D. (2001). *Surveillance society: Monitoring everyday life*. Philadelphia, PA: Open University Press.

Lyon, D. (2002). Surveillance studies: Understanding visibility, mobility, and the phenetic fix. *Surveillance & Society*, *1*(1), 1–7.

Lyon, D. (2003). *Surveillance after September 11*. Cambridge, UK: Polity Press.

Lyon, D. (2004). Surveillance technologies: Trends and social implications. In Barrie, S. (Ed.), *The security economy* (pp. 127–148). Paris: OECD Publishing.

Lyon, D. (2004). Surveillance technologies: Trends and social implications. In Stevens, B. (Ed.), *The security economy* (127-148). Paris: OECD.

Lyon, D. (2005). September 11, synopticon, and scopophilia: watching and being watched. In Haggerty, K., & Ericson, R. (Eds.), *The Politics of Surveillance and Visibility*. Toronto: University of Toronto Press.

Lyon, D. (2006). Why where you are matters: Mundane mobilities, transparent technologies, and digital discrimination. In Monahan, T. (Ed.), *Surveillance and Security: Technological Politics and Power in Everyday Life* (pp. 209–224). New York: Routledge.

Lyon, D. (2007). *Surveillance Studies: An Overview*. Cambridge, UK: Polity Press.

Lyon, D. (2009). *Identifying citizens*. Cambridge, UK: Polity Press.

Lyon, D. (2009). *Identifying Citizens: ID Cards as Surveillance*. Cambridge, UK: Polity Press.

Lyon, D. (2010). Why where you are matters: mundane mobilities, transparent technologies, and digital discrimination. In Firmino, R., Duarte, F., & Ultramari, C. (Eds.), *ICTs for Mobile and Ubiquitous Urban Infrastructures: Surveillance, Locative Media and Global Networks*. Hershey, PA: IGI Global.

Lyon, D., Marmura, S., & Peroff, P. (2005). *Location Technologies: Mobility, Surveillance and Privacy*. Report for the Office of the Privacy Commissioner, Ottawa, Canada. Retrieved from www. Queensu.ca/sociology/Surveillance/

Macek, S. (2006). *Urban Nightmares: The Media, the Right, and the Moral Panic over the City*. Minneapolis, MN: University of Minnesota Press.

Mack, M. P. (1969). *A Bentham reader*. New York: Pegasus.

MacKinnon, R. (2008). Flatter world and thicker walls? Blogs, censorship and civic discourse in China. *Public Choice*, *134*, 31–46. doi:10.1007/s11127-007-9199-0

Magedanz, T., Rothermel, K., & Krause, S. (1996). Intelligent agents: an emerging technology for next generation telecommunications. In *INFOCOM '96*, March 24-28, San Francisco.

Makagon, D. (2004). *Where the Ball Drops: Days and Nights in Times Square*. Minneapolis, MN: University of Minnesota Press.

Malecki, E., & Bous, C. (2003). Telecommunications Infrastructure in the South-eastern United States: Urban and Rural Variation. *Growth and Change*, *34*(1), 109–129. doi:10.1111/1468-2257.00201

Malecki, E., & Wei, H. (2009). A wired world: the evolving geography of submarine cables and the shift to Asia. *Annals of the Association of American Geographers. Association of American Geographers*, *99*(2), 360–382. doi:10.1080/00045600802686216

Mann, S. (1998). Reflectionism and diffusionism: New tactics for deconstructing the video surveillance superhighway. *Leonardo*, *31*(2), 93–102. doi:10.2307/1576511

Mann, S. (2004). Sousveillance: Inverse surveillance in multimedia imaging. In *Proceedings of the 12th Annual ACM International Conference on Multimedia*, (pp. 620-627). New York: ACM.

Manovich, L. (2002). The Poetics of Augmented Space. In Everett, A., & Caldwell, J. (Eds.), *Digitextuality*. London: Routledge.

Manovich, L. (2005). The Poetics of Augmented Space: Learning from Prada. *Noemalab*. Tecnologie e Società. Retrieved 10th May 2008, from http://www.noemalab.org/sections/ideas/ ideas_articles/manovich_augmented_space.html

Manovich, L. (2006). The poetics of augmented space. *Visual Communication*, *5*(2), 219–240. doi:10.1177/1470357206065527

Manovich, L. (2008). The practice of everyday (media) life. In Lovink, G. & Niederer, S. (Eds.), *Video Vortex Reader,* Responses to Youtube, (pp. 33-44). Amsterdam: Institute of Network Cultures. Retrieved May 15, 2006, from http://www.networkcultures.org/publications

Markoff, J. (2008). You're leaving a digital trail. What about privacy? *New York Times*, November 29. Retrieved from www.nytimes.com/2008/11/30/business/30privacy.html?_r=1&ei=5070&emc=eta1

Marris, P. (1998). Planning and civil society in the twenty-first century: An introduction. In Douglass, M., & Friedmann, J. (Eds.), *Cities for Citizens: Planning and the Rise of Civil Society in a Global Age* (pp. 9–17). New York: J. Wiley.

Marteleto, R. (2001) Análise de redes sociais – Aplicação nos estudos de transferência da informação. *Ci. Inf., Brasília, 30*(1, jan./apr), 71-81.

Marx, G. T. (1988). *Under cover: Police surveillance in America*. Berkeley, CA: University of California Press.

Marx, G. T. (2002). What is new about the new surveillance? Classifying for change and continuity. *Surveillance & Society*, *1*(1), 9–29.

Massey, D. (2005). *For Space*. London: Sage.

Massey, D. (2007). *World City*. London: Polity Press.

Mastrocolla, V. M. (2006). ARGS: Uma nova ferramenta de entretenimento, comunicação e Marketing. *Revista da ESPM, 13*(12-5), 94-103.

Mathiesen, S. A. (2001). You can ring, but you can't hide. *The Guardian*, 29 November, 2001. Retrieved from http://www.guardian.co.uk/print/0,3858,4309424-110837,00.html

Mathiesen, T. (1997). The viewer society: Michel Foucault's Panopticon revisited. *Theoretical Criminology*, *1*(2), 215–234. doi:10.1177/1362480697001002003

Mattelart, A. (2006). Para que "Nova Sociedade Mundial da Informação.". In de Moraes, D. (Ed.), *Sociedade Midiatizada*. Rio de Janeiro, Brazil: Mauad.

McAdams, A. J. (2005). Internet surveillance after September 11: Is the United States becoming Great Britain? *Comparative Politics*, *37*(4), 479–498. doi:10.2307/20072905

McCahill, M. (2002). *The Surveillance Web: The Rise of Visual Surveillance in an English City*. Cullompton, UK: Willan Publishing.

McCullough, M. (2004). *Digital Ground: Architecture, Pervasive Computing, and Environmental Knowing*. Cambridge, MA: MIT Press.

McGonigal, J. (2003a, November). A real little game. The performance of belief in pervasive play. In Raessens, J.R., Copier, M. (Eds.). *Proceedings of the Level Up DiGRA Conference,* Utrecht.

McGonigal, J. (2003b). *This is not a game: Immersive aesthetics and collect play*. Presented at the 5th International Digital Arts and Culture Conference (Melbourne, May).

McGonigal, J. (2006). *This Might be a Game*. Unpublished doctoral Dissertation, Berkeley University, Berkeley, CA.

McGonigal, J. (2007). Ubiquitous gaming. A vision for the future of enchanted spaces. In Borries, F. (Eds.), *Space Time Play: Computer Games, Architecture and Urbanism: the Next Level*. Basel, Switzerland: Birkhauser Verlag AG.

McLuhan, M. (1964). *Understanding Media: The Extensions of Man*. New York: Mentor.

McLuhan, M. (2003). *Undestanding me. Lectures and interviews*. Cambridge, MA: MIT.

McQuire, S. (2008). *The Media City: Media, Architecture and Urban Space*. London: Sage.

Merleau-Ponty, M. (1999). *Fenomenologia da Percepção. 2a. Edição*. São Paulo, Brazil: Martins Fontes.

Merleau-Ponty, M. (2005). *The Poetics of Augmented Space: Learning from Prada.* Retrieved May 27, 2006, from http://www.manovich.net/DOCS/augmented_space.doc.

Meyrovitz, J. (1985). *No Sense of Place: The impact of Electronic Media on Social Behavior*. London: Oxford University Press.

Michael, M. (2003). Between the mundane and the exotic: time for a different sociotechnical stuff. *Time & Society*, *12*(1), 127–143. doi:10.1177/0961463X03012001372

Mika, P. (n.d.). *Social Networks and the Semantic Web.* Disponível em wrg.upf.edu/WRG/seminarios/260407_aMika.pdf

Miles, J. C., & Walker, A. J. (2006). The Potential Application of Artificial Intelligence in Transport. *IEE Proceedings Intelligent Transport Systems*, *153*(3), 183–198. doi:10.1049/ip-its:20060014

Milligan, M.J. (). *Interactional Past And Potential: The Social Construction Of Place Attachment, 21* (1), 1–33.

Mitchell, W. J. (1995). *City of Bits: Space, Place, and the Infobahn*. Cambridge, MA: MIT Press.

Mitchell, W. J. (1999). *e-topia. 'Urban Life, Jim - But Not as We Know It.'* Cambridge, MA: MIT Press.

Mobile Operators Association. (2004). *Guide to Using Traffic Light Rating Model for Public Consultation*. London: MOA. Retrieved from http://www.mobilemastinfo.com/planning/UK-Guide-to-using-TLM-version-2-1.pdf

Mobile Operators Association. (2006). *Developing Mobile Networks Ten Commitments to best siting practice.* London: MOA. Retrieved from http://www.mobilemastinfo.com/planning/MOA_10_Commitments.pdf

Mobile Operators Association. (2006). *Mobile Phones and Base Stations*. London: MOA.

Mobile Telecommunications and Health Research Programme. (2007). *Report 2007*. London: MTHR Management Committee.

Mokey, N. (2009, January 28). Bill would ban silent camera phones. *Digital Trends.* Retrieved October 15, 2009 from <http://www.digitaltrends.com/photography/bill-would-ban-silent-camera-phones/>

Montolla, M. (2005). *Exploring the Edge of the Magic Circle. Defining Pervasive Games.* DAC 2005 conference, December 1-3, IT University of Copenhagen. Retrieved September 2008 from http://users.tkk.fi/mmontola/exploringtheedge.pdf

Montolla, M. Stenros & Waern. (Eds.). (2009). *Pervasive Games: Theory and Design*. San Francisco: Morgan Kaufmann.

Morellas, V., Pavlidis, I., & Tsiamyrtzis, P. (2003). DETER: Detection of events for threat evaluation and recognition. *Machine Vision and Applications*, *15*(1), 29–45. doi:10.1007/s00138-003-0121-6

Morgan, S. (2009, March 20). *Economy + Internet trends*. Retrieved September 29, 2009, from http://www.slideshare.net/misteroo/economy-tech-trends-in-2009-by-mary-meeker-morgan-stanley

Morin, E. (2002). *O método 3 – Conhecimento do conhecimento*. Porto Alegre, Brazil: Sulina.

Moroni, S. (2004). Towards a Reconstruction of the Public Interest Criterion. *Planning Theory*, *3*, 151–171. doi:10.1177/1473095204044779

Mosco, M. (2004). *The Digital Sublime: Myth, Power, and Cyberspace*. Cambridge, MA: MIT Press.

Moses, A. (2006). Wii breaks Xbox 360 sales record. *The Sydney Morning Herald*, 14/12/2006.

Moss, M., & Townsend, A. (2000). How Telecommunications Systems Are Transforming Urban Spaces. In Wheeler, J., Aoyama, Y., & Warf, B. (Eds.), *Cities in the Telecommunications Age: The Fracturing of Geographies* (pp. 31–41). London: Routledge.

Moss, M., & Townsend, A. (2000). The Internet backbone and the American metropolis. *The Information Society*, *16*(1), 35–47. doi:10.1080/019722400128310

Murakami Wood, D., & Graham, S. (2006). Permeable Boundaries in the Software-sorted Society: Surveillance and the Differentiation of Mobility. In Sheller, M., & Urry, J. (Eds.), *Mobile Technologies of the City* (pp. 177–191). London: Routledge.

Murdoch, J., & Lowe, P. (2003). The preservationist paradox: modernism, environmentalism and the politics of spatial division. *Transactions of the Institute of British Geographers*, *28*(3), 318–332. doi:10.1111/1475-5661.00095

Musil, S. (2008, September 9). NYC's 911 system upgraded to accept photos, video. *CNET News*. Retrieved October 20, 2009 from < http://news.cnet.com/8301-1035_3-10037418-94.html?tag=newsEditorsPicksArea.0>

Needham, B., & Louw, E. (2006). Institutional Economics and Policies for Changing Land Markets: The Case of Industrial Estates in the Netherlands. *Journal of Property Research*, *23*(1), 75–90. doi:10.1080/09599910600748675

Negroponte, N. (1995). Wearable computing. *OBS "Being Digital" Cyberdock*. Retrieved May 27, 2006, from http://www.obs-us.com/obs/english/books/nn/bd1201.htm

Neilson, L. (2002). Instruments of governance in urban management. *Australian Planner*, *39*(2), 97–102.

Neuman, M. (2006). Infiltrating infrastructures: On the nature of networked infrastructure. *Journal of Urban Technology*, *13*(1), 3–31. doi:10.1080/10630730600752728

Neuman, P. R. (2004). Why nobody saw 9/11 coming. *The New York Times*, March 27.

Newburn, T., & Hayman, S. (2002). *Policing, surveillance and social control: CCTV and police monitoring of suspects*. Cullompton, UK: Willan Publishing.

News, A. B. C. (n.d.). Retrieved from http://abcnews.go.com/video/playerIndex?id=3448815

Nicolescu, B. (1999). *O manifesto da transdisciplinaridade*. São Paulo, Brazil: Ed. Triom.

Nieuwdorp, E. (2007). The pervasive interface. Tracing the magic circle. In S. De Castell & J. Jensen (Eds.). *Proceedings of the DiGRA Conference*, Vancouver, June 2007.

Ning, L. (2009). *China's rise in the world ICT industry: Industrial strategies and the catch-up development model*. New York: Routledge.

Nolmark, H. (2007). *Re-thinking Sustainable Urban Development in an Era of Globalisation, Resource Constraints and Climate Change*. Centre for Sustainable Urban and Regional Futures, University of Salford, November 2007.

Nordvall, H. (2009). Making Sense of the Social Forum: On the Local Framing of a Fashionable Global Symbol. *Journal of Contemporary Ethnography*, *38*(4), 435–464. doi:10.1177/0891241608330355

Norman, D. (2002). *The design of everyday things*. New York: Basic Books.

Norris, C. (2003). From personal to digital: CCTV, the panopticon, and the technological mediation of suspicion and social control. In Lyon, D. (Ed.), *Surveillance as Social Sorting: Privacy, Risk, and Digital Discrimination*. New York: Routledge.

Norris, C., & Armstrong, G. (1999). *Maximum Security Society: The Rise of CCTV*. London: Berg.

Nowotny, H. (1998). *Time: The Modern and Postmodern Experience*. Oxford, UK: Blackwell.

NY1 News. (2009, September 1). *Port Authority fires bridge guards caught napping*. Retrieved October 20, 2009, from < http://ny1.com/1-all-boroughs-news-content/top_stories/105052/port-authority-fires-bridge-guards-caught-napping/?ap=1&=Flash

O'Brian, K. J. (2008). Still searching for profit in location-based services. *New York Times*, November 9. Retrieved from www.nytimes.com/2008/11/09/technology/09iht-wireless10.1.17649240.html

O'Brien, R. (1992). *Global Financial Integration: the End of Geography*. London: Pinter.

O'Brien, W., & Soibelman, L. (2004). Technology and Engineering Dimensions: Collecting and interpreting new information for civil and environmental infrastructure management. In Zimmerman, R., & Horan, T. (Eds.), *Digital Infrastructures: Enabling Civil and Environmental Systems through Information Technology*. London: Routledge. doi:10.4324/9780203357125_chapter_TWO

O'Connell, P. (2005). Korea's high-tech utopia, where everything is observed. *New York Times, 5 October 2005*. Retrieved from http://www.nytimes.com/2005/10/05/technology/techspecial/05oconnell.html?ex=1286164800&en=4a368c49e8f30bd2&ei=5088

O'Harrow, R. (2005). *No Place to Hide*. New York: Free Press.

Ofcom. (2009). *Communications Market Report 2009*. Retrieved September 13, 2009, from http://www.ofcom.org.uk/research/cm/cmr09/cmr09.pdf

Office of the Deputy Prime Minister. (2002). *Code of Best Practice on Mobile Phone Network Development*. London: ODPM.

Ohmae, K. (1990). *The Borderless World: power and strategy in the interlinked economy*. London: HarperCollins.

Okabe, D., & Ito, M. (2003, 28 August). Camera phones changing the definition of picture-worthy. *Japan Media Review*. Retrieved October 12, 2009 from http://www.ojr.org/japan/wireless/1062208524.php

Okabe, D., & Ito, M. (2006). Everyday contexts of camera phone use: steps toward technosocial ethnographic frameworks. In Hoflich, J., & Hartmann, M. (Eds.), *Mobile communication in everyday life: An ethnographic view* (pp. 79–102). Berlin: Frank and Timme.

OpenNet Initiative. (2009a). *Internet filtering in China*. Retrieved September 25, 2009, from http://opennet.net/sites/opennet.net/files/ONI_China_2009.pdf

OpenNet Initiative. (2009b). *China's Green Dam: The implications of government control encroaching on the home PC*. Retrieved October 5, 2009, from http://opennet.net/sites/opennet.net/files/GreenDam_bulletin.pdf

Örnenbring, H. (2007). Alternate reality gaming and convergence culture: The case of *Alias*. *International Journal of Cultural Studies*, 10.

Osborne, T., & Rose, N. (2004). Spatial phenomenotechnics: making space with Charles Booth and Patrick Geddes Environment and Planning D. *Society and Space*, *22*, 209–228.

Palazzi, C. E., Ferretti, S., & Roccetti, M. (2009). Communities on the road: Fast triggering of interactive multimedia services. *Multimedia Tools and Applications*, *44*(2), 229–247. doi:10.1007/s11042-009-0292-x

Palser, B. (2007, Oct/Nov). Mining the Web. *American Journalism Review*, *29*(5), 70.

Panic about Erdogan. (n.d.). *Milliyet*, October 18, 2006. Retrieved on November 12, 2009, from http://www.milliyet.com.tr/2006/10/18/guncel/agun.html

Park, H. W. (2003). Hyperlink network analysis: a new method for the of social structure on the web. *Connections*, *25*(1), 49–61.

Park, H. W., & Thelwall, M. (2003). Hyperlink Analyses of the World Wide Web: A Review. *Journal of Computer-Mediated Communication*, *8*(4).

Parker, J. (1999). Regulation of privatised public utilities in the UK: performance and governance. *International Journal of Public Sector Management*, *12*(3), 213–235. doi:10.1108/09513559910267387

Parker, J. (2001). *Total surveillance: Investigating the Big Brother world of e-spies, eavesdroppers and CCTV*. London: Piatkus.

Pereira, D. C. (2007). *Amazônia Transnacional: As redes ambientais na internet e a padronização da natureza*. Dissertation in Agricultural Extension, Department of Rural Economy, Federal University of Viçosa.

Pereira, D. C. (2008). *O encadeamento da imagem dos índios isolados da Amazônia na internet e a padronização da natureza*. In 1° Colóquio de Comunicação e Sociabilidade 'Comunicação Midiática: Instituições, Valores e Cultura', novembro de 2008.

Phillips, D. & Wiegerling, K. (2007). Introduction to IRIE Vol. 8. *International Review of Information Ethics*, *8*(12/2007), 5-6.

Pizzaro, N. (2004). *Un nuevo enfoque sobre la equivalência estructural: lugares y redes de lugares como herramientas para la teoría sociológica*. Redes: Revista hispana para el análisis de redes sociales.

Plant, S. (2001). *On the mobile. The effects of mobile telephones on social and individual life.* Motorola Inc. Retrieved May 27, 2006, from http://www.motorola.com/mot/documents/0,1028,296,00.pdf.

Pope, S. (2005). The Shape of Locative Media. *Mute Magazine, 29*. Retrieved 21st April 2008, from http://www.metamute.com/look/article.tpl?IdLanguage=1& IdPublication=1&NrIssue=29NrSection=10NrArticle=1477

Powell, W. W. (1990). Neither market nor hierarchy: network forms of organization. *Research in Organizational Behavior*, *12*, 295–336.

Pred, A. (1980). *Urban Growth and City Systems in the United States, 1840-1860*. London: Hutchinson.

Procopiuck, M., & Frey, K. (2009a). Articulações organizacionais em *redes de políticas públicas* no ciberespaço: o caso da política de difusão social de TICS em Porto Alegre e Curitiba. *Revista Organizações & Sociedade*, *16*(51).

Procopiuck, M., & Frey, K. (2009b). Redes de Políticas Públicas e de Governança e sua Análise a partir da *Websphere Analysis. Revista de Sociologia e Politica*, *17*(34), 131–144. doi:10.1590/S0104-44782009000300006

Pyatt, J. (2002). The plague of the phone masts. *The Sun (Baltimore, Md.)*, *15*(July).

Rabinow, P. (1992). Artificiality and enlightenment: from sociobiology to biosociality. In Crary, J., & Kwinter, S. (Eds.), *Incorporations* (pp. 234–252). New York: Zone Books.

Ramirez, C. (2003). *E-Parking: User friendly e-commerce to optimise parking space*. Paper presented at 10th World Congress and Exhibition on Intelligent Transport Systems and Services, Madrid.

Rasnake, D. (2008, August 6). Camera phone sales to double by 2012. *DigitalCameraReview.com*. Retrieved November 12, 2009, from <http://www.digitalcamerareview.com/default.asp?newsID=3612>

Reading, A. (2009). Mobile witnessing: Ethics and the camera phone in the 'war on terror.'. *Globalizations*, *6*(1), 61–76. doi:10.1080/14747730802692435

Recuero, R. (2009). *Redes Sociais na Internet*. Porto Alegre, Brazil: Sulina.

Regan, M., Oxley, J., Godley, S., & Tingvall, C. (2001). *Intelligent Transport Systems: Safety and Human Factors Issues*. Victoria, Australia: Royal Automobile Club of Victoria.

Repetti, A., & Desthieux, G. (2006). A Relational Indicator set model for urban land-use planning and management: methodological approach and application in two case studies. *Landscape and Urban Planning*, *77*(1), 196–215. doi:10.1016/j.landurbplan.2005.02.006

Rettie, R. M. (2005). Presence and Embodiment in Mobile Phone Communication. *PsychNology Journal*, *3*(1), 16–34.

Rheingold, H. (1993). *The Virtual Community: Homesteading on the Electronic Frontier*. Reading, MA: Addison-Wesley Pub Co.

Rheingold, H. (2000). *Smart Mobs: the next social revolution* (pp. 157–182). Cambridge, MA: Perseus.

Rheingold, H. (2005). *Mobile Phones, Ritual Interaction and Social Capital*. Retrieved June 01, 2006, from http://www.thefeaturearchives.com/topic/Culture/Mobile_Phones__Ritual_Interaction_and_Social_Capital.html.

Riviere, C. (2005). Mobile camera phones: a new form of being together in daily interpersonal communication. In Ling, R., & Pederson, P. E. (Eds.), *Mobile communications: Re-negotiation of the social sphere* (pp. 167–185). London: Springer.

Robbins, B. D. (1999). *Emotion, Movement & Psychological Space: A Sketching Out of the Emotions in terms of Temporality, Spatiality, Embodiment, Being-with, and Language*. Retrieved June 16, 2006, from http://mythosandlogos.com/emotion.html.

Robinson, W., & Robison, D. (2007). Tsunami mobilizations: Considering the role of mobile and digital communication devices. In Kavoori, A., & Arceneaux, N. (Eds.), *The cell phone reader: Essays in social transformation* (pp. 85–104). New York: Peter Lang.

Rodotà, S. (1995). *Tecnologie e diritti*. Bologna, Italy: Il Mulino.

Rodotà, S. (2008). *A vida na sociedade da vigilância. Privacidade hoje*. Rio de Janeiro, Brazil: Renovar.

Rosa, A., Frey, K., & Procopiuck, M. (2007). Redes virtuais de governança ambiental: análise de uma websphere ambiental a partir da cidade de Curitiba. *Revista Tecnologia e Sociedade*, *5*, 79–102.

Rose, N. (1999). *Powers of freedom. Reframing political thought*. Cambridge, UK: Cambridge University Press. doi:10.1017/CBO9780511488856

Rose, N. (2006). *Politics of life itself: biomedicine, power and subjectivity in the twenty-first century*. Princeton, NJ: Princeton University Press.

Rosello, M. (2008). *Culture de L'insecurité*. Keynote speech gave at Séminaire transdisciplinaire Cultures de l'(in)sécurité, Université de Montréal, Montréal. Retrieved 21st April 2008, from http://www.cerium.ca/Insecurite- linguistique-et

Rubinstein, D. (2005). Cellphone photography; The death of the camera and the arrival of visible speech. Retrieved October 28, 2009 from <http://lsbu.academia.edu/Daniel-Rubinstein/Papers/98273/Cellphone-photography--The-death-of-the-camera-and-the-arrival-of-visible-speech>

Rule, J. B. (1973). *Private Lives, Public Surveillance*. London: Allen-Lane.

Rule, J. B. (2002). From mass society to perpetual contact. In Katz, J. E., & Aakhus, M. (Eds.), *Perpetual contact: Mobile communication, private talk, public performance* (pp. 242–254). New York: Cambridge University Press. doi:10.1017/CBO9780511489471.019

Ruppert, E. (2003). Book review: Henri Lefebvre. The Urban Revolution. *Canadian Journal of Sociology*, (September-October), 1-3. Retrieved from www.arts.ualberta.ca/cjscopy/reviews/urbanrev.html

Russel, B. (1999). *A Headmap Manifesto*. In Headmap. Org. Retrieved August 28, 2009, from http://www.mutateweb.com/library/headmap.pdf

Rutherford, J. (2005). Networks in cities, cities in networks: territory and globalisation intertwined in telecommunications infrastructure development in Europe. *Urban Studies (Edinburgh, Scotland)*, *42*(13), 2389–2406. doi:10.1080/00420980500379529

Rutherford, J., Gillespie, A., & Richardson, R. (2004). The territoriality of Pan-European telecommunications backbone networks. *Journal of Urban Technology*, *11*(3), 1–34. doi:10.1080/10630730500064166

Ryan, M.-L. (2001). *Narrative as Virtual Reality: Immersion and Interactivity in Literature and Electronic Media*. Baltimore: The Johns Hopkins University Press.

Saint-Exupery, A. (2009). Internet of Things – Strategic Research Roadmap. Retrieved February 4, 2010, from http://www.sintef.no/upload/IKT/9022/CERP-IoT%20 SRA_IoT_v11_pdf.pdf

Salen, K., & Zimmermman, E. (2003). *Rules of Play. Game Design Fundamentals*. Cambridge, MA: MIT Press.

Santaella, L. (2002). *Semiótica aplicada*. São Paulo, Brazil: Thomson.

Santaella, L. (2007). A ecologia pluralista. In Oliva, F., & Rezende, M. (Eds.), *Comunismo da forma. Som, imagem e política da arte*. São Paulo, Brazil: Alameda Situações.

Santaella, L. (2007). *Linguagens líquida na era da mobilidade*. São Paulo: Paulus.

Santaella, L. (2008a). *A Estética Política das Mídias Locativas*, Nómadas, 28, April, Universidad Central, Colombia. Retrieved August 2009, from http://bibliotecavirtual.clacso.org.ar/ar/libros/colombia/iesco/nomadas/28/12-estetica.pdf

Santaella, L. (2008b). *A ecologia pluralista das mídias locativas Revista FAMECOS nº 37*. Porto Alegre, Brazil: Programa de Pós-Graduação em Comunicação Social da Faculdade de Comunicação Social / PUCRS.

Santaella, L. (2008c). *Mídias Locativas: A Internet Móvel de Lugares e Coisas Revista FAMECOS nº 35*. Porto Alegre, Brazil: Programa de Pós-Graduação em Comunicação Social da Faculdade de Comunicação Social / PUCRS.

Santaella, L. (in press). *A ecologia pluralista da comunicação. Conectividade, mobilidade, ubiqüidade*. São Paulo, Brazil: Paulus. Stalder, F. Opinion. Privacy is not the antidote to surveillance. *Surveillance & Society*, *1*(1), 120-124.

Santoro, M. A. (2009). *China 2020: How Western business can – and should – influence social and political change in the coming decade*. Ithaca, NY: Cornell University Press.

Santos, M. (1997). *A Natureza do Espaço: Técnica e Tempo, Razão e Emoção. São Paulo*. Brazil: Hucitec.

Santos, M. (1999). *A Natureza do espaço: Técnica e Tempo. Razão e Emoção, (3a Edição)*. São Paulo, Brazil: Editora Hucitec.

Santos, M. (2002a). *Por uma outra globalização: do pensamento único à consciência universal*. Rio de Janeiro, Brazil: Record.

Santos, M., & Marques, M. C. (2002b). *A natureza do espaço: Técnica e tempo, razão e emoção*. São Paulo, Brazil: Editora Science.

Sassen, S. (1991). *The Global City*. Princeton, NJ: Princeton University Press.

Sassen, S. (1991). *The Global City: New York, London, Tokyo*. Princeton, NJ: Princeton University Press.

Sassen, S. (1994). *Cities in a World Economy*. Thousand Oaks, CA: Pine Forge.

Sassen, S. (2002). Locating cities on global circuits. In Sassen, S. (Ed.), *Global networks, linked cities* (p. 368). New York: Routledge.

Sassen, S. (2007). *Una sociologia de la globalizacón*. Buenos Aires: Katz.

Schleifer, Y. (2009, June 19). Why Iran's Twitter revolution is unique. *Christian Science Monitor, 6*.

Schneider, J., & Kortuem, G. (2001). *How to host a pervasive game. Supporting face-to-face interactions in live-action role-playing*. Presented at the Workshop on Designing Ubiquitous Computing Games. Ubicomp, Atlanta, GA, September/October 2001.

Schneider, S. M., & Foot, K. (2005). Web Sphere Analysis: An Approach to Studying Online Action. In Hine, C. (Ed.), *Virtual Methods: Issues in Social Science Research on the Internet* (pp. 157–170). New York, NY, USA: Berg Publishers.

Schuler, D., & Stone, T. (Eds.). (1996). *New Community Networks: Wired for Change*. Reading, MA: Addison-Wesley Pub Co.

Schwartz, J. (2003). This car can talk. What it says may cause concern. *The New York Times*, December 29.

Scientific America. (2008, September). Who's watching you: The Future of Privacy. Retrieved 20th January 2009 from http://www.scientificamerican.com/sciammag/?contents=2008-09

Scottish Executive. (2001a). *National Planning Policy Guideline NPPG19: Radio Telecommunications*. Edinburgh, UK: Scottish Executive.

Scottish Executive. (2001b). *Planning Advice Note: PAN 62 Radio Telecommunications*. Edinburgh, UK: Scottish Executive.

Scottish Executive. (2004). *National Planning Framework for Scotland*. Edinburgh, UK: Scottish Executive.

Scottish Government. (2009). *National Planning Framework 2 for Scotland*. Edinburgh, UK: Scottish Government.

Security scandal, (2006, October 18). *Hurriyet*. Retrieved on November 12, 2009, from <http://hurarsiv.hurriyet.com.tr/goster/haber.aspx?id=5277220>

Segal, A. (2002). *Digital dragon: High technology enterprises in China*. Ithaca: Cornell University Press.

Sekula, A. (1986).The Body and the Archive. *October, 39*, 3-64.

Selznick, P. (1985). Focussing organizational research on regulation. In Noll, R. G. (Ed.), *Regulatory Policy and the Social Sciences*. Berkeley, CA: University of California Press.

Shafer, C., Lee, B., & Turner, S. (2000). A tale of three greenway trails: user perceptions related to quality of life. *Landscape and Urban Planning, 49*(1), 163–178. doi:10.1016/S0169-2046(00)00057-8

Shankland, S. (2007). Camera market to peak in 2010, IDC says. *Cnet News*. Retrieved January 5, 2010 from <http://news.cnet.com/Camera-market-to-peak-in-2010,-IDC-says/2100-1041 _3-6178950.html>

Sheller, M., & Urry, J. (2006). The new mobilities paradigm. *Environment & Planning A, 38*(2), 207–226. doi:10.1068/a37268

Shie, T. R. (2004). The tangled Web: Does the Internet offer promise or peril for the Chinese Communist Party? *Journal of Contemporary China, 13*(40), 523–540. doi:10.1080/1067056042000213382

Shields, R. (1992). *Lifestyle shopping: The subject of consumption*. London: Routledge.

Shiode, N. (2000). Urban planning, information technology, and Cyberspace. *Journal of Urban Technology, 7*(2), 105–126. doi:10.1080/713684111

Short, J., Kim, Y., Kuss, M., & Wells, H. (1996). The dirty little secret of word city research. *International Journal of Regional and Urban Research, 20*, 697–717. doi:10.1111/j.1468-2427.1996.tb00343.x

Simmel, G. (1971). The metropolis and mental life. In Levine, D. (Ed.), *George Simmel on Individuality and Social Forms*. Chicago: University of Chicago Press. [first published in German in 1903]

Sirt, T. (2007). Mobile phone sales reach 10 million in 10 months. *Sabah*, December 31, 2007. Retrieved on January 5, 2010, from <http://arsiv.sabah.com.tr/2007/12/31/haber218ACE9477514AA18D986FB64C1E300D.html>?>

Smith, N. (2005). Neo-Critical Geography, or, the Flat Pluralist World of Business Class. *Antipode, 37*(5), 853–1094. doi:10.1111/j.0066-4812.2005.00538.x

Solove, D. (2008). *Understanding Privacy*. Cambridge, MA: Harvard University Press.

Sousa e Silva, A. (2006). From Cyber to Hybrid: Mobile Technologies as Interfaces of Hybrid Spaces. *Space and Culture*, *9*, 261–278. doi:10.1177/1206331206289022

Spangenberg, J., Pfah, S., & Deller, K. (2002). Toward indicators for institutional sustainability: lessons from an analysis of Agenda 21. *Ecological Indicators*, *2*(1), 61–77. doi:10.1016/S1470-160X(02)00050-X

Spasojevic, M. (2005). *Camera phone use and its implications*. Retrieved October 19, 2009, from <http://www.spasojevic.org/pics/papers.htm>

Stevens, B. (2004). The emerging security economy. An introduction. In Stevens, B. (Ed.), *The security economy* (pp. 7–16). Paris: OECD Publishing.

Stone, B., & Cohen, N. (2009, June 16). Networks spread defiance online. *The New York Times, 11*.

Stubbs, M., Lemon, M., & Longhurst, P. (2000). Intelligent urban management: learning to manage and managing to learn together for a change. *Urban Studies (Edinburgh, Scotland)*, *37*(10), 1801–1811. doi:10.1080/00420980020080421

Surveillance Camera Players. (2003). *Ten predictions concerning cell phones*. Retrieved from http://www.notbored.org/cell-phones.html/

Surveillance Studies Network. (2006). *Report on the Surveillance Society*. London: Information Commissioner's Office. Retrieved from www.ico.gov.uk/SearchResultAsHtml.aspx?cid=zvXivWNGbIUJ&page=http://www.ico.gov.uk/upload/documents/library/data_protection/practical_application/surveillance_society_full_report_2006.pdf&keywords=report on the surveillance society

Szulborsky, D. (2005). *This Is Not A Game: A Guide to Alternate Reality Gaming*. New Fiction Publishing.

Tai, Z. (2006). *The Internet in China: Cyberspace and civil society*. New York: Routledge.

Tatsuno, K. (2006). Current trends in digital cameras and camera phones. *The Quarterly Review*, *18*, 35–44.

Taylor, N. (2002). State surveillance and the right of privacy. *Surveillance & Society*, *1*(1), 66–85.

Taylor, P. (1997). Hierarchical tendencies amongst world cities: a global research proposal. *Cities (London, England)*, *14*(6), 323–332. doi:10.1016/S0264-2751(97)00023-1

Taylor, P. J. (2001). Specification of the world city network. *Geographical Analysis*, *33*, 181–194. doi:10.1111/j.1538-4632.2001.tb00443.x

Taylor, P. J. (2001). Specification of the world city network. *Geographical Analysis*, *33*, 181–194. doi:10.1111/j.1538-4632.2001.tb00443.x

Taylor, P. J. (2004). *World City Network: a Global Urban Analysis*. London: Routledge.

Taylor, P. J. (2004). *World City Network: A Global Urban Analysis*. London: Routledge.

Taylor, P. J. (2005). Leading world cities: empirical evaluations of urban nodes in multiple networks. *Urban Studies (Edinburgh, Scotland)*, *42*, 1593–1608. doi:10.1080/00420980500185504

Taylor, P. J. (2008). World Cities in Globalization. *GaWC Research Bulletin 263*. Retrieved April 28, 2008 from http://www.lboro.ac.uk/gawc/rb/rb263.html.

Taylor, P. J. (2009). Urban economics in thrall to Christaller: a misguided search for city hierarchies in external urban relations. *Environment & Planning A*, *41*, 2550–2555. doi:10.1068/a42235

Taylor, P. J. (2009). Urban Economics in thrall to Christaller: A Misguided Search for City Hierarchies in External Urban Relations. *GaWC Research Bulletin 311*. Retrieved June 30, 2009 from http://www.lboro.ac.uk/gawc/rb/rb311.html

Taylor, P. J. (2010). Measuring the world city network. In Firmino, R., Duarte, F., & Ultramari, C. (Eds.), *ICTs for Mobile and Ubiquitous Urban Infrastructures: Surveillance, Locative Media and Global Networks*. Hershey, PA: IGI Global.

Taylor, P. J., & Aranya, R. (2008). A Global 'Urban Roller Coaster'? Connectivity Changes in the World City Network, 2000-04. *Regional Studies*, *42*, 1–16. doi:10.1080/00343400601145202

Taylor, P. J., & Lang, R. E. (2005). *US Cities in the world city network. Metropolitan Policy Program Survey Series*. Washington, DC: Brookings Institution.

Taylor, P. J., Catalano, G., & Walker, D. R. F. (2002). Measurement of the world city network. *Urban Studies (Edinburgh, Scotland)*, *39*, 2367–2376. doi:10.1080/0042098022008001 1

Taylor, P. J., Derudder, B., & Witlox, F. (2007). Comparing airline passenger destinations with global service connectivities: a worldwide empirical study of 214 cities. *Urban Geography*, *28*(3), 232–248. doi:10.2747/0272-3638.28.3.232

Taylor, P. J., Hoyler, M., & Verbruggen, R. (2010a). External urban relational process: introducing central flow theory to complement central place theory. *Urban Studies (Edinburgh, Scotland)*, 47.

Taylor, P. J., Ni, P., Derudder, B., Hoyler, M., Huang, J., & Witlox, F. (2010b). *Global Urban Analysis: a Survey of Cities in Globalization*. London: Earthscan.

Taylor, P. J., Walder, D. R. F., & Beaverstock, J. V. (2002). Firms and their global service networks. In Sassen, S. (Ed.), *Global networks, linked cities*. New York: Routledge.

Tekten, E. (2009, May 2). May 1 beatings by police. *Hurriyet.* Retrieved November 1, 2009, from <http://arama.hurriyet.com.tr/arsivnews.aspx?id=11564286>

Telecom Media Convergence. (2007). *Telecom Media Convergence*. Retrieved on 15 June 2009 from http://www.tmforum.org/TelecomMediaConvergence/4645/home.html

Telephony Online. (2009). *Simplifying fixed/mobile convergence (FMC) for businesses.* Retrieved on 15 June 2009 from http://telephonyonline.com/global/commentary/simplifying-fixed-mobile-convergence-0330/?cid=hcom

Teriman, S., Yigitcanlar, T., & Mayere, S. (2009). Urban sustainability and growth management in South-East Asian city-regions: the case of Kuala Lumpur and Hong Kong. *Planning Malaysia*, *7*(1), 47–68.

Thamel, P., & Evans, T. (2009, September 16). College stars run for cover from fans' cameras. *The New York Times*. Retrieved October 19, 2009 from <http://www.nytimes.com/2009/09/17/sports/ncaafootball/17colleges.html?_r=2&hpw>

Thompson, G. F. (2003). *Between Hierarchies and Markets*. Oxford, UK: Oxford University Press. doi:10.1093/acprof:oso/9780198775270.001.0001

Torpey, J. (2000). *The Invention of the Passport: Surveillance, Citizenship, and the State*. New York: Cambridge University Press.

Townsend, A. (2000). Life in the real-time city: mobile telephones and urban metabolism. *Journal of Urban Technology*, *7*(2), 85–104. doi:10.1080/713684114

Tuan, Y. (1977). *Space and place*. Minneapolis, MN: University of Minnesota.

Turok, I. (2009). The distinctive city: pitfalls in the pursuit of differential advantage. *Urban Studies (Edinburgh, Scotland)*, *41*, 13–30.

Tuters, M., & Varnelis, K. (2006). Beyond Locative Media: Giving Shape to the Internet of Things. *Leonardo*, *39*(4), 357–363. doi:10.1162/leon.2006.39.4.357

UNDP. (1997). *Participatory local governance*. New York: United Nations Development Programme Publications.

Urry, J. (2001). Inhabiting the car. In Larreta, E. R. (Ed.), *Collective imagination: limits and beyond* (pp. 277–304). Rio de Janeiro, Brazil: UNESCO.

Van Kronenburg, R. (2008). *The internet of things: A critique of ambient technology and the all-seeing network of RFID*. Amsterdam: Waag Societt/Institute of Network Cultures.

Vehovar, V., Sicherl, P., Husing, T., & Dolnicar, V. (2006). Methodological challenges of digital divide measurements. *The Information Society*, *22*(5), 279–290. doi:10.1080/01972240600904076

Velaga, N. R., Quddus, M. A., & Bristow, A. L. (2009). Developing an enhanced weight-based topological map-matching algorithm for intelligent transport systems. *Transportation Research Part C, Emerging Technologies*, *17*(6), 672–683. doi:10.1016/j.trc.2009.05.008

Velastin, S. A., & Remagnino, P. (Eds.). (2006). *Intelligent distributed video surveillance systems*. London: Institution of Engineering and Technology.

Vigarello, G. (1987). *Le Propre et le Sale. L'hygiène du corps depuis le Moyen Age*. Paris: Seuil.

Vigarello, G. (2004). *Histoire de la beauté, le corps et l'art d'embellir de la renaissance à nos jours*. Paris: Seuil.

Vigilante taxi drivers reporting crimes over 3G phones. (2009, September 22). *Cellular News*. Retrieved November 1, 2009, from http://www.cellular-news.com / story/39715.php

Virilio, P. (1991). *The Lost Dimension* (trans. D. Moshenberg), New York: Semiotext(e).

Von Stokar, T., Frick, R., Schultz, B., Keiner, M., Rey, M., & Mettan, N. (2001). *Planification Directrice Cantonale et Developpement Durable*. Berne, Switzerland: Publications de l'Office du Developpement Territorial.

Wacks, R. (1980). *The protection of privacy*. London: Sweet & Maxwell.

Walcott, S., & Wheeler, J. (2001). Atlanta in the telecommunications age: the fiber-optic information network. *Urban Geography*, *22*(4), 316–339.

Walton, W. (2002a). The changing regulation of mobile-phone mast development in a devolved United Kingdom. *Environment and Planning. B, Planning & Design*, *29*(5), 687–705. doi:10.1068/b12849

Walton, W. (2002b). Out of sight, out of mind? (mobile phone antennae). *Town and Country Planning*, *71*(12), 300–301.

Wang, H. (2001). Digital City and Urban Sustainable Development. *China Population Resources and Environment*, *11*(2), 114–118.

Wang, L., Wu, H., & Song, H. (2002). *A framework of integrating digital city and eco-city*. Wuhan, China: School of Business, Hubei University.

Warf, B. (1998). Reach out and touch someone: AT&T's global operations in the 1990s. *The Professional Geographer*, *50*(1), 255–267. doi:10.1111/0033-0124.00119

Wasserman, S., & Faust, K. (1994). *Social network analysis: Methods and applications*. Cambridge, UK: Cambridge Univ. Press.

Webber, M. N. (1964). The Urban Place and the Nonplace Urban Realm. In *Explorations into Urban Structure*. Philadelphia: University of Pennsylvania Press.

Weber, I., & Lu, J. (2007). Internet and self-regulation in China: The cultural logic of controlled commodification. *Media Culture & Society*, *29*(5), 772–789. doi:10.1177/0163443707080536

Webster, C. (2005). The New Institutional Economics and the Evolution of Modern Urban Planning. *The Town Planning Review*, *76*(4), 455–484. doi:10.3828/tpr.76.4.5

Webster, C., & Lai, L. W.-C. (2003). *Property Rights, Planning and Markets. Managing Spontaneous Cities*. Cheltenham, UK: Edward Elgar.

Weiser, M. (1991). The computer for the 21st century. *Scientific American*, *265*(3), 66–75. doi:10.1038/scientificamerican0991-94

Weiser, M. (1991). The computer for the 21st century. Scientific American. Retrieved February 4, 2010, from http://www.ubiq.com/hypertext/weiser/SciAmDraft3.html

Weiser, M. (1994). The world is not a desktop. *Interaction*, (January): 7–8. doi:10.1145/174800.174801

Weiser, M., & Brown, J. S. (1995). *Designing Calm Technology*. Xerox PARC. Retrieved May 16, 2006, from http://www.ubiq.com/weiser/calmtech/calmtech.htm

Weissberg, J. L. (2004). Paradoxos da Teleinformática. In Parente, A. (Ed.), *Tramas da rede: novas dimensões filosóficas, estéticas e políticas da comunicação* (pp. 113–141). Porto Alegre: Sulina.

Wellman, B. (2001). Physical space and cyberspace: the rise of personalized networking. *International Journal of Urban and Regional Research*, 25.

Welser, H. T., Gleave, E., Fisher, D., & Smith, M. (2007). Visualizing the signatures of social roles in online discussion groups. *Journal of Social Structure*, *8*(2).

Wertheim, M. Pearly (2000). *Gates of Cyberspace: A History of Space from Dante to the Internet*. New York: W.W. Norton & Company.

Westin, A. F., & Baker, M. A. (1972). *Databanks in a Free Society – Computers, Record-Keeping and Privacy. Report of the Project on Computer Databanks of the United States National Academy of Sciences*. New York: Quadrangle Books.

What did Akif Beki do to stop Milliyet reporter? *Medya Faresi*. (2006, October 19). Retrieved November 12, 2009, from <http://www.medyafaresi.com/haber/1545 / medya-akif-beki-balyoz-skandalini-goruntuleyen-milliyet-muhabirini-engellemek-icin-ne-yapti.html>

Whitacre, B., & Mills, B. (2007). Infrastructure and the rural–urban divide in high-speed residential internet access. *International Regional Science Review*, *30*(3), 249–273. doi:10.1177/0160017607301606

White, G. (2002). *Riding the tiger: The politics of economic reform in post-Mao China*. Stanford, CA: Stanford University Press.

White, J. G. (2003). *People, not places: A police framework for analysing location privacy issues. Masters memo prepared for the Electronic Privacy Information Center*. Terry Sanford Institute of Public Policy, Duke University.

Whittaker, J. (2002). *The Internet: The Basics*. London: Routledge.

Wieman, C. (1998). The high-tech transition: technology and the prospects for improving infrastructure performance. *Journal of Urban Technology*, *5*(2), 21–46. doi:10.1080/10630739883895

Williams, I. (2008). *Huawei pushes fixed-mobile convergence*. Retrieved on 15 June 2009 from http://identitymanagement.itweek.co.uk/vnunet/news/2230131/huawei-pushes-fixed-mobile

Willis, K. S. (2008). Places, Situations, and Connections. In Aurigi, A., & De Cindio, F. (Eds.), *Augmented Urban Spaces* (pp. 9–26). London: Ashgate Publishers.

Wilsdon, J., Wynne, B., & Stilgoe, J. (2005). *The Public Value of Science (Or how to ensure that science really matters)*. London: Demos.

Winseck, D. (2008). Information operations "blowback": Communication, propaganda and surveillance in the global war on terrorism. *International Communication Gazette*, *70*(6), 419–441. doi:10.1177/1748048508096141

Wolchok, S., Yao, R., & Halderman, J. A. (2009). *Analysis of the Green Dam censorware system*. Retrieved October 8, 2009, from http://www.cse.umich.edu/~jhalderm/pub/gd/

Wood, A. (2009). *City Ubiquitous: Place, Communication, and the Rise of Omnitopia*. Cresskill, NJ: Hampton Press.

Wood, D. (2005). Editorial: People watching people. *Surveillance & Society*, *2*(4), 474–478.

Wood, D. M. (Ed.). (2006). A report on the surveillance society. *Information commissioner by the surveillance studies*, September-2006.

Wood, D., & Graham, S. (2006). Permeable boundaries in the software-sorted society: surveillance and the differentiation of mobility. In Sheller, M., & Urry, J. (Eds.), *Mobile Technologies of the City* (pp. 177–191). London: Routledge.

Woods, M. (1981). Desert-like conditions hurt Sun Belt. *The Blade (Toledo, OH)*, 18 January 1981.

Woolgar, S. (Ed.). (2002). *Virtual Society? technology, cyberbole, reality*. Oxford, UK: Oxford University Press.

World Charter on the Right to the City. (2004). Retrieved September 12, 2009 from http://v1.dpi.org/lang-en/resources/details.php?page=124

World's favorite cell phones. (n.d.). *TelekomHaber.com*. Retrieved November 12, 2009, from <http://www.telekomhaber.com/haber.asp?haber_id=20404>

Wu, G. (2009). In the name of good governance: E-government, Internet pornography and political censorship in China. In Zhang, X., & Zheng, Y. (Eds.), *China's information and communications technology revolution: Social changes and state responses* (pp. 68–85). London: Routledge.

Yang, X., Liu, J., Zhao, F., & Vaidya, N. H. (2004). A vehicle-to-vehicle communication protocol for cooperative collision warning. In *Proceedings of MOBIQUITOUS 2004 - 1st Annual International Conference on Mobile and Ubiquitous Systems: Networking and Services*, (pp. 114-123).

Yar, M. (2003). Panoptic power and the pathlogisation of vision: critical reflections on the Foucaldian thesis. *Surveillance and Society, 1*(3), 254-271.

Yeung, Y. (2000). *Globalization and networked societies: urban-regional change in Pacific Asia*. Hawaii: University of Hawaii Press.

Yigitcanlar, T. (2009a). *Ubiquitous eco cities: a new sustainable city form?* Paper presented at the Urban Design Seminar, 11 February 2009, Gold Coast City Council, Australia.

Yigitcanlar, T. (2009b). Planning for smart urban ecosystems: information technology applications for capacity building in environmental decision making. *Theoretical and Empirical Researches in Urban Management, 3*(12), 5–21.

Yigitcanlar, T., & Velibeyoglu, K. (2008). Knowledge-based urban development: local economic development path of Brisbane, Australia. *Local Economy, 23*(3), 197–209. doi:10.1080/02690940802197358

Yigitcanlar, T., Han, J., & Lee, S. (2008c). Online Environmental Information Systems. In Frederic, A. (Ed.), *Encyclopaedia of Decision Making and Decision Support Techniques*. Hersey, PA: IGI Publishing.

Yigitcanlar, T., Velibeyoglu, K., & Baum, S. (Eds.). (2008a). *Knowledge-based urban development: planning and applications in the information era*. Hersey, PA: Information Science Reference.

Yigitcanlar, T., Velibeyoglu, K., & Baum, S. (Eds.). (2008b). *Creative urban regions: harnessing urban technologies to support knowledge city initiatives*. Hershey, PA: Information Science Reference.

Zhang, L. (2006). Behind the "Great Firewall": Decoding China's Internet media policies from the inside. *Convergence: The International Journal of Research into New Media Technologies, 12*(3), 271–291. doi:10.1177/1354856506067201

Zook, M., & Brunn, S. (2005). Regions, hierarchies and legacies: European Cities and global air travel. *Journal of Contemporary European Studies, 13*(2), 203–220. doi:10.1080/14782800500212459

Zook, M., & Brunn, S. (2006). From podes to antipodes: positionalities and global airline geographies. *Annals of the Association of American Geographers. Association of American Geographers, 96*(3), 471–490. doi:10.1111/j.1467-8306.2006.00701.x

About the Contributors

Rodrigo José Firmino is lecturer at the Postgraduate Program of Urban Management at the Pontifical Catholic University (PUCPR) in Curitiba, Brazil. He worked as Postdoctoral Fellow at University of São Paulo, Brazil, researching the co-development of urban and technological strategies for cities in developing countries. He obtained his PhD on Urban Planning from the School of Architecture, Planning and Landscape at the University of Newcastle upon Tyne, UK. He also holds an MPhil in Architecture and Urbanism from the University of São Paulo, and trained as architect and planner at State University of São Paulo.

Fábio Duarte is Professor at the Postgraduate Program in Urban Management at the Catholic University of Paraná (PUCPR) in Curitiba, Brazil. He is researcher of the National Council of Technological and Scientific Development (CNPq/Brazil). Duarte is urban planner, holds a PhD in Communications from the University of São Paulo, and a MPhil in Multimedia from the State University of Campinas. He has been guest researcher and lecturer at the Université Paris 1, Université Laval (Canadá) and Universidad Politécnica de Catalunya.

Clovis Ultramari is an architect and lecturer at the Postgraduate Program in Urban Management at the Catholic University of Paraná (PUCPR) in Curitiba, Brazil. He obtained his Ph.D. on Environment and Urban Development from the Federal University of Paraná, Brazil. He has a professional experience in state and non-governmental agencies in Latin America and Africa.

* * *

Luiz Adolfo Andrade is a researcher and game designer working on alternate reality games. Being a PhD Student at Federal University of Bahia, he is currently working on his thesis about games and the idea of production of space. He is member of both the collective of researchers 'Realidade Sintética' and the Urban Cultures, Leisure and Technology Laboratory.

Nelson Arteaga Botello is a professor and researcher in the Faculty of Political and Social Sciences at the Universidad Autónoma del Estado de México. He received his doctorate at the University of Alicante, Spain. He is a member of the National System of Investigators (SNI) in Mexico. His main research interests are public security and surveillance. Among many books and articles in Spanish, English and Portuguese, his publications include Pobres y Delincuentes: Estudio de sociología y genealogía (2006), and Sociedad de la vigilancia en el Sur-Global: Mirando América Latina (2009).

Andrew Boulton is a graduate student in the Department of Geography, University of Kentucky. His research is focused on locative annotative media and neogeographies (crowd-soured cartographies). His work deals with (i) the nature of contributor communities and the democratizing potential of Web 2.0 cartographic platforms, and (ii) the ways in which locative annotations reconfigure experiences of urban place.

Paolo Bruni is a PhD student at the Contemporary Communication and Culture Postgraduate Program of the Federal University of Bahia, connected to the Film Analysis Laboratory. He is also currently a member of the collective of researchers 'Realidade Sintética', and develops research on analytic methodologies that deal with videogames.

Stanley D. Brunn is Professor of Geography at the University of Kentucky. He has published on a wide variety of political, social, urban, economic, information/communication, and environmental topics. He has served as editor of the *Annals of the Association of American Geographers* and *The Professional Geographer* and guest-edited issues of other journals. His teaching experiences include the University of Florida and Michigan State University and a dozen of short-term assignments in European and Central Asian universities. Brunn's current research includes: a forthcoming (Springer) international edited volume on the impacts of megaengineering projects; innovative cyberspace cartographies; atlases of the US 2008 election and Greater Eurasia; geographies of contemporary religion; visual geographies (especially stamps).

Fernanda Bruno is Associate professor at the Federal University of Rio de Janeiro (UFRJ) - Post-graduate Program in Communication and Culture. She has a PhD in Communication from the Federal University of Rio de Janeiro. Bruno is researcher of the National Council of Technological and Scientific Development (CNPq/Brazil) and Founder Member of the Latin America Surveillance Studies Network.

Mario Viola de Azevedo Cunha is MD in Private Law and Specialist in Consumer Law (Universidade do Estado do Rio de Janeiro), Specialist in Private Law (Universidade Federal Fluminense), Master of Research and currently a PhD Candidate in law (European University Institute, Italy). He is also an attorney (on leave) of the Municipality of Saquarema, in the State of Rio de Janeiro.

Ben Derudder is Lecturer in Human Geography at the Geography Department of Ghent University, and Associate Director of the Globalization and World Cities research group and network (GaWC). His research focuses on (i) the conceptualization and empirical analysis of transnational urban networks, (ii) the (persisting) importance of business travel in the space economy, and (iii) spatial modelling techniques.

Lomme Devriendt has a doctoral degree in Geography at Ghent University. He is research assistant at the Geography Department of Ghent University and a research fellow of the Globalization and World Cities group and network (GaWC). His research is funded by the Flemish Fund for Scientific Research (FWO), and deals with the conceptualization and empirical assessment of the digital and physical accessibility of cities in the global economy.

Danilo Doneda is PhD in Civil Law (UERJ), lawyer and Law Professor. He also has a degree in Law (UFPR) and a Master in Law (UERJ). He taught at PUC-Rio, UERJ and UCAM. He was visiting researcher at Università degli Studi di Camerino (Italy) and at Max Planck Institute for Comparative and International Private Law (Germany). He is currently a member of the E-Commerce Commission and Consumer Protection of Brazilian Ministry of Justice and a counselor for the Brazilian Ministry of Science and Technology and UNESCO. He specializes in Data Protections and has several articles and books on this issue.

Susan J. Drucker, is a Professor in the Department of Journalism/ Media Studies, School of Communication, Hofstra University. She is the treasurer of the Urban Communication Foundation and a partner in Communication Landscapers, a consulting firm. She is an attorney, and Series editor of the Communication and Law series for Peter Lang Publishing Group. She is the author and co-editor of 9 books and over including The Urban Communication Reader I and II, Voices in the Street: Gender, Media and Public Space and two editions of Real Law @ Virtual Space: The Regulation of Cyberspace (1999, 2005) with Gary Gumpert. Her work examines the relationship between media technology and human factors, particularly as viewed from a legal perspective.

Thiago Falcão is a PhD Student at the Contemporary Communication and Culture Postgraduate Program of the Federal University of Bahia. He currently develops a research concerning human interaction through virtual worlds, besides being the chief-editor of the game research website 'Realidade Sintética' (www.realidadesintetica.com), which gathers different portuguese-language aligned researchers in the attempt of formally putting together the game studies area in Brazil.

Emmanoel Ferreira is a PhD student at the Communication and Culture Program of Universidade Federal do Rio de Janeiro (Brazil) and an Assistant Professor at the Media and Cultural Studies Department of Universidade Federal Fluminense (Brazil). He is a member of the 'Realidade Sintética' video game research group.

Klaus Frey is Professor at the Postgraduate Program in Urban Management and the bachelor courses in environmental engineering and sociology at the Catholic University of Paraná (PUCPR) in Curitiba, Brazil. He is researcher of the Brazilian National Council of Technological and Scientific Development (CNPq). He received a PhD in social sciences from the University of Konstanz, Germany (1997) and in 2007 he carried out his post-doctoral studies at the Institute of Urban and Regional Planning at the Technological University of Berlin. He has published on urban governance, local sustainable development, public policies, and socio-technical networks.

Maria Giaoutzi is Professor of Economic Geography and Regional Planning at the Department of Geography and Regional Planning, School of Rural and Surveying Engineering, National Technical University of Athens. Fellow of the Netherlands Institute of Advanced Studies (NIAS), the Royal Dutch Academy; Member of various International Research Networks; Elected Chancellor at the Steering Committee of the International Regional Science Association (1990-94); Elected Member of the Executive Committee of I.G.U-C18 (Telecommunications)/ CNFG, (1992-95); President of the Board of Directors of the Hellenic Tourism Organization Land Development Company (1998-2000); Consultant in International Organizations, such as OECD, EEC, ERT, ESF. She has experience on urban and regional planning and development, foresight methodologies, technology assessment, etc.

Gary Gumpert is Emeritus Professor of Communication at Queens College of the City University of New York and President of the Urban Communication Foundation. He is co-founder of Communication Landscapers, a consulting firm. Professor Gumpert's publications include: Talking Tombstones and Tales of the Media Age; three edited volumes of Inter/Media: Interpersonal Communication in a Media Age published by Oxford University Press. He is series editor of the Urban Communication book series of Peter Lang Publishing Group. His primary research focuses on the nexus of communication technology and social relationships, particularly looking at urban and suburban development, the alteration of public space, and the changing nature of community.

Jung Hoon Han's research interest focuses on the spatial and temporal changes in housing and urban system; in particular the dynamic changes occurring in response to constrains and opportunities in a socio-spatial context. While completing his PhD in the area of urban and regional planning at the University of Queensland, Australia he worked for the Australian Housing and Urban Research Institute (AHURI), one of the leading national research institutes in Australia. His researches were awarded in international and Australian research organisation, including the best written journal paper of the year (2004) by the Journal of Housing Studies Review and the best conference paper (2008) by Australia and New Zealand Regional Science International (ANZRSI). Dr Han is currently an editorial board member of the journal of 'City, Culture and Society' from Elsevier.

André Lemos has PhD in Sociology, Université Paris V, Sorbonne. He is Associate Professor at Faculty of Communication at Federal University of Bahia (UFBa), Brazil. He is former President of Brazilian Association of Communications PhD Programs (COMPÓS), and former director of PhD Program in Communication and Culture (PPGCCC/Facom/UFBa). He is Senior Researcher at the National Council of Technological and Scientific Development (CNPq/ Brazil). André Lemos has published 13 books and many articles in peer-reviewed scientific journals worldwide, and is member of editorial boards in scientific journals in Brazil and worldwide (Canadian Journal of Communication, Revue Society, Wi. Journal of Mobile Media, Herbert Dordick Award of Dissertations, among others). Visiting scholar at University of Alberta and McGill University, Canada, 2007-2008, he is now working on mobile communication and locative media studies.

Greg Lloyd AcSS, BA, MSc, FRSA, FIED, FHEA, MeRSA is Professor of Urban Planning and Head of the School of the Built Environment at the University of Ulster. Prior to this he held Professorial positions at the Universities of Dundee and Liverpool. His research includes land economy, public policy implementation and land use planning, institutional innovation in spatial planning practices, and the efficiency and effectiveness of new planning and regulatory arrangements. He is currently involved in the International Centre for Local and Regional Development in the island of Ireland. He was Ministerial Adviser to the Northern Ireland Assembly Government on its reform of land use planning. He is a member of the Scottish Government's National Planning Framework Advisory Group, and a member of the Best Commission which is examining the future of housing in Northern Ireland.

David Lyon FRSC, is Director of the Surveillance Studies Centre, Queen's Research Chair in Surveillance Studies and Professor of Sociology at Queen's University, Kingston, Canada. Author of many books and articles on surveillance, including most recently Identifying Citizens: ID Cards as Surveillance (Polity, 2009) and Surveillance Studies: An Overview (Polity 2007). He is a member of the international

'Surveillance Studies Network' and a co-editor of Surveillance and Society. His particular research interest at present is identification systems as surveillance, in both the global North and the global South.

Luisa Paraguai, researcher and artist, studied Civil Engineering and Computing at University of São Paulo, Brazil. She has a master and doctoral degree at the Department of Multimedia, Institute of Arts, State University of Campinas, Brazil. Paraguai has been teaching at the Master Design Program, Anhembi Morumbi University. Her current researches deal with the potential of mobile technologies as a mediator for body and space perception and experimentation.

Georgios Patris is an experienced transport engineer, having the degree of Civil Engineering from the National Technical University of Athens (NTUA), a Master in Business Administration (MBA) and a post-graduate degree in Project Management. Patris has participated in numerous traffic studies in Greece including traffic modelling, parking management, traffic management, road safety and public transport and he has prepared economic evaluations for a number of transport infrastructure projects in various European countries. He is a PhD candidate in the NTUA and his research field focuses on decision support systems in transport and in the applications of intelligent transport systems.

Deborah Peel BA, MATP, DipHE, MAHE, MRTPI, FHEA is Senior Lecturer in Planning Policy in the School of the Built Environment at the University of Ulster. Prior to this she held positions at the Universities of Westminster, Dundee and Liverpool. She has wide public sector experience in land use planning practice. She is Editor of the Journal of Education in the Built Environment. Her research interests include land use planning policy and practice; marine spatial planning; reform of planning policy and practice, decision-making and participation strategies; planning and pedagogy. She has undertaken research into mobile telephony for the Scottish and Welsh devolved governments.

Débora de Carvalho Pereira is a PhD researcher at the Federal University of Minas Gerais, Brazil, at the Centre of Media Studies and Social Uses of Knowledge and Information in Digital Environments. She is developing a research project entitled "Environmental Social networks on the Internet and the management of nature", to be completed in 2012. She earned her Master's in Rural Extension from the University Federal of Viçosa (UFV) with the dissertation "Amazon Cooperation: the environmental networks on the Internet and the standardization of nature ". Her areas of interest include: Social Networks, Environmentalism, Cyberculture and Semiotics.

Mario Procopiuck is judiciary analyst/administrator of the Federal High Court in Paraná State. He received a graduate degree in Administration at the Federal University of Paraná (1998) and a Master's degree in urban management at the Catholic University of Paraná (PUCPR) in Curitiba, Brazil (2007). Currently he is studying for a Doctorate degree in administration at PUCPR. He is evaluator of academic papers of the Brazilian Association of Post-graduation in Administration and for the Iberoamerican Academy of Management. His professional and academic experiences are in the field of administration and public organizations, with emphasis in the fields of bidding and contracts, human resources, public policies, socio-technical networks, the Internet, and urban governance.

Altair Rosa received a graduate degree in environmental engineering and a master's degree in urban management by the Catholic University of Paraná (PUCPR), and completed a professional specialization course in occupational health and safety at the Federal Technological University of Paraná (UTFPR), in Curitiba, Brazil. Currently, he works as technical assistant in environmental issues at ECOPARANÁ, an environmental non-governmental organization, and as associate professor at the bachelor course in environmental engineering at PUCPR.

Lucia Santaella is full professor at the Catholic University of São Paulo (PUCSP), PhD in Literary Theory (PUCSP) and professor in Communication Sciences (São Paulo University). Head of the Postgraduate Program in Technologies of Intelligence and Digital Design, Director of CIMID, Research Center in Digital Media, and also Director of the Center for Peirce Studies (PUCSP). Honorary President of the Latin American Federation of Semiotics. President of the Charles S. Peirce Society, USA, 2007. Guest professor at the Free University (Berlin, 1987), Valencia University (2004, Spain), Kassel University (Kassel, 2009). Jabuti Prizes (2002 and 2009) and Sergio Motta Prize (2005). She has published more than 30 books and scientific articles in peer reviewed journals.

Rob Shields' work spans architecture and cultural studies. He works on the identities of Places on the Margin (Outstanding Book of the Year 1991), on consumption and Lifestyle Shopping (ed. 1993), urban and architectural issues such as What is a City? Rethinking the Urban After Katrina (ed. 2008), and Building Tomorrow: Innovation in Construction (ed. 2005), theorists such as Lefebvre (1999), and the relevance of The Virtual (2003) and Cultures of Internet (ed. 1996) to Space and Culture, a refereed journal.

Zixue Tai is assistant professor in the School of Journalism and Telecommunications at the University of Kentucky. He holds a PhD in mass communication from the University of Minnesota as well as a MSS (Master of Software Systems) from the University of St. Thomas (Minnesota) and a MA from Shanghai International Studies University. His research interests focus on global communication with a special emphasis on the transformation of Chinese media in the new millennium as well as the individual/social impact of new media technologies. He is the author of The Internet in China: Cyberspace and Civil Society (Routledge, 2006). Additionally, his research has appeared in scientific journals worldwide.

Peter J. Taylor is Professor of Geography at Loughborough University (UK) where he is Director of the Globalization and World Cities (GaWC) Research Network. He researches city networks and their relation to territorial states as constructions of social space and social time. His recent books include World City Network (Routledge, 2004), Cities in Globalization (Routledge 2006, edited with B Derudder, P Saey and F Witlox) and Global Urban Analysis (Earthscan 2010, edited with P Ni, B Derudder, M Hoyler, F Witlox and J Huang). He is a Fellow of the British Academy and an Academician of the Academy of Social Sciences (UK).

Vassilios Vescoukis holds a Diploma in Electrical Engineering from National Technical University of Athens and a PhD in 'Software Engineering' from National Technical University of Athens. At present he is Assistant Professor at the School of Rural and Surveying Engineering of NTUA. He has participated in a number of EU and National projects on the strategic planning of information systems, applications and services, of e-commerce applications and frameworks, the use of new technology in education, as well as the design, management and certification of large information systems. He has published extensively in books and journals of his field of expertise. His research interests include knowledge bases for software evolution, distributed and multi-tier software architectures, network-based support for education and training, as well as social implications of globalization and new technologies in the continuing process of transformation of society.

Bilge Yesil has a PhD in Culture and Communication at the New York University with a research grant from the National Science Foundation. She is the author of Video Surveillance: Power and Privacy in Everyday Life (LFB Scholarly Publishing, 2009), and has published articles in Cultural Studies, Media History, Journal of Popular Culture and in online journals. Before joining CUNY-College of Staten Island, she taught media and communication at New York University, New School University, and Sabanci University (Istanbul, Turkey).

Frank Witlox is professor of economic geography at the Geography Department of Ghent University and Associate Director of the Globalization and World Cities group and network (GaWC). He is also a visiting professor at the Institute of Transport and Maritime Management Antwerp (UA-ITMMA).

Tan Yigitcanlar has a multi-disciplinary background and over two decades of work experience in private consulting, government and academia. Currently holding a senior academic position at the School of Urban Development, Queensland University of Technology, Brisbane, Australia, the main foci of his research are advocating and promoting knowledge-based urban development and sustainable urban, infrastructure and transport development in city-regions. Yigitcanlar researchers in the field of 'knowledge-based and sustainable urban development', and he has been responsible for research, teaching, training and capacity building programmes on urban and regional planning, transport modelling, environmental science, policy analysis and information and communication technologies in Turkish, Japanese and Australian universities.

Index

D

E

F

G

S

T

U

Breinigsville, PA USA
22 November 2010
249730BV00004B/149-210/P